THE ACADEMIC LIBRARY MANAGER'S

FORMS, POLICIES, *and* PROCEDURES HANDBOOK

with CD-ROM

Rebecca Brumley

Neal-Schuman Publishers, Inc.

New York   London

Published by Neal-Schuman Publishers, Inc.
100 William Street, Suite 2004
New York, NY 10038-4512

Printed and bound in the United States of America.

The paper used in this publication meets the minimum requirements of American National Standard for Information Sciences—Permanence of Paper for Printed Library Materials, ANSI Z39.48-1992.

ISBN-13: 978-1-55570-597-8
ISBN-10: 1-55570-597-9

Library of Congress Cataloging-in-Publication Data

Brumley, Rebecca, 1959–
The academic library manager's forms, policies, and procedures handbook with CD-ROM / Rebecca
  Brumley.
  p. cm.
  ISBN-13: 978-1-55570-597-8 (alk. paper)
  ISBN-10: 1-55570-597-9 (alk. paper)
  1. Academic libraries—Rules and practice. 2. Academic libraries—Forms. 3. Library rules and regulations—Case studies. I. Title.
Z675.U5B8527 2007
027.7—dc22   2006102714

In Loving Memory
Ruth D. Brumley
1925–1999

C. Wilson Brumley
1919–1998

"For I know the plans
I have for you,"
declares the Lord,
"plans to prosper you
and not to harm you,
plans to give you
hope and a future."

Jeremiah 29:11

DATE DUE

5/6/13	
MAY - 3 2013	
AUG 3 0 2013	
AUG 2 7 2013	
DEC 1 3 2013	
DEC 8 2013	
MAY - 2 2014	
APR 2 2 2014	

PRINTED IN U.S.A.

CONTENTS

PREFACE

The Academic Library Manager's Forms, Policies, and Procedures Handbook compiles the work and wisdom of my academic library colleagues from across the country. Inside these pages, you'll find over 600 proven and well-written forms, policies, and procedures on topics in more than 300 different areas. These can serve as inspirations, benchmarks, or reaffirmations for your institution. I hope that you, like me, will find many that have the perfect wording for trouble spots in your policies or manuals, as well as wonderful forms you really need. If you do, you can easily download the complete text or form from the companion CD-ROM (found on the inside back cover) to adapt for your own use.

Academic libraries have unique needs. While public libraries have only a few user categories, college and university libraries may serve administration, family members, faculty, alumni, undergraduates, graduate students, faculty, high school students, and community members. Effective library service may require variations in policy and procedure for many of these user groups.

I encourage you to compare your policy manual with the table of contents to identify areas in which you do not yet have policies. For example, when I visited a library recently, we discussed what to do with disruptive patrons. I asked, "What is your policy statement?" Much to my dismay, my colleague responded, "We don't need anything for that. Everyone knows what a disruptive patron is." From painful experience, I know that if a disruptive patron says, "Show me in writing that I am breaking the rules," the staff member had better be able to do so, or the institution won't have a leg to stand on. Anything that the library strives to do (or not do) is better served by a well-written and approved guideline.

I have tried to cover all the areas a library manager or dean faces. In compiling this guide, I read thousands of documents from two-year colleges, four-year liberal arts colleges, large universities and colleges, and research universities. I believe that the examples included will speak to most policy committees and directors/deans. Several unusual policies are also included because they are so creative that they can serve as a model for many libraries. I must thank all the contributing librarians for their willingness to share what works for them. Without these schools, there would be no book.

ORGANIZATION

The Academic Library Manager's Forms, Policies, and Procedures Handbook with CD-ROM is divided into 12 parts, each relating to a major function of the academic library.

- Part I, "Administrative Policies and Guidelines," includes materials that address administrative concerns, such as mission and vision statements, goals and objectives, gifts and donations, friends of the library, personnel, and library conduct guidelines.
- Part II, "Facilities and Equipment," highlights policies for library exhibits, displays, and notices; special-use rooms; equipment, furniture, and supplies; security and emergencies; and tours.
- Part III, "Collection Development," covers administrative guidelines for collection development, collecting guidelines for print and nonprint resources, preservation, collection of faculty-authored materials, deselection and weeding, and binding.
- Part IV, "Traditional Reference Service," focuses on administrative concerns for reference services, the reference collection, and service guidelines, including special services such as distance learning and telephone reference.
- Part V, "Virtual Reference Service," recognizes the importance of virtual reference with administrative and service guidelines specific to this area.

- Part VI, "Circulation," addresses the complex world of circulation with exemplary policies covering access, borrowing eligibility status, general circulation guidelines, loans, requests, renewals, reserves, and reproducing materials.
- Part VII, "Government Documents," explores the specific concerns of government document collections with policies for administration, collection development, reference and circulation, and providing internal revenue forms.
- Part VIII, "Legal and Ethical Concerns," provides guidance in establishing or updating your policies on copyright, privacy, and the Librarian's Code of Ethics.
- Part IX, "Information Literacy and Library Instruction," contains guidelines on library instruction in all areas of information literacy, including student involvement in information literacy.
- Part X, "Interlibrary Loan and Document Delivery," discusses requesting material, eligibility requirements, charges and fees, special services for faculty and staff, and borrowing guidelines for interlibrary loans, as well as document delivery.
- Part XI, "Internet and Electronic Resources," presents guidelines for the library Web site, subscription databases, and customer use of the Internet and other electronic resources.
- Part XII, "University Repositories," offers guidelines for managing and developing collections of materials produced by academic faculty, administration, and students.

The accompanying CD-ROM contains all of the policies, forms, and procedures in this book, along with some exclusive content. These documents can be downloaded into Microsoft Word and altered to fit your library's requirements, or even used as is. The electronic documents are a vital time-saver for managers updating a manual or creating a set of policies from scratch. Even if you don't want to download the text, the ideas in each section are invaluable. Take the time to thumb through the table of contents and index. I believe you will find many areas that you want to explore further. Take it. Use it. Make your work easier and your policies more responsive to your library's unique needs.

ACKNOWLEDGMENTS

I want to thank my Navarro College friends for their support and caring during the writing of this book. Thank you to my wonderful and brilliant editor, Michael Kelley, who helped make this book a useful resource for my fellow librarians, and to Charles Harmon, Director of Publishing, for all of his help. Thanks also to Miguel Figueroa and everyone else at Neal-Schuman.

This book is the proof that we as librarians share our hard work and wisdom with each other. Without the cooperation of the following libraries this book would not exist. My greatest thanks go to these libraries. Thank you for sharing.

Atlanta University
  Library of the Atlanta University Center, Inc.
  Robert W. Woodruff

Auburn University
  Auburn University Libraries
  Glenn Anderson

Augustana College
  Thomas Tredway Library

Ball State University
  Ball State University Libraries

Barton College
  Willis N. Hackney Library
  Rodney E. Lippard

Baylor University
  Moody Library
  Jeff Steely; Beth Tice

Bergen Community College
  Sidney Silverman Library

Bethel College
  Bethel College Library
  Gail Niles Stucky

Binghamton University
  Binghamton University Libraries
  Susan Currie

Brock University
  James A. Gibson Library
  Debbie Kalvee

Buena Vista University
  Buena Vista University Library
  James R. Kennedy

California State University, Long Beach
  University Library

Central Oregon Community College, Oregon State University
  Cascades Campus
  Campus Library

Central Washington University
  James E. Brooks Library
  Thomas Peischl

Centre College
  The Grace Doherty Library
  Stanley R. Campbell

Christopher Newport University
  Smith Library

College of Charleston
  Addlestone Library
  David Cohen

Colorado State University, Pueblo
  University Library
  Rhonda Gonzales

Columbia University
  Columbia University Libraries
  Janet Gertz

Connecticut College
  Charles E. Shain Library

Cornell University
    Cornell University Library

Crichton College
    J. W. and Dorothy Bell Library
    Pam Walker

Dartmouth College
    Dartmouth College Library

Drake University
    Cowles Library

Duke University
    Duke University Libraries
    Deborah Jakubs

East Carolina University
    J. Y. Joyner Library

Eastern Michigan University
    Bruce T. Halle Library
    Jui-Chung Chenge

Emory and Henry College
    Frederick Kelly Library
    Lorraine N. Abraham

Florida Atlantic University
    S. E. Wimberly Library

Florida International University
    Green Library and Biscayne Bay Campus
    Library

Framingham State College
    Henry Whittemore Library
    Librarians

Franklin and Marshall College
    Shadek-Fackenthal Library
    Pamela Snelson

Fullerton College
    Fullerton College Library
    Jackie Boll

Georgetown University
    Lauinger Library
    Mark Jacobs

Georgia State University
    University Library
    Laura Burtle

Gonzaga University School of Law
    Chastek Library
    June Stewart

Grand Valley State University
    Zumberge Library

Guilford College
    Hege Library
    Mary Ellen Chijioke

Hamilton College
    Daniel Burke Library

Henderson State University
    Huie Library

Hofstra University
    Joan and Donald E. Axinn Library
    Daniel R. Rubey

Hood College
    Beneficial-Hodson Library
    Jan Samet O'Leary, Director

Horry-Georgetown Technical College
    Horry-Georgetown Technical College
    Library
    Peggy Smith

Hudson Valley Community College
    Marvin Library
    Valerie Lang

Humboldt State University
    Sharmon H. Kenyon

Indiana University–Purdue University Fort Wayne
    Helmke Library
    Judith Violette

Indiana University
    Franklin D. Schurz Library

Indiana University Bloomington
    Herman B. Wells Library
    Garett Montanez

Johnson State College
    John State College Library
    Joseph Farara

Kalamazoo College
    Upjohn Library
    Stacy Nowicki

Kansas State University
    Kansas State University Libraries
    Sara K. Kearns

LaGuardia Community College
LaGuardia Community College Library,
Media Resources Center
Steven Ovadia

La Sierra University
The Library
Kitty J. Simmons, Library Director

Lake Sumter Community College
Library
Denise English

Lane Community College
Lane Community College Library
Nadine Williams

Lansing Community College
Lansing Community College Library

Los Angeles Valley College
Los Angeles Valley College Library
David May

Lynchburg College
Knight-Capron Library
Christopher Millson-Marula

Manatee Community College
Sara Scott Harllee Library

Marlboro College
Rice-Aron Library
Mary H. White

Milwaukee Area Technical College
Milwaukee Area Technical College Libraries

Monroe County Community College
Library

Neumann College
Neumann College Library
John M. Powell

New College of Florida
Jane Bancroft Cook Library
Joan M. Pelland

New Mexico State University
New Mexico State University Libraries
Library Instruction Program Task Force, Final
Report, May 21, 2002

New Mexico State University Alamogordo
David H. Townsend Library
Debra Teachman

New York University
New York University Library

Niagara University
Our Lady of Angels Library
David Schoen

Northern Arizona University
Cline Library

The Ohio State University
The Ohio State University Libraries
Joseph J. Branin

Oklahoma State University
Center for Health Sciences
Medical Library

Olin College of Engineering
Olin College Library
Dee Magnoni

Palo Alto College
Palo College Learning Resources Center
Colby O. Glass

Phoenix College
Phoenix College Library

Queens College (CUNY)
Benjamin S. Rosenthal Library
Robert A. Shaddy

Rockefeller University
Rockefeller University Library
Carol A. Feltes

Saint Charles Community College
Saint Charles Community College Library
Stephanie D. Tolson

Santa Monica College
Santa Monica College Library

Southern Illinois University Edwardsville
Lovejoy Library
Jay Starratt

State University of New York College at Cortland
Memorial Library

Stetson University
du Pont-Ball Library

Syracuse University
Syracuse University Library
Cynthia Cost

Tallahassee Community College
Tallahassee Community College Library
Cherry Alexander

Union College
Jones Learning Resource Center
Tara L. Cooper

University at Buffalo (SUNY)
University Libraries
Margaret R. Wells

University College University of Maine System
Campus Library Services
Susan Lowe

University of Alaska Anchorage
UAA/APU Consortium Library
University of Arizona Libraries and Center
for Creative Photography
Robert Mitchell

University of Arkansas Fayetteville
Mullins Library
Carolyn Allen

University of California Berkeley
The Library

University of California San Diego
University of California San Diego Libraries

University of California Santa Barbara
University of California Santa Barbara
Libraries

University of California Santa Cruz
McHenry Library
Virginia Steel

University of Colorado at Boulder
Jerry Crail Johnson Earth Sciences and Map
Library

University of Idaho
University of Idaho Libraries
Ron Force

University of Illinois at Urbana Champaign
University of Illinois at Urbana Champaign
Library
Robert Burger

University of Indianapolis
Krannert Memorial Library

University of Iowa
University Libraries
Nancy H. Seamans

University of Maryland Baltimore County
Albin O. Kuhn Library and Gallery

University of Michigan
University Library
Brenda Johnson

University of Michigan-Flint
Frances Willson Thompson Library
Dorothy Gae Davis

University of North Carolina Wilmington
William Madison Randall Library
Sue Ann Cody
Reprinted by permission of Randall Library,
University of North Carolina Wilmington

University of Pittsburgh
University Library System

University of Rochester
Rush Rhees Library
Ron Dow

University of Scranton
University of Scranton Libraries

University of South Alabama
University Library
Dr. Richard J. Wood

University of South Carolina Beaufort
Library
Ellen Chamberlin

University of Texas at Arlington
University of Texas at Arlington Library
Gerald Saxon

University of Texas Brownsville
Arnulfo M. Olivira Memorial Library

University of Texas at San Antonio
John Peace Library

University of Washington
University of Washington Libraries
Betsy Wilson

University of West Georgia
Irvine Sullivan Ingram Library
E. Lorene Flanders

University of Wisconsin River Falls
Chalmer Davee Library
Valeria Malzacher

Vanderbilt University
Jean and Alexander Heard Library
Paul Cherman

Ventura College
Evelyn and Howard Boroughs Library
Peter Sezzi

Virginia Tech
University Libraries

Washington and Lee University
University Library
Merrily E. Taylor

Wellesley College
Wellesley College Library
Eileen D. Hardy

Western Illinois University
Western Illinois University Libraries
Phyllis C. Self

Williams College
Williams College Libraries

Windward Community College
Library
Nancy A. Heu

Xavier University
McDonald Library
JoAnne Young

Yakima Valley Community College
Raymond Library
Joan Weber

Part I
Administrative Policies and Guidelines

Chapter 1

MISSION AND VISION STATEMENTS

MISSION STATEMENTS

Windward Community College
Kaneohe, Hawaii

Windward Community College Library is committed to providing exemplary services that foster information literacy and enhance teaching and learning, and to developing, organizing and maintaining resources that provide for diverse perspectives and styles of learning.

Tallahassee Community College
Tallahassee Community College Library
Tallahassee, Florida

The library, organized and managed for the user, serves as a learning resource center and, as such, provides the resources and services necessary to support the objectives of the College. The Library program exists to facilitate and improve learning and is an integral part of the instructional program. Its role in relationship to the educational objectives of the College is two-fold: (1) To provide an organized and readily accessible collection of materials and diversified forms of information and supportive equipment needed to meet the institutional, instructional, and individual requirements of the students and faculty. (2) To provide a variety of services to support and expand the instructional capabilities of the College. To accomplish its mission, the Division of Library Services does the following:

- Build collections (acquire, inventory, store, and make available), virtual and traditional, print and non-print materials which serve as resources for the College.
- Participate in networks, consortia and programs which promote resource sharing of collections and services.
- Provide instruction in research and information retrieval skills to prepare patrons for life-long learning.
- Offer services and hours which are responsive to the needs of the Campus community.
- Support the diverse research needs of the Campus community including specialized information services which are responsive to the diverse cultural and physical needs.
- Provide state-of-the-art facilities and other resources which utilize the latest development in instructional and information technology.
- Provide liaison services to faculty and other relevant groups and individuals within the Campus community.
- Serve as a center for life-long learning by providing information, activities and environments for independent study, self-directed, interactive and collaborative learning and professional development.

(For additional policies, please see the accompanying CD-ROM.)

VISION STATEMENTS

Emory and Henry College
Kelly Library
Emory, Virginia

Our vision is to provide life-long learning, information activities and environments for independent study and self-directed, interactive and collaborative learning. In partnership with the College faculty, we will support academic excellence for current and anticipated instructional programs. We will lead the College in the acquisition and management of information resources and in the creative and effective use of new technologies. We will serve as a student-centered library in which quality services and student success are primary goals recognized and shared by all staff.

Williams College
Williams College Library
Williamstown, Massachusetts

Vision Statement

Our Users:
- It is our goal to meet the educational and research needs of our primary users, Williams students, faculty, college departments and staff.
- We recognize the importance of sustaining mutually supportive relations with our secondary users, members of the community at large.
- We also recognize the value of nurturing productive reciprocal relationships with other libraries.
- As a depository for federal government publications, we recognize our obligation to make those materials fully accessible to the public.
- We respect the individuality of our users and acknowledge their cultural differences.

Our Collections:
- We value collections that facilitate and stimulate education and research.
- When selecting or retaining resources, we look for quality, utility, accessibility, stability and value.
- What we acquire and retain reflects the current curriculum as well as the selection choices of our predecessors and anticipates future intellectual inquiry.
- We seek to develop selective areas of strength and depth.
- Our collections represent a variety of viewpoints. We have a responsibility to acquire materials from alternative, non-mainstream publishers.
- We seek a balance between print and electronic resources. We understand that our historical print collections must continue to be developed even as we explore ways to best take advantage of electronic resources.
- Given the ever-expanding universe of information and the realities of limited space and budgets, we see shared, inter-institutional collection development and collaborative preservation initiatives as imperatives.

Our Services:
- We prize a welcoming atmosphere that is inviting to researchers and the enquiring community.
- We value the strength and depth of our collections and work proactively to encourage and facilitate their use.
- We want our users to be successful in their research and believe it is our mission to aid them in finding and accessing the information they require, both in our library and beyond.
- We believe in empowering the user—novice to expert—by providing assistance and instruction at the level required.

- We are interested in research as a process, and recognize that it is both a science and an art. We seek to provide the tools, the space and the moment for individuals and groups to pursue that process.
- We believe we should anticipate users' needs, and should take the initiative in informing them about the resources and services that are available.

Ourselves:
- We see ourselves, the library staff, as a vital resource and value personal contact with users.
- We value collaboration and rely on the varied knowledge and experience that individual staff members contribute.
- We strive to respond thoughtfully to innovations. We approach new ventures, systems and methods with an open yet critical mind.
- We seek to provide a physical environment that encourages research, quiet study, and learning.
- We understand the importance of continued learning and growth for all members of the staff. Opportunities for education and development are critical in ensuring that we provide the highest possible level of service.

Horry-Georgetown Technical College
Horry-Georgetown Technical College Library
Conway, South Carolina

Vision Statement

Horry-Georgetown Technical College Library strives to be an approachable, accessible organization that is sensitive to the needs of all users while providing a positive learning experience and fostering excitement in the process of discovery. The Library team of avid learners is highly trained, technologically sophisticated, and committed to the intellectual and structural life of the college. The Library promotes enlightenment, innovation and cooperation in the quest for excellence in our organization.

University of California Berkeley
University of California Berkeley Libraries
Berkeley, California

Collegiality and Cooperation

We work together to build a civil environment. We cooperate and support each other. We appreciate diversity.

We treat co-workers, clientele, subordinates and superiors the way we want to be treated, being mindful to respect cultural differences.

We show respect for each other by communicating in a friendly and courteous manner, listening attentively, encouraging the expression of differing points of view, and staying open to questions and opinions from others.

We work together by taking a library-wide perspective, basing discussions on facts rather than rumor, offering constructive criticism, seeking creative and practical solutions, committing ourselves to follow mutually agreed-upon methods and procedures and meeting agreed-upon deadlines.

Effective Communication

Regular and ongoing open communication occurs throughout the Library.

We are truthful, open and clear in our communication and respect confidentiality when appropriate.

We promptly report final decisions to those affected.

We respond to oral and written requests promptly, mindful that other's work may depend on our response.

We communicate information that is concise and accurate. Whenever possible, we make it available in time for those affected to have input.

We have a clear statement of the Library's ongoing and annual priorities.

We take responsibility for keeping apprised of what's happening in the Library (through reading committee and council minutes, CU NEWS, etc.).

We provide feedback on those issues that affect us or about which we have particular interest or expertise.

Excellence/Creativity

We pursue excellence and offer quality service within the context of the Library's stated needs and priorities.

We have clearly stated standards of excellence.

We regularly measure our performance against our standards of excellence.

We set realistic priorities among our tasks to ensure that the most important items can be performed to the Library's standards of excellence.

We develop and implement innovative models and standards in response to changes in our environment, providing leadership to the library and information community.

We recommend ways to improve policies and procedures that affect our work.

Fairness

Everyone is important and every part of the Library has an important function.

Within the Library, we seek to administer as equitably as possible the campus-based merit and bonus programs.

We conduct performance evaluations at least annually for all staff.

We evaluate performance based on clearly written standards.

We allocate resources according to the Library's stated priorities.

We expect the same standards of performance from library staff within the same personnel classification regardless of where they work.

We address behaviors inconsistent with the library standards and values in a respectful, constructive and straightforward way.

We have a clear system of appeal within the Library which an employee can use if s/he feels they have been treated unfairly.

Participatory Decision-Making

We value the opportunity to make decisions that directly affect our daily work.

As the environment changes (new projects, changes in personnel or workload, new decisions to be made,) we actively seek input from those who will be affected in order to both frame the problem and brainstorm potential solutions. Whenever possible, we allow time for give-and-take dialog on how best to proceed throughout the process.

We have a right to ask for the rationale behind decisions.

In making changes to workflow and workloads, we work together to adjust the priority on existing work.

Professional Growth and Development

We believe a highly skilled staff who are given opportunities and challenges are happier and more productive.

To support staff in being successful in their assigned duties, we provide training to all staff.

We have a professional development program to encourage all staff to obtain education needed to grow in our library careers.

As opportunities for career growth arise, eligible staff who are interested can apply and we supported their application.

Recognition

We value a clear and fair rewards policy and a competitive pay structure. We acknowledge each other's successes.

We wholeheartedly acknowledge jobs well done by individuals who excel in their work, regardless of their place in the hierarchy of the system.

We actively pursue a pay structure competitive with the market for all classifications represented in the Library.

We supplement campus compensation programs with celebrations and other forms of recognition to acknowledge outstanding achievements and longstanding contributions to the Library.

Safe, Comfortable and Healthy Work Environment

We provide a safe, comfortable and healthy environment for staff and users.

We have a clearly stated set of guidelines for what constitutes a safe and healthy work environment.

We have a library-wide program to regularly evaluate units and make corrections as needed.

We respond immediately and thoroughly to staff concerns about the work environment, taking action per advice of experts on campus when mitigation is needed.

(For additional policies, please see the accompanying CD-ROM.)

Chapter 2

Goals and Objectives

Cornell University
Cornell University Library
Ithaca, New York

GOAL I: Build the knowledge base of print, digital, and other materials using selection criteria that reflect 1) the academic priorities of the University, 2) significant research in all areas of study pursued at the University, and 3) current collection strengths.

1. Strengthen access to digital collections by:
   - allocation of funds and privileging electronic over print information when appropriate
   - innovative collaborations with information technology staff, publishers, consortia and other research institutions.

2. Expand and foster partnerships with the faculty to enhance access to scholarly information and to ensure the long-term preservation of that material.

3. Digitize library holdings.
   - Allocate annually a portion of the Library budget for digital conversion of analog holdings.
   - Select materials for digitization on the basis of their potential for broad utility, unique value of materials converted, reflection of core strengths of Cornell's holdings, and opportunities for building distinctive aggregations through national and international collaborations, with particular attention to projects that meet these criteria and have the potential to generate external support or to produce revenues from their use.
   - Investigate the extent and nature of use at Cornell and globally of Library digital collections currently available, incorporating these findings into the selection and design of new collections and the enhancement of existing sites.
   - Use evaluative tools to analyze and measure strengths and costs associated with various collections, taking into account the services (i.e. cataloging, digitization, etc.) associated with collection building.

GOAL II: Provide digital "life-cycle" production services.
   - Establish and maintain a central depository system capable of ensuring systematic management and long-term preservation and accessibility of digital collections.
   - Establish and operate a digitization service capable of converting a variety of textual, graphic image, and audiovisual objects to digital form and to contract for outside scanning when appropriate.
   - Establish and operate a "consulting to production" metadata service capable of producing metadata in a variety of formats to organize, manage, and preserve collections over time and to enable effective discovery and use.
   - Establish and operate a copyright service capable of ensuring adequate observance and protection of intellectual property rights and facilitating effective administration of our digital assets.
   - Instruct students, staff, and faculty in the use of available resources and tools facilitating the aggregation and organization of information and images.
   - Work with the university to establish a program to archive the university's electronic records.

GOAL III: Support electronic publishing, scholarly communication, and creative expression.

- Operate an electronic publishing program capable of systematic production and distribution of journals, monographs, and multimedia compositions and foster alternatives to conventional publishing.
- Build a discipline-based repository or repositories (math, physics, engineering, computer science, agriculture, law) that includes Cornell and non-Cornell resources, retrospective and current, commercial and nonprofit.
- Conduct a campus education program to increase awareness of issues relating to scholarly communication.
- Support innovative approaches to teaching, research, and creation, making the Library a site for exploration and experimentation.
- Selectively support Web authoring and electronic distribution and maintenance of information and image sources having broad educational use or unique value through collaborative endeavors.

GOAL IV: Support more effective organization and presentation of information for diverse audiences.

- Implement an integrated technological and methodological framework Library-wide, providing users with an integrated approach to discovery and use of Library resources and enhancing collection building and managerial efficiencies (e.g., Encompass).
- Make resources and services more visible and easier to find within Library buildings and on Library Web sites by employing appealing and engaging design techniques and intuitive navigational approaches.
- Pursue seamless linking between e-resources.
- Develop customized views and services for specific audiences, units, disciplines and genres.
- Integrate CU library sources, products and services into the CU information landscape.
- Provide users with the capability to create personalized views of the knowledge base.
- Develop enhanced services in support of social science and geospatial data.

GOAL V: Provide expert assistance, instruction, and an innovative suite of user services.

- Continue to build a distributed learning program supporting technology-based education.
- Expand document delivery capabilities, e.g., e-reserve, interlibrary loan and "borrow direct."
- Emphasize the role of librarians/information professionals/archivists as consultants and participants in the instructional and research programs of the University.
- Expand services in support of multimedia collections and production.
- Implement a system-wide chat reference service.
- Expand continuing education programs.
- Explore and develop 24/7 collaborative services.
- Implement software that supports push technologies so that users can get the information when and where they need it.
- Support the creation of an online version of every major exhibition mounted in the Library, incorporating additional materials, and instruction and exposition approaches not feasible in the physical exhibition.

GOAL VI: Create and maintain a physical environment that fosters learning and research through enhanced intellectual discourse and exploration.

- Agree on minimum standards and phase-in an implementation program to ensure all libraries provide a safe environment for both individuals and materials.
- Construct a second high-density storage module at the Library Annex in a timely manner, ensuring that this next module will be operational at the time it is initially needed.
- Phase in renovations in Olin and Uris libraries on the basis of the Shepley, Bulfinch, Richardson and Abbott reconceptualization study.

- Identify appropriate benchmarks for technological infrastructure needed to support multiple, and even unexpected, uses and provide resources to ensure that this level is available in all libraries.
- Create flexible spaces that by their size, furnishings, and orientation encourage exploration, innovation, and customization in all modes of information exchange, including individual, collaborative, and classroom.
- Conduct feasibility studies for unit libraries as appropriate.

GOAL VII: Foster an organizational culture that is agile, resilient and flexible, embraces change and encourages teamwork.

- Cultivate leadership skills that are focused and humane and that place a premium on cooperation across administrative lines.
- Identify the skills and resources needed for library innovation and develop new competencies by retraining and recruiting.
- Cultivate an understanding of CUL's goals and objectives and encourage staff participation in meeting these goals.
- Link performance evaluation system to achievements of master plan.
- Devise a more flexible reward system that recognizes both individual and team achievements.
- Revise CUL's organizational and committee structure to enhance effectiveness and to broaden participation.

GOAL VIII: Secure the resources to meet CUL's goals and objectives.

- Review current activities and expenditures to enhance efficiencies and to realign resources with new priorities.
- Determine the magnitude of the need—both one-time and ongoing—and establish a time frame for addressing it.
- Increase donor and external grant funding.
- Seek University financial support for selected new initiatives and building renovations.
- Establish a network of strategic partnerships to generate additional resources and share in the development and long-term maintenance of new services.
- Establish fee-based and cost-recovery mechanisms based on business plans and market assessments to support new services.

GOAL IX: Effectively market the library's products and services, and expand outreach to new and underrepresented constituencies.

- Conduct a needs assessment to understand our users and their needs and integrate the findings into annual planning process.
- Expand the number of programs, events, and exhibitions relating to authors, readers, and other library-related cultural activities that enhance the community's awareness of the Library's resources and services.
- Enhance user recognition of the Library as a virtual presence by "branding" the licensed resources and the digital collections made available through the Library.

GOAL X: Develop strategic alliances in support of CUL's goals and objectives.

- Expand joint initiatives and relationships with peer institutions.
- Expand relationships and joint projects with other Cornell University departments.
- Determine the strategic value of CUL's membership in regional, national, and international library consortia and organizations.

Ventura College
Evelyn and Howard Boroughs Library
Ventura, California

Library Goals and Objectives for 2003–2004

I. Support instructional programs and cultural activities of the college, both on and off campus, by providing excellent facility, collection, equipment, and staffing service.

A. Develop collection maximizing limited resources to 75,000 volumes by 2009

B. Build and equip new facility

- Continue working with contractor, architect, and project manager to solve construction problems as they arise
- Determine furniture and equipment to go into building
- Work with budget issues as they arise

C. Help students to become information literate

- Facilitate student access to information
- Move the library Web site to Library Corp to enhance its capabilities
- Create a single search engine for all VC library databases
- Computerize periodicals collection and tie into single search engine, putting entire periodical collection at the service of students
- Provide same resources to off-campus students as on-campus students
- Revise Library Orientation Course based on student and faculty evaluations
- Develop Web-based orientation for off-campus students
- Establish benchmarks and increase number of students who receive library orientation

D. Prepare for move to new facility

- Develop a self-check-out system for patrons
- Weed collection
- Decide what indexes, periodicals, etc. should be added, deleted, or moved to electronic vs. paper
- Plan for physical move and establish moving priorities
- Create a print vending plan
- Revise library card concept vs. ASB cards

E. Create operational East Campus Learning Resources Center

- Train staff
- Equip center
- Identify and move reference materials from campus library
- Provide online services to center-Smarthinking tutoring, electronic branch library services
- Create a benchmark to measure effectiveness of services in improving student learning

F. Spearhead cultural activities, including hosting Frankenstein exhibit

G. Stay abreast of technological changes in Learning Resources Areas

- Research latest technology and complete equipment list for new building and East Campus Learning Resources Center

II. Address budget shortfalls in Learning Resources Area to minimize impact on services

A. Attain outside resources for new facility

- VC Foundation campaign
- Book drive
- Grants and Endowments

B. Review current staffing and make adjustments as required

III. Evaluate library and learning resources services and use results in planning

A. Assess student learning in library

- Pilot classroom assessment technique after library orientations
- Do a student survey

B. Increase student satisfaction as measured on Student Perception Survey spring 2006 by 5 percent

C. Complete learning resources accreditation self study

Many of these goals have been accomplished through activities, which will be described throughout this self study.

Ventura College's learning resources include programs and services that support students and faculty. As described in the "Ventura College Learning Resources Brochure," they include the Library, the Tutoring Center, the Multimedia Resources Center (traditionally called Audio Visual Services), the Learning Center and the Staff Resource Center (IIC–3). The library and learning resources organizationally reside within the Liberal Arts and Learning Resources Division under the administration of the dean. Classified employees working in Learning Resources serve under the supervision of the learning resources supervisor. (Please see IIC–4 for the organizational structure of the college as a whole and IIC–5 for the library and learning resources organizational structure.)

Governance opportunities are defined by the organizational and committee structures of the College. Ventura College is committed to the full participation of students, faculty and staff in the governance of the college. Governance of the Library and Learning Resources reflects this philosophy and, according to the "Library Policy Manual," is executed by "three main entities which serve as an interactive network, working together to promote communication and to oversee operations, review policies, and improve library services and environment" (IIC–6). These include the library executive staff, which meets bi-weekly with the charge of providing leadership, managing daily operations, and initiating, implementing and evaluating policies, projects and procedures; the Library staff, which meets monthly with the charge of reviewing operational procedures, recommending policy, and providing frontline knowledge affecting the services of the library; and the Library Committee, which meets monthly with the charge of supporting and advocating for the library's overall interests and providing input on policies, procedures and services. The Library Committee is composed of faculty representatives from each division, student body representatives, and classified learning resources representatives.

GOALS IN STRATEGIC PLANNING

Augustana College
Thomas Tredway Library
Rock Island, Illinois

Strategic Plan

Objectives, Listed by Goal

Materials—Support and enrich each student's learning with the most educationally valuable resources in the most appropriate formats.

In response to changing curricular requirements (e.g. the Learning Communities and First Year Ages courses), select materials that support current and future needs.

Begin working internally and with faculty to determine additions to the collection that will be needed to support Senior Inquiry.

In consultation with the faculty, continue transition from paper to electronic format for many of our periodicals. Examine licenses for restrictions on ILL.

Develop a collection recovery plan.

Assess patrons' needs and quality of our collection building efforts by analyzing system reports of circulation and interlibrary loan data.)

Preservation of selected materials: migrate from obsolete to new formats.

Use statewide collection assessment data to establish a deselection plan.

Complete study of loss rate and security of materials

Organization—Make the library simple to use; describe and organize knowledge and information so that users can obtain resources in the most efficient manner.

Create online records of items in Special Collections.

Complete plan to reorganize and strengthen Special Collections, and submit to the Dean.

[Given the potential for increased use of Special Collections for Senior Inquiry projects, the two goals listed above have become even more important.]

Explore whether current or potential "pockets" in the collection should be changed. (e.g., Teaching Collection, video collection)

Implement link resolver and federated search software to increase ease of access to online journals.

Complete off-campus Web access for as many databases as possible.

Review the purpose, presentation, and development of research guides.

Implement improved "New Book" and video lists on the website.

Investigate open URL links to Google Scholar; implement if appropriate.

Service—Deliver coordinated, consistent, and high quality service that is responsive to the Augustana College community and to other library users.

Explore new ways of evaluating our services.

Collaborate with faculty and ITS staff regarding use of Moodle and reserve readings.

Analyze our Friday and Saturday open hours and our reference hours.

Provide an all-staff in-service activity on individual strengths and teamwork.

Establish library liaisons to non-academic departments (e.g., Career Center).

Develop Library award for inclusion in Honors Convocation.

Teaching—Collaborate with the faculty to teach each Augustana student to locate, evaluate, and use information effectively.

Integrate information literacy into upper level curriculum planning.

Begin working internally and with faculty to determine what kind of librarian teaching and consultation that will be needed to support Senior Inquiry.

Compile an online collection of information literacy assignments and other materials for faculty.

Conduct organized discussions of teaching on a regular basis.

Continue integration of Special Collections into courses.

With other faculty, develop a TRAC or similar program about our integration of information literacy into the curriculum.

Develop tutorial for training Circulation student workers and evaluate its success.

Explore ways in which the library can support lifelong learning and the liberal arts (e.g., Web site).

Place—Develop the library not only as a repository of resources or a gateway to information, but as a place where faculty, staff, and students communicate and collaborate intellectually, culturally, and socially; enhance the library to best support Augustana's goals of academic excellence and student growth.

Revise and update Library Safety Manual.

Revise method of doing patron count to identify how space is currently used.

Set up and announce 2nd floor periodical reading area.

Expand/improve use of technology and wireless access throughout the library.

As part of Augustana's strategic goal to enhance existing facilities: Investigate ways in which other libraries use their space in order to develop a plan for changing our space usage.

Community—Contribute to the development of the Augustana College community by participating in its curricular and co-curricular activities, and in its connections to the greater community.

Develop "Artful Library" and Jewish literature projects (05–06) and possibly "Year of the Book" (06–07) project.

Review campus community projects. (e.g., quotation contest, Week 7 seminar)

Collaborate with regional public libraries and historical societies via Upper Mississippi Valley Digital Archive project.

Maintain display of faculty publications.

Prepare for North Central Review in 2005 and organize evidence room.

Communication— Inform the college community what we do and why; engage the members of that community in using library services, thereby promoting the integration of intellectual inquiry, academic excellence, and respect for diversity into the fabric of Augustana College.

Use the library newsletter and Web site to communicate with the Augustana community.

Work with Office of Communication and Publications.

Develop a "marketing" plan, both internal and external.

Improve internal communication.

Develop Library annual report.

Develop online Library bulletin board.

Replace or fix signage in elevators and on 2nd floor.

Investigate use of blogs.

Investigate development of Web page on librarianship as career.

Professional Development—Participate in professional communities and activities in order to strengthen the services of the library and their support of academic excellence.

Attend Oberlin Group of Library Directors meeting.

Hold office in IL Association of College and Research Libraries.

Serve on boards of and advisory committees to IL library consortia.

Attend online and in-person professional seminars.

Attend numerous consortia committee and membership meetings, including CARLI (IL academic libraries), local system, OCLC, and others.

Submit publications and presentations to appropriate journals and groups.

(For additional policies, please see the accompanying CD-ROM.)

Chapter 3

GIFTS AND DONATIONS

ADMINISTRATIVE PROCEDURES

Acceptance Policy Statement

Queens College CUNY
Rosenthal, Library
Flushing, New York

Why Support the Library

Queens College, which former New York Governor George Pataki has hailed as the "Jewel of the City University," is committed to providing a first class education to talented students of all ethnic and socio-economic backgrounds. The College Library supports the liberal arts curriculum and professional studies with print and electronic resources, services, and instruction in information literacy.

Like most academic libraries in the U.S., we face many challenges, including:

- The rapid rise in the cost of Journals, books and electronic resources essential for the research needs of students and faculty.
- A continuous decrease in State funding.
- The need to incorporate emerging technologies.
- An aging and deteriorating print collection in need of replacement.

To meet these challenges, the Library depends on private donations from alums, members of the College community and the community at large. Donors may choose from the following giving opportunities: Cash gifts, donate for books, endowments, deferred gifts, or they can donate collections of books to the Library. However you choose to support the Library, whether you establish an endowment or donate for one book, you will become a member of the Queens College Community and will join in the educational process of generations of students.

Centre College
Grace Doherty Library
Danville, Kentucky

The Grace Doherty Library welcomes gifts of books and other library materials suitable to an academic library. In past years important additions to our collection have come through the generosity of donors. Also, the library welcomes direct donations of money to aid in collection and services development.

At the same time, we want prospective donors to understand why we cannot promise to add all gifts to the permanent collection. While some old books are valuable, most are not, especially in fields where information rapidly becomes outdated. Each book acquired costs a substantial sum to catalog and takes up expensive storage space in our automated catalog. Also, shelving space is limited and new shelving expensive. Thus we naturally wish to add to the collection only those books that students and faculty will find useful.

We request, therefore, that anyone who wishes to give books to Doherty Library will either allow a member of the library staff to examine the books first or will provide us with a list of authors, titles, and dates of publication. We can then select those books that will strengthen our holdings. If the donor wishes us to dispose of others we cannot use, we shall do so by selling or passing along the books to other libraries. As the last resort, we will discard them.

The library staff regrets that it does not have the time, expertise, or indeed the legal authority to appraise the value of gift books for tax deduction purposes. A letter of thanks, acknowledging the receipt of gift books, will be sent.

Similarly, we are generally unable to purchase specific books with gift money. If the donor expresses an interest in a specific subject area, we will make every attempt to purchase a scholarly title in that field.

All books purchased with gift money or with memorial gifts will be gift-plated appropriately. We will send a letter of thanks to the donor and identify the book or books purchased.

We trust that this statement of policy will in no way discourage library supporters from contacting the library about possible gifts. The college needs and appreciates the support of Centre friends and alumni in our common effort to make Doherty Library worthy of the institution it serves.

University of Pittsburgh
Pitt Digital Library
Pittsburgh, Pennsylvania

University Library System Gift and Exchange

The University Library System (ULS) seeks to provide access to the informational resources necessary to fulfill the academic, research, artistic, scholarly and community leadership objectives of the university. In seeking to meet its mission, the ULS tries to enhance collections and services through gifts of library materials, unique gifts-in-kind, and money for purchases and operations. The following guidelines for gifts of materials to the ULS have been developed to acquaint the potential donor with the policies of the library in accepting gifts, the federal regulations regarding gifts for tax purposes and appraisal of gifts of library materials.

The information contained in these pages is general in nature and does not constitute legal, tax or other advice. You should consult with your own legal, tax or other advisor(s) to obtain advice on how the applicable laws might affect you.

General Guidelines

The University Library System welcomes in-kind donations (books, journals, etc.), in good condition that fall within the scope of its collection and support its mission. For a description of items of interest to us as well as the types of material we will not accept, please see our Frequently Asked Questions page.

The University Library System understands all gifts to be unrestricted, and gift items are reviewed in accordance with the current policies for collection development. Gift items that are determined to be duplicate copies or outside the scope of our collections may be exchanged, sold, or discarded.

Consistent with federal law and to protect the interest of both donors and the institution, the staff members of the University Library System will not appraise gifts. Arrangements and costs for appraisals are the responsibility of the donor.

Georgia State University
Georgia State University Library
Atlanta, Georgia

The Georgia State University Library welcomes gifts of library materials—especially materials that fill existing gaps in our collection and support the curriculum. Donations of library materials to the University Library are made to the Georgia State University Foundation, Inc. The Collection Development Department of the University Library acts on the Foundation's behalf by receiving the gifts, overseeing their disposition, and providing donation records.

Donated materials are evaluated by the same standards and collecting policies as purchased materials. Because of space limitations and processing costs, many gift items are not added to our collection. These include:

- Textbooks
- Duplicate titles
- Previous editions
- Material in poor physical condition

Materials not added to the University Library are disposed of by some other means. We cannot guarantee to add unsolicited gifts. The University Library reserves the right to accept or decline any gift of materials.

Interested donors are requested to submit a list of the item(s) to be donated (including relevant information such as: author, title, publisher, edition and date of publication). The donor will be contacted as soon as the list has been evaluated, at which time they can bring the items that have been accepted to Collection Development. A gifts receipt form acknowledging the number of donated items is available at the time of donation, with one copy to go to the donor for her/his records.

Library staff cannot appraise donations as this must be done by book dealers or antiquarians to satisfy IRS guidelines. Ordinarily, the Collection Development Department cannot pick up donations, as we lack the equipment, staff, and time to perform this task. Donors should contact the Collection Development Office for details.

Acceptance Terms

Manatee Community College
Manatee Community College Library
Bradenton, Florida

Library Gift Policy

The authority to accept gifts rests with the Library Collection Development Committee.

Physical condition of materials will be a factor in the decision, as well as the other materials selection guidelines.

The Manatee Community College Library retains the right to dispose of gift material, including books, magazines, or audiovisuals, if after examination they do not meet selection guidelines.

Persons donating materials to the Manatee Community College Library may sign a release/acceptance letter at the time of donation. The Manatee Community College Library does not appraise gifts for tax purposes.

All monetary gifts to the Manatee Community College Library should be directed through the Manatee Community College Foundation Office.

University of Idaho
University of Idaho Libraries
Moscow, Idaho

Conditions

The Library becomes the owner of the gift upon receipt. UI Library reserves the right to determine retention, location, and other use or disposal of gifts. Gifts which are useful to the teaching, research and goals of the University, and which do not unnecessarily duplicate the library holdings, will be retained. Discarded materials are sold, transferred, or recycled.

Appraisal of Gift Value

Cornell University
Cornell University Library
Ithaca, New York

Appraisal

The Library encourages donors to consider, for their own interest, obtaining an appraisal of their gifts for income tax purposes. Such appraisals are the responsibility of the donor and should be made, if possible, before the gifts are transferred to Cornell in order to establish their fair market value. The Internal Revenue Service considers the Library to be an interested party which therefore precludes appraisals made or financed by Cornell. For this reason, donors must bear the costs of appraisal, but the costs may be deductible expenses. As income and estate tax laws are subject to frequent revision, Cornell recommends that donors discuss gifts-in-kind appraisals with their attorneys. The Library is willing to help by suggesting appropriate professional appraisers who might be consulted, or by arranging for third-party appraisals after receipt of the gift in the library. The acceptance of a gift which has been appraised by a disinterested party does not in any way imply endorsement of the appraisal by the Library.

University of Illinois at Urbana-Champaign
University Library
Urbana, Illinois

Appraisal of Donations

Potential donors must be advised that UIUC librarians cannot make a monetary appraisal of donated materials, because such an appraisal constitutes a conflict of interest. The AUL for Collections and the Rare Book and Special Collections Librarian can suggest outside agencies that potential donors may contact for an appraisal. In addition, donors can be advised that many services exist on the Internet that may help them place a value on their donations. The AUL for Collections, the Acquisitions Librarian or the Rare Book and Special Collections Librarian can provide current suggested sites and work with the donor as needed to guide him or her through the appraisal process. [Provide a link to the Collections Web site and a list of places to identify appraisers as well as general information on how donors can develop their own appraisals for gift less than $5,000.]

Although the Library does not provide appraisals of gifts in kind, the University does require an inventory of all gifts that are accepted for our collection, including an assessment of the value of the gift. For the many gifts that come to the Library in small lots, the Library Business Office uses a formula annually to account for the added value to the Library collections. For gifts that require a Deed of Gift, the AUL for Collections, in consultation with subject specialists, supplies an approximate assessed value.

In most circumstances, donors are responsible for sending gifts to the Library. In certain cases, the Library will pay for packing and shipping of gift items. These arrangements should be made through the Library Business Office, which works with the campus to identify the most cost-efficient and effective carrier for the donation. The AUL for Collections and the Rare Book and Special Collections Librarian can advise on situations when these costs should be borne by the Library.

Gift Transportation

Bethel College
Bethel College Library
North Newton, Kansas

Pick-up and Delivery of Donated Material

Library staff are available to pick up donations. If you would prefer to bring donations to the Library, you may come to the back (north side) of the building, park your car, and either bring the materials into the

Library yourself or request assistance at the Circulation Desk. We ask that you bring in donations during daytime hours (8 a.m.–5 p.m.) unless you have made prior arrangements with a librarian. Make sure you leave your name and address with library staff so that we can acknowledge your gift.

We will accept books on all subjects and in English, German, and Spanish. We also accept audio and videotapes, CDs, and periodicals. Please check with librarians, however, before delivering extensive periodical runs.

Brown University
Brown University Library
Providence, Rhode Island

Transportation and Arrangements

The Gifts Librarian can help a donor with the logistics of getting donated materials to Brown. Gifts arrive by mail, are hand-delivered to the Library, or in the case of large or very valuable gifts, arrangements can be made for a representative of the Library to pick them up. Instructions for packing gifts and making arrangements for their transportation can be obtained from the Gifts Librarian.

Tax Deduction

Brown University
Brown University Library
Providence, Rhode Island

Tax Deductions

As with most charitable donations, gifts to the Library are tax deductible to the extent of the law. The value of a monetary gift is self-evident, but an accountant or tax-preparer's advice is often useful in determining whether a gift in kind requires professional appraisal. As a rule, the value of small gifts and non-rare materials can be estimated for tax purposes; larger gifts and items or collections of significant value require appraisal by a qualified professional. Depending on the dollar amount at which the gift is valued, completion and signature of the IRS form 8283 may be required. In this case, the University fills out and countersigns section IV, attesting that the gift has been received.

Terms of Gift Acknowledgements

California State University Long Beach
University Library
Long Beach, California

Acknowledgement of Gifts

Donors must realize that the library is obligated by IRS regulations to adhere to strict guidelines with regard to donations of information resources to its collections.

The library can acknowledge only those items which it will catalog and retain in its collection for a minimum of two years. If a collection is donated, and only a portion of that collection is needed by the library, only those items which are needed will be cataloged and acknowledged.

Acknowledgement of a gift normally will be limited to a numerical count and very general description of materials received, e.g. "twelve volumes of U.S. History."

Gift value is established by the donor; no formal or informal valuation can be provided by the library; in accord with IRS regulations, gifts valued at $5000 and above should be independently appraised.

Eventual resale, exchange, donation, or recycling of unneeded materials (after the two year minimum retention period) is at the library's discretion.

There will be no acknowledgement of donations which are brought to the library without prior arrangements; such items will be disposed of in the most cost-effective manner possible.

University of Illinois at Urbana-Champaign
University Library
Urbana, Illinois

Acknowledgements

Donors are to be sent written acknowledgements in a timely fashion, unless they specifically request that no acknowledgement be made. Donors frequently use acknowledgements for tax purposes—this expectation along with the development of good donor relations requires that acknowledgements be made as soon as possible after a gift is received. For smaller gifts, the subject librarian or receiving unit may use the Gifts Receipt form to provide written documentation for the donor as well as the Library. The subject librarian may also choose to write an acknowledgement letter containing the same kind of information that is found on the form, including a listing or count of the donation, the date the items were received, information about the possible disposition of the material, and income tax issues. Acknowledgements should include a description of the material that has been donated, including quantity. The Office of the Director of Development and Public Affairs must be notified of all gifts accepted, and given a copy of any acknowledgement letters, as well as details of any agreements made with the donors. It is not necessary to provide the Office of Collections with a copy of acknowledgements, as this Office works closely with the Development Office on gifts. The AUL for Collections will notify the Director of Development and Public Affairs of materials accepted through his/her office.

University of Idaho
University of Idaho Libraries
Moscow, Idaho

Acknowledgments

A letter acknowledging each donation and specifying the number and type of items presented is sent to every donor. A copy of the letter is sent to the UI Foundation. Their response includes a "no stated worth" declaration unless the donor provides an estimate of worth at the time of donation.

Bookplates

Upon request a bookplate may be added to items recognizing the benefactor or honoree.

Donor Privileges

Queens College CUNY
Rosenthal, Library
Flushing, New York

Privileges

Anyone who donates $50 or more to the Library is entitled to borrowing privileges. Whether donations are made through the Queens College Foundation (for the Library), the Alumni Office, or in the Library, donors are asked to consult the Library Circulation Desk to receive their borrowing card.

Donors are invited to a special reception held annually in April, during National Library Week in their honor. Donors receive copies of Page Down, the Library Newsletter with updates on new services, print collections, electronic resources, and cultural events.

Gift Materials Disposition

Wellesley College
Wellesley College Library
Wellesley, Massachusetts

Disposition of Gift Materials

1. With the exception of some archival materials, all books added to the collection will bear a bookplate indicating the donor's name.
2. With the exception of some archival materials, all gifts added to the collection will be cataloged and listed in the Library's online public catalog.
3. Since all gift materials that are added to the general collections are shelved in the appropriate subject classification, the Library cannot maintain separate named collections.
4. Gifts that are not added to the collection may be disposed of in one of the following ways:

   • If it has been arranged in advance, they may be returned to donor.
   • If of artifactual value, they may be sold to a specialty book dealer, and the proceeds used to support future acquisitions.

   In cases where other institutions have teaching or collecting goals which the gift more appropriately supports, these institutions may be offered the gift. The first preference is to place the item in one of the member libraries of the Boston Library Consortium, to which Wellesley College belongs.
   All other unaccessioned gifts will be sold, at nominal prices, at the periodic books sales held for the students and faculty of the College. The proceeds will be used to support future acquisitions.
5. Donors who offer items or collections that Wellesley cannot accept may be referred to other libraries or to book donation programs such as the following:

   Hands Across The Water (www.surplusbooksforcharity.org/) is a Massachusetts book collection charity that promotes literacy and education. The organization provides books to needy schools, libraries and other community-based nonprofit organizations in the US and overseas. The Web site has a list of drop-off locations throughout the state.

   The University of Buffalo Health Sciences Library (http://ublib.buffalo.edu/libraries/units/hsl/ donationprograms.html) maintains a Web site that provides contact information on nonprofit agencies that manage donation programs that distribute books, journals and media in all subject areas to foreign countries.

University of Idaho
University of Idaho Libraries
Moscow, Idaho

Saleable books and journals that the Library cannot use are disposed of by:

Sales lists

Sales lists are organized by category. Categories include Monographs (mono77), Geology, Special, Serial, and Exchange (excgg). The sales lists are in Adobe PDF format.

Generally, these materials have a minimum bid of $2.00 for hardback and $1.00 for paperback, and are sold within a month to the highest bidder. Payments are made by check to the University of Idaho Library. Contact the Gift Supervisor to be placed on a mailing list of sales items.

UI Library Lobby Sales Shelf

Located south of the Reference Desk on first floor, the sales shelf contains books not wanted in the collection (books that do not sell on the Sales lists, withdrawals from the Library, and books in poor repair). Most of these books are priced below $1.00. Depending on supply, books are added daily. Also found on the sales shelf are boxes of free government documents and small publications. Payment is made at the Circulation Desk.

Other Sales or Free Items

A large selection of *National Geographic* magazines is for sale. *National Geographic* issues are $.25 apiece to individuals—free to schools and libraries. For further information contact the Gift Supervisor.

The Library provides a limited selection of free journals for projects requiring journal photographs or text. Patrons given discarded journals must agree to complete their projects elsewhere. No journals (including discarded journals) may be cut or defaced while in the library. For more information contact Periodical Service Center or the Gift Supervisor.

Goucher College
Julia Rogers Library
Baltimore, Maryland

Disposition of Out-of-Scope Materials

In order to make the most efficient use of library resources, donated materials will be evaluated for content that documents the college's history or supports its current and evolving curriculum and research needs. The library reserves the right to dispose of gifts that are duplicates or irrelevant to the collections, according to policies set by Goucher College. This may include sale, donation, transfer to another Goucher College department or academic institution or recycling.

Special Gift Categories

Endowments

University of Washington
University of Washington Libraries
Seattle, Washington

Endowments

Currently the University Libraries holds over 30 endowments, created at the direction of the donor, to support a variety of collections and interests relating to wide range of areas including the Pacific Northwest, Chinese studies, health sciences, business, art, Scandinavian studies, history, and music. Endowments are established in perpetuity: only the income generated from the endowment's principal is used by the Libraries. Benefits continue year after year, because the principal is invested while only part of the income generated is spent. This stable base of resources allows for a rich variety of activities such as support for distinguished Librarians and scholarships for talents students and support for the enhancement of new programs, collections and reference materials not otherwise funded.

Brown University
Brown University Library
Providence, Rhode Island

Making a Gift to the Brown University Library

Gifts to the Brown University Library are not only vital to the Library's excellence, but are easy to make and may carry distinct advantages for the donor. The following information will be of interest to those considering making a gift to the University Library. Monetary contributions of all sizes are welcome, from pocket change dropped into the 'cracked pots' on Carberry Day to the million-dollar endowment established to support a particular subject of study. Establishing an endowed named Library fund for any purpose requires a minimum gift of $25,000. Endowed funds are used in various ways, depending on the wishes of the donor and the needs of the Library. Endowments can be used for the unrestricted acquisition of books and other formats, or for the support of operating expenses and special projects. For example, this year a $100,000 endowment produced income of about $5,000, which translates into 100 books at $50, the average price of a scholarly imprint.

By the same token, a $1 million endowment generates approximately $50,000 annually, with which the Library might purchase 1,000 books at that price. Support for the collections has been the primary focus of the endowments, but funds aimed at capital projects provide necessary support for equipment and activities, as well as for staff. In addition to monetary gifts, gifts in kind also help support the collections. Books, manuscripts, maps, works of art, sound recordings and other media have found a welcoming home at Brown. Many people choose to remember the Library in their wills; a lawyer's advice and help is essential in this matter. The Library appreciates notice of a donor's intentions, either through a copy of the relevant clause in the will or through a letter stating this intention

(For additional policies, please see the accompanying CD-ROM.)

Monetary Donations

California State University Long Beach
University Library
Long Beach, California

Gifts of Money

The library welcomes gifts of money designated for the purchase of library materials. A donor may contribute to the Library Book Endowment, a large fund whose interest is used for new book purchases, or he/she may request that the gift be spent in a particular way: for the support of the Masback Science Fiction Collection, for example, or to buy books in British Colonial History. Memorial donations ("in honor of," "in memory of") are welcome and can be acknowledged through a bookplate placed in the items purchased. Checks should be made payable to "CSULB Foundation." Gifts of money designated for the purchase of information resources may grow out of a relationship between an alumnus/alumna or other benefactor and an academic department or program. Development credit for a cash gift accrues jointly and equally to the college which contacted or cultivated the donor and to the library. The library has sole discretion regarding the disposition of the funds donated, however, whenever the donor has stipulated that they are to be used to purchase library materials.

It also is possible to make money donations by credit card, using the CSULB Foundation's online form for this purpose: www.csulb.edu/divisions/urad/giving/transport.htm

Be sure to designate the University Library as the recipient of the donation.

Northern Arizona University
Cline Library
Flagstaff, Arizona

If Cline Library is to maintain its quality service programs and collections, financial support will be crucial. Gifts to the Library have a far-reaching impact. You can help ensure the preservation of a legacy of learning for future generations by making a monetary contribution to one or more of the following funds:

Library Fund

Supports the achievement of the Library's goals through providing funding for the materials, initiatives and activities of Cline Library.

Special Collections and Archives

Donations to this fund support access to the Library's Colorado Plateau and University Archives collections through the digitization and preservation of manuscripts, photographs, and historic film footage; the collection, transcription, and digitization of oral history interviews; the acquisition of archival collections and books which trace the history and development of the Colorado Plateau region; and the preparation of public exhibits.

Dean's Innovation Fund

Provides the Library with the flexibility to pursue emerging technologies and seed new projects that have the potential to greatly advance the Library's mission.

Library Book Fund

Provides funding for books in support of the University's curriculum and mission.

Make your gift online or send a cash gift by mail, designating a special fund if you wish.

In-kind Gifts

University of Washington
University of Washington Libraries
Seattle, Washington

In-kind Gifts

In-kind gifts of items such as books, journals, manuscripts, photographs, historic maps, unique materials, etc. are also welcome, as they help develop the size, depth and diversity of our resources. The donor may elect to have such contributions independently appraised to establish value for tax purposes. Please call for information on appraised gifts and collections.

In-kind Gifts (non-appraised)

If the donor is not interested in acquiring an appraisal for tax purposes, further information on how to contribute these in-kind gifts can be found at: www.lib.washington.edu/gifts/

Weber State University
Stewart Library
Ogden, Utah

The Stewart Library has, with great gratitude, accepted from various individuals materials in all formats for its collections. Although we are appreciative of any gift tendered to us, our general policy is to accept and add to the collection only those items which have relevance to our collections and the potential for use.

In most cases it is not possible for library personnel to inventory the items in a tendered gift prior to accepting it. Therefore, we must accept gifts with the express understanding that items not placed in the collection will be made available for return to the donor; and, if not returned, may be otherwise utilized or disposed of at the library's discretion. Most often, items not added to the collection are sold at the library's annual book sale. The funds from the sale are then used to purchase materials for the collections.

Normally, we cannot offer to donors estimates of monetary value (presumably for tax purposes) in exchange for gifts-in-kind. On the rare occasions when it appears that items have particularly high monetary value, together with relevance to the collections, a third-party or published estimate of monetary value may be given at the discretion of the University Librarian. In the cases of third-party estimates, the cost of obtaining an estimate may have to be borne in whole or in part by the donor.

The above does not in any way obviate our appreciation for the thoughtfulness and generosity of those considering a gift-in-kind to the Stewart Library.

Gifts Deeded

University of Illinois at Urbana-Champaign
University Library
Urbana, Illinois

Deeds of Gift

The Deed of Gift is a document that conveys the gift material to the Library without any encumbrances, including copyright or ownership issues. It spells out any terms or conditions of the gift and provides a clear title to the material. If a gift is potentially valued at $5,000 or more, a Deed of Gift is required. The Library Development can prepare these Deeds of Gift. For more information, check the Office of Collections Gifts Web site [www.library.uiuc.edu/administration/collections/gifts].

The unit accepting a gift that requires a Deed must notify the Library Development Office of the gift at the time the gift is accepted. In addition, the receiving library can work with the donor to identify an appropriate appraiser (contact the AUL for Collections, the Rare Book and Special Collections Librarian, or the University Archivist, as appropriate, for help in identifying appraisers.) The Library Development Office is responsible for issuing the Deed of Gift, in consultation with the University Librarian, the AUL for Collections and the Library faculty member in charge of the unit where the collection be will located. The Library Development Office keeps the master files on these gifts.

Gift Books

University of South Alabama
University Libraries
Mobil, Alabama

Gift Books

The University of South Alabama Library welcomes gifts of books, printed matter, and other materials which enhance the collection of the University Library, contribute to the store of scholarly knowledge, and aid instructional and research goals. Donations will be carefully reviewed by specialists for possible addition to the collection. All gifts become the property of the University Library for its disposal in the interests of the Library. They may be added to the collection, exchanged, sold or otherwise handled at the Library's discretion. However, the Library will take into account the owner's wishes.

If declining a gift should be necessary, the Library will make suggestions for alternative recipients such as libraries, schools, hospitals, charitable organizations, etc.

Donors may write or telephone the Coordinator of Collection Management when they would like to make a donation. The donor will be told where to deliver materials. Transportation to pick up boxed materials can be arranged.

Acknowledgments

The Dean of the University Libraries will send a written acknowledgment of the gift. Name, full address and phone number of donor should be included with the gift. The Coordinator of Collection Management is pleased to certify acceptance of a donor-prepared itemized list.

Donors frequently wish to claim income tax credit for their gift. The University is prohibited by law and policy from appraising such gifts. There are knowledgeable appraisers who may be able to help in establishing the value of materials. The Library may be able to assist in locating such people. Donors should see a tax expert for answers to questions concerning gifts. Internal Revenue publications, which may be obtained online, at the local office or by writing the IRS, will assist in these matters. Changes in tax law may affect previous practices and procedures.

FORMS
Library Donation Form

Grand Valley State University
Zumberge Library
Allendale, MI

Acquisitions Policy for Accepting Donations to GVSU Libraries Collection

Donations are accepted from the university community and the general public with the following restrictions:

- No textbooks
- No complimentary desk copies
- No trade paperbacks
- No sound recordings
- No outdated science or health material
- No sheet music
- No incomplete or broken sets
- No incomplete media kits
- No materials in poor physical shape

Donations requiring a letter for tax purposes must be received by November 1. Donations MUST be accompanied by a *Declaration Of Release* form.

Declaration of Release

Please fill in the following information and attach it to your donation.
Mr./Mrs./Ms.

Address:

hereby relinquish any and all claim to the following gift(s): *(listing items is optional)*

Number   Types of Items

Given to Grand Valley State University Libraries on
with the full understanding that:

1. According to IRS regulations, the University, including Library personnel, are unable to supply monetary evaluation of the gift; and
2. The donor will supply a valuation appraisal if the gift has value of $5000 or more.

I **do/do not** [*circle one*] want an acknowledgement of the gift. The University Libraries will provide a letter stating the actual items that were added to the collection.

I **do/do not** [*circle one*]want to be notified of the items not added to the collection so that I might pick them up.

Acquisitions Department _____

_____

[Donor's signature]

Transfer of Ownership Form

University of California Berkeley
University of California Berkeley Libraries
Berkeley, California

PRINT, FILL this form, & BRING with you to our office.

Architecture Visual Resources Library

Deed of Gift to Regents of the University of California

I (we)

Of (address)

Am (are) the owners(s) of the property described below (attach additional pages if needed):

I (we) desire to transfer said property as a gift to The Regents of the University of California for the benefit of the Architecture Visual Resources Library, University of California, Berkeley.

I (we) do hereby irrevocably assign, transfer, and give all my (our) copyright rights, title, and interest that I (we) possess in this materials to The Regents.

Should I (we) not agree to transfer and assign all copyrights, I do give permission to the Visual Resources Library to make this material available according to the established Visual Resources Library procedures for instruction, research, and other fair use purposes.

Are the materials restricted in any way? _____ No _____ Yes. If yes, please describe:

Date:_____

Signed:_____

Donor

Address:_____

City:_____

State, Zip:_____

Telephone: _____

Email:_____

The Architecture Visual Resources Library hereby gratefully accepts this gift to The Regents of the University of California subject to the conditions specified.

Date: _____   Signed: _____

Librarian, Visual Resources Library

Chapter 4

FRIENDS OF THE LIBRARY

GENERAL FUNCTIONS

University of Scranton
Weinberg Memorial Library
Scranton, Pennsylvania

The University of Scranton's Web site is changing, and policies will be separated from information on the updated site.

Friends of the Weinberg Memorial Library: To apply for membership in the Friends of the Weinberg Memorial Library Group, complete the membership form available at the Circulation and/or Reference Desks or online from the Friends of the Weinberg Memorial Library page. In addition to unlimited borrowing privileges, Friends receive invitations to Library programs and events; preview book sales; and have the opportunity to volunteer to work on special projects in support of Library programs and services. Student members of the Friends are limited to five (5) books out in Circulation at any one time.

Benefits to Members

Use of the Weinberg Memorial Library with circulation privileges.

Access to a variety of electronic databases.

Ten percent discount at the University of Scranton Bookstore (excluding textbooks).

Invitations to Friends of the Library programs and events throughout the year: lectures, exhibits, and cultural and social events.

Preview notices of Friends of the Library book sales.

Participation in the building of an endowment in the name of the Friends of the

Harry and Jeanette Weinberg Memorial Library to purchase special gifts for the Weinberg Library collection.

Receipt of Information Update, a quarterly newsletter of information about the Weinberg Memorial Library, books, authors, publishing, printmaking, bookbinding and the Friends.

Your membership listed in Information Update.

Recognition with a special bookplate for titles purchased for the Library by the Friends.

Distinctive keepsake bookmark for gifts of $100 or more.

Opportunity for volunteers to work in support of library programs and services.

Recognition in the annual Donor Report produced by the University of Scranton Institutional Advancement Office.

CONSTITUTION AND BYLAWS

Franklin and Marshall College
Franklin and Marshall College Library
Lancaster, Pennsylvania

The Friends of the Library at Franklin & Marshall College was organized in October 1986 as a prelude to the bicentennial celebration of the College. The purpose of the Friends is to advance the Library as a cultural and historical resource both within the College and in the larger community by providing support for development of library collections beyond the confines of the instructional program. We hope, moreover, to instill among the students who pass through its doors a sense of the Library as something more than a place to study and a warehouse of books.

Books, however, are uppermost on the agenda of the Friends. The primary use of membership dues is for books and manuscripts whose acquisition would not normally be possible using the funds supplied by the College for regular library purchases. These may include examples of contemporary book making from small presses, additions to established rare books and manuscript collections (such as the Unger-Bassler Collection of German Americana), or simply desirable works too expensive to be purchased otherwise.

The activities of the Friends include public lectures featuring speakers who address a variety of topics relating to books, libraries, collecting and preservation. Members of the Friends of the Library also receive borrowing privileges to all circulating library collections. In-library Internet access is limited to the domains .edu, .gov and .mil.

Friends must be 21 years of age. Membership is open to all who wish to consider themselves Friends of the Franklin & Marshall College Library in the following membership categories:

Active $25.00
Senior $5.00
Contributing $50.00
Sustaining $100.00
Patron $250.00 and above
F & M Student $5.00

The membership year begins January 1. Initial membership beginning after July will run until the second succeeding year.

MEMBERSHIP APPLICATIONS

University of Scranton
Weinberg Memorial Library
Scranton, Pennsylvania

The University of Scranton's Web site is changing, and policies will be separated from information on the updated sites.

Friends of Weinberg Memorial Library

Member Application

Title:_____

Given Name:_____   Family Name:_____
Address:_____
_____
Telephone (Home):_____   (Business):_____
Email Address:_____
would like to apply for (please circle):

- Student—$10/year
- Individual—$25/year
- Renewal

- Family—$35/year
- Corporate—$500/year
- Other

Make checks payable to Friends of the Library.

Chapter 5

PERSONNEL

STAFF COMPETENCIES AND TRAINING

Staff Standards

Rutgers University
Rutgers University Libraries
Newark, New Jersey

Librarian Competencies—All librarians providing reference service will attempt to adhere to the highest standards of knowledge and proficiency. All public service librarians must have knowledge of the following:

- The reference collection
- Library collection scope (local and system wide)
- IRIS and other networked electronic resources
- Major bibliographic networks (e.g., RLIN, OCLC, and the Internet)
- Libraries' Web site
- Local services and expertise and where to refer effectively within the Libraries systemwide
- Regional and national resources, especially in their areas of expertise
- Library and university policies
- Newly emerging technologies, such as the World Wide Web

Weber State University
Stewart Library
Ogden, Utah

The following performance expectations were developed to enable individuals providing reference service to better understand what is expected of them and to know on what they will be evaluated.

1. Knowledge of Role

Reference team members will have sufficient knowledge and understanding of the following to be able to effectively meet their reference responsibilities:

A. Role as a Member of the WSU Faculty or Staff: Reference team members are expected to demonstrate a clear understanding of their role as a member of the Weber State University Library faculty or staff and fulfill the responsibilities of their position in a professional manner.

B. Reference Theory and Practice: Reference team members are. expected to have, or to acquire, an understanding of current reference issues, theories, and methods of reference practice appropriate to an academic library.

In keeping with the Library's educational mission, reference assistance should stress providing guidance to users in their pursuit of information rather than retrieval of information for them.

2. Reference Service

To provide effective, high quality service, reference team members are expected to acquire and consistently demonstrate expertise in each of the following:

A. Knowledge of Sources:

To meet users' information needs effectively, reference team members must be able to remember, locate, use, and teach others to use, print and electronic resources in any discipline in the reference and government publications collections and to consult with colleagues and/or the appropriate subject bibliographer when necessary.

Reference team members must also be aware of and refer patrons to relevant print and electronic resources not available in the local collection.

B. Reference Collection Development:

To answer reference questions effectively, reference team members are expected to actively participate with subject bibliographers and the R&IS Librarian in evaluating and selecting relevant print and electronic resources, including a core collection of general sources and basic sources focused on disciplines currently taught by the University.

C. Question Negotiation Skills (Reference Interview):

To understand the user's information needs, reference team members are expected to develop and consistently employ excellent communication and question negotiation skills.

Reference team members are expected to make every reasonable effort to ascertain the nature of the user's immediate information need, to treat the user with courtesy and respect, to address the query in a serious, non-judgmental fashion, and to ascertain, when possible, whether or not the user's information need has been satisfactorily met.

D. Service Orientation:

To provide effective, high quality service, reference team members must consistently demonstrate a strong commitment to service within the context of the educational mission of the University.

Reference team members must be perceived by the patron as friendly, approachable, eager to assist, and strongly committed to helping each patron locate the information s/he needs.

Reference team members are expected to diplomatically assess the expertise of the patron and tailor the assistance to meet the patron's information needs and learning style.

3. Participation in the Reference Program

Reference team members are expected to demonstrate their commitment to and participation in the Reference Program by:

A. Understanding and being able to articulate to others the mission and goals of the Library and the Reference Program.

B. Serving as an advocate for the Library and the Program by displaying an attitude that demonstrates a strong commitment to reference service.

C. Serving their scheduled hours at the Reference Desk and consistently providing high quality reference service.

D. Regularly attending training sessions and using the training to improve their knowledge of reference sources and reference service skills.

E. Providing general library orientation tours as assigned.

F. Providing relevant training sessions for reference team members.

G. Actively participating in Program decision making by:

Keeping informed on reference issues, policies, and procedures.

Regularly attending and contributing to reference team meetings.

Serving on reference team committees.

Participating in the evaluation and selection of new team members.

4. Program Improvement/Problem Solving

To improve and further develop reference programs, reference team members are expected to:

A. Take the initiative in recognizing and constructively solving problems.

B. Make recommendations for program improvement.

C. Be collegial, consultive and supportive—consult and respect others and function as a team member. Attempt to understand the demands made on colleagues and, when possible, help them to meet those demands.

D. Assist in the training of new members of the Program.

Subject bibliographers are expected to provide reference training in their assigned subject areas for new reference team members.

5. Time Management Skills

To balance their many responsibilities, reference team members are expected to:

A. Demonstrate a positive work ethic and employ excellent time management skills.

B. Be able to prioritize responsibilities and activities.

C. Meet scheduled deadlines and commitments.

6. Interpersonal Relations/Communication Skills

A. With R&IS Librarian:

To carry out their responsibilities, reference team members must be able to communicate effectively with the R&IS Librarian and bring proposed solutions to problems to her/him.

B. With Colleagues:

Reference service is a conclusive process. The degree to which reference team members are effective is often determined by their ability to consult and communicate with colleagues. Reference team members are expected to demonstrate effective interpersonal and communication skills in working with colleagues.

C. With Faculty:

While subject bibliographers have primary responsibility for communicating with faculty, all members of the reference team need to understand faculty library needs and must be able to communicate effectively with faculty.

D. With Staff and Student Assistants:

To solicit support from staff and student assistants, reference team members must understand basic delegation and supervisory principles. In order to explain projects, they must possess good communication skills.

State University of New York Cortland
Memorial Library
Cortland, New York

General Responsibilities of Reference Librarians

Communication and Professional Development

The Librarian(s) in charge of Reference, in cooperation with reference librarians, is responsible for communicating in timely fashion appropriate information directly related to the reference function. Such communication includes the sharing of information and/or special short-term instructions that may be needed by the librarian on duty.

Reference librarians are responsible for maintaining ongoing awareness of new developments within the library, which, in any way, affect reference services. All reference librarians are expected to regularly attend library faculty meetings, etc., and to read all relevant library and college communications.

Reference librarians are expected to maintain ongoing awareness of trends and developments related to reference librarianship. The reading of relevant professional literature and the continuous review of new reference titles are essential to the provision of quality service. Reference librarians should be able to use computers for information retrieval. They should strive to attain a high level of competency in using the library's online catalog and databases, and a basic level of competency in utilizing other services to which the library subscribes or which the library utilizes, including government documents, online catalogs of other libraries, document delivery services, electronic mail, and other Internet resources.

Approachability and Attitude

Assistance to the individual library user is the chief responsibility of the librarian on duty at the reference desk. In order to encourage users to seek assistance, reference librarians must be approachable. Librarians may do other work at the reference desk (e.g., electronic mail, collection development activities, cataloging, etc.). Reference librarians, however, should not become so engrossed in other work that they fail to respond to users needing assistance.

Problem users will be dealt with in a polite but firm manner. If a user becomes abusive, appropriate action should be taken by calling University Police..

Reference staff members will exercise judgment when questions are asked at the reference desk at closing time. The user may be asked to return the next day if it appears that the question will require lengthy research.

The primary purpose of reference telephone lines is for reference service to off-site users. All other calls should be kept to a minimum.

Staff Continuing Education and Training

Rutgers University
Rutgers University Libraries
Newark, New Jersey

Development and Training—Professional development is the ongoing responsibility of all librarians to maintain current skills, develop new skills, and to implement the information services needed in a constantly changing environment. To support this development the Rutgers University Libraries will provide in-service training for librarians, encourage and support attendance at other professional programs, and provide the appropriate equipment suitable for service at the highest level.

The Libraries will continue to provide, on a systemwide basis, workshops and other formal programs designed to help librarians keep abreast of new technologies and other advances and to maintain traditional skills at a high level. Such programs should include both in-house and external experts.

Individual units will continue to provide local workshops and programs targeted to the needs of local librarians and their immediate constituencies.

All libraries will continue to foster an atmosphere of cordiality and collegiality that encourages colleagues to share their expertise with one another on a formal and informal basis.

Participation in formal and informal educational programs is recognized as a key part of scholarly development.

Teaching Classes Other than Library Instruction

University of Indianapolis
Krannert Memorial Library
Indianapolis, Indiana

Staff Class Teaching/Taking

Librarians with faculty or professional ("exempt") staff status are eligible by invitation to teach U of I classes in fields of their proficiencies or other educational background, and any university employee may take classes under guidelines enumerated in staff handbooks. In order to coordinate these opportunities with the library mission and daily work, the following guidelines apply:

Teaching University Classes

All opportunities to teach classes result from interactions between librarians and administrators from the teaching faculty; there is no library requirement to teach non-library courses; note—the university prohibits teaching at other institutions without permission.

A class taught at times outside a librarian's regular schedule of employment does not require the permission of the Library Director, but classes taught within regular employment hours must be approved in advance by the Library Director to arrange for make-up time.

If the librarian is paid for teaching a class, teaching preparations may not be made during library working hours (the salary is intended to pay the librarian's preparation and class time above and beyond the regular library work contract).

If the librarian is not paid for teaching a class, but the Library Director has given approval, library time may be used for class preparation and class time may be taken without compensatory library hours being worked; staffing coverage for unavailable periods should be worked out with the Library Director.

Taking University Courses

Any staff member may take a course outside his/her assigned working hours without permission from the Library Director.

A staff member wishing to take a course during working hours must obtain prior permission from his/her supervisor AND from the Library Director. Coverage of the absent time and plans for making up the missed time must be worked out.

PROMOTION AND EVALUATION
Core Values for Performance Appraisal

Princeton University
Princeton University Library
Princeton, New Jersey

Core Library Values

Excellence and Service

Taking action and direction to improve job performance in order to effectively meet the needs of patrons, staff, and other customers:

> Anticipates and responds to patron needs and the needs of internal customers.
> Assists all library patrons in a courteous, fair, and non-discriminatory fashion.
> Learns and applies new skills and procedures as established by individual action plans.
> Identifies areas for continuous process improvement.
> Learns about other library jobs or functions that relate to or support the work of the unit.
> Exercises sound and informed independent judgment when appropriate.
> Identifies work problems and moves them forward to resolutions in keeping with the expectations of the position and unit.
> Consistently meets clearly delineated deadlines.

Teamwork, Collaboration, and Communication

Working well with others:

> Cooperates with others toward the achievement of common goals.
> Seeks consensus and productive solutions to problems and conflicts.
> Actively contributes and fully participates in tasks of work unit and of the University and or Library committees.

> Builds and maintains constructive relationships with colleagues.
> Effectively expresses oneself in written and oral communications.
> Keeps others adequately informed.
> Displays respect, tact, diplomacy, sensitivity and composure when interacting with others.
> Exhibits active listening skills.

Technical Literacy

Effectively using the tools required for the job:

> Supports and adapts to changes in the technical environment of the Library.
> Maintains current knowledge of appropriate computer applications and procedures.
> Proficiently and safely uses the appropriate equipment, hardware, and software required to perform individual job duties.

Personal Responsibility

Being an informed and fully participating member of the workplace:

> Actively participates in Library education and training offerings that may enhance one's job performance.
> Demonstrates willingness to learn new tasks and procedures as required by the changing workplace.
> Displays initiative in organizing and prioritizing work, balancing needs for quantity and quality.
> Demonstrates awareness of the work unit's mission within the context of the Library's and University's missions.
> Keeps abreast of Library developments that may enhance one's job performance.
> Complies with all Library and University policies.

Documenting Personal Performance

Princeton University
Princeton University Library
Princeton, New Jersey

Documenting Your Performance

The main purpose of documenting your job performance is to help your memory at the end of the year and have a more productive performance appraisal dialog with your supervisor. There are many ways to keep a record of your job performance. Try experimenting with the ones that you feel most comfortable with and decide which works best for you. The following suggestions have been mentioned by both supervisors and staff at various workshops. If you need any technical assistance, contact Luisa Paster.

Portfolio—Keep a folder with samples of your best work. For example: printouts of your most complex cataloging, a description of your most difficult reference questions, messages of thanks that have been sent to you, statistics of how much you have accomplished on a monthly basis, etc.

Email—Send yourself email describing samples of your best work. You can save them in a special email folder labeled "performance". You can describe problems that you have solved, difficult patrons that you have dealt with, extra work that you have undertaken, committee work that you have done, etc.

Documents in MS Word—Keep a document on your hard drive called "performance." List samples of your best work. Every time you accomplish something out of the ordinary on your job, add it to the list with a date. Remember to save the document each time you add an item.

Calendars—Use your calendar to jot down information that might be useful for your performance appraisal. Keep a record of particularly difficult assignments, committee work, special projects, weekly or monthly statistics, etc. At the end of the appraisal period, go through your calendar to jog your memory.

Audiotape—If you don't like to write, you can borrow a tape recorder from the Staff Development Office to record your accomplishments. When you do something excellent at work, explain it on tape. Keep using the cassette to add to the list. Don't forget to state the date of each recording. At the end of the performance appraisal period, you will have to listen to the tape and transcribe the recording for your appraisal form.

Princeton University
Princeton University Library
Princeton, New Jersey

Policy Description:

The University's Performance Evaluation Program encourages ongoing communication between supervisors and employees in order to foster performance improvement and enhancement. Supervisors are required to hold an annual performance appraisal discussion with all employees whom they directly supervise. The appraisal must be summarized in a written memo or appraisal form. Performance evaluations are also used in determining merit increases.

Appraisal Period

Performance appraisal discussions should focus on the employee's performance during the previous twelve months. Generally, supervisors should complete their evaluation discussions during the first quarter of the calendar year. Supervisors of unionized areas should consult the union contract to determine the specific appraisal period.

Elements of the Appraisal Process

The core elements of the annual performance evaluation are summarized as follows.

1) Discussion, by supervisors, regarding performance with each of the administrative and support staff members who report directly to them. Each discussion includes:

   a) the supervisor's assessment of the employee's performance during the past twelve months, including specific reference to the accomplishments and contributions made by the employee and the areas where he or she should improve.

   b) a review of any changes to the employee's responsibilities which may have occurred, and a summary of the expectations of performance to which the employee will be held accountable, as determined by the supervisor with employee participation.

   c) an agreement between the supervisor and the employee on a plan designed to improve or enhance the employee's performance which may include workshops, conferences, course work, or special work projects.

   d) discussions which provide opportunities for the employee to suggest to the supervisor what additional guidance or support would enable the employee to do a better job.

2) A written summary of the discussion prepared by the supervisor with a copy to the employee. The employee can attach comments to the summary document. The supervisor and employee should try to resolve any disagreements regarding the summary prior to the employee's attaching his or her statement.

The supervisor, at the time of salary review, will provide feedback to the employee as to how his or her salary increase for the current year relates to the performance discussion.

Retention

The final performance evaluation document should be held in a confidential department/office file, or may be sent to the Office of Human Resources for placement in the employee's official personnel file. In either case, the performance evaluation document must be held in the appropriate file for a minimum of three years, or longer if there is a good business reason.

Employee Access

Employees have access to official evaluation documents upon request and may make copies. Employees may also use an official copy of the evaluation as part of their application materials for promotion/transfer opportunities at the University.

Referral

Office of Human Resources.

FORMS
Performance Appraisal Form

Princeton University
Princeton University Library
Princeton, New Jersey

Performance Appraisal Form

Princeton University Library is committed to building employee and departmental potential by developing and rewarding employee skills and efforts. The performance appraisal program rests on a basis of honesty, trust, and respect. The appraisal should be considered part of an ongoing dialogue between employee and supervisor.

Employee's Name:_____

Supervisor's Name:_____

Work Unit:_____

Type of review: Probationary_____   Interim_____   Annual_____

　　　　　　　　　Period covered:_____

I.   CORE LIBRARY VALUES (refer to "Core Library Values")

1.   Excellence and Service
Exceptional contributions_____Standards attained_____Improvement needed_____

Commentary with specific examples:

Action/Development Plan:

2.   Teamwork, Collaboration, and Communication
Exceptional contributions_____Standards attained_____Improvement needed_____

Commentary with specific examples:

Action/Development Plan:

3.   Technical literacy
Exceptional contributions_____Standards attained_____Improvement needed_____

Commentary with specific examples:

Action/Development Plan:

4.   Personal Responsibility
Exceptional contributions_____Standards attained_____Improvement needed_____

Commentary with specific examples:

Action/Development Plan:

II. POSITION SPECIFIC PERFORMANCE STANDARDS

Indicate 3–7 position specific standards as appropriate. Attach fully delineated standards on separate sheet if desired.

1.

Exceptional contributions_____Standards attained_____Improvement needed_____

Commentary with specific examples:

Action/Development Plan:

2.

Exceptional contributions_____Standards attained_____Improvement needed_____

Specific examples:

Action/Development Plan:

3.

Exceptional contributions_____Standards attained_____Improvement needed_____

Specific examples:

Action/Development Plan:

4.

Exceptional contributions_____Standards attained_____Improvement needed_____

Commentary with specific examples:

Action/Development Plan:

5.

Exceptional contributions_____Standards attained_____Improvement needed_____

Commentary with specific examples:

Action/Development Plan:

6.

Exceptional contributions_____Standards attained_____Improvement needed_____

Commentary with specific examples:

Action/Development Plan:

7.

Exceptional contributions_____Standards attained_____Improvement needed_____

Commentary with specific examples:

Action/Development Plan:

III.   **SUPERVISOR'S COMMENTS** (Required)

IV.   **EMPLOYEE'S COMMENTS** (Optional)

Signatures:
    Supervisor: **Date:**
    Employee: **Date:**
    Supervisor's supervisor: **Date:**

Annual Evaluation Form

Chapter 6

Library Conduct Guidelines

Permissible Use of Communication Devices
Cell Phones and Pagers

Indiana University-Purdue University Fort Wayne
Walter E. Helmke Library
Fort Wayne, Indiana

Rationale

The library is primarily committed to providing easy access to information and an atmosphere conducive to study and research. Noise of any sort detracts from the atmosphere that encourages study and research.

The Policy

Appropriate use of cell phones, pages, and similar electronic devices as well as any other noise, such as loud conversations, should be governed by common sense and courtesy to others using the library to study.

Cell phones, pagers, and similar electronic devices must be set at silent ring only in the library. Cell phone conversations should be limited to the snack lounge on the first floor or the stairwells.

The third floor of the library is designated as a "super quiet" floor.

A group study room with a networked computer is available and should be used for group meetings and projects. Tables on the first floor may also be used for group projects.

Auburn University
Auburn University Libraries
Auburn University, Alabama

Cell Phones: If ringing and talking appear likely to disturb other patrons, we ask that they go to another area of the library or outside to talk.

Tulane University
Howard-Tilton Memorial Library
New Orleans, Louisiana

Cell Phone Use Policy

Many people come to the library to find a quiet place to read and to study. Please respect others' need for quiet and observe these guidelines for cell phone use in the library.

Please turn the cell phone ringer off or to a non-noise setting upon entering the building.

Cell phone use is acceptable in:
- Elevator lobbies
- Snack lounge and telephone lobby in the basement

Cell phone use is prohibited in:
- All stack areas

- Reading room areas
- Study and seminar rooms
- Library Instruction Room
- Government Documents
- Microforms and Newspapers area
- Maxwell Music Library
- Latin American Library
- Service desks

Please use a low voice when using a cell phone in the acceptable areas. The library reserves the right to ask patrons to leave the building if they are using cell phones in restricted areas or disturbing others in any area of the library.

Paging in the Library

North Seattle Community College
North Seattle Community College Library
Seattle, Washington

Because the library does not want to unduly disturb patrons studying in the Library, the principle purpose of the library public address system is to announce library closing. The Library will refer all requests for paging patrons in the Library to Campus Security. The public address system will be used to page a patron only in extreme emergencies.

Guidelines

When asked to page a patron in the Library, give them the Campus Security phone number: 527–3636 or refer the requester to the Campus Security Office to help them locate the person.

A Librarian will decide if a situation is an extreme emergency and warrants using the public address system or walking around the library in search of the patron. If a Librarian is not available, a full-time Library Technician will decide.

Patron Use of Reference Desk Telephone

Auburn University
Auburn University Libraries
Auburn University, Alabama

Phones at the Reference Desk

Generally not to be used by patrons since we now have campus toll free phones as well as pay phones.

University of Texas at Austin
University of Texas Libraries
Austin, Texas

Public Use of Library Telephones

Telephones at the reference and information desks are for official library use only. Users are referred to the nearest pay phone for off-campus calls or the nearest on-campus phone for campus calls.

BEHAVIOR GUIDELINES
Code of Conduct

Brock University
James A. Gibson Library
Saints Catharines, Ontario, Canada

Code of Conduct

Preamble

The James A. Gibson Library is responsible for securing the Library's scholarly resources and safeguarding its collections and equipment against theft and abuse. The Library also aims to provide a suitable environment for research, study, instruction and reading for its authorized users.

In order to satisfy these goals, the Library has established the following Code of Conduct which addresses the use and protection of the collections: the use and protections of the building and library equipment; the library environment; library staff security procedures and formal disciplinary procedures.

Violations against persons are also noted in this document.

This code has been developed to augment, and is consistent with, the Code of Student Conduct and Disciplinary Procedures in Non-Academic Matters, as published in the Brock University Calendar.

The following behaviors are in conflict with the mission of the James A. Gibson Library and are cause for action by the library staff or a representative of the library staff:

Use and Protection of the Collections

Removing, or attempting to remove, library materials, equipment or property without checkout or other official library authorization.

Stealing or knowingly possessing stolen library property.

Defacing, mutilating, or otherwise damaging library property.

Concealing, or reserving without library authorization, material in the Library for the exclusive use of an individual or group.

Failing either to return or renew materials when due, or failing to clear delinquent accounts by payment of fines.

Not allowing search of possessions when the security alarm has been activated upon exit.

Use of the Building and Library Equipment

Being in non-public areas without authorization, or in library facilities during closed hours, or during emergency drills or evacuations.

Opening emergency exits, except in emergency situations, or blocking emergency exits or aisles.

Vandalizing or defacing the Library buildings, furniture or equipment, or engaging in behavior that could do so.

Unauthorized use of the library computers as specified in Section 9 of the Code of Student Conduct.

Refusing to show Brock or other identification upon request of library staff.

The Library Environment

Consuming food or drinking liquids in unapproved containers while in the Library.

Smoking or using illegal drugs while in the Library.

Engaging in disruptive or distracting behavior that interferes with library-related activities, or is potentially harmful or dangerous.

Using portable or cellular phones.

Bringing animals other than guide/assistance dogs inside the Library.

Library Staff Procedures

In order to satisfy the Library's mission to secure its resources and provide a safe working/study environment for staff and library patrons, library staff are authorized to:

Check all possessions of persons as they leave the Library.

Request to see the identification of any person in the Library.

Question any person if it appears that library regulations are being violated.

Request that any person in conflict with library regulations leave the Library.

Contact Brock University Campus Police and request that any person having been identified as violating library regulations wait until Campus Police personnel arrives.

Violations Against Persons

Violations against persons including Brock University library staff and library patrons, as well as authorized sanctions against violators are described in the Code of Student Conduct published in the Brock University Calendar under the section heading "Non-Academic Misconduct."

Formal Disciplinary Procedures

All the offences described above are considered sufficiently serious to warrant immediate and firm disciplinary action, and action will be taken depending on the nature of the offence. The Library may impose a sanction (including warning, fine, community service, restitution for damages, and temporary exclusion from the Library). Repeat offences and more serious offences will be referred for follow-up disciplinary measures to the Campus Police Office and the University Discipline Officer, with possible sanctions as noted in the University Code of Conduct. In addition, serious offences may also be referred by the Campus Police Office and the Associate Vice-President (Student Services) to Niagara Regional Police to be prosecuted through the criminal courts.

New York University
Bobst Library
New York, New York

Unacceptable Conduct

Users will refrain from engaging in behavior that leads to the denial of, or unreasonable interference with, the rights of others; or which disrupts the regular operations and activities of the Library. Behavior which is considered to be in violation of Bobst Library Conduct Code includes, but is not limited to:

- creating a disturbance or behaving in a manner which interferes with normal use of the Library (including rowdiness, noise, offensive interpersonal behavior, and the use of laptops and cellular phones in designated quiet study areas)
- removing or attempting to remove Library materials or property from the building without authorization
- damaging Library property (including mutilating Library materials by marking and/or underlining pages, tearing or cutting out pages or sections thereof, removing binding and staples, removing or tampering with security tags)
- refusing to honor Library regulations regarding overdue items, materials recalled by the Library, and the payment of fines and/or fees for lost or damaged Library materials
- concealing Library materials in the building for the exclusive use of an individual or group
- leaving personal materials and library books that have not been checked out unattended in stacks and study areas for extended periods of time or overnight

- refusing to abide by regulations (as specified in Responsibilities of All New York University Computer and Network Users) guiding access to and use of computing and networking resources at New York University, including Bobst Library, failing to adhere to copyright laws and/or University policies on copyright
- smoking anywhere in the building
- eating or drinking in the building, except in designated areas
- being in an unauthorized area of the Library, or remaining in an area after its closing
- staying in the building when requested to leave during emergency situations or drills sharing an NYU ID, Consortium, Friends of Bobst or reader's card to allow unauthorized users entrance to the library

Violations of the Bobst Library Conduct Code may be referred for disciplinary action under applicable Library and/or University disciplinary processes. Where appropriate, instances of misconduct may be referred to local, state or federal law enforcement officials.

Fragrance Use

North Seattle Community College
North Seattle Community College Library
Seattle, Washington

Fragrance Use

In compliance with the North Seattle Community College Indoor Air Quality Policy and to provide a facility conducive to concentrated and effective use of library materials and services, the Library encourages a fragrance-free environment. The Library Staff has the responsibility to intervene courteously, but firmly, when the use of chemical scents interfere with the rights of others.

Guidelines:

1. The Library Classroom (2238A), Electronic Classroom (2236B), and the Typing Room (2233A) are designated Fragrance-Free classrooms.
2. When a Library patron complains of another patron in the Library wearing a heavy scent (cologne, perfume, etc.), approach the individual, introduce yourself, explain the problem, and ask for consideration or changes in behavior that can improve the situation. Offer the offender a copy of the handout provided by the Educational Access Center (located on the Reference Desk shelves).
3. When a Library Staff person detects a patron in the Library wearing a heavy scent (cologne, perfume, etc.), approach the individual, introduce yourself, explain the problem, and ask for consideration or changes in behavior that can improve the situation. Offer the offender a copy of the handout provided by the Educational Access Center (located on the Reference Desk shelves).
4. Direct the complainant to a designated fragrance free Library classroom.
5. If the problem persists then students may report the problem to Student Complaint Officer.

Photography in the Library

Syracuse University
Syracuse University Library
Syracuse, New York

Introduction

These guidelines apply to all facilities of the Syracuse University Library: E.S. Bird, Science and Technology, Math, Geology, and Physics Libraries, the Belfer Audio Laboratory and Archive, and the Architecture Reading Room.

Visitors to the campus or the Library are welcome to take a few photographs for their personal use without formal authorization from the Library Administration, providing Library staff and users are not inconvenienced in any way. All other photography, video, or filming requests must be approved by the Library Administration according to the guidelines and procedures below. Photography, videotaping, or filming for commercial or news media purposes also must be cleared through the Syracuse University Office of News Services and Publications.

Guidelines

Use of photographic, videotape, or film equipment within the libraries:

- must not interfere with the study, research, privacy, or safety needs of Library users
- must not violate any Syracuse University policies, rules, or regulations
- may not hinder access to exits, stairways, corridors, doorways, and other library facilities
- may sometimes be restricted during midterms or near final examinations.

Those wishing to make extensive use of photographic, video, or film equipment, use lights or tripods, or shift (or otherwise make use of) Library materials or furniture, must also:

(1) schedule the project for a period of low library usage;
(2) minimize disturbance to library staff and users;
(3) minimize re-arrangement of furniture or library materials, return any furniture used to its original location, and place library materials in designated locations for re-shelving
(4) keep in mind that library staff prefer not to be filmed or photographed when working.

Procedures

Individuals or groups wishing to photograph, videotape, or film within the library must:

(1) complete the Request to Photograph/Videotape/ Film in Syracuse University Library Facilities form on the reverse side of this page. This form also is available in the Library's administration offices, at the circulation desk at the Science and Technology Library in the Carnegie Building; or at library.syr.edu/policies
(2) submit the completed request form for review at the Library Administration Office (Monday-Friday, 8:00 a.m.–5:00 p.m.) as far in advance of the requested time as possible
(3) receive a copy of the approved and signed request form
(4) be prepared to present the approved request form to Library staff upon request at any time in which photography/videotaping/filming is taking place
(5) obtain the prior consent of any individual who is to be the subject of the photography/videotaping/filming.

Right to Terminate

The Library reserves the right to terminate any photography, videotaping, or filming that causes an undue disturbance, violates Library or University policies or regulations, or endangers the health and safety of participants, Library patrons, and Library staff.

University of California Berkeley
University of California Berkeley Libraries
Berkeley, California

Filming in the UC Berkeley Library

Filming or photographic work must be coordinated carefully so that it does not disturb students, faculty, other library users or staff.

Special arrangements must be made with the Librarian's Office in advance to film in study areas such as Morrison Library or the North Reading Room. The Library Administration reserves the right to disallow proposals which will disrupt or inconvenience normal library use.

Common sense and consideration should be used in photographing individuals. Photographs of individuals, particularly close-ups, may be taken only with the person's express permission.

When photographs or film are used for any commercial purpose, and certain other purposes, The Library requires credit, in print, in any finished product, as well as a copy of the publication or film for inclusion in The Library's collections.

A service fee is normally charged. For non-profit and UC Berkeley-affiliated organizations, the charge is $50 per hour for the filming session; if the request is made by a commercial organization and/or appears complex, we will charge $500 per hour. For questions, please telephone Library Administration,

Eating and Drinking

Brock University
James A. Gibson Library
Saints Catharines, Ontario, Canada

Food and Drink Policy

In the interest of providing a comfortable and positive learning atmosphere for our users, the James A. Gibson Library allows the consumption of snack food and non-alcoholic beverages in most areas. To maximize the continuing value of the Library's collections, equipment, furnishings, and carpet, please adhere to the following guidelines:

Allowable areas: At study tables, chairs, study carrels and in group study rooms.

Non-allowable areas: Special Collections and Archives, the e-classroom, Sound and Video Collection, Map Library, and at computers.

Non-allowable items: Hot food of any kind, and open drinks. Deliveries of food are prohibited. Library-authorized deliveries for sponsored events are not subject to this policy.

Please dispose of trash in the refuse baskets or recycling bins located throughout the Library.

Please report spills and/or waste issues to Library staff.

Thank you very much for your cooperation in maintaining the Library and in reducing litter.

Gonzaga University School of Law
Chastek Library
Spokane, Washington

Food and Beverage Policy

Beverages in spill-proof containers are permitted in all areas of the Library. Please use extra care in handling beverages in the Computer Labs so as to avoid damaging any equipment.

Eating food or using tobacco products is not allowed in the Library.

Problem Students

University of Indianapolis
Krannert Memorial Library
Indianapolis, Indiana

Patrons causing disruptions or public nuisance can be asked to leave by library staff at their discretion; if the offence is egregious or appears dangerous, library staff may call Campus Police to handle it.

University of Illinois at Urbana-Champaign
University Library
Urbana, Illinois

Disruptive Behavior

Disruptive behavior is detrimental to the Library's mission and to staff and patron safety. Disruptive behavior includes, but is not limited to, the following:

Abusing, threatening, or intimidating Library staff or patrons through language or actions.

Fighting or other behavior that creates excessive noise or commotion.

Bringing weapons, simulated or real, into any Library facility.

Playing musical instruments or audible electronic devices.

Using bicycles, skateboards, or skates.

Refusing to leave a Library unit at closing time.

Entering areas of the Library marked "Staff Only."

Engaging in sexual harassment and/or overt sexual behavior.

Displaying overt signs of substance abuse, including drunkenness.

Petitioning, conducting unauthorized surveys, or direct distribution of any non-library materials.

Soliciting goods, services, or donations.

Bringing bedding into any Library facility.

Staff will take appropriate action to remedy disruptive behavior.

Noise in the Library

Brock University
James A. Gibson Library
Saints Catharines, Ontario, Canada

Study and Work Space in the James A. Gibson Library

Campus libraries are places for learning. People need quiet places to study and work as well as space for group learning and collaboration. Libraries are also centers for teaching, where library staff instruct individuals and groups in the use of information resources and materials.

To create an environment that serves each of these needs, we have designated three distinct types of library areas:

Common Areas—Usually busy with high traffic levels. These areas are intended for group study and or instruction and include library service desks. Here, conversational noise is to be expected. Most of the main floor of the Gibson Library is designated a common area. The common areas are near the Reserve, Circulation and Reference/Information Desks, and in the northwest area of the floor where the group study rooms and tables are located. A quiet study is available on the southwest side of the main floor where individual carrels are provided.

Quiet Areas—Intended to serve as quiet space for readers and students. In these areas only low-level talking is permitted. Floors 5, 6, 7, and 8 are quiet areas.

Silent Areas—Intended to serve as silent, individual study space for readers and students who need to concentrate. No talking is permitted. Floor 9 and 10 are now silent areas.

Each floor of the Gibson Library has signage indicating designated areas.

College of Charleston
College of Charleston Libraries
Charleston, South Carolina

5.0 Noise Policy

5.1 Patrons may use the main floor of the library for collaborative work and quiet conversation. Students may also use one of the many group study rooms for these activities. (Some of the other areas of the library—the second and third floors—are designated quiet areas. With the cooperation of everyone, these areas should be kept free of excessive noise.

5.2 Use of cellular phones is prohibited throughout the interior of building, except in the cafe. Please read Policy #33 regarding the use of cellular phones.

5.3 Audio equipment may only be used with headsets and should not be audible by others.

5.4 If a patron reports a noise or disturbance to a staff member, the staff member will ask the person(s) involved to move or be quiet. If a staff member receives a second complaint, the person(s) making the noise will be asked to leave the building.

Gonzaga University School of Law
Chastek Library
Spokane, Washington

Noise Policy

As an academic law library, we seek to provide a scholarly environment that allows for quiet study. All three floors of the Library, including the Computer Labs, are quiet study areas. Although we recognize that certain library activities (such as reference and circulation) or patron activities (such as the use of computers) generate some noise, we ask that all patrons and staff work cooperatively to minimize the noise level in the Library. If you must talk in the Library, please respect the needs of those who seek a quiet place to study by keeping your voice to a whisper and your conversation to a minimum. Students are asked to use the common areas outside of the Library for telephone calls and general conversation.

The third floor of the Library is intended to be the quietest of the three floors. It has more study space than other floors and is located furthest from the Circulation Desk and the Computer Labs. Please make a special effort to maintain the quiet on the third floor by not talking in the open areas. Conversations are allowed in the third floor study rooms, however, please note that the rooms are not soundproof. When using a study room, keep the door closed and talk in a normal tone of voice so as not to disturb those who are studying outside the room.

Sleeping in the Library during Finals

University of Texas at El Paso
University Libraries
El Paso, Texas

Sleeping in the Library during Finals

The Library is open 24 hours for one week at the end of each semester to provide a place for students to study and prepare for final exams. It is understood that students will be working long hours, exhaustion occurs and falling asleep while studying in the Library is understandable; however "camping out" in the Library is not permitted. Any kind of bedding including pillows, blankets, and sleeping bags is not permitted. Library staff and/or security guards will patrol the library and enforce this library use policy.

Unattended Children

Augustana College
Thomas Tredway Library
Rock Island, Illinois

Children Disruptions Policy

Although we welcome all of the community to use our facility for study and research purposes, the Thomas Tredway will not tolerate disruptions from children in the library. If children are in the library and are creating a disruption:

  A supervisor or librarian will ask the parent to please have the children stop doing whatever is creating the disruption and remind them that the library is a place for quiet study and research.

  In the absence of a parent, the children themselves will be told.

  If the disruption continues, campus security will be called.

Olin College
Olin College Library
Needham, Massachusetts

Campus facilities are designed for use by members of the campus community. The campus community includes students, faculty, staff, and sanctioned visitors. The Olin College Library welcomes children of the community sufficiently mature to not disturb others' study and accompanied by a parent or adult caregiver.

Children 13 years and younger must not be left unattended in the library.

The safety and security of children is very important and is the responsibility of the parent or adult caregiver. The Olin College Library is open to the public, a situation that can present risks to children. Staff cannot assume responsibility for children's safety and comfort when they are unattended.

Please note:

A child 13 and under must be under the supervision of an adult who assumes responsibility for him or her while in the library.

Parents and adults must monitor all activities and behavior of their children while they are in the library and are responsible for any damage to property done by the child.

Olin students, faculty, and staff have priority use of computers and group study rooms.

If a child is left unattended in the library, or in the event of an emergency situation, staff will notify security.

Adapted from College of St. Catherine Libraries: March 30, 2005.

Part II
Facilities and Equipment

Chapter 7

EXHIBITS, DISPLAYS, AND NOTICES

GUIDELINES FOR EXHIBITS AND DISPLAYS

University of North Carolina Wilmington
William Madison Randall Library
Wilmington, North Carolina

Who May Hold an Exhibit or Display?

Only those persons, groups and organizations affiliated with UNCW may have exhibits in Randall Library. Faculty and staff members, departments, groups and organizations are welcome to request to have displays that are class, research, campus life or curriculum related.

Please note that all requests must be approved by the Exhibits and Displays Committee of Randall Library.

Schedule

Our exhibits calendar is arranged one year in advance. The Exhibits Committee requires that your request for exhibit space be received 6 months in advance of the approximate date you hope to install your display.

Installation and dismantling dates must be adhered to.

Exhibit Spaces

The Exhibits Committee is responsible for overseeing three display venues: the glass cases near the front door and the portable display walls.

Your display will be assigned to one of these locations, based on availability. Please work completely within the space provided.

Exhibitors' Responsibilities

Work with the Randall Library Exhibits and Displays Committee to design and plan the exhibit.

Publicize the exhibit (e.g. by sending press releases, contacting the Campus Communiqué, and/or contacting Mimi Cunningham, [962-3171], etc.). Contact information must be provided to allow any questions that arise to be directed to the proper person.

Install and dismantle the exhibit.

The Committee can answer any questions you may have and make suggestions to improve the quality of the display.

Create a professional quality sign for the exhibit that states the sponsor's name (the Committee can make some recommendations).

Clean the glass cases once exhibit is dismantled.

Locating and relocate any fixtures and equipment that you may need to supplement your exhibit (tables, carts, etc.).

Any supplemental fixtures and equipment must be approved beforehand by the exhibits committee.

Accessories available from Randall Library upon request

Fabric (limited number of colors)	Bookstands
Poster frames	Easels

Do's and Don'ts

In order to offer a more polished appearance, the Exhibits Committee strongly suggests that you keep in mind the following "do's and don'ts" when planning your exhibit.

DO
- Use both glass cases if you are assigned them.
- Have a professional sign created
- Ask for assistance from the Committee if you need help or have questions

DON'T
- Use tape to secure items in the case
- Use any materials to that are not easy to remove to secure items in the cases
- Create signs with construction paper and magic markers

The display materials and Velcro walls are only available for use within the library.

We support exhibits and invite you to submit an application for a display. We will work with you within these guidelines to help you create a quality display.

Ferris State University
Ferris Library
Big Rapids, Michigan

Display Space Policies and Guidelines

FLITE has display spaces throughout the building that are available for the display of materials of interest to the Ferris State University community.

Displays should reflect educational, intellectual, social, artistic, or cultural subjects. If possible, library materials should be included as part of each display.

Generally, a display duration will be one month for 1st floor cases and two months for all others.

Displays MUST be set up no later than two days after the start date, and must be removed by the last day of the reserved time. If a display is not set up within two days of start date the reservation may be forfeited at the discretion of the Display Team.

Displays not removed on time will be removed by the Display Team and stored for one month. If the removed display materials are not picked up within one month, they will be disposed of at the discretion of the Display Team.

No organization may set up a display more than twice a year, and displays must be at least six months apart.

To ensure enough time for review, planning, and set-up, display spaces should be reserved at least 30 days in advance. Due to high demand, it is advised that 1st floor displays be reserved at least 90 days in advance.

The approval for displays will be at the sole discretion of the Library Display Team. Displays proposed by the staff of FLITE or from University-affiliated groups or individuals will receive preference over external groups.

The Display Team will assign display cases in consultation with the organization/individual requesting the display.

Stands and other display items such as rods, drapes, etc. are available from the Display Team, and will be provided upon request.

The identification of the sponsor/provider/creator of a display must be clearly indicated within the display, along with the date of set-up and date to be removed.

Neither the Display Team nor the Library will be held responsible for the loss of, or damage to, materials on display.

The group or individual setting up and dismantling the display will be held responsible for damage caused to the display space(s), shelving units, light bulbs, or other items used to support the display if they caused the damage.

Public areas in FLITE (other than display cases) where displays might be set up must be discussed in detail with the Display Team.

Display Space Reservation Request forms are available online as well as at the Check-Out Desk on the 1st floor of FLITE.

Non-compliance

The Library reserves the right to refuse or to remove any display that does not comply with the policies and guidelines herein presented.

Failure to comply with the FLITE Display Space Policies and Guidelines may cause your organization to be banned from displaying within FLITE for one full year following the date of non-compliance.

Prohibited Uses and Practices

Library display facilities may not be used to promote or advertise, whether directly or indirectly, a commercial product or service; urge support or opposition to any political candidate or issue; or urge support of or opposition to any religion or religious belief.

Material that is obscene, defamatory, invades a particular person's privacy, or directly incites violence will not be posted or displayed.

Prices may not be affixed to any material on display, although an exhibitor's name, address and telephone number may be posted.

Material and equipment that, in the opinion of the Display Team, are potentially dangerous to FLITE users, staff, or property will not be presented in displays.

Banners are not allowed to be hung from the exterior walls and balconies of FLITE. Banners may not be displayed in the interior of FLITE unless expressly approved by the Dean of the Library.

Solicitations

Displays announcing or promoting fundraising programs or activities sponsored by not-for-profit, noncommercial organizations will be permitted, provided the requirements stipulated in this policy statement are met.

People may not solicit money or donations in FLITE, nor may any receptacle be placed in FLITE for the purpose of soliciting donations.

Sponsorship or Endorsement

Use of FLITE display space by an organization or individual does not constitute Library sponsorship or endorsement of that organization, individual, or the viewpoints or activities they are promoting. Statements that either directly or indirectly imply otherwise will not be permitted.

Appeal Process

Decisions by the Display Team to refuse or to remove a display may be appealed. Such an appeal must be made in writing to the Dean of the Library no more than 10 days after formal notification of the Display Team's decision is delivered.

After the written appeal is received, the Dean will appoint a committee of Library staff members to review the matter.

The committee will make its recommendations to the Dean within 10 days, and the Dean will make a final determination about the appeal.

Questions not directly answered by these policies/guidelines may be forwarded to [staff member].

SPECIAL GUIDELINES FOR STUDENT ARTWORK

Marlboro College
Rice–Aron Library
Marlboro, Vermont

Displaying Student Artwork

- Interested artists must submit a completed application (attached) to the Library Director.
- The Marlboro College Art Committee and the Library Director may refuse a display if the work is not acceptable for presentation and installation.
- Approved shows will be displayed on a first-come, first-served basis.
- The artist is responsible for installing and taking down the display.
- All artwork not removed by the designated date will be disposed of and the student will be billed
- $100 for staff time and trash removal costs.
- Each display will last approximately one month.
- The artist must accept all responsibility for theft or damage.
- Holes may NOT be made in walls.
- Art must be attached to walls with materials that do not leave a residue or peel the paint.

Application Form

Name: _____ Date: _____

E-mail: _____ Phone: _____

Location in library for show: _____

Total number of 2-D items: _____

# of items—matted only: _____

# of items—framed: _____

Total number of 3-D items: _____

# of items on stands: _____ Stands must be provided by the artist.

Approximate dimensions of each: # of items on floor: _____

Approximate dimensions of each:

SPECIAL GUIDELINES FOR DISPLAY CASES

Indiana University South Bend
Franklin D. Schurz Library
South Bend, Indiana

Display Case Policy   Search Schurz Library:

The Schurz Library makes display cases and display areas available for exhibit of materials which support the university's mission, programs and services. Of special interest are exhibits which promote the library's collection, services and programs.

Displays and exhibits should :

- contribute positively to the library's environment
- highlight, when possible, the collections of the library

- publicize resources and services of the university
- enrich the life of the university and the community it serves or
- provide a means of strengthening ties between the library, university and the community.

Materials accepted for display in the library display cases or display area should satisfy the following criteria:

- relate to the mission of the library and/or the university
- be sponsored by the library or by a university faculty member, staff member or administrator
- promote the materials, services and functions of the library (or the functions and services of the university).

Procedures

Permission for use of the display case or area must be obtained from the Office of the Director of Library Services at least two months in advance of the proposed date of the exhibit. Requests must be submitted in writing and contain the following information: sponsoring person or group, a brief description of the proposed display, requested dates, number of display cases and/or area requested. The library reserves the right to deny requests for displays that do not meet the above criteria.

Responsibility for the installation and removal of displays rests with the individual or group.

NOTE: Materials on display have the same security as the library collection, however, there are no special security features for display areas outside of the first floor locked display cases.

Phoenix College
Phoenix College Library
Phoenix, Arizona

The Phoenix College Library provides space for exhibits or displays using any combination of the following selection criteria:

The display....

1) Promotes the library and its collection
2) Meets the curricular needs of Phoenix College
3) Contributes to ongoing campus events
4) Provides information about an individual, group, or theme that would be of interest to the local community

Other factors considered include the availability of space and library staff to facilitate the work involved in the setting up and taking down of the exhibit.

The Phoenix College Library is an institution which supports the free expression of diverse points of view and will not exclude works based on the "origin, background, or views of those contributing to the work." Furthermore, "materials should not be proscribed or removed because of partisan or doctrinal disapproval" (Articles I & II of the American Library Association's Library Bill of Rights (www.ala.org/ala/oif/statementspols/statementsif/librarybillrights.htm).

ACCEPTABLE CONTENT AND PLACEMENT FOR POSTED NOTICES

Duke University
Duke University Libraries
Durham, North Carolina

Posting Notices in Perkins Library

Posting of non-library notices (including posters, notes, announcements, flyers, advertisements, signs, handbills, cards, etc.) in the public areas of the library, with the exception of the designated bulletin boards, is prohibited. Public areas include study rooms, lobbies, seminar rooms, doors, elevators, hallways, windows, restrooms, stairwells, book stacks and the public building entrances. Notices posted in these areas will be removed.

The library provides two areas for the posting of notices:

- Two bulletin boards in the elevator/stairwell area on the first floor, near the Circulation Desk
- A large bulletin board in the first floor hallway of the old building, outside the Deryl Hart Room.

Priority for space on the bulletin boards is given to the university community. Out-dated and duplicated notices will be removed.

This policy is intended to:

Maintain the library as an attractive and uncluttered environment.

Increase the effectiveness of notices and signs posted by library staff, which are intended assist and inform those who use our resources.

Chapter 8

SPECIAL USE ROOMS

GUIDELINES FOR STUDY AREAS

Group Study Rooms

Atlanta University
Robert W. Woodruff Library
Atlanta, Georgia

Room Reservations

Group Study

The Robert W. Woodruff Library currently has eight rooms available to be reserved for group study. Faculty and students are strongly encouraged to reserve rooms at least one day in advance of the date needed. Reservations are not accepted over the phone.

Main Level

Atlanta University Center (AUC) faculty and students may reserve any one of the group study rooms located on the main level for up to three hours at a time during normal hours of operation. Persons seeking to reserve a room will be asked to present a valid AUC campus photo ID at the Reference Desk on the Main Level. NOTE: Rooms must be occupied within fifteen (15) minutes of the onset of the reservation. After fifteen minutes have passed, the rooms may be occupied on a first-come, first-served basis until the next reservation goes into effect. Capacity: 12

Upper Level

Atlanta University Center (AUC) faculty and students may also reserve Rooms A, B and C located on the Upper Level (near the Virginia Lacy Jones Exhibition Hall) for up to three hours at a time between 8:30 a.m. and 5:00 p.m., Monday through Friday. After 5:00 p.m. Room D will also be available for use. Persons seeking to reserve a room will be asked to present a valid AUC campus photo ID at the Reference Desk on the Main Level. NOTE: Rooms must be occupied within fifteen (15) minutes of the onset of the reservation. After fifteen minutes have passed, the rooms may be occupied on a first-come, first-served basis until the next reservation goes into effect. Capacity: 10

Faculty Study Areas

Eastern Michigan University
Bruce T. Halle Library
Ypsilanti, Michigan

Six study rooms on the second floor of the Library (205M, 205N, 214B, 214C, 214D and 214E) can be "checked out" by faculty on a daily, first-come, first-served basis. Interested faculty can sign-in in the Library's Client Services Office (Room 116), and in exchange for their Eagle Card will be given a key to one of the study rooms for the remainder of the day. Upon return of the room key their Eagle Card will be returned to them.

Six study rooms on the third floor of the Library (307E, 307F, 312C, 312D, 312E, 312F) can be shared (minimum two people per room) on a semester basis. Occupants can renew or return keys at the end of each term. To request space in a shared faculty study room contact [staff member].

University of Arkansas
University of Arkansas Libraries
Fayetteville, Arkansas

Policy for Mullins Library Faculty Studies Eligibility

All members of the University teaching and research faculty (including non-tenure-track faculty), as well as emeritus faculty, are eligible for faculty studies.

Graduate students may apply for a graduate carrel. Carrel assignments are governed by a separate policy (contact the Circulation Department).

Faculty applicants must be working on a specific research project in order to be assigned a study.

Applicants may print out the application online (PDF) or stop by the Dean's Office (Mullins, Rm. 206) and pick one up.

Applications must be approved by the relevant college dean and department head, and must be submitted to the library Dean's Office no later than May 15 each year.

Disbursement of Assignments

Of the 66 available faculty studies, 60 percent (40 studies) will be assigned to tenure-track faculty members. Approximately 30 percent (20 studies) will be set aside for tenured faculty. Approximately 5 percent (3 studies) will be set aside for non-tenure-track faculty, and 5 percent (3 studies) for emeritus faculty. Faculty in all these categories will be assigned studies on a first-come, first served basis within their category.

Length of Assignments

The length of assignment for appointed tenure-track, tenured, and non-tenure track faculty is two years, maximum. These faculty may go through the application process again at the end of the second academic year, and their application will be reconsidered at that time.

The length of assignment for emeritus faculty is one year, maximum. These faculty may go through the application process again at the end of the academic year, and their application will be reconsidered at that time.

Occupants are asked to notify the library Dean's Office if they no longer need their study before the designated maximum period has ended. Doing so will allow another applicant on the waiting list to make use of the study.

Study Policies

Occupants may not unofficially sublease studies assigned to them. However, occupants may formally request to share a study with another eligible occupant (see above for eligibility). If a key is lost, the occupant assigned to that key must pay for the key replaced at the University's Key Office.

Smoking, food, and small appliances (including electrical space heaters) are prohibited in faculty studies. Commensurate with library policy, drinks in spill proof metal or plastic containers may be used in the studies.

Scholar Study Rooms

Dartmouth College|
Dartmouth College Library
Hanover, New Hampshire

Scholar Studies Information

Eligibility

The Baker-Berry Library assigns scholar studies to individuals in support of their scholarly activities. The majority of scholar studies are assigned on a term-by-term basis to eligible faculty, visiting faculty, visiting scholars with appointments, faculty spouses/partners, and administration, as well as a few select graduate and undergraduate honors thesis writers. Having a quiet, separate and secure location to leave research materials within the Baker-Berry Library is a wonderful privilege.

General Expectations

Scholar studies are very popular spaces and there can be a waitlist for studies. Lockers are available throughout Baker-Berry and Sherman libraries for anyone assigned to the waitlist.

Because of limited space, the studies are assigned for given periods of time with an expiration date for each occupant. All occupants have certain obligations and responsibilities that are outlined in an agreement that is signed prior to occupancy.

A $25 refundable key deposit is collected from each occupant at the time the agreement is signed.

All studies are equipped with a desk, chair, bookcase and light. There are Ethernet ports but phone usage (cell or land line) is not allowed in the study areas. The studies are only open during regular library hours.

All library material must be checked out prior to being housed in the studies. Library staff will occasionally enter the studies to ensure that library materials are checked out to the study occupant.

Usage of the studies is monitored one week at random each term. Each occupant is expected to return monitoring sheets within a one week time frame to confirm that they are using the study.

Studies are not meant for multi-media projects that would increase noise in the area. There is a no smoking, no dog and no food policy in effect for the library studies.

Faculty/Visiting Faculty/Administrators

These are mostly term use studies. A select few year long assignments are available to those agreeing to use it regularly over the course of a full year.

Scholar studies are not substitute offices and are assigned only to the individual signing the agreement. They may not be secondarily reassigned by the occupant without consultation with the library. Spouses/partners must apply separately for study spaces and are never automatically guaranteed space in a study.

Recalled items will not be retrieved from the study for the occupant. The faculty member is responsible for returning books prior to leaving the area for extended periods of time.

A faculty member who is planning to be away on a foreign study program or a leave of absence must relinquish the study prior to leaving the area. All library and personal materials must be removed from the study by the faculty member. The faculty member's department will be contacted regarding any needed arrangements for materials left in a study. The library will not be responsible for moving the contents of the study.

Visiting Scholars

Visiting scholars must have official appointment letters and be eligible for a Dartmouth library card.

Graduate and Undergraduate Thesis Writers

Thesis studies are shared by 2 occupants to better serve the graduate and undergraduate population.

The coordinator will e-mail a letter of application to the thesis advisor after a request is made by a student. Upon receipt of the returned form, the student will be put on a waitlist for a study. Studies are only assigned for one term at a time. In order to make it equitable for all, those who have not had a study before, will be given preference over those that have had a study. These assignments are for the approved occupants only and may never be reassigned or shared with a non approved occupant.

Individual Study Carrels

Binghamton University
Binghamton University Libraries
Binghamton, New York

Guidelines for Locked Study Carrels

Library study carrels are available to registered students based upon an agreement by the Library and the Senate Library Committee. *Assignments are based on the following priority groups.*

Priority Groups

- First: PhD students who are designated as ABD by Binghamton University
- Second: PhD students who have already completed their master's degree
- Third: Graduate students

Occupants are expected to adhere to the guidelines, including vacating the carrels at the expiry date. Failure to comply with study carrel guidelines will result in termination of study carrel privileges.

1. The Library does not assume any responsibility for personal property, including private computers, left in study carrels by occupants.
2. All study carrels have been provided with a connection to the Binghamton University network. All computers located in study carrels must be powered off when the occupant is not present. Computers that are left on may be powered off by Library staff. Due to security concerns, private computers may not be configured to function as a server or host server-type services to remote users. Study carrel occupants are expected to comply with the Binghamton University Computer and Network Use Policy. Violations will result in immediate suspension of services.
3. All Library materials in study carrels must be charged out to the carrel occupant. Study carrels will be checked regularly; books and periodicals not charged will be removed. A notice will be left for materials not properly charged to patrons. A second notice will constitute grounds for automatic termination of carrel assignment during a semester.
4. Smoking, food or drink, appliances, heating and cooling devices are prohibited in all study carrels. New York State Public Health Law 13-E prohibits smoking in the Library.
5. Objects are not to be attached in any manner to study carrel walls, doors or glass panels. Due to safety and security considerations, any material covering glass panels will be removed.
6. Carrel occupants must indicate use of the carrel by initialing sign-in sheets. If the indications are that the person to whom the study carrel is assigned is not using the carrel at least once a week, it may be reassigned to another patron. Reassignments will not be made without notice. When, under special circumstances, a carrel occupant will not be using the carrel for an extended period (two weeks or more), the occupant must notify the Head of Circulation Services.
7. Study carrels are not to be shared without prior approval. Carrel occupants who allow unauthorized use of their carrels are subject to termination of their carrel privileges.
8. If a carrel occupant reports (s)he has lost their carrel key, a $35.00 lock change fee will be assessed to reimburse fees charged to the Library.
9. If a carrel is not vacated by the date the assignment expires, occupant will be assessed a $35.00 lock change fee and a hold will be placed on Library and Registrar records. This procedure is necessary to protect each occupant's privacy and personal property.

Atlanta University
Robert W. Woodruff Library
Atlanta, Georgia

Individual Study Carrels

Individual study carrels may be rented for the semester by faculty and students who are presently engaged in ongoing research. The study carrel application must be completed, signed by the appropriate university officials, and submitted to the Office of the Director for approval. For a copy of the study application form, click here.

Baylor University
Moody Library
Waco, Texas

Types of Carrels and Assignment Priorities

Faculty

A limited number of keyed carrels are available for faculty members.

Graduate Students

A limited number of keyed carrels are available for graduate students.

Because of the limited number of keyed study carrels, all graduate double carrels must be shared.

Graduate carrels will be assigned on a first-come, first-served basis. If all graduate carrels are full, students will be placed on a waiting list.

Honors College students

Honors students obtain study carrels by contacting the Honors Program Coordinator.

Open Carrels and Group Study Rooms

There are nine carrels without doors on the second floor of Moody Library that are available to anyone.

Also on the second floor of Moody Library are four large, glassed-in group study rooms. These rooms accommodate 6–8 persons, and include dry erase boards and projection screens. Computer projectors are available for checkout in the Prichard Information Commons. Contact the Prichard Information Commons to reserve the use of a group study room.

There are numerous "Quiet Study" carrels located on the second and third floors of Moody Library. These carrels, identifiable by green signs on the doors, are available on a first-come, first-served basis. Please do not leave any materials or personal items in these carrels as they can not be locked.

Procedures and Policies

Assignment and Renewal

Carrels are assigned to clients (faculty and graduate students) for a period of one semester. Carrels may be renewed, but the number of renewals is limited. Master's students may have a carrel for a maximum of one academic year (one fall term, one spring term, and one summer term). Doctoral students may have a carrel for a maximum of two academic years (two fall terms, two spring terms, and two summer terms). Faculty may have a carrel for a maximum of two academic years. Faculty who have exhausted their two years may request to be added to the end of the faculty waiting list at the end of the two year period. It is important, therefore, to plan ahead and request a carrel for the period when its use will be most beneficial.

Renewal notices are automatically distributed via email. If a study carrel is not formally renewed or released, fines will be assessed and the carrel will be made available to the next person on the waiting list.

Library Materials

Library materials kept in keyed carrels must be properly checked out. Carrels are monitored weekly by library staff. Library materials found that are not properly checked out will be removed. Journal issues and bound volumes are not to be left in carrels, and they will be removed.

Furniture and Maintenance

Carrels are furnished with a chair, desk, shelves, and a bulletin board. Library furniture from other areas of the building may not be moved into the carrels. Smoking and eating are not permitted in the carrels.

Security

Keyed carrels should be locked at all times when not in use. The Baylor University Libraries assume no responsibility for the loss of or damage to personal possessions that are kept in closed carrels.

Disregard of any study carrel policies will be cause for withdrawal of the carrel assignment. Study carrel policies are posted in each study carrel.

(For additional policies, please see the accompanying CD-ROM.)

Student Lockers

Marlboro College
Rice-Aron Library
Marlboro, Vermont

Lockers Policy

Thirty lockers are available for off-campus students only. Lockers are located on the ground level of the Rice Library.

Locker assignments are made at the Rice-Aron Library Service Desk.

Students must fill out this form and return it to library staff.

All lockers must be emptied at the end of the semester, even if the student will be returning the following semester.

Lockers not emptied by students will be emptied by library staff. Items left in lockers will be placed on the lost and found shelves in the Recycling Closet that is located on the middle-level connecting corridor.

Reference materials, periodicals, reserve materials, or uncharged items may not be kept in lockers.

Food and drink may not be kept in lockers.

The Library Director reserves the right to open lockers if necessary to remove reference materials, periodicals, reserve materials, uncharged items, food, and illegal or dangerous items. Illegal or dangerous items stored in lockers will be confiscated and the student will be reported to the appropriate authorities.

Failure to comply with the above regulations may result in loss of locker privileges.

Dartmouth College
Dartmouth College Library
Hanover, New Hampshire

Steel lockers in Berry are on the Lower Level (south wall, near the elevator) and Level 4 (south wall near the east elevator), and in Baker on Levels "A" and 5 (southeast corner, near the smaller elevator). There are also some steel lockers in Sherman Art Library, in the southwest corner of the east room on the main floor. The steel lockers have combination locks, whose combinations will be given out as lockers are assigned.

Cabinet lockers are reserved for students working on theses. They are in Berry Levels 3 and 4 along the north walls. Keys may be obtained at the Circulation Desk on application, and must have verification by the signature of the student's instructor. The user must keep his key connected with its barcoded tag. Both key and tag are to be returned to this desk when vacating the locker. The paper tags are susceptible to being torn by accident; please exercise care to avoid this. A replacement fee of $25.00 (see LOST KEYS below) may be applied if the key cannot be properly checked in due to a missing barcode tag.

All library materials in lockers MUST be checked out, using the personal ID card of the locker holder. The loan period will be determined by the privileges of the user's borrower category. Please remember to renew items, if necessary, even when stored in the locker. If needed by another patron, materials may be recalled after the first two weeks. Personal belongings (except food and beverages) may be stored in the lockers. Food and beverages are not permitted in Baker/Berry Stacks at any time. The library staff retains the right to periodically inspect locker contents; any library books found not properly checked out will be returned to the stacks, and the borrower may forfeit the privilege of using a locker.

Please note, occupancy and use of a locker does not supersede the library's policies on recalled materials. In the event of a recalled item, borrowers are obligated to return it within the due date specified on the recall notice.

Lost Keys

A replacement charge of twenty-five dollars ($25.00) will be levied if one's key is lost. Students must take the responsibility for having their keys when needed. Library staff will not open lockers by request in the event of a forgotten key.

How to Apply

Fill in this application and submit it to a staff person at the Baker-Berry Circulation Desk. We will attempt to assign lockers to all applicants. If there are more applicants than lockers, senior class students will have priority.

Library Responsibility

Locker assignments are confidential. The library staff will not divulge your name, locker number or combination. In the case of a forgotten combination, library staff will provide the combination only after checking your ID against the list of locker assignments. As noted above, the claim of a forgotten key for the cabinet lockers will not permit unlocking.

Quiet Study Areas

Tulane University
Howard-Tilton Memorial Library
New Orleans, Louisiana

Quiet Study Area Policy

The library should be a place conducive to study, but its space limitations and lack of study rooms often make it difficult to find a quiet spot to study. Therefore the 3rd floor stack area of the Howard-Tilton Memorial Library has been designated as a quiet study area.

Patrons should refrain from talking or working in groups on the 3rd floor.

Students who wish to work in groups should use the designated group study rooms available on the 1st and 2nd floor.

Cell phone use is prohibited in this area.

Staff and student assistants who work in this area should refrain from loud talking in and around study areas.

Patrons whose quiet study is disrupted are strongly encouraged to contact the Circulation Desk. A stacks phone is available on the 3rd floor for this purpose.

Library patrons who fail to abide by the quiet study policy will be asked to leave the 3rd floor reading area.

University of Texas Brownsville
Arnulfo L. Oliveira Memorial Library
Brownsville, Texas

Study Rooms

A valid library card is needed to use one of the eleven study rooms available for quiet study.

Students may pick up the key at the Circulation Desk. There will be a $10 fee for lost keys.

Circulation staff assign study rooms on a first-come, first-serve basis.

Study rooms may be occupied for one two-hour period per day.

All study rooms have chalkboards. Chalk and erasers are available at the Circulation Desk.

No individuals may reserve a study room in advance of the day on which he/she intends to use it.

Food and drink of any kind are not permitted in any study room.

Study room privileges may be suspended if these rules are not followed.

Note: During the final exam period, the demand for study rooms is overwhelming. Room renewals will not be allowed. The two-hour policy will be strictly enforced to allow equal access to the study rooms.

GUIDELINES FOR MULTI-USE ROOMS

Audiovisual Rooms

Henderson State University
Huie Library
Arkadelphia, Arkansas

Audio-Visual Room Policy

Only Henderson State University and Ouachita Baptist University faculty/staff and students are eligible to reserve the AV Room.

Valid Henderson State University or Ouachita Baptist University or other ID cards will be retained at the Reference Desk.

The AV Room may be booked one week in advance.

The AV room may be booked for a two-hour period. Booking periods may be extended if no person or group is waiting.

The video, listening equipment, and the Adaptive Technology computer may be reserved simultaneously.

Community patrons may use the AV Room, but only on a non-priority basis. Henderson State University and Ouachita Baptist University students and faculty/staff will have priority use of the room.

Any video from the circulating collection may be viewed in the Audio-Visual Room.

No food or drink is allowed in the AV Room.

Music Listening Rooms

Binghamton University
Binghamton University Libraries
Binghamton, New York

Music Listening Room

The Music Listening Room is located in the Fine Arts Library LN–1606. The collection consists of phonodisks and audio CDs. Listening services are available to the general public. Borrowing is limited to Binghamton University staff and students. Hours of operation vary according to the time of year. During semester breaks and summer session, the Music Listening Room is open by appointment. For assistance, please call the Circulation desk

SETUP FOR MULTI-USE ROOMS
Criteria for Using Rooms

University of Maryland Baltimore County
Albin O. Kuhn Library
Baltimore, Maryland

General Criteria for Booking 7th Floor Rooms

These spaces are reserved for meetings which require prestige and elegance. Also, Library, Humanities Center and Honors College meetings which would not fit in other Library spaces may take place on the 7th floor.

Types of meetings which may be booked:

- President's and Provost's meetings, and other meetings sponsored by the campus administration
- Fundraising for UMBC; Institutional Advancement events
- Alumni or Community Relations
- Campus-wide lectures and forums with possible off-campus involvement provided that they fall within normal Library hours, e.g. Humanities Forum Recruitment of special groups of potential students, faculty or staff
- Library, Humanities Center or Honors College meetings, including meetings of campus
- Honors associations and classes invited for bibliographic instruction or to view special collections materials.
- Campus senates, department chairs meetings, and other governance-related meetings.
  The 7th floor spaces must be kept clear for meetings which meet the above criteria and fall within the above categories.

Examples of meetings which would NOT qualify:

Routine staff meetings, club meetings, course seminars, departmental meetings, lunches for job candidates, social events and brown-bag lunches except when sponsored by the groups or offices listed above; vendor or employment fairs, meetings with purposes more suited to The Commons, the University Center, the Faculty/Staff Dining Hall, or another campus location; events whose noise would disturb Library users in stacks or study areas; meetings with anticipated attendance of fewer than 20 people. If meetings do not require the high profile of the Library spaces, they should be booked into other spaces.

Room Setup

University of Maryland Baltimore County
Albin O. Kuhn Library
Baltimore, Maryland

Preparation/Setup:

Setup and breakdown fees are charged to event sponsors by Student Work Force. Forms for specified set ups should be completed accordingly.

At the present time the default (standard) setup in 767 is Conference Style with 8 tables with 30 chairs around the table and a total of 54 chairs are available.

Note: Library staff is NOT responsible for setup or general event support merely by their presence in the building. Event sponsors should arrange for event support from the Student Work Force, Food Services, Audio Visual Services, etc.

If the room for a scheduled event is locked, event sponsors may sign out room keys from the Library Security Desk on the first floor.

Drake University
Cowles Library
Des Moines, Iowa

Room setup decisions need to be made at time of reservation. Furniture available includes the study tables/chairs in the Reading Room and the large table in the atrium. If the event requires more or different furniture, they will need to be rented at the expense of the event's organizers. Delivery and setup of the additional furniture need to be coordinated with the Library Event Coordinator. Decorations or attachments to the walls, ceilings, floors, etc. require prior approval from the Library Event Coordinator and the Library Dean.

Catering

Drake University
Cowles Library
Des Moines, Iowa

Catering needs require using the University's vendor Sodexho (sodexho.catering@drake.edu). Delivery and setup of the food/equipment need to be coordinated with the Library Event Coordinator. Because of the academic nature of the facility, serving alcoholic drinks is not encouraged. At the time of making the room reservation, a separate written request to allow alcohol must be submitted to the Library Dean for approval.

Book Signings

Drake University
Cowles Library
Des Moines, Iowa

Book Signings require using the University's vendor, University Book Store (www.drakebookstore.com or Bookstore Manager). Delivery and setup of the books need to be coordinated with the Library Event Coordinator.

FORMS

Form to Request Faculty Study-Carrel

University of Arkansas
University of Arkansas Libraries
Fayetteville, Arkansas

Application for a Faculty Study at Mullins Library

Name _____ Department _____

Title _____ Campus Address/Phone/Email _____

/_____/_____

_____ Original application (give floor preference: 3rd _____ 4th _____)

_____ Renewal application (indicate Study number _____)

INDICATE YOUR FACULTY STATUS:

Tenured _____ Tenure-track _____ Non-tenure-track _____ Emeritus _____

* PLEASE DO NOT MARK SUMMER IF YOU DO NOT PLAN TO USE A FACULTY STUDY FOR THE SUMMER.

INDICATE TIME PERIOD REQUIRED:

Summer 2006_____ Fall 2006_____ Spring 2007_____ Other_____

APPLICATIONS MUST BE RENEWED ANNUALLY: IT IS THE RESPONSIBILITY OF STUDY OCCUPANTS TO NOTIFY THE DEAN'S OFFICE WHEN THE STUDY WILL BE VACATED PRIOR TO THE EXPIRATION OF THE ASSIGNED PERIOD.

Describe briefly your research project and explain why this project requires the use of a faculty study. (Continue on the back of the sheet if more space is needed.)

I have read and agree to comply with the regulations and procedures in the attached Policy Statement on the Assignment and Use of Faculty Studies. I understand that I must remove all materials from the study and return the key to the University Key Office within one week after the expiration date. I understand that I will be charged a fee to cover the cost of rekeying the lock if the key is not returned. I also understand that violation of these regulations may result in the revocation of faculty study privileges.

_____

Signature of Applicant   Date

_____

Departmental Chairperson   Date

_____

Dean   Date

Return to: Dean of Libraries,

Locker Request Form

Marlboro College
Rice–Aron Library
Marlboro, Vermont

Library Locker Policy

- Thirty lockers are available for off-campus students only. Lockers are located on the ground level of the Rice Library.
- Locker assignments are made at the Rice-Aron Library Service Desk.
- Students must fill out attached form and return it to library staff.
- All lockers must be emptied at the end of the semester, even if the student will be returning the following semester.
- Lockers not emptied by students will be emptied by library staff. Items left in lockers will be placed on the lost and found shelves in the Recycling Closet that is located on the middle-level connecting corridor.
- Reference materials, periodicals, reserve materials, or uncharged items may not be kept in lockers.
- Food and drink may not be kept in lockers.
- The Library Director reserves the right to open lockers if necessary to remove reference materials, periodicals, reserve materials, uncharged items, food, and illegal or dangerous items.
- Illegal or dangerous items stored in lockers will be confiscated and the student will be reported to the appropriate authorities.
- Failure to comply with the above regulations may result in loss of locker privileges.

PLEASE PRINT CLEARLY

I have read and agree to the terms and conditions of the locker policy.

Name:

_____

Off-campus contact info:

Street: _____ State: _____ Zip: _____

Phone with area code: (_____) _____

E-mail: _____

Signature: _____ Date: _____

FOR STAFF USE ONLY:

Locker number: _____ Lock code: _____ Staff Initials: _____

September 2004

Dartmouth College
Dartmouth College Library
Hanover, New Hampshire

Application for Patron Locker Baker/Berry Library Stacks

(*This part to be retained by the Library*)

Name Class: _____

Address (local) _____

Telephone: _____ Hinman Box: _____

E-mail: _____

Student major: _____

Date:_____ Applying for term(s): F W S X Year: _____

Instructor's signature (required for thesis writers): _____

Instructor's name (*please print*): _____

Location choice: Berry Stacks Level: Lower *or* 4 (steel lockers) Baker Stacks Level: A *or*

   5 (steel lockers) *available to thesis writers only*: Berry Stacks Level: 3 *or*

   4 (cabinet lockers) *available to Art Department affiliates only*: Sherman Art Library
          ########
       for staff only

Assignment Date: Initials:
       use if required

Key replacement fee (amount) Date: _____ Initials: _____

Key replacement fee (amount) Date: _____ Initials: _____

Reminder to staff: We will not open lockers by request in the event of a forgotten key.

Chapter 9

EQUIPMENT, FURNITURE, AND SUPPLIES

FAX MACHINES

University of Scranton
Weinberg Memorial Library
Scranton, Pennsylvania

The University of Scranton's Web site is changing, and policies will be separated from information on the updated sites.

Fax Service

A fax service is available at the Circulation Desk on the First Floor. Within the United States, the cost for outgoing fax pages is $1.00 per page; international faxes are $4.00 per page. Incoming faxes are $.50 per page.

Macon State College
Macon State College Library
Macon, Georgia

The MSC Bookstore has a fax machine available for student use. During the times the Bookstore is closed, students may send a fax from the Library's fax machine at the following cost:

Local . . . . .50 cents per page

Long Distance . . . . $1.00 per page

MICROFORM MACHINE

Lake Sumter Community College
Lake Sumter Community College Libraries
Sumterville, Florida

Microforms

The Library provides self-operating microform copiers and readers for the use of government documents microforms within the Library. One microfiche reader-printer is available in the government documents area.

LAPTOP LOANS

Florida International University
Florida International University Libraries
Miami, Florida

Laptop Borrowing Policy

Laptop computers are available for in-library use at the Circulation Desk. The laptops represent a significant investment in providing University users with a technology service. Your respect for the equipment and the rights of other patrons will be appreciated. If you have any questions please feel free to ask.

Borrowers

Laptop computers are available for currently enrolled FIU students, faculty, staff, retired faculty, alumni, and currently enrolled consortium students from other SUL libraries and SEFLIN libraries.

You must have a current Panther ID (Library) Card for the checkout process

Loan Guidelines

Laptops must be used in the Library.

The loan period is 3 hours.

Late charges will be imposed. Overdue fines are set at $30 for the first hour overdue, and $30 per hour thereafter, until billed for replacement. Partial hours count as a full hour overdue. Laptop clocks are not accurate and are not to be used to calculate due time. A replacement charge of $2,200 will be imposed if the laptop is not returned after 24 hours from time due.

If damage occurs to any components or accessories, charges will be imposed as appropriate. Never leave a laptop unattended—you are responsible for the laptop until you have returned it and it is checked in. Billing charges will be assessed if the laptop is lost or stolen while checked out to you.

Return Procedures

Return the laptop to a library staff member at the Circulation Desk. Do not place the laptop in the Return slot.

Connections and Printing

Each laptop is equipped with a battery that will last approximately 2 to 3 hours, and with a network card for access to the wireless network in public areas of the library building. You may print from the laptop to any of the public networked printers in the library. Regular printing charges will apply.

Software Applications
- Microsoft Office Suite
- Adobe Acrobat Reader
- Netscape Communicator
- Internet Explorer
- Accessories

A limited number of accessories are available for checkout. Each accessory is separately checked out. Accessories may only be used with library laptops.
- Power (A/C) Adaptor
- ZIP Drive for 100MB or 250MB ZIP disks (ZIP disks are not available from the Library)
- Optical Mouse

FURNITURE AND EQUIPMENT USE

University of Texas at El Paso
University Libraries
El Paso, Texas

Use of furniture and equipment. Library furniture is for the exclusive use of patrons who are reading or studying. Furniture should not be relocated or used for sleeping, as footrests, etc. Computers, copiers, fax machines and telephones located at public service desks and in offices are for the use of Library staff; patrons are referred to the equipment in the building available for public user.

University of Indianapolis
Krannert Memorial Library
Indianapolis, Indiana

Equipment for Staff Use—Computers, Copier/Fax Machine, Printers

Persons other than staff to whom specific pieces of equipment are assigned are not permitted to use staff equipment.

Students workers may only use staff equipment to fulfill job assignments—not for personal purposes.

Staff may not use library equipment for personal purposes without the permission of the library director.

Staff telephones and computers are to be used for work related purposes; game playing, shopping, Web 'surfing', political lobbying, conversations with friends, family business, etc. for personal use may not be done during working hours.

Staff telephones and computers are not to be used for economic gain; home businesses, stock trading, auction sales, product or service advertisement, etc. are not to be conducted on library time or with university equipment; staff should not load private files for storage on university computers.

No one is to use a staff computer to access, upload, download, transmit, or otherwise distribute defamatory, abusive, obscene, profane, sexually oriented, threatening, harassing, racially offensive, illegally discriminatory, or other illegal materials, files, etc. unless in the course of appropriate library work or research.

No one shall violate any university, local, state, or federal statute, rule, regulation, code, or ordinance; no one shall access another person's computer materials, information, or files, except with permission.

Staff may not commit the library to any unauthorized financial obligation online or by telephone.

Staff should remember that neither telephone conversations nor files stored on library computers are private and may be reviewed by the administration at any time.

STUDENT BORROWING OF LIBRARY SUPPLIES

University of Wisconsin River Falls
Chalmer Davee Library
River Falls, Wisconsin

Supplies

Generally, reference staff will provide small amounts of supplies to patrons. Scrap cards and pencils are routinely supplied at public workstations. Small amounts of paper clips, rubber bands, white-out, etc. are provided. A stapler, scissors, and three-hole punch are provided for public use at the Reference Desk. A typewriter for public use is available in the Reference Area.

Multimedia Equipment Checkout

York College
Schmidt Library
York, Pennsylvania

Multimedia Checkout

The following equipment is available for personal use by YCP faculty, staff, and enrolled students.

- Calculator 1 day loan
- Camcorder 1 day loan
- Digital camera 1 day loan
- Digital video recorder 1 day loan
- Easel 3 day loan

- Flipchart 3 day loan
- Laptop (students, in-library use) 2 hour loan
- LCD projector (use with laptops in Group Study rooms) 3 hour loan
- Slide cassette projector 3 day loan
- Slide projector 3 day loan
- Tape recorder 3 day loan

The equipment listed below is available for faculty and staff checkout at Information Services. Reserve at ext. 1345 or via email infoservices@ycp.edu.

- Calculator 3 day loan
- Digital camera 3 day loan
- Digital video recorder 3 day loan
- Laptop 1 week loan
- LCD projector 3 day loan

Chapter 10

SECURITY, EMERGENCIES, AND TOURS OF THE LIBRARY

SECURITY
Lost and Found

University of South Alabama
University Libraries
Mobil, Alabama

Lost and Found

Items found and turned in at the Circulation Desk are kept there approximately until the end of each academic term. USA Picture IDs are ultimately forwarded to USA Student Services, Room 110 in the Student Center. When identification permits, we try to contact owners concerning recovered items.

University of Texas at Arlington
University Libraries
Arlington, Texas

UTA Libraries Lost & Found

Each UTA Library has a Circulation Desk repository for lost and found items. Inexpensive, replaceable articles are retained for approximately two weeks, then passed along to a charitable organization, recycled, or discarded. Campus Police are called immediately for pick-up of valuable items found in the libraries. Items sent to Campus Police can be claimed at the Campus Police Office, 700 South Davis Street.

Please do not leave personal items, materials checked out to you, or private information left lying unattended in the libraries. It is also advisable to have possessions marked with your name and phone number in case of loss.

Unattended Student Belongings

University of Illinois at Urbana-Champaign
University Library
Urbana, Illinois

Personal Property

Theft is an unfortunate reality in the Library. Please take every precaution to ensure the security of your personal belongings, especially that of purses, wallets, backpacks, books, portable computers, and other electronic devices. In addition, sleeping in the Library increases the potential for theft of personal belongings. For this reason, library staff will wake sleeping persons.

The University Library has no facilities to store personal property, and will not under any circumstances take responsibility for theft, damage, or loss of property.

University of Scranton
Weinberg Memorial Library
Scranton, Pennsylvania

The University of Scranton's Web site is changing, and policies will be separated from information on the updated sites.

Security Warning

Please, do not, under any circumstances, leave our laptops or your valuables unattended. You are responsible for the laptop and peripherals charged out to you. The Library is not responsible for its loss or the loss of your personal possessions if they are left unattended.

Parking Passes

Florida Atlantic University
S.E. Wimbrely Library
Boca Raton, Florida

Volunteer/Vendor

Parking Spaces were constructed using money donated by the Friends of the Libraries, and are exclusively for the use of regular, long-term library volunteers for whom parking elsewhere on campus would be a physical hardship due to age or infirmity. Parking spaces are also reserved for vendors who must make short service visits or bring heavy parts and equipment into the Wimberly Library building.

Parking stickers will be available for those volunteers with no other affiliation with FAU. A volunteer who is an able-bodied staff member, faculty member or student, may use their normal FAU student/faculty staff parking privileges. They will not be issued a volunteer hang-tag for parking.

Drake University
Cowles Library
Des Moines, Iowa

Parking passes for the Olmsted Lot (approximately a block west of the library) can be purchased by the event's organizers in advanced from the Olmsted Parking Lot Supervisor (271-4046). Street parking is also available. The day of the week, time of day and part of the year makes a difference on how much street parking is accessible.

EMERGENCIES
General Guidelines

University of Indianapolis
Krannert Memorial Library
Indianapolis, Indiana

Security Gates, Theft, False Alarms

All non-Information Services staff entering into the library are required to exit through either the security gate at the Circulation Desk or the gate into Media Services.

The security gates sound an alarm if an item owned by the library is carried through it. At the Circ. Desk a sign is clearly posted in front of the exit pathway telling patrons to "Please present all library materials" to the staff person at the Circulation Desk; this procedure permits staff to pass the item(s) around the security gate and avoid setting off the alarm. At the Media Services gate, a sign warns patrons not to take library materials through the gate.

Note: Occasionally, the alarms are triggered by items other than library materials, including books from other libraries, tagged items from commercial establishments, certain beepers, or certain types of ID cards. Computers, cell phones, and other electronic devices will not set off the alarms, and the security system will not damage photographic film or digital data storage devices. Because staff cannot know whether the alarm is from library materials or one of these other reasons, any alarm is handled in the same way.

If the gate into Media Services sounds, Circ. Desk staff ensure that the person returns into the library; if the Circ. Desk alarm sounds, library staff working at the Circ. Desk act according to the following procedures:

Ask the patron to return to the desk (on the exit side of the gate).

If the patron fails to comply, again ask the patron to return to the desk. If the patron persists in exiting or refuses to return to the desk, call Campus Police immediately to report a possible theft of library materials is in progress.

Ask the patron if he/she has any library materials on his/her person or in a carried container or bag. If so, make sure that they have been checked out by looking at their due dates and keep them on the exit side of the gate. Ask the patron to pick up all other items he/she has and walk back through the gate to be sure that the library materials already presented were the only ones setting off the alarm. If the alarm does not sound, permit him/her to recover all materials and exit. If the alarm does again sound, follow the next procedures:

   a. If the patron states that he/she has no library materials, ask him/her to remove all items from his/her bag and, assuming none are library materials, ask him/her to carry the bag through the gate again to ensure that something previously removed was setting off the alarm. If this is the case, explain that sometimes the system picks up a non-library item, apologize for the inconvenience, and allow the patron to exit.
   b. If the patron should refuse to empty his/her bag or to permit a staff person to do so, warn him/her that you will have to call Campus Police to resolve the matter. If the patron still refuses, call Campus Police and let them handle it.
   c. If a search of a patron's belongings reveals unchecked-out library materials, and the person claims it is a mistake or oversight, a judgment must be made whether the person is telling the truth. If you deem so, ask him/her to return to the other side of the Circulation Desk and properly check out the item(s). If the patron admits an attempt to steal or otherwise seems very suspicious, ask the person for his/her U of I identification card and use it to fill out a Security Incident Form which is forwarded to the Office of Student Services for processing.

Attitude and Enforcement

Any person who sets off a security alarm is likely to be embarrassed or upset which may result in inappropriate defensive actions and/or words. It is important that library staff maintain composure and not argue with patrons but, instead, focus on implementing the above described procedures.

Staff should keep voices calm and low in volume to minimize the levels of concern and to avoid making the incident into a public scene. It may be helpful to point out to the patron the sign asking for all library materials to be presented.

Emergency Alarms

If an alarm sounds for the emergency exit door in the basement, first floor west end, or second floor into Sease Wing, an attempt will be made to catch the person violating the door and to ask them to return to the library and exit properly through the front door; an explanation of their violation of the door will be provided; if it appears likely that the person has attempted a theft or other unlawful activity, Campus Police are called.

If the weather emergency radio sounds, staff will listen to ascertain whether there is a true emergency; if so, an evacuation of all staff and patrons to the basement is initiated using the intercom and rounding up people by foot—all persons in the library must either comply with the evacuation to basement order or leave the building at their own risk.

If the building fire alarm sounds, everyone in the building will automatically be evacuated outside through use of the intercom and by foot; do not use the elevator; staff and patrons are required to stay out of the building until the "all clear" signal is given by fire department personnel or university administrators.

Emergency Closings

University at Buffalo SUNY
University at Buffalo Libraries
Buffalo, New York

James A. Willis, Interim Executive Vice President for Finance and Operations, has issued a revised memo (November 30, 2005) concerning "changes in scheduled operations," including closings, class cancellations, and early departures for the University. Announcements regarding a change in scheduled operations will be made on:

- WBFO-FM 88.7, the official UB information station
- www.buffalo.edu/aboutmyub/, MyUB, a Web-based personal portal
- 645–NEWS (645-6397), the UB information line local broadcast media.

If an announcement is made that UB is making a change in scheduled operations, obviously the Libraries will follow suit. Such announcements will be posted on the staffWEB at http://libweb.lib.buffalo.edu/sw and issued via email to UBLIB-L.

As University policy indicates, even though the University may be closed, no one who chooses to report to work and is able to do so will be deprived of that opportunity. Arrangements have been made for those library staff who wish to report to work, to do so either at the Health Sciences Library in Abbott Hall on the South Campus or at the Undergraduate Library in Capen Hall on the North Campus.

However, rather than assign the responsibility for opening those facilities to individuals who may be unable to reach them, we have again secured the cooperation of the University Police. Those procedures require that you contact University Police informing them of your estimated time of arrival and at which library; prior notice is essential. University Police will open the facility for you, if it is not already opened at the time you call. Near the end of your work day, you must contact University Police again to arrange for them to close the library upon your departure.

According to State policy, should you not report for work, your absence will be charged to accrued credits for personal leave, vacation, or compensatory time. If you do not have sufficient credits, you may borrow from future accruals. Also, you may take a day without pay if you wish.

If you do report to work only to find your own library closed because the University is closed, you have the following options:

- call University Police to open either the Health Sciences Library or the Undergraduate Library to provide you with an alternate work site
- or return home and charge your absence to appropriate accruals
- or take leave without pay.

On days on which the University Libraries are opened and then subsequently close, you are not required to leave at that moment; you may leave then or any time thereafter. If you leave early, you should charge the remaining time to appropriate leave credits.

Please note that these procedures do not apply to student assistants. Unit directors should alert student employees of the need to determine whether the University is closed before reporting for work; student employees cannot be paid for lost time. Of course, they are welcome to any shelter the library or the University can provide, but once the University is closed, student employees are ineligible for payment.

Wilkes University
University Libraries
Wilkes-Barre, Pennsylvania

Emergency Closings

At times, emergencies such as severe weather, fires, power failures or floods can disrupt the institution's operations. In extreme cases, these circumstances may require the closing or delay the opening of Wilkes University. In the event that such an emergency occurs during non-working hours, this information will be disseminated on campus and to the local radio and television stations who will be asked to broadcast notification of the closing. Employees may also contact 408–SNOW or the Wilkes University Service Center, 408–2FIX for University closing or delayed opening information.

When operations are officially closed due to emergency conditions, the time off from scheduled work will be paid. An employee who is on an authorized leave of absence such as disability or FMLA leave will remain on such leave.

In cases where an emergency closing is not authorized, employees who fail to report for work will not be paid for the time off. An employee may request available paid leave time such as unused personal or vacation leave. An employee must report off work on or before the official start of the employee's shift and notify the supervisor to assess the time off as either personal or vacation leave.

Some essential services and functions must remain in operation regardless of Wilkes University closing conditions. Employees in "essential" operations may be asked to work on a day when operations are officially closed. Certain "essential" personnel may be required to report earlier than their designated shift. Media announcements will indicate the need for "essential" personnel to come to work. In these circumstances, exempt and non-exempt employees who work will receive double time for the hours worked. The following is a list of positions/departments that have been officially designated as "essential" for operational purposes:

- Public Safety Officers
- Service Center Personnel
- Residence Life Director (when classes are in session)
- Health Services Personnel (when classes are in session)
- Payroll Personnel
- Facilities Personnel
- Technology Personnel
- Library Personnel (when classes are in session)
- Any other positions as designated by the University

Each employee is expected to use discretion in determining if travel is safe and plan accordingly. If the University remains open during certain conditions, and the employee determines that it is too dangerous to come to campus or remain on campus, they are expected to notify the supervisor of their intentions as soon as possible. The employee may opt not to be paid for missed time or may elect to use available vacation or personal leave time.

TOURS
Library Tours

University of California Berkeley
University of California Berkeley Libraries
Berkeley, California

Library Tours

Many libraries offer tours of their buildings and collections at the beginning of each semester, and some offer tours throughout the year. Tours of the Doe/Moffitt Libraries begin in the north lobby of Doe Library (floor 1) at 10 a.m. on the first Tuesday of each month and at 2 p.m. on other Tuesdays. A comprehensive list of library tours is available on the Library's Web site. Visitor Services provides information and assistance for your visit to the campus.

University of Texas at El Paso
University Libraries
El Paso, Texas

Tours

Teachers, parents and community organizations may bring student or other groups to the Library for a tour under the following conditions:

All tours must be scheduled and approved by the staff of the Reference Department, libraryref@utep.edu, or call 747-5643. Staff may not be available to conduct tours for groups that arrive without making the prior arrangements. Groups without reservations may be asked to leave the building.

The UTEP Library is a place for quiet study. It is disruptive and generally inappropriate to bring large numbers of pre-school or grade school children to the Library during the school semester. Therefore, the preferred time for these tours is during intersession. Tours should be scheduled at least two weeks in advance to ensure proper scheduling. The maximum suggested size for a tour group is 25. Groups of young children should have a ratio of one adult for every 8 children.

No tours will be given during the week prior to finals, or finals week.

FORMS
Library Incident Form

Princeton University
Princeton University Library
Princeton, New Jersey

PRINCETON UNIVERSITY
LIBRARY INCIDENT REPORT

Date of Incident: _____ Time of Incident: _____

Location of Incident: _____

Nature of Incident:

☐ Building Problem   ☐ Computer
☐ Heating/Cooling   ☐ Theft
☐ Electrical   ☐ Harassment
☐ Flood/Water Leak   ☐ Accident/Illness
☐ Suspicious Odor   ☐ Problem Patron
☐ Pest Control   ☐ Patron Complaint
☐ Carrel   ☐ Vandalism/Damage
☐ Door/Fire Alarm   ☐ Other: _____

Incident Description

Action Taken:
- ☐ Public Safety Notified (x8–3134)
- ☐ Library Security Notified (x8–3221)
- ☐ Custodians Notified (x8–3226)
- ☐ Maintenance Notified (x8–6691)
- ☐ Systems Office Notified (x8–5580)
- ☐ Preservation Notified (x8–5591 or 8–2451)
- ☐ Paged
- ☐ Other: _____

Person Reporting: _____

COMPLETED REPORT SHOULD BE SENT TO DOTTIE PEARSON, FIRESTONE LIBRARY

Part III
Collection Development

Chapter 11

LIBRARY COLLECTION DEVELOPMENT GUIDELINES

GOALS AND OBJECTIVES

Guilford College
Hege Library
Greensboro, North Carolina

Goals and Objectives

The Hege Library's collection development policy supports the mission of Guilford College as a liberal arts institution for undergraduates. In the development of a collection, the staff of the library and the faculty selectors strive to support the goal of academic excellence while seeking diversity of intellectual matter—a diversity which reflects traditional as well as non-traditional thinking.

The primary objectives of collection development are to gather materials which will support and enhance the curriculum and which will reflect the values of Guilford College's Quaker and liberal arts heritage. In the building and management of the collection, attention will be given to materials consonant with the multicultural, interdisciplinary, international, and pluralistic interests of the institution. Materials will be collected in the most appropriate and most durable format. Careful consideration will be given to items reflecting current technologies, and content, not format, will be the deciding factor in acquiring materials.

Christopher Newport University
Captain John Smith Library
Newport News, Virginia

I. Purpose

The purpose of Smith Library is to provide access to knowledge and information resources needed by the faculty, students, and staff of the university. Adequate resources from all major subject fields will be accessible by students in support of the curriculum they choose. Materials for the cultural enrichment and recreational interests of the faculty and students will also be provided. Specialized research needs of faculty and graduate students will be considered on an individual basis.

The goals for selected areas in the Library collection are:

A. To maintain a reference collection designed to meet the reference and research needs of the students and faculty of the university. The collection shall consist of the standard works of general reference and important specialized reference works in fields covered by the curriculum.

B. To provide a periodical collection of general interest titles as well as titles that support instruction and faculty research. Appropriate indexes for accessing periodical materials will be available. Backfiles of currently received periodicals are provided when feasible and are added as funds permit.

C. To provide media materials in a variety of formats to support instruction. Emphasis is on current and developing formats.

D. To support a reserve collection of material requested by the faculty, for use by their students, organized to maximize use.

E. To provide browsing collections of popular books and audiovisual materials for the recreational needs of students, faculty and staff.

II. General Collection Guidelines

Christopher Newport University recognizes the responsibility of the library to keep in its collection materials on all matters of interest to its users, including materials that support all sides of controversial subjects. Materials will not be excluded from the collection solely on the basis of the frankness of language, or the controversial manner an author may use in dealing with religious, political, sexual, social, economic, racial, scientific, or moral issues.

The Library follows the principles of ALA's Library Bill of Rights. In handling criticisms of material or attempts at censorship, the librarians in consultation with other members of the library staff will reply to the person or group, quoting or referring to the above policy. Persistent or repeated criticisms will be referred to the library's administration, who, with the advice of the Library Advisory Committee, will respond to the matter. All decisions on disposition of challenged materials remain with the library.

COOPERATIVE COLLECTION DEVELOPMENT AND RESOURCE SHARING

Hudson Valley Community College
Dwight Marvin Library
Troy, New York

Resource Sharing

The Library provides faculty and students access to the resources of other libraries through the Inter-Library Loan (ILL) System. The SUNY Open Access Program allows students and faculty to borrow items from all SUNY libraries. Additionally, the Library is a member of the Capital District Library Council (CDLC), a consortium that includes college, university, public and special libraries located in the counties of Albany, Rensselaer, Saratoga and Schenectady. Items from these collections are listed on a database called CaDiLaC. Local library collections are available to our faculty and students through the Direct Access Program (DAP). Using their DAP card, students and faculty may go to other academic, public, and special libraries in the Capital District and borrow books as they would at our Library. The Hudson Valley Community College is also a member of OCLC. This organization maintains WorldCat, an international database containing 46 million records of book and non-book items cataloged by the Library of Congress and member libraries around the world. WorldCat helps facilitate resource sharing through its on-line interlibrary loan subsystem.

Illinois College
Schewe Library
Jacksonville, Illinois

If Schewe Library does not have an item that you need, you may be able to find it at one of the libraries with which we have a reciprocal borrowing agreement. By these agreements, Illinois College students may borrow from MacMurray College Library and ten other college libraries in the area. Students with Jacksonville addresses (including the dorms!) can also apply for a free library card at the Jacksonville Public Library. If these libraries do not have the needed materials, you may request the materials through interlibrary loan by filling out a form at the circulation desk. Usually interlibrary loan is free, but there may be a charge for photocopies of long periodical articles. An interlibrary loan takes two to three weeks to arrive, so you need to plan ahead in order to use this service.

Lake Sumter Community College
Lake Sumter Community College Libraries
Sumterville, Florida

Cooperative Collection Development

Due to the libraries' limited budgets and diminishing ability to physically collect even a small percentage of the world's information, access rather than ownership has become the reality of collection development. Increasing numbers of information resources are available only in online electronic formats. The worldwide development of electronic information systems such as online library catalogs, abstracting and full-text databases have made it possible for libraries to direct users to vast quantities of information resources. While the libraries cannot keep all of the material relevant to the users in their collections, they can provide access to the vast amount of information available for use in other collections. This type of access requires that libraries engage in cooperative collection development, resource sharing, and document delivery systems. When it is determined that access on demand is more economically feasible in terms of storage, projected use, and cost, this option can enhance the libraries' abilities to expand the information base available to their primary users.

Every possible effort will be made to cooperate with Lake County Library System, the Sumter County Library system, regional and statewide organizations, particularly the Central Florida Library Cooperative, the College Center for Library Automation, and the Florida State Community College Library Standing Committee to share resources and engage in cooperative acquisitions projects.

(For additional policies, please see the accompanying CD-ROM.)

CLASSIFICATION AND ORGANIZATION

Olin College
Olin College Library
Needham, Massachusetts

Items in the library catalog are assigned locations and call numbers.

Most items are located in the stacks (lower level) or in reference or reserves (upper level).

Maps (upper level and lower level) are available to help you find specific locations. The Library uses the Library of Congress (LC) call numbering system. Each book in our collection is assigned a unique call number, and these call numbers appear on the spine of books. Materials are arranged in the stacks by these call numbers.

A good tutorial on reading LC call numbers is available at:

http://geography.miningco.com/library/congress/blhowto.htm?pid=2820&cob=home. Several posters providing an overview of the LC classification system are posted in the library. The full Library of Congress outline can accessed at: www.loc.gov/catdir/cpso/lcco/lcco.html.

University of Scranton
Weinberg Memorial Library
Scranton, Pennsylvania

The University of Scranton's Web site is changing, and policies will be separated from information on the updated sites.

The Collection

The Weinberg Memorial Library is classified on the Library of Congress (LC) scheme. LC Subject Headings are used to establish correct terms for subject searches on the OPC.

Library books are shelved as follows:

Oversized	5th Floor
Curriculum Materials (Ed Lab) and G to PQ	4th Floor
PR to Z	3rd Floor
Science Reference (REF QB to QZ) and Indexes	3rd Floor
Reference Books	2nd Floor

Library non-print materials are shelved on the first floor in the Media Resources Collection.

LIBRARY LIAISONS

College of Charleston
College of Charleston Libraries
Charleston, South Carolina

1.0 Purpose

This policy describes the responsibilities of the Library Liaison including their relationships with academic departments, the Collection Development Committee, and the Collection Development Department. Library Liaisons are defined as members of the library faculty who have collection maintenance responsibilities for various subject areas. Library Liaisons are expected to serve as the primary mechanism for communication to academic departments usually through departmental liaisons concerning all aspects of library services.

2.0 Selection of Library Liaisons

The Collection Development Committee recommends appointments for Library Liaisons to the Dean of Libraries. An effort will be made to integrate areas of expertise and interest and especially other work responsibilities with liaison assignments. The Marine Resources Librarian is the liaison to the Graduate Marine Biology faculty.

3.0 Acquisitions Responsibilities
    3.1 Firm Orders
        3.1.1 At the beginning of the budget cycle, liaisons in consultation with the academic departments, shall prepare budget requests for each of their assigned areas.
        3.1.2 Liaisons will review all faculty orders prior to ordering by the Collection Development Department.
        3.1.3 Liaisons will prepare orders in the assigned areas especially in areas especially in areas where faculty make few selections.
        3.1.4 Liaisons are responsible for monitoring fund encumbrances and expenditures to ensure adequate spending levels.
        3.1.5 Liaisons will review all returned duplicate orders prior to them being forwarded to the faculty.
    3.2 Approvals
        3.2.1 Liaisons will work with the Collection Development Committee and the Collection Development Department to monitor and develop an approval profile which meets the academic department needs.
        3.2.2 Liaisons review and approve acceptance of approval books on a weekly basis.
    3.3 Serials
        3.3.1 Liaisons will participate in the ordering and canceling of serial titles as defined in Policy #4 Serial Order Request and Cancellation Policy, Section 4.2.
    3.4 Gifts
        3.4.1 At the request of the Dean, Assistant Dean for Technical Service, Assistant Dean of Public Services, or Head, Collection Development, liaisons may be asked to evaluate and negotiate for the acceptance of gifts (see Gift Policy and Procedures, Policy #2).

4.0 Public Services Responsibilites

    4.1 Liaisons are responsible for communicating library services and policies to the academic departments.

    4.2 Bibliographic Instruction/Specialized Lectures

        4.2.1 An effort will be made to match liaison responsibilities with specialized lectures.

        4.2.2 Technical Service librarians with liaison responsibilities may be required to participate in Bibliographic Instruction with the approval of the Assistant Dean for Technical Services, the Dean of Libraries and coordinated by Public Services.

5.0 Training Responsibilities

    5.1 Acquisitions training is provided by the Head of Collection Development as coordinated by the Assistant Dean for Technical Services.

    5.2 Public service orientation and training is provided by the Assistant Dean for Public Services.

    5.3 Liaisons will be responsible for participating in the ongoing orientation and training program of the library.

    5.4 Budget preparation training will be provided by the Head, Collection Development as coordinated by the Assistant Dean for Technical Services.

Hudson Valley Community College
Dwight Marvin Library
Troy, New York

Library and Media Center Liasion Program

The Liaison Program is designed to maintain lines of communication between professors, the Media Specialist, and Faculty Librarians. A Liaison Librarian and Media Specialist are assigned to work with each department. The role of the liaison is to collaborate with faculty in the selection, evaluation, and utilization of Library/Media resources. Liaison services offered include acquisition of materials, bibliographies, handouts, guides, projects, enrichment reading, audio-visual programs, as well as class instruction. Professors are encouraged to suggest books and media for the circulating and reference collections that will support their curriculum or their own research needs. Instructors who plan to introduce a new course are required by the Curriculum Committee to collaborate with their Liaison Librarian and the Media Specialist, so that they may suggest materials or acquire items to support the course.

Retention of Materials

Lane Community College
Lane Community College Library
Eugene, Oregon

Retention

    A. Base retention on indexing and physical format of the subscription.

    B. Guidelines for retention

        1. Current issue:

            Newspaper subscriptions—retain current issues (which have microfilm subscription) until receipt of microfilm.

        2. Current & previous month:

            Newspaper subscriptions—discard newspapers (when not receiving microfilm) after current & previous month.

        3. Current & previous year:

            a. Keep periodicals that are not indexed in a source accessible by LCC clientele at the LCC Library for current & previous year.

    b. Generally retain indexed periodicals for which the Library receives microfilm for current & previous year.

    c. Retain indexed periodicals in "newspaper format" (maintenance difficulty), but for which Library does not receive microfilm, for current & previous year.

4. Current five years:

    Indexed periodicals—when their LCC print or electronic indexes are retained or provide coverage for approximately five years.

5. Current ten years:

    Indexed periodicals—when their LCC print or electronic indexes are retained or provide coverage for approximately ten years.

6. Open-ended holdings:

    a. Periodicals providing curriculum-related (freshman or sophomore level) material college-wide support, such as community college and higher education information, some historical background exceptional visual documentation.

    b. Periodicals in this category are indexed LCC print or electronic indexing covers the time for which the publication is available at LCC.

    c. Generally microfilm holdings are in this category.

7. Closed holdings:

    a. Ceased publications are in this category.

    b. Periodicals with Library-dropped subscription are in this category.

    c. Retain periodicals in this category if LCC available indexing provides coverage and usage warrants.

    d. Generally this category is microfilm.

C. Request a change in retention by using the Periodical Request form.

University of Illinois at Urbana-Champaign
University Library
Urbana, Illinois

Retention Policies in the Digital Age

A Guide for the University of Illinois Library

This document describes the policies and procedures governing the retention of material in our Library collections. It applies to decisions to retain or withdraw material, as well as to decisions relating to the replacement of lost material. It covers both multiple and single copies, monographs and serials, in all formats.

General Principles

The Library has as a central element of its mission the obligation to retain the materials that record and represent our intellectual and cultural heritage, and which form the history of disciplines, and to make these materials available through resource sharing to the state of Illinois and beyond. The publication of new editions does not mean earlier editions should be discarded. Special care should be taken in subject areas where outdated works cannot be used for current research but are invaluable to historians.

In general, last/single copies are retained. When both print or microform and electronic versions exist, print/microform copies are the copy of record. When material is electronic only, assure perpetual access and best possible provisions for interlibrary loan. The number of print/microform copies retained of any one item may vary based on the professional judgment of the individual subject specialist, however it is expected that no more than two print or microform copies will be retained except under special circumstances.

The subject specialist makes the decision of how many print copies to retain. The online catalog, other internal records, and the materials themselves must be consulted before making withdrawal decisions.

Consultation among our faculty and other members of our user community, as well as with librarians at UIUC is necessary. When appropriate, consultation with CIC and other consortial schools should occur. Decisions should take into consideration: subject, including interdisciplinary impact; language; rarity; provenance; format; projected use; physical condition; licensing restrictions on resource sharing; accessibility of electronic formats; and completeness.

The Circulation/Bookstacks Librarian oversees consultation with the appropriate subject, language, and area specialists before any withdrawal takes place from the Stacks. Consultation with the AUL for Collections, the Preservation Librarian and subject specialists regarding items in poor condition will be done as needed.

As a regular part of collection maintenance, lists of missing items should be reviewed on a regular basis and evaluated for replacement, both in the bookstacks and in the departmental library collections. When missing interdisciplinary items are identified, consultation with other librarians should occur.

Care should be taken not to transfer unnecessary multiple copies to the bookstacks or the storage facility.

Retention Decision Guide

Last copy (print copy)

May be transferred to Stacks or Remote Storage. The last copy is considered to be the archival copy. If in poor condition it should be repaired or replaced before any transfer. Withdrawal of the last copy must be approved by the Associate University Librarian for Collections, who will consult with librarians as needed to consider the availability of copies in other libraries as well as the impact on resource sharing.

Damaged: Have repaired if possible, or keep as is if it has intrinsic value or is difficult to repair. Otherwise, consult with subject specialist to see about the acceptability of replacement with another copy, including another format. If the material is replaced with another format, the decision to retain the original lies with the subject specialist, who should consider the impact of the format choice on resource sharing.

Missing: Serials: replace print or microform copy missing volumes with like copy, depending on availability, cost, use, and access to the item via ILL. Monographs: Selectors should consider replacement in the same or another format.

Last copy (electronic copy)

In certain cases, material is "born digital" with no printed copies in existence. Purchase or license terms should assure perpetual access to all material for which the Library has paid a fee even if a continuing subscription has not been maintained.

Bookplated Material: Care should be taken to retain material with bookplates which indicate that the item was a gift purchased with endowed funds. Consult appropriate selector or the Library Development Office as necessary.

Disposition of Withdrawn Material

A. Materials purchased on State funds and non-State funds, including endowment funds, are the property of this collection and have the following restrictions placed upon their disposal, unless other restrictions are imposed from outside agencies, such as federal granting agencies:

1) May not be sold, offered for credit or given to private individuals.
2) May be transferred to the following entities located in Illinois:

- another agency covered by State Property Control Act 605a state-supported university library a tax-supported public library, including a library established by a public library district
- a library system organized under the Illinois Library System Act or any library that is a member of such system Illinois Library
- items that are disposed of in these ways must be submitted on an itemized list to the Library Business Office, along with an estimated cost of the material. This may be done using established procedures for withdrawing items from the online catalog. Library with-

drawals are reported by the Library Business Office to Campus Property Accounting on an annual basis.

3) May be withdrawn and recycled as scrap. Recycling should be pursued and withdrawn items must be sent to an approved local Illinois recycling program if the material is recyclable. Scrap may not be used for private purposes or private gain.

4) May be offered for credit or exchange for library materials of equal value to a reputable agent or vendor, through the Office of Collections.

5) May be used in another part of the University.

6) May be kept for office use. Later disposal of this material must follow the procedures set forth here.

7) May be transferred to an out-of-state library if not needed by any other state library and only after receipt of approval from the Property Accounting Section who, on behalf of the Library, will first pursue approval from the Illinois Department of Central Management Services. A list of items and their estimated original costs, estimated current value, acquisition dates, and original funding sources must be provided to the Library Business Office.

B. Materials received as gifts:

1) May be added to the collection if needed. Once a gift is added to the Library collection, it becomes University property and the procedures outlined in the Disposition of Library Materials apply.

2) If not needed, it may be sold in the Library book sale or used for exchange with reputable agents for additional Library collection materials, unless the donor has stipulated the gift may not be used in this way.

C. Materials received through external funding sources:

1) Items acquired with restricted external funding, such as grants and federal depository items, must follow the disposition procedures prescribed by the funding agency. If the external sponsor does not stipulate procedures for disposition, then procedures outlined in Disposition of Withdrawn Procedures then applies.

ALLOCATION OF FUNDS IN A BOOK BUDGET

Centre College
Grace Doherty Library
Danville, Kentucky

Book Budget Allocation

Generally, the Director of the Library, with the help of the librarians, is responsible for the overall balance and quality of the library collection. Academic programs, generally, are responsible for selecting materials and resources appropriate for their program needs. This process requires consultation between the faculty and the librarians.

Accordingly, the Committee on Instructional & Technology Resources adopts the following guidelines and procedures:

The Director of the Library shall report to Division Chairs the results of the book budget allocation; The Division Chairs shall allocate the divisional book budget to programs (Division Chairs may wish to set aside some small portion of the divisional book budget as discretionary book funds); Program Chairs assume responsibility for the supervision of the program book budget, approving and forwarding program book orders to the Director of the Library or Acquisitions Librarian; The library staff shall maintain up to date acquisition records and provide regular reports to the Division Chair or, when necessary, to Program Chairs;

The Director of the Library shall establish bi-annual book order deadlines. Orders arriving past the deadlines will be charged to the next year's book budget or will be returned to the Program Chair;

The Director of the Library will maintain discretionary book funds for special requests;

The Director of the Library and other librarians will be available for consultation with faculty.

The annual library book budget shall be allocated in the following manner:

The Director of the Library will allocate a portion of the book budget to the library general fund, which supports purchases in reference, general reading, special requests, etc. The recent amount has been 30% of the book budget.

The Committee on Instructional & Technology Resources, made up of faculty, staff, librarian, and student representatives, will allocate the remainder of the book budget among the three divisions according to a formula which gives equal weight to four factors:

- average cost per book purchased during the previous fiscal year in each division;
- average number of majors in each division over the previous five years;
- total circulation in each division during the previous fiscal year;
- total instruction load in each division during the previous fiscal year.

These variables are applied to the statistical totals of each academic division. For each variable, the lowest number among the divisions is assigned a value of "1," and the totals for remaining divisions are weighted accordingly. The division's four weighted variables are then totaled. The three divisions' totals are then totaled to provide a number that represents 100%. Each division's total is then figured as a percentage of the grand total and the resulting number is the division's share of the total book budget.

University of South Carolina Beaufort
USC Beaufort Library
Beaufort, South Carolina

Allocation of Funds

The Library Director is responsible for the expenditure of all library funds. A percentage of those funds designated for the purchase of library materials is allocated to each academic discipline each fiscal year according to a formula approved by the Faculty Library Committee. It is library policy for each department to pay for all periodical subscriptions and standing orders in its particular subject area from its allocation. A general fund under the jurisdiction of the library staff is reserved for the following: reference materials, materials needed to fill in gaps in the collection, materials in subject areas that are not represented in the curriculum, materials that have been damaged or lost, and materials to be bound.

COLLECTION EVALUATION

University of South Carolina Beaufort
USC Beaufort Library
Beaufort, South Carolina

Evaluation

Evaluation of the collection, as the word implies, is exercised continually by judging it against qualitative standards, that is, through consultation with knowledgeable people and through comparison of the collection with standard general and specialized bibliographies as Books for College Libraries, Choice, Best Books for Academic Libraries, Magazines for Libraries and, where available, subject lists for college libraries prepared by learned associations.

Saint Philips College Learning Resource Center
Alamo Community College District
San Antonio, Texas

Evaluation of the Collection

The continual review of library materials is necessary as a means of maintaining an active library collection of current interest to users. Evaluations will be made to determine whether the collection is meeting its objectives, how well it is serving its users, in which ways it is deficient, and what remains to e done to develop the collection. This process requires the same attention to quality and authority as the original selection of materials.

SPC LRC faculty and/or staff will evaluate portions of the collection on a regular basis, using a combination of standard, qualitative and quantitative methods.

Access/Ownership Statement

With the Library's diminishing ability to own even a small percentage of the world's information, the economics of access has become a crucial issue.

Integrating access as a part of the collection development policy is a modern necessity and provides some decided advantages to the library as an information provider.

Developments in electronic information systems have made it possible for libraries to provide their patrons with an awareness of the vast amount of information available for use. While the library cannot keep all of the material relevant to its users in its collection, it can provide access to the vast amount of information available for use in other collections. This type of access requires that the library engage in cooperative collection development, resource sharing, and document delivery systems.

The trend is toward availability of information in electronic format only. When it is determined that access on demand is more economically feasible in terms of storage, projected use, and cost, this option can enhance the library's ability to expand the information base available to its primary users.

The SPC LRC's goal is to move toward a logical combination of traditional collections and access to materials that cannot be owned.

The LRC will incorporate cost-effective models to guide decisions concerning access to information in all formats used for book purchases as well. Because the commitment to serials is over a long period and expensive, the library has in place a separate review process for the addition or deletion of titles.

(For additional policies, please see the accompanying CD-ROM.)

INTELLECTUAL FREEDOM STATEMENT

Centre College
Grace Doherty Library
Danville, Kentucky

Intellectual Freedom Statement

Library Intellectual Freedom Policy

As an academic institution, The Grace Doherty Library seeks to uphold the tradition of intellectual freedom and to create an atmosphere conducive to research and learning.

Further, the Grace Doherty Library shall provide books and other library resources for the education and information of all members of the Centre College Community. The library shall attempt to provide materials and information representing a variety of points of view on current and historical issues. Materials shall not be proscribed or removed because of partisan or doctrinal disapproval.

University of South Carolina Beaufort
USC Beaufort Library
Beaufort, South Carolina

Intellectual Freedom

The library adheres to and supports the American Library Association's position on the freedom to read. It is important in modern society that knowledge and a diversity of ideas, regardless of point of view, be readily available in order to promote critical thinking and increase student learning.

The principles of intellectual freedom as outlined in the Library Bill of Rights and the Freedom to Read Statement of the American Library Association shall be followed in the selection of library materials. The USC Beaufort libraries do not act as agents for or against particular issues but seek to maintain a free flow of information in the selection of books. The disapproval of a book by one group should not be a means for denying that book to all groups if, by library selection standards, it belongs in the collection. The procedure for challenged materials follows:

> The library receives the complaint; staff members react politely and make no personal comment regarding the challenge of materials.

> The patron is asked to complete the "Request for Reconsideration of Library Materials" form available at the Circulation Desk and return it to the Director of the Libraries.

> The Library Director receives the form and activates a Review Committee (consisting of the members of the Faculty Library Committee) to study the complaint and make a recommendation.

> The Library Director places the challenged material on reserve so that members of the committee may read, reread, or study it. The Director also checks reviews of the challenged material to ascertain the general feelings of the reviewers.

> The Review Committee meets. After evaluating the material, the charge, relevant reviews, and the views of professionals in the field, the Review Committee weighs the values and faults of the challenged material very carefully and then makes a recommendation to the Library Director. A copy of the recommendation is sent to the Executive Vice Chancellor for Academic Affairs.

> The Executive Vice Chancellor meets with the Library Director to verify the recommendation of the Review Committee. Results of this meeting are forwarded to the Chancellor.

> The complainant is notified of the decision by the Library Director.

Until the time that a decision is reached, no action shall be taken by the library to remove the challenged material.

SELECTION RESPONSIBILITIES

The College of Saint Catherine
College of Saint Catherine Libraries
Minneapolis, Minnesota

Authority

Final responsibility for selection rests with the Library Director. The Director delegates to staff members the authority to interpret and guide the application of selection policy and procedures in making day-to-day decisions. Unusual problems and requests for reconsideration of library materials are referred to the Director.

Guilford College
Hege Library
Greensboro, North Carolina

Responsibility for Selection

Library staff, faculty, staff, and students share the privilege and responsibility for selection of books, periodicals, and other library materials. Any member of the Guilford College Community may initiate requests. The library staff encourages faculty to order materials to meet curriculum needs and for faculty and librarians to work together to maintain collections within appropriate subject areas. Final responsibility to insure that the collection meets its stated goals, objectives, and priorities rests with the library.

Responsibility for selection of monographic materials:

The library staff will submit requests where the collection has an identifiable need or where critically acclaimed items supplement priorities as listed above.

Faculty should submit requests for materials to the person designated by their department head, or to the department's collection development liaison in the library.

Other members of the College community may submit requests to the library. Students are encouraged to make recommendations for the collection either through the library or through the department in which they are studying. Questions may be addressed to the Library Director.

Responsibility for selection of periodical materials (newspaper, journals, indexes, etc.):

Any member of the Guilford College community may initiate requests for new titles. Those requests should meet the priorities listed under the acquisition of materials above. The Library Director will consult with all relevant departments and the Library Liaison of the Committee on Educational Support before making a commitment to periodical subscriptions costing more than $200 per year.

Cancellation decisions on periodicals are made by the Library Director in consultation with faculty members from the department(s) most affected by the cancellation(s). The library staff will attempt to monitor use and costs for specific titles. They will review periodicals consistent with the policy for standing orders and may make recommendations for cancellations. Availability of electronic journals and full-text online will be part of these decisions.

Responsibility for selection of materials on standing order:

Standing orders should be approved by the Library Director, in consultation with librarians, relevant departments, and the Library Liaison of the Committee on Educational Support. Standing orders should be reviewed periodically by the library staff who may propose titles for withdrawal.

Responsibility for selection of electronic materials:

The Library Director will oversee the selection of electronic resources. In the case of electronic materials costing more than $200 per year, the Library Director will consult with relevant academic departments, the Library Liaison of the Committee on Educational Support, and, as appropriate, the Department of Information Services and Technology.

Christopher Newport University
Captain John Smith Library
Newport News, Virginia

A. The responsibility for selection of library materials is shared between the university instructional faculty and the library. The professional library staff select works not requested by faculty including reference works, bibliographies, general interest materials and interdisciplinary works.

The librarians, serving as liaisons to academic departments, utilize their professional judgment and academic backgrounds to fill gaps in the library collection. Librarians should also be guided by their knowledge of courses taught, student research needs, and general and specialized subject expertise.

Approval plans are utilized to obtain monographic materials in a timely manner.

As new programs of study are developed and implemented, collections to support those programs will be acquired. Responsibility for developing these collections will be shared between the university instructional faculty and the library.

Crichton College
Crichton College Library
Memphis, Tennessee

Responsibility for Selection

The Library Director is responsible for the selection of all library materials. The Vice President for Academic Affairs (representing the College Administration) retains the right to consider each item selected by the Library Director and to approve or disapprove of its purchase on the basis of cost and/or the administration's view of the item's appropriateness to the library collection.

The recommendations and advice of the College faculty as to materials selection is actively sought by the Library Director and forms a major portion of the selection process. Publisher's catalogs and published subject bibliographies are regularly sent to faculty subject specialists so they may aid in the selection of materials. Books for College Libraries is also available for faculty to consult so they may indicate priorities for purchase. Book reviews are provided by the Library Director upon request.

The Library Director also relies on such selection tools as Choice, Katz's Magazines for Libraries, Sheehy's Guide to Reference Books and book reviews contained within subject journals to guide in selection. In addition, recommendations are also received from staff and students.

CHALLENGES/OBJECTIONS TO MATERIALS

Crichton College
Crichton College Library
Memphis, Tennessee

Position on Censorship and Procedure for Complaints

The basic function of the academic library is to aid the institution in carrying out its programs which are reflective of its Biblical, theological, philosophical and educational viewpoints.

It follows, then, that within this setting there are certain built-in philosophies which serve as basic restrictions in the acquiring of library materials.

Furthermore, limitations as to clientele and budget endemic to a small college demand that library materials selection be implemented by means of a very carefully formulated selection policy. The key questions to be asked of any item which presents itself are:

A. If the work is fiction, does it compare favorably with the criteria employed in the selection of fiction works? (also see section V and VI)
B. If the work is non-fiction, does it compare favorably with the criteria employed in the selection of non-fiction works? (also sections V and VI)

Disclaimer: An item's presence in our collection does not imply institutional endorsement of the positions expressed therein.

Procedure for Complaints

A. In the event that a particular item in the library's collection is challenged by a patron, the following steps will be taken:
B. Director shall invite the complainant to fill out the request for Reconsideration of Library Materials' form (a copy of which is included in the appendix).

C. This form will be filled out by the complainant and returned to the Library Director, who will then inform the Vice President for Academic Affairs regarding the complaint.

D. The Library Director will fill out the "Library Book Evaluation Form" (or check in the files to see if such a form was filled out for the item at the time it was added to the collection).

E. The Library Committee will receive both of the above forms. It will also:

1. Read or examine the material in question.

2. Read reviews (supplied by the Library Director) regarding the item, consult standard bibliographic sources, and possibly consult with other libraries regarding the item.

3. On the basis of the above, the committee will attempt to judge the item as a whole, which avoids judging the item on the basis of passages pulled out of context.

4. Meet to discuss the material and prepare a written report on it.

5. File a copy of the report in the College Administrative office and submit a copy to the Vice President for Academic Affairs.

6. The Vice President for Academic Affair's office shall notify the complainant in writing concerning the administrations' final decision regarding the item.

F. Any item which is rejected by the Library Committee after careful consideration will be removed form the library Collection.

ACCESS VERSUS OWNERSHIP

Indiana University–Purdue University Fort Wayne
Walter E. Helmke Library
Fort Wayne, Indiana

Access/Ownership Statement

With the library's diminishing ability to own even a small percentage of the world's information, the economics of access has become a crucial issue. Integrating access as a part of the collection development policy is a modern necessity and provides some decided advantages to the library as an information provider. First, the developments in electronic information systems have made it possible for libraries to provide knowledge of the vast amount of information available for use. While the library cannot keep all of the material relevant to its users in its collection, it can provide access to the vast amount of information available for use in other collections. This type of access requires that the library engage in cooperative collection development, resource sharing, and document delivery systems. The trend is toward availability of information in electronic format only. When it is determined that access on demand is more economically feasible in terms of storage, projected use, and cost, this option can enhance the library's ability to expand the information base available to its primary users.

The Helmke Library's goal is to move toward a logical combination of traditional collections and access to materials that cannot be owned.

The library will incorporate cost-efficient models to guide decisions concerning access to information in all formats used for book purchases as well. Because the commitment to serials is over a long period and expensive, the library has in place a separate review process for the addition or deletion of titles.

FORMS

Objection to Material Forms

Crichton College
Crichton College Library
Memphis, Tennessee

REQUEST FOR RECONSIDERATION OF LIBRARY MATERIAL

Title _____ Book _____ Periodical _____ Other _____

Author _____

Publisher _____

Request initiated by (Full name) _____

Address _____

City _____ State _____ Zip _____ Phone _____

Do you represent:

_____ Yourself

_____ An organization (name) _____

_____ Other group (name) _____

1. To what in the work do you object: (Please be specific; cite pages)

2. Did you read the entire work? _____What parts?

3. What do you feel might be the result of reading this work?

4. For what types of readers might you recommend this work?

5. What do you believe is the theme of this work?

6. Are you aware of judgments of this work by literary critics or subject specialists?

7. What would you like this library to do about this work?

_____ Do not lend it to anyone.

_____ Return it to the staff selection committee/department for reevaluation

_____ Other (Please explain)_____

8. In its place, what work would you recommend that would convey as valuable a picture and perspective of the subject treated?

Signature_____ Date_____

Lane Community College
Lane Community College Library
Eugene, Oregon

Statement of Concern About Materials in Lane Library

Because of the Library's commitment to the principles of intellectual freedom, there may be materials in the Library's collection which are of concern to some individuals or groups. The acquisition of such materials does not imply approval or endorsement of their contents or opinions, but enables the Library to fulfill its role in providing curriculum support and presenting a diversity of perspectives. For additional information on how the library selects materials, please read our collection development policy.

The Library also has a commitment to those we serve to respond to concerns expressed about materials in the collection, and has developed a process for reconsidering materials that reflects the seriousness with which these concerns are treated. Please complete the form below if you wish to make a formal request for reconsideration of materials.

REQUEST TO REEVALUATE LIBRARY MATERIALS

Top of Form

Name [＿＿＿＿＿＿＿＿＿＿＿＿]

Address [＿＿＿＿＿＿＿] City: [＿＿＿＿＿＿＿] State: [＿＿] Zip: [＿＿＿＿＿]

Phone [＿＿] [＿＿] [＿＿]

Email [＿＿＿＿＿＿]

1. Resource on which you are commenting: *required
   ○ Book
   ○ Magazine
   ○ Audiovisual
   ○ Newspaper
   ○ Online Resource
   Other: [＿＿＿＿＿＿＿＿]

2. Title: [＿＿＿＿＿＿＿＿＿＿＿] *required

3. Author/Producer: [＿＿＿＿＿＿＿＿＿]

4. What brought this title to your attention?
   [＿＿＿＿＿＿＿＿＿] *required

5. Did you review the entire item? ○YES ○NO
   If not, what sections did you review?
   [＿＿＿＿＿＿＿＿＿]

6. Please comment on the resource as a whole, as well as being specific on the matters which concern you. For example, are there specific pages, scenes, words, etc. that you find offensive or disturbing?
   [＿＿＿＿＿＿＿＿＿] *required

7. What do you think would be a satisfactory resolution to your concern?
   [＿＿＿＿＿＿＿＿＿] *required

This form will be submitted to a Library Review Committee composed of the librarian responsible for selecting this material, the Library Director, and a member of the Library staff. This committee shall consult with faculty from the affected discipline(s) if appropriate. The material will be reviewed objectively, and with the best interests of the students, the community and the College in mind. The Committee will notify you of the results of its review within 7 days.

> Submit Form

Central Washington University
Brooks Library
Ellensburg, Washington

Request for Reconsideration of Library Resources

If you wish to request reconsideration of library material or resources, please return the completed form to: Dean of Library & Media Services, Central Washington University. (Attach additional pages if needed.)

Name _____

Date _____

City _____ State_____

Zip Code_____ Phone_____

Are you a CWU student_____ or employee _____ of Central Washington University? Do you represent yourself? _____ your organization? _____

1. Resource on which you are commenting:

Title:

_____

Author/Producer:

_____

Book ___	Textbook ___	Video ___	Other (please specify): _____
Magazine ___	Library ___ Program	Audio Recording ___	Electronic information/ network (please specify):_____
Newspaper_____	Display_____		

2. What brought this resource to your attention?

3. Have you examined the entire resource?

4. What concerns you about the resource? Please be specific:

5. What of value is there in this work?

6. Are you aware of the reviews of this work by critics?

7. What do you believe is the theme or purpose of this work?

8. What do you feel might be the result of reading, viewing, or listening to this work?

9. Are there other resources you suggest which might provide additional information and/or other viewpoints on this topic?

10. What action do you request the Library to take?

Chapter 12

SCOPE OF COLLECTION

COLLECTING AND PURCHASING GUIDELINES

Scope of Collection

Crichton College
Crichton College Library
Memphis, Tennessee

Minimal Level

A subject area which is out of scope for the library's collection, and in which few selections are made beyond very basic reference tools and individual titles. Recreational reading materials and novels are collected at this level.

All acquisitions, whether purchased or donated, are considered in light of the following criteria:

The needs of the current curriculum, as well as long-range development of the college with reference to its degree programs. Included within this factor is the library's need to "fill in the gaps" of its current collection. This need will necessarily change focus with time.

The number of students majoring in each subject area

The research needs and literary production of the faculty (supplemented by Interlibrary Loan and borrowing agreements with local libraries)

Cost of the item and budget funds available

The item itself

Non-Fiction

Qualifications of the writer (education, experience, significance in field)

Scope of treatment (appropriate to intended reader; popular versus scholarly)

Accuracy

Timeliness or permanence of either the subject matter or its treatment

Date of publication

Presence of index, bibliography, glossary, illustrations, etc.

Reputation of publisher

Inclusion of the work in bibliographies, indexes and selection tools, such as Books for College Libraries

Authority of work

Physical condition of the item

Appropriateness of the format to our collection needs

Subject is presented in a balance, well-organized, thoughtful manner

Fiction

Representative of important movements, genres, trends or national cultures

Originality

Exemplifies good literary style, structure, characterization and plot

Has lasting appeal

Authenticity of historical or social setting

Inclusion of the work in selection tools

Physical condition of the item

Special Concerns for Community College Collections

Saint Philips College Learning Resource Center
Alamo Community College District
San Antonio, Texas

Selection and Evaluation Tools

Criteria

Literary merit, enduring value, accuracy, authoritativeness, social significance, importance of subject matter to the collection, timeliness, popular demand, cost.

Scarcity of material on the subject and availability elsewhere, quality and suitability of the format,(other considerations may be applicable in specific subject areas). Selectors should choose materials that will build a well-rounded collection which includes all viewpoints and opinions and which will meet the patrons' needs.

Tools

Professional journals, trade journals subject bibliographies, publishers' catalogs and promotional materials, reviews from reputable sources, lists of recommended titles and sales representatives for specific materials. Purchase suggestions from faculty and students are also an important source.

Levels of Collection Development by Subject Classification

Librarians are responsible for assessing collection strengths. Guidelines exist for determining levels of collection density and collecting intensity designations. Such guidelines are used to identify the existing strength of the collection, the actual current level of collection activity, and the desirable level of the collection to meet program needs.

In general, collecting will be at one of the following levels:

Out of Scope

Library does not intentionally collect materials in any format on this subject.

Minimal Information Level

To support minimal inquiries about this subject, the following are included:

A very limited collection of materials including monographs and reference works

Periodicals directly dealing with this topic and in-depth electronic information resources are not collected

The collection should be frequently and systematically reviewed for currency of information. Superseded editions and titles containing outdated information should be withdrawn. Classic or standard retrospective materials may be retained.

Basic Information Level

To introduce and define a subject, to indicate the varieties of information available elsewhere and to support the needs of general library users through the first two years of college instruction, the following are included:

A limited collection of monographs and reference works

A limited collection of representative general periodicals

Access to a limited number of owned or remotely accessed electronic bibliographic tools, texts, data sets, etc.

The collection should be frequently and systematically reviewed for currency of information. Superseded editions and titles containing outdated information should be withdrawn. Classic or standard retrospective materials may be retained.

Study or Instructional Support Level

To provide knowledge about a subject in a systematic way, but at a level of less than research intensity and to support the needs of general library users through college students, the following are included:

An extensive collection of general monographs and reference works

An extensive collection of general periodicals and a limited collection of representative specialized periodicals

Limited collections of appropriate foreign language materials, e.g., foreign language learning or foreign language material about a topic like German history

Extensive collections of the works of better-known writers and selections from the works of less well-known writers

Access to an extensive collection of owned or remotely accessed electronic bibliographic tools, texts, and data sets

The collection should be systematically reviewed for currency of information and to assure that essential and significant information is retained including significant numbers of classic retrospective materials.

Houston Community College System
Houston Community College Libraries
Houston, Texas

1.6 Criteria for Selection of Materials

    1.6.1 The library selects print and non-print materials from a number of professional selection tools. These include:
- Professional journals.
- Popular review sources.
- Standard bibliographies.
- Publishers' and producers' catalogs.
- Also from requests submitted by faculty, staff and students.
- The library also accepts gift materials (see separate policy for gift materials).

    1.6.2 When selecting materials, an overriding consideration is appropriateness for community college use. Most materials should be written or produced on a level that the average community college student can use or benefit from, or at a level that students in a particular field are expected to attain.

    1.6.3 Selection is also conditioned by the Library Bill of Rights and the Freedom to Read Statement as ratified by the American Library Association, and approved by the HCCS Board of Trustees (10–20–75), by the Statement of Academic Freedom and Responsibilities which is published yearly in the Houston Community College Faculty Handbook, and by HCCS policy regarding Internet and use.

    1.6.4 In addition to the above, the following criteria are used to evaluate materials considered for acquisition and inclusion in the collection.
- Relevance to instructional needs.
- Correlation to the existing collection.
- Appropriateness of the medium/compatibility with hardware already owned.
- Timeliness/permanence of contents.

- Quality
- Reputation of author, director, publisher, producer.
- Scarcity of materials on subject matter.
- Demand.
- Age.
- Cost in relation to other costs and other relevant materials.
- Storage needs.
- Availability elsewhere.

1.6.5 Due to budgetary and space limitations, duplication of materials between libraries within a college is made judiciously. Less heed is taken of duplication between colleges.

1.6.6 Titles are not automatically purchased in large quantities or as single copies, but what seems to be the best combination of quantity and anticipated needs.

1.7 System Collection

1.7.1 A major goal of collection development is to provide at least one full-service general resource center at each college.

1.7.2 Space and budget limitations will usually preclude large independent collections at each library within a college.

1.7.3 Through the use of the on-line catalog, students and faculty have access to materials throughout the system.

1.7.4 Each campus, however, is different, has its own unique needs and capabilities based on its courses, students, faculty, as well as its particular location and size.

1.8 Materials Formats

1.8.1 This section describes the various types of materials and formats purchased by the library.

1.8.2 Print materials

1.8.2.1 Books
- Hardbound materials are preferred for inclusion in the cataloged collection, except in the case of subject areas where materials become out-of-date quickly.
- If a choice is available between a hardbound or paper edition of the same title (and edition), the hardbound should be purchased, unless the cost difference is so great as to prohibit purchase in hardbound format.
- Textbooks adopted for courses are not customarily purchased by the library. Exceptions to this can be made on a case-by-case basis.
- Workbooks or any other work that consists primarily of pages to be filled in are considered consumables and are not purchased.
- Paperbound materials may be purchased for inclusion in the collection if a hardbound edition is not available.
- Mass market paperbacks are purchased for recreational reading. They are regarded as a browsing collection and are not cataloged or classified.

1.8.2.2 Serials

A serial is defined as a publication "issued in successive parts bearing numerical or chronological designations and intended to be continued indefinitely." (ALA Glossary, 1983) The Library recognizes two different categories of serials:
- Unclassified serials include magazines, journals and newspapers.
- Unclassified serials are issued more frequently than annually.
- Unclassified serials are purchased on a subscription basis.

Selection Criteria

Decisions about specific titles, numbers of copies and locations are made by the library chairs. These recommendations are based on information provided by librarians and faculty.

The quantity and specific titles at any one campus library depend on a number of variables: course offerings, enrollment, faculty and student requests, library use, space and budgetary limitations. The goal is to provide basic coverage at most campus libraries to support specific courses being taught as well as to provide both general interest and news magazines of international, national and local interest.

Format

Unclassified serials may be purchased in hard copy, microform or an electronic format.

The hard copy is replaced by the microform when it becomes available. This is done either annually or, preferably, on a quarterly basis.

Because of space and cost, some periodicals are only purchased in microform or electronic format.

Classified serials are publications issued in successive parts at an annual or lesser frequency. The include such items as almanacs, yearbooks, directories, indexes, and loose-leaf services.

Selection responsibility resides with the librarians under the coordination of the Library Chair.

1.8.3 Non-Print Materials

1.8.3.1 Audio-visual software
Formats currently in use:
- Videocassette (1/2 VHS) (VTC)
- 16 MM Film (Film)
- Audiocassette (CAS)
- Slide/Cassette (SLC)
- Filmstrip/Cassette (FSC)
- Filmloop (FL)
- Slide (SLI)
- Filmstrip (FS)
- Transparency (TRS)
- Map
- Phonograph record (PHO)
- Videodisk (VDD)

Selection Criteria

Materials must be compatible with equipment owned by the library.

Whenever a choice is available, preference should be given to media which is closed captioned over media which is not closed captioned..

There should be a definite commitment by the requesting instructor to use these items. (See also 1.6. Criteria for Selection of materials).

Because of cost, software is ordered on a 'Preview' basis and must be previewed by faculty. Faculty must indicate a willingness to use media in the classroom as a precondition for purchase.

Items costing under $50 may be purchased outright.

(For additional policies, please see the accompanying CD-ROM.)

Guidelines for Print Collections

Autographed or Signed Material

Columbia College
Columbia College Library
Chicago, Illinois

Autographed or Signed Copies

Autographed or signed copies of monographs or other materials will generally not be added to Special Collections unless the item meets one or more of the following conditions:

1. The author is determined to be of literary, artistic or historic significance, and has been or can be verified as authentic.
2. The work itself has increased in value due to the significance of the signature.
3. The work has been acquired specifically because of the presence of the signature.

Works that have been inscribed to an individual or individuals will generally be added to the main circulating collection unless the inscription is to a person of literary, artistic or historic significance. If there is a question regarding location placement of a specific item or items, each will be treated on a case-by-case basis in consultation with the appropriate selector and the Special Collections Librarian.

Hardbound Bindings

Christopher Newport University
Captain John Smith Library
Newport News, Virginia

Hardcover bindings are preferred because of their durability. Paperbacks are purchased when a suitable hardcover edition is not available, or when the price of paperback is at least $25 less than the hardcover and high use is not anticipated. Paperbacks of lasting value may be bound.

Honors Papers

University of North Carolina Wilmington
William Madison Randall Library
Wilmington, North Carolina

Randall Library serves as the repository for UNCW Honors Papers. Students must submit two copies of their papers to the Honors Program Office. One of the two copies must be the original copy.

The papers must be printed on 100% cotton fiber paper and placed in a heavyweight two-piece report cover. These may be purchased at the University Bookstore. The first page should show the title of the paper and the author's full name.

If all requirements are satisfied, the papers will be delivered by the Honors Program Office to the Library Administrative Office for addition to the collection. The original copy becomes part of the University Archives. The second copy is added to the General Collection.

Language

Christopher Newport University
Captain John Smith Library
Newport News, Virginia

Language

English is the primary language of collection. Materials in other languages are acquired to support the curriculum, including French, Latin, German, and Spanish. Material in other languages will be acquired to support the international studies programs of the university. English translations of major works are also acquired.

New York University
Bobst Library
New York, New York

Language

By the very nature of its core collections, the Library collects literature almost exclusively in English. The primary language of biographies, memoirs, and collected critical works is also English. This in large part also applies to the Downtown Collection and current efforts at Bobst to document the Downtown movement. Due, however, to the ethnic diversity of the area-particularly that work relating to the Nuyorican Poets Café in the Lower East Side (Losaida), some Spanish language materials are also collected.

Columbia College Chicago
Columbia College Library
Chicago, Illinois

Language

English language publications are preferred for acquisition, however these exceptions apply:

Books that are primarily pictorial in content (art, photography, graphic design, architecture, etc.) may be purchased without language restrictions.

Foreign language materials may be purchased in other subject areas if there is sufficient demand by students and / or faculty.

Where foreign language programs exist or are added to the curriculum, materials will be acquired with the assistance of faculty from those departments.

Materials in Process

Columbia College Chicago
Columbia College Library
Chicago, Illinois

If a Columbia student or faculty member urgently needs an item that is labeled No Holdings Available—check at Circulation Desk or Order Received in our Library catalog, they may submit a request for expedited processing of the material by Library staff from our Technical Services Department.

Next Steps

Please complete a Request Form for Material in Process available at the Reference or Circulation Desk. Attach to it a printout from our Library Catalog for the item in question. If you need assistance with completing the form or if you have questions, please check with staff at the Reference or Circulation Desk.

Library Technical Services staff will investigate and confirm the item's actual status. If there is a problem, we will contact you right away.

Library Technical Services staff will locate the in-process item within the department.

Library Technical Services staff will process the needed material within 48 hours after the item has been located.

When processing has been completed, the item will be brought to the Circulation Desk where it will be placed on the HOLD shelf under your name. Whoever placed the request for the material will be "first in line" to consult or check out the material (if permitted). Rush processing of an item does not grant circulating status to those already classified as non-circulating.

The Circulation Desk staff will notify you that the requested item is now available for use and it will remain on the HOLD shelf at the Circulation Desk for 24 hours only.

University of South Alabama
University Libraries
Mobil, Alabama

Rush Processing

If you need an item that the catalog indicates is "In Process," you may request that processing be expedited. Ask the Circulation Staff for a Rush Request Form and have the exact information from the SOUTHcat screen available to transcribe onto the form. Please be aware, however, that items listed as "In Process" are not always available. Materials listed as "On Order" or "In Pre-Order Process" have not yet been received.

Monographs

New Mexico State University Alamogordo
David H. Townsend Library
Alamogordo, New Mexico

Books/monographs are collected in clothbound editions unless cost is significantly higher than a paper edition. Books that must be frequently updated (nursing/medical texts, computer manuals, test preparation materials) will be purchased in paper formats. No attempt is made to support research needs of faculty pursuing advanced degrees. Interlibrary loan is regularly provided in a timely manner to meet faculty and administrative research requirements for books.

Eastern Michigan University
Bruce T. Halle Library
Ypsilanti, Michigan

Monographs

Monographs are selected to cover, as broadly as possible, all fields relating to the curriculum of the University, while also supplying deeper coverage in those fields where advanced degrees are offered. Monographs are added to the collection based on the following criteria: positive reviews in renowned review sources; author's and publisher's reputations; format; language (English is preferred in most cases); cost; recommendations by faculty and students; local interest; the quality and extent of the existing collection on the subject; and whether the edition has been revised or is merely a reprint.

A collection of books published for preschool through high school levels is maintained to support the education curriculum. This collection includes fiction, nonfiction and picture books.

In most disciplines, the library does not purchase textbooks; however, textbooks that are requested by a faculty member or received as gifts and that meet selection criteria will be added to the collection.

The library acquires fiction to support the University's curriculum and does not aspire to provide such a collection for leisure reading.

The library normally purchases only one copy of a title but exceptions may be made for archival purposes or to meet high demand.

Electronic format is preferred for most indexes, abstracts and reference materials.

Newspapers

University of South Carolina Beaufort
USC Beaufort Library
Beaufort, South Carolina

Newspapers

The library subscribes to representative local, regional and national newspapers. Due to limited storage space, backfiles of newspapers are not kept beyond three months.

The College of Saint Catherine
College of Saint Catherine Libraries
Minneapolis, Minnesota

Newspapers

The Libraries maintain subscriptions to selected local and regional newspapers. National newspapers are acquired on a highly selective basis. International newspapers are also acquired on a highly selective basis to support the curriculum. Selected newspaper backfiles are retained permanently on microfilm in the St. Paul Campus Library. Indexed newspapers are given priority in making backfile decisions.

Paperbacks

Crichton College
Crichton College Library
Memphis, Tennessee

Paperback Books

Paperback books may be purchased for any of the following reasons:
    a. The title has never appeared in a bound edition.
    b. The title is out of print and otherwise unobtainable in a better format.
    c. It is more economically feasible to purchase the paperback edition as opposed to the hardback edition (see above).

If a paperback book is selected, the quality of the paperback binding should be such that pages are not apt to come loose easily. This is particularly important when considering items that will remain permanently unbound. Paperback books may be bound at the discretion of the librarians, depending on quality, anticipated use and wear and other factors.

University of South Carolina Beaufort
USC Beaufort Library
Beaufort, South Carolina

Paperbacks

When there is a choice between hard cover and paperback, the paperback will be purchased unless the work is one expected to stand up to frequent and heavy use.

Indiana University–Purdue University Fort Wayne
Walter E. Helmke Library
Fort Wayne, Indiana

Paperbacks

Paperback monographs for the regular collection will be acquired only when hardback editions are not available or when there is a significant price difference between the hardback and paperback editions. When making a choice between paperback and hardback, the long-term value and expected use of the title will be considered.

Popular Fiction

Lake Sumter Community College
Lake Sumter Community College Libraries
Sumterville, Florida

Popular fiction having short-term interest among readers is not purchased. Established literary works and new works receiving critical acclaim in the literary field are considered, especially those works that support literature course offerings. Literary prizewinners are purchased when funds permit.

Indiana University-Purdue University Fort Wayne
Walter E. Helmke Library
Fort Wayne, Indiana

The library will not buy fiction that is anticipated to have only short-term interest among readers, but will attempt to select established literary works and new works of promise in the literary field, especially those works which would support literature course offerings. As part of the selection process librarians will evaluate the work in terms of the author's earlier writings and current reader interest.

Second Copies

The College of Saint Catherine
College of Saint Catherine Libraries
Minneapolis, Minnesota

Duplication of Materials among the Libraries of the College of St. Catherine

Duplicate copies of titles are not normally purchased for an individual library. Exceptions may be made, but will be reviewed carefully. Duplication of titles among the libraries will be reviewed to insure the best use of available resources.

Guidelines for Duplication:

Duplication of resources between the St. Paul and Minneapolis libraries is most likely to occur in the Reference collections.

Access tools (e.g. indexes and abstracts) will be duplicated as needed, if sharing electronically is not cost effective.

Circulating materials will not be duplicated as a general rule. Exceptions will be reviewed carefully.

Indiana University–Purdue University Fort Wayne
Walter E. Helmke Library
Fort Wayne, Indiana

Duplicates

Duplicates are not normally purchased. Duplicate materials will be added to the collection if warranted by heavy usage of copies already held by the library.

Serials

New Mexico State University Alamogordo
David H. Townsend Library
Alamogordo, New Mexico

Serials/periodicals/journals/newspapers are publications issued in successive parts bearing numeric or chronological designations and intended to be continued indefinitely. Serials are issued in print, microform, and electronic formats. All formats will be considered in the library's purchase and/or access decisions.

Serials are acquired via subscription. Individual issues or reprints will rarely be purchased.

The selection of serials requires a continuing commitment to the cost of the title, including maintenance, viewing and reproduction equipment, and storage space.

The escalating cost of serials subscriptions demands that requests for serials subscriptions be carefully reviewed before they are purchased for the collection and that an ongoing evaluation of current subscriptions be conducted.

Since it is becoming more cost-efficient to purchase electronic access or document delivery services for serials instead of acquisition through print subscription, this method of delivery will be chosen when fiscally prudent. Cooperative acquisition (regional and statewide) of electronic serials databases is actively pursued.

Electronic serials subscriptions licensing contracts may limit access to currently enrolled students, faculty and staff. The professional library staff reviews local serials collections and accessibility of online titles annually.

The serials collection supports the research needs of the NMSU-A curriculum.

No attempt is made to support research needs of faculty pursuing advanced degrees.

Interlibrary loan is regularly provided in a timely manner to meet faculty and administrative research requirements. Factors to be considered are:

- Support of academic programs
- Cost, including rate of price increases, cost of storage, and/or access costs
- Uniqueness of subject coverage for the college libraries
- Accessibility within resource sharing groups, consortia, and/or through document delivery or courier services
- Full-text availability via electronic access
- Professional reputation
- Usage or projected usage
- Indexing and abstracting in sources accessible to library users
- Demand for title in interlibrary loan or document delivery requests
- Intended audience including special users (2 + 2 or joint-use programs).

Crichton College
Crichton College Library
Memphis, Tennessee

Periodicals

Periodicals are purchased or accepted as gifts for one or more of the following reasons:
  a. To keep the library's collection up-to-date with current thinking in various fields
  b. To provide information not available in books.
  c. To provide some measure for the research needs of advanced students and faculty.
  d. To keep the faculty informed of developments in their field
  e. To serve the staff as book selection aids, book reviewing media, and professional reading. Individual titles are chosen for the following reasons:
     Accuracy and objectivity
     Accessibility of content through indexes
     Ease of consultation
     Demand
     Need in reference work
     Representation of a point of view or subject needed in the collection
     Cost of the subscription in relation to its use.
  f. In an age of limited resources and resource sharing, the library will also consider maintaining periodicals subscriptions which are requested through ILL even if not often used by CCL patrons.

Lake Sumter Community College
Lake Sumter Community College Libraries
Sumterville, Florida

Serials/periodicals/journals/newspapers are publications issued in successive parts bearing numeric or chronological designations and intended to be continued indefinitely. Serials are issued in print, microform, and electronic formats. All formats will be considered in the libraries' purchase and/or access decisions. Serials are acquired via subscription. Individual issues or reprints will rarely be purchased.

The selection of serials requires a continuing commitment to the cost of the title, including maintenance, viewing and reproduction equipment, and storage space. The escalating cost of serials subscriptions demands that requests for serials subscriptions be carefully reviewed before they are purchased for the collection and that an ongoing evaluation of current subscriptions be conducted.

Since it is often becoming more cost-efficient to purchase electronic access or document delivery services for serials instead of acquisition through print subscription, this delivery method will be chosen when fiscally prudent. Cooperative acquisition (regional and statewide) of electronic serials databases is actively pursued. Electronic serials subscriptions licensing contracts may limit access to currently enrolled students, faculty and staff. The professional library staff reviews local serials collections and accessibility of online titles annually.

The serials collection supports the research needs of the Lake-Sumter Community College curriculum. No attempt is made to support research needs of faculty pursuing advanced degrees. Interlibrary loan is regularly provided in a timely manner to meet faculty and administrative research requirements. Factors to be considered in the acquisition of serials are:

   Support of academic programs

   Suitability for intended audience including special users (2 + 2 or joint-use programs)

Uniqueness of subject coverage for the college libraries

Cost, including rate of price increases, cost of storage, and/or access costs

Professional reputation

Usage or projected usage

Indexing and abstracting in sources accessible to library users

Demand for title in interlibrary loan or document delivery requests

Accessibility within resource sharing groups, consortia, and/or through document delivery or courier services

Full-text availability via electronic access

Cost, including rate of price increases, cost of storage, and/or access costs

Textbooks

University of South Carolina Beaufort
USC Beaufort Library
Beaufort, South Carolina

Textbooks

Except in extraordinary cases, no textbooks in current use on the USCB campuses are purchased for the library collection. Textbooks are purchased, and free copies are accepted, when they supply information in areas in which they may be the best or the only source of information on the subject.

Lake Sumter Community College
Lake Sumter Community College Libraries
Sumterville, Florida

Textbooks are not selected unless recommended by faculty as exceptional resources. Exceptions are those that have earned a reputation as "classics" in their fields, or which are the only or best sources of information on a particular topic, or for a particular user group. Their high cost, frequent revision, and generally poor bindings make most textbooks a poor investment for the libraries' permanent collections.

The College of Saint Catherine
College of Saint Catherine Libraries
Minneapolis, Minnesota

The libraries do not collect textbooks. Exceptions are made, however, when textbooks are the best or only source of information on the topic. Some test preparation books are purchased in academic fields for which our students will pursue advanced studies. Other test preparation books will not be purchased.

Christopher Newport University
Captain John Smith Library
Newport News, Virginia

Although CNU course textbooks are not generally purchased, they may be acquired for the collection when they provide information in subject areas in which they may be the best or only source of information. Textbooks published within the preceding five years may be added when received as gifts.

Theses and Dissertations

University of North Carolina Wilmington
William Madison Randall Library
Wilmington, North Carolina

The Graduate School requires that each student submit three (3) copies of his/her thesis for binding at Randall Library. Each copy must be on white, 8.5 x 11", 20 or 24 lb. 100% cotton bond paper, and each copy must contain a title page bearing the original signatures of all members of the thesis committee. These copies must be delivered to the Technical Services Department of Randall Library. Please include copies of supplementary materials, i.e. slides, photographs, CD's, disks, videos, etc. All copies must be in correct page order. Library and bindery staff members do NOT check page order. The Library will pay binding costs for these three copies.

After binding, one copy will be cataloged for the University Archives and another copy will be cataloged for the library's circulating General Collection. The third copy will be sent to the appropriate academic school or department.

Students and faculty may want additional copies bound for personal use. State contracts for library binding prohibit the binding of personal materials, but students and faculty may contact a professional bindery to arrange for binding personal copies. The following binderies are currently on the state binding contract, and although personal copies do not qualify for state contract rates, students and faculty may negotiate for a higher quality binding for their personal copies.

College of Charleston
College of Charleston Libraries
Charleston, South Carolina

1.0 Purpose

The purpose of this policy is to establish the responsibilities and procedures for the Library acquiring and preserving copies of the College's bachelor's essays and theses. The Library attempts to collect and preserve all significant documents produced at the College of Charleston.

2.0 Definitions

These are formal treatises written by candidates for advanced degrees and approved by the appropriate academic department. Bachelor's essays are papers written by undergraduates either enrolled in the Honors Program or approved by the appropriate faculty member.

3.0 Responsibilities

3.1 Each department and school at the College of Charleston will send at least two copies of each thesis and one copy of each bachelor's essay to the Library's Collection Development Department.

3.2 The Collection Development Department will have each thesis bound and bill the Graduate School for the cost of binding. The Library will absorb the cost of the binding of bachelor's essays.

3.3 Each item will be cataloged by the Cataloging Department and entered into the Library's online catalog.

3.4 One copy of each item will be placed in the Library's Special Collections Department for archival purposes. A second copy of theses will be placed in the Library's circulating collection.

3.5 Three copies of theses from the graduate program in Marine Biology will be sent to the Library; the additional copy will be bound and cataloged for the Marine Resources Library.

GUIDELINES FOR NONPRINT COLLECTIONS

Criteria for Nonprint Material

Crichton College
Crichton College Library
Memphis, Tennessee

Criteria for Selection of Nonprint Materials
Points of Quality
- Accurate facts
- Facts impartially presented
- Up-to-date information up-to-date
- Other acceptable works by producer
- Vocabulary at user's level
- Concepts at user's level
- Useful data
- Media/subject correlation (e.g. art prints to art, specimens to science)
- Titles, captions, etc. relates to subject
- Narration, dialogue, sound effects related to subject
- Individual and/or group use suitable
- Full coverage as indicated
- Superior concept development by this means
- Content to satisfy demands for current subjects
- Relationship to user's experiences
- Intellectual challenge
- Curiosity satisfaction
- Credibility
- Imagination appeal
- Human appeal
- Sensory appeal
- Logical development
- Pertinence of all sequences
- Balance in use of narration and dialogue, music and sound effects, background elements
- Tone fidelity
- Clarity
- Intelligibility
- In-focus pictures
- True size relationships
- Unified composition
- Effective color use
- Complete synchronization of sound and image
- Descriptive notes, teacher's and/or user's guide, script
- Pertinent accompanying material
- Ease in handling, for user, for storage
- Minimum instruction for individual use
- Attractive packaging
- Durability
- Ease of repair

- Recommendation in evaluation sources
- Conformity to budget
- No less expense for satisfactory substitutes
- Inexpensive or already purchased equipment
- Economic if purchased
- Average supplemental costs for replacement, repair, physical processing, storage

From: Hicks, W.B., & Tillin, A.M. *Developing Multi-Media Libraries*. New York: Bowker, 1970.

Saint Philips College
Alamo Community College District
San Antonio, Texas

Nonprint Material

Normally, the library will not add materials in obsolete formats to the library collection. Any addition of such materials to the collection will be at the discretion of the subject area specialist. The primary criteria for adding these materials will be the availability of equipment to use the material and the availability of storage space.

Decisions to withdraw nonprint items will be based upon the obsolescence of the format and the condition of the equipment necessary to use it. If funds are available and the contents warrant preservation, materials may be transferred to another format instead of being deselected.

Audiovisuals

University of South Carolina Beaufort
USC Beaufort Library
Beaufort, South Carolina

Audio-Visual Media

The library acquires a limited number of recordings, CDs, DVDs and videos. These are selected on the basis of course needs and general interest to the Library's clientele, largely on the recommendation of the faculty. As for adding other A-V materials to the collection, the general policy is to select materials which will best serve the purposes of USCB.

Lansing Community College
Library at Lansing Community College
Lansing, Michigan

Audiovisual Selection

Refer inquiries and requests to the Audiovisual Coordinator. Recommendations for purchase of materials are accepted for consideration from instructors, from other LCC Librarians, and LCC students. The "Library Materials Request" (LMR) form may be used.

Guidelines to Facilitate Selection:

1. Reviews are consulted from such sources as Library Journal, Choice, Publishers' Weekly, Quality Books' non-print notification cards, and "recommended holdings" lists appearing in academic or popular literature.

2. Refer film and laserdisc requests to LCC AV-Media Services. With videocassette requests check the current Library Information Services—Media Services Videotape, Laserdisc and Film Catalog.

3. At the present time, three formats are being selected:

Cassette Tapes—books on tape (abridged or unabridged), dramatizations, lectures, panel discussions.

VHS Videotapes & DVDs—mostly documentary or instructional in nature; feature films only when directly supportive of a current course.

Music CDs—evenly divided between classical and popular, and representative of established musical genres. No attempt is made to keep up with the "latest on the charts".

4. If possible, the Library AV budget is evenly divided among the stated three major formats. Instructors recommending titles significantly more costly than the average may be referred instead to LCC AV Services or to the LCC Media department. In addition, Instructional Programs or Departments on campus have their own budget amounts for the purchase of instructional materials that may then be housed by Library or Media Services.

Audiovisual selection for the Library collection follows Collection Development principles and guidelines as stated. The purpose of nonprint materials in the Library is to provide collateral support to current LCC curricula and to accommodate varying learning styles. Consider compatibility with available hardware when choosing AV, nonprint, compact disc, recordings (spoken or music), or electronic information formats. Give special consideration to the format's appropriateness for LCC Library use or circulation. Library selectors will regard availability through LCC Media Services' Video Distribution and consult the Library Information Services—Media Services Videotape, Laserdisc and Film Catalog.

No discrimination by format is intended. The Library selects to be consistent with generally available listening-viewing equipment and meeting LCC instructional-course related Library needs.

Refer clients to special audiovisual collections within the Lansing area through use of the Lansing Area Library Information Guide when appropriate.

(For additional policies, please see the accompanying CD-ROM.)

CD-ROM

Christopher Newport University
Captain John Smith Library
Newport News, Virginia

Compact Discs (CD-ROMs) that are acquired should be relevant to the curriculum at CNU. They should contain information not already found in the print collection or present information in a simplified or more current manner. An example of the former would be a more comprehensive periodical index which allows a faster and more useful way to search for relevant information. An example of the latter would be statistics that are available on CD ROM that are updated monthly instead of a print version of the same statistics which is updated annually.

Databases and Electronic Books

University of Texas at Arlington
University Libraries
Arlington, Texas

Aggregated Databases

The stability and continuity of coverage in aggregator services is often unpredictable. Aggregated databases take many forms. For the purpose of this policy, aggregated databases will refer to those products that provide indexing to information sources produced by different publishers that include some full-text articles. Services will primarily be judged on indexing features and full-text coverage to a significant number of sources or journals that are not duplicated in other electronic products. Overlap in coverage should not exceed 40%.

Licenses

The creation and dissemination of digital information has resulted in a number of unique challenges. One of the more complex aspects of electronic resources is the license agreement. A license is a contractual agreement between the rights holder and the University of Texas at Arlington. It is used to define who and how the data may and may not be used. A license grants only the rights spelled out in the agreement. Any rights not specified in the license belong to the information owner. The information provider's terms are often not beneficial to the libraries long-term interests or to those of the scholarly community. The library has a responsibility to try to negotiate agreements that respect the rights and privileges of users as well as the provider. The UTA Libraries will abide by all terms within vendor licensing agreements. The Libraries will also promote observance by educating staff and users about restrictions and permissible uses.

Over-Riding Principles

The Libraries will follow principles consistent with the organization's values and the following guidelines developed and endorsed by six leading, national organizations that are embodied in Principles for Licensing Electronic Resources1 and are excerpted and reproduced here.

A license agreement should state clearly what access rights are being acquired by the licensee—permanent use of the content or access rights only for a defined period of time.

A license agreement should recognize and not restrict or abrogate the rights of the licensee or its user community permitted under copyright law. The licensee should make clear to the licensor those uses critical to its particular users including, but not limited to, printing, downloading, and copying.

A license agreement should recognize the intellectual property rights of both the licensee and the licensor.

A license agreement should not hold the licensee liable for unauthorized uses of the licensed resource by its users, as long as the licensee has implemented reasonable and appropriate methods to notify its user-community of use restrictions.

The licensee should be willing to undertake reasonable and appropriate methods to enforce the terms of access to a licensed resource.

A license agreement should fairly recognize those access enforcement obligations which the licensee is able to implement without unreasonable burden. Enforcement must not violate the privacy and confidentiality of authorized users.

The licensee should be responsible for establishing policies that create an environment in which authorized users make appropriate use of licensed resources and for carrying out due process when it appears that a use may violate the agreement.

A license agreement should require the licensor to give the licensee notice of any suspected or alleged license violations that come to the attention of the licensor and allow a reasonable time for the licensee to investigate and take corrective action, if appropriate.

A license agreement should not require the use of an authentication system that is a barrier to access by authorized users.

When permanent use of a resource has been licensed, a license agreement should allow the licensee to copy data for the purposes of preservation and/or the creation of a usable archival copy. If a license agreement does not permit the licensee to make a usable preservation copy, a license agreement should specify who has permanent archival responsibility for the resource and under what conditions the licensee may access or refer users to the archival copy.

The terms of a license should be considered fixed at the time the license is signed by both parties. If the terms are subject to change (for example, scope of coverage or method of access), the agreement should require the licensor or licensee to notify the other party in a timely and reasonable fashion of any such changes before they are implemented, and permit either party to terminate the agreement if the changes are not acceptable.

A license agreement should require the licensor to defend, indemnify, and hold the licensee harmless from any action based on a claim that use of the resource in accordance with the license infringes any patent, copyright, trade-mark, or trade secret of any third party.

The routine collection of use data by either party to a license agreement should be predicated upon disclosure of such collection activities to the other party and must respect laws and institutional policies regarding confidentiality and privacy.

A license agreement should not require the licensee to adhere to unspecified terms in a separate agreement between the licensor and a third party unless the terms are fully reiterated in the current license or fully disclosed and agreed to by the licensee.

A license agreement should provide termination rights that are appropriate to each party.

Make or Break Contract Features for UTA Libraries

Site—UTA's site encompasses all physical or virtual locations administered by the President of the University of Texas at Arlington. Licenses that attempt to define an institution's site geographically (within x mile radius or located in the city of Arlington) are unacceptable.

Authorized users—Our minimum acceptable definition is current faculty, staff and students, including distance learners? The preferred definition of users is currently employed faculty and staff, currently registered students, including distance learners and walk-in users at any of the Libraries' facilities?

Acceptable uses—Electronic resource licenses should permit use for non-commercial educational and research purposes. Licenses should not restrict fair use rights granted by copyright law.

Indemnification/Liability—A license must not hold UTA liable for actions of third parties.

User confidentiality and privacy—The license must be consistent with applicable privacy laws and provide confidentiality in gathering usage information.

Desirable Features

Archival access.

Use data that is appropriate to the content and can be used for evaluative purposes.

Termination rights for both parties.

Notification of license violations with appropriate time allowed for correction.

New Mexico State University Alamogordo
David H. Townsend Library
Alamogordo, New Mexico

Electronic books will be considered when they provide the most current and/or cost-effective format, or when they provide collections in support of distance education courses and programs. Cooperative lease/purchase of electronic books will be pursued as a cost-effective method of providing access to book collections. In addition to general selection criteria and online resources/Internet-based materials selection criteria, consideration must be given to the availability of an archival copy of electronic texts purchased in perpetuity.

Columbia College Chicago
Columbia College Library
Chicago, Illinois

Introduction

For the purpose of this policy, electronic resources are defined as reference or indexing sources, whether full-text or citation only, which require computer access.

The Library of Columbia College Chicago subscribes to electronic resources in support of the educational needs of students, faculty and staff of the College. The Library's current collection development policy governing the selection of library materials and information resources also applies to electronic resources and can be found at: www.lib.colum.edu/learn/policies/collectiondevelopment.htm.

Due to the high cost of electronic resources subscriptions, the Electronic Resources Committee (in consultation with appropriate library personnel) is charged with making cost-effective and balanced purchase decisions based on institutional needs. At the same time, a major goal of acquiring electronic resources is the provision of access both on and off campus in the most affordable manner possible.

The Library will pursue partnerships in cooperative acquisitions and cost-sharing both within and outside of Columbia College Chicago including consortia such as Illinois Digital Academic Libraries, Illinois Cooperative Collection Management Program and the Missouri Library Network Corporation.

Selection

General Criteria

Subject matter covered is relevant to the Columbia curriculum and needs of primary users (students, faculty and staff)

Appropriate intellectual level, depth of coverage and quality of information for user population

Reputable, reliable, and authoritative producer

Information and updates are current, accurate and complete

Electronic format provides greater accessibility to information over other formats

Uniqueness of Information

Formats

Citation/abstract databases

Full text article databases

Full text reference sources online

Graphics and multimedia files

Ebooks (selective)

Access

The following are the preferred methods of access:

Delivery via the Web

Authentication by IP address (rather than passwords or logins)

Compatibility with the Library's existing proxy server and software

User-Friendliness

Electronic resources should adhere to conventional user expectations such as:

Availability of on-screen help and/or tutorials

Basic and guided/advanced searching

Helpful error messages (i.e., error message indicates specific problem(s) and provides possible alternatives)

Ability to print, save, and email results and/or articles

Cost Considerations

Cost-effectiveness (including the availability and cost of updates and backfiles when appropriate)

Ability to sustain cost for the foreseeable future

Potential usage and/or uniqueness of information justifies cost

Vendor Considerations

Provides responsive customer service and technical support that is available during library working hours

Availability and quality of training programs

Reputation and business record suggests continued support for the product via updates or new versions

Documentation is thorough and clear

Technical Considerations

Meets usual and customary technical standards in the industry

Allows for local customizations via system administration access for the Library

Product is compatible with the Library's existing and/or future hardware

Product is compatible with standard web browsers if accessible via the web

Usage statistics are readily available in a user-friendly format (preferably COUNTER** compliant).

**For more information about COUNTER see: www.projectcounter.org

Special Considerations for Online Reference Sources or Subscriptions to Individual Online Journals

A subscription to or purchase of an individual online reference or journal title will be considered if:

The electronic format offers value-added enhancements to make it preferable over, or a significant addition to, its print equivalent. Examples of such enhancements include wider access, flexibility in searching, and frequent updates.

It contains or covers the equivalent information compared to the print format.

Acquiring the electronic version is cost-effective (e.g., the cost differential is justified by demonstrated or expected increase in use) and provides greater access to users

If an electronic resource is acquired in the electronic format, especially with perpetual ownership rights, the Electronic Resources Committee (in conjunction with appropriate Library staff) should determine if the print equivalent should be canceled.

License Agreements

The Columbia College Chicago Library purchases access to or data from publishers who require signed license agreements. When negotiating license agreements, the Library keeps the interests of the user in mind and refrains from purchasing products where use restrictions would seriously impede research or be impossible to enforce. The Head of Collection Management coordinates the review of license agreements and submits the signed license agreement as part of the ordering procedure. The Library will consult with General Counsel to amend vendor license agreements on a case-by-case basis to ensure use is granted to the fullest extent possible.

Decision-Making Process

Requesting New Subscriptions/Acquisitions

All new electronic acquisitions must be requested through the Electronic Resources Librarian and the Electronic Resources Committee.

In consultation with faculty, liaisons, appropriate library staff and others (as needed), the Electronic Resources Committee will consider whether or not the product meets the selection criteria outlined in the Electronic Resources Collection Development Policy.

The Electronic Resources Librarian will request pricing for the product and investigate consortial purchase options.

The Electronic Resources Librarian will request a trial of the product. All trials should be coordinated through the Electronic Resources Librarian. This will ensure that the trial is appropriately timed and publicized when necessary.

In consultation with faculty, liaisons, appropriate library staff and others (as needed), the Electronic Resources Committee will solicit feedback and evaluate the product based on the trial.

The Electronic Resources Committee will consult reviews of the product.

The Electronic Resources Committee will consult other subscribers to the product.

Based on cost, perceived need, usage, and the degree to which the electronic resource meets the selection criteria, the committee will: 1) decide whether or not to acquire and 2) if a decision to acquire is made, prioritize its purchase in relation to other electronic resources requested within budgetary constraints.

Review of Electronic Resources for Cancellation

A subscription to a product may be cancelled if:

Usage statistics are consistently low over a significant period of time.

The product is no longer cost-effective.

The content provided is no longer meeting the needs of Columbia College Chicago users.

A competitive or better product becomes available.

The vendor fails to hold up their end of the agreement and/or provides poor service.

A product's price inflates such that it no longer is considered affordable.

The product's content is found to duplicate content in another database.

A new vendor can deliver a superior product, including a more user-friendly search interface, providing greater and more reliable access at a reasonable cost, or meet other key criteria not being met by current database provider.

Lake Sumter Community College
Lake Sumter Community College Libraries
Sumterville, Florida

Electronic books are considered when they provide the most current and/or cost-effective format, or to support distance education courses and programs. Cooperative lease/purchase of electronic books via CCLA, SOLINET and other cooperatives are pursued as a cost-effective method of providing access to book collections. Duplication is considered for electronic books provided by such cooperative lease/purchase. In addition to general selection criteria and online resources/Internet-based materials selection criteria, consideration is given to the availability of an archival copy of electronic texts purchased in perpetuity.

Dartmouth College
Dartmouth College Library
Hanover, New Hampshire

Selection Criteria

Making the Decision to Acquire Information in Electronic Format

Selecting an electronic information resource is similar to selecting other formats for the Library's collection. Bibliographers base selection decisions, regardless of format, on relevance to Dartmouth programs, the curriculum, and faculty and student research.

Cost is always a consideration because bibliographers must fund purchases from their respective materials budget, and they must continually balance the cost of information against importance and relevance to the collection.

Several bibliographers may share the cost of a purchase when they conclude a resource is relevant yet too expensive for one bibliographer's budget. Electronic information sources are often more expensive than print and may be appropriate candidates for central funding or split funding.

Points to Consider Before Purchase

If there is a choice of formats, consider the advantages and disadvantages to be sure the electronic form is the most useful. Frequency of updates, inclusion of additional information, ability to manipulate data, and the ability to network all add value to the product.

Consider only fully-documented products with well-known system requirements. Helpful sources in this regard: comments from relevant listservs, vendor presence in the Library community, vendor's reputation, other products owned by the Library from the same publisher or vendor.

Consider whether the Library has the necessary staff resources and expertise to support the hardware and software, including installation, maintenance, troubleshooting etc.

From a user services perspective, consider the staff time that may be needed to prepare user guides and to teach faculty and students how to use the product.

Specify the type of hardware (Mac, IBM or compatible) and hard disk and RAM capacity required.

Note any video or audio requirements.

Based on any knowledge of the product gained from the literature, product reviews, conferences etc., evaluate the user interface, any additional product features (downloading, for example) and users' familiarity with the software.

Investigate potential for saving and manipulating search results (i.e. printing, saving to a disk, to a hard disk, e-mail, or ftp). Also, can the results be imported into a word processing program?

Check possible exposure to computer viruses resulting from a choice of media and access.

Look at ways to access archival issues.

Investigate ways to assure compliance (is monitoring software provided?) with license agreement or copyright requirements.

Consider the level of access most appropriate for the product (should it be on the campus network? on a lan? etc.) and consult appropriate people or groups.

In the case of compact disk databases, consider possible obstacles or constrictions: network speed, CD reader speed, printing bottlenecks.

Note stability and adequacy of hardware; for example, high-capacity disk drives will be needed to read high-density disks.

Decide on a location and necessary furniture for optimum access and use; investigate ergonomic considerations in setting up the workspaces.

If an electronic acquisition duplicates a print product currently received, consider whether the print subscription can be cancelled.

If the product exists in electronic form in the library system, consider whether it could be networked instead of duplicated.

The Product

> Are product reviews available?
> Do relevant listservs exist to query colleagues?
> Is the product user-friendly?
> Can product quality and database content be easily appraised? (can one request a demo?)
> What workspaces are necessary and appropriate?
> What is the currency of content and frequency of updating?
> Could information be supplied by other vendors? If so, what are the advantages and disadvantages of each, including cost?

The Vendor

> What is the reputation of the vendor?
> Do we have other products from the vendor and if so, what are bibliographers' impressions?
> Are terms and conditions of contracts and access arrangements negotiable enough to meet Dartmouth's needs?
> Is customer service and support available?

Necessary Equipment

What equipment—hardware, printer(s), specialized accessories such as a math co-processor—is needed to run the product?
Is existing hardware adequate or will new purchase(s) be necessary?
What software is needed?
What technical expertise and support is available?
Is new furniture needed to adequately house the product?

Service After the Sale

Is equipment maintenance/support/service available?
Is vendor support available after the sale?
What is known about hardware reliability?
Is documentation included and is it adequate?

The Bibliographer's Communication and Decision-Making Environment

Bibliographer and colleagues with whom he/she consults

Bibliographer's means of learning about electronic resources

listservs
newsgroups
product reviews
colleagues
faculty and student recommendations
Library committees and departments
Library groups: LOSC, Internet Resources Subcommittee, Automation, Tecor
Computing Services: IBM Specialists, Academic Computing Coordinators
College Attorneys

Budget

As noted previously, bibliographers fund purchases for the collection from their respective budgets. As the cost of electronic information may exceed the ability of one bibliographer to fund it, several bibliographers may collaborate on a purchase. In addition, the Director of Collection Services may be consulted to explore other funding possibilities. In the case of bibliographers working in a library associated with the professional schools, operating with acquisitions budgets separate from Arts and Sciences, these decisions rest with the Department Head, who may in turn consult with the Director of Collection Services.

Information Format and Type

CD-Rom Databases

___ hardware and software requirements
stand-alone systems
networked for one location
networked across zones
terms and conditions of use, including licensing and contracts

Magnetic Tape Databases

___ hardware and software requirements
constituencies served
terms and conditions of use, including licensing and contracts

Remotely-Accessible Files

___ files are accessible using various tools, including ftp,

Gopher, Mosaic

___ text, images and data—software and hardware
requirements at the requestor's workstation

128

Types of Information Content
___ bibliographic, text, numeric, graphic and multimedia

Augmented Collection Services
___ tables of contents providers and/or document delivery services

Information Access

Local Access

Fileserver Resources

Dartmouth Gopher

DCLOS, DCIS

Remote Access
___ Internet-accessible resources such as newsgroups

Commercial online services
___ pricing options: discounted for educational use, fixed-price, off-peak pricing

Access Tools
___ ftp, Mosaic, Gopher, Wais, WWW, Veronica, etc.
hardware and software requirements to gather and receive data

(For additional policies, please see the accompanying CD-ROM.)

Digital Resources

University of Texas Austin
University of Texas Libraries
Austin, Texas

Purpose

Digital library materials are collected to support the mission of The University of Texas at Austin

Categories

Digital library materials currently collected by The University of Texas Libraries consist of three broad categories:

1. Purchased or licensed material such as electronic journals or databases. These are generally acquired from a commercial source, a government entity, a non-profit organization, a professional society, or an institution engaged in furthering scholarly research. In many cases this material is not "physically owned" by the library in the same sense that a printed book or journal may be owned, but instead the library has acquired specific rights to the material on behalf of the library's clientele.

2. Material that has been reformatted (digitized) by The University of Texas Libraries or the University from non-copyrighted print or analog sources, or has been reformatted from copyrighted sources with appropriate permission. In some cases the library may also serve as a repository for material digitized by other libraries, universities, institutions, or individuals. Typically, this material consists of resources from special collections that have been selected for digitization in order to make them more widely available, or deteriorating materials that have been reformatted for preservation reasons. As the use of digital material expands in higher education, the library will increasingly digitize materials on a programmatic basis in order to support the mission of the University and The University of Texas Libraries.

3. Links and pointers to Internet resources of significant scholarly value which are added to the library's catalogs, databases, and networked resources as appropriate.

Selection Considerations

Selection criteria for digital library resources comprises four levels of review: is the content appropriate to the library mission; are the format and information delivery medium appropriate to the content and commensurate with the library rationale for acquiring the resource; is the acquisition practical within existing budgetary, technical, legal and other constraints; and is the resource compatible with the library's overall strategic digital library vision and current infrastructure.

1. Content. Is the content intellectually significant? Is the content relevant to the University of Texas at Austin? Measures of intellectual significance include authority, uniqueness, timeliness, breadth or depth, and demand.

2. Is the format appropriate for the content? Is the format appropriate to achieve the underlying rationale for the acquisition of the resource? Print may be the appropriate format for a unique item with a low rate of expected usage; while high-use general undergraduate-level information resources, distance education resources, or frequently used reference material, may be more appropriately acquired in a network able digital format. In a similar vein, special collection material with wide potential interest might benefit from re-selection for digitization to increase its utility and to make it available to a wider audience. An analysis of the advantages and disadvantages of a particular format, along with considerations of audience, intended use of the material, archival and access issues, and overall cost—are all factors to be used in determining which format would be most appropriate for the library collection.

3. Practical issues. Does the library have the overhead resources (equipment, staff, space, etc.) necessary to support the resource? Do library users have the necessary resources to utilize the content (computers, players, plug-ins, etc.)? Does the license or contract for the resource meet the library, university, and state requirements? Is the vendor reliable, is the format stable, and can we utilize the resource (linking, archiving, etc.) in the ways our users need? Does the digital product adhere to the best prudent practices of current library collection management (including, but not limited to, appropriate retrieval software, a well-designed interface, appropriate format and linking options, a properly reliable delivery mechanism, authentication and security designs that meet library needs, a library-friendly approach to fair use and copyright, quality statistical reporting, appropriate technical support, assurances of rights to permanent access, and appropriate licensing terms).

4. Strategic Considerations. Is the resource compatible with the library/university/state information technology plans? Is the product compatible with the library's overall digital library vision and the library's current infrastructure in terms of its discovery, access, organization, and technical components? Does the product comply with the digital guidelines established by the International Coalition of Library Consortia? Is the product design and delivery consistent with the best practices of digital libraries?

Goals

Within this framework, it is the objective of the library to collect scholarly digital materials in order to provide broad access to relevant scholarly information at every level of granularity including articles, monographs, and large databases. As with all formats, digital material should meet the same subject, chronological, geographical, language and other guidelines as outlined in the library's subject collection policies; and possess the same standards of excellence, comprehensiveness, and authority that the library expects from all of its acquisitions. The library recognizes that different disciplines utilize different formats and different types of information in different ways, and that no one solution is appropriate for every subject or area of study. The ultimate goal of The University of Texas Libraries digital library collection development planning—is to provide seamless cross-linkages between all elements of the digital library whether commercially licensed or locally created, and whether the resources are locally or remotely mounted and serviced.

Priorities

Priorities should be given to those digital materials that offer significant added value in supporting teaching and research over similar materials in traditional formats, that offer significant opportunities for cost containment, and whose license terms are reflective of the University's academic values. Measures of added value might include: additional content, greater functionality, greater accessibility, improved resource sharing ability, improved linkages with other information tools, ease of archiving, and the enabling of more efficient uses of limited faculty and student time and resources. Licenses should allow the library the flexibility to develop collections that match the University's needs without contractually forcing entangling ties to unwanted products, and without restricting the rights of fair use or the values of academic inquiry. License terms should also be financially sustainable and address achival rights to the resources in question. Materials that meet these and other selection needs, will be given priority over digital material of a more problematic nature.

Observations and Qualifications

Electronic Journals

Goals: To license access to a critical mass of high quality electronic journals throughout all subject areas.

Observations: Because the acquisition of any particular electronic journal is staff-intensive and involves the work of many people over a period of months—initial collecting efforts will focus on acquiring a solid core of proven e-journals from respected publishers.

Qualifications: E-journal publishers vary greatly in their familiarity with electronic publishing issues, and in their familiarity with needs of the scholarly and library community. In some cases e-journal publishers have unrealistic expectations as to the prices libraries can afford, and in the technical and format barriers they expect libraries to scale in order to access their journals. The library has limited funds and staff time that can be devoted to problematic publishers. In those cases where the content is desirable, but the price and practical barriers are too formidable, we will not pursue the electronic versions of the journal, but will provide access through other formats or delivery mechanisms.

Indexing and Abstracting Databases

Goals: To acquire the primary database in each subject area, and secondary and tertiary databases as needed by local programs.

Observations: Indexing and Abstracting databases provide valuable discovery tools both for material owned and licensed by The University of Texas Libraries and for other material which may be obtained through Inter-Library Loan or Document Delivery. In some instances these services also provide valuable links and online access to actual data and full-text resources.

Qualifications: The number of databases relevant to UT-Austin programs is multiplying faster than the library's ability to fund them. Selection of secondary and specialty databases will continue to be limited by available funds for the foreseeable future. The usefulness of a particular database to a discipline or audience group will be measured database by database, particularly against other types of resources that might be purchased with the available funds, and against how it fits in with the library's overall mix of resources and technical platforms, and the database's prospects for long-term utility.

Full-Text Databases

Goals: To acquire a complete range of full-text databases that serve the university's general and specialized scholarly interests.

Observations: Full-text databases are notable for their ease of use and cost-effectiveness. They typically receive high use and are the least expensive means of providing access to information covered by the database.

Qualifications: These databases must be constantly monitored as the specific resources covered by each database change as publishers renegotiate contracts with the vendor. By their very nature, full-text databases directed at different audiences and designed for different purposes may also have significant overlap in coverage.

Primary Resources

Goals: Identify selected content that has value for teaching and research at the university, that would benefit from being more widely available in digital form.

Observations: The nature of primary resources used in different disciples varies significantly. The original primary resources may be manuscripts, pamphlets, books, official records, photos, paintings, audio clips, data sets, lab reports, digital files, etc. With all of recorded human history to draw upon, the reformatting of primary resources into digital form presents a wealth of potential material.

Qualifications: This material is available in a number of ways including licensing via commercial vendors, free via the Internet, or via resource sharing agreements with other institutions. The potential use and value of the material must be weighed against its cost and the amount of resources its provision requires. Consultation with faculty, and consideration of the experiences of other institutions with the material is especially valuable in considering selection. When possible, outright purchase of the digital primary resource material should be considered as an option, instead of paying ongoing subscription and maintenance fees. In many cases this primary resource material is being republished from another easily available published format such as microfilm; in these cases the cost of digital primary research materials must be carefully weighed against the potential usage and convenience of digital access.

Digitization of Local Materials

Goals: Identify local materials whose wider availability would aid university teaching and research, promote scholarship, enrich the arts and sciences, deepen our understanding of human culture, and benefit the citizens of Texas.

Observations: Local materials are digitized both to provide wider access, and to preserve them for future generations.

Qualifications: Digitization projects require a significant investment of local resources and are not undertaken lightly. Long-term value to the academic community, congruency with the library and university mission and areas of interest, and significance to worldwide users of the Internet are all important considerations. Digitization projects are planned in consultation with the Electronic Information Programs Division and the Research Services Division.

Online Books

Goals: To contract with vendors for permanent online digital rights to selected current academic and trade books.

Observations: These services are new but growing in number. Initially The University of Texas Libraries will purchase rights to reserve items, high circulating popular scholarly items, and convenience books such as reference items or items that are frequently consulted but not pondered at length nor read in depth.

Qualifications: Until these services become reliable, The University of Texas Libraries will continue its general policy of fiscally conservative experimentation.

Alerting and Profiling Services

Goals: To subscribe to services and databases that can supply e-mail alerts to new articles, publications, and digital resources in a library user's area of interests.

Observations: These types of automated notification services are a way of extending the library's collection development activities outward to encompass newly published material that the library does not yet own, and to more fully involve faculty and students in the dialogue that is the library's collection building effort.

Qualifications: The amount of faculty and student interest in well-developed alerting and profiling services is not known. Current e-mail alerting services are little used.

Electronic Document Delivery and Pay Per View Service

Goals: To contract with vendors for the seamless delivery of material on a cost-per-use basis, that the library does not own and has not previously licensed.

Observations: For the immediate future these electronic services will be mediated through Inter-library Services in order to insure efficiency and to control costs. In the future, unmediated delivery of electronic information directly to the user is a realistic possibility, though access would be controlled via computerized rationing or accounts.

Qualifications: The lines between services such as these, and full-text databases, and electronic journals and books, is likely to continue to blur.

Archiving of Non-University of Texas Web Sites

Goals: To undertake archival responsibilities for non-University of Texas Web-based information carefully and with proper consideration for all the issues involved.

Observations: There are considerable intellectual property, copyright, technical, and resource issues involved with archiving a Web site. The issues pertaining to serving data that was created on another hardware/software platform are legion, and any archival consideration needs to begin with a finding of whether or not archiving the site in question is technically possible. Consideration for local archiving of a Web site also includes obtaining signed legal permission for The University of Texas Libraries to archive and serve the data, and a consideration of whether the library has the resources (staff/hardware/software/etc.) to undertake the project.

Qualifications: Other archival options, such as printing out screens from the Web site, cataloging them, and making them available in the library; or relying on national Web archival options such as the Alexa project or Library of Congress should also be explored.

Integration of Print and Electronic Resource

Goals: To promote the integration of print and digital items through bibliographer subject pages, conversion of finding aids into digital form, and through the licensing of resources that intermix citations to multiple formats.

Observations: Integration of formats can be achieved technically through improved discovery and access mechanisms, as well as through the efforts of individual librarians via the creation of bibliographer subject pages, the addition of digital resources to the online catalog, and similar activities.

Qualifications: For the foreseeable future, print and digital resources will both be essential in a successful research library. Collection planning needs to consider both formats.

Overall Multiple User Profiling and Alerting Capability

Goals: To ensure that the various digital library products are capable of responding to profiling and alerting services that the library may create or contract with, so that users may be automatically notified of new information of personal interest.

Observations: Integration of the variety of vendor based products of this nature is currently problematical

Qualifications: Campus usage of these services is low, and whether or not library users would find these services truly useful is unclear.

Tulane University
Howard-Tilton Memorial Library
New Orleans, Louisiana

Digital Collections Policies

The Howard-Tilton Memorial Library at Tulane University is committed to providing its users with access to up-to-date digital resources. Preference in the selection of digital resources is given to arrangements with the widest access, e.g., those accessible via the campus network. Purchase arrangements for access-only versus ownership are considered. However, ownership is preferred when online access would replace print subscriptions currently held in the Library; this is considered important to retaining the fundamental value of libraries in the digital age.

Purchase of subject-specific digital resources such as online journals, e-books, and specialized databases may be made by individual librarians from the subject-specific funds they manage (see sidebar to the right). Librarians may make recommendations for expensive or multi-disciplinary purchases from the general electronic serials fund to the Library's Selection Committee on Electronic Databases. License agreements should meet the Library's licensing criteria adopted from the Association of Research Libraries (ARL) Principles for Licensing Electronic Resources.

Online Journals: It is the general practice of the Library to routinely seek Internet access to its journal subscriptions, whenever such access is offered at no extra cost, and to provide links to them in the Local Catalog. Exceptions would include free trials with eventual added costs. The Library will selectively consider the purchase of online access to its journal subscriptions when added costs are required. Online access will not be substituted for print issues unless ownership and adequate archival provisions can be assured.

Digital Archiving: The Howard-Tilton Memorial Library shares with other research and educational institutions the responsibility to determine the most effective methods for the long-term preservation of the digital materials accessed by the Library but not stored locally. Resources lacking fixed responsibility for long-term preservation are considered only selectively and under special circumstances. The Library has a special preservation responsibility for digital resources it may develop that are unique to its collections.

Consortial Purchasing: The Library participates in a number of library corsortia—including the LOUIS/LALINC, LAICU, SOLINET, and the Association of Southeastern Research Libraries—in order to take advantage of aggregated purchasing agreements for digital library resources. It seeks other consortial licensing opportunities whenever they serve the best interests of Tulane University.

Selection Criteria

The potential purchase of each digital library resource should be considered using the criteria listed in the following sections.

Policy Criteria

Overall, the selection of digital formats should reflect the Library's other practices for collection development and acquisitions. More specifically, potential purchases should be assessed with regard to the following:

Consortia availability, through which purchase is preferred.

Licensing or other limitations on the use of the database.

User and academic program needs and demands. Special attention should be given to resources that provide coverage of high-priority or under-represented areas.

Reputation of the producer and vendor.

Comprehensiveness, scope, and indexing accuracy.

Timeliness of updates or accumulations.

The relative difficulty of using the print version versus the digital version.

Cost in relation to value (see Cost Criteria below).

Service Criteria

Overall, the selection of a digital resource should conform with Tulane University's general plans for establishing a computerized information environment. Staffing and training levels should be considered. Specifically, potential purchases should also be assessed with regard to:

The potential effect that the product would have on the demand for interlibrary loan.

The potential impact the product would have on the demand for user assistance from librarians at the reference desk.

The potential impact the product would have on the need for additional user education or printed literature guides.

The potential impact the product would have on the need for set-up or maintenance.

Any need for restrictions on access to the database as required by licensing, sales agreements, or the requirements of Tulane students, faculty, or staff.

The availability of built-in user education features such as tutorials and help screens.

Technical Criteria

Overall, the selection of electronic databases should reflect the Library's current or planned level of technical resources, as well as its current or planned level of in-house technical support. More specifically, potential purchases should also be assessed with regard to the following criteria that apply mostly to non-internet formats such as CDs or computer software:

The necessity of technical support and maintenance for the product.

Software issues that include: menu-driven versus command-driven features; database complexity for end users; security features that protect against tampering, viruses, or theft; and, flexibility for networking.

Hardware issues including: reliability, maintenance, compatibility with peripherals, flexibility for networking, and security from tampering or theft.

Compatibility with existing systems in the Library and with systems currently or planned at Tulane University.

Environmental and space requirements for equipment and work stations.

Cost Criteria

Costs are an important concern and potential purchases should also be assessed with regard to the following:

The relative value of the format considered versus access through some alternative means.

Availability of options or price differences relative to consortia, lease, or specified number of users.

The likelihood of additional costs for updates or upgrades.

The possibility of unseen startup or maintenance costs.

The shelf life of the product and its replacement costs.

Availability of packages, credits for canceled print, or other special deals.

Licensing Criteria

A license agreement should state clearly what access rights are being acquired by the Library—permanent use of the content or access rights only for a defined period of time.

A license agreement should recognize and not restrict or abrogate the rights of the Library or its user community permitted under copyright law. The Library should make clear to the licensor those uses critical to its particular users including, but not limited to, printing, downloading, and copying.

A license agreement should recognize the intellectual property rights of both the Library and the licensor.

A license agreement should not hold the Library liable for unauthorized uses of the licensed resource by its users, as long as the Library has implemented reasonable and appropriate methods to notify its user community of use restrictions.

The Library should be willing to undertake reasonable and appropriate methods to enforce the terms of access to a licensed resource.

A license agreement should fairly recognize those access enforcement obligations which the Library is able to implement without unreasonable burden. Enforcement must not violate the privacy and confidentiality of authorized users.

The Library should be responsible for establishing policies that create an environment in which authorized users make appropriate use of licensed resources and for carrying out due process when it appears that a use may violate the agreement.

A license agreement should require the licensor to give the Library notice of any suspected or alleged license violations that come to the attention of the licensor and allow a reasonable time for the Library to investigate and take corrective action, if appropriate.

A license agreement should not require the use of an authentication system that is a barrier to access by authorized users.

When permanent use of a resource has been licensed, a license agreement should allow the licensee to copy data for the purposes of preservation including the creation of a usable archival copy. Uses would include interlibrary loan. If a license agreement does not permit the Library to make a usable preservation copy, a license agreement should specify who has permanent archival responsibility for the resource and under what conditions the Library may access or refer users to the archival copy.

The terms of a license should be considered fixed at the time the license is signed by both parties. If the terms are subject to change (for example, scope of coverage or method of access), the agreement should require the licensor or Library to notify the other party in a timely and reasonable fashion of any such changes before they are implemented, and permit either party to terminate the agreement if the changes are not acceptable.

A license agreement should require the licensor to defend, indemnify, and hold the Library harmless from any action based on a claim that use of the resource in accordance with the license infringes any patent, copyright, trade-mark, or trade secret of any third party.

The routine collection of use data by either party to a license agreement should be predicated upon disclosure of such collection activities to the other party and must respect laws and institutional policies regarding confidentiality and privacy.

A license agreement should not require the Library to adhere to unspecified terms in a separate agreement between the licensor and a third party unless the terms are fully reiterated in the current license or fully disclosed and agreed to by the Library.

A license agreement should provide termination rights that are appropriate to each party.

A license agreement should define clearly the terms used and should use those terms consistently throughout.

Decision to Purchase

Digital resources are purchased under a variety of scenarios that include selections of relatively low cost discipline-specific resources by individual librarians and higher cost or cross-disciplinary resources requiring broader review.

Lower cost discipline-specific resources: Generally available through serial subscriptions, librarians may select these resources individually using the established selection criteria listed on this page, submitting orders with license and access information to the Assistant Dean for Collections & Information Services. Once approved, these are forwarded to the Acquisitions Department and handled as permanent transfers from book funds to digital serials.

Higher cost or cross-disciplinary resources: Requests for higher cost (generally more than $500) digital serials are reviewed by the Library's Selection Committee for Electronic Databases, which oversees the distribution of budget increases for these types of resources. Requests for higher-cost "monographic" digital resources, i.e., those available with one-time payments for ownership of content are reviewed along with other one-time big expense items by the Collection Coordinators group.

Internet Resources

Stetson University
duPont-Ball Library
DeLand, Florida

Purpose: The Stetson University Libraries collect electronic resources to support the instructional and research activities of Stetson students, faculty, and staff. The Library Web site is the primary vehicle used to distribute Library information, databases, and e-collections electronically to the Stetson community. While the primary audience is the Stetson University community, much of the site is open to non-Stetson Internet users.

Administration: The Library Web site is administered by a Web Team that includes the Library Web Master (currently the Associate Director), the Library Director, the Head of Technical Services, and the Electronic Services Librarian. Team membership may change at the discretion of the Library administration. The team is responsible for Web site design, content, organization, maintenance, updates, and assessment. Web team members, and others designated by the web team, are the only Library staff members authorized to upload Web pages to the Library's Web site.

Content & Organization: Collected electronic resources may include, but are not limited to, contents of the Library's OPAC, library-produced informational resources, electronic serials or collections of serials, commercial databases, electronic reference material, electronic monographs, and free external Internet resources.

The Web site content is divided into the following categories:

Informational: Pages that provide information on Library operations such as calendar, hours, map, staff, directions, policies, procedures, membership, gifts, departments, how to do interlibrary loans, how to access databases from off campus, etc.

Publications: Includes such items as the Library Mission Statement, department Mission Statements, Annual Reports, Research Guides, Library Newsletter, New Employee Welcome Packets, Library Faculty Publications, ILL forms, etc.

Databases: Subscription databases, including the Library's WebCat Online Catalog are included on the Web site. Those databases on the database page (excluding WebCat) are the only links on the Library's Web site that are restricted to the Stetson University DeLand & Celebration campus communities.

External Internet Resources: Links to search engines and non-Stetson external Internet resources are included in the Library's Web site. See External Link Selection Criteria below.

Selection: Selection decisions are made by the Library Web Master with significant contributions from the Library Web Team and the Library faculty. In case of disagreement, the Library Web Team, in consultation with the Library Administration, will make the final decision on content. Specific selection criteria include the following:

Internal Library Link Selection Criteria: Internal Library links refers here to informational links created by librarians and library staff (such as department pages, research guides, announcements, etc.). Links created for the Library should be consistent with the Library's Mission Statement and/or have value to the Library and/or University. All library links must be approved by the Web master for inclusion on the Library's Web site.

Commercial Link Selection Criteria: Commercial links refers here to commercially purchased databases and e-books. Database and e-book selection should be consistent with the Library's General Collection Development Policy and the Library's Reference Collection Development Policy. See specifically the section on "Electronic Reference Sources" in the Reference Collection Development Policy.

Librarians will meet each summer to consider databases to be purchased for the following academic year. Many of the databases and e-books considered will be based on the Independent Colleges & Universities of Florida's (ICUF) database offers from the annual May ICUF meeting. Other databases, however, may also be considered for purchase. Public Services librarians will test, evaluate, and suggest databases for purchase in order of importance to the collection and with consideration to available funding. Database purchase recommendations are forwarded to the Head of Technical Services and the Library Director. Databases may be considered for purchase at other times of the year, but funding may not be available until the next fiscal year begins in June.

Database quality is essential, but other factors must also be considered:

- Cost (related to both the cost of the material and the available budget)
- Technical considerations (IP recognition, hardware/software requirements, compatibility with existing systems)
- Full-text content or availability of full-text through traditional library sources if database is strictly an index
- Currency and update schedules
- Interface and ease of use
- Vendor reliability
- Availability of usage statistics
- Acceptable licensing terms

External Link Selection Criteria: External links refers here to Web sites freely available on the Internet. External link selection should be consistent with the Library's general Collection Development Policy, and links are chosen to best support the current Stetson University curriculum. Factors taken into consideration in selection include quality, relevance, currency, authority, organization, accessibility, reliability, and stability. The Library has chosen to offer only a small number of highly selective external links for each discipline or subject area included (most corresponding to Stetson majors and/or minors). Sources chosen reflect the mission of the Library, the curricular and research interests of the students and faculty, and include educational value.

In order to provide wide access to the Internet, links to search engines, and other sites offering evaluation and/or review of Web sites are also provided. The Library does not use blocking or filtering software, however, and certain Internet sites can be accessed that may be inappropriate for minors.

The Library reserves the right to refuse to link to any Internet resource that is not an official Stetson Web resource.

Maintenance & Updates: All external links shall be verified for accessibility and content monthly if possible, but at least quarterly. Dead, out-dated, or changed linked should be reported to the Web Master. Although links are checked and verified regularly and all attempts are made to ensure that the links provided remain relevant to our collection policies, the Library is not responsible for the content of external sites to which we have provided links.

All internal Library-related links (department pages, staff home pages, library-created material) shall be checked by the responsible librarian or staff member at the beginning of fall and spring semesters to ensure currency and accuracy. The Web Master is responsible for updating staff changes throughout the year. The Web Master will update the copyright in January each year.

Data will be kept on the following:

1. Number, names, URL, format, of all Web pages (Ryan–Excel spreadsheet)
2. Database contacts, licensing agreements, payment schedules etc. (Johnson/Dinkins)
3. Databases linked from each subject Web page (Ryan–Excel spreadsheet)
4. Databases linked from Reference Guides & Research Aids (Bradford)

Assessment: The Library Web team will utilize available tools to assess the utilization and success of the Web pages, including page usage statistics analysis, user surveys, literature studies, etc.

Deselection: All electronic resources are subject to deselection if they no longer meet the needs of the Stetson community or if other factors affect the continued subscription to or access to the material, including, but not limited to:

Unacceptable increased cost or cost not commensurate with use

Content changes or data is no longer relevant

Lack of updates or data is no longer reliable

Duplication by other resources

Material is obsolete

Policy Review: This policy shall be reviewed and revised as needed to address changes and reflect current practices in the evolving electronic information environment.

New Mexico State University Alamogordo
David H. Townsend Library
Alamogordo, New Mexico

Online Resources/Internet-based materials will be considered when they provide the most current and/or cost-effective resources. The following online resources will be actively selected. Licensed commercial, fee-based resources and databases will be selected when they provide cost-effective means of providing resources for the library.

These resources may include electronic books, citation, abstracting and full-text databases providing periodicals, newspapers or reference materials, or databases providing information portals for specific subject areas. In additional to general selection criteria, the following criteria will be used:

- Material has broad appeal to large number of Townsend Library users or will serve special needs of a user group
- Good technical support is available
- The interface is user-friendly
- Appropriate online help is available
- The license agreement allows normal rights and privileges accorded libraries under copyright law
- The availability of usage statistics is highly desirable
- The library is not required to subscribe to both print and electronic versions of the product
- The vendor allows a trial of the actual product
- The license agreement gives the library indemnification against third party copyright infringement
- The product compares favorably with similar products
- Multiple user access is preferred

The library will attempt to balance print, electronic and online resources without unnecessary duplication. Print, audiovisual, or electronic resources may be duplicated with fee-based online resources when:

- The resource has significant historical value
- One format is unstable
- A cost benefit for purchasing multiple formats exists
- Multiple formats meet the different needs of user groups

Freely linkable World Wide Web resources and other freely available resources, services and databases will be selected and provided as links from the Library Web page, the library's Web-based subject directory of Internet resources.

In addition to resources located via Internet directories and search engines, several sources are consulted for current reviews of Internet resources. These sources of selection include Choice, CRL News, American Libraries, Library Journal, and The Scout Report. Several high-quality subject indexes are also regularly consulted, such as the Internet Public Library and The WWW Virtual Library. Duplication of print resources is acceptable for free Internet resources since it provides an additional point of use.

In addition to general selection criteria, the following criteria will be used for selecting general and subject-specific Internet resources for the library Web page directory:

- The resource may support the curriculum, faculty research interests, or the reference collection.
- The resource may enhance the library's collections for community users or specific groups or organizations.
- Access and design considerations include:
  - Size of files; how long do the pages take to load?
  - Is the site open to everyone or does access to most of the site require membership and/or fees?
  - Is it usually possible to reach the site or is the server often down or overloaded?
  - Must you download software to navigate the site?
  - Is the purpose of the site clearly stated?
  - Are author and title information clearly identified?
  - Are there clear instructions for use?
  - Does the site employ navigation buttons or links, enabling the user to return to an index page or easily locate a particular page?
  - Do all parts of the site work?
  - Is the page stable, or do features frequently disappear or move between visits?
  - Can the user back out of the site, or does one get stuck

Lake Sumter Community College
Lake Sumter Community College Libraries
Sumterville, Florida

Online Resources/Internet-based materials will be considered when they provide the most current and/or cost-effective resources. The following online resources will be actively selected:

Licensed commercial, fee-based resources and databases will be selected when they provide cost-effective means of providing resources for the three campus libraries. These resources may include electronic books; citation, abstracting and full-text databases covering journals, magazines, newspapers or reference materials; and databases providing information portals for specific subject areas. In additional to general selection criteria, the following criteria will be used:

The product has broad appeal to a large number of LSCC library users or will serve the special needs of a user group

The product compares favorably with similar products

Multiple user access is preferred

The interface is user-friendly

Appropriate online help is available

Good technical support is available

The availability of usage statistics is highly desirable

The vendor allows a trial of the actual product

The libraries are not required to subscribe to both print and electronic versions of the product, unless this is desired

The license agreement allows normal rights and privileges accorded libraries under copyright law

The license agreement gives the libraries indemnification against third party copyright infringement

Products available via LINCCWeb are preferred

The libraries will attempt to balance print, electronic and online resources without unnecessary duplication. Print, audiovisual, or electronic resources may be duplicated with fee-based online resources when:

The resource has significant historical value

One format is unstable

A cost benefit for purchasing multiple formats exists

Multiple formats meet the different needs of user groups

Usage justifies additional copies

Freely linkable World Wide Web resources and other freely available resources, services and databases will be selected and provided as links from the Cyberlibrary, the libraries' Web-Based subject directory of Internet resources.

In addition to resources located via Internet directories and search engines, several sources are consulted for current reviews of Internet resources. These sources of selection include Choice, CRL News, American Libraries, Library Journal, and The Scout Report. Several high-quality subject indexes are also regularly consulted, such as the Internet Public Library and The WWW Virtual Library. Duplication of print resources is acceptable for free Internet resources since it provides an additional point of use.

In addition to general selection criteria, the following criteria will be used for selecting general and subject specific Internet resources for the Cyberlibrary directory:

The resource supports the curriculum, faculty research interests, or the reference collection

The resource enhances the libraries' collections for community users or specific groups or organizations

Access and design considerations include:

Is the purpose of the site clearly stated?

Are author and title information clearly identified?

Is the page stable, or do features frequently disappear or move between visits?

Is it usually possible to reach the site or is the server often down or overloaded?

How large are the files; how long do the pages take to load?

Is the site open to everyone or does access to most of the site require membership and/or fees?

Must you have or must you download software to use the site?

Are there clear instructions for use?

Do all parts of the site work?

Does the site employ navigation buttons or links, enabling the user to return to an index page or easily locate a particular page?

Can users back out of the site, or do they get stuck looping between pages?

Maps

Indiana University–Purdue University Fort Wayne
Walter E. Helmke Library
Fort Wayne, Indiana

The map collection contains selected topographic, demographic, navigation, raised-relief, and political maps available from the U.S. government through its depository library program. Collection priority is given to maps of the Midwest and Indiana.

Eastern Michigan University
Bruce T. Halle Library
Ypsilanti, Michigan

Maps

Depository maps and non-depository maps covering all geographic and subject areas are collected.

Microform

Crichton College
Crichton College Library
Memphis, Tennessee

Microform

Though microform as a physical format is considered an audiovisual item, its content is that of a book or periodical. This section will treat microform only as to its physical format. Microfilm are selected for any of the following reasons:

a. Material is not available in the original format
b. Low cost
c. Reduced physical bulk
d. Original is too fragile

Microforms being considered for addition to the Library's collection should be of standard dimensions and be capable of being read on standard equipment. The microform should possess a high quality of reproduction (i.e., contrast, clarity of print and illustrations), and be of a film type that is not highly flammable. When purchasing large sets of microform, care should be taken that the library does not already possess a large number of the titles in the set. Ease of access to the information contained in the set should be considered as well (Is there an index to contents? Should the library catalog each item in set and how much staff time will be involved with this as opposed to the need for the set?) At this time, the majority of the microforms in the collection are in periodicals.

Lansing Community College
Library at Lansing Community College
Lansing, Michigan

Microfilm Subscriptions

A. The Library subscribes to microfilm as long as print or electronic indexes are available for that title and are readily accessible by clientele of the LCC Library.

B. The LCC Library will not duplicate any microfilm subscription.

C. Periodicals with difficult storage and maintenance format, and those for historical research, are candidates for microfilm subscription providing they remain indexed at LCC.

FORMS

Form to Request a Purchase of New Materials

Framingham State College
Henry Whittemore Library
Framingham, Massachusetts

Request a Purchase of New Materials

Please check the Whittemore Library Online Catalog to verify library holdings before submitting a request for purchase.

*Name: [   ]

*E-mail: [   ]

Phone No: [   ]

Status:

○ Undergraduate Graduate Student

○ Staff

○ Faculty

○ Other

Bibliographic Information

Please supply us with as much information as possible. Use the Tab key to proceed to the next column.

*Author: [   ]

*Title: [   ]

Publisher: [   ]

ISBN (or ISSN): [   ]

Publication Date: [   ] Price: [   ]

Type of Material: ○Book ○Journal ○Audiovisual ○Electronic Resource ○E-Journal

Comments (and where you saw this item was mentioned) on purchase.

Chapter 13

PRESERVATION PROCEDURES

GENERAL PROCEDURES PRESERVATION OF MATERIALS

University of Iowa
University of Iowa Libraries
Iowa City, Iowa

Mission Statement

The Preservation Department supports the University research mission to acquire, organize and deliver information by maintaining collection resources in useable condition. The Preservation department will respond promptly to any concerns with the physical care of collections.

Overview

The Conservation Department was established in 1984. The Preservation department was established in 1987, drawing together various preservation activities previously carried out in other departments. In the mid 90's Preservation and Conservation were merged into a single department as a part of a library wide reorganization. The current Preservation Department consists of three units; Conservation, Assessment/Reformatting and Binding/Marking all under the administrative head of the Preservation Librarian.

The Preservation Department is responsible for activities that relate to the care and handling of Library materials, both circulating and non-circulating. Services include commercial and in-house binding, repair, marking, attaching security tapes and in-house and vended reformatting. The Conservation unit provides specialized treatments. The Preservation department also provides services aimed at improving the storage condition of the collections including environmental monitoring, emergency planning and preparedness and staff and user education. In 2003, the department assumed the responsibility of directing the activity of the statewide digital collections initiative and is an integral part of digital initiative planning and production.

University of Texas at Austin
University of Texas Libraries
Austin, Texas

Philosophy

The collections of the University of Texas Libraries, in addition to their intellectual and aesthetic value, represent an enormous economic investment. The University of Texas Libraries is committed to providing a comprehensive preservation program for these collections, consistent with the goals and objective of the Library and the University and with the Library's stature as a major national research collection

A comprehensive preservation program encompasses a system of plans, policies, procedures, and resources required to properly care for and prolong the life of these collection for the use of the educational and research community. An active preservation program encourages respect for the library and its collections, reduces the loss of materials through neglect or carelessness, and conserves resources through the application of preventive and corrective measures. Preservation, in fact, is an essential component in any activity involving introduction of library materials into collections (selection, acquisition, and cataloging) and handling by library staff and users.

The success of the University of Texas Libraries preservation program to a large extent depends on staff understanding and observance of good preservation practices. Because library materials are handled extensively by library staff, and because library users look to staff as exemplars in library matters, the observance of good preservation practice is extremely important. Active participation and leadership in the preservation program is the responsibility of all staff.

Definitions

"Preservation" is the set of actions taken to prevent, stop or retard deterioration of library materials through the management of: storage environment; housing materials and techniques; security; handling practices; as well as through user and staff education. Replacement is a form of preservation, as is changing the format of materials in order to preserve the intellectual content. "Conservation" implies the actions taken to prevent, stop, or retard deterioration of individual items through treatment level intervention into the physical state of the item. "Preservation" is used here as the broader term encompassing both preservation and conservation.

Administration

Responsibility for directing the preservation program rests with the Head Librarian, Preservation Services, who, with appropriate consultation, formulates, implements, and coordinates preservation policies and activities on a library-wide basis. The Head Librarian also maintains active liaison with the preservation programs of other campus agencies, such as the Harry Ransom Humanities Research Center, the Tarlton Law Library, the Archer M. Huntington Art Gallery, and the Texas Memorial Museum.

Program Objectives

Within the limitations imposed by budget and staffing levels, the University of Texas Libraries strives to provide a comprehensive preservation program that includes the following elements:

Adheres to nationally and professionally accepted preservation standards and techniques. This includes limited conservation treatment of library materials using permanent, nondestructive materials.

Evaluates and improves the physical care of library materials. This includes handling and storage, environmental conditions, collections security, and up-to-date disaster prevention and preparedness planning.

Ensures that the most effective preservation options are implemented. Present options include commercial binding and rebinding, in-house repair and binding, protective enclosures, replacement, limited preservation photoduplication and microfilming and, in rare instances, conservation.

Identifies materials requiring preservation measures. Items in poor condition are identified through general stack maintenance, circulation, and physical surveys of collections. In cases of non-routine treatment, bibliographers recommend preservation options appropriate to the material under review.

Conducts an on-going program of staff training and awareness. In addition to the use of Preservation of Library Materials: A Manual for Staff, this includes an orientation session held each semester for new professional and classifies staff, on-going training in minor book repair for public service units, video and slide/tape presentation, demonstrations, and exhibits. The Head Librarian, Preservation Services, and Conservator are available for staff consultation on any preservation concern. All supervisors are responsible for directing staff to appropriate preservation training resources.

Carries forward a user education program on preservation. Elements included in the program are book flags, posters, exhibits, videotapes, and direct appeals to faculty and students.

PROCEDURES SPECIFICALLY FOR PRINT RESOURCES

Southern Illinois University Edwardsville
Lovejoy Library
Edwardsville, Illinois

Preservation Policy

The faculty and staff of Lovejoy Library are committed to an ongoing preventive preservation program designed to maximize the natural life cycle of all library materials, equipment, and furnishings. We appreciate the financial investment that the university makes in providing SIUE faculty, students, and staff with an excellent library facility and with authoritative library and information resources essential to the fulfillment of our teaching, research, and service obligations. The faculty and staff of Lovejoy Library invite the understanding and active participation of the university community in the implementation of our preventive preservation program.

We strive to foster an environment conducive to rigorous intellectual inquiry and quiet contemplation. Such a learning environment is characterized by respect—respect for the rights of other researchers, respect for appropriate conduct in the university classroom, and respect for library resources. In their own best interests, patrons are encouraged to become sensitive to preservation issues, to handle library materials carefully, and to behave responsibly within the library facility. Without positive participation by our patrons, our preventive preservation program cannot succeed. The Lovejoy Library Patron Conduct Policy explains to library users their responsibilities with respect to preventive preservation.

All formats of library materials possess inherent limitations in their chemical or physical structures. In addition, a number of external factors such as careless handling of materials, theft, vandalism, light, pests, pollutants, extreme variations in temperature and relative humidity, water, and fire can greatly accelerate the normal process of deterioration. Fortunately, a comprehensive program of preventive preservation can significantly reduce or even prevent premature deterioration. Lovejoy Library's preventive preservation program is primarily concerned with the following interrelated issues. This summary of issues is based upon the document Assessing Preservation Needs: A Self-Survey Guide prepared by the Northeast Document Conservation Center.

Environmental Control—providing a moderate, stable temperature and humidity, and controlling exposure to light and pollutants

Disaster Preparedness—preventing and responding to damage from water, fire, or other emergencies

Security—protecting collections from theft and/or vandalism

Storage and Handling—using non-damaging storage enclosures; using proper storage furniture; cleaning materials and storage areas; using care when handling, exhibiting, or reproducing materials

Reformatting—reproducing (microfilming, photocopying, or digital imaging) onto stable media fragile, damaged, valuable, and/or heavily-used materials

Binding and Repair—using library binding for appropriate materials (those that are not valuable as artifacts), performing minor in-house repairs (encapsulation, surface cleaning, minor paper repair)

Conservation Treatment—having valuable items such as manuscripts, journals, maps, and drawings treated by a qualified conservator

1. Building Characteristics and Condition
2. Building Environment
   A. Climate Control

      Relative Humidity

      Temperature

      Stability

      Storage Areas

      Monitoring
   B. Control of Pollutants
      Air Circulation Filtering
      Vacuuming
   C. Control of Light
      Intensity and Length of Exposure
      Filtering of UV Light

    D. Pest Control/Housekeeping
       Food, Drink, Refuse
       Systematic Cleaning of Dust/Dirt
       Integrated Pest Management
       Economics of Neglect

3. Protecting Collections from Loss
    A. External Threats
       Acts of Nature
       Manmade
    B. Water Protection
       Roof/Drainage
       Pipes, Restrooms, HVAC
       Materials Shelved Off Floor
    C. Fire Protection
       Detection Systems
       Prevention Education
       Sprinkler Systems
       Extinguishers
    D. Disaster Planning
       Evacuation
       Disaster Recovery Plan
       Education for Response
       Insurance
    E. Building Security
       Education for Prevention of Theft, Vandalism, Arson
       Monitoring
    F. Controlling Access to Collections

4. Individual Storage and Exhibition Areas

5. General Storage and Handling Practices
    A. Storage Furniture
    B. Archival Enclosures
    C. Handling and Processing of Collections
    D. Cleaning Collections

6. Storage and Condition of Specific Formats

7. Exhibition of Materials
    A. Light Levels
    B. Duplicates or Facsimiles
    C. Exhibit Case Environment

8. Reformatting
    A. Microfilm
    B. Photocopy
    C. Photographs
    D. Audio
    E. Digital Imaging
       Expense
       Metadata
       Quality Control

      Storage
      Obsolescence
      Migration/Refreshment

9. Binding
10. Repair and Treatment
    A. In-house
    B. Specialist

University of Illinois at Urbana-Champaign
University Library
Urbana, Illinois

Preservation Policy Statement

Preservation, as it applies to library and archive material, can be defined as: "all managerial and financial considerations including storage and accommodation, provision, staffing levels, policies, techniques and methods involved in preserving library and archive materials and the information contained therein."

As an institution committed to building collections for the use of students, faculty, scholars, and the public long into the future, the University of Illinois Urbana-Champaign is obligated to ensure long-term access to those materials and their intellectual content. With an estimated replacement value in excess of $1.5 billion, the Library's collections represent a significant investment—one that can hardly be reconstructed. The university must care for this investment or risk losing access to significant portions of it. To this end, the Library develops relevant preservation and conservation policies that will address institutional concerns.

As a research institution, the University of Illinois Urbana-Champaign's Library selects most of its materials on the basis of their permanent value to the individual collections, the scholars and students who use them, and the institution as a whole. Subject specialists are responsible for developing and maintaining collections that will meet the needs of users and the institution long into the future. Consequently, preservation activities are best undertaken by the subject specialists in consultation with their peers, the Preservation and Conservation Offices, and other members of the academic community when necessary.

Through such consultation, the Preservation and Conservation Offices help subject specialists choose the most appropriate treatments for their materials. Using available options, the Preservation and Conservation Offices work to preserve physical and intellectual access through careful consideration of an item's value to both the institution and the larger research community.

Through cooperative collection management and evaluation of institutional workflow, the Preservation and Conservation Offices also work with other units within the Library as they select, process, and make accessible new acquisitions in the most timely manner possible.

University of North Carolina Wilmington
William Madison Randall Library
Wilmington, North Carolina

One of Randall Library's stated goals is:

To identify, select, acquire and preserve informational resources, including print, electronic, visual, and sound formats, relevant to current and anticipated curriculum, scholarly practice, research, and creative activities.

This policy explains how the library operates to meet its preservation goal.

The state of North Carolina has made a significant investment in information resources and it is the obligation of all library staff to steward the resources. Library resources are expensive to acquire. Additional labor and funds must be expended to process, house and preserve the materials for current and future generations. Randall Library takes this charge seriously, and fully endorses the American Library Association Preservation Policy.

Preserving informational resources is a multi-faceted endeavor, requiring both division of labor and collaboration among various library units and outside vendors.

General preservation objectives:

Training staff and users on proper handling of the materials

Maintaining proper storage and environmental controls

Providing security (theft prevention) for the resources

Repairing, reformatting, or replacing damaged materials

Responding to disasters that threaten the collection

Specific measures to accomplish these objectives are:

Training staff and users on proper handling of the materials

Cataloging processes materials to provide uniform labeling, while paying attention to minimize masking useful information on the covers.

Circulation Department trains student assistants in proper handling of materials.

Public Services staff include instruction on handling materials for users at appropriate times, e.g., loading microform. Exhibits are also used to educate the public on preservation issues.

The Circulation staff person responsible for repair is provided additional training. Ideally, this person should be sent to the Fundamentals of Book Repair Workshop, offered by Solinet.

Maintaining proper storage and environmental controls:

New materials are considered for special protection upon initial processing, and may receive one of the following treatments:

In-House Binding

Technical Services staff perform in-house binding for most pamphlets, music scores, and materials with accompanying items such as maps and charts. Acid-free pressboard binders are used for most in-house binding.

Professional Binding

Library materials that require professional binding are sent to one of the professional binderies included on the North Carolina Library Binding State Contract TC–130. The products of these binderies conform to binding industry standard ANSI/NISO/LBI/ Z39.78–2000.

Technical Services staff make most binding decisions for books and periodicals, using the following criteria:

Books

Paperback books are bound if original binding is poor quality or if high use is predicted.

Rebind if cost of rebinding damaged materials is cheaper than purchasing a new copy.

Custom boxes are made if paper is too brittle to bind and material cannot be replaced.

Theses

3 copies are bound, 1 for the University Archives, 1 for the General Collection, and 1 for the academic department.

If electronic copies of theses are available, 1 copy will be bound for the University Archives.

Periodicals

Most periodicals are routinely bound on a schedule based on the frequency of publication.

Periodicals that are available via an electronic subscription may not be bound and are stored in periodical boxes in the Bound Journal Collection.

Newsletters and newspapers that are valuable only for current information are discarded, newsletters after 1 year and newspapers after 1 month.

Newspapers and other periodicals published in formats that aren't suitable for binding are purchased in microform. Print issues are discarded when microform is received.

Newspapers that are not available in microform may be preserved by binding.

Media

CDs accompanying books will be shelved, if possible, in the book. When this is not feasible, these CDs will be given a separate item record and stored at the Reserve/Media Desk. Security targets will be applied to CDs.

Magnetic media accompanying books (e.g., diskettes) are stored at the Circulation Desk. These items may be checked out, but must not be desensitized.

As videocassettes and audiocassettes need to be replaced, DVD and CD formats will be the preferred format.

Splicing equipment and supplies are used to repair damaged microfilm.

The Stack Maintenance Supervisor and Circulation Department Supervisor have primary responsibility for ensuring there is sufficient stack space for collections and that items are properly shelved or filed. Librarians in charge of specific collections, e.g., Reference, Documents, CMC, Special Collections, manage this effort for their areas of responsibility. The Associate University Librarian for Public Services provides overall, long-range planning for most stack and cabinet acquisitions.

Exhibit cases are equipped with UV filters on lights to minimize damage to materials.

Special Collections takes extra care with rare and fragile materials. Items are housed in a specially climate-controlled environment. The climate control system is separate and distinct from the rest of the building. It has separate humidity and temperature controls that allow for distinct temperature variation from other areas of the library. Materials are kept in low or no light environments, in acid free folders and/or containers. Access is limited. Items are only handled by staff or professionals on an as-needed basis.

Photo copying is not encouraged, to prevent further deterioration of items.

Temperature and humidity is controlled through continuous monitoring by the Physical Plant. Problems detected by library staff are reported to the library administrative office, which forwards requests for service to the Physical Plant.

Providing security theft prevention for the resources:

The Cataloging Department applies labels and security targets to new items added to all open-stack collections.

The Circulation Department monitors the security gate and complies with written procedures for responding to the alarm.

Special Collections allows for very limited access. Keys are held by department head and assistant only. The rarest and most valuable items are housed in a vault. Within the vault there is a safe for the most valuable smaller items. Access to vault is via a key that is held by the department head and by the library director.

Patrons coming into special collections are required to register and include their names, email address, regular address and purpose of visit. Patrons are given a secure locker to house their personal belongings while they conduct research. Only paper and pencil are allowed in the main reading room. All storage areas and stacks are behind locked doors. Student workers and staff are encouraged to lock and close doors to areas when not in use. Access to Special Collections when it is closed to the public is via a door with a doorbell, so there is ample notice when someone wishes to enter special collections.

Repairing, reformatting, or replacing damaged materials:

Items in need of repair are identified in a number of ways, including users bringing damaged items to the staff's attention, items identified upon checkout/check-in, and items identified during shelf-reading and inventory. The Circulation Department provides the initial review and if the repair is minor, it is performed in the department. Items damaged beyond the repair abilities of the Circulation Department are forwarded to Technical Services. Technical Services will decide whether to rebind, box, or replace the material.

The following criteria are used when making replacement decisions:

Availability of additional copies in the collection

Material is available for purchase (new or high-quality used copies)

Cost of rebinding versus replacement

Circulation statistics

Availability of newer editions

Coverage of the subject matter in the collection

During the time materials are unavailable for circulation, their status will be changed in the online system to indicate this, e.g., Damaged, To Bind, Lost, etc.

Items not in hand that have been determined to be lost, either by the user or in inventory will be reviewed by creating a list in the online system. Technical Services will review the list and decide upon replacement or withdrawal. When items are withdrawn, they will be deleted from the online system and from the OCLC database. Some materials are designated to be retained for a specific period, such as newsletters. Notations of the retention period are noted in the catalog record and discards are managed by Technical Services.

Replacements are purchased from a separate line in the budget. When library users lose materials, the replacement costs they pay are deposited in this account.

Responding to disasters that threaten the collection:

The library has a separate Disaster Policy, mainly designed to prepare for and respond to hurricanes, the greatest threat we face.

New York University
Bobst Library
New York, New York

Preservation of Library Books

Books must be returned to the library in the same condition in which they were borrowed. Fees will be assessed for books which are damaged. Replacement costs plus processing fees will be assessed for books which are damaged beyond repair.

Please avoid the following common sources of damage to library books:

Moisture (including rain and spilled beverages)

Using inappropriate materials as bookmarks:

Paperclips and post-its cause great damage to pages and should not be used.

Pencils (or anything thicker than a piece of paper) wedged between pages causes great damage to the spine.

Rubber bands leave damaging residue on pages and should not be used to hold pages back.

Animals (especially dogs)

Stuffing books into an overfull book drop (if they don't go into the chute easily, return them at the Circulation desk instead).

Please do not ever write in library books, even in pencil. Everyone's cooperation is required in order to keep the collection in the best condition possible.

(For additional policies, please see the accompanying CD-ROM.)

PROCEDURES SPECIFICALLY FOR ELECTRONIC RESOURCES

Columbia University
Columbia University Libraries
New York, New York

Statement of CUL policy for preservation of digital resources

According to the Columbia University Libraries' Mission Statement (7/22/93):

The Columbia University Libraries provides Columbia faculty, students, and staff with access to information in all subject areas related to the University's academic mission and its goals. The Libraries embraces its time-honored obligations of collecting, preserving, and providing access to collections, not only for the Columbia community but also for scholars and students from throughout the world who require access to the Libraries' unique materials.

Policy

Digital resources are part of the CUL collections and subject to the same criteria for selection and retention decisions as other media. As such, they are included under the central CUL preservation policy: ensuring that the collections remain available over the long term, through prevention of damage and deterioration; reversing damage where possible; and, when necessary, changing the format of materials to preserve their intellectual content.

As with other parts of the collections, decisions about preservation are made by selectors, curators, and bibliographers as experts on the value of the content, in consultation with the relevant technical experts, including Academic Information Systems, the Library Systems Office, and Preservation. Priorities for preservation action are based on this Policy, the CUL Strategic Plan, and available resources. When possible, decisions about the need for long-term retention are made at the time of creation, acquisition, or licensing of digital resources.

For digital resources that are deemed to be of long-term value, preservation can be defined as the actions needed to assure enduring access to the full content of those resources over time. Content has wider implications than simply assuring that a given image can be accessed. Thus, hierarchical and structural relationships among the files (e.g. the pages of a book) and metadata that make the files usable must be preserved as well as the files themselves,

Digital resources may exist in multiple versions. CUL is committed to preserving the archival version: the fullest, highest-quality available version of the resource, whenever possible; and the descriptive, structural, and administrative metadata associated with it.

Scope of Preservation Responsibility

Responsibility for internal long-term retention and management by CUL/AcIS of:

Digital resources created by CUL for which no other versions exist, and deemed to be of long-term value.

Digital versions of resources reformatted by CUL, and deemed to be of long-term value in digital form.

Unique digital resources which are acquired by CUL (through donation or purchase) as parts of archival/manuscript collections and which are unlikely to be preserved anywhere else.

Digital records (e.g. bibliographic records, personnel records) deemed of long-term value and/or essential to CUL's functioning, and not preserved through any other arm of the university.

Responsibility for working externally through consortial action, licensing agreements, etc. to assure that someone (possibly but not necessarily CUL/AcIS) carries out preservation of appropriate commercially available digital resources to assure that CU faculty, staff, and students will have adequate ongoing access to these resources. Particular emphasis should be given to resources which exist in digital form only.

Responsibility for informing, consulting, and as appropriate coordinating with other units of Columbia University in the preservation of administrative and other digital resources to assure that CU faculty, staff, and students will have adequate ongoing access to these resources. Included here are digital resources created at CU outside of the Libraries but considered to be part of the digital library (EPIC ventures, others) and of long-term value.

Frequency with which preservation/retention policy for digital materials will be updated:

This policy will be reviewed at the beginning of each academic year to assure timely updates as technology and experience mature, or more often if need arises.

Statement of CUL's Commitment to Lifecycle Management

CUL is committed to lifecycle management of its digital resources. Guidelines and procedures for each stage have been or are being developed, and are reviewed as technology changes or other need arises. CUL will participate actively where appropriate in research, development, and implementation of new practices for preservation of digital resources.

Development of preservation strategies, including consideration of:

  Degree of integration with storage, backup, and preservation for non-digital library resources.

  Development and use of decision-making tools (e.g., risk analysis, usage monitoring, probability of loss calculations, cost models, etc.).

  Maintenance strategies (backups—online and/or offline, monitoring, refreshing, redundancy through mirror sites or caching, etc.).

  Survival strategies (migration, emulation, archeology, etc.).

  Reliance on outside consulting and archiving services, if any, contract negotiation, etc.

  Selection for long-term retention at time of digitization, acquisition, or licensing; and later reselection for retention if this decision was not made initially:

Primary criteria: based on institutional mission, needs, priorities, and reasons for creating or acquiring the resources (related to long-term institutional mission and linked to conversion guidelines): see Selection Criteria for Digital Imaging Projects, www.columbia.edu/cu/libraries/digital/criteria.html

Secondary criteria: based on regional, national, consortial, and international responsibilities.

Conversion Guidelines

CUL follows relevant standards where they have been established and best practice for digital conversion, as documented by Library of Congress, the Research Libraries Group (RLG), the Digital Library Federation (DLF), and other relevant bodies.

See: Technical Recommendations for Digital Imaging Projects, www.columbia.edu/acis/dl/imagespec.html

Metadata Creation and Management (unique IDs and other descriptive, structural and administrative metadata, including ownership/rights management)

CUL follows relevant standards where they have been established and best practice for metadata creation and management, as documented by Library of Congress, RLG, DLF, and other relevant bodies.

Digital resources deemed to be of long-term value are tracked through the Master Metadata File (MMF). See: CU Master Metadata File, www.columbia.edu/cu/libraries/inside/projects/metadata/

Storage (online, offline, redundancy recommendations, etc.)

CUL follows relevant standards where they have been established and best practice for storage, as documented by Library of Congress, RLG, DLF, and other relevant bodies.

The archival version of the digital resource is preserved in a lossless, non-proprietary format, whenever possible.

Storage Plan for Primary Responsibility Materials

Resources currently in use: kept online with regular backup, refreshment, and migration.

Whether online or not, all archival versions (highest resolution, fullest capture, lossless compression) are written to approved storage media and stored off-line in the Library Systems Office (LSO), with a schedule for regular refreshment, and migration.

For archival versions which are not currently online: a duplicate off-line copy is created for storage at a different site.

All versions, online and offline, are tracked through the MMF.

Access Arrangements (database management, Web interface, access reliability, etc.)

CUL follows relevant standards where they have been established and best practice for access arrangements, as documented by Library of Congress, RLG, DLF, and other relevant bodies.

Statement of CUL's Resource Management Policies and Plans

As stated in the Six-Year Plan for the Libraries and AcIS (May 1999), the digital library is the primary online information interface for the University, delivering scholarly, instructional, research, administrative and personal information. The University is committed to supporting all of the operations of the digital library, including preservation. Resource management for preservation of digital resources includes:

Technical infrastructure (equipment purchases, maintenance and upgrades, software/hardware obsolescence monitoring, network connectivity, etc.).

Financial plan (strategy and methods for financing the digital preservation program, commitment to long-term funding).

Staffing infrastructure (including hiring and ongoing training).

Rights management.

Statement Related to Regional, National, Consortial, and International Responsibilities

Whenever it is proposed that digital resources created or acquired by CUL as part of a cooperative or consortial effort, and deemed to be of long-term value, should be preserved by another institution or organization, CUL will evaluate their capacity to provide long-term access to digital files, metadata, and functionality in order to assure that the resources will be preserved at least as well as they would be by CUL. Issues which must be taken into account include:

Shared obligations and cooperative preservation.

Information sharing.

Technology support (e.g., reuse of same migration paths and strategies by others; following emerging common/recommended practice).

Development of minimal standards for capture, management, and maintenance (to enable efficient strategies).

Chapter 14

COLLECTION SELECTION GUIDELINES FOR FACULTY

MATERIALS BY FACULTY

Eastern Michigan University
Bruce T. Halle Library
Ypsilanti, Michigan

EMU Publications

The library purchases two copies of each monograph authored by University faculty and staff. One copy goes to the main collection and the other to Archives.

Columbia College
Columbia College Library
Chicago, Illinois

Faculty Publications

The Library attempts to acquire and maintain, whether through purchase or donation, present and retrospective works by current Columbia full-time faculty in all formats for use by the College community and as a record of scholarship. These include, but are not restricted to: monographs (works/collections of essays, poems, stories, research), laboratory guides, textbooks, supplemental texts, audio, electronic and visual materials. Works by part-time faculty, visiting lecturers or full-time faculty with prolific publishing histories will be acquired selectively based upon input from the Department Chair and/or the individual faculty member.

Two copies will be obtained as appropriate; one copy for the circulating collection if it falls within the library's collection development parameters, and a second for the College Archives, regardless of subject matter or reading level. Laboratory guides and supplementary materials will be added only to the College Archives.

Works in which a faculty member is an editor or contributor may be purchased on a case-by-case basis, depending upon its appropriateness for the main library collection. Single poems, essays, chapters, or stories appearing in books or journals will not be purchased or subscribed to unless the entire content falls within collection guidelines. A copy of the individual work is acceptable for placement in the College Archives.

FACULTY PURCHASE REQUESTS

Columbia College Chicago
Columbia College Library
Chicago, Illinois

Faculty

Acquisitions FAQ for Faculty

How do I request a book to be purchased for the library? Is there a limit on the number or dollar amount?

Submit an Online Library Purchase Request Form. Paper forms (yellow) are available in the library and can be sent to your office upon request. While there is no limit on the number or dollar amount faculty can request at this time, the library reserves the right to take into consideration whether or not potential use justifies cost, and whether the item is appropriate for the collection.

I need the library to purchase textbooks for reserves ASAP. Can you do this?

Please submit reserve requests as soon as your syllabus is finalized. The earlier you inform us of your reserve needs, the better we are able to accommodate you and your students. Duplicate copies are discouraged due to space considerations. Use statistics reveal that one copy is usually sufficient. The library does NOT automatically order textbooks for our collection. We will not process textbook requests from students but we do honor textbook requests from faculty. Another quick solution would be to submit a personal copy for Reserve.

How long does it take for a book to be ordered?

Faculty requests are treated as priority orders. Turnaround time is generally 6–8 weeks. Some requests may take longer if item is out-of-stock or out-of-print. Every effort is made to accommodate your request, but for items out-of-print or which we cannot otherwise obtain, you are encouraged to borrow the book through Interlibrary Loan.

How am I notified when a requested book or video comes in?

Once a requested item is cataloged, you will receive a request notification card with call number information on the back. This will be the only notification you receive. You will also be notified if your item is unavailable, unobtainable or already in the collection.

I am teaching a history class and I would like to use videos that discuss specific topics in American history. What videos does the library have in this area?

Search our online catalog using the Guided Keyword screen. Click on More Limits and chose Primary Format: Films/Videos. After clicking on Set Limits, enter your term(s) as "subject words" and click on search. For help with choosing appropriate subject terms, please check with a librarian at the Reference Desk. Contact your liaison to assist you in your lesson planning.

I submitted several video requests recently and would like to use them in the next several weeks. I checked the online catalog and didn't find them. How can I find out if they have been ordered or received?

Titles that are currently on order do not display in the online catalog. You may check the status of your request at any time by contacting Library Acquisitions at If the item has been received but is not cataloged, you may still use it in your class; please provide at least 48 hours for processing. Contact the AV Desk. Audiovisual requests with show dates are given priority processing.

I'd like the library to subscribe to a journal? How do I notify you?

The procedure for requesting journals is similar to that of requesting books. Please complete a either an online or paper Library Purchase Request/Notification Form and forward it to Library Acquisitions. If you would like the library to begin the subscription with a specific date, please indicate this on the form.

Students

If you would like to suggest a purchase, fill out an Online Purchase Request Form or a Library Purchase Recommendation card available at the 2nd floor Reference Desk. Student recommendations are subject to approval by Library staff. Please allow at least 6–8 weeks for processing.

FORMS

Faculty Request to Purchase Material Form

Columbia College Chicago
Columbia College Library
Chicago, Illinois

Library Purchase Request Form

REMINDER: Please allow at least 6–8 weeks for processing.

*REQUIRED FIELDS

YOUR INFORMATION

Name: * _____

Department or Major: * _____

Status: * Faculty _____ Undergraduate Student _____ Graduate Student ___ Staff ___

Email address: * _____

Phone number:* _____

ITEM INFORMATION

Please supply as much information as possible for your request.

Author/Editor/Director: _____

Title:* _____

Publisher or Distributor:_____

ISBN/ISSN (if known): _____

Publication Year:_____

Material Type:* Book _____ DVD/VHS _____ Journal/Periodical _____ Audio _____ CD _____

Date Needed:* _____

The item I am requesting is:* New Copy _____

Additional Copy _____

FOR FACULTY ONLY:

Would you like this item to be held for you when it becomes available for check out?
_____

(All items are held at the 1st floor Circulation Desk.) Yes _____ No _____

Would you like for this item to be placed on reserve for a course? Yes ___No __

If you answered "yes," please provide the course number:

_____

Comments:

Chapter 15

Collection Deselection Guidelines

Material Removal Methods

Guilford College
Hege Library
Greensboro, North Carolina

Weeding the Collection

Maintaining a useful and current collection requires the deletion of no longer appropriate materials as well as the addition of new acquisitions. Criteria for weeding will be consistent with priorities in acquiring materials. Candidates for withdrawal are those items not recently circulated, those with superseded, dated or obsolete information, or materials in poor condition. Surveys of usage and opinions of public service librarians and teaching faculty should determine the retention of any titles in question. An ongoing process of review, evaluation, and replacement will aid in these decisions.

Houston Community College System
Houston Community College Libraries
Houston, Texas

Weeding

Weeding is an integral and important aspect of the collection development/management process. It is an ongoing process, reflecting changing needs and current developments in every area.

Responsibility for weeding rests with library faculty.

The following are general guidelines that may be applied to the weeding process both generally and within each subject area. Subject Specialists may provide more specific guidelines in their areas as need indicates. The general guidelines are valid for print and non-print materials except where otherwise indicated.

Multiple copies—Generally there should not be more than one copy per title on any campus. Additional copies should be either reassigned or withdrawn. Exceptions are heavy use of a title, but this should be monitored closely, and as soon as the demand lessens, additional copies should be weeded.

Editions—In most cases, a later edition will replace an earlier edition of a work. When 2d, 3d, 4th, etc., editions are received, older editions should be examined closely and weeded if appropriate.

Erroneous or outdated information—especially applicable in the sciences and technical areas. Works that may contain out-of-date information should be weeded. This is an area where consultation with appropriate faculty may be necessary. Generally, works over five years old should be looked at carefully.

Discontinued programs or courses—print materials supporting programs or courses that are no longer offered on a particular campus or in the system should be examined for general relevance. Materials should be moved to the corresponding campus when a program or course moves, or may need to be withdrawn if areas are no longer covered at all by the system.

Use patterns—materials that have not been checked out for 4–5 years should be considered for withdrawal. For whatever reason these materials are not meeting students' needs.

Serials/Annuals—When newer editions of serials or annuals are received, the older editions should be withdrawn. Generally, these are reference materials, and if the Librarians determine that the need exists, the older editions may be placed in the circulating collection, but these also should be withdrawn as they are replaced.

Textbooks—Although the library tries to avoid acquisition of textbooks, this is not always possible. However, all textbooks should be examined carefully whenever newer texts become available or when a course no longer uses a text or is no longer taught.

Age—Except in some areas of the humanities and social sciences materials of a certain age have a very limited value and should be withdrawn or replaced with new materials. Generally, any title over ten years old should be looked at carefully to determine its continuing value.

Physical condition—Materials that have been damaged or are missing some part should be either replaced or withdrawn entirely.

Level of materials—Level of materials should be that which is most accessible to student body. Advanced works may need to be replaced by more basic works appropriate to a community college setting or basic works may need to be replaced or supplemented by more in-depth, comprehensive coverage if the need exists.

Audiovisual media weeding should be done in conjunction with the appropriate instructional personnel.

1.9.1 Inter-college cooperation.

Materials weeded from one college collection may still be of use or value at another college within the HCCS system. Before materials are discarded, each college will notify the other HCCS college libraries about the availability of materials and transfer to other colleges any that are requested.

Los Angeles Valley College
Los Angeles Valley College Library
Valley Glen, California

Recommendations for specific titles may be made to the acquisitions librarian by filling out an order card; just ask one of the librarians for one. We encourage faculty members to review the collection in their discipline for possible discarding (weeding) of dated or obsolete materials. Additionally, professional development credit is given for "review and assessment of library holdings in your discipline."

New Mexico State University Alamogordo
David H. Townsend Library
Alamogordo, New Mexico

Deselection (Weeding)

Deselection of library materials (the process of removing items from the collection) is essential for the maintenance of a current, academically useful library collection.

Deselection provides quality control for the collection by elimination of outdated, inaccurate, and worn-out materials. Librarians are responsible for conducting an ongoing deselection effort. Faculty members are regularly consulted when specific items are recommended for deselection.

- Print and audio-visual resources deselection:
  - Superseded editions are routinely deselected from the collection.
  - Materials which cannot be repaired or rebound or for which the cost of preservation exceeds the usefulness of the information contained are deselected.
  - Because currency of information is extremely important in some fields such as health sciences, technology, and business, older materials must be regularly deselected so that outdated or inaccurate information is eliminated.
  - Material that has not been used, based on circulation and browsing statistics, may be deselected after five to ten years of inactivity. However, some library materials, such as items

considered classic works in their field, have long-term value and should be kept in the collection despite lack of use.

- The title may be retained if it is included in a standard list or bibliography such as Books for College Libraries or if the author has a reputation for being an authority on the topic.
- Online resources deselection:

  Ongoing deselection of Internet resources is a necessity because of the dynamic nature of such resources. The following guidelines are used:
  - An Internet resource is no longer available or maintained
  - The currency or reliability of the resource's information has lost its value
  - Another Internet site or resource offers more comprehensive coverage
  - A comparable fee-based or free resource provides more affordable access
- Serials Deselection:
  - Incomplete and short runs of a title may be withdrawn, particularly when the title is not received currently.
  - Titles which contain information that is not useful long-term, such as newsletters and trade magazines, usually have automatic discard patterns established such as "Library retains one year only"
  - Annuals, biennials, and regularly updated editions of guidebooks, handbooks, almanacs, and directories have a deselection pattern established depending on the value of the information contained in earlier editions. Often one or two older editions are retained in the reference and/or circulating collections or the latest edition is retained at the Townsend Library.

Lansing Community College
Library at Lansing Community College
Lansing, Michigan

Deselection (Weeding)

A. Generally, consider "drop" titles on a one-by-one basis.

B. Request form

1. Use a separate Periodical Request for each title considered for deselection.
2. With assistance of a LIS staff member, a requester should thoroughly document their reason for suggesting a periodical deselection. See also Request for Reconsideration—Attachment A.
3. LIS staff member assisting requester or initiating a "drop" request complete as much of the form as possible.
4. Send a completed Periodical Request and a sample issue from the collection to Periodicals Coordinator.
5. Coordinator checks for current subscription price and verifies completeness of the "drop" request.

C. Routing the request

1. Coordinator routes drop request form and sample issue to Reference staff soliciting their comment.
2. Upon completing routing, the Coordinator forwards drop request to Library Director with a summary recommendation based on Reference staff comment.
3. Library Director returns drop request form to Periodicals Coordinator with final decision. Coordinator notifies the requester, LIS staff member assisting requester, and DCM.

D. Reference staff review a portion of the Periodicals Collection, or perhaps the entire collection, as may become necessary. Reviews of this type may result in deselection and weeding of a number of titles at one time.

LCC Library is Curricula Based

Lansing Community College Library Information Services will remove obsolete materials to maintain a quality and current collection best meeting the needs of currently enrolled LCC students. To keep the collection up to date Librarians will remove older materials that no longer contain current information and duplicate copies of once popular items where demand has diminished. A purpose of the LCC Library is to have books that students use. If shelves have become crowded and shifting potential remains limited, are all the present books in the topic currently serving LCC needs? Materials taking space that ought to be used more profitably are subject to re-evaluation and weeding when warranted. Replace titles withdrawn due to physical condition, loss, or damage, if they meet current selection criteria and are in Books in Print plus with Book Reviews.

Weeding, an ongoing part of Collection Development work, is a regular responsibility of each Reference Librarian in areas where they are Selector & Liaison. Other areas may be agreed upon from time to time with the Collection Development Coordinator.

Criteria for removal correspond to the "Guidelines for Selectors" (II. B). Current principles for deselection are essentially the same as for selection. Procedure is the deselector places a self-stick red dot on the "spine" call-number label signaling the item is a candidate for withdrawal from the collection at a later time. DCM (Database & Collection Maintenance) will call for the red-dotted items to be pulled by Circulation.

Weed an item when it is not wanted by LCC clientele. If someone wants items from the collection these items should not, therefore, be weeded. Such desire for the material indicates apparent continued usefulness for LCC.

Remove unused materials from the general collection when the topic is otherwise adequately represented. Systematic discarding is important to keep the collection alive. Predominantly older less attractive books that just sit on the shelves may divert clientele away from more currently useful materials. Re-evaluate materials continuously when selecting new or replacement materials. Weed obsolete materials. Newer editions replace superseded editions. When possible, place a "red dot" on superseded non-reference materials.

Different types of libraries will retain different materials. In awareness of this, and with encouragement, resource sharing in the LCC service area shall continue. Refer LCC clients to scholarly and historical depositories as necessary. Use LCC's comprehensive "reference" sources for coverage of many specific information requests. Use available periodical publications and electronic delivery of information for current data.

Guidelines for Deselectors

Consider the following when suggesting material for deletion from the Library:

1. Check the current Lansing Community College Catalog. Do the subject matter and scope of the material suit the purpose of the LCC curriculum currently being supported?

2. Be aware of recent reading-level test results, LCC student profile, etc., when this information is shared. Does the treatment of the subject suit the needs of LCC students studying in the discipline? Does the item serve student interests in more than one LCC curriculum? Be aware of current LCC enrollment trends. Freshmen-Sophomore students find introductory works, surveys of the topic, study guides, handbooks, manuals, to be very useful. Is the item a partial or more extensive coverage? LCC Library clientele look for very specific information material that is often found within more encyclopedic sources. Is the item speculative?

Is it contemporary or retrospective in nature? Historical coverage of a subject is in relatively lesser demand. What emphasis occurs in the curricular areas that the item supports?

Is the item a scholarly, technical, or popular work? While instructors seem to want LCC student use of research level materials, Library Information Services Librarians must continue an awareness of student readiness in introductory level courses.

3. What is the original publication date; if revised, how extensively? What is the reputation of the publisher? What are the author's qualifications? Does the item under consideration have an index? Does the item draw on primary or secondary sources? Is the information based on observation or research?

4. Does the item contribute to pro and con interpretations of current issues? Is the point of view partisan or sectarian? Does it present fact or opinion? Does it show unredeemable bias? Is it a contribution to community values, citizenship, cultural diversity? Does it challenge and promote critical thinking skills?

5. What elements of quality identify the item as among the best of its type, for retention in the LCC Library? What degree of creativity is represented? Is there a freshness in the presentation? Is the material aimed at community college students and adult amateurs? Is the format of the material suitable for the message? What is the quality of illustration? Are there more appropriate similar publications in the LCC Library collection?

6. Is the physical format (introductory material, print, indexing, paper quality, binding) of the item attractive? Is it unusual in size? Are standard format items available that may effectively substitute?

7. In weeding works of literature, does the item add to an understanding of cultural diversity, personality, human nature, and the human condition? Retain works that are representative of an author or of a genre of current and lasting interest. Retain works of minority authors. Is the item among the best in representing its author or genre? When available, give preference to study editions containing notes. Give preference to anthologies of poetry, drama, etc., over individual works. As in other curricular areas, non-usage is a criterion for consideration when weeding.

Procedure:

1. Physical presence

Check the physical condition of the material. Is the cataloging adequate? Does the Library own a newer edition? Check for other works by the same author. Check the quantity of other works in the same subject headings.

2. Usage

Check the acquisition date (this appears in various forms in the book). "Last activity dates" (LAD) appear in the catalog for the input or updating of a bibliographic record and again for the inputting or updating of an item record. Check the last date of circulation. Consider weeding an item if it has not circulated in ten years. When possible, check frequency of recent circulation. If duplicates are present, consider frequency of circulation among the duplicate items. Be aware of usage within the classification area where the item is shelved. If the work is now out-of-date, individual item usage might be disregarded.

3. Networking

Keep in mind that LCC is but part of a network of resources. Be ever ready to refer to other library and information services in the LCC area. Additional developments in electronic "document delivery" and automated information services will have an impact on materials retention. Be familiar with and ready to use Interlibrary Loan procedure.

(For additional policies, please see the accompanying CD-ROM.)

DAMAGED AND LOST MATERIALS REPLACEMENTS

New Mexico State University Alamogordo
David H. Townsend Library
Alamogordo, New Mexico

Replacement of Materials

Decisions must be made regarding the replacement of lost, damaged, missing, or worn-out materials, based on the following criteria:

- Does the material being replaced meet the general library collection policy?
- Does the frequency of use justify replacement?
- Is the item used for class reserve reading or is it on a faculty recommended reading list?
- Is the item listed in Books for College Libraries or other recommended book list?
- Is an electronic version available that would provide remote access for users?

Lake Sumter Community College
Lake Sumter Community College Libraries
Sumterville, Florida

Replacement of Materials

Decisions are made regarding the replacement of lost, damaged, missing, or worn-out items, based on the following criteria:

Does the item being considered meet the general library collection policy?

Does the frequency of use justify replacement?

Is the item used for class reserve reading or is it on a faculty recommended reading list?

Is the same item available in another format that would better meet the needs of users or is the content better covered by another title?

Is an electronic version available that would provide remote access for users?

University of Texas at Austin
University of Texas Libraries
Austin, Texas

Library materials are normally replaced when lost, missing, worn, mutilated or defective. It is the responsibility of the appropriate subject bibliographer to decide, within the guidelines of the Collection Development Policy, whether to replace such materials and in what form.

Status of Materials

Officially lost or missing materials: Review should be made by the appropriate bibliographer in accordance with the schedule stipulated in Procedures for Implementation of the Withdrawal Policy. Usually a title reported lost in circulation will be needed, and a replacement copy should be purchased immediately. Likewise, once a title is officially declared lost, it should be considered for immediate replacement. The decision whether to replace may be affected by the replacement, or because of the provisions of current collection policy.

Worn, mutilated, or defective materials: Materials requiring other than routine repair should be referred to the appropriate bibliographer as they are identified. If the decision is made to retain, the material may be repaired or rebound, and additional copies may be acquired. Defective, in-print titles may be returned to publisher.

Guidelines for Replacement

Replacement is always preferred over rebinding for inexpensive in-print titles. Current editions are preferred over previous ones unless the earlier edition has special distinguishing characteristics.

Replacement in part, by insertion of bindable photocopied pages, may be employed for mutilated or defective serial and monograph titles, especially for those out of print.

It is usually desirable to replace monographs or serials in their same format; however, microform rather than hard copy should be considered for extensive serial replacements.

Chapter 16

BINDING MATERIALS

LIBRARY MATERIALS

College of Charleston
College of Charleston Libraries
Charleston, South Carolina

1.0 Purpose

The purpose of this policy is to give guidelines concerning the binding of library material housed at the Robert Scott Small Library (excluding Special Collections) and the Marine Resources Library.

2.0 Binding Standards

All binding performed by the commercial binder will be by a certified binder in accordance with the Library Binding Institute Standard for Library Binding (see Attachment 1).

3.0 Types of Materials Which Are Bound

All library materials which are expected to be retained in the Library indefinitely and are received in paper format should be bound. This includes all serials (not replaced by microform) and all monographs (approval plan, firm order, gift, or government document). The only exceptions are materials designated as Special Collections materials (send returned items to Collection Development Department for a binding decision). The Reference Department is responsible for notifying the Collection Development Department when material they request should not be bound due to its immediate need.

4.0 Monographs

Generally all monographs should be bound after receipt and prior to cataloging. It is the responsibility of the Collection Development Department to determine when materials should be sent to the commercial binder or bound in-house. Items requested for RUSH processing will normally be bound after the item is returned by the patron (Circulation should send returned items to the Collection Development Department for a binding decision). The Reference Department is responsible for notifying the Collection Development Department when material they request should not be bound due to its immediate need.

    4.1 The Collection Development Department will determine upon receipt whether the item is of significant size where it can not be handled in-house. The Collection Development Department is responsible for maintaining adequate records to identify items sent to the commercial binder.

    4.2 When the Collection Development Department determines that items are of modest size (less than fifty pages), these items should be forwarded to the Cataloging Department for cataloging and in-house binding. It is the Cataloging Department's responsibility to bind all items designated for in-house binding.

5.0 Serials

All Serials (not replaced by microform and expected to be retained indefinitely) will be bound by the commercial binder. It is the responsibility of the Collection Development Department to maintain proper records of the pulling of completed volumes, recording of the binding titles and volumes designations. Completed volumes (normally yearly) will be pulled and sent to the commercial binder based on the individual characteristics of the title under consideration. Normally, serials will be pulled when the first issue of the new volume arrives in the library. Serials will be bound incomplete only after all avenues of issue replacement have been explored or usually after one year. (The Marine Resources Library is responsible for the binding of serials which are housed in their library.)

6.0 Repairs

Bound volumes with loose boards or pages should be charged out and sent to the Cataloging Department where minor repairs will be performed or routed to the Collection Development Department for sending to the commercial binder. Anyone other than the Cataloging Department should refrain from making repairs to library materials.

7.0 Rebinding

Library staff identifying items in need of rebinding should forward the item to the Collection Development Department where determination will be made as to whether they can be rebound. Items physically capable of rebinding will be sent to the commercial binder or rebound in-house.

8.0 Replacements

The Collection Development Department should forward items which are in need of rebinding, but physically incapable of being rebound, to the appropriate Library Liaison who will determine if the item is worthy of replacement. Items worthy of replacement should be ordered by the library Liaison. Items not worthy of replacement will be withdrawn from the collection. The Library Liaison should forward the item to the Cataloging Department for the withdrawal processing.

DISSERTATIONS AND THESES

University of South Alabama
University Libraries
Mobil, Alabama

Library Binding

Library Binding is located in Collection Management/Serials on the First Floor South. Library Binding consists of Thesis/Dissertation binding, periodical binding, and special book binding. For more information, call 6–2835.

Thesis/Dissertation distribution, format and style, including binding, follows the USA Graduate requirements. The Collection Management/Serials Thesis/Dissertation binding procedure includes:

> Binding is paid for in the USA Graduate Office
> Cost is $10.00 per copy
> Library gets 2 copies
> Major professor gets 1 copy
> Books for binding are picked up on a monthly basis, approximately every 28 days
> Notification of Thesis/Dissertation is made by e-mail or telephone to the person listed on the receipt to pick up copies

Part IV
Traditional Reference Service

Chapter 17

REFERENCE DEPARTMENT GUIDELINES

PURPOSE OF REFERENCE POLICY STATEMENT

University at Buffalo
University at Buffalo Libraries
Buffalo, New York

Purpose Statement

The purpose of this policy statement is to provide the staff with a compendium of information policies that promote a uniform standard of service of the highest possible quality consistent with available resources.

This statement is designed both to orient new staff and be an information resource for more experienced staff. The statement may be made available to any library user if s/he has a question concerning the service policy of the Department.

University of Texas Austin
University of Texas Libraries
Austin, Texas

Purpose of Guidelines for Reference and Information Services

These guidelines describe the levels and forms of reference and information services that are offered by the University of Texas Libraries and are intended to insure a uniform standard of the highest quality in all public service units, despite the diverse size, resources, staff, and clientele of the various units. They are also a source of information concerning library policy and procedures. They are to be used in conjunction with the Reference Collections Policy and other related policies and publications of the University of Texas Libraries.

PHILOSOPHY OF SERVICE

University at Albany
University Libraries
Albany, New York

Philosophy of Service

The provision of high quality, individualized reference services to any library user who asks for assistance is central to our philosophy. In carrying out this philosophy, we adhere to the following principles:

A helpful and welcoming attitude is essential to the provision of quality reference service.

Accuracy of information: Accuracy is an important goal of reference service, but the accuracy of published information cannot be guaranteed due to the limitations of available resources and the subject knowledge of individual librarians. It is the library user's responsibility to use judgment in interpreting and using information provided by a reference librarian.

Medical and legal questions: Reference librarians assist users to find the information they need. They do not interpret the law, nor advise library users on legal matters or medical matters.

Intellectual freedom: Reference librarians provide assistance without bias.

Equity of library users: In general, each individual asking a question will be treated equally in terms of thoroughness and attention. If a library user who is not affiliated with the University requires extensive assistance at a time when other users need assistance, the librarian must use judgment to ensure that the needs of affiliated users are being met.

Privacy: The privacy of users' queries is respected. Discussion among reference librarians of users' queries is appropriate when seeking a colleague's advice on best sources, or when a question and its answer are instructive for other librarians who work at the reference desk.

Rutgers University
Rutgers University Libraries
Newark, New Jersey

Service Definitions

Information Service—Basic/general information can be provided by librarians, staff, or trained student assistants—in person, by telephone, by electronic mail either to individual librarians or staff or through Ask a Librarian, or by the use of signs, printed or online finding aids and guides, and such electronic resources as IRIS, online indexes and other basic reference tools, and the Libraries' Web pages. It addresses the more routine information needs of patrons, including:

> Library holdings and bibliographic citations
> Library policies (e.g., Admission to the libraries, borrowing, interlibrary loan)
> Library hours/directions
> Ready reference (e.g., Brief definitions, brief statistical data, other concise factual information)

Reference Service—Reference service is provided by all the Rutgers libraries. Professional librarians provide the most in-depth service; highly trained staff or graduate assistants under the supervision of professional librarians may provide other levels of service. Reference Service may take place at the reference desk, in private consultations with reference specialists, by telephone, by correspondence, or by electronic mail either to individual librarians or staff or through Ask a Librarian.

Reference Service also includes the development and implementation of printed and online finding aids and research guides, computer systems, and user interfaces to support independent research and end-user searching.

Since the Rutgers University Libraries are part of an educational institution, reference service is often appropriately instructional in nature, fostering the client's information literacy and self-sufficiency by instruction in the methods of research, the tools of research (both printed and electronic), and the ability to evaluate the quality and relevance of the research material retrieved. Reference Service includes instruction in the use of bibliographic sources, assistance in developing research strategies, assistance in locating complex data, the retrieval of data through electronic means, etc.

At other times, especially in the smaller and more specialized of the Rutgers Libraries, or in cases involving clients with special needs, reference service might more appropriately take the form of providing factual answers or retrieving and packaging bibliographic or statistical data. In many instances, reference assistance involves the use of electronic resources available on either networked or standalone workstations or from such fee-based vendors as Dialog or STN. See Appendix 2 for detailed information about the Rutgers Online Automated Retrieval Service (ROARS).

The mission of the library, the needs of the client, and the professional judgment of the reference librarian will usually determine the appropriate level of service.

Whom We Serve, and Why

The primary community served by the Rutgers University Libraries consists of current faculty, faculty emeritus, students, staff, and administrators of Rutgers University.

The Libraries' reference and information services are available to all individuals on site, by telephone, by correspondence, and through the online Ask a Librarian service.

The Libraries may engage in mutually beneficial contractual arrangements. These include referral services for the New Jersey Library Network, METRO libraries, OCLC, and the Research Libraries Group. These reciprocal arrangements provide the needed services for Rutgers users who cannot have their needs met within the Rutgers libraries. The Libraries also provide services to certain university affiliates.

Reference service provided by a Rutgers library as a professional courtesy to outside users (other librarians, independent researchers, etc.) does not take the place of services provided by their primary library—whether school, public, academic, or special. In many instances, it will be appropriate to ascertain that outside users have already exhausted the resources of those libraries, or to refer such clients to other appropriate libraries, especially when we do not have the specialized resources needed or the professional expertise to handle their queries.

(For additional policies, please see the accompanying CD-ROM.)

MISSION STATEMENT

University at Albany
University Libraries
Albany, New York

Mission Statement

The primary goal of reference service is to provide excellent services to assist users with their educational and research needs. To achieve this goal, reference librarians provide research assistance and answer reference questions, both to users in the library, and remotely through telephone and e-mail services.

The objectives of the service are:

    To provide individual assistance and instruction
    To provide and maintain an appropriate collection of reference resources, both print and electronic
    To educate users concerning resources and research techniques in order to help the users to
        become information literate

State University of New York Cortland
Memorial Library
Cortland, New York

Library Mission Statement

The library collects, organizes, disseminates, and facilitates access to information related to the intellectual and academic needs of the College community. The Library's services and educational programs promote information literacy and develop research skills. The Library's primary goal is to meet the curricular needs of undergraduate and graduate students. The Library uses both traditional means and new technologies to implement its programs and services, and to access and deliver information from all available sources.

GOALS AND OBJECTIVES

Lane Community College
Lane Community College Library
Eugene, Oregon

Library Purpose and Goals

In support of the stated goals and objectives of the College, the Library is developing a unified program of library-media resources and services. The purpose of this program is to enhance instruction and learning in a manner consistent with the philosophy and curriculum of Lane Community College. The Library is guided by the principles of the Library Bill of Rights in the development of its programs and services.

The goals of the Library are:

To provide organized collections of print and non-print resources which will meet institutional and instructional requirements as well as the individual needs of students.

To create an environment in which resources are made readily accessible, not only through the provision of appropriate facilities, furnishings, equipment, and supplies, but particularly through the provision of adequate staff.

To facilitate learning and community services by providing services, resources and facilities which encourage and stimulate individualized instruction, independent study and effective use of resources by students, faculty and the community.

ACCESS ELIGIBILITY

State University of New York Cortland
Memorial Library
Cortland, New York

Service to Non-SUNY Cortland Users

Although SUNY Cortland faculty, students, and staff are the library's primary user group, Cortland community and other non-SUNY Cortland users may use the library's collections and services, as stated in general library policy. In the case of unusually time-consuming inquiries, or at times when the reference area is busy, the librarian may ask the user's affiliation, and may give priority to SUNY Cortland users. Generally, however, no distinction should be made, especially when the library has unique resources in staff and material which meet the information needs of the user. The library's agreement with the Federal Library Depository Program requires that reference service be provided to all library users seeking information about or assistance in using government documents.

University at Albany
University Libraries
Albany, New York

Clientele

The University at Buffalo Arts & Sciences Libraries provide reference services for patrons affiliated with the University and patrons from the general public. No distinctions are made among different categories of library users when providing routine reference services. However, priority is given to UB-affiliated users when library resources, staffing, space, or funding are inadequate to meet the demands for reference services at any time. As participants in the depository program of the United States government, the University Libraries also fulfill their statutory obligation as a depository library by providing equal access to all documents materials for all users, without distinction and regardless of affiliation. The Arts & Sciences Libraries take primary responsibility for anticipating and meeting the research and information needs of constituents in the following University at Buffalo schools, colleges and programs:

School of Architecture & Planning
College of Arts & Sciences
General Education Program
Graduate School of Education
School of Engineering & Applied Sciences
School of Informatics
School of Management
School of Social Work

ASL services and collections are also intended to work within the University Libraries to serve the needs of faculty, staff and students from: Cora P. Maloney College , the University Honors and Scholars Program, selected UB Research Centers and Institutes and the Graduate School.

PATRON USE STATISTICS

University of Indianapolis
Krannert Memorial Library
Indianapolis, Indiana

Statistics

Routine statistics kept by the library:

> Book titles and volumes owned, added, and withdrawn—total and by Dewey category
> Active periodicals subscriptions
> Media owned, added, and withdrawn—by format
> Items circulated, both outside and as Reserves
> Library classes given and number of student participants
> ILL borrowing and lending requests and fills
> Bound/volumes of periodicals
> Microforms, by format

Other statistics may be generated using Aleph reports or manual counts.

University of Wisconsin River Falls
Chalmer Davee Library
River Falls, Wisconsin

Reference Desk Statistics

A. A daily record is maintained of all questions answered by reference staff at the Reference Desk. Three types of questions are recorded: reference, ready reference, and directional.

B. Reference Questions. An extended information contact which involves the use, recommendation, interpretation, or instruction in the use of one or more reference sources, or knowledge of such sources, by a reference staff member.

C. Ready Reference Questions. A reference question which can easily be answered by consulting one source, which generally can be completed in a short amount of time.

D. Directional Questions. A simple question that can be answered without consulting any library resource.

ROLE OF REFERENCE COLLECTION

State University of New York Cortland
Memorial Library
Cortland, New York

The Reference Collection
General Statement

The library will maintain an up-to-date, relevant, and accessible collection of reference materials, including both traditional print materials and electronic resources. The in-house Reference Collection includes resources such as encyclopedias, dictionaries, handbooks, statistical sources, periodical abstracts and indexes, and other primary sources and finding tools commonly regarded as "reference tools." These reference tools are increasingly available in electronic formats, which will be made available whenever ease of use, cost, and accessibility permit.

The in-house Reference Collection is supplemented by external resources such as electronic databases available from commercial vendors and library agencies, online catalogs of other libraries, resources available through interlibrary loan, and other sources available through the Internet and other networks. Judgments about whether to purchase materials for in-house use or to rely on remote access are based on such factors as available resources, purchase cost, anticipated use, currency, and ease of use. Refer to the Collection Development Policy for further explanation. Reference bibliographers are responsible for evaluating reference materials and resources, and for recommending which should be acquired and which should be made accessible through external sources. The Librarian(s) in charge of Reference works with the bibliographers to evaluate and select materials and resources.

University at Albany
University Libraries
Albany, New York

General Purpose

The Reference collection is selected and acquired to support the research, teaching and information needs of the University at Albany community with emphasis placed on support of the academic programs in the social sciences and humanities at the main campus. This policy offers guidelines for the acquisition, retention, and scope of materials housed in the collection. The Reference collection includes sources that index or summarize information usually contained in the general circulating collection. All formats will be considered for inclusion in the Reference collection. The Reference collection is non-circulating.

Usefulness to reference librarians and to members of the University community is the principal criterion for inclusion of materials in the Reference collection. Highly esoteric, narrowly focused, and seldom used sources should not ordinarily be included in the collection, even though they may be arranged in a reference type of format. In order to provide accurate and current information, reference sources are continuously withdrawn and updated.

This Collection Development Policy also applies to the Libraries' Web-based Reference Collection, the contents of which reflect the research, teaching and information needs of the University Library as well as the Dewey and Science Libraries. Sites are primarily selected which are academic in nature. Overly commercial sites are excluded as well as those which duplicate the content of the Libraries' subscription databases. Subject areas not related to the University Curriculum are normally not included although a selection of recreational sites is also offered. An effort is made to make this collection usable by limiting the number of web titles on any given subject. An effort is made to exclude titles which substantially duplicate other web-site sources already contained in this collection.

REFERENCE COLLECTION COMPONENTS

University at Albany
University Libraries
Albany, New York

Description of Materials Collected:

The Bibliographer for the University Library's Reference Collection makes decisions concerning selection, retention, and location of materials, in both hardcopy and electronic format, consulting with other bibliographers as appropriate. The Bibliographer consults with counterparts at the Dewey and Science Libraries when necessary, concerning the purchase of expensive and/or electronic resources in order to avoid the duplication of purchases.

Types of Materials Collected:

Almanacs, Annuals, and Yearbooks. Generally only the latest year is placed in the Reference collection. Foreign country almanacs are designated "latest issue in Reference." Earlier issues are sent to the general stacks of the University Library. Exceptions are made for backfiles of encyclopedic yearbooks and some annual review publications of a bibliographic nature.

Completed sets of the World Almanac and Statistical Abstract of the United States are retained in the Reference collection.

Bibliographies. Bibliographies that are general in nature and cover broad topics are housed in Reference. Single-author bibliographies and others that are narrow in scope are housed in the circulating stacks. Exception will be made for those bibliographies on topics in great demand or those of major literary figures, such as Shakespeare.

Only the latest year of United States and foreign trade bibliographies are retained.

Biographical Sources. Major international works, major national works and current biographical works (Who's Who) of every country from which they are available are retained in the Reference collection. Specialized dictionaries are considered on their individual merits and degree of use. Usually the most recent editions of biographical dictionaries are maintained in the Reference collection.

Concordances. Only concordances to the Bible and Shakespeare are kept in Reference.

Dictionaries. Most unilingual, bilingual and polyglot dictionaries for major languages are placed in Reference. Some local and regional language dictionaries are only housed in the general collection and are usually designated "building only." Historical dictionaries and specialized dictionaries, such as dictionaries of slang and subject dictionaries, may also be included in the Reference collection depending on their degree of use.

Directories. The Reference collection contains the latest edition of various types of directories which support Albany's academic programs and meet general information needs. Directories are acquired selectively. Older editions of some directories are shelved in the general collection.

Encyclopedias. Major foreign language encyclopedias and the latest significantly revised editions of all major English-language encyclopedias, both single-volume and multi-volume, are housed in the Reference collection. Selected earlier editions of some foreign language encyclopedias are housed in the general collection. An attempt is made to update the general encyclopedias on a yearly rotating basis. The latest editions of frequently-consulted, single-subject, encyclopedias are maintained in Reference. If an older edition is considered to have significant value, it may be retained in the Reference collection beyond its period of currency.

Geographical Sources. A representative collection of major comprehensive atlases, gazetteers, and bound maps are included in the Reference collection including historical atlases, sources on major countries of the world and those sources which meet state and local information needs. Highly specialized sources will not ordinarily be included. Superseded editions of some atlases are housed in the general collection.

Handbooks, Manuals and Guides. A selection of up-to-date handbooks, manuals, and guides which meet general information needs or relate to the University's academic disciplines are retained in Reference. Amount of use is a key consideration in determining which titles are placed in the Reference collection and which are placed in the general collection.

Indexes and Abstracts. The Reference collection includes indexing and abstracting services relevant to the teaching, research, and general information needs of the University community. Many of these are provided in electronic format.

Services. Loose-leaf services on taxation, law and business are subscribed to and maintained in the Reference collection.

Law. The collection contains a selection of statute and case law for the United States and New York State.

Other Materials:

Telephone Books. Selected current telephone books are maintained in the Reference Collection including a large collection for New York State. Other U.S. and foreign directories are provided in electronic format.

College Catalogs. The collection includes a select hardcopy collection of local and regional college catalogs. Access to U.S. and foreign catalogs is provided electronically.

Ready Reference. A small number of materials within the Reference collection have the special designation, "Ready Reference," because they receive such frequent use and it is convenient to have them near the Reference Desk. Ready Reference materials which frequently disappear are housed in the Reserve Reading Room. Some titles are duplicated.

University of West Georgia
University Library
Carrollton, Georgia

Types of Materials Included in the Reference Collection

Reference collection materials shall be supportive of the Library Collection Development Policy and shall be pertinent to the chronological, geographical, and subject scope of courses taught at the University of West Georgia. Supplemental materials outside these guidelines are also collected to maintain a viable information resource for the University community. Much of the Reference Collection is in the English language, but emphasis will also be placed on appropriate materials in any language which support the curriculum of the University of West Georgia.

The following list, which is illustrative not exhaustive, represents the types of materials collected for reference.

Almanacs, Annuals, and Yearbooks: Major national and international publications

Bibliographies: General, national, and trade bibliographies; Bibliographies with narrow subject scope are usually placed in the circulating collection.

Biographical Sources: National, international, and professional biographies, retrospective and current

Dictionaries: Unilingual, bilingual, polyglot and specialized

Encyclopedias: Selected general and subject encyclopedias

Genealogy: Selected sources with a concentration on Georgia history

Geographical Sources: Selected authoritative country, specialized, and historical atlases, and gazetteers

Heraldry: A limited number of selected sources

Handbooks: Various subject areas that support the University curriculum

Indexes and Abstracts: Numerous subject and general indexes and abstracts with emphasis given to subjects which support the University curriculum

Legal Materials: Legal sources that support courses taught in business, education, and constitutional law; basic United States and Georgia legal materials

Quotations: Major collections in English

State and Local Information: Georgia and Carroll County

Statistical Sources: Selected national and international materials

Style Manuals: Recent editions of selected manuals

Other Materials: Information sources based on usefulness to primary users and perceived need.

State University of New York Cortland
Memorial Library
Cortland, New York

Ready Reference

The Ready Reference Collection, located at the reference desk, consists of materials that need to be consulted on a frequent and regular basis. The Librarian(s) in charge of Reference, in consultation with the reference bibliographers, selects materials for placement in the Ready Reference Collection.

Chapter 18

REFERENCE SERVICE GUIDELINES

GENERAL SERVICE GUIDELINES

Referrals to Outside Resources

State University of New York Cortland
Memorial Library
Cortland, New York

Referrals

The reference librarian may find it necessary or advisable to refer users to other collections, services, or sources of information within or external to the library.

Referrals to Other Library Faculty

A referral to another member of the library faculty may be necessary when the librarian on duty does not possess the in-depth expertise or knowledge needed to answer a detailed reference query. When making a referral to another librarian, the librarian on duty should notify the colleague of the referral and outline the sources already checked.

Referrals to Other Libraries, Institutions, Departments, Faculty, or Other Services

Referrals to outside sources may be made based on the librarian's knowledge of resources, services, or information available from other libraries, institutions, or departments. It is appropriate to confirm in advance the availability of the needed information, service, or material from the institution or individual recommended. Availability of needed materials may be confirmed in various ways, such as searching other online library catalogs. It may also be appropriate for the librarian or user to phone ahead to verify availability of services and materials.

Referrals to Interlibrary Loan

Referrals to Interlibrary Loan (ILL) should only be made after determining that the requested item(s) are not owned by the library and are not available online. The reference librarian should make sure that the user has a complete bibliographic citation, and should assist the user, if necessary, in properly filling out the Interlibrary Loan Request Form. When a user is in urgent need of an item not owned by the library, fax service, Ariel or alternate document delivery service may be recommended by the Librarian on the ILL form.

University of Texas at Austin
University of Texas Libraries
Austin, Texas

Referrals

Staff members should recognize their own limitations and ask colleagues within the unit for advice and assistance as necessary. They also refer users to others who are better qualified to serve particular needs. Staff members confirm that other units, libraries, or special collections can be of assistance before referring users to them. Staff members do not recommend specific fee-based information services. They refer users to standard directories. Referrals to other libraries or agencies off campus are made whenever appropriate.

Reference Appointments

Indiana University–Purdue University Fort Wayne
Walter E. Helmke Library
Fort Wayne, Indiana

Rationale

There are two types of reference appointments available at Helmke Library, walk-in and scheduled. Both types of appointments are available at the library's reference consulting areas—general reference on the first floor and Science Information Center on the fourth floor. The library maintains statistics on reference appointments and its performance is judged on such indicators, so it is important to make and record appointments accurately. This document outlines the policies and procedures governing the provision of reference and information services on a walk-in and scheduled basis.

Policies

The library's basic and in-depth reference and information services and two-tiered instructional services are described in detail on the library's homepage under Reference & Instruction. Any librarian, library staff member, or student worker may respond to a patron's request for information by scheduling a reference appointment with a librarian.

Appointments are recorded by library staff in separate appointment books kept at the Service Desk. The Science Information Center's appointment book will be transferred to the fourth floor during the Center's normal hours of operation (2–4 p.m., Monday–Thursday, during Fall and Spring semesters), and it will be returned to the Service Desk when the Center is closed.

The Science Information Center schedule provides eight (8) hours in addition to the regular general reference schedule's 60 hours, for a total of 68 hours of reference appointments per week. Extra Saturday hours are also added during the peak mid-semester schedule to accommodate demand.

It is important for library staff to convey the message to patrons that a librarian is available to assist them. Patrons who seek assistance on a walk-in basis should be assigned to the next available librarian working in (1) the first-floor general reference area, followed by (2) the fourth-floor Science Information Center, according to the procedures below.

Procedures for Recording Walk-in Appointments

When an appointment is for the next available time, and the patron does not ask to meet with a particular librarian, write "walk-in," "student," or "patron" in the appointment book next to the initials of the librarian on duty.

Schedule all walk-in appointments for the general reference consulting area first, then assign patrons to the next available Science Information Center librarian (whether the question is science related or not).

Procedures for Recording Scheduled Appointments

When the patron asks to meet with a particular liaison librarian or subject specialist (e.g., "the education librarian," "psychology librarian," etc.), write the patron's full name in the appointment book next to the librarian's initials. See the posted list of Library Fund Managers by Subject or Department to identify the appropriate librarian.

When scheduling an appointment hours or days in advance, also record the patron's name, even if the patron does not request the librarian by name.

Procedures for Making Referrals to Librarians

Staff should encourage patrons to meet with the next available librarian, who will help them begin their search and perhaps make a referral to a subject specialist for further help. When a patron clearly needs specialized assistance, make an effort to schedule an appointment with the appropriate librarian.

If the librarian's hours listed on the reference appointment schedule do not suit patrons' schedules, encourage them to contact the librarian by phone or e-mail to arrange a more convenient appointment time. Do not convey the message that a librarian is not available if he or she does not have a regular shift listed on the schedule. Make every effort to offer the librarian's business card and allow the patron to use a library telephone to reach the librarian or to leave a message with their name, brief reference question, phone number, and/or e-mail address.

Librarians are responsible for keeping their business cards stocked at the Service Desk, the first-floor reference consulting area, the Science Information Center, and the Electronic Information Training Center (EITC).

Librarians who are called to respond to a patron's immediate need should negotiate a convenient time to meet if they are busy with other obligations.

Please direct questions about reference and information services policy or reference-appointment procedures to [staff member's name].

Xavier University
Xavier University Library
Cincinnati, Ohio

Education Services

Research Consultations

Appointment required!

Consultation services are available by appointment at times convenient for you. Contact a specific librarian or your department's librarian liaison (see right menu). Consultation services are available in-person, over the telephone or through online chat. Faculty, staff and students may take advantage of consultation services.

To access an online chat consultation, follow the instructions below:
First, make an appointment with the appropriate librarian liaison (see right menu)
Then, click the online chat consultation icon which will take you to the consultation waiting room

The library encourages students to use this service for:

Automatically sending the results of search strategies to your email address periodically

Developing search strategies for senior research papers, dissertations or theses

General library orientation (using research databases, XPLORE, OhioLINK, electronic journal locator and document delivery services)

Preventing plagiarism with TurnItIn

Saving search strategies to run at another time

Using RefWorks (creating perfect bibliographies and in-text citations with the click of a button)

The library encourages faculty and staff to use this service for:
Adding library resources to Blackboard's main menu
Adding library resources to your courses in MyXU, the campus portal
Automatically sending the results of search strategies to your email address periodically
Creating electronic reading lists
Do-it-yourself electronic reserves
General library orientation (using research databases, XPLORE, OhioLINK, electronic journal locator and document delivery services)
Keeping current with RSS (Really Simple Syndication) feeds
Painless publishing with RefWorks or creating perfect bibliographies and in-text citations with the click of a button
Preventing plagiarism with TurnItIn
Saving search strategies to run at another time

Remember! You must make an appointment with your librarian liaison first.

Service Priorities

State University of New York Cortland
Memorial Library
Cortland, New York

Service Priorities

General Statement

While on duty at the reference desk, librarians will give priority to activities involving direct service to individual users, as outlined below. The librarian on reference duty at night or on weekends may also be in charge of overall building operations; thus, building emergencies or other urgent situations may of necessity occasionally take priority over reference service. The librarian on duty is also responsible for monitoring and directing the activities of any reference assistants on duty.

Users in the Reference Area

Service to library users in the reference area takes priority over any other activity. Reference librarians, assigned to specifically scheduled hours, are expected to arrive and be ready to offer service at their scheduled times. Scheduled reference hours take priority over other work obligations.

Librarians on duty must balance the needs of all users in the area and must use judgment in determining how best to serve the users simultaneously needing assistance. Generally, extended reference queries are not answered when other users are waiting.

Telephone Queries

Responding to telephone calls receives a lower priority than responding to users in the reference area. Generally, the reference librarian will provide only brief responses on the telephone, and usually will give no more than three serial or catalog verifications for an individual telephone user. When the reference area is busy, the librarian answering a telephone query should do one or more of the following as appropriate to the circumstances:

> Put the caller temporarily on hold;
> Take the caller's name and telephone number and call him/her back;
> Encourage the caller to come to the library for reference assistance.

Guidelines for Answering Specific Questions

University at Buffalo
University at Buffalo Libraries
Buffalo, New York

In the Library

Respond to ready reference inquiries, which generally require the use of a single source to answer a quick, factual question

Provide access to and instruction about remote bibliographic, full-text, and numeric databases

Offer help in clarifying research problems, developing good search strategies and finding and evaluating information

Introduce students and faculty to the use of new technologies in information access

Validate/check citations

Locate known items

Respond to directional questions

Help users navigate the Libraries' website (http://ublib.buffalo.edu/)

Help library users evaluate information sources

Refer people to other libraries or agencies when appropriate

Refer people to subject specialists (http://ublib.buffalo.edu/libraries/staff/specsubj.html)

Teach information literacy at levels appropriate to library users

Help library users perform basic technical operations, such as downloading, uploading, sending articles and using databases

Offer in-depth consultations by appointment

Rutgers University
Rutgers University Libraries
Newark, New Jersey

Service Definitions

Information Service—Basic/general information can be provided by librarians, staff, or trained student assistants—in person, by telephone, by electronic mail either to individual librarians or staff or through Ask a Librarian, or by the use of signs, printed or online finding aids and guides, and such electronic resources as IRIS, online indexes and other basic reference tools, and the Libraries' Web pages. It addresses the more routine information needs of patrons, including:

> Library holdings and bibliographic citations
> Library policies (e.g., Admission to the libraries, borrowing, interlibrary loan)
> Library hours/directions
> Ready reference (e.g., Brief definitions, brief statistical data, other concise factual information)

Reference Service—Reference service is provided by all the Rutgers libraries. Professional librarians provide the most in-depth service; highly trained staff or graduate assistants under the supervision of professional librarians may provide other levels of service. Reference Service may take place at the reference desk, in private consultations with reference specialists, by telephone, by correspondence, or by electronic mail either to individual librarians or staff or through Ask a Librarian.

Reference Service also includes the development and implementation of printed and online finding aids and research guides, computer systems, and user interfaces to support independent research and end-user searching.

Since the Rutgers University Libraries are part of an educational institution, reference service is often appropriately instructional in nature, fostering the client's information literacy and self-sufficiency by instruction in the methods of research, the tools of research (both printed and electronic), and the ability to evaluate the quality and relevance of the research material retrieved. Reference Service includes instruction in the use of bibliographic sources, assistance in developing research strategies, assistance in locating complex data, the retrieval of data through electronic means, etc.

At other times, especially in the smaller and more specialized of the Rutgers Libraries, or in cases involving clients with special needs, reference service might more appropriately take the form of providing factual answers or retrieving and packaging bibliographic or statistical data. In many instances, reference assistance involves the use of electronic resources available on either networked or standalone workstations or from such fee-based vendors as Dialog or STN. See Appendix 2 for detailed information about the Rutgers Online Automated Retrieval Service (ROARS).

The mission of the library, the needs of the client, and the professional judgment of the reference librarian will usually determine the appropriate level of service.

Whom We Serve, and Why

The primary community served by the Rutgers University Libraries consists of current faculty, faculty emeritus, students, staff, and administrators of Rutgers University.

The Libraries' reference and information services are available to all individuals on site, by telephone, by correspondence, and through the online Ask a Librarian service.

The Libraries may engage in mutually beneficial contractual arrangements. These include referral services for the New Jersey Library Network, METRO libraries, OCLC, and the Research Libraries Group. These reciprocal arrangements provide the needed services for Rutgers users who cannot have their needs met within the Rutgers libraries. The Libraries also provide services to certain university affiliates.

Reference service provided by a Rutgers library as a professional courtesy to outside users (other librarians, independent researchers, etc.) does not take the place of services provided by their primary library—whether school, public, academic, or special. In many instances, it will be appropriate to ascertain that outside users have already exhausted the resources of those libraries, or to refer such clients to other appropriate libraries, especially when we do not have the specialized resources needed or the professional expertise to handle their queries.

(For additional policies, please see the accompanying CD-ROM.)

Reference Service Evaluation

University at Albany
University Libraries
Albany, New York

Evaluation of Reference Service

All librarians will be involved periodically in the collection of statistics and records of reference inquiries. Statistics and record keeping are essential in providing a factual base for review of reference service, staffing levels, and/or government-required statistical counts.

Periodic evaluation of reference services will be conducted under direction of the Librarian(s) in charge of Reference. Evaluations will measure and examine the quality of reference service, success of users in finding needed information, and/or user satisfaction. Data gathered through the evaluation process may also be used to analyze staffing levels and determine where improvements can be made.

Types of Queries Answered

University at Buffalo
University at Buffalo Libraries
Buffalo, New York

Limits to Reference Services

Reference staff will not:

- Perform research. Generally, users asking ready reference questions will have the information provided to them, while users with more difficult and involved questions will be instructed in how to conduct their own research.
- Interpret materials. Reference staff do not interpret information, such as medical, legal, financial, statistical, tax information, or class assignments.
- Offer legal, medical, tax, or financial advice.
- Violate the copyright law.
- Knowingly act in a manner that violates the Code of Ethics of the American Library Association (www.ala.org/Content/NavigationMenu/Our_Association/Offices/Intellectual_Freedom3/ Statements_and_Policies/Code_of_Ethics/Code_of_Ethics.htm).
- Recommend purchases of sources or other materials. Reference staff refer patrons to standard reviews of the work in question and advise the patron to examine the library copy, if available. Staff do not make recommendations regarding such purchases.

- Appraise books or artifacts. Reference staff do not appraise the private property of patrons. Patrons are advised to consult a professional appraiser.
- Perform genealogical research. Genealogical searches are not undertaken by reference staff. Catalog assistance and help locating standard reference sources are offered. The Business/ Government Documents Reference Center assists with queries about the Census. City directories? Most genealogy questions are referred to the public library (see www.buffalolib.org/).
- Compile bibliographies. Reference staff will not compile or check bibliographies. Staff do assist patrons in the use of bibliographical tools and in identifying, interpreting, and verifying citations.
- Answer contest, quiz or trivia questions. No searching is done for answers to contests, puzzles, quizzes, etc. Assistance is limited to advising individuals about where they might locate such information.
- Lend reference materials. Reference materials generally do not circulate, however if the situation warrants, a special loan may be approved. See Section _____ for details.
- Interpret or complete class assignments. Staff members help patrons locate information for class assignments. When a class assignment creates a concern, the appropriate subject librarian is responsible for contacting the instructor. In some cases, the librarian on duty may initiate the contact with the instructor and then provide information to the subject specialist. Assignment information should be posted to the ASL "Reference Alerts" page and also sent to [specialty service]. Students with questions about the assignment itself should be referred to their instructors.
- Retrieve materials in the book stacks. Reference staff generally will not pull an item from the stacks and hold it for a patron who is calling on the phone.
- Proofread or edit student papers. Students are advised to consult The Learning Center's Writing Center for assistance (http://tlc.buffalo.edu/lcwrite.htm).

Phoenix College
Phoenix College Library
Phoenix, Arizona

Legal Reference Questions

Library users with legal questions will be directed and taught how to use legal books, databases, and the Internet. Legal advice will not be provided.

Medical Reference Questions

Library users with medical and/or drug questions will be directed and taught how to use medical books, the databases, and the Internet. Medical and drug advice will not be provided.

Tax Reference Questions

Library users with tax questions will be directed to relevant books, databases, and the Internet for information. Tax advice will not be provided.

Rutgers University
Rutgers University Libraries
Newark, New Jersey

Legal, Medical, or Pharmaceutical Advice—The Libraries cannot provide legal, medical, or pharmaceutical advice in response to reference queries. Specific information may be read from manuals, but in most circumstances patrons will be referred to sources of information from which to draw conclusions.

University of Texas at Austin
University of Texas Libraries
Austin, Texas

Special Inquiries

Class Assignments

Staff members help users locate information for class assignments. When a class assignment creates a problem for students and staff, the appropriate subject specialist is responsible for contacting the instructor about the present and possible future class assignments.

Bibliographies

Although staff members do not prepare bibliographies for individuals, they do assist users in compiling their bibliographies.

Interpretation of Material

Staff members do not interpret legal, medical, financial, or statistical information.

In-Process Materials

Users are not referred to Technical Services departments.

Staff members may use the online acquisitions database to check order and receipt status for books, serials, and other library materials. For more information about in-process materials, staff members contact the appropriate Technical Services section. When these areas are closed, questions are deferred until the next working day. Users are contacted as soon as the information is located.

Circulation of Reference Materials

Reference materials are for library use only. Permission to borrow them is given only at the discretion of the reference staff member on duty following guidelines set by the specific library unit.

Recommendations to Users on Personal Purchase of Books

When asked for recommendations, staff members refer users to standard reviews of the work in question or advise the user to examine the library copy, but they do not make recommendations.

Appraisal of Books and Artifacts

Staff members do not appraise items. Users are advised to consult appropriate reference materials or a professional appraiser, but specific appraisers are not recommended.

Genealogical Questions

Genealogical searches are referred to the Texas State Library and Center for American History, as appropriate. Staff members offer help in locating standard genealogical sources in the University of Texas Libraries and through the Libraries Web site.

Contests, Puzzles, and Scavenger Hunts

Staff members, when they have evidence that a contest is behind a question, suggest appropriate sources but do not locate the information.

Proctoring Exams and Signing Attendance Forms

Reference staff does not proctor exams. The Division of Continuing Education Testing Center proctors exams. Staff does not sign attendance forms for required study hall attendance.

SPECIAL SERVICE GUIDELINES

Mediated Database Searches

University of North Carolina Wilmington
William Madison Randall Library
Wilmington, North Carolina

In addition to the CD-ROM databases available for patron use, the Reference Department also provides a mediated search service. This service provides access to remote commercial database services, i.e., Dialog Information Service, EPIC (OCLC) and STN (American Chemical Society). Because these services charge the Library for connect-time and records printed, and because familiarity with the command languages is important for cost-effectiveness, librarians conduct these searches. Request forms for this service are available at the Reference Desk.

At the reference librarians' discretion, and with certain limitations, searches will be provided to UNCW students, faculty, and staff at no charge. Search charges which exceed the limitations specified in the Online Search Services guidelines may be charged to the individual's account. With proper authorization, fees may be charged to departmental or grant accounts.

For users not affiliated with UNCW, a 15% surcharge is added to the total cost of a mediated search. These searches are performed only if the demand for other reference services has been met, and a librarian is able to schedule this additional service.

Vassar College
Learning and Teaching Center
Poughkeepsie, New York

Mediated Database Searching

The purpose of the mediated database searching service is to support the academic and scholarly research needs of Vassar faculty and students by supplementing the readily available indexes and abstracts. Request forms for database searches may be filled out at the Reference Desk. Please allow 3–5 days for processing of the request. There is no charge for this service

Distance-Learning Students

North Seattle Community College
North Seattle Community College Library
Seattle, Washington

The Seattle Community College

The Seattle Community College District Libraries strive to meet the special information needs of students in distance learning programs. Within the limit of our resources, we intend to provide library services to the distance learning programs equitable with that provided to the on-campus programs. These guidelines are intended to embody the philosophy of the Guidelines for Extended Campus Library Services prepared by the Association of College and Research Libraries.

The Seattle Community College District is developing distance learning programs unique to each campus. These programs have different histories, goals, and student populations. However, these programs are growing and will in the future have a significant impact on library resources and services. The following guidelines are meant to help the District Libraries provide services to these students built upon the Library programs and collections already in place. These collections and services will increasingly require further development off already established regional and state cooperative agreements among academic and public libraries to share resources. Continued development to meet the expanding needs of these programs will require specially allocated revenues outside of existing library budgets.

Guidelines

Library Support Services: A district-wide committee comprised of library faculty, in cooperation with the District Distance Learning Committee, shall be responsible for gathering information, developing proposals, and bringing that information to the District librarians for approval. This committee shall recommend the development of services to distance learning faculty and students appropriate to the modes of instructional delivery offered by these programs. The recommendations will take into consideration the changes in delivery mode, information technology, and development of new programs. Each campus library representative will maintains communication with the distance learning programs on their own campuses to inform this progress.

Reference Services: Each campus library Reference Desk and Circulation Staff will provide points of service to distance learners and instructors. The level of service provided should be consistent with that provided to all on-campus students. The establishment and maintenance of e-mail reference service and a shared toll-free telephone number, for use by distance learning students, should be a priority for the district libraries. We should also investigate new possibilities, such as virtual reference service.

The service we are able to provide will be spelled out in a brochure for instructors and students to be included in their orientation and course packets. Students must understand that our role is to help them become independent information uses. We will not do research for them, but help them use the resources available to them wherever they are by helping locate resources and making referrals.

Bibliographic Instruction: Instruction on how to conduct library research should be consistent with the mode of instruction of the program in which they are enrolled. The instruction may take the form of printed, recorded, or electronic media. The development and delivery of this instruction will require the support of the parent institution's distance learning programs for students requiring services and materials not already included in the current library budget. Distance learning programs must take these costs into consideration when developing new programs.

Access to Resources: The libraries will attempt to accommodate students who require resources which are not available remotely and will encourage instructors to consider access to resources as they develop distance learning courses. Students will be encouraged to make use of local community college and public library resources, including Interlibrary Loan services.

Materials may be provided on a case-by-case basis, depending on circumstances of individual students. Any document delivery—e-mail, fax, or conventional mail—will be consistent with current copyright law. Students who are close enough to use District libraries in person will receive the same level of service provided to all campus students.

Students enrolled in courses through SCDD will have access to online databases on campus or through a password, consistent with services provided to on-campus students. Passwords will be made available to distance learning faculty for distribution to students on a quarterly basis. Individual students will be given passwords upon request when they provide their last name and last four digits of their student identification number. Requests may be made by phone, e-mail, or in person.

Service Agreements: Whenever distance learning programs develop courses, they must take the costs of library resources and services into account in their budgets. When geographically concentrated distance learning students require library services beyond those which are normally available through Seattle Community College Libraries and local public libraries, library service agreements should be established with local libraries to compensate for services provided to students registered at Seattle Community Colleges.

User Surveys: Surveys should be conducted on a regular basis to get information from faculty and students to discover: where students are located, what kinds of information and technical help they need, and how well the library services and resources are meeting their needs.

Additional Services: Proctoring is not a regular library service and will be available at the discretion of individual campus libraries. This service may be referred to the campus testing center.

University of Scranton
Weinberg Memorial Library
Scranton, Pennsylvania
The University of Scranton's web site is changing and policies will be separated from information on the updated sites.

Eligibility Policies

As a student, you are eligible for services when:

- you are currently enrolled in University of Scranton credit courses being delivered either off-campus or via the Internet OR you are completing an independent study or internship off-campus, AND
- you currently reside off-campus, AND
- you have registered for a Distance Learning Library Services account.

As a faculty member, you are eligible for services when:

- you are teaching all of your University of Scranton credit course(s) at off-campus locations or via the Internet, AND
- you do not have office hours on campus, AND
- you have registered for a Distance Learning Library Services account.

Note: A Distance Learning Library Services account must be established by completing the online Registration Form prior to receiving distance library services. The Library reserves the right to refuse services to those individuals whose information it cannot verify.

General Information

Register online using the Distance Learners' Registration Form—or print the registration form and either fax or mail the completed form.

The following services are available ONLY to Registered students and faculty:

Delivery of articles from the Weinberg Memorial Library—Articles from newspapers, magazines, or journals that are unavailable online are either faxed or mailed to you. You will be billed $1.50 for each article sent to you. A total bill for all articles sent during the semester will be added to your library account at the end of the semester.

Delivery of books from the Weinberg Memorial Library—Books are shipped to you by UPS. You are responsible for returning all books to the Weinberg Memorial Library at your own expense, using UPS Ground (contact us first if you must use other shipping options). Use the return label that is provided.

The following services are available to all University of Scranton students and faculty:

Remote Access to the Weinberg Memorial Library's Catalog via any standard Web browser with Internet access. The catalog contains books and other materials owned by the Library.

Remote Access to full-text articles from over 15,000 electronic periodicals (newspapers, magazines, and journals) contained in over 100 electronic databases to which the Library subscribes via a standard Web browser with Internet access using a Proxy Server.

Options to Get Books

Search the Weinberg Memorial Library's Catalog.

If the book you want to borrow is available, then complete the Document Delivery Book Request Form. If you have registered for a Distance Library Services account, the book(s) will be sent to you. Allow 5–7 working days for delivery.

Search WorldCat from the Library's list of databases to find a library located near you that has the book that you want.

Once you've identified some libraries near you, contact them to see whether or not they will allow you to check out books.

Search the PALCI Catalog. PALCI is a joint catalog for a consortium of academic libraries mainly located in Pennsylvania. Allow 2 weeks for delivery.

You may directly request books found in the PALCI catalog by using your Royal ID as your login password. IMPORTANT: You must select Weinberg Memorial Library as your "Pick-Up Location" option.

If you do request a book, you will receive a confirmation e-mail from PALCI. Forward this e-mail to the ILL Department staff (interlibrary-loan@scranton.edu) at the Weinberg Library to notify them that you have requested a book.

When the book arrives, it will be sent to you at no charge, but you are responsible for returning the book to the Weinberg Memorial Library by the due date at your own cost using UPS Ground. Use the return label that is provided and send the book back to the Weinberg Memorial Library.

Please do not remove the blue band around the front cover of the PALCI book.

IMPORTANT: Do NOT return books to the original lending library. The book will remain on your University of Scranton account until we receive the book. If it is not returned to us, you may be charged for a lost book.

If the book you want is not owned by the University of Scranton and is not available from PALCI, request it by using the Electronic Interlibrary Loan Book Request Form. Be sure to select the Borrower Status of "Distance Student" from the drop-down menu. Allow 3–4 weeks for an Interlibrary Loan book to be delivered to you.

When the book arrives, it will be sent to you at no charge, but you are responsible for returning the book to the Weinberg Memorial Library by the due date at your own cost using UPS Ground. Use the return label that is provided and send the book back to the Weinberg Memorial Library.

Please do not remove the yellow band around the front cover of the Interlibrary Loan book.

IMPORTANT: Do NOT mail books back to the original lending library. The book will remain on your University of Scranton account until we receive the book. If it is not returned to us, you may be charged for a lost book.

Options to Get Articles

Full-Text Articles via databases on the Weinberg Memorial Library's Web page.

Articles available in Print format at the Weinberg Memorial Library.

Articles not available in any format at the Weinberg Memorial Library may be ordered through Interlibrary Loan.

Search for Articles

You may search for articles by topic in one of the Library's databases. If you already know which database you want, begin at the Databases by Title page. Note that the letter F in the column to the right of the name of the database indicates that there are full-text articles available in that database, the letter P indicates that there are only some full-text articles. If you're not sure which database to use, begin at the Databases by Subject page and then click on your subject area for a list of databases in that subject.

To access the databases remotely:

From the list of databases, click on either the "Off Campus" or the "Remote Access" link.

You will need to enter your User ID (Royal ID) and a Password (your birthday in the DDMMYY format), for example, if your birthday is April 7, 1984, then your Password is 070484.

Choose the database that you wish to search from the Database Menu.

For detailed instructions with screen shots, see Remote Access Instructions.

To search a database:

Enter your search terms. In databases where full-text is available, you have the option to limit your search to those articles for which the full text is available electronically.

If an article is full-text, then you have the option to print, e-mail, or save it.

If an article is not full-text, there may be a link to the full-text, or there may be a link to the Library's catalog.

To get articles from journals in the Weinberg Library:

Check to verify that the Library has the issue and year that you want. To request the article, complete the Document Delivery Journal Article Request Form. The article will be delivered to your desktop. You will receive an e-mail notice containing a clickable link that takes you to a login page. To login, you must enter your complete e-mail address and the PIN that is in the e-mail. Save the article to a disk. You can print the saved document. You will be billed $1.50 for each article sent to you.

To get articles from journals NOT available in any format at the Weinberg Library:

Request the article by completing the Electronic Interlibrary Loan Journal Article Request Form. Select the Borrower Status of "Distance Student" from the drop-down menu. The article will be delivered to your desktop. You will receive an e-mail notice containing a clickable link that takes you to a login page. To login, you must enter your complete e-mail address and the PIN that is in the e-mail. Save the article to a disk. You can print the saved document. You will be billed $1.50 for each article sent to you.

Research Help

The Librarians in the Reference Department are your main contact for most questions. Check the List of Reference Librarians for one who has subject expertise in your area.

Telephone the Reference Department directly at (570) 941-4000. If you are calling long distance, a Reference Librarian will call you back. Call in advance to schedule an extended appointment. The Librarian with whom you have made the appointment will call you at the telephone number that you provide at the scheduled time.

E-mail your questions to the Reference Department by using the e-mail reference service, Ask A Librarian. E-mail reference questions are generally answered within 24 hours; however, response time may vary according to the academic calendar and library hours of operation.

Chat with us online using Virtual Live Chat during posted hours to get real-time help. Virtual Live Chat is monitored by librarians from the American Jesuit Colleges and Universities (AJCU) and Tutor.com librarians to provide 24/7 virtual chat reference.

*Check the technical requirements for optimal performance on your computer.

To chat with specifically with a University of Scranton Librarian, login during the following hours: Monday 8–9 p.m.; Tuesday 10–11 a.m. and 8–10 p.m.; Wednesday and Thursday 3–4 p.m.

Research Guides

Research guides are not meant to answer specific questions. Rather, they are guides to library resources to aid you in your research. Research Guides are available for selected fields only. Within each guide, electronic indexes available through the Library are listed first, print sources second, and internet resources last. Please consult a librarian for more detailed assistance.

Extended Reference Questions and Reference Service

University of Texas at Austin
University of Texas Libraries
Austin, Texas

Extended Reference Questions

When it becomes apparent that a question will require extensive searching, staff members on desk duty may offer to search further and make arrangements for reporting results. Reference staff members work on extended reference questions as time permits and consult other staff in their own or other units as necessary.

Weber State University
Stewart Library
Ogden, Utah

Extended Reference Service

A. Definition

This type of service encompasses the unusual in terms of the time, effort, complexity, number and types of sources involved, and so forth.

B. Patron Classes and Priorities

Priority groups for extended service are, in order: WSU administration (deans and above), WSU faculty/staff, and WSU students. In general, extended service will not be given to those patrons who are not officially affiliated with WSU. Such patrons should be referred to those libraries or institutions specially established and equipped to meet the needs of these people.

C. The Extended Question

Individual judgment must be exercised by public services personnel as to what constitutes extended service or what the time and resource limitations are in any given situation while keeping in mind the patron class priorities established.

I. Bibliographies

Bibliographies of materials housed in the Stewart Library collections may be compiled on request of campus faculty and administration. These may be used as class handouts or for workshops, discussion groups, seminars, etc.

Bibliographies may be annotated or not annotated depending on the given need and the amount of time available for completion. Costs of photocopying or printing will be charged to the department or the faculty member originating the request.

Bibliographies needed for projects funded by outside agencies may also be produced on request, provided appropriate funding for "library research" is allocated to the Stewart Library. Arrangements, for such projects are to be made through the Director of Information Services. Two copies of all bibliographies will be placed in the University Archives and twenty copies will. be sent to the State Library Depository System for distribution to other institutions and agencies. The library, however, does not compile bibliographies to fulfill personal needs but in this case assists patrons in the use of the necessary bibliographical tools. Bibliographies produced to patron specifications may be printed from the DYNIX online catalog (see full description of this feature under Circulation, sec. VI.E.6).

2. Genealogy Requests

Genealogical searches are not undertaken. However, assistance is offered in the location of standard reference sources or genealogical service agencies.

3. Specialized Advice, Interpretation

Personnel serving at the reference desk may not offer interpretations or advice regarding legal, medical, financial, or "how to" information.

4. Reciprocal Exchange

The library supports reciprocal exchange of reference information among libraries of all types in pursuit of patron satisfaction. Incoming correspondence should be sent to the chair of the Reference Services Committee who will refer it to an appropriate person for reply. All replies should be made within one week of receipt of the original request. A copy of all correspondence should be kept in the Reference Services Committee files. As a general rule, several pages of photocopied material may be supplied free as part of a response so long as it complies with copyright law.

D. Private Requests

Requests for extended research service coming from patrons outside the priority groups stated in section 2 above cannot be honored on library time by Stewart Library personnel. However, the Stewart Library has no policy prohibiting any library employee from privately contracting with patrons to do research or prepare custom bibliographies for a fee so long as that employee pursues the work on his/her own time. However, in this case the Stewart Library assumes no responsibility for the quality of the results.

E. Special Services

Special services are unusual services in the sense that they go beyond the normal, required services provided the request for this type of special treatment usually comes from the faculty. An example of this is a request for the library to photocopy the tables of contents each month from selected journals in a certain discipline for distribution to a specific academic department on campus. Each request for special service shall be reviewed on a case-by-case basis by the library committee most affected. Since any decision has the potential of impacting the library image at large, the appropriate committee, after studying the request and the library's ability to meet it, shall offer a recommendation to the body of the library faculty who will make the final decision on the request. Primary considerations in each decision are the human, financial, and information resources available and the real or potential return benefits to be realized.

F. Handling the Time-Consuming Question

For this type of question, the following options might be considered:

A subject specialist may be called in or referred to.

The patron could be informed of the time needed to answer the question and asked to return or check in later.

Special Services

Golden Gate University
Golden Gate University Library
San Francisco, California

Research Services and Support for Faculty via GGU University Library

How can University Library Staff Support Faculty and Faculty Use of Technology?

When you are developing curriculum guidance or planning a course, librarians can help you identify resources needed for the course—including textbooks, recommended readings, Web sites, etc.

We can help you design research assignments for students, and we can help ensure resources will be available so students can have a successful research experience.

We can order library resources needed to support your courses. (Please give us as much lead time as possible, so materials will arrive and be processed in time.)

Circulation Staff can arrange to put library materials on reserve for your class, so the materials will be available to all the students. If you wish to put some of your own materials on reserve, she can arrange for that, as well, and she can arrange to place materials on electronic reserves. It is ideal if you can make arrangements with Sylvia two weeks before the course begins, so materials will be ready when your students request them. Additional lead time is always welcome!

We can develop pathfinders, guides, and/or Web sites for your courses. Check out our Web site. Bookmark Library site for future reference. We'll work with you to create a guide for your course. By working with you, we are always learning new ways to create more effective guides. Some examples of guides we have created in the past include:

Web sites tailored to syllabi, such as:

Guides tailored to course assignments, such as:

- Current Business News
- Business Valuation for Accountants especially
- Researching U.S. National Economic Information and
- Researching U.S. Regional Economic Information
- Nonprofit Organizations Research Strategy Summary
- Theater and Society

We can provide research sessions in the library, in labs, or via Cyberconference for your students, so they can do their research most effectively. Although we also give workshops throughout the term, a seminar designed specifically for your course is the most effective way of ensuring that students will get the most out of their research experience. We'll tailor the seminar to meet your needs and the course assignments. Please give us as much advance notice as you can, so we can reserve the time you want, and so we can prepare an effective presentation. Contact sessions in library or in labs in San Francisco; contact . . . . to schedule research sessions in regional campuses or via Cyberconferences.

We can help you locate resources you need for your courses and your academic activities here at GGU. If we do not have the resources you need here, we can help you identify where they are located and Dolores Neese can request them through Interlibrary Loan (ILL) for you. ILL charges will be billed to your account or to your department.

We can show you how to search Internet or commercial online and CD-ROM resources effectively, and how to locate and subscribe to professional discussion lists of interest on the Internet. Please contact Janice Carter if you cannot access the commercial databases from your offices at GGU campuses.

If you wish to access databases from other locations, stop by the Circulation Desk to have a Library Barcode placed on your faculty ID card. Please bring your faculty ID card with you whenever you come to the University Library, as you will be asked to show your faculty ID card when you enter the Library. If you do not have a faculty ID card, please check with staff in your academic department.

If you are teaching through the regional campuses, you can obtain a barcode from Steven Dunlap. Instructors in the Regional Campuses and Cybercampus may also want to consult Regional Campus Library Information a guide to services for students and faculty at Regional Campuses and Cybercampus, compiled by Steven Dunlap.

Virginia Tech
Virginia Tech University Libraries
Blacksburg, Virginia

The University Libraries offer a range of instructional opportunities designed to help faculty and students maximize their effectiveness in using information resources. Our goal is to ensure that all students are information literate.

Personalized services research aids:

- college librarian program
- tips (on effective library assignments)
- liveref & askus (online reference)
- course specific web pages
- subject pages

Seven steps to library research:

- evaluate Web information
- information skills online (self-paced)
- glossary of library terms
- citation guides
- copyright guidelines
- FAQ (frequently asked questions)
- handouts (research/databases/services, etc)

Classes & tours distance education:

- library instruction options
- schedule library instruction
- library tour options (individuals or classes)
- self-guided tours (PDF brochure)
- library maps
- Addison classes (effective searching instruction)
- instructional services
- distance education (information & contact)
- your college librarian
- contact information:
- your college librarian

TELEPHONE AND CORRESPONDENCE GUIDELINES

Telephone Reference

Rutgers University
Rutgers University Libraries
Newark, New Jersey

Telephone Service—Information or reference assistance given by telephone will generally be quite brief. Users in need of more extensive assistance may be advised to visit the library or referred to a subject specialist.

More extensive telephone service will be provided to other Rutgers Libraries, other institutions, and, when possible, to Rutgers faculty and students. In most such instances, these clients will be advised that librarians will call back with the desired information, as instant responses will not normally be feasible.

University of Texas at Austin
University of Texas Libraries
Austin, Texas

Telephone Reference Service

Telephone reference service is an integral part of reference and information service; however, priority is given to users who come to the library for assistance.

Information given over the phone is limited to short, factual answers, such as directory entries, or statistics quoted directly from the source; information about UT Austin library holdings; or information about UT Austin. Callers needing assistance with long or complex research questions are urged to come to the library for in-person assistance.

Training

The unit head is responsible for assigning and training staff members to answer the telephone. Staff members who answer the telephone should be courteous and efficient. Staff members should be familiar with University of Texas Libraries policies for telephone reference.

Priorities

General information calls which can be answered quickly are responded to as they are received. When telephone calls come at a busy time or when questions will take more than a few minutes to answer, staff members take down the question and the name and telephone number of the caller. Staff members identify themselves and inform the individual that the call will be returned, giving an approximate time.

In-person priority is given to calls from staff in other library units who are assisting waiting users.

Types of Questions Not Answered

Library staff members should not interpret statistical, medical, or legal information for patrons either over the phone or in person. No more than three titles are checked in the library catalog. Staff in a unit may find it necessary to set limits on telephone assistance relating to special materials held only in that location.

Long Distance Calls

If an inquiry received by long distance cannot be answered immediately, arrangements are made to respond at a later time. For out-of-state telephone calls, the individual may be asked to call back. The name and telephone number of the staff member handling the inquiry as well as an approximate time to call back are given. In the event that it is difficult to estimate the time needed to prepare a response, the staff member will return the call.

Photocopying

A maximum of eight pages may be photocopied from hard copy without charge when answering a long distance telephone call. If photocopying exceeds eight pages, the citations are given to the inquirer with instructions to request the items through his/her local library from Inter-Library Service or to request the item through the University of Texas Libraries Document Express service.

Telefacsimile

Telefacsimile may be used when time is of utmost importance, particularly when information is for another state agency. A maximum of eight pages from hard copy materials may be sent by telefacsimile without charge.

(For additional policies, please see the accompanying CD-ROM.)

Correspondence Reference

University of Texas at Austin
University of Texas at Austin Libraries
Austin, Texas

Correspondence Reference Service

Correspondence is an integral part of reference and information services and every effort is made to answer written requests for information within a week of receipt.

Routing Incoming Correspondence

All units of the University of Texas Libraries route letters to the appropriate library unit for reply.

The unit head is responsible for correspondence reference service. The responsibility for answering letters may be delegated.

Referral form letters may be used when sending an inquiry to another unit on campus for the information requested. One copy of the form letter is sent to the inquirer; one copy of the form letter and the original letter requesting information are sent to the unit receiving the referral and one copy of the form letter is retained as a record of the referral.

Types of Questions Answered

Letters requesting bibliographic information about University of Texas at Austin theses and dissertations are answered in detail. If the number of titles concerned is large, e.g., theses concerning Mexican-Americans in Texas, a printout from the library catalog or photocopies of the thesis catalog cards involved should be made.

Letters requesting information about publications written by UT Austin faculty or staff members, sponsored by UT Austin departments or institutes, or published by campus bureaus are answered as completely as possible.

Letters requesting broad subject information require only a brief indication of sources with an invitation to visit the University of Texas Libraries for personal assistance or with a referral to a library near the correspondent.

The Perry-Castañeda Library uses form letters to refer requests for genealogical searches to appropriate libraries. Requests for information about Texas residents are referred to the Center for American History and the Texas State Library.

Photocopying

A maximum of eight pages is photocopied from hard copy without charge when a letter is being answered. If photocopying exceeds eight pages, the citations are sent to the inquirer with instructions to request the items through their local public library from our Inter-Library Service.

Telefacsimile

Telefacsimile may be used when time is of utmost importance, particularly when information is for another state agency. A maximum of eight pages may be sent by telefacsimile without charge.

Reply

Most replies are by mail. However, an electronic response is appropriate if the requestor includes an e-mail address.

Record of Correspondence

Each letter received and a copy of the reply are retained in the unit for one year.

FORMS

Fee-Based Data Request Form

University of South Alabama
University Libraries
Mobile, Alabama

Patron Information (Required fields marked with an *)

If you cannot provide the required information, write "unknown." Otherwise, if these fields are not filled in, your request will be returned to you. To keep your patron information, hit your browser's **BACK** button after you've submitted a request. The just enter the new search information and resubmit the request. **When using a public workstation, delete your patron information by clicking the Clear This Request button.**

*First Name [_____]

*Last Name [_____]

*Full Mailing [_____]
Address   Include Zip Code

*Phone Daytime [＿＿＿＿＿] Fax [＿＿＿＿＿]

        Include area code.

E-Mail [＿＿＿＿＿＿＿＿＿＿＿]

*Status [＿＿＿＿＿＿＿＿＿＿＿]

      Select a Status

USA ID #, Library [＿＿＿＿＿＿＿＿＿＿＿]

Card # or Phone

Search Information (Required fields marked with an *)

If you cannot provide the required information, write "unknown." Otherwise, if these fields are not filled in, your request will be returned to you. To keep your patron information, hit your browser's BACK button after you've submitted a request. The just enter the new search information and resubmit the request. When using a public workstation, delete your patron information by clicking the Clear This Request button.

Database(s) to   ○ USA-Subscribed

be searched   ○ Dialog or STN—Please Specify if known [＿＿＿＿＿]

                       ┌────────────────────────┐
                       │   │

*Search Topic   │   │
                       └────────────────────────┘

In narrative form, explain what you hope to find. List key terms or phrases—include both scientific and common terms.

Purpose of Search [＿＿＿＿＿＿＿＿＿]

      Thesis, class assignment, grant proposal, etc.

Number of Citations to be Retrieved [＿＿＿＿＿]

               Select a number

Years to be Covered   ○ Current Five Years

                   ○ Other Time Period—Please Specify [＿＿＿＿＿]

Language [＿＿＿＿＿]

Other Restrictions [＿＿＿＿＿＿＿＿＿]

        Please specify

Delivery Method [＿＿＿＿＿]

      Select an option.

* I am aware that no guarantee as to to results can be made prior to search. The maximum cost acceptable to me is $[＿＿＿＿]

* ○ Please check box to indicate acceptance of disclaimer and maximum cost.

         [SEND this request]   [CLEAR this request]

To keep your patron information if you've made an error or wish to submit a new request, hit the browser's BACK button after you've submitted a request. Then just enter the new search information and submit the request. When using a public workstation, delete your patron information by clicking the Clear This Request button.

Part V
Virtual Reference Service

Chapter 19

SERVICE GUIDELINES

ADMINISTRATIVE GUIDELINES

Purpose of Virtual Reference

University of California Davis
University Library
Davis, California

UC Davis General Library Policy on Electronic Reference Service

Through e-mail reference, UC Davis General Library provides prompt assistance with a variety of types of inquiries, such as library holdings information, search strategy in the use of the Melvyl Catalog or CDL-hosted databases, factual questions, statistical data, or questions about UCD General Library's unique resources, services and facilities. E-mail reference may not be appropriate for questions which are more complex in nature or require more research time. The library does not provide financial, legal, medical, or veterinary advice. Requests to check citations or holdings will be limited to no more than five. Interlibrary loan requests should be forwarded to the appropriate ILL unit.

For questions requiring more research time to resolve, individuals are advised to come to the library for onsite consultation. UC faculty, students or staff, or outside scholars or researchers needing information on UCD unique collections may be referred to a Librarian Subject Specialist for further consultation by phone or e-mail.

The UCD electronic reference service is intended to support the learning, research and continuing education needs of UC Davis faculty, students and staff. Queries from individuals not affiliated with UC must be limited to the unique collections and resources of the UCD General Library. Some electronic information sources are limited to use by faculty, staff and students of the University of California, Davis.

The library will provide a response to electronic reference queries as soon as possible, with a goal of no more than two working days (holidays excepted).

If you have any comments on this service, please contact us at [contact information].

Service Definition

University of Maine Off Campus Library Services
University College
Augusta, Maine

Ask a Librarian Live

This service is similar to a chat session which allows a patron and librarian to "talk" live via a computer. This is especially helpful to patrons who wish to get instruction on how to use library services and only have one telephone line. We are able to instruct the patron while he/she is still connected to the Internet.

Ask a Librarian E-Mail

This service allows patrons to send us their questions via e-mail. The patron will receive a reply within 24 hours (except for weekends and holidays). This service is helpful to patrons when the live mode is unavailable or if the question is a more lengthy research question. A reply may only acknowledge receipt of your email. A full answer to your question may be sent later.

University of Pittsburgh
Pitt Digital Library
Pittsburgh, Pennsylvania

About Ask-A-Librarian Live

Ask-a-Librarian Live is the interactive Digital Reference Service offered by the University Library System at the University of Pittsburgh. Ask-a-Librarian Live offers online, real time research assistance to University of Pittsburgh students, faculty, and staff. This service complements other reference service points throughout the ULS (consultation, email, and telephone reference services) that have been traditionally available.

About Ask-A-Librarian

Ask-a-Librarian is the email version of the Digital Reference Service offered by the University Library System at the University of Pittsburgh. This service is open to anyone with a question concerning the research and teaching mission of the University of Pittsburgh. In responding to these requests, priority will be given to University of Pittsburgh affiliated students, faculty and staff. You must have a valid email address to receive a response. If you are a University of Pittsburgh student, faculty or staff you can also receive reference assistance using the Ask-a-Librarian Live service, in person at any ULS library reference desk, by telephone, or through reference consultation.

Response Time

University of Pittsburgh
Pitt Digital Library
Pittsburgh, Pennsylvania

When will I receive an answer?

Typically, you will be contacted within 24 hours, excluding holidays and term breaks. At that point we may provide you with an answer, ask for more information, or let you know when you may expect to hear from us again.

University of Texas at Austin
University of Texas Libraries
Austin, Texas

How long will it take a librarian to answer my question?

Email is checked several times a day, Monday–Friday, 8am–5pm. Responses are usually sent within two business days, excluding weekends and University holidays.

Questions are answered in priority order:

- Questions from currently enrolled UT students, faculty, and staff
- Requests for information about UT Austin libraries and special collections holdings and services
- Requests for information about the University
- Request for information about Texas
- Requests for other information

Chat requests will be answered during service hours. At peak times, users may have to wait in a patron queue for the next available librarian. Chat sessions typically take 15 minutes or less. If your question requires more time, the librarian may ask if they can research your question and send a response to your e-mail address.

Terms and Conditions of Service

University of Maine Off Campus Library Services
University College
Augusta, Maine

Terms and Conditions

Before using our services you need to read the applicable rules and policies pertaining to the Live and E-mail modes of Ask-A-Librarian. By using these services, we understand you have read the applicable rules and policies regarding the Live and E-mail modes of Ask-A-Librarian and have agreed to these rules and policies.

Rules pertaining to the questions submitted to our services:

1. We may refuse to answer questions.
2. We may refuse services to you if we determine you are not using our services in the way in which they were meant to be used. This includes, but not limited to, questions that are: illegal, harassing, libelous, threatening, harmful, obscene or objectionable, or that violates any applicable local, state, national, or international law or regulations.
3. You agree that your question will enter the public domain, and you will retain no ownership rights to your question.

University of Southern California
University Libraries
Los Angeles, California

Terms & Conditions

The following terms and conditions apply to USC's Ask-A-Librarian services. At our discretion, we may refuse to answer any question. In using our E-mail and chat services, users agree to send only questions that meet ordinary standards of decency and legality.

Ownership of Materials

E-mail questions sent to us are in the public domain. This means that anyone, including the library, can freely reproduce, copy, modify or otherwise use an E-mail question without permission. For example, questions asked and answered will be saved and will be accessible in our local Knowledge Base within the QuestionPoint database. As part of its public service mission, the University Libraries provide and use information for non-commercial, educational or research use only.

Excerpts of materials provided in answer to E-mail questions may be subject to copyright restrictions. It is the responsibility of the user to determine the existence of such rights and to obtain any permissions, and to pay any associated fees, which may be necessary for any proposed use. The library may also provide links to non-USC Web sites and is not responsible for that content, for changes in content of the sources to which the library pages link, or for the content of sources accessed through secondary links.

Disclaimer

Please note the following disclaimer: While every effort is made to provide accurate information, the University of Southern California Libraries shall have no liability for any damages arising out of or relating to use of this Web site or the information and materials provided herein.

203

ASK A LIBRARIAN REFERENCE SERVICE

Eligible Users

Auburn University
Auburn University Libraries
Auburn University, Alabama

Who may use this service?

This service is intended for the faculty, students, and staff of Auburn University. These requests will be handled first within 48 hours. Requests from those not affiliated with Auburn University will be handled in a timely manner.

University of Idaho
University of Idaho Libraries
Moscow, Idaho

Who may use this service?

E-mail reference service is provided primarily for current students, faculty and staff to the University of Idaho, including those students who are currently enrolled in a distance education class or off-campus course offered by this university. Questions about unique resources or collections of the University of Idaho Library are welcome from the general public.

Guidelines for Determining Acceptable Questions

University of Maine Off Campus Library Services
University College
Augusta, Maine

Which kinds of questions we answer:

The types of questions best handled in Live Mode are ready reference (quick research and answer) and instruction in the use of our URSUS book catalog, the Mariner indexes and databases, and other resources. For reference questions that take a longer time to research and cannot be answered during a chat session, we will either reply through e-mail or call you, providing you leave us a daytime phone number where you can be reached.

The types of questions we handle in e-mail mode are the same for live mode. In addition, we can answer more extensive reference questions.

Examples of the types of questions we cannot answer but may be able to provide a source:

    Medical or law-related advice

    Product evaluations, appraisals

    Legal questions, tax questions

University of Pittsburgh
Pitt Digital Library
Pittsburgh, Pennsylvania

What sort of questions can I ask Ask-a-Librarian?

Any question you'd ask at a physical reference desk. In some cases we might give you the answer. In other cases, we'll direct you to a source, or suggest that you come into the library. We will not, however, respond to medical, legal, tax-related or genealogical questions, as we do not have extensive resources in these areas.

Auburn University
Auburn University Libraries
Auburn University, Alabama

What can it be used for?

Use this service to ask any question you might ask at the AU Libraries' Reference Desks: help with an incomplete citation, identification of a historical fact, biographical information, a quotation, or a suggestions for a source to use. Inappropriate requests include asking the librarian to research topics, forward messages to other staff members, interlibrary loan requests, or obtain books for patrons.

Staff Responsibility for Answering Questions

University of Pittsburgh
Pitt Digital Library
Pittsburgh, Pennsylvania

Who answers the questions?

A University of Pittsburgh librarian will answer your question.

University of Scranton
Weinberg Memorial Library
Scranton, Pennsylvania

The University of Scranton's Web site is changing, and policies will be separated from information on the updated sites.

Who answers the questions?

Reference staff of the Weinberg Library at the University of Scranton will answer all phone and e-mail reference questions. Virtual live chat will be monitored by the librarians of the American Jesuit Colleges and Universities (AJCU) and Tutor.com librarians to provide 24/7 virtual chat reference.

Anonymous Questions

University of Texas at Austin
University of Texas Libraries
Austin, Texas

Can I ask a question anonymously? Who else sees my question?

Questions can be submitted anonymously. It is not necessary to include a name in the question or chat request form. However, an email address is required. Answers to email questions will be sent to the email address you provided in the question form. After your chat session, a transcript of your chat will be sent to your email address.

This service will make every attempt to respect and preserve your privacy. Only library staff members have access to questions submitted to this service. Questions will be retained for 90 days. After that time, any identifying information, such as names and e-mail addresses, will be edited from questions and deleted. Questions may be added to a database of frequently asked questions accessible to librarians for training and evaluation purposes.

FORMS

E-Mail Query Forms

Xavier University
Xavier University Library
Cincinnati, Ohio

Reference Services: Email Request Form   Monday, June 12, 2006

Hours Today: 8am to 10pm

Use the request form below for assistance any time of the day or night. For more information see email reference policies and procedures.

Name: [   ]

Email: [   ]
if different

Phone: [   ]

Course: [   ]

Status: Undergraduate○   Faculty/Staff ○
            Graduate ○   Other ○

Course
Department: [   ]

Assignment
Type: [   ]

Assignment
Description:
[   ]

What You
Have Done
Already
[   ]

[Submit]

[Clear]

Policies and Procedures

During fall and spring semesters questions are downloaded at 9am, 12pm, 3pm, 6pm, and 9pm. Times may vary during weekends, breaks, and summer sessions.

Professional librarians will respond to questions on a "first come, first served" basis, with precedence given to patrons actually visiting the library.

Responses are returned via e-mail within 1 working day.

Although the librarians will not do your research for you, they will suggest resources, search strategies, and subject headings.

LaGuardia Community College
LaGuardia Community College Library Media Resources Center
Long Island City, New York

Ask a Librarian by Email

The more information you provide on this form, the better we can serve you.

* Required field

* Name: [   ]

* Your Affiliation: ○ Student ○ Faculty ○ Staff

Faculty/Staff only: Department: [   ]

Phone: [   ]

* Email address: [   ]

Your email address MUST be accurate for us to deliver information to you.

Information to be   ○ Research paper
used for: ○ Classroom assignment
                           ○ Oral presentation / speech
                           ○ Thesis / dissertation
                           ○ Personal interest
                           ○ Other: [   ]

* Ask your brief reference question here (in 50 to 75 words or less):

[   ]

We will make every attempt to respond to your inquiry within 72 hours.

(Responses will take longer over weekends and holidays)

Questions are answered in the order in which they're received.

Reference Consultation Form

* Required field

* Name: [   ]

* Your Affiliation: ○ Student ○ Faculty ○ Staff

Faculty/Staff only: Department: [   ]

* Email address: [   ]

Your email address MUST be accurate for us to deliver information to you.

*Phone number: [   ]

*Best time to call: [   ]

*Dates available: [   ]

*Times available: [   ]

*For students—Class assignment is for:
(for example, ENG101, HUS200)   [   ]

*For students—Professor assigning this project: [   ]

*Your research topic (please be as specific as possible):

[   ]

Monroe County Community College
Monroe County Community College Library
Monroe, Michigan

Ask a Librarian

Reference desk

E-mail

Fill out the form below

Please note that we cannot provide answers to all questions via e-mail. We will do our best to respond to every question in the most timely manner, and we encourage you to come into our campus facility for full service.

Student Name   Telephone

Email Address   Are you enrolled this semester?
                                                       ○ Yes ○ No

Course (include name and number)

Instructor's Name

Assistance with this question is need no later than

○ Today
○ Tomorrow
○ This week
○ Specific date this semester

Please explain your question in as much detail as possible:

Have you discussed this question with any of the MCCC librarians?

○ Yes ○ No

Have you tried finding information on our databases?

○ Yes ○ No

Specifically, which databases have you tried?

○ FirstSearch   ○ EBSCO
○ InfoTrac   ○ JSTOR
○ Hoovers   ○ Facts.com
○ NetLibrary   ○ SIRS Discoverer
○ Oxford Reference Online   ○ eLibrary Elementary
○ Harper's Weekly   ○ Ulrich's
○ LearnATest   ○ Books In Print
○ Newsbank   ○ All of the above
                               ○ None of the above

When is the best time to contact you? [   ]

Is there any other information related to your question?

| Submit Form | | Reset Form |

Please note: If you experience any difficulties using this form, email your questions directly to Ask a Librarian or call [contact info].

Part VI
Circulation

Chapter 20

CIRCULATION PRIVILEGES

GENERAL GUIDELINES

Access Eligibility

Central Oregon Community College
Central Oregon Community College Campus Library
Bend Oregon

Who can use the Campus Library:

The Campus Library serves primarily COCC and OSU-Cascades students, faculty, and staff. A current COCC or OSU-Cascades ID is required to check out materials.

The Campus Library is also open to the public at no charge for on-site use of collections. All Oregon residents 16 years of age or older may check out materials from the circulating collection after they acquire a library card. A photo ID and proof of a current Oregon mailing address are required for community or other Oregon patron cards. In addition, Oregon residents outside the library's immediate service area need to provide a forwarding address of a friend or family member for library mail in case the patron moves unexpectedly.

The library does not issue library cards to children younger than 16 years old unless they are currently enrolled in COCC courses.

Oregon corporations may also have up to five Oregon patron cards under the corporate name for use by employees. A completed Corporate Borrower Application, available at the circulation desk, signed by an authorized representative of the corporation is required together with a signed letter of authorization on corporate letterhead.

(For additional policies, please see the accompanying CD-ROM.)

STUDENT ELIGIBILITY STATUS

Undergraduate Students

Georgetown University
Georgetown University Library
Washington, D.C

How many? You may borrow as many books as you need from the Lauinger, Blommer Science and Woodstock Theological libraries.

Loan Period. The loan period is four weeks.

All books are subject to recall after four weeks if requested by another borrower, two weeks if needed for Course Reserves.

For renewal policies, see Renewing books.

Your library record responsibilities. You are responsible for all activity that takes place on your library account record.

Report lost GOCards immediately to the GOCard office.

You must notify the Registrar of changes to your address and phone number. Notify the library of changes to your email address.

If you have any questions about your record or our borrowing policies and procedures, please ask to speak to the Circulation Desk Supervisor. You may call us or email.

Checking out books. You must present your Georgetown University GOCard every time you borrow books.

Only you may use your GOCard.

Bring materials to the circulation desk of the department to check out.

Recalls. You may recall any book charged out to another patron. To recall a book use GEORGE to locate the book you want and select the option.

You will receive an email or a print notice when an item you recalled is ready for pickup.

You can check the status of your requests by selecting "Display held items" option while viewing your circulation record in GEORGE.

Remember, as a borrower, all your books are subject to recalls and holds.

You will receive an email and a print notice if a book you borrowed is recalled for another patron. Return the book by the new due date on the notice.

If you do not return a recalled item by the new due date, a block will be placed on your circulation record and you will not be able to borrow additional items or renew checked out items. Overdue recall fines are $5.00 a day.

Searches and Paging You may request that library staff search for a book that you could not find on the shelf or have a book paged that has an "in library" status in GEORGE. To place a search or page request use GEORGE and select the option. You will be notified via email when books searched or paged are available for pickup at the location you have selected.

Items will be held at the Circulation Desk for eight days.

Off campus storage. You may request items located at the off campus storage facility to be retrieved. To place a request use GEORGE and select the option.

The material arrives within two business days.

You will receive an electronic and a print notice when the material is ready for pick-up. You may also view your circulation record to see when material arrives.

Items will be held at the Circulation Desk for eight days.

Riggs retrieval. Items stored in Riggs must be requested through the main circulation desk of either Lauinger or Blommer Science libraries.

Request forms are kept at the circulation desk.

If you have Adobe reader, you may print the request form and submit it to the main circulation desk at either library.

Items will be held at the Circulation Desk where the request was submitted for 8 days before sent back to the Riggs library.

Renewing books. You may renew your books up to three times, if they have not been requested by another borrower.

Books can be renewed online through GEORGE at the "View Your Circulation Record" option (enter name and ID number, then click on "Items currently checked out"), by phone (202) 687-7607, in person at the Circulation/Reserve Desk, or by responding to the electronic overdue notice.

Fines will accrue on all materials renewed three days or more beyond the listed due date.

Reserves. A maximum of three Reserve items may be checked out at one time.

Reserve items are available on a first come, first serve basis. Reserve items cannot be held, recalled, or renewed.

Check the Course Reserves for items available electronically.

Electronic reserves can be accessed 24/7 by clicking on the title and then "view document".

Please report any Reserve problems to reserves@georgetown.edu or by phone (202) 687-7644.

A replacement fee of $200.00 will be assessed after a reserve item is 4 days overdue. This amount will be adjusted to $40.00 if the item is returned after 4 days. To avoid fines and to be considerate of other students, please return reserve readings on time.

Late fees will accrue on all late materials.

Checking out. Media Media items are checked out and returned at the Gelardin New Media Center's circulation desk.

Please see Gelardin's borrowing policies for a complete listing of loan periods and fines.

Media is not renewable on-line or by phone.

For more information about the Gelardin New Media Center, please visit www.library.georgetown .edu/dept/gelardin/index.htm, or call [number].

Media owned by other WRLC libraries in the WRLC Catalog, does not circulate, but you can listen to or view these materials at the owning WRLC library.

Borrowing from WRLC Libraries. You can borrow materials (excluding media) through the Consortium Loan Service (CLS) or at any of the Washington Research Library Consortium (WRLC) libraries.

Use your myALADIN account to keep track of due dates, renewals, and status of requested materials.

Use your Georgetown University GOCard to check out materials at WRLC libraries.

Complete WRLC borrowing policies can be viewed at www.wrlc.org/polill.html.

Requesting books and journal articles via the CLS Books and journal articles not available in GEORGE may be requested through the WRLC catalog. The items will be delivered via WRLC's Consortium Loan Service (CLS).

Article requests may be retrieved via web delivery if your email address is listed in your myALADIN account.

Books will be held for ten days at the Circulation Desk, 3rd floor, Lauinger Library.

To request items:

Access the WRLC catalog.

Once a title has been selected, check that the status is "available." Click on "request" in the dark blue tool bar located at the top of the page.

Follow instructions on screens.

Material will be delivered to Georgetown (GT) unless specified otherwise.

At the "barcode field," enter the nine digit number located on the front of your GoCard.

Access myALADIN for account information to track the status of your request(s). Enter your email address if it is not in your MyAladin account.

Books may be returned to any WRLC library.

Complete WRLC borrowing policies can be viewed at www.wrlc.org/polill.html.

Interlibrary Loan. If a book or journal is not available in GEORGE and not able to be requested via CLS from the WRLC catalog, order via Interlibrary Loan.

Interlibrary Loan (ILL) request forms are online and accessible 24/7.

A limit of six requests will be processed per day during periods of high activity in ILL.

Borrowed items must be returned on time.

ILL cannot borrow materials that are owned by the Main Campus Libraries, regardless of whether they are checked out or currently not found on the shelves.

You will be notified by email when your material is available; the pick up location is the ILL Office on the third floor of Lauinger Library.

After office hours, ILL materials may be obtained from the Lauinger circulation desk on the third floor.

For more information about ILL, please visit www.library.georgetown.edu/service/ill.htm

Returning books. Return books to inside or outside book drops at Lauinger or Blommer Science libraries.

Do not leave books on the Circulation counters.

Do not return overdue items in outside book drops when the library is open.

You may request a receipt for books discharged from your account at the time you return them.

Returning Media. Please return media to the Gelardin New Media Center on the first floor.

Do not leave media sitting unattended on the Gelardin Service desk.

If the Gelardin Service desk is closed, please return media to the media return drop bin, located on the far right corner of the desk.

Do not return media in any book drop.

Lost or Damaged Materials Book replacement options:

1) $57 replacement cost

30 processing fee

and any fine charges up to a maximum of $10,

or

2) A copy of the material may be brought to the Circulation Desk (on the 3rd floor) by the patron for replacement consideration by the Library. If accepted, there will be a $15 processing fee and any fines accrued up to a maximum of $10.

Multimedia:

Replacement costs and options for multimedia can be found at: www.library.georgetown.edu/dept/gelardin/borrowing.htm

Reserves:

Please contact Reserves for replacement options.

Overdue Fines. Overdue notices are sent to your Georgetown e-mail address as a courtesy. Failure to receive notices of overdue items is not grounds for dismissing fines.

Fines are levied against all overdue items.

Circulating items: $0.25 / per day

Interlibrary Loan items: $0.25 / per day

Media: $1.00 / first hour; $0.50 each additional hour

Recalled items: $5.00 / per day

Reserve items: 2, 4 or 24 hour loan period $1.00 / first hour; $0.50 each additional hour

Reserve items: 3 day loan period $2.00 / first day; $1.00 each additional day

A block will be placed on your circulation record if you owe $100.00 or more in fines.

All unpaid fines will be sent to Student Accounts four weeks after date of assessment.

University of Iowa
University of Iowa Libraries
Iowa City, Iowa

Undergraduates, Merit Staff, and Most Permit Holders

In all but the Hardin Library for the Health Sciences, books are due in 4 weeks, unless recalled earlier. (At the Hardin Library, these users may check out books for 2 weeks.) Renewals are unlimited. Renewals may be done from My Account within InfoHawk or requested by phone, list, or mail. (Phone renewals are limited to five or fewer items per call.) The last nine digits of the barcode number (the number beginning with 31858...) is what staff need for a phone or mail renewal. In addition, your University ID number (or permit barcode number) is required. A fine of $10.00 is assessed only if a book is kept so overdue that its replacement cost must be charged. Recalled books are fined at the rate of $2.00 per day overdue.

University of Texas at Arlington
University Libraries
Arlington, Texas

Undergraduate Students

"Undergraduate Students" are people currently enrolled at UT Arlington in an undergraduate program of study, as defined by the UT Arlington Registrar's Office.

Undergraduates can:

*   Have up to 50 items checked out at one time
*   Check out books for 21 days
*   Check out special materials
*   Renew materials 2 times for 21 days each time, unless an item has been placed on hold for another user
*   Undergraduates cannot check out current or bound periodicals

People enrolled in an undergraduate program of study at UT Arlington but who are also in the UT Arlington Honors College or the McNair Fellows Program receive the library privileges of UT Arlington graduate students, as outlined below.

Graduate Students

University of Iowa
University of Iowa Libraries
Iowa City, Iowa

Graduate Students

In all but the Hardin Library for the Health Sciences, books are due twice a year—on specified dates in January and June—unless recalled earlier. (At the Hardin Library, graduate students may check out books for 4 weeks and medical, dental, and pharmacy students may check out books for 2 weeks.) Renewals are unlimited but books must be brought in to one of the libraries to be renewed. Renewals begin on the first Monday in December and May. A Fine of $10.00 is assessed only if a book is kept so overdue that its replacement cost must be charged. Recalled books are fined at the rate of $2.00 per day overdue.

University of Texas at Arlington
University Libraries
Arlington, Texas

Graduate Students

"Graduate Students" are people currently enrolled at UT Arlington in an graduate program of study, as defined by the UT Arlington Registrar's Office.

Graduate students can:

- Have up to 50 items checked out at one time
- Check out books for 30 days
- Check out special materials
- Check out current or bound periodicals for 2 hours, with no renewals
- Renew materials 3 times for 30 days each time, unless an item has been placed on hold for another user

Graduate students holding an appointment as a Graduate Teaching Assistant or a Graduate Research Assistant receive "Graduate Student" privileges at the UT Arlington Library.

Graduate students whose research or teaching assignments require that they receive the borrowing privileges of UT Arlington Faculty should apply for those privileges at the Central Library Circulation Desk. Contact us for more information, or print and submit the Faculty Borrowing Privileges application available here in PDF format.

(For additional policies, please see the accompanying CD-ROM.)

Continuing Education Students

Bergen Community College
Sidney Silverman Library
Paramus, New Jersey

Students Enrolled in Non-Credit Courses
(ILIR, EOF, Continuing Ed)

Students enrolled in non-credit courses at Bergen Community College may request borrowing privileges by presenting proof of registration and another valid form of identification at the Circulation Desk.

Borrowing privileges are extended for the period of time in which an individual is enrolled in the non-credit course/program.

Periodicals, Reference works and Reserve items are for in-library use only.

There is a limit of 3 items that may be charged out to an individual at any one time.

Loan period is 14 days.

A loan may be renewed unless another borrower has requested the item; renewals may be made in person, or by calling the Circulation Desk .

Some restrictions may apply.

Bergen County residents enrolled in non-credit courses are encouraged to apply for borrowing privileges under the BCCLS reciprocal borrowing program. (BCCLS patrons have borrowing privileges for one year or the expiration date on their public library card whichever occurs sooner.)

Georgetown University
Georgetown University Library
Washington, D.C

How many? You are allowed a maximum of six books checked out to your account at any given time.

Loan Period. The loan period is four weeks.

All books are subject to recall after four weeks if requested by another borrower, two weeks if needed for Course Reserves.

If your privileges expire four weeks before the due date, your books will be due on the expiration date.

All CED privileges expire on the last day of class.

For renewal policies, see Renewing books.

Your Library Record Responsibilities. You are responsible for all activity that takes place on your library record. Notify the library immediately if you lose your Special Borrower library card.

You must inform the library of any changes to address, email, and phone number.

If you have any questions about your record or our borrowing policies and procedures, please ask to speak to the Circulation Desk Supervisor. You may call us at (202) 687-7607 or email accessservices @georgetown.edu.

Checking Out Books. You must register for borrowing the first time you borrow books from the library.

Faculty must present a letter from SSCE with start and end date of courses taught to register.

Students must present the registration form from SSCE to register.

After you are issued a Special Borrowing library card, you must present this card and a picture ID (driver's license, passport, college ID, military ID, etc.) when checking out books.

Only you may use your Special Borrower library card.

Bring the materials to the circulation desk to check out.

Recalls. You may recall any book charged out to another patron. To recall a book use GEORGE to locate the book you want and select the option.

You will receive an email or a print notice when an item you recalled is ready for pickup.

You can check the status of your requests by selecting "Display held items" option while viewing your circulation record in GEORGE.

Remember, as a borrower, all your books are subject to recalls and holds.

You will receive an email and a print notice if a book you borrowed is recalled for another patron. Return the book by the new due date on the notice.

If you do not return a recalled item by the new due date, a block will be placed on your circulation record and you will not be able to borrow additional items or renew checked out items. Overdue recall fines are $5.00 a day.

Searches and Paging. You may request that library staff search for a book that you could not find on the shelf or have a book paged that has an "in library" status in GEORGE. To place a search or page request use GEORGE and select the option. You will be notified via email when books searched or paged are available for pickup at the location you have selected.

Items will be held at the Circulation Desk for 8 days.

Off Campus Storage. You may request items located at the off campus storage facility to be retrieved. To place a request use GEORGE and select the option.

The material arrives within two business days.

You will receive an electronic and a print notice when the material is ready for pick-up. You may also view your circulation record to see when material arrives.

Items will be held at the Circulation Desk for 8 days.

Riggs Retrieval. Items stored in Riggs must be requested through the main circulation desk of either Lauinger or Blommer Science libraries.

Request forms are kept at the circulation desk.

If you have Adobe reader, you may print the request form and submit it to the main circulation desk at either library.

Items will be held at the Circulation Desk where the request was submitted for 8 days before sent back to the Riggs library.

Renewing Books. You may renew your books up to three times, if they have not been requested by another borrower.

Books can be renewed online through GEORGE at the "View Your Circulation Record" option (enter name and ID number, then click on "Items currently checked out"), by phone (202) 687-7607, in person at the Circulation/Reserve Desk, or by responding to the electronic overdue notice.

Fines will accrue on all materials renewed three days or more beyond the listed due date.

Returning Books. Return books to inside or outside book drops at Lauinger or Blommer Science libraries.

Do not leave books on the Circulation counters.

Do not return overdue items in outside book drops when the library is open.

You may request a receipt for books discharged from your account at the time you return them.

Using the Gelardin New Media Center. Although your Special Library card does not entitle you to check out material from the Gelardin New Media Center, with a photo ID you are welcome to view or listen to media while the center is open (please see library hours)

Please note only GU faculty, students, and staff have access to the Picchi Multimedia Room and the Audio and Video Editing Rooms.

For more information about the Gelardin New Media Center, please visit www.library.georgetown .edu/dept/gelardin/index.htm, call (202) 687-7410, or email gelardin@georgetown.edu.

Replacement costs and options for multimedia can be found at: www.library.georgetown.edu/dept/ gelardin/borrowing.htm.

Lost or Damaged Materials. Book replacement options:

1) $57 replacement cost

$30 processing fee

and any fine charges up to a maximum of $10,

or

2) A copy of the material may be brought to the Circulation Desk (on the 3rd floor) by the patron for replacement consideration by the Library. If accepted, there will be a $15 processing fee and any fines accrued up to a maximum of $10.

What you cannot do with these borrowing privileges Continuing Education borrowing privileges do not entitle you to:

- borrow course reserves
- borrow Gelardin New Media Center material
- off-campus access to selected reference databases
- use the GU Interlibrary Loan service
- use the Picchi Multimedia Room and the Audio and Video Editing Rooms

Overdue Fines. Overdue notices are sent via e-mail (or postal mail if there is not an e-mail address on your account) as a courtesy. Failure to receive notices of overdue items is not grounds for dismissing fines.

Fines are levied against all overdue items.

Circulating items: $0.25 / per day

Recalled items: $5.00 / per day

A block will be placed on your circulation record if you owe more than $25.00.

Joint Degree Programs

Bergen Community College
Sidney Silverman Library
Paramus, New Jersey

Students Enrolled in Joint Degree Programs

Non-BCC students enrolled in Degree programs offered jointly by BCC and other New Jersey community colleges may request borrowing privileges by presenting their college ID at the BCC circulation desk.

Borrowing privileges are extended for the semester in which the student is enrolled in the program.

There is a limit of 10 books which may be charged out to an individual at any given time.

Loan period is 21 days.

A loan may be renewed unless another borrower has requested the item; renewals may be made in person, or by calling the Circulation Desk.

Some restrictions may apply.

Proxy Borrowing

Northern Arizona University
Cline Library
Flagstaff, Arizona

Proxy Card Information

Northern Arizona University faculty and staff who wish to authorize their research assistants to charge out library materials for them may apply for a Cline Library Proxy Card by completing the application below. The proxy card will be attached to the instructor's or staff's personal library record and that person assumes full responsibility for all materials checked out according to the Cline Library Circulation Policy.

Each faculty or staff member may receive one or more proxy card(s) and may designate student assistant(s) to use those card(s). Materials charged out on the proxy card will receive the usual faculty or staff loan period. The faculty or staff member will receive all correspondence for the card.

The Ohio State University
The Ohio State University Libraries
Columbus, Ohio

Faculty/Staff Authorization

OSU faculty and staff may authorize one or more persons to borrow and request library materials under the authorizing person's name; the authorizing person is responsible for all transactions done by the designated individuals. To make such an authorization, print off a Faculty Authorization Request Form, supply the requested information, and submit the form to any OSU Libraries Circulation Desk. Please contact any OSU library if you have questions or would like further information.

Western Illinois University
Western Illinois University Library
Macomb, Illinois

Surrogate Checkout Procedure
Library Materials Checkout and Photocopying
of Periodicals by Graduate Assistants

This is the procedure which allows faculty to appoint a Graduate Assistant to checkout library materials and photocopy library materials. It is initiated when the attached form is returned to the Access Services

Librarian from a faculty member to name the Graduate Assistant and include ID numbers for both the student and professor. The student ID # is required for identification and the items are checked out to the faculty ID #.

The checkout service includes books, audiovisual materials (not equipment) and government publications in the online catalog, which may be checked out for the normal borrowing period. Periodicals may be checked out for three days only. Checkout of materials takes place at the circulation desk on the 2nd Level of the Malpass Library.

The photocopy service covers material in print format designated for Library use only. Material is to be given to staff at the Periodicals Desk located on the 3rd Level of the Malpass Library.

For requests exceeding 100 pages, the Library has the right to limit the number of photocopies, which can be accommodated on a daily basis. There is a limit of 50 pages from any one reference book. It is expected that the Graduate Assistant will complete all "Citation Slips" for the articles to be copied, as well as an Address Label. The Graduate Assistant will present a University ID, which will be checked against the letter on file. Photocopies will be returned to the faculty member's office via Campus Mail.

STAFF AND FACULTY ELIGIBILITY STATUS

Staff and Faculty

Colorado State University Pueblo
Colorado State University Pueblo Library
Pueblo, Colorado

Faculty and administrative staff with proper identification may check out books for a semester with all items due the last day of finals. Government documents, vertical file materials and materials from any of the four high school libraries in School District 60 may only be borrowed for a three-week period. Audiovisual materials may be borrowed for a one-week period. Family of CSU faculty and administrative staff who are not participants in the Colorado Library Card with proper identification may check out four items. Materials are subject to recall after three weeks. Materials not returned after recall are subject to a lost book charge.

Binghamton University
Binghamton University Libraries
Binghamton, New York

Faculty and University Staff, Clinical Campus Faculty, Emeritus/Emerita Faculty, Management Confidential, University Council, Volunteer: Limit of 100 items at any one time. Books, microforms, and government documents may be borrowed for one year. Bound periodicals may be circulated for three days; current periodicals are due at 5 p.m. the day borrowed.

Los Angeles Valley College
Los Angeles Valley College Library
Valley Glen, California

Faculty may check out books by obtaining a library card, available at the circulation desk. Books circulate for two months, but are due at the end of each semester. They may be renewed. Faulty are not subject to fines, but are held responsible for lost materials and must keep their records current.

University of North Carolina Wilmington
William Madison Randall Library
Wilmington, North Carolina

Active and retired FACULTY and STAFF, and TRUSTEES of the University of North Carolina at Wilmington may borrow materials from the collections upon presentation of a valid identification card.

We ask that you observe the following regulations:

1. Present your UNCW One Card at the Circulation Desk with the items that you wish to borrow.

2. Faculty and staff borrowing privileges are not transferable, with two exceptions.

   Faculty may authorize a research assistant to check out materials for them. Contact the Circulation Desk to set up the authorization in the library's patron database. By authorizing this assistant, the faculty member assumes responsibility for the return of all materials and the payment of any charges assessed for damage. To check out materials to a faculty member's account, the authorized research assistant must present the faculty member's card and their own UNCW identification card.

   Faculty and staff may add their high-school children enrolled in grades 9–12 as authorized users. Contact the Circulation Desk to add this authorization to the library's patron database. By sponsoring their child, the parent or guardian assumes responsibility for the return of all materials and the payment of any charges assessed for damage. To check out materials, the high school student should present their parent's or guardian's UNCW identification card and their high school identification card or driver's license.

3. Faculty and staff are responsible for each item borrowed on his/her card until the material is returned to the Library. Lost or damaged materials must be paid for. When materials are declared lost, we charge the replacement cost.

4. Borrowed materials should be returned and/or renewed at the end of each semester or second summer session. Unless overdue or requested by another user, materials may be renewed by telephone or using: http://library.uncwil.edu

Loan Period

The loan period is to the last day of the semester or second summer session for general collection materials and government documents; two days for bound journal volumes; and seven days for audiovisual materials. Items on reserve may be borrowed for periods specified by the course instructor. Reference materials should be used in the Library; however, faculty and staff may borrow some items for a negotiated period (please check with the reference librarian on duty).

A/V Renewals

Renewals for videos, DVDs, CDs and audiobooks are limited to two (2) per item.

Borrowed items are subject to recall when requested by another user. A revised due date will be set. As a courtesy to other library users, please return recalled items as soon as possible.

Overdue Charges

Faculty and staff are not charged for overdue materials. If items are long overdue however, you will receive a bill for the replacement cost. UNCW faculty and staff will have their borrowing privileges blocked when:

- Their debt for Randall Library materials exceeds $100.00
- Their debt for borrowing from UNC system libraries or interlibrary loan transactions exceeds $50.00.

We hope that you will enjoy using the Randall Library. Your suggestions concerning our services are always appreciated.

Hamilton College
Burke Library
Clinton, New York

Spouses and Children of College Employees, and Alumni

Spouses and children of college employees and Alumni have the same borrowing privileges as college employees, and may borrow up to 50 books. Fines for overdue books and recalls are the same as those for Hamilton students.

University of North Carolina Wilmington
William Madison Randall Library
Wilmington, North Carolina

Welcome to the William Madison Randall Library. Faculty/staff spouses may be issued a Borrower's Card without charge by visiting the Circulation Desk to get registered for the card.

Loan Period

The loan period is 21 days for books and government documents. The loan period for audiovisual materials is 7 days. Reserve materials, reference items, and periodicals must be used in the building.

A/V Renewals

Renewals for videos, DVDs, CDs and audio books are limited to two (2) per item.

Restrictions

Items in the Reserve Collection may not be checked out. These materials are in high demand for students enrolled in UNCW courses.

No holds (i.e. requests for items already checked out) are allowed.

You are not eligible for UNCW's Interlibrary Borrowing services. Please use your local public library for this service.

Faculty/staff spouses are not eligible for computer lab use or laptop checkout.

Overdue Charges

Overdue charges accrue at $.25 per item per day, to a maximum of $6.00 per item. The overdue charge for audiovisuals is $1.00 per item per day, to a maximum of $10.00 per item. Borrowing privileges are revoked if a user has overdue books or owes overdue charges. When borrowing materials, please observe these regulations:

1. Present your Randall Library Borrower's Card for each transaction.
2. Borrowing privileges are not transferable, with one exception. High school students enrolled in grades 9–12 may be added as an authorized user to an adult parent's or guardian's borrower's card. By sponsoring their child, the parent or guardian assumes responsibility for the return of all materials and the payment of any charges assessed for damage or overdues. To check out materials, the high school student should present their parent's or guardian's borrower card and their high school identification card or driver's license at the Randall Library Circulation Desk.
3. Borrowers are responsible for materials borrowed until they are returned to the Library. Lost or damaged material must be paid for; we charge the replacement cost and accumulated overdue fines.
4. Most materials may be renewed by bringing them to the Circulation Desk. Unless overdue or requested by another user, materials may also be renewed by telephone (962-3272), or by using the Library's online system.

The Library's catalog is available on the Web at http://library.uncw.edu. Access to this system provides a record of the library's collection and serves as a gateway to a wide variety of other electronic resources, including full-text article databases and indexing and abstracting services.

Please inquire at the Reference Desk for assistance in using the Library. We hope that you will enjoy using the Randall Library.

Visiting Scholars

Georgetown University
Georgetown University Library
Washington, D.C

How Many? You may borrow as many books as you need from the Lauinger, Blommer Science and Woodstock Theological libraries.

Loan Period. The loan period is six weeks

All books are subject to recall after four weeks if requested by another borrower, two weeks if needed for Course Reserves.

For renewal policies, see Renewing books.

Your Library Record Responsibilities. You are responsible for all activity that takes place on your library account record.

Report lost GOCards immediately to the GOCard office.

You must notify the library of any changes to your address, email, and phone number.

If you have any questions about your record or our borrowing policies and procedures, please ask to speak to the Circulation Desk Supervisor. You may call us at or email

Checking Out Books. The first time you borrow, you must present your University invitation letter that states the term of your contract.

You must present your Georgetown University GOCard every time you borrow books.

Only you may use your GOCard.

Bring materials to the circulation desk of the department to check out.

Recalls. You may recall any book charged out to another patron. To recall a book use GEORGE to locate the book you want and select the option.

You will receive an email or a print notice when an item you recalled is ready for pickup.

You can check the status of your requests by selecting "Display held items" option while viewing your circulation record in GEORGE.

Remember, as a borrower, all your books are subject to recalls and holds.

You will receive an email and a print notice if a book you borrowed is recalled for another patron. Return the book by the new due date on the notice.

If you do not return a recalled item by the new due date, a block will be placed on your circulation record and you will not be able to borrow additional items or renew checked out items. Overdue recall fines are $5.00 a day.

Searches and Paging. You may request that library staff search for a book that you could not find on the shelf or have a book paged that has an "in library" status in GEORGE. To place a search or page request use GEORGE and select the option. You will be notified via email when books searched or paged are available for pickup at the location you have selected.

Items will be held at the Circulation Desk for 8 days.

Off Campus Storage. You may request items located at the off campus storage facility to be retrieved. To place a request use GEORGE and select the option.

The material arrives within two business days.

You will receive an electronic and a print notice when the material is ready for pick-up. You may also view your circulation record to see when material arrives.

Items will be held at the Circulation Desk for 8 days.

Riggs Retrieval. Items stored in Riggs must be requested through the main circulation desk of either Lauinger or Blommer Science libraries.

Request forms are kept at the circulation desk.

If you have Adobe reader, you may print the request form and submit it to the main circulation desk at either library.

Items will be held at the Circulation Desk where the request was submitted for 8 days before sent back to the Riggs library.

Renewing Books. You may renew your books up to three times, if they have not been requested by another borrower.

Books can be renewed online through GEORGE at the "View Your Circulation Record" option (enter name and ID number, then click on "Items currently checked out"), by phone, in person at the Circulation/Reserve Desk, or by responding to the electronic overdue notice.

Fines will accrue on all materials renewed three days or more beyond the listed due date.

Reserves. A maximum of three Reserve items may be checked out at one time.

Reserve items are available on a first come, first serve basis. Reserve items cannot be held, recalled, or renewed.

Check the Course Reserves for items available electronically.

Electronic reserves can be accessed 24/7 by clicking on the title and then "view document".

Please report any Reserve problems to reserves@georgetown.edu or by phone (202) 687-7644.

A replacement fee of $200.00 will be assessed after a reserve item is 4 days overdue. This amount will be adjusted to $40.00 if the item is returned after 4 days. To avoid fines and to be considerate of other students, please return reserve readings on time.

Late fees will accrue on all late materials.

Checking Out Media. Media items are checked out and returned at the Gelardin New Media Center's circulation desk.

Please see Gelardin's borrowing policies for a complete listing of loan periods and fines.

Media is not renewable on-line or by phone.

For more information about the Gelardin New Media Center, please visit www.library.georgetown.edu/dept/gelardin/index.htm

Media owned by other WRLC libraries in the WRLC Catalog, does not circulate, but you can listen to or view these materials at the owning WRLC library.

Checking Out Bound Periodicals. Visiting researchers may borrow up to six bound periodicals at a time for two hours.

Bound periodicals cannot be renewed.

Fines for bound periodicals will be $1.00 for the first hour overdue and $0.50 for each additional hour.

A notice will be sent after the first day overdue and the borrower will be billed for the replacement cost ($100 or actual replacement cost, whichever is higher, plus overdue fines) after the fourth day.

Borrowed bound periodicals must be returned to a circulation desk staff member. You may request a receipt verifying the material has been returned.

Borrowing from WRLC Libraries.

You can borrow materials (excluding media) through the Consortium Loan Service (CLS) or at any of the Washington Research Library Consortium (WRLC) libraries.

Use your myALADIN account to keep track of due dates, renewals, and status of requested materials.

Use your Georgetown University GOCard to check out materials at WRLC libraries

Complete WRLC borrowing policies can be viewed at www.wrlc.org/polill.html.

Requesting books and journal articles via the CLS Books and journal articles not available in GEORGE may be requested through the WRLC catalog. The items will be delivered via WRLC's Consortium Loan Service (CLS).

Article requests may be retrieved via web delivery if your email address is listed in your myALADIN account.

Books will be held for ten days at the Circulation Desk, 3rd floor, Lauinger Library.

To request items:

   Access the WRLC catalog.

   Once a title has been selected, check that the status is "available." Click on "request" in the dark blue tool bar located at the top of the page.

   Follow instructions on screens.

   Material will be delivered to Georgetown (GT) unless specified otherwise.

   At the "barcode field," enter the nine digit number located on the front of your GoCard.

   Access myALADIN for account information to track the status of your request(s). Enter your email address if it is not in your MyAladin account.

   Books may be returned to any WRLC library.

Complete WRLC borrowing policies can be viewed at www.wrlc.org/polill.html.

Interlibrary Loan. If a book or journal is not available in GEORGE and not able to be requested via CLS from the WRLC catalog, order via Interlibrary Loan.

Interlibrary Loan (ILL) request forms are online and accessible 24/7.

A limit of six requests will be processed per day during periods of high activity in ILL.

Borrowed items must be returned on time.

ILL cannot borrow materials that are owned by the Main Campus Libraries, regardless of whether they are checked out or currently not found on the shelves.

You will be notified by email when your material is available; the pick up location is the ILL Office on the third floor of Lauinger Library.

After office hours, ILL materials may be obtained from the Lauinger circulation desk on the third floor.

For more information about ILL, please visit www.library.georgetown.edu/service/ill.htm

Returning Books. Return books to inside or outside book drops at Lauinger or Blommer Science libraries.

Do not leave books on the Circulation counters.

Do not return overdue items in outside book drops when the library is open.

You may request a receipt for books discharged from your account at the time you return them.

Returning Media. Please return media to the Gelardin New Media Center on the first floor.

Do not leave media sitting unattended on the Gelardin Service desk.

If the Gelardin Service desk is closed, please return media to the media return drop bin, located on the far right corner of the desk.

Do not return media in any book drop.

Lost or Damaged Materials Book replacement options:

1) $57 replacement cost

$30 processing fee

and any fine charges up to a maximum of $10,

or

2) A copy of the material may be brought to the Circulation Desk (on the 3rd floor) by the patron for replacement consideration by the Library. If accepted, there will be a $15 processing fee and any fines accrued up to a maximum of $10.

Bound journals:

Patron will be charged either

1) $100.00 plus $60.00 processing fee and $40.00 fine charge

or

2) actual cost of journal plus $60.00 processing fee and $40.00 fine charge,

whichever amount is higher

Multimedia:

Replacement costs and options for multimedia can be found at: www.library.georgetown.edu/dept/gelardin/borrowing.htm

Overdue Fines. Overdue notices are sent to your Georgetown e-mail address as a courtesy. Failure to receive notices of overdue items is not grounds for dismissing fines.

Fines are levied against all overdue items.

Bound periodicals: $1.00 /first hour, $0.50 each additional hour, replacement charge after 4 days overdue

Circulating items: $0.25 / per day

Interlibrary Loan items: $0.25 / per day

Media: $1.00 / first hour; $0.50 each additional hour

Recalled items: $5.00 / per day

Reserve items: 2, 4 or 24 hour loan period $1.00 / first hour; $0.50 each additional hour

Reserve items: 3 day loan period $2.00 / first day; $1.00 each additional day

A block will be placed on your circulation record if you owe $100.00 or more in fines.

University of Washington
University of Washington Libraries
Seattle, Washington

Borrowing Information for Visiting Scholars

Getting Visiting Scholar Status

To obtain borrowing privileges as a "Visiting Scholar" individuals must be designated as such by a University of Washington academic department. See the UW's procedures for visiting scholars for information on obtaining a Husky Card, used as a library card within the University of Washington Libraries system.

Access

Most libraries and sections have open stacks with selected materials kept in closed areas, not accessible for browsing. Auxiliary and storage stacks; Special Collections, and the Media Center are examples of closed stacks, materials that are unavailable for public browsing. Most reserve materials are also in closed stacks. Access to these materials is acquired through the appropriate public service desk. Requests for storage materials may be placed online through the UW Libraries Catalog. Some materials are restricted to Library Use Only. Typical items include most reference materials, Special Collections and archival theses.

Loan Periods

Loan periods vary among libraries and may be determined by the status of the borrower, type of material and individual collection policy.

Holds, Searches and Retrieval

Any borrower may place a hold for a non-reserve item that is on loan. The item will then be recalled from the current borrower. Borrowers may initiate a search for missing materials at the appropriate circulation desk. Some libraries have remote storage facilities for less-used material. Requests for such items can be made at any circulation desk or through the online catalog.

Returning Materials

Non-reserve library materials (except for fragile items) may be returned to any UW library or bookdrop. A drive-up bookdrop is available south of the dental wing of the Health Sciences Center. Reserve items must be returned to the service desk where they were checked out.

Change of Address

Report address changes to the Library Cashier.

Fines

Circulation policies are designed to provide equal access to the collection for all University borrowers. The borrower must be aware of the policies. Overdue notices are sent as a courtesy, but the borrower is responsible for accumulated fines whether or not the overdue notice is received. Library fines may be paid online, by mail, or in person at the Library Cashier. Delinquent accounts may result in the revocation of borrowing privileges and/or referral to a collection agency.

Appeals

If a borrower feels that a fine has been levied in error, or has questions as to why a fine has been levied, he or she should contact the library unit that issued the bill. The Library Fines Appeals Committee, made up of faculty and students, meets quarterly to adjudicate any appeals of library charges. Library charges must be appealed within 6 months of the billing date.

ALUMNI

Framingham State College
Henry Whittemore Library
Framingham, Massachusetts

Alumni may obtain free borrowing privileges upon request. There is a limit of 3 curriculum library items that may be checked out at a time. There will be no expiration of alumni privileges unless the curriculum library restriction is not respected.

Georgetown University
Georgetown University Library
Washington, D.C

Alumni Borrowing

The library is pleased to offer several ways for Georgetown University Alumni to continue their lifelong studies in an environment outside the classroom.

The University collections and resources located in the Lauinger and Blommer Science libraries are available for the general public to view. Please read the Entrance and Building Use Policies for important information regarding the access to and use of materials within the Georgetown University Main Campus libraries.

Niagara University
Niagara University Library
Niagara University, New York

Alumni

You are an alumnus if you actually graduated from Niagara University. You can obtain a Library Card at the Circulation Desk that allows you to check out up to 10 books for 28 days at a time. You can also use any Library database on-site. Research Assistance is available to you, but Interlibrary Loan Services are not. If you took courses at Niagara University, but did not actually graduate, then see the Local Residents category below.

The library invites Georgetown University Alumni to become a member of the Library Associates. New alumni are offered a free, one year membership upon graduation. Membership includes borrowing privileges, invitations to special events, and an informative quarterly newsletter about the library. Please see Alumni borrowing privileges for more information.

The library also offers LibraryLink, a portal designed especially for Georgetown University Alumni, to assist with the access and use of information resources and technology.

NON-AFFILIATED ELIGIBILITY STATUS

Visitors and Community Members

Guilford College
Hege Library
Greensboro, North Carolina

Non-Guilford Patrons/Guest Patrons

PALS Consortium Institution's faculty and students—Bennett, Elon, Greensboro, and Salem College, and Salem Academy are permitted to borrow circulating materials by requesting items through the PALS system or by presenting current ID cards at the desk. The Consortium rules limit borrowing to a total of 15 items at one time from all Consortium schools and allow one renewal per item.

Students from UNCG, High Point University and NCA&T State University may borrow books with a letter or request form from their home institution's Reference Librarian.

Guests of Hege Library who have paid the $50.00 guest fee for individual or family use ($25.00 for Senior citizens, $25 for Guilford Alumni) receive borrowing privileges that allow them to borrow up to ten books at one time. They may also borrow CD's, videos, recordings and Juvenile books that are circulating materials. Retired Guilford College faculty members receive the same privileges as the Guests of Hege Library. Residents of Friends Homes at Guilford may also apply and receive limited library borrowing privileges from Hege Library.

Members of the groups above are subject to the same regulations and fines that apply to all library patrons.

Colorado State University Pueblo
Colorado State University Pueblo Library
Pueblo, Colorado

Community patrons are welcome to check out books and audiovisual materials at the University Library. They may check out two (2) items with a valid driver's license or four (4) items with a public library card. Books, government documents and vertical file materials check out for a three-week period and audiovisual materials check out for one-week with renewal privileges. Library materials are subject to recall after ten (10) days.

The University Library also offers community patrons the option of purchasing a Library ID (LID) card for $1.00, which allows the patron to check out four (4) books. The LID card also offers a patron printing privileges when money is added to the card at either of the Card Value machines in the Library. To purchase an LID card the patron must fill out an application form at the circulation desk.

University of Texas at El Paso
University Libraries
El Paso, Texas

Community User Cards

Residents of El Paso County, 18 years of age or older, may secure borrowing privileges by acquiring a Community User Card. The fee is $50 per year. Fines are charged for books returned late, lost, or damaged. The library also honors the TexShare card, which may be obtained at the El Paso Community College, Public Library, and other Texas libraries, to borrow specific items.

Loan periods:

- Main Stack Collection: 28 days
- Documents: 28 days
- Textbook Collection: 28 days
- Loan Policies:
- Maximum number of items allowed to be borrowed concurrently: 10
- Maximum number of renewals: 3 per item
- Borrowing is not permitted from the following collections:
- Browsing, Children's, Special and Reference
- Periodicals do not circulate.

Fines:

- Overdue fines: $ .25 per day
- Recall fines: $ 1.00 per day

Cause for suspension of library privileges:

- 5 or more items overdue concurrently
- $25 or more owed the Library in bills or fines
- Not returning overdue items which have been recalled

Renewals

Renewals may be done through the Web, or in person at the Library. They cannot be done over the phone or by email.

Staff at the Circulation Desk on the main (2d) floor of the Library can provide detailed information concerning circulation policies, email librarycirc@utep.edu, or call 747-5672.

Interlibrary Loans

Interlibrary loan services are available to community users holding a valid Community User card. There is a handling charge of $5.00 per transaction, in addition to any charges accessed by the sending library.

Reference Services

Reference and other information services are provided to all patrons on a first-come, first-served basis. However, at all times, priority is given to UTEP students and faculty.

Instruction

Instruction in the use of Library resources is available only to University classes. Occasionally exceptions are made for high school honors classes and groups with special needs. Class instruction is provided strictly by appointment. Contact the Reference Department (747-5643) for additional information

Telephone Queries

Short reference questions are answered by telephone as time permits. In-house users are given priority.

Electronic Resources

The equipment and services of the Collaborative Learning Center are exclusively for the use of currently enrolled UTEP students. Community users may access the Library's electronic resources using the computers in the Media & Microforms Department on the first floor.

UTEP students, faculty, and staff have priority in the use of the Library's Internet, CD-ROM and related electronic products. Community users may be asked to relinquish use of Library computers in order to allow UTEP users access. Certain databases are not available to community users due to licensing agreements. Remote access to the Library's databases is not available to community users.

Library computers must be used for their assigned purpose. Computer use is restricted to databases authorized by the Library. Web "surfing," "chatting," e-mailing, or other personal use of this equipment is not permitted.

Meeting Rooms

The Library's meeting and instruction facilities may only be used by University affiliated groups. They are not available to community groups or individuals.

Walk-in ILL

Framingham State College
Henry Whittemore Library
Framingham, Massachusetts

Students who are currently enrolled at any of the Massachusetts public institutions of higher education may borrow from the library through the W.I.L.L. (Walk-in Interlibrary Loan) program. A validated student ID with a current semester sticker must be presented in order to check out materials.

Area Colleges and Universities

Lynchburg College
Knight-Capron Library
Lynchburg, Virginia

College Students:

Students at Randolph-Macon Woman's College and Sweet Briar College are welcome to borrow materials on a reciprocal basis and to use services and materials available on-site.

Central Virginia Community College students, upon the recommendation of the CVCC librarian, may apply for loan privileges and may use services and materials available on-site.

Students at Virginia University of Lynchburg may apply for loan privileges and may use services and materials available on-site.

Students at other colleges and universities may use the library, on an occasional basis, as a resource that supplements the services and materials provided by their home institution. As such, the Lynchburg College Library does not act as their principal provider of library and information services and resources. The library does not extend borrowing privileges to this category of visitor.

Hamilton College
Burke Library
Clinton, New York

Area Residents, Area College Students and Summer Programs

Area residents, area college students and most summer program participants may check out up to 20 books for a period of 28 days. Books may be renewed twice. These patrons may not recall a book from another borrower. Fines are assessed at $.50 per day per book up to the maximum of $40.00 per book. Recalls are fined at $5.00 per day per book up to the maximum ($40.00).

University of California Berkeley
University of California Berkeley Libraries
Berkeley, California

Currently enrolled California State University or community college students who need the UC Berkeley collections for research may purchase a six-month Library borrowing privileges card by presenting a current student registration card showing an expiration date or a copy of their current class schedule. The fee is $25.

High School Students and Youth

Niagara University
Niagara University Library
Niagara University, New York

High School Students

If you are a high school student participating in Niagara University's NUSTEP program, you can obtain a Library Card that allows you to check out a maximum of 10 books for 28 days. To do this, you must bring two documents to the Library:

- Your NUSTEP ID card, which you obtained from the NUSTEP Office. This will serve as your Library Card.
- The slip called Request for Borrowing Privileges, also obtained from the NUSTEP Office. Your teacher must sign it first, but you only need to present this slip the first time you check out books.

High School students not participating in the NUSTEP program can still use the Library but can not check out books. In either case, you can use any Library database on-site. Research Assistance is available to you, but Interlibrary Loan Services are not.

University of Texas at Arlington
University Libraries
Arlington, Texas

UTA Libraries Youth Access Policy and Consent Form
Policy:

Persons under 18 years old who are not in the University of Texas at Arlington database may get a UTA library card to check out materials, provided a Parental Consent Form form is completed and filed at the circulation desk of the UTA Central Library. A card can be acquired through:

- The purchase of a guest borrower's card
- Participation in the UTA Libraries' K12 Connections Program

- Participation in the TexShare program
- The request of a UTA faculty or staff member for their children.

Youth may check out up to 5 books at a time for 21 days with the option of up to 2 renewals if the material is not needed by someone else. Honors, Advanced Placement, International Baccalaureate Students have extended privileges.

Academic Freedom Statement:

A strong intellectual freedom perspective is critical to the development of academic library collections and services that wish to meet the needs of the entire academic community. The Libraries at the University of Texas at Arlington purchase information resources aimed at adult, university-related curricula. In the interest of research and learning, it is essential that we make available information that represents a variety of perspectives on subjects that may be considered controversial.

It is our policy not to act *in loco parentis*, in keeping with the principles of equal access to information and materials for all customers. Therefore, the UTA Libraries do not restrict any customer, including children, from access to any type or class of materials or from any information in the Libraries. If a parent or guardian does not wish his or her child to access particular materials, the parent or guardian should discuss restrictions with his or her child in the context of their parent-child relationship.

Consent:

The purpose of the attached form is three-fold:

- The parent or guardian agrees to accept responsibility for the materials checked out by their child or young adult.
- The parent or guardian recognizes that the UTA Libraries are adult academic facilities and as such practice academic freedom of information for all registered library users and are not responsible for the topics of the materials chosen by their users.
- The parent or guardian understands that at the UTA Libraries academic freedom of information includes unfiltered and unmonitored access on the internet. For further information, see the UTA Libraries Internet Policy.

Failure to provide a completed consent form means that the youth will be unable to check out materials from the UTA Libraries.

Santa Monica College
Santa Monica College Library
Santa Monica, California

High School Students:

High school students may apply for a free courtesy library card. Application requires a signature from one parent of the applicant, and applicant must show current high school identification. Library card is valid until end of SMC's Spring semester. High school students may borrow up to five items at one time. Borrowing privileges will be terminated if fines owed to the Library exceed $10.00.

Colorado State University Pueblo
Colorado State University Pueblo Library
Pueblo, Colorado

District 60 and District 70 high school students with proper identification may check out four (4) items. Books, government documents and vertical file materials check out for a three-week period and audiovisual materials for a one-week period with renewal privileges. Students are not allowed to check out materials on another person's ID.

District 60, District 70, and PSAS (Pueblo School for the Arts and Sciences) faculty and staff with proper identification may check out four (4) items. Books, government documents, and vertical file materials check out for a three-week period and audiovisual materials for a one-week period with renewal privileges. Faculty members are not allowed to check out materials on another person's ID. Substitute teachers and family of faculty may check out four items with a picture ID.

University of Texas at Arlington
University Libraries
Arlington, Texas

K–12 Students and Teachers

Participants in the K12 Connections program are area high school students enrolled in Advanced Placement or Honors classes and local teachers and librarians for grades K–12.

K12 Connections participants can:

- Have up to 5 items checked out at one time
- Check out books for 21 days
- Check out special materials
- Renew materials 2 times for 21 days each time, unless an item has been placed on hold for another user

FORMS

Parental Consent for Minors' Use of Library Materials

University of Texas at Arlington
University Libraries
Arlington, Texas

The University of Texas at Arlington Libraries
Parental Consent for Youth Access to the Libraries

In keeping with increased computer security and the protection of minors in an open information environment, persons under the age of 18 who wish to access the computers in the Libraries and/or borrow books must file a completed Parental Consent Form with the Central Library Circulation Desk. This form serves as an application for a library card and gives permission for minors to register for a temporary computer account to access the Internet. Libraries' policies can be found at

http://library.uta.edu/Main/policies.uta.

Today's Date _____

Youth's Name _____

Last First MI

Age _____ Social Security No. _____

Youth is an Advanced Placement, International Baccalaureate, or Honors Student? ○Yes ○ No

Youth's School _____

City_____ State_____

Parent/Guardian Name _____

Last First MI

Parent/Guardian Address _____

City _____ State _____ Zip_____

Parent/Guardian Daytime Phone _____

Evening Phone _____

Parent/Guardian E-Mail _____

The minor above has my permission to use and check out materials owned by the UTA Libraries and to use the Internet in any of the UTA Libraries. I understand that there is a variety of information available in the Libraries and that some of that information is of an adult nature. I understand that at the UTA Libraries' policy of academic freedom means that Library use includes unfiltered and unmonitored access to the Internet. I agree that I will not hold the UTA Libraries or its staff responsible for the material my charge chooses to check out, use or view at the facilities. I also acknowledge that I am responsible for my charge's actions and for any fines or fees incurred by my charge while using UTA materials. I am aware that this form is valid for the current academic year (Fall thru Summer).

I have read the above statements and the Libraries' Academic Freedom Statement and Internet Policy on the reverse side of this document. I understand my responsibilities and the responsibilities of my charge.

Parent/Guardian Signature_____

Date _____

Present completed form along with applicant's photo ID at the Central Library Circulation Desk

You may be entitled to know what information UT Arlington (UTA) collects concerning you. You may review and have UTA correct this information according to procedures set forth in the UT System BMP#32. The law is found in sections 552.023 and 559.004 of the Texas Government Code.

Rev. 08.16.04

Staff Use Only _____ Voyager Staff Initials:

_____ OIT Database Date:

_____ BR06 Notes:

_____ UR17

UTA Libraries Academic Freedom Statement

A strong intellectual freedom perspective is critical to the development of academic library collections and services that wish to meet the needs of the entire academic community. The Libraries at the University of Texas at Arlington purchase information resources aimed at adult, university-related curricula. In the interest of research and learning, it is essential that we make available information that represents a variety of perspectives on subjects that may be considered controversial.

It is our policy not to act in loco parentis, in keeping with the principles of equal access to information and materials for all customers. Therefore, the UTA Libraries do not restrict any customer, including children, from access to any type or class of materials or from any information in the Libraries. If a parent or guardian does not wish his or her child to access particular materials, the parent or guardian should discuss restrictions with his or her child in the context of their parent-child relationship.

UTA Libraries Internet Policy

Information Philosophy: The University of Texas at Arlington Libraries respect the rights of users and ensure their means to have free and open access to ideas and information, which is fundamental to the learning process and the university experience. To this end, the UTA Libraries will protect intellectual freedom, promote information literacy, encourage lifelong learning, and develop collections, resources, and services that meet the informational and educational needs of the University's diverse user community. The UTA Libraries respect the users' rights to privacy in accessing information so long as users obey applicable policies and laws.

The Internet: The Internet, as an information resource, enables the UTA Libraries to provide information beyond the confines of its own collections. It allows access to ideas, information, and commentary from around the world. While the Internet offers a wealth of material that is personally, culturally, and professionally enriching to individuals of all ages, it also enables access to some material that may be offensive, disturbing, inaccurate, or illegal under U.S. law. The UTA Libraries cannot police this global network and takes no responsibility for its content. Rather, each individual user must take responsibility for his or her own activities on the Internet.

The use of the Internet must be consistent with the mission of the UTA Libraries, the policies of the University, and the laws of the State of Texas. These policies and laws include but are not limited to:

- UTA's policy on sexual harassment, www.uta.edu/eoaa/broc.html
- UTA's computer usage policy, www.uta.edu/uta/wwwteam/citup.html
- Chapter 43, section 21, subchapter B of the Texas Penal Code, referring to the display of obscene materials, www.capitol.state.tx.us/statutes/pe/pe0004300.html#pe007.43.21
- The Digital Millennium Copyright Act (U.S. Copyright Office Summary), www.loc.gov/copyright/legislation/dmca.pdf

Access to the Internet over library computers is a privilege granted to users, and the Libraries reserve the right to suspend or amend this privilege if a user:

- Violates Texas obscenity laws
- Violates campus computer usage policies
- Harasses others including, but not limited to, sexual harassment
- Intentionally damages or destroys equipment, software, or data belonging to the Libraries or to other users, including adding, altering, or deleting files on library workstations or other library computer equipment
- Copies materials protected by copyright law beyond the bounds of fair use
- Violates software or database license agreements
- Violates or attempts to violate computer system or network integrity, including attempts to bypass network security functions, obtain restricted passwords, or alter the configuration of library workstations in any way
- Uses the Internet for any illegal activity

The decision to suspend or limit a patron's use will be made at the discretion of the Dean of Libraries. Use of the Libraries' workstations will be on a first-come, first-served basis.

Proxy Borrowing Form

Northern Arizona University
Cline Library
Flagstaff, Arizona

Required fields are indicated with an asterisk (*).

Please set up a proxy card for me:

*First Name: [ ]   *Last Name: [ ]

Email: [ ]

* Library Barcode # (format 60138100–xxxxxxxx): [ ]

Campus Department and P.O. Box:

[ ]

Campus Telephone No.: [ ]

* Full name(s) of research assistant(s) authorized to use the card:

* Student ID number(s) of assistant(s):

The proxy card should expire on:

○ Last day of Spring Semester
○ Last day of Summer Session
○ Last day of Fall Semester

Pick up method:

○ Please mail card to my campus address
○ I or my assistant will pick up card at the Circulation Desk

Questions? Contact

Western Illinois University
Western Illinois University Library
Macomb, Illinois

Permission for a Graduate Assistant to Checkout
Library Materials and Pull Periodical Articles

Please allow _____ ID#_____
(Name of Graduate Assistant)

To checkout library materials and pull periodicals to be photocopied on my behalf.

I agree to abide by the following conditions:

A. Conditions for Checkout of Library Materials

- All materials are to be checked-out in my name and I take full responsibility.
- Periodicals may be checked out for 3 days.
- Other library materials may be borrowed for the normal checkout period.
- Only circulating items are available for checkout (no Archives, Reference, etc.).
- The student will locate and bring the items to the Circulation Desk for checkout.

B. Conditions for Pulling Periodical Articles

- My Graduate Assistant will pull the volumes and bring them to the Periodicals Desk.
- My Graduate Assistant will fill out each citation slip.
- I will not submit more than 100 pages per day to be photocopied.
- My Graduate Assistant will fill out the address label.

(Photocopies will be returned via Campus Mail to the Faculty Member.)

_____   Name: _____
(Faculty signature)   (Faculty member, please print legibly)

Date: _____ ID#: _____

Dep't: _____ Phone: _____

I understand all the above points: _____
(Graduate Assistant signature)

Send completed form via Campus Mail.

HOLDS AND RECALLS

Requests for Holds and Recalls on Material

Binghamton University
Binghamton University Libraries
Binghamton, New York

Recall Policy

Library books may be recalled, immediately, if needed for Reserve, after two weeks, if requested by another patron. A recall automatically reduces the loan period for a book and a notification of the new due date is sent to the borrower. Material must be returned by the date given on the recall notice regardless of the original due date. A $1.00 per day fine is assessed for the late return of recalled books. The maximum recall fine per book is $15.00.

Hudson Valley Community College
Dwight Marvin Library
Troy, New York

Holds and Recalls

Faculty may place a hold on books that have been checked out. Once the items are returned to Circulation, they will be put aside for the faculty member and that member will be notified. Books are then held for three days. If the faculty member has not picked up the items after three days they are then re-shelved. Faculty loans are subject to recall after the initial three-week checkout period.

New York University
Bobst Library
New York, New York

Holds and Recalls

If you need a book that is not currently available, you may request that a Recall be placed on the book. The user who has the book will be sent a notice alerting them that the book has been requested. When the book becomes available, we will notify you by email and hold the book for 14 days. Requests for recalls may be placed at the Express line at the Circulation desk, or directly through BobCat by clicking on the "Recall/Request" button on the left-hand side of the item record.

If you request a recall on a book that is not already due within 14 days, the book will become due in 14 days. The notice sent to the patron will specify the new due date.

Note that items that have been recalled from you must be returned by the due date specified in the recall notice, regardless of the original due date or the due date stamped in the back of the book. Recalled books which become overdue accrue fines at the rate of $1/day and block your record so that you cannot check out or renew any books until the recalled items are returned.

Also keep in mind that you are responsible for responding to recall notices even if you are out of town or otherwise indisposed at the time that the notice is sent, or when the book becomes due. Books may be recalled between semesters and over the summer; this often occurs when a book is required for course reserve.

Remember that all books are subject to recall at any time.

Santa Monica College
Santa Monica College Library
Santa Monica, California

Holds on Students' College Records

When a student accrues over $15.00 of charges (overdue fines and/or lost material, a hold will be placed on the student's college record, preventing the student from registering for future classes, obtaining grades, transcripts, etc. The hold from the student's record will be removed when the library materials are returned and/or fines are paid.

FINES, FEES, BLOCKS, SUSPENSIONS, AND LIBRARY CARDS

Library Cards/ID Cards

Illinois College
Schewe Library
Jacksonville, Illinois

To check out any item, you will need your student I.D. The first time you check out an item, the library staff will activate the barcode on the back of your I.D. This barcode will not only allow you to check out, it will also allow you to check your own patron record at any terminal in the library. THE LIBRARY CANNOT CHECK ANYTHING OUT TO YOU WITHOUT YOUR I.D.!

New York University
Bobst Library
New York, New York

Identification Cards

You must present a current school ID card in order to check out or renew books. There are no exceptions.

If your card is lost or stolen, be sure to let us know immediately. You will be held responsible for any items checked out on your card if you do not inform us that it is missing.

Any time you obtain a new or replacement ID card, you must activate it for library use in person at the library's main circulation desk.

FINES AND FEES

Binghamton University
Binghamton University Libraries
Binghamton, New York

Fines and Fees

Fine Structure:

A fine structure for the late return or Renewal of library materials has been established to assure all patrons maximum access to Library materials. Repeated, flagrant violations will be considered cause for suspension of borrowing privileges.

Circulating books: $0.10 per day per book to a maximum of $10.00 per item.

Recalled books: $1.00 per day per book to a maximum of $15.00 per item.

Reserve Material: 1–hour & 2–hour loans: $0.02 per minute to a maximum of $50.00 per item. 1–Day & 2–Day loans: $3.00 per day to a maximum of $50.00 per item.

Videos & DVD's: $3.00 per day to a maximum of $50.00 per item.

Interlibrary Loan Materials: $1.00 per day per item.

La Sierra University
La Sierra University Library
Riverside, California

Regular books: When a book is 14 days overdue a bill of $50.00 per book will be generated and sent to the user. This includes $40.00 for the cost of the book and a $10.00 non-refundable processing fee. In the event that the cost of an item not returned significantly exceeds the standard fee, the library reserves the right to charge a fee based on the actual replacement cost.

If materials are returned prior to the generation of the bill no charge will be incurred. This means you have a 14 day grace period, which begins on the due date. If materials are returned after the generation of the bill, the $10.00 fee per book will stand.

Reserve materials: Fines for overdue reserve materials have increased and are as follows:

- 2 hour reserve $1/hour or fraction thereof 15 minutes grace period
- 1 day reserve $1/hour or fraction thereof 30 minutes grace period
- 3 day reserve $5/day No grace period
- 7 day reserve $5/day No grace period

Periodicals: Fines for overdue periodicals are $1.00 an hour or fraction thereof. If fines are not paid, a bill of not less than $5.00 will eventually be submitted to the Student Accounts Office. When materials are not returned, a bill of $20.00 will also be included with any fine forwarded to the Student Accounts Office.

All fines: Any bill left unpaid will be posted to the user's student account 4 weeks from the generation date.

If fines are not paid, a bill of not less than $5.00 will eventually be submitted to the Student Accounts Office.

When materials are not returned, a bill for the cost of the materials will also be included with any fine forwarded to the Student Accounts Office.

Milwaukee Area Technical College
Milwaukee Area Technical College Library
Milwaukee, Wisconsin

Library Fines

Library fines, either from overdue items or from lost materials, apply to all MATC students, faculty, and staff. To help insure that each MATC patron has equal access to library resources, return loaned materials promptly by their due date to the appropriate MATC campus library.

Fines are NOT handled by the library

When an item is overdue:

- Bring in the item(s) as soon as possible to the library.
- Ask the Circulation staff for an overdue fine slip.
- Take the overdue fine slip to the MATC campus Cashier's office to pay the fine.
- Until all fines are paid, student transcripts or grades will not be released.
- No fines are charged over weekends and holidays when the library is closed.

Overdue Fines for Books from the General Stacks

There is a one week grace period.

After the one week grace period, the overdue fine for a book is $.40 per day, per item.

The maximum overdue fine for a book is $10 unless the item is declared lost (see Fine for Lost Items).

Overdue Fines for Videocassettes and Reserve Items

There is NO grace period.

The overdue fine for all videocassettes and reserve items is $1 a day per item.

The maximum overdue fee for a videocassette and reserve item is $10.

Fines for Lost Items

Any item that is not returned five weeks from its due date is declared lost by the library. Also, any item that has been stolen is treated as a lost item. Fines for lost items are:

Books from the General Stacks:

A total of:

The current book price listed in "Books in Print" or $35, whichever is higher

Plus a non-refundable $10 processing fee

And the maximum overdue fee of $10.

Videocassettes and Reserve Items: $10.

Refunds

Colorado State University Pueblo
Colorado State University Pueblo Library
Pueblo, Colorado

If the charge has been paid for a lost book and the book is later returned, the money will be refunded or credited to the patron's account at the accounting office, minus the fine which is computed on the basis of the day the material is returned. Maximum fines are $15.00 for books, $10.00 for government documents and vertical file items and $35.00 for audiovisual materials. Fines for lost government documents and vertical file materials cannot be refunded.

Santa Monica College
Santa Monica College Library
Santa Monica, California

Refunds

If a lost and paid for item is found and returned to the Library in good condition within three months of payment, the Library will issue a refund, minus the $15.00 processing fee. Receipt of payment must be presented to receive the refund.

Overdue Fines for Various Media

Colorado State University Pueblo
Colorado State University Pueblo Library
Pueblo, Colorado

Library Materials: Policy for Overdue and Lost Items

Library patrons will be mailed four overdue notices, a final notice, a lost notice and a billing notice.

Fines are 25 cents per day for each overdue book, government document, and vertical file item. Once an item is two weeks overdue, the fines will begin accumulating and must be collected.

Audiovisual fines are $5.00 for the first day overdue and $1.00 for each succeeding day.

Reserve fines are $1.00 for the first hour and 50 cents for each succeeding hour. There is no maximum fine for reserve items. If a reserve item is overdue and it is the only copy available at the Circulation desk, the fine will be DOUBLED. Faculty and staff are not charged daily fines, although they are required to pay for lost materials. Reserve fines are non-refundable. NO patron is immune from video fines. (Additional video policies are enumerated in another document.)

Final overdue notices for all patrons are sent when an item is 60 days overdue. A lost notice is sent approximately 3 days after the final notice is sent. The billing notice is the last notice generated. The lost notice encumbers the patron with the CSU-Pueblo accounting office for the cost of replacing the item.

Houston Community College System
Houston Community College Libraries
Houston, Texas

2.108.1 Book Overdues

2.108.1.1   A book has a loan period of two weeks. All books become overdue if not returned or renewed by the due date.

2.108.1.2   Overdue notices will be sent the day following the due date and again one week following the due date if material is still not returned. When overdue letters are returned because of an incorrect address, library staff is to insert a message in the INNOPAC patron record that reads: Overdue Notice Returned. Verify Address—date, initials.

2.108.1.3   Books may be renewed within 4 days following the due date for a total of 14 days from the original due. Books can also be renewed online via the HCCS library catalog.

2.108.1.4   Penalties for books overdue at the end of the semester will be assessed as follows:
• cataloged book—$40.00 per book
• uncataloged paperback—$8.00 per book

2.108.1.5   HCCS student records will receive negative service indicators for any items overdue at the end of the semester.

2.108.2 Audio-Visual Media Overdues

2.108.2.1   Media is loaned for a 4 day period to instructors and Training and Development members. Media becomes overdue if not returned or extended by the date due.

2.108.2.2   If not returned on the date due, the patron will be contacted immediately, followed by a written overdue letter.

2.108.2.3   The library reserves the right to suspend borrowing privileges for anyone who abuses the system and deprives others of their access to audio-visual materials.

2.108.2.4   Penalties for media materials overdue at the end of the semester will be assessed as follows:
• media—actual cost of each item
• overdue videotapes—$1.00 per day for overdue developmental math/algebra tapes (The total amount due should be determined by the Library/LRC Department Chair.)

2.108.3 Equipment Overdues

2.108.3.1   If library equipment is not returned on time, a phone call must be made to check up on the return of the equipment. If still overdue a week following the telephone call, an overdue letter should be sent. If the equipment is not returned within two weeks following the letter, the circulation supervisor should make sure that a second letter is sent, with a copy to the person's immediate supervisor. If the equipment is not returned within one week of this second letter, the matter should be referred to the appropriate chair.

2.108.3.2   The library reserves the right to suspend privileges for anyone who abuses the system and deprives others of their access to audio-visual equipment.

2.108.4 Reserve Materials Overdues

2.108.4.1   If library reserve material is not returned on time, a phone call must be made to check up on the return of the item(s).

2.108.4.2   An overdue notice will be sent the day after material becomes overdue.

2.108.4.3   If material is not returned after 5 days a second overdue notice will be sent and the student will be blocked from further library checkouts and will receive a negative service indicator in SPIN.

Blocking Records

Hudson Valley Community College
Dwight Marvin Library
Troy, New York

Overdue Materials

At the end of each semester, faculty overdue notices are mailed to those faculty members who have failed to return books to the library. Instructors and professors are not charged fines, however faculty borrowing privileges may be suspended when materials have not been returned after one academic year. In addition, borrowing privileges may be suspended for gross failure to observe regulations.

New York University
Bobst Library
New York, New York

Blocks

Your account will be blocked, so that you cannot check out or renew any items, for any of the following reasons:

- You owe a total of $5.00 or more in fines and fees.
- Any book on your record has become "lost" (50 days overdue).
- Any book which has been recalled from you has not been returned by the new due date.
- Any mail we send you is returned by the post office.

Xavier University
Xavier University Library
Cincinnati, Ohio

You may be blocked from borrowing or placing a hold for the following reasons:
- Charges to your library record have exceeded the maximum amount.
- Borrowed items exceed the maximum number of allowed.
- Holds placed exceed the maximum number of allowed.
- The item has been recalled by a Xavier or OhioLINK faculty member.

There are limits to the number of items that can be placed on hold, the amount charged to a library record, and the number of items borrowed. These limits vary for Xavier (XU) and OhioLINK (OL) materials as well as by patron type. Once these limits have been reached, your library record may be blocked from borrowing and placing holds.

University of California Berkeley
University of California Berkeley Libraries
Berkeley, California

Autoblock Policy

The Library implemented an automated blocking policy for all categories of patrons. This policy
- ensures that more of the Library's materials are available in-house for browsing, consultation and circulation,
- elicits a timely response to Library requests for return of materials from its patrons, and
- reduces administrative overhead.

Borrowers who do not return materials by their original or renewal due date are blocked from enacting any circulation functions once a grace period has expired. Notices generated by the GLADIS Autocirc System advise borrowers of pending block activity; e.g., overdue and recall notices state that failure to return items by a specified date may result in blocking of circulation privileges. Specific functions which are blocked include: checkout, recall, search, and page from storage.

Upon return of the overdue item(s), the patron is automatically unblocked and normal circulation privileges restored.

Note:

To further assist borrowers in avoiding blocks, the GLADIS circulation systems allows any patron to run an inventory of all materials charged to their library ID. (See "help inventory" on GLADIS.) In the event that a patron has already been blocked, these on-line inventories indicate which unit's materials are causing the block(s).

Automated block does not replace and is separate from a manual block input at the Library Privileges Desk in Doe Library.

Each Library unit may elect a special password enabling override of blocked status at any point.

Appeals on blocking follow regular procedures; i.e. unit head, AUL.

Replacement billing is not affected by this policy.

Payment Methods for Fines and Fees

University of South Alabama
University Libraries
Mobil, Alabama

Forms of Payment: Payments may be made by cash, check, money order, Visa or MasterCard. To obtain immediate clearance of a hold so that a transcript may be issued, payment should be made by cash, money order or credit card. A two-week delay is required when payment is made by personal check. A fee will be assessed for a returned check.

The University prohibits check cashing, and change cannot be given on checks made out for an amount greater than what is to be paid. Cash advances on credit cards are also prohibited by the University.

The Ohio State University
The Ohio State University Libraries
Columbus, Ohio

Lost and Billed Items

Long overdue items are assumed lost, and a lost item charge will be added to the borrower's record. The charges are $140 for books and $170 per volume for bound journals (these charges include a $40 processing fee, plus a billing charge, which will usually be $10 for OSU items). If the items are returned, the replacement/processing cost will be waived, but the billing fee will be retained (Note: OhioLINK books have a billing fee of $50.00). Patrons with lost and billed items are blocked from borrowing until the charges are settled with the Library Business Office.

In lieu of Lost and Billed charges, the Libraries provide the option to accept purchase of a replacement book with payment of the processing and billing fees noted above. OhioLINK replacements must be approved by the owning institution; please contact the Library Business Office prior to purchasing a replacement book.

Items reported as returned will be searched for promptly in all library locations. If the items are not found, you will be charged a replacement cost.

Payment of Fines

All other Patron Fines and charges can be paid by cash, check (made payable to the Ohio State University Libraries), or major credit card. Payment may be made in person during regular office hours (M–F, 8:00am–4:30pm, closed holidays) at the Thompson (Main) Library Business Office, Room 107; by phone

(292-2400) during office hours (credit cards only), and by mail (no credit cards) at 1858 Neil Ave., Columbus, OH 43210.

Payment plans are available; contact the Business Office for additional information.

Patrons of the Health Sciences Library, Law Library and Regional campus Libraries, should pay fines at those locations.

Appealing Suspension of Library Privileges

Ball State University
Ball State University Library
Muncie, Indiana

Appeal of Fines and Costs

Appeals of library fines and costs must be initiated within ninety calendar days following the date the borrowed material was due for return to the Library. Appeals of assessments must first be directed to the designated personnel at the service location where the material was borrowed. If unresolved at the service location level, appeals may be continued through successive levels of supervision within the Library's Public Services. If unresolved within the Library's Public Services, appeals may be directed to the University Senate Library Subcommittee. (Staff at the service location will, on request, identify the designated personnel, who will explain the route of appeal.)

Appeals once begun must proceed at the borrower's initiative in a timely and reasonable fashion. If a borrower fails to initiate and pursue an appeal within the prescribed time period, penalties approved by the Board of Trustees will result. Appeals made to the Library Committee will be judged on behalf of the University community; the Committee's judgments will be advisory to the Library administration.

The Ohio State University
The Ohio State University Libraries
Columbus, Ohio

Appealing Library Charges

Please try to resolve non-OhioLINK fine questions or problems first at the items's owning location. Request to speak to the circulation supervisor at the specific library.

Unresolved problems may be sent to the Library Business Office, Main Library. Appeals must be presented to the Business Office in person or in writing within six (6) months of the fine date to be considered and should include copies of receipts, library notices, and other useful documentation.

All reasonable concerns related to Library charges will be considered; however, the following are NOT considered reasons on which an appeal can be based:

Lack of understanding of Library policies. Circulation policies are available on the web and are the responsibility of the patron to read and understand.

Unwillingness to take responsibility for materials checked out to you which you loaned to another person or allowed others to use.

Non-receipt, late receipt, or inattention to library mail. Renewal reminders are sent as a courtesy by the Libraries; therefore, it is the patrons' responsibility to monitor their circulation records and ensure prompt renewal of items with or without these reminders. Patrons not reading e-mail due to conferences, vacations, holidays, quarter breaks, etc, are still responsible for responding. It is the patron's responsibility to make arrangements for maintenance of their account during these times of absence.

Central Oregon Community College
Central Oregon Community College Campus Library
Bend, Oregon

You may appeal COCC library charges, if you believe they have been mistakenly assessed or if extenuating circumstances may warrant reduction or cancelation of the charges. Appeals should be made within 30 calendar days of the original billing by Student Enrollment. You may complete an Appeal of Library Charges form, also available at Circulation. You will be notified of the outcome by email.

Q: What are reasons for which an appeal will be denied?

A: The following reasons are generally not regarded as valid for canceling or reducing charges:

- Lack of knowledge of library policy
- Disagreement with library fine or fee structure
- Inability to pay fees and charges
- Material loaned to a third party
- Non-receipt or late receipt of library reminder notice
- Returning items to libraries other than the COCC library
- Being out of town
- Forgetting the due date
- Term breaks, illness, leaves, vacations, exams, car problems, etc.

FORMS

Form to Appeal Lost-Book Charges or Fines

Virginia Tech
Virginia Tech University Libraries
Blacksburg, Virginia

Newman Library Fine/Book Appeal Form

Patron Information

* = Required fields

Patron ID# * [_____] (usually the ID# on your Hokie Passport, VA Drivers License or Library Borrower Card)

Name * [_____]

Address * [_____]

Phone No. [_____] E-mail * [_____]

Item(s) in Question

Call No.	Item No.	Title	Due Date	Date Returned	Fines on Item

Why should these items and/or fines be removed from your account?

*The information I have given in this form is true to the best of my knowledge.

Submit   Reset

Chapter 21

LOANS, RENEWALS, AND REQUESTS

LOANS AND RENEWALS OF MATERIAL

Standard Loan Periods

East Carolina University
Joyner Library
Greenville North Carolina

Joyner Material Types (Books, Videos, etc.) & Loan Periods

Joyner Stacks Books, Joyner North Carolina Collection Books, and Government Documents

- ECU Undergraduate students—4 weeks
- ECU Graduate students—fixed due date at the end of the semester
- ECU Staff—4 weeks
- ECU Faculty—fixed due date in May

TRC Curriculum Books

- Undergrads—2 weeks
- Grads—2 weeks
- Staff—2 weeks
- Faculty—Fixed due date in May

TRC Basal Books (NO RENEWALS TO ANYONE)

- Undergrads—2 days
- Grads—I week
- Staff—2 days
- Faculty—I week

Audiovisuals* (Videos, DVD's, etc.) (NO RENEWALS TO ANYONE)

- Undergrads—I week
- Grads—I week
- Staff—I week
- Faculty—I week

Joyner Reference Collection Books

- DO NOT CIRCULATE

Joyner Periodicals

- Undergrads—DO NOT CHECK OUT
- Grads—DO NOT CHECK OUT
- Staff—DO NOT CHECK OUT
- Faculty—Overnight (Current Periodicals see Reference Desk)

For material not listed as at Circulation: (252) 328-6518

FINES for late Audiovisuals are $1.00 per item, per day

Henderson State University
Huie Library
Arkadelphia, Arkansas

What Can Be Checked Out & Length of Checkout Period

All books (except bestsellers) and music scores from the circulating collection may be checked out for 28 days. Renewals must be made in person. There are no renewals for items with a hold on them.

Bestsellers check out for 14 days. Renewals must be made in person.

Students may have a maximum of three audio books checked out at any given time. Checkout period is for 14 days. No renewals.

Henderson State University students may check out any video. Ouachita Baptist University students may check out only videos from the popular collection. Students may have a maximum of three videos charged out at any given time. Checkout period is 3 days. No renewals.

Ouachita Baptist University students who need to view educational videos may do so only in the Audio-Visual Room at Huie Library.

Videos from the Reserve Collection are checked out for the period of time specified by the instructor.

All other material may not be checked out.

Henderson State University and Ouachita Baptist University students have reciprocal borrowing privileges.

Henderson State University faculty may check out any book (except bestsellers) from the circulating collection for 80 days. Ouachita Baptist University faculty may check out books for 80 days.

Faculty/staff may have a maximum of three audio books checked out at any given time. Checkout period is for 14 days. No renewals.

Faculty/staff may check out any video in the collection. A maximum of three videos may be checked out at any given time. Check out period is for three days. No renewals.

Henderson State University and Ouachita Baptist University dependents may borrow books from the circulating collection for a period of 28 days. Renewals must be made in person.

Henderson State University and Ouachita Baptist University dependents may have a maximum of three audio books charged out at any given time. Loan period is for 14 days. No renewals.

Dependents may have a maximum of three videos charged out at any given time. Only videos from the popular collection may be checked out to dependents. These are videos in the bin near the circulation desk that have a plastic coated description. No renewals.

Community patrons may have a maximum of three items checked out at any given time. This can be a combination of any of the following: bestsellers, books, scores, audio books, and popular videos/DVDs. Renewals must be made in person.

Community patrons may only check out videos from the popular collection. Popular videos are those with plastic coated descriptions that are kept in bins near the circulation desk. Any video/DVD can be viewed in the Audio-Visual room.

Checkout period for videos is three days. No renewals.

Loan Periods for Faculty

New York University
Bobst Library
New York, New York

Loan Periods

The due date will be stamped in each book at the time of checkout. Media loans will be accompanied by a printed receipt with the due date and time clearly stamped. Note that because due dates may be changed by remote renewal or when an item is recalled (see below), the stamp will not always reflect the actual due date. To check the due date of any item checked out to you, you may view your library record online (instructions on viewing your record and renewing books online). You may also request a printout of your record from the Full Service line at the Circulation desk when you visit the library.

Loan type	Standard Loan Period
General Collection	120 days
Items with Holds on them	14 days
Special loans	Set by Reference or Avery Fisher Center
Interlibrary Loans	set by ILL
Journal Loans	1 day
Leisure Collection	14 days

General Collection refers to circulating books from the stacks. Circulating books are located on floors 2, 4, 5, 7, 8, 9, and 10. Non-circulating books and bounds journals, also found on these floors, may not ordinarily be checked out.

Special loans refer to non-circulating books or media items that have been approved for short-term checkout by a librarian in the appropriate reference center: General & Humanities (1st floor); Avery Fisher Center for Music & Media (2nd floor); Business & Government Documents (6th floor); or Science (9th floor). The loan period is set by the librarian, and is usually overnight or shorter. For current media loan periods see http://library.nyu.edu/afc/faculty.html

Interlibrary Loans may be checked out until the due date set by the Interlibrary Loan department.

Journals Loans: Bound journals may be checked out overnight.

Leisure Collection refers to the current titles in fiction and non-fiction for recreational reading, shelved on Lower Level 2.

Loan Periods for Retired Faculty

Florida International University
Florida International University Libraries
Miami, Florida

Library Services available to FIU Retired Faculty:

- Use of Library resources and services in-house.
- Use of the Intercampus Loan and Interlibrary Loan Services.
- Checking-out library materials (use your FIU I.D. card).
- Recall, Renew, and In-Process requests—both online and in person at the Circulation Desk.
- Full use of photocopiers (copy card purchase is required).
- Full use of networked printers for library computers (copy card purchase is required).
- Access to all library databases, including the library catalog and full-text resources.

Additional information:

- Your FIU ID card is your permanent library card. Please retain this card after you have retired.
- There is no limit to the number of checkouts you may have at any time.
- The loan period is for 3 months; renewals allowed unless there is a recall or hold request for the item.
- Audio-Visual materials are available, with some restrictions.
- Remote access to some electronic databases maybe restricted because of licensing and contractual agreements with vendors.

Questions?

Please contact the Circulation Desk.

Noncirculating Material Loans

University of Scranton
Weinberg Memorial Library
Scranton, Pennsylvania

The University of Scranton's Web site is changing, and policies will be separated from information on the updated sites.

Reference books and current and bound periodicals do not circulate. Reference books, journals, and reserves must be used in the building. "In-Library use only" materials must be returned to the Circulation Desk before the Library closes. Most media materials do not circulate and must be used in the viewing/listening area. Music CDs, if not on Reserve, may be charged out for 3 days. Students may make special arrangements to use media in classroom presentations.

Buena Vista University
University Library
Storm Lake, Iowa

Non-Circulating Materials

The following item types do not circulate (except as noted above): Reference Materials, Journals, Microforms, Special Collections.

Copies of pertinent pages can be made, but the item itself cannot be checked out. Change is available at the Circulation Desk for the library copiers. A scanner is also available.

Georgia State University
Georgia State University Library
Atlanta, Georgia

Circulation of Materials Designated as Reference and General Collection Non-Circulating Policy

Reference materials by their nature are commonly used to retrieve relatively short, specific pieces of information, rather than to be read cover-to-cover. The primary purpose of having a reference collection is to make such convenient sources of specific information readily available when needed by library patrons and by library personnel assisting patrons and carrying out other library operations. Non-circulating items in the General Collection have been designated as such in order to insure that they are available when needed by library patrons; the majority of these items are reference materials. For these reasons, reference materials and those designated as non-circulating, generally do not circulate. Any decision to allow a reference or non-circulating book to circulate is an exception to customary policy, and as such, should be made only in circumstances that warrant such an exception.

The decision to circulate a reference or non-circulating item is made according to the professional expertise of a librarian working at the reference desk. If the item is allowed to circulate, it will be authorized for a checkout period of no more than 3 hours. Only the appropriate subject librarian(s) or head of collection development can authorize a checkout period of more than 3 hours. If the subject librarian or head of collection development is not available to make this determination, for example on nights and weekends, a checkout period of greater than 3 hours will not be authorized.

In deciding whether or not to make an exception and allow a reference or non-circulating book to circulate, consideration will be given to faculty, staff, graduate students and undergraduate students, in that order. In addition, the following criteria will be considered:

- Can the patron's information need be met by an item in the circulating collection, such as a different book on the topic, a circulating dictionary, or a superseded edition of the same item?
- Can the need be met by an Internet site or library database?

- Is this a standard reference item that does or is likely to receive frequent or regular use and if so, should remain in the library?
- Is the item part of a set, and if removed, would negate the usefulness of the remaining items in the set?
- Is the item needed for a class assignment, so that others are likely to need the item?

University of Wisconsin River Falls
Chalmer Davee Library
River Falls, Wisconsin

Special Permission Checkout

A. Materials from the Reference Collection do not circulate outside of the library. Permission to check-out general non-circulating materials (e.g., reference books, periodicals, Curriculum Materials Center materials) to UWRF faculty, students and staff will be granted by librarians at the Reference Desk. Special permission to checkout non-circulating materials from the Reserve, Government Document and Archives collections will be granted by authorized staff in those departments.

B. The length of time that materials may be kept is determined by the librarian, based on the needs of the library user. The time period should be as short as possible.

Reference Materials Loans

Ferris State University
Ferris Library
Big Rapids, Michigan

Policy for Circulation of Reference Items

For a variety of reasons, materials designated as and housed in Reference collections represent a valuable, discrete portion of a library's overall holdings. Containing the most up-to-date statistical and informational resources, items in Reference collections traditionally do not circulate in order to help ensure access to these items by patrons at the time when they need to consult them.

Items may circulate from Reference, however, on a limited basis at the discretion of the Librarian or Library Associate on duty. Conditions which may warrant circulation of Reference materials include if a suitable substitute is not found within the circulating collection or if the information needed is too long to be photocopied easily. Whereas individual situations in which a patron may want to borrow a reference item will differ, circulation of Reference materials should remain a rare occurrence.

As a guideline, Reference materials may be checked-out to a Ferris State University faculty or staff member for a period that should not exceed an overnight or 24–hour period and to a Ferris student for a period that should not exceed 2 hours. A permission slip, delineating the duration of the check-out period and signed by a Librarian or Library Associate, is required for the Check-Out Desk to circulate Reference material.

Fines on Reference materials will be assessed at the highest rate currently allowed by the university for library items not returned on time. No "Grace Period" is accorded overdue Reference material.

Items located in Ready Reference and the Legal Collection, items currently in heavy demand due to a class assignment, and items which comprise part of a set should never circulate.

This policy applies to personal use by library patrons. Classroom or administrative use is considered on a case-by-case basis.

Hood College
Beneficial-Hodson Library
Frederick, Maryland

Overnight Reference Books Policy

At the discretion of the evening Reference Librarian, a reference book will be allowed to circulate one hour before the Library closes. The book must be returned one hour after the Library opens.

The following restrictions apply:

- "Ready-reference" titles kept at the Reference Desk do not circulate.
- Materials which are being heavily used for a class assignment do not circulate.
- Individual volumes from sets of reference books do not circulate.
- Students may borrow only one reference book at a time.

These books must be returned directly to a staff member at the Reference Desk. Do not place them in the outside book drop. Overdue fines will accrue at the rate of $1.00 per hour for each hour or fraction thereof until the books are returned.

Media Loans

La Sierra University
La Sierra University Library
Riverside, California

Media Materials Circulation

Audio tapes, compact discs, video tapes, slides, and films are available from Media Services. Video and audio tapes, as well as the Music CD Library, are maintained here, and may be checked out by faculty for use on campus, and by students for use in the library and outside with instructor approval. Students may watch video tapes and listen to audio cassettes in the carrels near our department.

We wish to urge the faculty to use our video tape library to store and maintain tapes they purchase for use in their department. We wish to improve the university's collection here in the library, and these materials are most beneficial when they are available to others, here in the library, rather than stored somewhere where no one maintains them or catalogues them

Illinois College
Schewe Library
Jacksonville, Illinois

CDs and Records

CDs are located in a cabinet across from the new book shelf, to your right as you enter the building. The cabinet is locked, so request a CD at the circulation desk. Records are housed on the lower level. You may request headphones at the circulation desk to use in the library or check the CDs or records out for three days.

Florida International University
Florida International University Libraries
Miami, Florida

Sound & Image AV Resources—Circulation Loan Periods

Circulation Services	Faculty/Staff/Adjunct/ Grad/PhD/Honor	Undergrad	Alumni/Associates/Certificate/Seflin/ Consortium/Other SUS/UM	Elders Institute
Videos (VHS & DVD)	2 weeks/6 titles	3 DAYS—6 TITLES AT A TIME		
Laser Discs VL	2 weeks/6 titles	2 hrs. class pre-sentations	IN-HOUSE USE ONLY NOT AVAILABLE FOR CHECKOUT	
Classroom/ Home Viewing FF	2 weeks/6 titles	3 DAYS—HOME VIEWING ONLY— NO IN-HOUSE USE		
Non-Circulating uvid, rest	2 weeks	2 hrs. class pre-sentations	IN-HOUSE USE ONLY NOT AVAILABLE FOR CHECKOUT	
3/4" Videos VT	Sent to Classroom (UP only)	2 hrs. class pre-sentations	IN-HOUSE USE ONLY NOT AVAILABLE FOR CHECKOUT	SENT TO CLASSROOM
AV Reserves	2 hrs; 24 hrs; 3–days	2 hrs; 24 hrs; 3–days	NOT AVAILABLE	
Distance Lear. & Feeds	N/A	2 HRS RESERVE—FOR STUDENTS REGISTERED IN COURSE ONLY		
Books-On-Tape AC or CD Kits KT	2 Weeks/2 Titles			
Films—16 mm	Sent to Classroom (UP only) or 2 weeks chkt	2 hrs class pre-sentations	IN-HOUSE USE ONLY NOT AVAILABLE FOR CHECKOUT	SENT TO CLASSROOM
Music CDs & LPs	2 Weeks—6 Titles			
Art Slides	3 months/unlimited	3 days/25 slides	IN-HOUSE USE ONLY NOT AVAILABLE FOR CHECKOUT	
CD-ROMs	2 Weeks/2 items			
AV Desk	3 months	3 Weeks		

Accompanying Materials

Gen. Col.	Yes
Reference	IN-HOUSE USE ONLY—NOT AVAILABLE FOR CHECK OUT
Periodicals	IN-HOUSE USE ONLY—NOT AVAILABLE FOR CHECK OUT
Gov. Documents	IN-HOUSE USE ONLY—NOT AVAILABLE FOR CHECK OUT

Circulation Services

Holds	Yes	For Class Presentations	NOT AVAILABLE
Intercampus ICL	Yes		
Interlibrary ILL	Yes	Yes	NOT AVAILABLE (Alumni-YES)

University of Texas at Arlington
University Libraries
Arlington, Texas

Borrowing Media Items

Media items owned by the UTA Libraries are kept at the Reserves Desk, but they have different borrowing rules from Reserves items.

Media items found at the Reserves Desk are:

- Videocassettes
- Audiocassettes
- LPs
- Filmstrips
- Slides
- CD-ROMs
- Other computer disks

Media Loan Periods:

- 4 days/1 renewal for an additional 4 days

Media Overdue Fines:

- $1.20 per day/$30 maximum fine
- When the maximum overdue fine is reached, we will bill you for the replacement of the item.

Bill-for-replacement charges consist of 3 parts:

- The replacement cost of the item, as determined by the Libraries' Collections & Information Resources Manager
- The overdue fine
- A processing fee of $35.00

Renewals

Milwaukee Area Technical College
Milwaukee Area Technical College Library
Milwaukee, Wisconsin

Renewal Policies

Renewals are granted to library users unless another library patron has placed a hold on the given item.

To renew materials from either the general stacks or the reserve collection:

Bring the item(s) to the library's Circulation and Reserve desk.

Renewals are not accepted over the telephone, through regular mail, or e-mail.

To request a hold for a library item, contact the library staff in person.

Oklahoma State University Center for Health Sciences
Medical Library
Tulsa, Oklahoma

Renewing Materials

Library items may be renewed once, providing they are not recalled, "lost," interlibrary loan materials, or reserve items. Center faculty may request a semester checkout with no renewals. Materials can be renewed via phone, fax, or in-person.

(For additional policies, please see the accompanying CD-ROM.)

Returns

New York University
Bobst Library
New York, New York

Returns

All books borrowed from Bobst Library must be returned to Bobst on or before the due date.

Interlibrary Loans and Special Loans must be handed directly to a Circulation assistant; they may not be returned to a book return bin.

Other books may be placed in a book return bin or handed directly to a Circulation assistant. Books that have not been returned in one of these manners are not considered to have been returned.

You are responsible for returning your library books by the due date even if you are out of town or otherwise indisposed on that date.

Remember that books cannot be checked in if they don't come to the Circulation desk; books which are left in the library without being properly returned will most likely remain on your record, becoming overdue.

Only items belonging to Bobst Library may be checked out, renewed, and returned at Bobst. Items belonging to other libraries (including Consortium libraries) must be returned to the owning library.

Oklahoma State University Center for Health Sciences
Medical Library
Tulsa, Oklahoma

Returning Materials

Collection materials may be returned to:

Circulation desk, or outside book drop in hall near Library entrance.

All reserve materials must be returned to the Circulation Desk.

Tulane University
Howard-Tilton Memorial Library
New Orleans, Louisiana

To Return a Book

When the library is open, a book should be returned to the drop at the Circulation Desk. Ask for a receipt, as proof that you returned the book.

When the library is closed, a book depository is available to the right of the main entrance for your convenience. However, General Reserve books are still subject to fines if not returned to the General Reserve counter.

Do not return a checked-out book to the shelf or place it on any of the book trucks throughout the building as the loan record is not cancelled until the book is returned to the Circulation Desk from which it was borrowed (or until it is dropped in the after-hours Book Depository.) A book will be subject to fines for any delay involved in its return to the Circulation Desk if it has been placed incorrectly in one of these areas.

Books may be returned to the bins located in the library lobby near the photocopiers on the first floor. However, patrons are strongly urged to bring the books to the circulation desk to get a receipt. A receipt is your proof that you returned the library material. When the library is closed you may return library material in the outdoor bin adjacent to the front door of the Howard-Tilton Memorial Library. If the bin is full (especially over long weekends or holidays), do not leave the library material on the ground or garbage cans. You may return them on the next day the library is open. You will not be charged fines for such a delay.

Renewals, Returns, and Recalls for Faculty

New York University
Bobst Library
New York, New York

Renewals

Renewal guidelines:

Books from the General Collection may be renewed remotely, or at Circulation.

Special loans may not usually be renewed. To request a renewal, bring the Special Loan item to the appropriate reference department.

Journal loans and books from the Leisure collection may not be renewed.

To request an interlibrary loan, log in to the Interlibrary Loan system.

Books from the General Collection may be renewed in person at Circulation (to renew in person, you must bring the books to the Circulation desk), by turning in a signed overdue notice or remotely on the web. Books may be renewed as many times as you wish as long as they have not been requested by other users or for course reserve. You might not be aware that a Hold has been placed on an item until the time you try to renew it.

Holds and Recalls

If you need a book that is not currently available, you may request that a Recall be placed on the book. The user who has the book will be sent a notice alerting them that the book has been requested. When the book becomes available, we will notify you by mail and hold the book for 14 days. Requests for recalls may be placed at the Express line at the Circulation desk, or directly through BobCat, by clicking on the "Recall/Request" button on the left-hand side of the item record..

If you request a recall on a book that is not already due within 14 days, the book will become due in 14 days. The notice sent to the patron will specify the new due date.

Note that items that have been recalled from you must be returned by the due date specified in the recall notice, regardless of the original due date or the due date stamped in the book. Recalled books which become overdue accrue fines at the rate of $1/day and block your record so that you cannot check out or renew any books until the recalled items are returned.

Also keep in mind that you are responsible for responding to recall notices even if you are out of town or otherwise indisposed at the time that the notice is sent, or when the book becomes due. Books may be recalled between semesters and over the summer; this often occurs when a book is required for course reserve.

Remember that all books are subject to recall at any time.

Returns

All books borrowed from Bobst Library must be returned to Bobst on or before the due date.

Interlibrary Loans and Special Loans must be handed directly to a Circulation assistant; they may not be returned to a book return bin.

Other books may be placed in a book return bin or handed directly to a Circulation assistant. Books that have not been returned in one of these manners are not considered to have been returned.

You are responsible for returning your library books by the due date even if you are out of town or otherwise indisposed on that date.

Only items belonging to Bobst Library may be checked out, renewed, and returned at Bobst. Items belonging to other libraries (including Consortium libraries) must be returned to the owning library.

REQUESTS FOR MATERIALS

Materials in Process

Columbia College
Columbia College Library
Chicago, Illinois

Requesting Materials In Process

If a Columbia student or faculty member urgently needs an item that is labeled No Holdings Available—check at Circulation Desk or Order Received in our Library catalog, they may submit a request for expedited processing of the material by Library staff from our Technical Services Department.

Next Steps

Please complete a Request Form for Material in Process available at the Reference or Circulation Desk. Attach to it a printout from our Library Catalog for the item in question. If you need assistance with completing the form or if you have questions, please check with staff at the Reference or Circulation Desk.

Library Technical Services staff will investigate and confirm the item's actual status. If there is a problem, we will contact you right away.

Library Technical Services staff will locate the in-process item within the department.

Library Technical Services staff will process the needed material within 48 hours after the item has been located.

When processing has been completed, the item will be brought to the Circulation Desk where it will be placed on the HOLD shelf under your name. Whoever placed the request for the material will be "first in line" to consult or check out the material (if permitted). Rush processing of an item does not grant circulating status to those already classified as non-circulating.

The Circulation Desk staff will notify you that the requested item is now available for use and it will remain on the HOLD shelf at the Circulation Desk for 24 hours only.

Boston College
Boston College Libraries
Boston, Massachusetts

On Order/In Process Requests

A request placed in Quest or at a circulation desk for an item designated on-order or in-process will automatically assign a rush status to the item and processing is expedited. Delivery time varies depending on whether the item is on site or still on order with a vendor.

Materials in Book Stacks

University of Washington
University of Washington Libraries
Seattle, Washington

Access

Most libraries and sections have open stacks with selected materials kept in closed areas, not accessible for browsing. All visitors are free to use materials in the library.

Auxiliary and storage stacks, Special Collections, and the Media Center are examples of closed stacks, materials that are unavailable for public browsing. Most reserve materials are also in closed stacks. Access to these materials is acquired through the appropriate public service desk. For those without UW borrower cards, service desks accept requests for daily retrieval of storage materials. For those with UW borrower cards, requests may be placed online throughout the UW Libraries Catalog.

University of Illinois at Urbana-Champaign
University Library
Urbana, Illinois

Bookstacks Access

In the interest of preserving an environment conducive for scholarship and research, the UIUC Library limits entrance to its Main Bookstacks primarily to faculty, staff, and students currently employed by or enrolled in the University of Illinois at Urbana-Champaign. UIUC faculty, graduate students, and staff are granted entrance upon presentation of a valid I-Card; UIUC undergraduate students should request a Bookstacks pass at the Main Circulation Desk or in Room 203 Main Library.

The following types of unaffiliated users with research needs, upon presentation of appropriate identification, may be issued a pass to enter the Main Bookstacks:

- Visiting U.S. or international scholars who are being hosted by a unit of the University of Illinois at Urbana-Champaign.
- UIUC emeritus faculty.
- Members of the University of Illinois President's Council and the University Librarian's Council.
- UIUC doctoral students who are currently not enrolled in classes.
- Faculty of other CARLI libraries in the state of Illinois.

Written requests for temporary exceptions to this policy should be addressed to Head of Central Circulation and Book stacks, Main Library.

Upon request, persons who currently hold a Book stacks pass, but who will become ineligible for entrance with this revised policy, will have their entrance privileges extended temporarily for two months from the date on which their current pass expires.

Please note that upon presentation of valid identification any resident of the state of Illinois, as well as many unaffiliated users not mentioned above, may request to have materials retrieved from the Book stacks for them. Please inquire about this service at the Main Circulation Desk or in Main Library.

Materials in Remote Stacks

University of Washington
University of Washington Libraries
Seattle, Washington

Access

Most libraries and sections have open stacks with selected materials kept in closed areas, not accessible for browsing. All visitors are free to use materials in the library.

Auxiliary and storage stacks, Special Collections, and the Media Center are examples of closed stacks, materials that are unavailable for public browsing. Most reserve materials are also in closed stacks. Access to these materials is acquired through the appropriate public service desk. For those without UW borrower cards, service desks accept requests for daily retrieval of storage materials. For those with UW borrower cards, requests may be placed online throughout the UW Libraries Catalog.

University of Illinois at Urbana-Champaign
University Library
Urbana, Illinois

Bookstacks Access

In the interest of preserving an environment conducive for scholarship and research, the UIUC Library limits entrance to its Main Bookstacks primarily to faculty, staff, and students currently employed by or enrolled in the University of Illinois at Urbana-Champaign. UIUC faculty, graduate students, and staff are granted entrance upon presentation of a valid I-Card; UIUC undergraduate students should request a Bookstacks pass at the Main Circulation Desk or in Room 203 Main Library.

The following types of unaffiliated users with research needs, upon presentation of appropriate identification, may be issued a pass to enter the Main Bookstacks:

- Visiting U.S. or international scholars who are being hosted by a unit of the University of Illinois at Urbana-Champaign.
- UIUC emeritus faculty.
- Members of the University of Illinois President's Council and the University Librarian's Council.
- UIUC doctoral students who are currently not enrolled in classes.
- Faculty of other CARLI libraries in the state of Illinois.

Written requests for temporary exceptions to this policy should be addressed to Head of Central Circulation and Book stacks, Main Library.

Upon request, persons who currently hold a Book stacks pass, but who will become ineligible for entrance with this revised policy, will have their entrance privileges extended temporarily for two months from the date on which their current pass expires.

Please note that upon presentation of valid identification any resident of the state of Illinois, as well as many unaffiliated users not mentioned above, may request to have materials retrieved from the Book stacks for them. Please inquire about this service at the Main Circulation Desk or in Main Library.

Materials at Bindery

Auburn University
Auburn University Libraries
Auburn University, Alabama

Binding and Receiving: If a volume has just been sent to Binding and a patron needs it, call to ask if it has indeed been sent. If the item is still in Binding, personnel in that department will find the item in the box and bring it to the reference desk for the patron. Ask the patron to return the volume to the Reference Desk; the librarian should return it to Binding. If Binding can't find record for the item, place a missing trace on it.

Library Courier Service

Virginia Tech
Virginia Tech University Libraries
Blacksburg, Virginia

What is the Library Courier Service?

The Library Courier Service delivers materials owned by University Libraries to the on-campus Virginia Tech branch libraries.

Requests for materials that are located at Newman Library are processed by the courier service and delivered to the appropriate branch library for pick up.

Library Courier Service also retrieves books from the return bins located across campus. The bins are checked several times a day and books are checked in as they are received.

Questions, comments, or suggestions regarding Library Courier Service can be directed to delivery. . .

How Do I Request Materials?

To request items from Storage or the branch libraries, complete and submit a Library Courier Service Request Form on-line. There is a limit of 15 items per person per day that can be requested. The request will be electronically mailed to the library where the requested item is located. Once received, the item will be searched, pulled, and delivered to the library pickup location of your choice.

Who Can Use the Courier Service? / What Materials Can I Request?

The Library Courier Service is open to all patrons of the Virginia Tech Libraries. This includes all Virginia Tech Faculty, Staff, Students (Undergraduates and Graduates), Virginia Tech Extension Agents and Virginia Residents.

Library material that can be checked-out (i.e. circulates) can be delivered to you at one of the library pickup locations. Items that can be requested vary for the branch libraries and Storage, depending on which library department owns the item. The Storage facility contains books, journals, Special Collections items, and media items. Items that are currently checked-out can be requested using the Place Request feature in Addison.

How Long Does It Take? / What is the Delivery Schedule?

Storage material requests and on-campus branch library requests usually require a 48 hour processing time to be delivered to the selected on-campus pick up location. Occasionally requests may take up to 5 business days to process due to request volume or citation problems. There are no deliveries on Saturday or Sunday.

Items delivered from the Resource Center at the Northern Virginia Center in Falls Church usually take 7–10 days to be delivered to the on-campus pick-up locations.

Deliveries are made to Newman Library and the other on-campus branches once a day with all deliveries completed by 5:00 pm.

Where Can I Have My Requests Delivered To?

Courier requests can be delivered to the Circulation Desk at any of the branches listed below.

On-Campus Library Branches:

- Carol M. Newman Library. Located between the on-campus University Bookstore and Squire's Student Center on The Mall.
- Veterinary Medicine Library. Located in the Virginia-Maryland Regional College of Veterinary Medicine on Duck Pond Drive.
- Art and Architecture Library. Located in room 302 on the third floor of Cowgill Hall.

Off-Campus Library Branch:

Resource Center at the Northern Virginia Center. Located in Falls Church, Virginia. Items requested from this branch are delivered via UPS. Patrons who wish to have materials owned by other branch libraries delivered to the Northern Virginia branch need to submit their requests using ILLiad.

Information on Library Materials

Books, Journals

Books that are located at any Virginia Tech branch library and are listed as Available on Addison can be delivered from one branch library to another branch library. Items that are checked out can be requested.

Journals that are located in Newman library, the Vet-Med library, the Art/Architecture library, and the Northern Virginia Center library are not allowed to circulate. As a result, these items must remain in their respective buildings. The branch libraries do not offer a photocopy service, so patrons must use these materials at the appropriate branch library.

Storage Material

Books and journals that are located at Storage can be delivered to any University Libraries branch for checkout. For more information about the Storage Facility, please visit the Storage Facility Web page.

Special Collections Material

Items from Special Collections that are housed at Storage can be requested using the Library Courier Request Form. These items are not allowed to circulate and must be viewed in the Special Collections area.

Media Items

There are media materials such as filmstrips, multimedia kits and phono records housed at Storage. Filmstrips and multimedia kits can be requested by faculty only. Phono records may be requested by faculty, staff, and students.

(For additional policies, please see the accompanying CD-ROM.)

Searches Requests

University of California Berkeley
University of California Berkeley Libraries
Berkeley, California

Searches

Borrowers may place a search request for materials not found on the shelf and not checked out. Borrowers will be notified of the status of the search request within one to two weeks.

Barton College
Willis N. Hackney Library
Wilson, North Carolina

Searches for Books

If you do not find a book in the stacks area, ask at the Circulation Desk. The staff will try to find out where the book is located. If the book can not be located at that time, they will assist you in placing a Search Request. Staff members will make three thorough searches for the book. You will be notified of the book's status after the first search. If the book is not found, you will be contacted only if a subsequent search is successful.

Books found will be held for one week after patron notification.

In the case that a Search Request is unsuccessful, the item will be considered for replacement at the discretion of the library director.

When dealing with items that are claimed to have been returned, and the Search Request has been unsuccessful, then the item will be designated as LOST. In this case, the patron who checked the item out will be responsible for replacement costs and billing fees or for replacing the item with an acceptable copy, unless there is a receipt stating the item was returned.

FORMS

Request Form for Audiovisual Materials

Columbia College Chicago
Columbia College Library
Chicago, Illinois

Audiovisual Reserve Form

Use this form to reserve AV materials for classroom use.

FACULTY USE ONLY.

READ THIS:

Requests for AV reserves received after 4:00PM CANNOT be processed for the next day.

ALL FIELDS ARE REQUIRED

After completing the form, please scroll to the bottom and click on "Submit."

Instructor Name: [_____]

Email: [_____]

Phone Number: [_____]

Department: [_____]

Course Title: [_____]

Course Number: [_____]

Semester: [_____]

Requested Reserve Materials

NOTE: Fields below starting with (*) are required.

Failure to fill in these fields may result in a delay or failure to fill your request.

If you would like to request more than the allotted 5 items on this form, please complete and submit an additional form.

The call number for av materials always begins with a V, VD, DVD, or FILM (i.e. DVD4571).

```
Title:
Director:
Year:
Call Number:
Date Needed:
Title:
Director:
Year:
Call Number:
Date Needed:
Title:
Director:
Year:
Call Number:
Date Needed:
Title:
Director:
Year:
Call Number:
Date Needed:
```

Additional Comments:

[Submit]

Request Form for In-Process Materials

Columbia College
Columbia College Library
Chicago, Illinois

Request Form for Material in Process

This service is only available for the Columbia College Chicago community.

Date: _____

Title of item: _____

Please attach a printout from the **Library Catalog** of the item's full record to this form.

In order to process your request, we need the following information from you.

Your Name: _____

Your Phone Number: _____

Your Email Address: _____

Your Affiliation: ○Columbia student   ○Columbia faculty   ○Columbia staff Library staff

The Library will contact you **as soon as possible** if we are unable to process the material. We will rush process your item **within 48 hours** after the request has been submitted, the status of the item has been confirmed and it has been located. You will be notified when the item is available for use. It will placed **ON HOLD** for you at the Library's Circulation Desk for **24 hours only**.

Request for Search Form

Virginia Tech
Virginia Tech University Libraries
Blacksburg, Virginia

Library Material Search Request

Use this form if you are having trouble locating specific library items. Library staff will begin a search to locate the missing items.

Search requests may take up to 2 business days to complete. You will be notified ASAP at the completion of the search. If the item is located, it will be held for you at the circulation desk unless it does not circulate. Otherwise, it will be set to status missing, and you are encouraged to consult InterLibrary Loan. There are no searches on Saturday or Sunday.

Call Number: [＿＿＿＿＿＿]

Author: [＿＿＿＿＿＿＿＿＿＿＿＿]

Title: [＿＿＿＿＿＿＿＿＿＿＿]

Volume: [＿＿＿＿＿＿] Issue/No: [＿＿＿＿＿＿]

Month/Season: [＿＿＿＿＿＿] Year: [＿＿＿＿＿＿]

Location of Item:
- ○ Newman
- ○ Art/Arch
- ○ Northern VA Library
- ○ Vet Med

Type of Item: ○ Book ○ Bound Journal ○ Current Periodical

Patron name: [＿＿＿＿＿＿＿＿＿＿]

Patron Number: [＿＿＿＿＿＿]

Patron type: ○ Graduate ○ Undergrad ○ Faculty ○ Staff ○ VA Resident

Email address: [＿＿＿＿＿＿]

Phone: [＿＿＿＿＿＿]

Chapter 22

PROTECTION OF LIBRARY MATERIALS

GENERAL PROTECTION GUIDELINES

Cornell University
Cornell University Library
Ithaca, New York

The university intends its libraries to serve all its students, faculty and staff members. Materials are to be shared for the common good, and we encourage you to use university property carefully so that future Cornellians may also enjoy it.

Lost, stolen, and missing books and other materials significantly damage our ability to provide the resources that students and faculty members need. Replacing items is expensive, and often it is impossible to buy even recent books and periodicals at any price. The seriousness of the problem will probably not be apparent to you until you make the unpleasant discovery that an item you want is no longer available in the collections.

To protect books and periodicals from theft, most libraries have installed security systems at exits and in other areas. Materials that are not properly checked out will set off an alarm. If the alarm sounds when you leave the library, you will be asked to return to the circulation desk and identify any library material you are carrying. Any CUL materials not properly checked out to you will be kept by library staff. As university officials, library staff have the authority to ask you for your identification and to search book bags, knapsacks, or other containers for library materials. These procedures are in accordance with the CUL Library Security Policy, which is available at circulation desks in each library.

Members of the library staff are also conscious of the need to handle library materials with care. No one wants to discourage you from using the collections, but we ask you to join with the staff in protecting the collections from damage. Eating, drinking, and smoking are generally not permitted anywhere in the libraries. You can also help by being careful not to handle books roughly—especially older items and those that have brittle pages. Books taken out of the library should be protected from hazardous environments such as basements likely to flood or food preparation areas. Please do not get library materials wet in the rain or snow or leave them where they will be exposed to extreme temperatures. Patrons are asked to report damage to books without delay, especially books that have been damaged by water or fire.

Willful damage to library material by theft and mutilation denies information to others. Anyone involved in such activity, which is a violation of the Code of Academic Integrity, is subject to disciplinary measures as described in The Code of Academic Integrity and Acknowledging the Work of Others, available from the Office of the University Faculty, 315 Day Hall. Violations of the code include stealing materials from the library, not returning library materials promptly when asked to do so, hoarding scarce copies of material needed by others in order to advance one's own position, deliberately damaging library material (for example, cutting pages out of books or magazines), and helping another person steal, hoard, or damage library material.

University of California Santa Cruz
McHenry Library
Santa Cruz, California

Food and drink stains can damage library materials and make them unusable. Damaged materials may need to be removed from the collection and we don't have funds to replace them. There are similar issues with damage to furniture and equipment.

In addition to the direct damage to materials, food and drink attract insects and other pests which feed on the paper, starches, and other munchable components of books and paper. Liquid spills also promote mold growth, which damages materials and is unhealthy for people. Once pests and mold get a foothold, removal is difficult and may require the use of chemicals which we would prefer not to have to use. Good housekeeping—keeping food away from books—helps us avoid using chemical pesticides.

While we want to acknowledge the social aspect of libraries, we haven't yet found a balance that allows us to loosen the food and drink policy and protect the collection. Until then we will hope users will understand the consequences while we maintain a strict policy prohibiting food and drink in the library.

Georgia State University
Georgia State University Library
Atlanta, Georgia

Relating to Library Collections & Practice:

- Failing to comply with existing Library policies on time limitations for use of equipment or space.
- Removing or attempting to remove library materials or property without checking them out or without proper authorization.
- Mutilating library materials in any way, including by marking, underlining, or removing pages or portions of pages; removing binding or electronic theft detection devices; injuring or defacing library materials or property, including furniture or equipment, in any way; tampering with or harming library computers or computer systems.
- Concealing library materials in the Library for the exclusive use of an individual or group.
- Being in an unauthorized area of the Library or remaining in the Library after closing or when requested to leave during emergency situations.

A person who commits or attempts to commit offenses enumerated in the University Code of Conduct or in this Library Conduct Policy, whether a member of the Georgia State University community or not, may be asked to leave the campus by library staff, campus security, campus police, or university officials; may be subject to the sanctions of warning, suspension, expulsion; forfeiture, prosecution, and/or making restitution; and may be accountable to both civil authorities (city, state, or federal) and to the university.

(For additional policies, please see the accompanying CD-ROM.)

SECURITY SYSTEMS

North Seattle Community College
North Seattle Community College Library
Seattle, Washington

Book Security System

The library utilizes a book security system to enable the circulation system to work more efficiently. The system provides better library service for all users by ensuring the proper charging out of library materials and discouraging theft of learning resources. The library reserves the right to inspect handbags, backpacks, briefcases, parcels, and all other carry-in items when the patron exits the library.

Guidelines

Personal books and other objects may trigger the system if there is a security system device in the item itself. If the alarm on the security system goes off when a patron is exiting, the turnstile will lock. A library employee will ask the patron to step back to the Circulation Desk and unlock the turnstile to let other patrons exit. Items from other libraries, personal books, and other objects may also trigger the system.

The patron is asked to hand any library items to the employee then walk through the security system again carrying their backpack, briefcase, etc. If the system is triggered again, they are asked to repeat the procedure and check their pockets, coats, etc. for any other items that may trigger the alarm.

If the item that triggered the security system is an NSCC library item, the employee will check the due date. If not overdue, it will be handed back to the patron after they have passed through the security system. If the item is overdue or not properly checked out, they will be asked if they wish to renew the item, check it out, or return it. If the item was not a circulating item, it will be retained by the employee.

All library patrons are expected to enter and leave the library through the designated entrance/exit turnstiles. Patron authorized to exit by the disabled gate are to pass their carry in items to an employee at the circulation desk to pass through the security system.

University of Illinois at Urbana-Champaign School of Law
Albert E. Jenner, Jr Memorial Law Library
Champaign, Illinois

Security System

The library electronic security system monitors material exiting the Library. When a library book has not been properly checked out and is passing through the system, the alarm sounds and the exit gate locks.

If the system reacts as you leave the Library, step back from the gate and return to the circulation desk.

The security system does not interfere with pacemakers, hearing aids, tape recorders, or any other electronic devices, but users of walkman-type earphones are advised to remove them when approaching the system.

LOST MATERIALS

Colorado State University Pueblo
Colorado State University Pueblo Library
Pueblo, Colorado

The current lost book charge is $75.00 or a current replacement cost as determined by the Catalog/Circulation Librarian. The Catalog/Circulation Librarian will select an acceptable replacement if a book is no longer in print. The replacement charge for each lost government document and vertical file item is $20.00. The charge for lost or damaged audiovisual materials is the current library replacement cost. Patron charges for lost items are automatically placed on accounts receivable at the CSU-Pueblo accounting office. Fines totaling $20.00 or more are also placed on accounts receivable.

Ferris State University
Ferris Library
Big Rapids, Michigan

Lost Books or Materials

Lost books or materials should be reported promptly.

Cost of Lost Items:
- Actual replacement cost if known or average replacement cost (according to Bowkers Annual) will be charged for all lost materials.
- $20.00 processing fee charged.
- $20.00 service fee charged.

Refunds:
- If a book is returned six months or later, no refunds are made.
- The cost of the book and the processing fee are refunded if you return it within six months.
- Service fees will not be refunded.

STOLEN AND MUTILATED MATERIALS

University of South Carolina Beaufort
USC Beaufort Library
Beaufort, South Carolina

Theft/Mutilation of Library Materials

All library users are subject to state law regarding theft, damage, and failure to return borrowed library materials.

Persons who are apprehended mutilating or stealing library materials may be punishable by a minimum fine of $50.00, plus the cost of replacing any defaced material. In the case of student violators, such violations may constitute grounds for further disciplinary action which may include suspension, expulsion, and/or referral to the civil authorities for appropriate legal action. Alleged student violators have the right of appeal to the Vice Chancellor for Student Development and the Honor Court.

Procedure

Theft/Mutilation of Library Materials

In the event of suspected theft of library materials, the following procedure should be followed:

USC Beaufort student

- Ask for suspect's name and ID card.
- Report alleged violator to Library Director.
- Contact Vice Chancellor for Student Development.

K–12 student

- Report alleged violator to Library Director.
- Contact Executive Vice Chancellor for Academic Affairs.
- Contact parent or guardian to come to library.
- Release alleged violator to custody of parent or guardian.

Other non-USCB users

- Report alleged violator to Library Director.
- Inform alleged violator that his/her library privileges may be revoked and that a fine may be imposed.

(Note: Sections 16–13–330, 16–13,331, 16–13,332, 16–13,340, 16–13–350, 16–13–370 of the Code of Laws of South Carolina 1976 reinforce such policy.)

Ball State University
Ball State University Library
Muncie, Indiana

Theft or Mutilation

The University Libraries may suspend library privileges and/or seek criminal prosecution or civil sanctions in cases of theft or mutilation of library materials.

Barton College
Willis N. Hackney Library
Wilson, North Carolina

Lost, Stolen, or Mutilated Materials

Patrons are responsible for the materials that they borrow and will be fined for lost, stolen, or mutilated items. Patrons will be responsible for paying the replacement cost and billing fee of such items. Patrons may pay the total lost item bill, or replace the item with an acceptable copy and pay only the billing fee or overdue fine, whichever is greater. Items that have been billed for replacement and have not been returned, replaced, or paid for within 30 days of the billing date, will be designated as LOST. Lost items are not subject to appeal. Unpaid student bills may result in blocks on registration, graduation ceremony, and transcripts.

Magazines and Journals

Magazines and journals may only be checked out by college faculty and staff. Any other removal of such material from the library will be considered as theft. Mutilation or the tearing out of pages from a magazine will also be considered as theft. When the library identifies a student as having stolen or mutilated a magazine or journal, he/she will be billed for the cost of a single issue of that periodical or if that cannot be determined, $10.00. Unpaid student bills of this nature will result in blocks on registration, graduation ceremony, and transcripts.

In the event that a student refuses to pay for the magazine or denies having stolen the magazine, evidence of the theft will be turned over to either the Dean of Students or the Student Life Personnel Enforcing Campus Mutilating and Theft Committee. It will be their responsibility to determine whether the student is indeed guilty of theft and whether any disciplinary action is called for.

In the event that a community patron steals or mutilates a magazine or journal or refuses to pay for a lost book, his/her library privileges will be immediately revoked.

DAMAGED MATERIALS

Los Angeles Valley College
Los Angeles Valley College Library
Valley Glen, California

Lost and Damaged Materials

All library users are responsible for lost library materials.

The replacement policy is:

- books—regular books: $40 (specialized materials such as textbooks and art books have a significantly higher replacement cost), plus a $10.00 processing fee
- periodicals, newspapers, pamphlets: the cover price of the issue plus a $5.00 processing fee
- reserve material: the current price of the item plus a $10.00 processing fee
- ITV videocassettes: $20.00

Damaged materials: Items the Library judges to have been damaged by the borrower shall be evaluated by the circulation department and repair or replacement fees will be assessed based on the extent of the damage.

Lynchburg College
Knight-Capron Library
Lynchburg, Virginia

Lost and Damaged Items

Lost items should be reported to the circulation desk at once and the fine, if any will stop at that time. The charge for a lost book is determined by the library's cost for replacement.

Patrons will be charged for materials which are returned damaged. If an item is repairable, the patron will be charged for the cost of the repairs only. If an item is beyond repair, the replacement cost will be charged. All materials remain the property of the library.

Items returned without a barcode will result in the patron being assessed a fee of $1.00 per barcode.

Marlboro College
Rice-Aron Library
Marlboro, Vermont

Fines, applied to student accounts, will be assessed for lost or stolen items, items returned in unsatisfactory condition, or damage to library furniture or equipment. Patrons will be charged the replacement value of the item if it exceeds the cost below. If a patron believes that a fine has been assessed or privileges suspended in error, they should contact the Library Director as soon as they become aware of the situation.

Material Types and Replacement Costs for Missing or Damaged Items

- Books 25.00
- Reference Books 100.00
- Art Books 50.00
- Periodicals 15.00
- Microfilm 25.00
- Computer software 25.00
- Musical Recordings 25.00
- Audio Books 40.00
- Video Cassette 25.00
- Video Disc 25.00
- Special Collection & Archive Materials 50.00

RESERVES

COURSE RESERVES

Framingham State College
Henry Whittemore Library
Framingham, Massachusetts

Reserve Policy

Placing Materials on Reserve:

1. Books and photocopies may be placed on reserve by faculty only in order to facilitate their use for specific assignments. Students are not allowed to place materials on reserve for their instructor.
2. Personal items belonging to the instructor may be placed on reserve. The instructor may request these items may be sensitized for the security system.
3. Requests must be submitted three days prior to when they are needed because of the large number of items used each semester.
4. Materials are kept on reserve for one semester only. No reserve items will be held from semester to semester.
5. The instructor informs students of what has been placed on reserve, as we have no knowledge of course assignments or requirements.
6. Articles and sections of books may be photocopied in the library.
7. All Reserve Materials placed on Open or Closed Reserve may not leave the library.

There are three distinct types of reserves.

1. Closed Reserve: Material on closed reserve is used in the library only and for a period not to exceed two hours. The library recommends this type of reserve as it provides maximum access and security where specifically assigned readings must be available. Student must have their ID card with them in order to borrow a reserve item.
2. Overnight Reserve: Material on overnight reserve may be used in the library for a two hour period during the day and may be taken out of the building after 4 PM to be returned by 10 AM the following day. On weekends the materials may be checked out at noon Friday and are due back by 10 AM Monday.
3. Open Reserve: Materials on open reserve are available for students for use within a supervised area. Multi-volume sets, items on comprehensive reading lists, and similar materials that require constant access to be successfully used, should be placed here. Materials are currently housed in the Reference foyer.

University of Pittsburgh
Pitt Digital Library
Pittsburgh, Pennsylvania

Guidelines for Using Print Course Reserve Materials

Borrower must have a valid ID card.

Only two reserve items may be checked out at one time.

Items placed on two-hour reserve may be checked out overnight two hours before the library closes, and must be returned the following morning when the library opens.

Personal copies of reserve materials provided by instructors may not leave the library under any conditions unless the instructor so designates.

Fines for reserve items are $1.80 per hour per item for two-hour loans and $1.00 per day per item for 3-day and 7-day loan periods.

Textbook Reserves

Los Angeles Valley College
Los Angeles Valley College Library
Valley Glen, California

As the Library does not buy textbooks, instructors are encouraged to put their own extra copies of the texts they are using on reserve. To put a book on reserve, simply bring it to a librarian. (If you are requesting the Library buy a book, you must order it the semester before you wish to use it to allow for processing time.) Books will be kept on reserve until you take them off. Other materials such as photocopies, past tests, and journal issues may also be placed on reserve.

Hofstra University
Joan and Donald E. Axinn Library
Hempstead, New York

The University Library and your Student Government Association are pleased to announce a collaborative effort to make some of your more expensive textbooks available in the Axinn Library's Reserve Department, on the main floor of the library, just inside the doors off the unispan.

We have selected textbooks that cost over $100, and were assigned for classes with more than one section. All available textbooks are listed in our online catalog, and a list may be viewed below. A printed list of the available textbooks is available at the Axinn Library Circulation Desk. Textbooks are available for 2-hour checkout. We hope that this new service will contribute to your success in your studies at Hofstra.

Removing Reserves

University of South Carolina Beaufort
USC Beaufort Library
Beaufort, South Carolina

Removing Reserve Items

All materials will be removed from Reserve at the end of each semester. Renewal for the following semester must be requested prior to the end of the course. If needed, copyright permission should be secured for these materials. Library material not renewed will be returned to the stacks. Items owned by faculty will be returned to the faculty member.

Southeastern Louisiana University
Linus A. Sims Memorial Library
Hammond, Louisiana

Guidelines for Removing Reserve Materials

All materials will be available on reserve for no longer than the end of one semester. All Electronic Reserve materials will be removed from the system at the end of semester.

At the end of each semester, faculty with items on Reserve will be sent a letter notifying them of the request for removal of items. Faculty may respond that non-copyrighted materials or library-owned materials remain on the reserve for the next semester. Copies of copyrighted materials may not remain on reserve for subsequent semesters unless copyright permission has been granted by the copyright owner (see policies about "Repeated Reserves" above).

In order to remove photocopied or personal items from reserve, a signed Reserve Retrieval Form, which is available at the Reserve Desk and on the Library's web page, must be presented to the Reserve staff. For security reasons we prefer that all photocopy and personal reserve items be retrieved for removal in person by the instructor. However, materials may be retrieved by graduate assistants or other persons designated by the instructor, if a written letter of permission signed by the instructor is presented with the signed Reserve Retrieval Form.

Books and other materials owned by the Library will be returned to the shelves if they will not needed for classes in the next semester and/or if the faculty member does not respond to the reserve notification letter.

Photocopies that are not picked up by faculty member by the end of the semester will be discarded.

FACULTY RESERVES

Neumann College
Neumann College Library
Aston, Pennsylvania

1. Faculty should try to bring all required reserve materials in as soon as possible, in order for them to be processed in a timely manner. All requests are processed on a first come, first served basis.
2. Photocopied materials will no longer be available in the Library. Articles will, however, be available through the Electronic Reserves (E-Res) system. Faculty must have an E-Account before placing photocopies on Reserve. To set up an appointment, contact the Faculty Reserves Desk. Remember: No account, no Reserves. See the Faculty Electronic Reserves Policy for more information.
3. Faculty must fill out a Reserves Request form available at the Library's Circulation Desk. This form must be completely filled out, in order for materials to be cataloged into the Library's computer system or placed in E-Reserves.
4. Faculty must have a valid Neumann College photo ID with a barcode, in order to place items on reserve. Barcodes can be obtained from the Circulation Desk. Be prepared to complete a Library record, if you do not already have an existing one. This is necessary for attaching reserve materials to instructors in the computer system.
5. To remove items from Reserves, faculty members must completely fill out the Reserves Deletion form obtainable from the Circulation Desk. Please be sure to remove all personal items from the Library at that time.
6. Materials will be automatically deleted from the Reserves holdings, at the end of each Semester, unless prior arrangements have been made with the Reserves Librarian. Exception: Nursing, P.T., and INT202 materials.

Phoenix College
Phoenix College Library
Phoenix, Arizona

Faculty may place library materials or their own personal materials on Course Reserves so they will be accessible to students for classroom assignments.

A Course Reserves Room Request Form may be picked up at the Library Circulation Desk, or you may call the number below, or email reserve@pcmail.maricopa.edu to have a form faxed or e-mailed to you. The form should be filled out completely so that the material will be correctly entered into the Course Reserves Room for easy access.

The material will be placed on Course Reserves under the Instructor Name, Subject Code and Course Number. The instructor may specify the length of time the material is to be left on Course Reserves (if not specified the material will be removed at the end of the current semester). You may also specify how long the material may be checked out (In Library Use Only is generally 2–4 hours use. If material is to be taken out of the library the loan period is generally Overnight—1 week).

University of Pittsburgh
Pitt Digital Library
Pittsburgh, Pennsylvania

Instructors: Guidelines for Placing Print Materials on Reserve

For Books:

Book reserve request forms must be filled out completely. Retrieving the books from the stacks and submitting them with your completed form will allow us to process your reserve list more efficiently and in less time. Reserve request forms can be picked up at the Lending/Reserve Desk or you can use the online Reserve Book Request Form or print the form and submit to Hillman Library Reserves, G–2 Hillman, or via campus mail.

Books that are not currently in our collection can be ordered. Please allow 4–6 weeks for us to process book orders.

The deadline for submitting reserve lists in order for the items to be available for the first day of the term, is one month before the semester starts.

Items can be placed on two-hour, three-day, or seven-day reserve. Please indicate the length of time you would like items on reserve for your course to circulate.

There is a 60 item limit to the number of books and/or photocopies placed on reserve per instructor per course per term.

Personal copies of books will be returned to the instructor at the end of the term unless other arrangements are made.

For Photocopies:

Instructors are responsible for copyright compliance related to the materials they place on reserve. Please familiarize yourself with the ULS policy. The ULS fully expects that instructors are following the U.S. Copyright Act of 1976.

The instructor must supply all photocopies of copyrighted material, along with a Photocopy Reserve Form (PDF) which includes complete citations. This form can be printed, filled out, and should accompany the photocopies.

Instructors should provide only as many copies as are absolutely required to meet the demands of the class. Traditionally, this has been defined widely as one copy for every twenty students except in extraordinary cases. Please indicate projected enrollment for the class.

No more than one chapter of any given book may be photocopied and placed on reserve, although multiple copies of such chapter or excerpt may be placed on reserve.

There is a limit of three (3) photocopies per periodical volume per course per term.

It is illegal to repeatedly place the same photocopies on reserve each semester. Therefore the library will return all photocopies to the instructor at the end of each term.

Instructors: Guidelines for Submitting Material for Electronic Reserves NEW!

The library will scan reserve materials and make them available through Pittcat.

Please note what you can do to help:

Reserve staff in Hillman Library will scan individual articles and book chapters if the copy submitted is of good quality and printed on a single side. Clean copies of articles and chapters make legible scans. Single-sided copies scan faster.

The instructor must supply a completed copy of the Electronic Reserve List (PDF) form.

Course Packs are NOT eligible for scanning.

If the article is available from any of our electronic resources, please provide the URL and we will link directly to the e-version. Do not bother to print it out.

Please provide the full citation when possible.

Please read the Library's statement on Copyright and Course Reserves.

As with print reserves it is first come, first served. Please give us your reserve materials as soon as possible.

University of Idaho
University of Idaho Libraries
Moscow, Idaho

Fill out online Request Form or come to the library.

Must include all information on form.

Reading lists may be sent separately as an email attachment, but the professor will still need to supply copies of source pages.

Each item must be identified by a complete citation:

- Author
- Title
- Item title (if appropriate)
- Date of publication (including month and year, if appropriate)
- Volume, issue, page numbers (if appropriate)

We would prefer a copy of the title page for each item.

Requests lacking any of this information will take longer to process, pending citation verification.

During peak periods, processing may take up to two weeks; so please plan accordingly.

Appropriate types of materials for electronic reserves

- Full text articles (or links) from electronic journals or aggregators licensed by the University of Idaho Library
- Original materials created by the instructor where the instructor owns the copyright (test files, lecture notes, solutions files, syllabi)
- Book chapter (single chapter or 10 percent, whichever is LESS)
- Journal article
- Student papers with written permission of the student author
- Links to websites with materials that are covered under copyright law

Inappropriate

- Multiple chapters from the same book
- More than two articles from the same issue of a journal
- Materials not in compliance with the copyright law
- Commercially produced workbooks or instruction manuals with answer keys, or similar products that are excluded from the principles of Fair Use as designated by copyright law
- Student papers without written permission of the student author
- Links to websites that post materials that are not in compliance with the copyright law
- Materials lacking bibliographic citations or copies of the title page

Submitting materials in electronic format

- MSWord, ASCII, or PDF files acceptable
- File size is important: Reduce size by scanning from clean copy (original preferred)
- Complete bibliographic citation (author, title, vol., no., mo., yr, pp.) required for copyright compliance

Submitting materials for scanning

- Original copy is preferred or clean, single-sided copies (no marks, lines) to avoid large file size
- Supply a copy of the title page and the verso of the title page, required for copyright compliance.
- Send to:

Passwords

Scanned articles are only accessible by passwords. You will be given a password that must be communicated to your students so that they can access the electronic reserve readings. These passwords will change every semester and are different for each class.

Limits

Five articles per week may be submitted for scanning. More than this will be scanned as time permits. If no priorities are indicated, library staff will use its discretion to avoid further delays.

Processing time

- Typically, first come, first served; may, at the discretion of the library, be arranged to serve the largest number of students for the least effort.
- Plan for two weeks, particularly if you expect the library to scan and/or pull materials.
- Remember that everyone needs to have his materials available for the first day of the semester. Do not expect this to happen if you have not submitted your material two weeks before the first day of the semester.
- You will be notified by email when your material is available. At this time, you will be given the password for your students to use to gain access to scanned documents.
- If you would like to check on the availability of your class, please visit the Web site: www.lib.uidaho.edu

Successive use

Materials can be used for one semester under provisions of the Fair Use sections of the copyright law. Subsequent use requires that the library purchase rights to re-use the item. In the event that these rights are denied or deemed to be beyond reasonable costs, the library will remove the item from reserve and contact the professor about securing different readings.

PRINT RESERVES

Vanderbilt University
Heard Library
Nashville, Tennessee

Print Reserves

Please complete the Reserve form available at the Reserve Desk or use the Web Form. If books are requested for reserve, Reserve staff will be happy to pull the books from our stacks. If it is a book owned by another Vanderbilt Library, we will get it sent to the Reserve Room. Any books requested for reserve that are not owned by the Library will be ordered with the exception of textbooks. If you do not want to make other readings available electronically, the Reserve Room will be happy to accept the photocopied materials provided and place them on print reserves. If requesting a journal article from a periodical volume that we don't own at Central, a photocopy will have to be supplied since most libraries will not send us their journals. If it is a journal article for a journal that we do own, we will be glad to put the periodical on reserve if you do not wish to provide a photocopy of the article. Materials such as old tests, homework solutions, book chapters, and journal articles should be supplied in manila folders. If material is over 1" thick, please supply a 3-ring binder for the materials. The recommended guideline is 1 copy on reserve for every 10 students in the class. Length of circulation options: Restricted (room use only), 1 hour, 2 hours, 4 hours, overnight, 1 day, 3 days and 1 week. Current lists of the available print reserves may be searched by Instructor name, course name or course number in the Acorn catalog. The Reserve Room also maintains a paper list of materials on print reserve.

FAQS FOR INSTRUCTORS

University of Washington
University of Washington Libraries
Seattle, Washington

Electronic Reserves and Course Paks FAQ Instructor's Guide to Reserves, Ereserves and Course Paks—Frequently Asked Questions

I would like my students to read a wide range of material that is not in one textbook. What are the options?

If the material does not require copying (e.g. the library puts a book on reserve) the material can be placed on reserve for any number of quarters. Copying for library reserves is governed by the fair use section of the copyright law. Typically journal articles and book chapters are placed on reserves or electronic reserves for one quarter. The Libraries will not accept copies of entire books or place more than 30 articles on reserve per class. You can also request that material be put in a Course Pak and copyright permissions paid.

What are my options if I want to use material for more than one quarter?

Course Paks are currently the best option for ongoing use of copyrighted materials. The UW's Copyright Permission Center can handle the work of getting permissions from publishers and creating the Course Paks.

What about my syllabus, class notes, tests and papers?

As long as you own the copyright you can place material on library reserves or electronic reserves. Students own the copyright for papers they write for your class so you should get permission before placing material on the Web.

What are economics of electronic reserves and Course Paks?

The Libraries will put materials on reserve or electronic reserves for free if the instructor provides clean copy for scanning. Students pay for Course Paks. Electronic reserves may seem cheaper but if you consider the cost of downloading and printing all of the readings the cost difference between reserves and Course Paks is much less. Over time, as the Libraries buys more online full text resources, the cost of Course Paks should decrease.

Can I put readings on my course Web?

Yes, but the same copyright limits apply if you don't get permission. If you already have material in a digital format (for example, Microsoft Word) you can fairly easily put it on the Web. To scan a document and put it on the Web so that it is legible and small takes some effort. It is helpful to have material all in one place or linked from one place so if you have material on a course Web and on reserve make sure that the Libraries has your course Web URL and that your course Web has the link to library reserve readings.

What about using UW-licensed full text databases to provide course content?

Links can be made to these databases (e.g., Research Library) from your course Web or Libraries reserve list. Some of the URLs in the databases are not fixed. The Health Science Library has developed some information about linking to online journals and linking to online book chapters.

Chapter 24

NONPRINT RESERVES

GENERAL GUIDELINES

Audiovisual Reserves

Vanderbilt University
Heard Library
Nashville, Tennessee

Video Reserves

Non-book materials such as CD-ROMs, CDs, Slides, Cassettes and Videos must be placed on reserve in the Government Info/Media Desk on the 4th floor. This facility has the equipment for the students to access this type of material. These materials can be placed on reserve using the Online Video Reserve Request Form.

Whether using print or electronic reserves, new lists must be submitted each semester. In the case of electronic reserves, copyright permissions are granted for one semester at a time only. Reserve lists and materials from previous semesters cannot be stored in the Reserve Room. Personal copies of books or articles placed on reserve for a semester need to be picked up by the last day of exams if possible. If that is not convenient and an alternate pickup time needs to be arranged or if there are any questions about placing materials on Reserve, call [staff contact].

Milwaukee Area Technical College
Milwaukee Area Technical College Library
Milwaukee, Wisconsin

Videocassettes on Reserve:
- College of the Air (TV College) videocassettes may be checked out for two hours within the library.
- No more than two College of the Air videocassettes per course can be loaned at one time.
- College by Cassette videos loan period is four weeks.
- Only one tape per course can be loaned at one time.

University of Iowa
University of Iowa Libraries
Iowa City, Iowa

Reserving video material will help ensure the availability of a video within the Media Services room during the hours the unit is open. Reserved videos may not be checked out from the Media Services unit except to be shown in a class by an instructor.

There are three categories of reserve:

1. Weekly Reserve: For example, an instructor may put a video on reserve for a week or so depending on need to ensure the availability of the video for the class. We will also need a date that the video will be shown in class. While a video is on reserve it may not leave the Media Services Department unless approved by the Instructor placing the reserve.

2. Semester Reserve: Instructors may put video material on reserve to use all semester. This material can be checked out by other instructors but not by students. Please remove the material from reserve if you find that you no longer need it for the whole semester.
3. 16MM Films: Instructors may check out 16mm films for class only and must be returned after the class is finished. These films are reserved the same way as VHS and DVDs. CIC films must have approval from the Films Studies Department and forwarded to us so that we can put it in the computer and also bill the department. If department isn't open you will need to drop the film at the North entrance.

The Media Services unit will accept instructor- or student-owned videos for reserve use. Those placing their own video material on reserve must inform staff regarding the category of reserve and must retrieve the material at the end of the reserve period. Media Services staff cannot accept responsibility for the return of the video material nor responsibility for damage to or theft of the material while it is in reserve status. Video material not retrieved will be disposed of eventually. Exceptions to these guidelines are made in consultation with the Media Services Supervisor.

Scanning Materials

University of Texas at El Paso
University Libraries
El Paso, Texas

Policy Statement: Library Scanning Policy for Electronic Reserves

The mission of the Library is to provide all faculty, students and staff access to the various book collections and electronic resources housed or maintained in the library. Use of electronic reserve materials is restricted to students currently enrolled in a class whose instructor requested the access of his information through electronic means.

The copyright law (Title 17, United States Code) sets strict limits on making copies of copyrighted works. Exceeding these limits may subject the individual to liability for infringement with damages up to $100,000 per work.

The Library reserves the right to refuse either to accept a copy request that would involve a violation of copyright law or to make available through course reserve materials that might have been duplicated in violation of copyright law. The library can make no more than five copies of an article or portion of a book in accordance with "fair use" guidelines as outlined in Section 107 of US Copyright Law.

Section 107 Fair Use:

For institutions of higher education, the cardinal portion of the Copyright Act is Section 107 of the Copyright Act, the fair use provision. This section sets forth the factors that must be evaluated in determining whether a particular use, without prior permission, is a fair and, therefore, permitted use. The legitimate and lawful application of fair use rights provides the necessary and constitutionally envisioned balance between the rights of the copyright holder versus societal and educational interests in the dissemination of information.

Section 107 is as follows:

Notwithstanding the provisions of sections 106 and 106A, the fair use of a copyrighted work, including such use by reproduction in copies or phonorecords or by any other means specified in that section, for purposes such as criticism, comment, news reporting, teaching (including multiple copies for classroom use), scholarship or research, is not an infringement of copyright. In determining whether the use made of a work in any particular case is fair use the factors to be considered shall include:

The purpose and character of the use, including whether such use is of a commercial nature or is for nonprofit educational purposes;

The nature of the copyrighted work;

The amount and substantiality of the portion used in relation to the copyrighted work as a whole;

The effect of the use upon the potential market for or value of the copyrighted work.

Electronic Reserves is an extension of traditional library services and will be provided in a manner that respects fair use rights, the right of copyright holders, and current copyright law. The electronic copying and scanning of copyright protected works for library reserve service and distance learning are unsettled areas of the law which may be addressed by courts and/or legislation. The UTEP library will continually monitor legal developments that may affect the fair use analysis of Electronic Reserves to ensure that library services are in compliance with the letter and spirit of the U.S. copyright law.

(For additional policies, please see the accompanying CD-ROM.)

Electronic Reserves

Colorado State University Pueblo
Colorado State University Pueblo Library
Pueblo, Colorado

Policy for Electronic Reserves

Access to Published Copyrighted Materials

The University Library Circulation Department bases its electronic reserve policy on the fair use provisions of the United States Copyright Act of 1976, Section 107, which permit making multiple copies for classroom use, and is one of six examples of uses which do not require the permission of the copyright owner, nor the payment of a royalty if the circumstances of use are fair as assessed by the four factors listed in section 107 of the Copyright Act. The text of this section follows:

"Notwithstanding the provisions of sections 106 and 106A, the fair use of a copyrighted work, including such use by reproduction in copies or phonograph records or by any other means specified in that section, for purposes such as criticism, comment, news reporting, teaching (including multiple copies for classroom use), scholarship or research, is not an infringement of copyright.

In determining whether the use made of a work in any particular case is a fair use the factors to be considered shall include the following:

1. the purpose and character of the use including whether such use is of a commercial nature or is for nonprofit educational purposes;
2. the nature of the copyrighted work;
3. the amount and sustainability of the portion used in relation to the copyrighted work as a whole; and
4. the effect of the use upon the potential market for or value of the copyrighted work."

An item for reserve must conform to the above fair use factors based on an analysis using the following widely used interpretations:

1. the material is to be used for nonprofit educational use;
2. is a published and copyrighted work;
3. uses an appropriate amount, not including the "heart of the work";
4. is lawfully acquired and cannot replace the sale of a copyrighted work.

The collections of the Colorado State University–Pueblo Library are purchased for the nonprofit educational use of our students and faculty, with the understanding that there will be multiple uses of a limited number of copies. Libraries frequently pay premium institutional subscription prices for journals, expressly for the privilege of supporting multiple academic users. The sole purpose of Electronic Reserves will be to facilitate the making of multiple copies for classroom use by students.

The University Library will adhere to the following procedures in order to insure that items placed on reserve conform to the spirit and letter of the 1976 Copyright Law, and the fair use provisions therein:

- Materials will be placed on Electronic Reserves solely at the initiative of Colorado State University–Pueblo faculty for the non-commercial, educational use of their students.
- Materials not owned by the University Library will be purchased whenever possible; if purchase is not possible, a licensing fee will be paid to the publisher.
- No more than one article per journal issue per course may be scanned for placement on Electronic Reserves.
- No more than 25% of an entire book may be scanned for placement on Electronic Reserves.
- There will be no charge for students to access Electronic Reserves. A nominal per page fee to cover the cost of printing within the University Library may be charged in the future.
- A copyright notice will appear on screen and must be acknowledged before the student is permitted to access materials on Electronic Reserves.
- Materials on Electronic Reserves will be accessible only by faculty name or course number.
- Students may access materials on Electronic Reserves only by using a course password.
- Electronic documents will be deleted from the E-reserves system when they are no longer used for course instruction.
- At the end of each semester, Electronic Reserve materials will be archived.
- The University Library will adhere to the principles of Fair Use when placing materials on Electronic Reserves.

The electronic copying and scanning of copyright-protected works for library reserve service are unsettled areas of the law which may be addressed by the Supreme Court or in future revisions of the copyright law.

CSU-Pueblo Library will continually monitor legal developments which may affect the fair use analysis of electronic reserve services to ensure that library services are in compliance with the letter and spirit of the United States Copyright Law.

The University Library reserves the right to refuse any material submitted that does not comply with copyright guidelines. However, users of reserve materials assume all risk for purposes of copyright.

I have read and agree to the University Library's Electronic Reserve Collection Policy

_____   _____
Faculty Signature   Date

Please retain a copy for your files and return the signed original to the Library Circulation/Reserve Desk.

University of Scranton
Weinberg Memorial Library
Scranton, Pennsylvania

The University of Scranton's Web site is changing, and policies will be separated from information on the updated sites.

Electronic Reserves

Electronic Reserves are available over the Internet. Access is restricted through the use of a password distributed by the faculty member who is teaching the course. For an item to be placed on reserve, it must comply with copyright restrictions.

University of Texas at Austin
University of Texas Libraries
Austin, Texas

Electronic Reserves

Instructors are responsible for placing course materials on electronic reserve. Materials on electronic reserve are available online through the University of Texas Libraries Web page and are restricted to the students enrolled in each course. Electronic reserves are available from Internet-connected computers and may be accessed simultaneously by any number of students. Therefore, no loan periods are associated with electronic reserves.

Because instructors control their own electronic reserve materials, they may add and remove materials at any time during the semester. Instructors are responsible for complying with The University of Texas System Policy Statement on Use of Copyrighted Materials.

The University of Texas Libraries staff are responsible for maintaining the electronic reserves software and server, issuing electronic reserves accounts to instructors, and training instructors to use the software. Library staff may limit the number of electronic reserve items which can be posted for each course to accommodate space constraints on the reserves server.

E-RESERVE COPYRIGHT CONCERNS

Library's Responsibilities

Towson University
Albert S. Cook Library
Towson, Maryland

Cook Library Responsibilities Regarding Copyrighted Works Placed on E-Reserve

Materials will be included solely at the request of Towson University course instructors. Cook Library will not charge for access to e-reserves, nor will patrons making single copies for private study, scholarship, or research be charged beyond the actual cost of such photocopies or printouts.

Access to materials will be restricted via password-protection to students, instructors, instructional support staff, or course administrators for the specific course for which the materials were requested.

Access to materials will be disabled at the end of the semester or when students have completed the course.

Appropriate citations or attributions to sources will be included for each item.

Any notice of copyright that appears on the original item will be reproduced on the copy posted in e-reserves.

A copyright warning will be included on a preliminary or introductory screen for all e-reserve course pages notifying patrons that U.S. copyright law governs the making of photocopies or other reproductions of copyrighted material and that patrons may be liable for infringement if they engage in uses which exceed fair use.

Material will be linked to, copied, or scanned for inclusion in e-reserves only from copies of the work that have been legally acquired by the library, the requesting instructor, or some other unit of the University.

Repeat use of material by the same instructor for the same course may require permission of the copyright owner; instructors must indicate on the e-reserves submission form whenever their use of a given work is a repeat use. Cook Library will research and request permission from the copyright owner for such uses when necessary.

"Consumable" copyrighted instructional materials (e.g., standardized tests, exercises and workbooks, lab manuals, etc.) will not be placed e-reserve under a claim of fair use.

Materials placed on e-reserve under a claim of fair use will generally meet the following limits as to amount and substantiality of the portion used from the original copyrighted work:

Short works: One item may be included in its entirety from a given collective work (e.g., an article from a particular issue of a journal issue; a chapter from a book; a poem, short story, or essay from an anthology or compilation), so long as the item is of customary length to be considered a small part of the collective work and so long as it could not be considered the "heart" of the collective work.

Longer works: Articles, chapters, poems, and other works that are of such length as to constitute a substantial portion of the journal issue, book, or other collective work-or which, regardless of length, could be considered the "heart" of the work-will only be included as excerpts in e-reserve under a claim of fair use.

Note: Uses of works of an imaginative or highly creative nature (e.g., fiction, poetry, plays, essays) are more restricted under the second fair use factor (nature of the work) than factually based works (e.g., journal articles). Accordingly, regardless of length, instructors should request only as much from such works as would be necessary to meet their desired teaching goal.

Materials posted on e-reserve under a claim of fair use that exceed these amount limits may still qualify as fair use, depending on the specific circumstances involved. Cook Library will make these determinations as warranted, but faculty who would like more information may consult with the library's copyright liaison

Instructor's Responsibilities

Towson University
Albert S. Cook Library
Towson, Maryland

Instructor Responsibilities Regarding Copyrighted Works Placed on E-Reserve

The materials placed on e-reserve will only be used for non-profit educational activities relating to specific courses or educational programs.

The password required to access the course e-reserve page will only be distributed to students, instructors, instructional support staff, or course administrators for the specific course for which the materials are requested.

The total amount of material placed on e-reserve is reasonable in relation to the total amount of material assigned for one term of a course, taking into account the nature of the course, its subject matter and level. E-reserves are not intended to substitute for coursepacks or commercially available textbooks, anthologies, or other compilations. In some cases, Cook Library may request a copy of the course syllabus before e-reserve requests can be processed.

The requested material is not already included in a coursepack created for the course.

Determining Fair Use

Towson University
Albert S. Cook Library
Towson, Maryland

What is Fair Use?

The fair use statute (Sec. 107, Title 17, U.S. Code) serves as one of several limitations on the exclusive rights granted by federal law to copyright owners. Sec. 107 specifies that use of a copyrighted work for purposes such as "teaching (including multiple copies for classroom use), scholarship, or research" is not an infringement of copyright when the following four factors are taken into consideration in regard to the proposed use:

- the purpose and character of the use;
- the nature of the copyrighted work used;
- the amount and substantiality of the portion used in relation to the copyrighted work as a whole; and
- the effect of the use upon the potential market for or value of the copyrighted work.

In any fair use analysis, consideration must be given to all four factors-the factors must be weighed in the aggregate and no single factor is solely determinative of a finding for or against fair use. The fair use statute contains no definitive limits beyond consideration of the four factors, so each use must be addressed on a case-by-case basis.

The faculty and library responsibilities included in these guidelines apply to all materials placed on e-reserve at Cook Library, but they are also intended to address one or more of the four factors described in Sec. 107 for those materials placed on e-reserve under a claim of fair use.

For more information about fair use, see "Fair Use Issues," on the IUPUI Copyright Management Center's site.

Copyright Owner's Permission

Towson University
Albert S. Cook Library
Towson, Maryland

Cook Library will research any permissions necessary for materials included in e-reserves in excess of fair use.

In cases where payment of a royalty is required and the cost of such payment is prohibitive, Cook Library will consult with the requesting instructor about alternatives to including the material in e-reserves.

Similarly, in cases where permission to post material in e-reserves is requested but denied by the copyright owner, Cook Library will explore alternatives to e-reserves with the requesting instructor. One alternative to including such material in e-reserves may be to place the item on print reserve in Cook Library if the library already owns a legally acquired original copy (as opposed to a photocopy) of the work, or if the library can purchase a commercially available copy of such works when they are not already in its collection.

Chapter 25

REPRODUCTION OF MATERIALS

GENERAL GUIDELINES FOR PRINTING

Duplex Printing

Indiana University–Purdue University Indianapolis
University Library
Indianapolis, Indiana

Is Duplex printing available?

Currently we have one printer available for duplex printing which it is located in the 2nd floor Philanthropic Studies area (2110 cluster). The charge to IU affiliates for a double sided page will be 8¢ (4¢ per printed side).

Can I save money by duplex printing?

No. Duplex printing is very hard on printer hardware, resulting in frequent paper jams and hardware problems. The increase in maintenance costs outweighs the savings in paper.

Can I save money by printing on both sides of the paper (duplex printing)?

While duplex printing conserves paper, it does not reduce printing costs because the cost of paper is a very small part of the cost of printing. In fact, overall waste from unnecessary printing far exceeds any savings from everyone using duplex all the time. Duplex printing also reduces overall printer reliability.

Required Use of University Paper

Indiana University–Purdue University Indianapolis
University Library
Indianapolis, Indiana

Can I bring my own paper?

No. Changing paper quality levels and types is hard on the printers, resulting in higher printer maintenance costs and there is no good way for the library to charge users with their own paper.

On the 4th floor (to your left as you exit the elevator) is a printer designated for Custom Paper. The only custom paper allowed is résumé laser jet paper and colored laser jet paper. The sheets of paper must be no larger than 8 1/2" x 11."

Can I use my own paper?

Paper quality varies greatly and not all paper is well suited for use in laser printers. Therefore, users cannot supply their own paper. You can, however, print using your own paper on the fourth floor of University Library (to your left as you exit the elevator) on a printer designated for custom paper. However, the only custom paper allowed however is standard (8.5"x11") laser jet paper and colored laser jet paper. Use of this service does not reduce the per-page cost of printing.

Rationale for Printing Charges

Indiana University–Purdue University Indianapolis
University Library
Indianapolis, Indiana

Answers to Frequently Asked Questions

Why charge for printing?

Over 4.5 million pages were printed on University Library (UL) public printers last year. Every year the number of pages printed has grown, along with the costs of paper, toner, printers and maintenance. Meanwhile the library has not received any additional funding to cover these rising costs.

Haven't I already paid for printing in my technology fees?

The IUPUI University Library does not receive any technology fees specifically for printing. Printing costs are covered by the University Library budget. While printing costs have increased each year, the University Library budget for printing has not.

Why 4 cents per page?

University Library is charging the minimum per page to assist us with rising printing costs. UL will still incur the bulk of the printing costs for students, faculty and staff.

University Library is hoping this small charge per page will not deter users from printing necessary materials at UL, but will help curb unnecessary printing. Every day of every semester, library staff members remove stacks of printouts abandoned at our printers. Many times, the user only wanted one page of a document, but printed the entire document to save steps. Hopefully, this small charge will encourage users to print only what they require.

How was the cost per page determined?

Because Indiana University is a not-for-profit institution, the cost per page was established on a cost-recovery basis. The four cents per page will help recover costs associated with the entire print process, including toner, paper, replacement printer parts, personnel, hardware and software support, as well as database and server management of the systems which support the print process. This price is below that of commercial laser printing services and below the cost-per-page of ink used in personal inkjet printers.

University of Wisconsin Green Bay
Cofrin Library
Green Bay, Wisconsin

Self-service Copying
$.10 per image for paper records; $.25 per image for microfilm and microfiche records

FEES FOR SPECIAL SERVICES

Fees for Reproducing Nonprint and Special Print Materials

Georgia State University
Georgia State University Library
Atlanta, Georgia

Policy

    1. In order to ensure the careful handling of Special Collections & Archives materials, all copying is done or arrangements made by Special Collections & Archives staff. Personal duplication/reproduction equipment is not allowed in the reading room without prior permission.

2. Special Collections & Archives will not reproduce entire manuscript or archival collections or extensive sections of collections.

3. Reproduction of audio or visual tapes will be done on a case-by-case basis. This determination will be based on preservation issues, donor restrictions or copyright restrictions imposed upon the item. When copy negatives must be made, they become the property of Special Collections & Archives. Original materials from the Special Collections & Archives collections will not be lent to researchers.

4. Items so fragile that they would be damaged in the process of duplicating them will not be reproduced. Materials will not be reproduced if the procedure will in any way injure the material, for example: Bound newspapers, tightly bound volumes, early manuscripts, or rare books. The decision to prohibit reproduction will be made by the staff member at the reference desk; this decision is final.

5. Certain materials cannot be copied because of restrictions placed upon the item by the donor or agency of origin. In every case, copyright law (Title 17 of the U.S. Code) and the doctrine of educational fair use (Section 107 of H.R. 2223) applies.

6. Copies of materials housed in Special Collections & Archives are to be used solely for scholarly research. The department reserves the right to request the return of photocopies. Copyright is not conveyed with the copies. The researcher must not quote from, publish, reproduce, or display any material in the copy, in whole or in part, without written permission from the copyright holder and from Special Collections & Archives. Transfer of copies to another library or repository is prohibited, except with written permission of the Head of Special Collections.

7. Materials which Special Collections & Archives has obtained from other institutions or projects cannot be copied unless the researcher has obtained written permission of the original institution. The researcher assumes all responsibility for questions of copyright and invasion of privacy that may arise in copying audio-visual materials and in the use made of the copies.

8. Researchers may contact the department for a list of freelance researchers who can be employed to examine the collections and select relevant items for reproduction.

Please contact the Head of Special Collections with any questions concerning this policy.

Approved July 2003.

Procedures

All services must be pre-paid. Payment may be made either by cash, check, or money order. Checks and money orders should be made payable to "Georgia State University Library." Inter-departmental payments may be made via account transfer.

Georgia State University
Georgia State University Library
Atlanta, Georgia

Prices

Photocopies: 25 cents for letter and legal size

50 cents for 11 X 17

Some photocopy requests may require 24 hours or more for completion, such as: Requests for 25 pages or more, documents that require special handling, or requests placed after 4:00 p.m.

Service Fee: $15.00 per order for work done by an outside facility.

B&W Photographic Prints: $6.75 for 5 X 7

$8.25 for 8 X 10

$14.00 for 11 X 14

$25.00 for 16 X 20

When a 4X5 copy negative must be made there will be an additional charge of $20.00. Copy negatives and transparencies will remain the property of Special Collections.

Duplicating items with own equipment: Setup and handling fee of $25.00 and $1.00 per image

Slides: $6.50 each

Digital Scans:		
	Medium-resolution image scan (1,200 X 1,500 pixels)	$5.00 each
	High-resolution image scan (<1,200 X 1,500 pixels)	$20.00 each
	Digital copy of an existing scan	$2.00 each
	Computer diskettes	$1.00 each
	CD-ROM	$3.00 each
	Digital black & white laser print	50 cents each
	Digital print, glossy photo quality paper, black & white or color	$2.00 each

Computer diskettes: Finding aids and scans on diskette are $5.00 for each disk.

Audio Tapes and CDs: $12.00 per cassette or CD

Video Tapes: $13.00 for duplication onto VHS

Faxes: $5.00 for sending every 10 pages (no charge for providing introductory information at time of initial contact).

Postage and Handling:		
	Total order cost is $10** or less	add: $2.00
	Total order cost is between $10 & $20	add: $3.00
	Total order cost is $20 or more	add: $4.00
	Certified mail (Large orders)	add: $7.00

On request, we can accommodate rush mailings. There is a $25.00 rush fee plus other applicable fees.

Please allow at least 10 working days for the completion of all photographic or audio reproduction orders. Requesting a faster completion time may incur rush charges (depending on our present work load). Times are computed on business day hours. For 8–16 hours add 100%; less than 8 hours add 200%.

A deposit is required on all large orders. The amount for deposit will be approximately half of the total estimated cost.

There will be an additional charge of $30.00 per item for commercial projects and a charge of $10.00 per item for University Press projects.

**For Photocopy orders over 40 pages there is a $2.00 postage fee for each additional 40 pages.

Payment

Advance payment is required for all orders. Checks should be made payable to "GSU Library" and mailed to the archivist assisting your order at:

Special Collections & Archives

The University Library

Cash payments may be made by on-site researchers.

Georgia State University employees may request that Accounting Services expense their Department's speedtype and transfer these funds into LIBS4. Please send a copy of your transfer request to the archivist assisting your order.

University of California Santa Cruz
University of California Santa Cruz University Library
Santa Cruz, California

How much does photocopying cost?

McHenry Library:

Photocopies cost $0.15 per page when paying with cash, $0.08 per page when using a copy card (Slug Card) from the UCSC Copier Program.

Science & Engineering Library:

Photocopies cost $0.15 per page when paying with cash, $0.08 per page when using a copy card (Slug Card) from the UCSC Copier Program.

Georgia State University
Georgia State University Library
Atlanta, Georgia

Photocopies:

Requests for photocopies should be made of the staff member at the reference desk. Every attempt will be made to complete photocopy requests in a timely manner. Orders will not be completed on a while-you-wait basis. The normal turnaround time is 24 hours. Exceptions are granted for requests of 7 pages or less. Large orders may take several days to process. The cost is 25 cents per page. Photocopies can be picked up or mailed; if mailed there is a shipping and handling fee.

The procedure for photocopy reproduction is as follows:

1. Please complete the Photocopy Request Form (available here for offsite researchers).
2. Please be sure archives staff is aware of what needs to be copied.
3. Please do not remove original material from folders. Turn the Photocopy Request Slip (yellow form) perpendicular and in front of the materials you would like copied in the folder. This will ensure the materials remain in order. For bound volumes (if it is permissible for the volume(s) to be copied) write the pages you would like copied on the Photocopy Request Form.

Fees for Copying Archival Documents

North Park University
Archives and Special Collections
Chicago, Illinois

Copies: Patrons may make photocopies of documents on the provided copy machine, at the discretion of the Archivist. To help us prolong the life of the documents, please ask for assistance when working with fragile items.

Cost: 10 cents per page.

Off-site patrons not able to visit the Archives may request photocopies of previously identified records up to the amount of 50 pages, per semester. Please note that the Archives staff can not provide any research within the identified records. Cost: 10 cents per page, plus postage. The order will be filled upon the receipt of money and as staff time allows.

Fees for Notary Service

University of Wisconsin Green Bay
Cofrin Library
Green Bay, Wisconsin

There will be a $5.00 handling fee for all notarizing of documents.

All responsibility for questions of copyright that may arise in copying and in the use of copies will be assumed by the user. A signed Indemnification Agreement is required for all publication and production use.

Fees for Searching and Copying Records

University of Wisconsin Green Bay
Cofrin Library
Green Bay, Wisconsin

Copying Services

A $5.00 advance payment will be required for each name searched in each of these types of records: Vital records (birth, marriage, death); citizenship records; census records; court records; probate records; tax rolls; other public records; manuscript collections and published sources (books, maps).

If the record requested is found and is less than 5 pages in length, a copy will be provided at no additional charge. If the record is found and is more than 5 pages in length, a cost estimate will be provided using the following guidelines:

- $.50 per page for copies from paper records
- $.60 per page for copies from microfilm records

If you would like us to proceed with the copy job after you have received our cost estimate, you must pay that amount in advance.

Search & Copy Request Forms for the various types of records are available on-line to print, fill out, and mail in with your check. At this time, we are unable to accept credit card payments, online, or phone requests.

Fees and Guidelines for Scanning

North Park University
Archives and Special Collections
Chicago, Illinois

Scanning: Patrons may scan textual documents, if the condition of the document allows. Scanning of tightly bound papers or fragile items is prohibited. Upon discretion of the Archivist, on-site patrons may scan up to 5 documents per visit, using their own equipment. Also upon discretion of the Archivist, the Archives may scan up to 5 documents with our scanner. The charge for the latter service is $1.00 per image, and computer disks must be provided by the patron. Copy and Request form for each document must be signed before scanning

University of Wisconsin Green Bay
Cofrin Library
Green Bay, Wisconsin

Scanning

Many of the materials in the Special Collections Department can be scanned. All responsibility for questions of copyright that may arise in scanning and in the use of copies will be assumed by the user. A signed Indemnification Agreement is required for all publication and production use.

- Scan to laser printer—$1.00 per image
- Scan to disk/CD—$1.00 per image and $2.50 disk/CD fee
- Scan to e-mail: $1.00 per image.

Each scanning job will also have a $15.00 processing charge. Normal delivery time is 2 weeks.

University of Wisconsin Green Bay
Cofrin Library
Green Bay, Wisconsin

Self-service Scanning

- Scan to laser printer: $1.00 per image
- Scan to disk/CD: $1.00 per image + $2.50 disk/CD fee
- Scan to e-mail: no charge

Fees for Duplicating Photographs

North Park University
Archives and Special Collections
Chicago, Illinois

Photographs

Copies: Patrons may request copies of photographs. The costs are as follows:

- Black and White, 5" x 7" $10, if copy negative available
- Black and White, 5"x 7" $25, if copy negative unavailable
- Black and White, 8"x 10" $12, if copy negative available
- Black and White, 8" x 10" $27, if copy negative unavailable
- Color, 5" x 7" $20, if copy negative available
- Color, 5" x 7" $40, if copy negative unavailable
- Color, 8" x 10" $23, if copy negative available
- Color, 8" x 10" $43, if copy negative unavailable

The Archives retains any copy negatives. Copy and Request forms must be signed for each photograph ordered. The order will be processed by Archives staff upon the receipt of money and form.

Scanning: Upon discretion of the Archivist, on-site patrons may scan up to 5 photos per visit, using their own equipment. Also upon discretion of the Archivist, the Archives may scan up to 5 images with our scanner. The charge for the latter service is $1.00 per image, and computer disks must be provided by the patron. Copy and Request forms for each image must be signed before scanning.

University of Wisconsin Green Bay
Cofrin Library
Green Bay, Wisconsin

Photographic Prints

When ordering media reproductions, please include identification numbers, any published references, and photocopies of the images. Also, please state the intended use of the materials requested. Any special copying, handling or mailing instructions should be included with the order. Negatives are not provided for photographic orders. All fees are subject to change. All sales are final. Some material may not be available for copying due to restrictions. All responsibility for questions of copyright that may arise in copying and in the use of copies will be assumed by the user. A signed Indemnification Agreement is required for all publication and production use.

If a negative is on file:

- 4 x 5—$5.00
- 5 x 7—$7.50
- 8 x 10—$7.50

If a negative is NOT on file:

- 4 x 5—$7.50
- 5 x 7—$10.00
- 8 x 10—$12.50

Prices for other sizes available upon request. Each reproduction job will also have a $5.00 processing charge. Normal delivery time is 2 weeks.

Georgia State University
Georgia State University Library
Atlanta, Georgia

Photographic Reproductions

Photographic reproductions may be provided from selected pages of books, manuscripts, or original photographs. Please consult the staff member at the reference desk for the proper procedure.

A photographic reproduction, under normal circumstances, will take from 7 to 14 business days. Orders can be expedited but there is an additional fee for this service.

Fees for Color Printing and Copying

University of Wisconsin Madison
Memorial Library
Madison, Wisconsin

Color Photocopies

Color photocopier with a cost of 58¢ per image.

York College
Schmidt Library
York, Pennsylvania

Color Printing (available for YCP faculty, staff, and enrolled students)

A full color laser printer is available for printing paper copies or transparencies. Items can be scanned and printed or printed from a CD, USB drive, or your network drive. This service requires a YCP network account and assistance from Information Services staff. The cost is $0.50 for paper and $1.00 for a transparency.

FEES FOR SPECIFIC FORMATS

Oral History Recordings

University of Wisconsin Green Bay
Cofrin Library
Green Bay, Wisconsin

All reproductions are produced on audio cassettes. If the original is on a reel-to-reel tape there is a $8.00 set up fee. Fees are based on number of minutes copied:

- 0–30 minutes—$7.50
- 30–60 minutes—$8.00
- 60–90 minutes—$9.00

All responsibility for questions of copyright that may arise in copying and in the use of copies will be assumed by the user. A signed Indemnification Agreement is required for all publication and production use.

Each reproduction job will also have a $15.00 processing charge. Normal delivery time is 2 weeks.

Architectural Drawings

University of Wisconsin Green Bay
Cofrin Library
Green Bay, Wisconsin

Charges for reproductions of videos, film, and filmstrips are available upon request. Architectural drawings are $5.00 each.

Lamination

York College
Schmidt Library
York, Pennsylvania

Lamination

The cost for lamination is $0.05 an inch. The laminator is 24" wide. Ask for assistance at Information Services to laminate larger items.

Overhead Transparencies

York College
Schmidt Library
York, Pennsylvania

Overhead Transparencies

Thermal transparencies are made from a carbon-based original source, such as a photocopy, from the scanner or from a file on a disc or your network drive.

Price list:
- Write-on $0.10
- Black on clear $0.50
- Red on clear $0.50
- Purple on clear $0.50
- Green on clear $0.50
- Yellow on blue $0.50
- Yellow on purple $0.50
- Yellow on green $0.50
- Full color $1.00

Printing Computer Graphics as Posters

York College
Schmidt Library
York, Pennsylvania

Full Color Poster Printer (available for YCP faculty, staff and enrolled students)

This printer will create full color posters, up to 41" x 70", from graphic programs such as PowerPoint. The cost is $0.30 per inch. This service requires staff assistance and a YCP network account. Ask for assistance at Information Services

Single Color Poster Printer

This printer will enlarge an 8 1/2 x 11 piece of paper to larger sizes of 17" or 23" wide. The background is white with a variety of colors available for the print. The cost is $0.12 per inch.

Microforms

University of California Santa Cruz
University of California Santa Cruz University Library
Santa Cruz, California

Can I print from Microforms or Microfiche (and how much does it cost)?

McHenry Library:

Yes. There are three microfilm/microfiche readers with printing capacity in Microfilms. Printed pages cost $0.20. For this, Library Print Cards can be purchased from a vending machine located near the Government Publications desk, 2nd floor, McHenry Library.

Science & Engineering Library:

Yes. There is one microfilm/microfiche reader with printing capacity on the Lower Level by the Map Room. Printed pages cost $ 0.20 with a Library Print Card (Xerox card) available from the vending machine in the S.H. Cowell Room.

FORMS

Request for Photocopies from Special Collections

Special Collections Department

University Library

Georgia State Library

Photocopy Request Form

The Special Collections Department furnishes photocopies as an aid to private study, scholarship, or research. The Department reserves the right to refuse copying because of the physical condition of the material, restrictions on the material, or copyright laws. The amount of copying may be limited at the discretion of the Department or the donor; copying for other than scholarly purposes may be limited at the discretion of the Department or the donor. When unusually large or complicated photocopy orders and requests for copying for purposes other than scholarly research are accepted, additional fees may apply.

Notice: Warning Concerning Copyright Restrictions

The copyright law of the United States (Title 17, U. S. Code) governs the making of photocopies or other reproductions of copyrighted material. Under certain conditions specified in the law, libraries and archives are authorized to furnish a photocopy or other reproductions. One of these specified conditions is that the photocopy or reproduction is not to be "used for any purpose other than private study, scholarship, or research." If a user makes a request for, or later uses, a photocopy or reproduction for purposes in excess of "fair use," that user may be liable for copyright infringement. This institution reserves the right to refuse to accept a copy order if, in its judgment, fulfillment of the order would involve violation of the copyright law.

Please Sign the Following Statement

I assume all responsibility for complying with U.S. copyright restrictions applicable to these materials and agree to indemnify and hold harmless the Board of Regents of the University System of Georgia, Georgia State University, and their officers and employees, from and against any claims for invasion of privacy, copyright infringement, or any other claims, suits, costs, and liabilities arising out of any use of the material copied. I understand that receipt of copies does not constitute permission to publish, and that I am responsible for obtaining such permission.

Name (printed) _____

Signature: _____

Date:_____ Copies to be mailed _____ (postage to be paid by researcher)

Mailing address (please print legibly):

_____

_____

_____

_____

Instructions

1. **DO NOT REMOVE ITEMS FROM FOLDERS OR FOLDERS FROM BOXES. DO NOT REARRANGE THE CONTENTS OF ANY BOX OR FOLDER**. If you find that the contents of a box or folder are out of order, please bring the problem to the attention of the reading room archivist.
2. **Please fill out and attach a copy slip to each item you select for copying.** Copy slips are available from the reading room archivist. Attach the copy slip to item in such a manner that the slip protrudes from the long side of the folder; leave the material to be copied in its original place in the folder; and return the folder to the box.
3. **List each copy slip on this form,** including the collection name or book title, the box and folder number or call number, and the number of pages. Leave the last column ("Amount Owed") blank.
4. Researchers must pay for their copies before receiving them.

COLL. NAME/ BOOK TITLE	BOX/CALL #	FOLDER/PAGE #	NO. PAGES	AMOUNT OWED

Reference Person(s) _____ Previous Balance _____

Copy Person(s) _____ Total Due _____ ( ) Paid

Date paid _____

Part VII
Government Documents

Chapter 26

GOVERNMENT DOCUMENTS GUIDELINES

ACCESS TO THE COLLECTION

Lake Sumter Community College
Lake Sumter Community College Libraries
Sumterville, Florida

General Access Policy

Physical access to the LSCC government documents collection is available to any member of the general public. The Library is open to the general public, and the documents collection is freely available in open stacks, which are centrally located and clearly marked with library signage. Any library user may physically handle and use any government document at the Library without impediments.

Government documents are cataloged in the Library's online public access catalog, LINCC. Through its memberships in the Central Florida Library Cooperative, SOLINET, and OCLC, the resources of the depository are shared on local, state, regional, national, and international levels. The Central Florida Library Cooperative's Government Documents Interest Group publishes an annual union list of item numbers, which facilitates access and referral on a regional level.

INTERLIBRARY LOAN PROCEDURES

University of Iowa
University of Iowa Libraries
Iowa City, Iowa

Interlibrary Cooperation

1. The University of Iowa recognizes its depository resource sharing responsibilities and will loan most government publications in accordance with existing University Libraries' interlibrary loan policy.
   a. As the library of last resort, publications will be loaned directly to other libraries within the state, regardless of any statewide protocols that may be in place.
   b. When conditions permit and necessity dictates, materials may be faxed to other depository libraries.
2. As the Federal Depository Library Program Regional library, the University of Iowa Libraries recognizes its responsibility to consult with and advise Iowa selective depositories.
3. As a member of various library consortia, The University of Iowa Libraries will, whenever contractual agreements permit, contribute appropriate bibliographic records, including records of government documents, to such utilities such as OCLC, RLIN, and SILO.

Chapter 27

GOVERNMENT DOCUMENTS COLLECTION AND RESOURCE GUIDELINES

COLLECTION DEVELOPMENT POLICY

University of Iowa
University of Iowa Libraries
Iowa City, Iowa

Collection Development

1. Depository material in tangible formats will be retained as a resource for the State of Iowa and in accordance with depository program requirements. Access will be provided to electronic information resources released through depository programs.
2. Other materials will be acquired selectively as needed for instruction and research purposes in support of the depository collections and the research mission of The University of Iowa Libraries. Gifts will be added to the collection at the discretion of the appropriate documents specialist.
3. Every attempt will be made to fill gaps in serial holdings in order to maintain the integrity of publication titles.
4. The collection managers/documents specialists will acquire and maintain the reference works considered essential to the effective use of the collection.

Collection Management

1. Collection management activities will be divided among documents specialists according to responsibilities outlined in corresponding job descriptions.
2. Maps will generally be housed in the Map Collection or the Geoscience Library.
3. Microforms, audiovisual materials, CD-ROMs, diskettes, and other alternative formats will be treated in a similar manner to print publications wherever possible.
4. Shelflist records via InfoHawk will be maintained concerning receipt and placement of materials.
5. Materials are arranged using several classification schemes including Superintendent of Documents Classification System (SuDocs), Library of Congress, Dewey, United Nations and Swank systems. Reclassification when possible to reduce the number of publications in non-standard classification systems is a desired goal.
6. Acquisition of missing serial volumes, revised editions, and active supplementation in strong collection areas will be the responsibilities of documents specialists collaborating with Bibliographers when appropriate.
7. Supplements will be filed/interfiled with the parent publications in a timely manner.
8. The collection will be weeded according to the collection scope and stated collection levels (see Appendix).
9. Only the latest cumulative volumes will be retained.

Johnson State College
Johnson State College Library
Johnson, Vermont

Collection Policy

United States Government Documents Depository

I. Mission

The John Dewey Library of Johnson State College, which is located in the U.S. Congressional District At Large, was the first of the Vermont State Colleges to become a Senate-designated Federal Depository in 1955. The mission of the Library is to serve the 1,700 students who comprise the undergraduate and graduate populations of Johnson State College and to meet the scholarly and professional development needs of its faculty and staff. By Virtue of the Library's location in rural north central Vermont, it also functions as a public library for Lamoille County, population 19,735 (Census 1990). As such, we promote free access to our collections for all segments of our user population.

II. Mandate

In accordance with requirements defined in the Federal Depository Library Manual Supplement 2: Guidelines for the Federal Depository Library Program, February, 1996, the Library collects government documents to support the interests of the general public as will as the academic community it serves. Citizens in Lamoille County are either employed in the tourism and service industries, agriculture, or engaged in the provision of health services and schooling on various levels, with Johnson State College representing the high end of the educational spectrum. Small business ownership is perceived as critical to economic stability in this and the other 13 counties throughout the state.

Although we tend to think geographically with respect to our community of users, it must be noted that as a State College library, we encourage access by Vermonters who are often willing to travel long distances to use our collections. It is not uncommon to extend borrowing privileges to citizens outside of our county's boundaries.

III. Methods and Objectives

To meet the needs of our constituents and to help fulfill our role as a public library presence in Lamoille County, collection development activities are concentrated in these subject areas: Agriculture, health, business, education, environment, legislation, consumer affairs. Consequently, special attention will be paid to publications issued by the following agencies, departments, and government establishments:

- Department of Agriculture
- Department of Commerce
- Department of Education
- Department of Energy
- Department of Health and Human Services
- Department of the Interior
- Department of State
- Environmental Protection Agency
- National Archives and Records Administration
- National Foundation of the Arts and the Humanities
- Small Business Administration

Future revisions of this policy will delineate subject areas, collection development intensity levels, and publication types/formats as suggested in Section 4 "Subject Areas and Collection Arrangement" in the Federal Depository Library Manual Supplement: Collection Development Guidelines for Selective Depositories, September 1994.

Selection responsibility is distributed among reference staff who serve all segments of the user population and who are knowledgeable of patron needs and the resources available in this library and elsewhere. In addition to annual reviews of item selections using the List of Classes of the United States government

Publications Available for Selection by Depository Libraries, the "Suggested Core Collection Annotated for Small to Medium Public Libraries and Academic Libraries and for All Law Libraries", the Publications Reference File and Subject Bibliographies, librarians will respond to GPO surveys, selecting new items as they are available and when they meet collection development goals. Non-depository selection tools include these sources:

Sears, M.K. and Moody, J.L. *Using Government Information Sources: Print and Electronic*, 2nd ed., 1994.

PAIS International in Print

Library Journal's "Notable Documents of (Year)" sponsored by ALA's GODORT

The Library currently selects all item numbers listed in the "Basic Collection" in Appendix C in the FDLP manual. Moreover, the top 200 item selection checklist has been used in the past as a comparative measure to gauge the viability of our collection.

Our objective is to maintain an instructional or working collection with an emphasis on selecting current materials. Referrals to area depositories will be made for research and use of historical or retrospective sources.

IV. Weeding and Maintenance

The Library adheres to the guidelines in the Instructions to Depository Libraries and strives to maintain the Federal Depository material entrusted to its care. All depository items are marked with a three part stamp and SuDoc number. Separate shelving arrangements for selected reference sources that are catalogued in DDC are listed in the procedures manual. Annotations on the shelflist cards for those sources indicate location and disposition while they are temporarily available at the reference desk. A separate file cabinet for pamphlets has been purchased an the item location is noted on SCOLAR. Replacements for heavily used documents or nondepository items will be made through the use of an established GPO Deposit Account #122632–3.

Items will be withdrawn from the collection according to this plan:

1) Superseded documents after receipt of new edition or update and according to the "List of Superseded Documents," Appendix C of Instructions to Depository Libraries.
2) SIRSI reports based on the item inventory date, and thus meeting the five-year holding date, may be requested from the Vermont State College Bibliographic Database Coordinator to generate a list for possible deselection.
3) Documents held five years that no longer meet collection development criteria will be itemized on discard lists and sent to the Regional Depository at the University of Maine, Orono, Maine.

V. Resource Sharing and Access

Linked through SIRSI, our online library system, to the collections of the other Vermont State Colleges, the University of Vermont, Norwich University, Middlebury College, St. Michael's College, Trinity College of Vermont and the State of Vermont Department of Libraries, the Library engages in very high volume ILL transactions utilizing electronic mail requests placed between libraries via the SIRSI software that most in-state libraries use. On a national and international level, the Library has participated in interlibrary loan as a member of OCLC since May 1985. Within this networked external environment, identification, location and retrieval of documents not held by this library has improved increasingly as more libraries have gone online, helping us to meet our obligation as a Depository Library in supplying government information to other libraries and depositories—a function of our resource sharing imperative. Currently, the ILL code for the Vermont Resource Sharing Network is under revision, and forthcoming changes will be incorporated into our policy.

Contacts are maintained with the local USDA Agricultural Extension Agent in Morrisville and the Lamoille County Planning Commission a referral sources for mapping and industry statistics for the area.

Public services staff monitor the GOVDOC-L listserv, attend meetings of the Government Publications Libraries of New England (GPLNE) when possible and visit depository libraries in the region to help keep abreast of access issues, collections, and personnel.

Internet access is maintained with the development of pathfinders and guides to the literature incorporating vital document sources necessary to the search process; promotion of the Library's status as a Federal Depository is expected and delivered in the bibliographic instruction sessions offered by librarians. Area teachers are encouraged to bring classes on field trips during semester breaks so that their students are exposed to the realm of academic libraries.

The Depository collection is housed in state-of-the-art compact moveable shelving in open stacks accessible to the public. With the exception of standard reference sources (designated Ref. Doc. material code) and periodicals, government documents circulate without restriction to primary user groups and the community. The new Library/Learning Center scheduled to open August 1, 1996 will be fully ADA compliant with abundant signage and a floor plan describing the location of the separate stack arrangement for the documents collection but with ready access to the reference/ information desk.

With the impending, ubiquitous electronic delivery of government information, continuous revision of this policy will be necessary to incorporate new technologies that will undoubtedly see libraries emerging as clearinghouses and directing patron inquiries to appropriate sources regardless of format. The move to a new library should help position us with the equipment we will need to meet and even exceed the "Recommended Minimal Technical Guidelines" (January 1995 revision) set forth by the Library Programs Service of the GPO and reiterated in Administrative Notes, December 15, 1995. With hardware in place, the shift to software decisions based on knowing what formats—and what content is available in those sources—will be essential in the selection decisions made by government documents librarians in the future.

INTERNAL REVENUE DISTRIBUTION GUIDELINES

Florida Atlantic University
S. E. Wimbrely Library
Boca Raton, Florida

Internal Revenue Forms

Approximately in August or September of every year, the Internal Revenue Service will send the Florida Atlantic University Library a "Request for Federal Income Tax Forms for Miscellaneous (or BPOL) Accounts" (Form 9161). This survey will reflect the Library's request for public distribution of general IRS tax forms and related instructions for the previous year. The Documents Librarian should review the survey, complete it, and return it promptly to the Internal Revenue Service to ensure the forms are received.

The forms and accompanying instructions will be shipped in late December. When received, they are placed out in the Documents area for patrons to help themselves. If additional forms are needed, the Documents Librarian may decide to order more depending on time of year, availability of staff, etc.

No assistance is provided to patrons in filling the forms out. Patrons may be referred to local libraries providing that service, to the IRS offices, to private companies or accountants.

INTERNAL AND ELECTRONIC RESOURCE SYSTEM GUIDELINES

Lake Sumter Community College
Lake Sumter Community College Libraries
Sumterville, Florida

Electronic Access Policy

LSCC Library adheres to the Depository Library Public Service Guidelines For Government Information in Electronic Formats. As a result, the LSCC Government Documents Department offers free public access to electronic information provided by the Government Printing Office. A workstation in the Government Documents Department provides access to many CD-ROMs available through the GPO. These sources provide access to government statistics, maps, patent information and other useful products. Internet access to government information is available via computer workstations in the main library and at branch campus libraries, and through the computer workstation in the Government Documents Department.

The LSCC Library also adheres to FDLP's Internet Use Policy Guidelines. LSCC's Internet Acceptable Use Guidelines specifically state that as a participant in the Federal Depository Library Program, the LSCC Library must provide access to federal government documents to any requestor. In addition any LSCC library user, at any campus library, may access the Internet to retrieve government publications for personal or commercial use. Acceptable use guidelines preventing e-mail, chat, downloading to any hard drive, etc. apply to government documents users as well. Downloading any government publication to a floppy disk is allowed at all stations, and Adobe Acrobat readers are installed on all Internet capable computers to assist with access and printing. Printing is also available at all public workstations.

Librarians provide assistance in accessing government information on the Internet by using the Library's homepage as a gateway to many government sources. The Government Documents section in the Cyber-library, provides links to many government web sites by department. A Subject Directory of government sites helps users find information on specific topics.

PRESERVING GOVERNMENT DOCUMENTS

University of Iowa
University of Iowa Libraries
Iowa City, Iowa

Preservation Policy

The goal in establishing a preservation policy for the Government Publications collection is to ensure the usability, durability and longevity of government information resources and hence, access to government information in varying formats to all library users in accordance with the American Library Association Preservation Policy. In close partnership with and guidance of the Preservation Department, the Government Publications collections will be preserved through various methods including but not limited to the following:

1. routine utilization of commercial binding services for serials and monographic publications.
2. appropriate and non-damaging storage including use of pamphlet shelving, non-acid pamphlet boxes, shrink wrap, binders to house loose-leaf materials, archival quality envelopes and slings for small or fragile pamphlets, and the use of non-damaging shelving methods.
3. remedial treatment of damaged and fragile items such as hinge tightening, and shrink wrapping of fragile infrequently used material.
4. preservation of materials in their original format when possible (paper to paper, fiche to fiche, electronic to electronic).
5. replacement or reformatting of deteriorated materials using methods such as photocopying on acid free paper or possible digitization.
6. application of appropriate security measures such as the use of security strips and standardized circulation practices to help assure collection accountability.
7. creation and/or supplementation of bibliographic records to enhance security, access, and preservation, and to facilitate collaborative efforts to protect government information.

REPLACING GOVERNMENT DOCUMENTS

Florida Atlantic University
S. E. Wimbrely Library
Boca Raton, Florida

Replacement of Lost Government Documents By Patrons

"Depository materials which are lost, tattered or damaged, etc., should be subject to the same replacement policy that the library maintains for non-government materials." Instructions to Depository Libraries

A government document in the Florida Atlantic University is defined as that product which bears an identifying stamp of the Florida Atlantic University Government Documents Department or which in its uniqueness would identify it as an official product of a federal or state government agency. This would include U.S. and Florida documents in a variety of formats (i.e., paper, microform, floppy diskette, or compact disk).

If a patron requests to replace a lost government document at the patron's own expense and effort, the decision to accept this request will be made by the Government Documents Librarian. Should a document be replaced by the patron, there will be a $10.00 processing charge. This charge approximates the costs incurred for bibliographic verification, physical processing, online corrections, etc. completed by library staff (e.g., cataloging, documents, circulation). Any replacement should be exact in bibliographic detail and quality of the original document. If a document can be replaced by the library, the patron will be assessed the cost of the replacement and the $10.00 processing charge. Replacement costs may vary from costs listed in the Sale Product Catalog (online), ILL photocopy charges, NTIS Government Reports Announcements, the CIS Documents on Demand program or a price quote from the producing agency (federal or state). Charges for compact disks vary from $35 to several hundred dollars.

If a government document is returned damaged, the Government Documents Librarian will determine whether the document should be repaired or replaced.

Chapter 28

GOVERNMENT DOCUMENTS REFERENCE AND CIRCULATION GUIDELINES

REPLACING LOST MATERIALS

Florida Atlantic University
S. E. Wimbrely Library
Boca Raton, Florida

Replacement of Lost Government Documents By Patrons

"Depository materials which are lost, tattered or damaged, etc., should be subject to the same replacement policy that the library maintains for non-government materials."

Instructions to Depository Libraries

A government document in the Florida Atlantic University is defined as that product which bears an identifying stamp of the Florida Atlantic University Government Documents Department or which in its uniqueness would identify it as an official product of a federal or state government agency. This would include U.S. and Florida documents in a variety of formats (i.e., paper, microform, floppy diskette, or compact disk).

If a patron requests to replace a lost government document at the patron's own expense and effort, the decision to accept this request will be made by the Government Documents Librarian. Should a document be replaced by the patron, there will be a $10.00 processing charge. This charge approximates the costs incurred for bibliographic verification, physical processing, online corrections, etc. completed by library staff (e.g., cataloging, documents, circulation). Any replacement should be exact in bibliographic detail and quality of the original document. If a document can be replaced by the library, the patron will be assessed the cost of the replacement and the $10.00 processing charge. Replacement costs may vary from costs listed in the Sale Product Catalog (online), ILL photocopy charges, NTIS Government Reports Announcements, the CIS Documents on Demand program or a price quote from the producing agency (federal or state). Charges for compact disks vary from $35 to several hundred dollars.

If a government document is returned damaged, the Government Documents Librarian will determine whether the document should be repaired or replaced.

REFERENCE SERVICES

Florida Atlantic University
S. E. Wimbrely Library
Boca Raton, Florida

The Reference Desk is the primary reference service point for assistance using basic government documents (federal and state). Depositories are located in libraries so that members of the general public will have access to reference tools, knowledgeable librarians and other library resources. Reference service offered to members of the general public using the depository will be comparable to the reference service given to the library's primary patrons. Competent ready reference service, indexes and other tools to locate government information in the collection, need to be available to all depository patrons.

Patrons will be able to locate specific documents in the depository by title and/or class number or other access points. At a minimum, staff should be able to locate and mount electronic products and its documentation on the proper workstation. Since most depository libraries are selective and, therefore, not recipients of all government documents disseminated through the Federal Depository Library Program, and since the Federal Depository Library Program functions best as a system of cooperating libraries, the documents staff should be familiar with resources of neighboring depositories and be able to make appropriate referrals.

Assistance is provided in finding resources in the collection, including specific titles; location of requested publications in the library; answers to reference questions or a referral to a source or place where answers can be found; guidance on the use of the collection, including the principal available reference sources, catalogs, abstracts, indexes, and other aids; availability of additional resources in the region; information regarding borrowing documents from a regional or other library. Self-operating photocopiers are provided for patron convenience. Because of the limited number of staff and the complexity of the retrieval of certain types of questions, patrons with inquiries of a legal, medical, or statistical nature will usually be referred to appropriate sources in which they may research their question.

Statistical information where the information is straight forward from a table and easily retrieved may be given. The requestor of lengthy statistical questions will be encouraged to come into the Library to retrieve the answer(s). Limited funding and number of staff also preclude the Government Documents Department from extensive searches, specialized bibliography compilations, or software programming assistance. These same limitations encourage appointments for consultations, where the information sought requires more in-depth instruction and assistance in the use of the Government Documents collections.

Lake Sumter Community College
Lake Sumter Community College Libraries
Sumterville, Florida

Reference Services

The government documents reference desk is the primary reference service point for government documents assistance when the reference/government documents librarian is on duty. At all other times the library is open, the reference/circulation desk is the service point for government documents. Reference staff are periodically familiarized with basic government publications and access methods with in-house workshops conducted by the reference/government documents librarian.

Reference services offered to students and members of the general public using the depository are comparable to the reference services given to the library's primary patrons. Competent ready reference services, indexes and other tools to locate government information in the collection are available to all depository patrons.

CIRCULATION

Florida Atlantic University
S.E. Wimbrely Library
Boca Raton, Florida

Circulation of Government Documents

Paper

Most federal and state government publications circulate through the Library's online circulation system and according to the Library's policies and procedures. Non-circulating publications are those with "DOC PER" prefacing the documents call numbers or those stamped "FOR REFERENCE USE ONLY". The general public not affiliated with Florida Atlantic University (and not having a valid FAU Library card) may use the materials in-house or will be referred to their respective libraries for interlibrary loan service. Self-service photocopiers are located throughout the Library.

Microform

Microforms do not circulate. The Library has provided self-service microform photocopiers. Documents on microfilm do not circulate.

Maps

USGS/NIMA (DMA) topographic/quadrangle maps do not circulate. USGS maps received in the manila/brown folders do circulate.

Electronic Products

Selected electronic products (i.e., floppies, compact disks) circulate. Older issues of serial electronic products and those serial electronic products not identified for permanent retention may be allowed to circulate at the discretion of the Documents Librarian. A copy of the floppy diskette, NOT THE ORIGINAL, will be allowed to circulate.

Special Exceptions

Should a special exception be given to circulate non-circulating government publications, the "Non-Circulating Items Release" form must be completed and filed at the Reference Desk. For electronic products, the "Non-Circulating Items Release" form must be completed and kept by the Government Documents Department.

Reserve

For reasons of security and/or heavy demand, selected documents are removed from their normal location on the government document shelves and placed on RESERVE. These publications do not circulate outside the library building. They are for in house use only and time limits may be placed on their use (i.e., 3 hrs, etc).

While most publications on Reserve require the patron to present a library card to use them, government documents do NOT have this restriction. "Free access to the resources of the documents collection by the general public is a fundamental obligation that all Federal Depository Libraries share." Instructions to Depository Libraries. This means that even documents on Reserve must be accessible to all who wish to use them. To ensure that basic obligation, a slip stating that "Government Documents on Reserve are available for use in-house by the general public, FAU staff, students faculty without or with an FAU library card" shall be placed in every federal document placed on Reserve. This shall serve as a reminder to staff and patrons of this federal depository obligation of free access to government documents without barriers. Documents on Reserve can be identified in the Library's online public access catalog. The document will be barcoded (even if a serial) to facilitate Reserve personnel in "checking it out" to Reserve.

Examples of government documents placed on RESERVE:
- Census of Population and Housing—Florida maps
- CFR titles that are frequently stolen
- IRS tax form reproducibles (GPO and IRS copies)
- Occupational Outlook Handbook
- North American Industry Classification System (formerly SIC)

The Documents staff must fill out a "Reserve Form" for placing any documents on Reserve. A "Removal of Reserve Materials Form" must also be filled out to remove a document from Reserve.

University of Michigan Flint
Frances Willson Thompson Library
Flint, Michigan

Circulation of Documents

The majority of documents in the separate Documents Collection may be checked out. Some publications of reference value are marked "Does Not Circulate." These publications can leave the building only with permission of the Documents Librarian or a Reference Librarian.

All depository publications are marked "Depository Document." Any publication so marked can circulate to any person resident in the State of Michigan, provided that the primary clientele of the Frances Willson Thompson Library can also check out the publication.

Persons not affiliated with the University of Michigan system who do not have a valid card on our Mirlyn online system, if residents of the State of Michigan, may be issued a free Special Permission Card, valid for checking out depository publications only. The Special Permission Card may be issued by the Documents Librarian or by a Reference Librarian. It is valid for four months from the date of issue and may be renewed providing there are no outstanding fines or overdues on the card. Loan terms are as for undergraduate students of the University of Michigan-Flint.

Periodicals, including depository publications transferred to the periodicals collection do not circulate except briefly to UM-Flint faculty. They may not be checked out on a Special Permission Card.

Depository publications transferred to the circulating book collection (identified by a "Depository Documents" notation on the front or flyleaf) may be checked out on a Special Permission Card.

Part VIII
Legal and Ethical Concerns

Chapter 29

COPYRIGHT

GUIDELINES FOR COMPLYING WITH LEGAL REQUIREMENTS

Policy Statements

University of Washington
Seattle Washington

The University encourages the publication of scholarly works as an inherent part of its educational mission. In this connection, the University acknowledges the right of faculty, staff, and students to prepare and publish, through individual initiative, articles, pamphlets, and books that are copyrighted by the authors or their publishers and that may generate royalty income for the authors.

The variety and number of copyrightable materials that may be created in the university community have increased significantly in recent years as have the author-university-sponsor relationships under which such materials are produced. Therefore, the following statement of University policy on ownership and use of copyrightable materials is provided to clarify the respective rights of individuals and the University in this increasingly important area. The policy will be administered by the University's Office of Intellectual Property and Technology Transfer.

General Statement of University Policy on Ownership and Use of Copyrightable Materials

University faculty, staff, and students retain all rights in copyrightable materials they create, including scholarly works, subject to the following exceptions and conditions:

Grant and Contract Limitations. Conditions regarding rights in data or restrictions on copyright privileges contained in sponsored grants, contracts, or other awards are binding on the University and on faculty, staff, or student authors. Copyright works, with the exception of routine progress reports, prepared as required elements of such sponsored grants, contracts, or other awards shall be reported to the Office of Intellectual Property and Technology Transfer for review prior to any external dissemination of the work. If necessary to fulfill grant and contract limitations, authors shall execute an appropriate written assignment of copyrights to the University.

University-Owned Materials. Materials shall be "University-owned" within the meaning of this policy statement if the work is a "work for hire" under copyright law or the author was commissioned in writing by the University (or one of its colleges, schools, departments, or other divisions) to develop the materials as a part of the author's regularly compensated duties, as for example, released time arrangements in the case of faculty members. As to a faculty member, "commissioned in writing" specifically does not refer to his or her general obligation to produce scholarly works.

University-Sponsored Materials. Materials shall be "University-sponsored materials" within the meaning of this policy statement if the author developed the materials in the course of performance of his or her normal duties and utilized University staff, resources, or funding to develop the work. As to a faculty member, "normal duties" does not include his or her usual scholarly activity unless it involves extensive uncompensated use of University resources.

Written Agreements. It is desirable to reach agreement in writing as to the rights of the University and of participants before work begins whenever (1) a question exists as to whether the materials will be

University-owned or University-sponsored, or (2) copyrightable materials are likely to result from the joint efforts of persons in academic departments and University service departments. As to jointly-developed materials, determination of rights in written form shall be accomplished no later than prior to sale of the materials in question. Questions concerning the interpretation and administration of this policy shall be resolved in accordance with Section 3.

Proportional Ownership. In case of materials developed in substantial part under commission and in substantial part through other means, the materials shall be regarded as "University-owned" in an appropriate proportion. In the case of materials developed in substantial part during the course of normal duties and with use of University staff, resources, or funding the materials shall be regarded as "University-sponsored" in an appropriate proportion.

Royalty-Free Privileges to University. The University retains a right to royalty-free use of any copyrightable materials developed by University employees (other than books and materials available from a publisher through normal distribution channels) when the development of such materials was advanced through the use of University facilities, supplies, equipment, or staff services. This right exists even though the materials do not constitute University-owned or University-sponsored materials as defined above (e.g., where use of facilities by a faculty member was not extensive).

Student Writings. Students employed by the University in any capacity are covered by the terms of this policy. In addition, where a student receives financial aid or remuneration under a sponsored research, training, or fellowship program, his or her rights in copyrightable materials are limited by the terms of the University agreement with the sponsoring agency. The University has no ownership rights in copyrightable materials developed by students who are not employees of the University or in materials unrelated to their employment.

University of Minnesota Duluth
UMD Library
Duluth, Minnesota

As an institution devoted to the creation, discovery, and dissemination of knowledge to serve the students and public, the University of Minnesota Duluth is committed to complying with all applicable laws regarding intellectual property.

That commitment includes the full exercise of the rights accorded to users of copyrighted works under the "Fair-Use" provision of federal copyright law.

It is, therefore, the policy of UMD to facilitate the exercise in good faith of full Fair-Use rights by faculty, librarians, staff, and students, in furtherance of their teaching, research, and service activities.

To that end, the University of Minnesota Duluth shall:

1. inform and educate its faculty, librarians, and staff about their Fair-Use rights and the application of the four factors for determining those rights set forth in United States Code Title 17, Chapter 1 Sec 107;
2. develop and make available resources concerning Copyright, Fair-Use and intellectual property laws generally and the application of Fair Use in specific situations;
3. avoid adopting or supporting policies or agreements that would restrict Fair-Use rights; and
4. defend and indemnify faculty, librarians, and staff in the event of an infringement allegation when the member of the University community acts in the best interest of the Regents and within the scope and course of his or her university duties. University staff making copyright decisions consistent with established policy will, in making such decisions, be considered to be acting in the best interests of the Regents for the purpose of the Regents Policy on Indemnification.

Copyright Act

New Jersey City University
Jersey City, New Jersey

Definition of Copyright

Federal law Title 17 (United States Code), automatically gives copyright protection to "original work authorship" at the moment the work is "fixed in a tangible medium."

Generally, copyright belongs to the person, who authors or creates an original work that is fixed in a tangible medium of expression. Works of authorship include the following:

a. Literary works;
b. Musical works, including any accompanying words;
c. Dramatic works, including any accompanying music;
d. Pantomimes and choreographic works;
e. Pictorial, graphic, and sculptural works;
f. Motion pictures and other audiovisual works; and
g. Sound recordings.

Because a copyright notice is not required for copyright protection of works published after March 1, 1989, most works (except those authored by the US Government) should be presumed to be copyright protected, unless the copyright holder makes known, usually by clear notice, that he/she intends the work to be in the public domain. Original work consists of the creator's unique way of expressing something and actually requires only a minimum amount of creativity to establish authorship. Copyright ownership and protection does not extend to underling ideas or facts, thereby leaving facts and ideas free for public use.

A useful guide to determine whether or not a "work" is protected is to analyze a work according to the following:

a. Works that lack originality are not protected, e.g., compilations such as the phone book; unoriginal reprints of public domain works.
d. US Government works are not protected.
e. Facts are not protected.
f. Ideas, processes, methods and systems described in copyrighted works are not protected with some caveats.

A copyright holder under the law is viewed as holding a "bundle of rights" including the owner's exclusive right to

(1) make a copy (reproduce),
(2) use a work for the basis of a new work (derivate work),
(3) electronically distribute or publish copies (distribute work),
(4) publicly perform music, prose, poetry, a drama, or play a vide or audio tape or CD ROM, etc (publicly perform a work), and
(5) publish display an image on computer screen or otherwise (publicly display a work).

Digital Copyright Millennium Act

Albion College
Albion, Michigan

Compliance with the Digital Copyright Millennuim Act

As an Online Service Provider (OSP), Albion College is required by the Digital Copyright Millennium Act of 1998 to establish limitation of liability for copyright infringement by:

- designating an agent to receive statutory notices from copyright owners about infringements and to send statutory notices to affected subscribers;
- advising the Copyright Office of the agent's name and address and posting that information on the OSP's Web site;
- developing and posting a policy for termination of repeat offenders and providing network users with information about copyright laws;
- complying with "take down" and "put back" notice requirements;
- ensuring that the system accommodates industry-standard technical measures used by owners to protect their works from unlawful access and copyright infringement.

As an OSP, Albion College has limited liability for copyright infringement by third parties, which may include faculty under some circumstances. Limitation of liability applies to the college as an institution, not to individuals. The Act determines that the knowledge or actions of a faculty member will not be attributed to the institution when all of the following conditions are met:

- the faculty member's infringing activities do not involve providing online access to course materials that were required or recommended during the past three years;
- the institution has not received more than two notifications over the past three years that the faculty member was infringing;
- the institution provides all of its users with information describing and promoting compliance with copyright law.

The statutory rules do not require the College actively to monitor material on the Internet. The limitation requires an OSP to take action when it has "actual knowledge" of an infringement (by facts brought to its attention or by notice from the copyright owner), but it does not impose the burden on the OSP to monitor or discover infringing behavior. The law also gives immunity from third party user claims, provided there is good faith compliance with the statutory rules.

Fair Use

13.2 Fair Use Guidelines
University of California Policy on the Reproduction of Copyrighted Materials for Teaching and Research

UC Guidelines for Determining "Fair Use"

Educators including representatives of higher education developed, along with publishers, a set of minimum standards of fair use which were set forth in the "Agreement on Guidelines for Classroom Copying in Not-for-Profit Educational Institutions" (the Ad Hoc Committee Guidelines).

These standards are reproduced in their entirety in Appendix 1 and can be used as a practical approach to determine fair use. Any copying that falls within the Ad Hoc Committee Guidelines is considered to be fair use and permissible.

Since these standards are often not realistic in a University setting, the following Guidelines should be used to judge if intended photocopying of copyrighted materials constitutes fair use in teaching and research at the University of California.

(See below for Single and Multiple Copies of works.)

The limitations shall not apply to current news periodicals and newspapers and current news sections of other periodicals.

The following shall be prohibited:

    (a) There shall be no copying of or from works intended to be "consumable" in the course of study or of teaching. These include workbooks, exercises, standardized tests and test booklets, answer sheets, and like consumable materials.

    (b) Copying shall not:

(1) substitute for the purchase of books, publishers' reprints, or periodicals;

(2) be directed by higher authority;

(c) No charge shall be made to the student beyond the actual cost of the photocopying.

C. Situations Not Specifically Covered by UC Guidelines

The doctrine of "fair use" may permit reproduction of copyrighted works in excess of the word limit restriction specified in the UC Guidelines.

1. Since this is an area of unclear legal definition, you should use caution and discretion in such copying and should seek advice from the General Counsel's Office for a legal opinion, or request prior written permission directly from the copyright owner to perform copying substantially the limits enumerated in the Guidelines.

2. Any questions regarding the application of the Guidelines in specific cases, whether a work is covered under copyright protection, or the ways to secure permission from publishers should also be referred to the General Counsel.

Permission to Reproduce Material

Washington and Lee University
Leyburn Library
Lexington, Virginia

Copying for Which Permission Must Be Obtained

The guidelines prohibit the following:

1. Course Packs—Primary Course Materials

Copying shall not be used to create, replace, or substitute for, anthologies, compilations, or collective works. Such substitution copying is prohibited unless permission is obtained whether copies or various excerpts are accumulated as course packs or reproduced and handed out separately. Copying shall not be a substitute for the purchase of books or periodicals.

2. Consumable Works

There shall be no copying of or from works intended to be "consumable" in the course of studying or teaching. These include workbooks, exercises, standardized tests, test booklets and answer sheets, and similar consumable material.

3. Repetitive Copying

Copying of the same material by the same teacher from term to term is not legal without explicit permission.

SUNY
Cortland Memorial Library
Cortland, New York

SUNY Examples of When Permission Is Required

7.1 Commercial Uses: Any commercial use including the situation where a nonprofit educational institution is conducting courses for a for-profit corporation for a fee such as supervisory training courses or safety training for the corporation's employees.

7.2. Dissemination of Recorded Courses: An institution offering instruction via distance learning under these guidelines wants to further disseminate the recordings of the course or portions that contain performance of a copyrighted work.

7.3 Uncontrolled Access to Classes: An institution (agency) wants to offer a course or program that contains the performance of copyrighted works to non-employees.

Requiring Permission

University of California Policy on the Reproduction of Copyrighted Materials for Teaching and Research

How to Obtain Permission

When a proposed use of photocopied material requires a faculty member to request permission, communication of complete and accurate information to the copyright owner will facilitate the request. The Association of American Publishers suggests that the following information be included to expedite the process:

1) Title, author and/or editor, and edition of materials to be duplicated; 2) Exact material to be used, giving amount, page numbers, chapters and, if possible, a photocopy of the material; 3) Number of copies to be made; 4) Use to be made of duplicated materials (including time period or duration if copying on an on-going basis is desired); 5) Form of distribution (classroom, newsletter, etc.); 6) Whether or not the material is to be sold; and 7) Type of reprint (ditto, photocopy, offset, typeset).

When the copyright owner is the publisher of the work, the request should be sent, together with a self-addressed return envelope, to the permissions department of the publisher in question. If the address of the publisher does not appear at the front of the material, it may be obtained from The Literary Marketplace (for books) or Ulrich's International Periodicals (for journals), both published by the R.R. Bowker Company. When the copyright owner is the author, the request should be directed to the author either in care of the publisher's permissions department, as set forth above, or at the author's address. For purposes of proof, and to define the scope of the permission, it is important that the permission be in writing. Many publishers have registered with the Copyright Clearance Center, 21 Congress Street, Salem, MA 01970. This organization can facilitate obtaining permission to copy. Check with your campus library about the use of this service.

The process of requesting permission directly from the publisher requires time, as the publisher must check the status and ownership of rights and related matters, and evaluate the request. It is advisable, therefore, to allow sufficient lead time. In some instances the publisher may assess a fee for permission, which may be passed on to students who receive copies of the photocopied material.

GUIDELINES TO TYPES OF MATERIAL COVERED BY COPYRIGHT

Audiovisual

Albion College
Albion, Michigan

Classroom Use of Films and Videotapes:

Possession of a film or video does not confer the right to show the work. The copyright owner specifies, at the time of purchase or rental, the circumstances in which a film or video may be "performed." For example, videocassettes from a video rental outlet usually bear a label that specifies "Home Use Only." However, whatever their labeling or licensing, use of these media is permitted in an educational institution so long as certain conditions are met. Section 110(1) of the Copyright Act of 1976 specifies that the following is permitted:

Performance or display of a work by instructors or pupils in the course of face-to-face teaching activities of a nonprofit educational institution, in a classroom or similar place devoted to instruction, unless, in the case of a motion picture or other audiovisual work, the performance or the display of individual images is given by means of a copy that was not lawfully made . . . and that the person responsible for the performance knew or had reason to believe was not lawfully made.

Additional text of the Copyright Act and portions of the House Report (94–1476) combine to provide the following, more detailed list of conditions [from Virginia M. Helm, What Educators Should Know about Copyright (Bloomington, IN: Phi Delta Kappa Educational Foundation, 1986)]:

- They must be shown as part of the instructional program.
- They must be shown by students, instructors, or guest lecturers.
- They must be shown either in a classroom or other school location devoted to instruction such as a studio, workshop, library, gymnasium, or auditorium if it is used for instruction.
- They must be shown either in a face-to-face setting or where students and teacher(s) are in the same building or general area.
- They must be shown only to students and educators.
- They must be shown using a legitimate (that is, not illegally reproduced) copy with the copyright notice included.

Further, the relationship between the film or video and the course must be explicit. Films or videos, even in a face-to-face classroom setting, may not be used for entertainment or recreation, whatever the work's intellectual content.

Use Outside the Classroom:

The Library has a license from the Motion Picture Licensing Corporation (MPLC) which permits videocassettes in its collection which are covered under that license to be viewed by students, faculty or staff at workstations or in small-group rooms inside the Library. These videos may also be viewed at home (e.g., in a dorm room), so long as no more than a few friends are involved. Larger audiences, such as groups that might assemble in a residence hall living room, require explicit permission from the copyright owner for public performance rights. No fees for viewing a video are permitted even when public performance rights are obtained.

Copying Films or Videotapes:

Permission from the copyright holder must be obtained prior to copying any copyrighted film or videotape. College departments will not duplicate any film or videotape without written authorization indicating that the copyright holder possesses all applicable rights to the work, including literary rights upon which the work is based; music rights (composition and performance); rights to all visual and graphic elements (slides, graphs, still photographs) contained in the work; and performing artists' releases. When you obtain written authorization, make sure that the number of copies of the work that can be made and the length of time they can be retained is indicated. You should also request that the copyright holder indemnify the College against any infringement actions pertaining to the work.

One copy of a purchased foreign-standard videotape may be made to transfer the program to NTSC (U.S.) format. One copy of a purchased U.S. format videotape may be made for use by Albion faculty use while teaching in a foreign country.

Copying Television Programming Off the Air for Classroom Use:

In 1981, an Ad Hoc Committee on Copyright Law negotiated guidelines for off-air recording of broadcast programming for educational purposes. These guidelines represent the committee's "consensus as to the application of 'fair use' to the recording, retention, and use of television broadcast programs for educational purposes. They specify periods of retention and use of such off-air recordings in classrooms and similar places devoted to instruction and for homebound instruction. The purpose of establishing these guidelines is to provide standards for both owners and users of copyrighted television programs."

These guidelines are not embedded in the Copyright Act and it is unclear how courts may choose to apply them. In the absence of explicit legislative or judicial acts, strict adherence to the guidelines may serve as some protection should the issue of infringement arise. See Appendix F, "Guidelines for Off-Air Recording of Broadcast Programming for Educational Purposes."

Filmstrips and Slide Sets:

Copying filmstrips and slide sets in their entirety, or altering a program, requires written permission. Transferring a program to another format (e.g., filmstrip to video, filmstrip to slides) also requires permission. Copying a few frames or slides may be a fair use, if the four fair use criteria are met.

St. Charles Community College
St. Charles Community College Library
St. Peters, Missouri

Video

An instructor may use a videotape at any time if the following is true:

- It a legal copy, professionally made.
- It supports the curriculum being taught.
- It is documented (in the syllabus or lesson plan).
- It is used in a face-to-face educational situation.

An instructor may not copy a video from VHS to DVD format without copyright permission (this will require a major change for SCC).

The performance of a musical or play can be videotaped for instructor evaluation only without copyright permission; no copy can be placed in the library's collection. A video reproduction that does not support curriculum is not covered under fair use. (Instructional Media currently tapes and provides copies to parents for Children's theater programs which is a violation).

Off-air taping is defined as television programs provided without charge by local television stations for reception by the general public (e.g., ABC, NBC, CBS, etc.). An off-air taping may be captured if:

- It is used to support the curriculum being taught, only at the instructor's request–fair use.
- It is used within the first consecutive 10 class days following taping and used no more than 2 times–fair use.

The instructor may retain (but may not show to students) an off-air tape for a period not to exceed 45 consecutive calendar days following the date of recording.

Educators may continue to use only those off-air recordings from cable and satellite programs that have been designated and cleared for educational use; use programs with all class sections within the course for which the recording was requested.

University of Pittsburgh
University Libraries
Pittsburgh, Pennsylvania

Audiovisual Material

Pictorial, graphic, or sculptural works, motion pictures and other audiovisual material may be reproduced by the Library or University Center for Instructional Resources (UCIR) for the following purposes:

- For preservation and security, provided the original work is currently in the collection of the library or owned by UCIR and the work is unpublished.
- For replacement of a damaged, deteriorating, lost or stolen published material, providing an unused replacement cannot be obtained at a reasonable price.
- The library may make one archival tape for each tape purchased, unless specifically forbidden by the supplier.
- Only one copy, either the original or archival, may be used or circulated at any given time.
- If multiple copies are needed, they must be purchased.
- Reproduction for other purposes, with exception of classroom use (See below), is prohibited without permission from the Copyright owner.

Bibliographic Instruction

University of Minnesota Duluth
UMD Library
Duluth, Minnesota

Bibliographic Instruction

The copyright law may affect materials chosen for use in bibliographic instruction. The use of copyrighted materials in the classroom is governed by a determination of Fair Use [US Code Title 17 Chapter 1 Sec 107]. Responsibility for making copyright decisions and determining fair use will lie with the librarians and staff using the copyrighted materials.

Library staff using copyrighted material for bibliographic instruction are encouraged to complete a "Fair Use Worksheet" for each copyrighted item and retain a copy for their records.

All distributed duplications of copyrighted works will include the notice of copyright as it appears on the original work. If no notice appears on the original, then the copy must include "a legend stating that the work may be protected by copyright."

Course Reserves

University of Central Florida
University of Central Florida Libraries
Orlando, Florida

The UCF Libraries' Circulation Department, including the main library and other branches of UCF Libraries, provide course reserve services to support the teaching activities of the University. All reserve materials must comply with copyright laws. Any item for which the UCF faculty or staff has obtained written permission from the copyright holder, materials that fall within fair use, and any work in the public domain may be placed on reserve. Current fair use guidelines do not cover the use of material beyond one semester. At the end of each semester, all materials on reserve will be removed from reserve.

Faculty or staff placing materials on reserve are responsible for verifying that those items are copyright compliant. To assist in determining whether copyright permission is required, please consult the UCF Libraries Copyright Decision Tree. When required, written permission must be obtained. UCF Libraries' staff may require proof that materials placed on reserve do not violate copyright guidelines.

To date, there is no university-wide infrastructure for the University to process and/or pay for copyright permissions. Individual faculty members may check with their departments, or obtain permissions on an individual basis.

University of Texas at Arlington
University of Texas at Arlington Libraries
Arlington, Texas

Built upon "UT System Rules of Thumb for Reserves"

Reserve copies should be a small part of the materials required for a course and obtained legally by the faculty member or the library through purchase, license, interlibrary loan, fair use, etc. CONFU (Conference on Fair Use) guidelines stipulate that reserve articles should not substitute for the purchase of a textbook.

Copies of copyrighted materials placed on reserve can be: a single article or chapter; a short story, poem or essay; or a few graphs, charts or pictures.

Reserve copies should include any copyright notice on the original, complete citation and attributions to the source, and a section 108(f)(1) notice that reads, "Copying, displaying and distributing copyrighted works may infringe the owner's copyright."

Access to copies, whether paper or electronic, should be limited to students enrolled in the class and administrative staff as needed. Access is to be terminated at the end of the class term.

Copies of copyrighted materials that will be used repeatedly by the same instructor for the same class requires permission from the copyright holder. Generally the first semester a copy is placed on reserve, permission will not be required unless there is some factor that negates it falling under fair use guidelines.

If permission has to be sought, one (1) copy will be placed on reserve (either electronic or paper—the faculty member may choose). Once permission is received additional paper copies may be placed on reserve if so desired. The following credit line should go on copied material authorized by the Copyright Clearance Center: "Reproduced with permission of the copyright holder via the Copyright Clearance Center."

If permission is denied or the royalty charge excessive, the copy will be removed from reserve and returned to the faculty member. If the original work is owned by the Library, it may be placed on reserve in place of the copy.

If the original work is placed on reserve (a book or journal issue for example) then copyright permission does not have to be sought.

If an article to be placed on reserve is already available electronically and our licensing agreement allows, we will point to that location from the reserve list instead of scanning and posting the article.

Photocopies of entire works and coursepacks will not be placed on reserve.

E-Reserves

University of Minnesota Duluth
UMD Library
Duluth, Minnesota

Reserve—Electronic

Duplications made for Electronic Reserve are governed by the US Code Title 17 Chapter 1 Sec. 107 Limitations on exclusive rights: Fair use. Reserve Processing staff, acting in the best interest of the Library, reserves the right to refuse a processing request if, in their judgment, fulfillment of the request would involve violation of the copyright law.

The UMD Library Reserve Processing staff will, at the request of UMD faculty or staff, place on electronic reserve duplications from copyrighted materials owned by the library since library materials are acquired with the understanding that there will be multiple uses of a limited number of copies.

Requests for duplications from materials not owned by the UMD Library will be placed on reserve as "fair use" as determined by the requesting faculty or staff or with proof of copyright clearance from the copyright holder. Faculty and staff will be encouraged to complete a Fair Use Worksheet, which is available on the Campus Copyright Information Site. Use of duplications determined to be in excess of fair use will require a purchase of the original by the UMD Library, permission from the copyright holder or payment of copyright fees.

Reserve Processing staff will assist in obtaining copyright permission and/or arranging for the payment of copyright fees for duplications determined not to be fair use. Copyright clearance will be sought using the Copyright Clearance Center ECCS (Electronic Course Content Service) account. In instances when the cost is prohibitive, a single copy will be placed on traditional reserve with payment through the CCC TRS (Transactional Reporting Service) account.

Duplications of lecture notes, exams or items in the public domain will be placed on electronic reserve.

Papers submitted for course work will be placed on electronic reserve when accompanied by a written permission form signed by the student. They will remain on reserve for the time period indicated by the requesting faculty unless an earlier time period is specified on the permission form.

A copyright statement will be placed on each electronic reserve item to indicate the material may be protected by the copyright law.

Electronic files will be removed from the reserve system as soon as time permits following the end of the term indicated by the requesting faculty or staff.

University of Texas System
Austin, Texas

Introduction

Many college, university, and school libraries have established reserve operations for readings and other materials that support the instructional requirements of specific courses. Some educational institutions are now providing electronic reserve systems that allow storage of electronic versions of materials that students may retrieve on a computer screen, and from which they may print a copy for their personal study. When materials are included as a matter of fair use, electronic reserve systems should constitute an ad hoc or supplemental source of information for students, beyond a textbook or other materials. If included with permission from the copyright owner, however, the scope and range of materials is potentially unlimited, depending upon the permission granted. Although fair use is determined on a case-by-case basis, the following guidelines identify an understanding of fair use for the reproduction, distribution, display, and performance of materials in the context of creating and using an electronic reserve system.

Making materials accessible through electronic reserve systems raises significant copyright issues. Electronic reserve operations include the making of a digital version of text, the distribution and display of that version at workstations, and downloading and printing of copies. The complexities of the electronic environment, and the growing potential for implicating copyright infringements, raise the need for a fresh understanding of fair use. These guidelines are not intended to burden the facilitation of reserves unduly, but instead offer a workable path that educators and librarians may follow in order to exercise a meaningful application of fair use, while also acknowledging and respecting the interests of copyright owners.

These guidelines focus generally on the traditional domain of reserve rooms, particularly copies of journal articles and book chapters, and their accompanying graphics. Nevertheless, they are not meant to apply exclusively to textual materials and may be instructive for the fair use of other media. The guidelines also focus on the use of the complete article or the entire book chapter. Using only brief excerpts from such works would most likely also be fair use, possibly without all of the restrictions or conditions set forth in these guidelines. Operators of reserve systems should also provide safeguards for the integrity of the text and the author's reputation, including verification that the text is correctly scanned.

The guidelines address only those materials protected by copyright and for which the institution has not obtained permission before including them in an electronic reserve system. The limitations and conditions set forth in these guidelines need not apply to materials in the public domain—such as works of the U.S. government or works on which copyright has expired—or to works for which the institution has obtained permission for inclusion in the electronic reserve system. License agreements may govern the uses of some materials. Persons responsible for electronic reserve systems should refer to applicable license terms for guidance. If an instructor arranges for students to acquire a work by some means that includes permission from the copyright owner, the instructor should not include that same work on an electronic reserve system as a matter of fair use.

These guidelines are the outgrowth of negotiations among diverse parties attending the Conference on Fair Use ("CONFU") meetings sponsored by the Information Infrastructure Task Force's Working Group on Intellectual Property Rights. While endorsements of any guidelines by all conference participants is unlikely, these guidelines have been endorsed by the organizations whose names appear at the end. These guidelines are in furtherance of the Working Group's objective of encouraging negotiated guidelines of fair use.

This introduction is an integral part of these guidelines and should be included with the guidelines wherever they may be reprinted or adopted by a library, academic institution, or other organization or association. No copyright protection of these guidelines is claimed by any person or entity, and anyone is free to reproduce and distribute this document without permission.

A. Scope of Material

1. In accordance with fair use (Section 107 of the U.S. Copyright Act), electronic reserve systems may include copyrighted materials at the request of a course instructor.

2. Electronic reserve systems may include short items (such as an article from a journal, a chapter from a book or conference proceedings, or a poem from a collected work) or excerpts from longer items. "Longer items" may include articles, chapters, poems, and other works that are of such length as to constitute a substantial portion of a book, journal, or other work of which they may be a part. "Short items" may include articles, chapters, poems, and other works of a customary length and structure as to be a small part of a book, journal, or other work, even if that work may be marketed individually.

3. Electronic reserve systems should not include any material unless the instructor, the library, or another unit of the educational institution possesses a lawfully obtained copy.

4. The total amount of material included in electronic reserve systems for a specific course as a matter of fair use should be a small proportion of the total assigned reading for a particular course.

B. Notices and Attributions

1. On a preliminary or introductory screen, electronic reserve systems should display a notice, consistent with the notice described in Section 108(f)(1) of the Copyright Act. The notice should include additional language cautioning against further electronic distribution of the digital work.

2. If a notice of copyright appears on the copy of a work that is included in an electronic reserve system, the following statement shall appear at some place where users will likely see it in connection with access to the particular work:

"The work from which this copy is made includes this notice: [restate the elements of the statutory copyright notice: e.g., Copyright 1996, XXX Corp.]"

3. Materials included in electronic reserve systems should include appropriate citations or attributions to their sources.

C. Access and Use

1. Electronic reserve systems should be structured to limit access to students registered in the course for which the items have been placed on reserve, and to instructors and staff responsible for the course or the electronic system.

2. The appropriate methods for limiting access will depend on available technology. Solely to suggest and not to prescribe options for implementation, possible methods for limiting access may include one or more of the following or other appropriate methods:

    (a) individual password controls or verification of a student's registration status; or
    (b) password system for each class; or
    (c) retrieval of works by course number or instructor name, but not by author or title of the work; or
    (d) access limited to workstations that are ordinarily used by, or are accessible to, only enrolled students or appropriate staff or faculty.

3. Students should not be charged specifically or directly for access to electronic reserve systems.

D. Storage and Reuse

1. Permission from the copyright holder is required if the item is to be reused in a subsequent academic term for the same course offered by the same instructor, or if the item is a standard assigned or optional reading for an individual course taught in multiple sections by many instructors.

2. Material may be retained in electronic form while permission is being sought or until the next academic term in which the material might be used, but in no event for more than three calendar years, including the year in which the materials are last used.

3. Short-term access to materials included on electronic reserve systems in previous academic terms may be provided to students who have not completed the course.

Feature Films and Broadcasts

SUNY
Cortland Memorial Library
Cortland, New York

Classroom Performance of Films and Videotapes

The Copyright Act protects audiovisual works such as films and videotapes. The law creates a legal distinction between classroom performances and other public performances or reception of programming in the privacy of one's home. In-classroom performance of a copyrighted film or videotape is permissible under the following conditions:

a) the showing must be by instructors (including guest lecturers) or by students;
b) the showing of the video tape is in connection with face-to-face teaching activities;
c) the entire audience is involved in the teaching activity;
d) the entire audience is in the same room or same general area;
e) the teaching activities are conducted by a non-profit education institution;
f) the showing takes place in a classroom or similar place devoted to instruction, such as a school library, gym, auditorium or workshop; and
g) the videotape is lawfully made; the person responsible had no reason to believe that the videotape was unlawfully made.

Home Copied Videotapes for Classroom Use

The law makes a distinction between the act of recording a program on videotape in the privacy of one's home and the act of displaying that program in a public space such as a classroom. It is not clear that if a faculty member tapes a program on his/her VCR and shows it in the classroom, such an act would constitute a violation of fair use in an educational setting. Decisions would have to be made on a case-by-case basis, weighing the circumstances of each case against fair use criteria.

Reformatting Films and Videotapes for Classroom Use

Making a derivative copy of a copyrighted work (for example changing the format of a 16mm film to videotape) is also a problematic area for higher education. Creating a derivative work under current law is an important exclusive right of the copyright owner. Educators, media specialist librarians, and others often want to change the format of audiovisual materials for convenience of use, purposes of preservation or ease of multiple access. Although some flexibility has been granted to libraries for purposes of archival preservation, it is probably best to assume that the making of derivative works should be done only with prior permission from the copyright owner, or if permission is granted as a written condition of a sales contract.

(For additional policies, please see the accompanying CD-ROM.)

General Print Material

St. Charles Community College
St. Charles Community College Library
St. Peters, Missouri

Printed Material

An instructor can request that a photocopy of an item be placed on reserve for a single (one-time) semester without copyright permission (after this time reserve items can only remain with the copyright permission). Items that do not receive copyright permission will be returned to the instructor at the end of each semester.

Educators have a fair use right to make:

Single copy—made of any of the following by or for an educator at his or her individual request for scholarly research, or use in teaching or preparation to teach a class:

- A chapter from a book
- An article from a periodical or newspaper
- A short story, short essay, short poem
- A chart, graph, diagram, drawing, cartoon or picture from a book, periodical or newspaper.

Multiple copies—(not to exceed, in any event, more than once copy per pupil in a course) for classroom use or discussion, provided that:

- The copying meets the tests of brevity and spontaneity as defined below,
- Meets the cumulative effect test as defined below,
- Each copy includes a notice of copyright.

Brevity

Poetry—a complete poem if less than 250 words and if printed on not more than two pages.

Prose—either a complete article, story or essay of less than 2,500 words, not greater than 10 percent of the work which ever is less.

Illustration—one chart, graph, diagram, drawing, cartoon, or picture per book or per periodical issue.

Spontaneity—in order to meet the fair use test of spontaneity, the inspiration and decision of the individual to use the work and the time of its use (for maximum teaching effectiveness) are so close together, that it would be unreasonable to expect a timely reply to a request for permission.

Cumulative Effect—

Copying the material for only one course in the school in which the copies are made.

One short poem, article, story, essay or two excerpts may be copied from the same author.

Three short poems, articles, stories or excerpts from the same collective work or periodical volume may be copied during one class term.

A limit of nine instances of multiple copying for one course during one class term.

Educators may not:

- Copy to avoid purchase of materials,
- Copy from consumable materials (workbooks, activity books, exercises, standardized test, answer sheets, etc.),
- Make illegal copies on direction from higher authority,
- Copy the same item from term to term,
- Use materials copied by another educator without securing written permission,
- Alter a copyrighted image (cartoon, graph, chart, photograph, diagram, etc.) by modifying the original to create a derivative work,
- Copy the same item for more than one course. Copies may be made for each section of the course,
- Charge students more than the actual cost of the authorized copies.

Government Documents

University of Pittsburgh
Pittsburgh, Pennsylvania

Government Publications

Most U.S. government publications may be copied without restrictions except to the extent they contain copyrighted materials from other sources.

U.S. Government publications are documents prepared by an official or employee of the government in an official capacity, and include:

- The opinions of courts and legal cases
- Congressional reports on proposed bills
- Testimony offered at congressional hearings
- Works of government employees in their official capacities

Works prepared by outside authors on a contract of the government may or may not be protected by copyright, depending on the specifics of the contract.

State Government works may be protected by copyright, and should be checked for notice of copyright before making copies of such material.

University of South Florida

U.S. Government Documents: Most U.S. government publications may be photocopied without restrictions except to the extent that they contain copyrighted material from other sources. Certain works prepared for the U. S. government by outside authors may be protected by separate copyright. If a copyright notice cannot be found, it is reasonable to assume that these works can be photocopied without restriction.

State Government Documents: Unlike most U.S. government publications, state government works may be protected by copyright. If a copyright notice is specifically set out in a state government document, the work may be photocopied or reproduced only according to the guidelines set out in this policy. Note that if a copyright notice is not found, copyright protection may still be afforded to the work, and you may wish to contact the state agency responsible for the document

Images

Washington and Lee University
Leyburn Library
Lexington, Virginia

Guidelines for the Use of Images

The current state of understanding among visual resources people about the Conference on Fair Use guidelines is one of intense dissatisfaction, not with the idea of fair use per se, but with the fair use guidelines, specifically. The guidelines are regarded as having been drafted primarily for the protection of the vendors, and primarily in the context of printed materials rather than visual images. The controversy concerns the extent to which a photograph or slide of a public domain art work or scientific drawing is protected by copyright.

The proposed CONFU guidelines, the committee believes, place unnecessary restrictions on what is currently permitted as fair use. For example, none of the fair use factors puts time limits on use, but the guidelines do.

Given the lack of consensus on this matter among visual resources professionals, many issues remain unsolved. Since there is no consensus for using copyrighted images, the University recommends that copying be done pursuant to the fair use factors.

A. Definitions

1. Visual image is a unique photographic representation of an object (e.g., an "original" 35 mm slide) or a photographic reproduction of an object ("duplicate" slide), usually issued in multiple copies. The term "visual image" is used here to refer to representations or reproductions of works of art (painting, sculpture, decorative or craft objects, graphics media, drawings, collages, mixed media, and electronic media) and architecture, and also includes maps, diagrams, charts, and scientific drawings. Images are typically surrogates for the represented works; their intrinsic value is primarily as documentation of the original

object (e.g., a slide representation of the Mona Lisa, a photograph of the Eiffel Tower, a color reproduction of an anatomical chart).

2. Image archive is a collection of images, acquired and maintained by an organization such as a non-profit library, museum, or school. An image archive can be a collection of collections in different formats, of which slides and CD-ROMs are but two examples. Images in archives derive from numerous sources: From commercial vendors of images, from work-for-hire, from donation by amateur and professional photographers, and from copy photography.

3. Copy photography is making slides from reproductions in books or journals. This widespread and long-standing practice in the community has been a necessity for teaching, and frequently is a reason for the purchase of a book rather than an interference with the market for a book.

4. An electronic image is a digital representation or reproduction of a photographic representation or reproduction of an object described above (under visual image). Electronic (digital) images are essentially the same as analog images. The content is the same; only the format for delivery and the ease with which they can be copied are different.

5. Electronic image archives is a collection of electronic (digital) images of art and architecture or other subjects that may be part of a larger image archives.

B. Fair Use and Image Archives

Visual images are typically sold by image brokers (commercial vendors) who have made photographic reproductions pursuant to a non-exclusive right with the creator of the object, or who have acquired a reproduction license to market images made from public domain objects owned or controlled by museums or corporations.

Visual images made from reproductions in books and journals for purposes such as teaching or research are understood to be fair use when photographic representations of the objects are no longer available or reasonably accessible from commercial vendors, the object's creator, or the owner of the work. The practice of reproducing images included with copyrighted text for the uses specified above is a long-standing practice in education and the subject of vigorous debate within the community, although there have been no cases addressing this practice.

Current practice recognizes the need to use large quantities of projected images in a classroom (a typical art history lecture requires an average of 25–50 different images per class period). It is not uncommon for various images to be used the next time the course is offered. Multiple versions of the same object are commonly also presented. In practice, images are typically arranged in sequences or sets for comparison or contrast.

Assuming a fair use of copyrighted materials in providing images for the purposes listed above, permissions are not necessary. Permission is required only if the use of the copyrighted image is for other purposes, such as publication, or in circumstances where profit and/or commercial advantage is the motive for the use.

1. Image photocopying

The photocopying of images for classroom use or in the preparation of class assignments or papers is acceptable under the fair use guidelines.

2. Slides

    a. Purchase, whenever possible. Subsequent duplication of purchased slides is not acceptable.

    b. Guidelines for copy photography, when a purchase is not possible: Follow fair use factors (see statement at the beginning re Fair Use Guidelines).

Make only one copy of a reproduction; making multiple copies is not acceptable.

Shooting every plate in a book is not acceptable.

Slides made in this way are to be used for educational purposes.

Once a slide has been added to the slide collection of an academic department, by either purchase or copy photography, it becomes the property of Washington and Lee University. If a slide is loaned, it may not be duplicated in any form. It is implicit in the lending that the borrower agrees not to authorize duplication or reproduction of these slides and assumes all responsibility for that restriction.

3. Clip art

Clip art is sold to be copied; use it, taking care to note any limitations that accompany it (e.g., some clip art may be used in printed works, but the license expressly forbids digital distribution; therefore, it may not be used to liven up Web pages).

4. Fair use and electronic images

    a.   Fair use is inadequately defined for images in general, and thus poorly understood for most transmissions of images.

    b   During transmission, a copy of the image is made. This adds another layer to the already multi-layered ownership issues surrounding an image. Is the image of an artwork the property of the creator (if still under copyright) or the photographer or the repository maintaining it? This is never as self-evident as it is with a text object such as a book or a journal article.

    c.   It is in the immediate and long range interests of Washington and Lee that digitized images be readily and inexpensively available for teaching and research.

5. Copying which is permitted

    a.   One or a small number of images is retrieved from a large collection and used so that the intrinsic value of the original collection is in no way diminished.

    b.   Use of "thumbnail-size" images, for no purpose other than as a reference or as a mnemonic device.

6. Copying which requires permission

    a.   Using without compensation any sizable archive that someone else has collected with considerable expenditure of time, energy, and money.

    b.   Acquiring images that are free or quite inexpensive, and then charging an unreasonable amount for their use.

7. Notice

    a.   Check for the copyright symbol ("copyright" or "<©>") and the name of the copyright owner (which should be attached directly on, under, or around a digital work); it should be visible to anyone who will be using the excerpted material. Works 1989–present, may be under copyright whether or not a copyright symbol is present; no copyright symbol has been required since 1989.

    b.   Put the copyright symbol, name, and date on each copy, even if the material is only being used once for a class presentation or project; this is important in case you change your mind and decide to use material for commercial or extended purposes; you would then have a record of the copyright information and of when and where you found the material.

SUNY
Cortland Memorial Library
Cortland, New York

X. Digital Images, Distance Learning and Multimedia

Digital imagery, distance learning and multimedia technologies have pushed the limits of copyright and fair use. In 1994 the Conference on Fair Use (CONFU) was formed to present guidelines on fair use in these areas. Below are those guidelines, revised December 1997.

1. Educational Fair Use Guidelines for Digital Images

Fair use is a legal principle that provides certain limitations on the exclusive rights of copyright holders. The purpose of these guidelines is to provide guidance on the application of fair use principles by educational institutions, educators, scholars and students who wish to digitize copyrighted visual images under fair use rather than by seeking authorization from the copyright owners for non-commercial educational purposes. These guidelines apply to fair use only in the context of copyright.

There is no simple test to determine what is fair use. Section 107 of the Copyright Act sets forth the four fair use factors which should be assessed in each instance, based on the particular facts of a given case, to determine whether a use is a "fair use": 1) the purpose and character of the use, including whether such use is of a commercial nature or is for nonprofit educational purposes, 2) the nature of the copyrighted work, 3) the amount and substantiality of the portion used in relation to the copyrighted work as a whole, and 4) the effect of the use upon the potential market for or value of the copyrighted work. While only the courts can authoritatively determine whether a particular use is fair use, these guidelines represent the endorsers' consensus of conditions under which fair use should generally apply and examples of when permission is required. Uses that exceed these guidelines may or may not be fair use. The endorsers also agree that the more one exceeds these guidelines, the greater the risk that fair use does not apply.

The limitations and conditions set forth in these guidelines do not apply to works in the public domain—such as U.S. government works or works on which copyright has expired for which there are no copyright restrictions—or to works for which the individual or institution has obtained permission for the particular use. Also, license agreements may govern the uses of some works and users should refer to the applicable license terms for guidance.

Those who developed these guidelines met for an extended period of time and the result represents their collective understanding in this complex area. Because digital technology is in a dynamic phase, there may come a time when it is necessary to review the guidelines. Nothing in these guidelines should be construed to apply to the fair use privilege in any context outside of educational and scholarly uses of digital images. These guidelines do not cover non-educational or commercial digitization or use at any time, even by non-profit educational institutions. These guidelines are not intended to cover the fair use of copyrighted works in other educational contexts such as educational multimedia projects, distance education, or electronic reserves, which may be addressed in other fair use guidelines.

This Preamble is an integral part of these guidelines and should be included whenever the guidelines are reprinted or adopted by organizations and educational institutions. Users are encouraged to reproduce and distribute these guidelines freely without permission; no copyright protection of these guidelines is claimed by any person or entity.

1.2 Background: Rights in Visual Images

As photographic and electronic technology has advanced, the making of high-quality reproductions of visual images has become easier, cheaper, and more widely accessible. However, the fact that images may be easily available does not automatically mean they can be reproduced and reused without permission. Confusion regarding intellectual property rights in visual images arises from the many ways that images are created and the many sources that may be related to any particular image. Clearing permission, when necessary, requires identifying the holder of the applicable rights. Determining all the holders of the rights connected with an image requires an understanding of the source of the image, the content portrayed, and the creation of the image, both for original visual images and for reproductions of images.

Visual images can be original works or reproductions of other works; in some cases, original works may incorporate reproductions of other works as well. Often, a digital image is several generations removed from the visual image it reproduces. For example, a digital image of a painting may have been scanned from a slide, which was copied from a published book that contained a printed reproduction of the work of art; this reproduction may have been made from a color transparency photographed directly from the original painting. There may be intellectual property rights in the original painting, and each additional stage of reproduction in this chain may involve another layer of rights.

A digital image can be an original visual image, a reproduction, a published reproduction, or a copy of a published reproduction. An original visual image is a work of art or an original work of authorship (or a part of a work), fixed in digital or analog form and expressed in a visual medium. Examples include graphic, sculptural, and architectural works, as well as stills from motion pictures or other audiovisual works. A reproduction is a copy of an original visual image in digital or analog form. The most common forms of reproductions are photographic, including prints, 35mm slides, and color transparencies. The original visual image shown in a reproduction is often referred to as the "underlying work." Digital images can be reproductions of either original visual images or of other reproductions. A published reproduction is a reproduction of an original visual image appearing in a work distributed in copies and made available to the public by sale or other transfer of ownership, or by rental, lease, or lending. Examples include a plate in an exhibition catalog that reproduces a work of art, and a digital image appearing in a CD-ROM or online. A copy of a published reproduction is a subsequent copy made of a published reproduction of an original visual image, for example, a 35mm slide which is a copy of an image in a book.

The rights in images in each of these layers may be held by different rightsholders; obtaining rights to one does not automatically grant rights to use another, and therefore all must be considered when analyzing the rights connected with an image. Rights to use images will vary depending not only on the identities of the layers of rightsholders, but also on other factors such as the terms of any bequest or applicable license.

1.3 Applicability of These Guidelines

These guidelines apply to the creation of digital images and their use for educational purposes. The guidelines cover (1) pre-existing analog image collections, and (2) newly acquired analog visual images. These guidelines do not apply to images acquired in digital form, or to images in the public domain, or to works for which the user has obtained the relevant and necessary rights for the particular use.

Only lawfully acquired copyrighted analog images (including original visual images, reproductions, published reproductions, and copies of published reproductions) may be digitized pursuant to these guidelines. These guidelines apply only to educational institutions, educators, scholars, students, and image collection curators engaging in instructional, research, or scholarly activities at educational institutions for educational purposes.

1.4 Definitions

Educational institutions are defined as nonprofit organizations whose primary purpose is supporting the nonprofit instructional, research, and scholarly activities of educators, scholars, and students. Examples of educational institutions include K–12 schools, colleges, and universities; libraries, museums, and hospitals. Other nonprofit institutions also are considered educational institutions under this definition when they engage in nonprofit instructional, research, or scholarly activities for educational purposes. Educational purposes are defined as non-commercial instruction or curriculum-based teaching by educators to students at nonprofit educational institutions, and research and scholarly activities are defined as planned non-commercial study or investigation directed toward making a contribution to a field of knowledge and non-commercial presentation of research findings at peer conferences, workshops, or seminars.

Educators are faculty, teachers, instructors, curators, librarians, archivists, or professional staff who engage in instructional, research, or scholarly activities for educational purposes as their assigned responsibilities at educational institutions; independent scholars also are considered educators under this definition when they offer courses at educational institutions. Students are participants in instructional, research, or scholarly activities for educational purposes at educational institutions.

A digital image is a visual work stored in binary code (bits and bytes). Examples include bitmapped images (encoded as a series of bits and bytes each representing a particular pixel or part of the image) and vector graphics (encoded as equations and/or algorithms representing lines and curves). An analog image collection is an assemblage of analog visual images systematically maintained by an educational institution for educational purposes in the form of slides, photographs, or other stand-alone visual media. A pre-existing analog image collection is one in existence as of [December 31, 1996]. A newly acquired analog visual image is one added to an institution's collection after [December 31, 1996].

A visual online catalog is a database consisting of thumbnail images of an institution's lawfully acquired image collection, together with any descriptive text including, for example, provenance and rights information that is searchable by a number of fields, such as the source. A thumbnail image, as used in a visual online catalog or image browsing display to enable visual identification of records in an educational institution's image collection, is a small scale, typically low resolution, digital reproduction which has no intrinsic commercial or reproductive value.

2. Image Digitization and Use by Educational Institutions

This Section covers digitization by educational institutions of newly acquired analog visual images and Section 6 covers digitization of pre-existing analog image collections. Refer to the applicable section depending on whether you are digitizing newly acquired or pre-existing analog visual works.

2.1 Digitizing by Institutions: Newly Acquired Analog Visual Images

An educational institution may digitize newly, lawfully, acquired analog visual images to support the permitted educational uses under these guidelines unless such images are readily available in usable digital form for purchase or license at a fair price. Images that are readily available in usable digital form for purchase or license at a fair price should not be digitized for addition to an institutional image collection without permission.

2.2 Creating Thumbnail Images

An educational institution may create thumbnail images of lawfully acquired images for inclusion in a visual catalog for use at the institution. These thumbnail images may be combined with descriptive text in a visual catalog that is searchable by a number of fields, such as the source.

2.3 Access, Display, and Distribution on an Institution's Secure Electronic Network

Subject to the time limitations in Section 2.4, an educational institution may display and provide access to images digitized under these guidelines through its own secure electronic network. When displaying digital images on such networks, an educational institution should implement technological controls and institutional policies to protect the rights of copyright owners, and use best efforts to make users aware of those rights. In addition, the educational institution must provide notice stating that digital images on its secure electronic network shall not be downloaded, copied, retained, printed, shared, modified, or otherwise used, except as provided for in the permitted educational uses under these guidelines.

2.3.1 Visual online catalog: An educational institution may display a visual online catalog, which includes the thumbnail images created as part of the institution's digitization process, on the institution's secure electronic network, and may provide access to such catalog by educators, scholars, and students affiliated with the educational institution.

2.3.2 Course compilations of digital images: An educational institution may display an educator's compilation of digital images (see also, Section 3.1.2) on the institution's secure electronic network for classroom use, after-class review, or directed study, provided that there are technological limitations (such as a password or PIN) restricting access only to students enrolled in the course. The institution may display such images on its secure electronic network only during the semester or term in which that academic course is given.

2.3.3 Access, display, and distribution beyond the institution's secure electronic network: Electronic access to, or display or distribution of, images digitized under these guidelines, including the thumbnail images in the institution's visual online catalog, is not permitted beyond the institution's own electronic network, even for educational purposes. However, those portions of the visual online catalog which do not contain images digitized under these guidelines, such as public domain images and text, may be accessed, displayed, or distributed beyond the institution's own secure electronic network.

2.4 Time Limitations for Use of Images Digitized by Institutions from Newly Acquired Analog Visual Images

An educational institution may use and retain in digital image collections images which are digitized from newly acquired analog visual images under these guidelines, as long as the retention and use comply with the following conditions:

2.4.1 Images digitized from a known source and not readily available in usable digital form for purchase or license at a fair price may be used for one (1) academic term and may be retained in digital form while permission is being sought. Permission is required for uses beyond the initial use; if permission is not received, any use is outside the scope of these guidelines and subject to the four-factor fair use analysis (see Section 1.1).

2.4.2 Where the rightsholder of an image is unknown, a digitized image may be used for up to three (3) years from first use, provided that a reasonable inquiry (see Section 5.2) is conducted by the institution seeking permission to digitize, retain, and reuse the digitized image. If, after three (3) years, the educational institution is unable to identify sufficient information to seek permission, any further use of the image is outside the scope of these guidelines and subject to the four-factor fair use analysis (see Section 1.1).

3. Use by Educators, Scholars, and Students

Subject to the time limitations in Section 2.4, images digitized under these guidelines may be used by educators, scholars, and students as follows:

3.1 Educator Use of Images Digitized Under These Guidelines

3.1.1 An educator may display digital images for educational purposes, including face-to-face teaching of curriculum-based courses, and research and scholarly activities at a nonprofit educational institution.

3.1.2 An educator may compile digital images for display on the institution's secure electronic network (see also, Section 2.3.2) to students enrolled in a course given by that educator for classroom use, after-class review, or directed study, during the semester or term in which the educator's related course is given.

3.2 Use of Images for Peer Conferences

Educators, scholars, and students may use or display digital images in connection with lectures or presentations in their fields, including uses at non-commercial professional development seminars, workshops, and conferences where educators meet to discuss issues relevant to their disciplines or present works they created for educational purposes in the course of research, study, or teaching.

3.3 Use of Images for Publications

These guidelines do not cover reproducing and publishing images in publications, including scholarly publications in print or digital form, for which permission is generally required. Before publishing any images under fair use, even for scholarly and critical purposes, scholars and scholarly publishers should conduct the four-factor fair use analysis (see Section 1.1).

3.4 Student Use of Images Digitized Under These Guidelines

Students may:

- Use digital images in an academic course assignment such as a term paper or thesis, or in fulfillment of degree requirements.
- Publicly display their academic work incorporating digital images in courses for which they are registered and during formal critiques at a nonprofit educational institution.
- Retain their academic work in their personal portfolios for later uses such as graduate school and employment applications.

Other student uses are outside the scope of these guidelines and are subject to the four-factor fair use analysis (see Section 1.1).

4. Image Digitization by Educators, Scholars, and Students for Spontaneous Use

Educators, scholars, and students may digitize lawfully acquired images to support the permitted educational uses under these guidelines if the inspiration and decision to use the work and the moment of its use for maximum teaching effectiveness are so close in time that it would be unreasonable to expect a timely reply to a request for permission. Images digitized for spontaneous use do not automatically become part of the institution's image collection. Permission must be sought for any reuse of such digitized images or their addition to the institution's image collection.

5. Important Reminders and Fair Use Limitations under These Guidelines

5.1 Creation of Digital Image Collections

When digitizing copyrighted images, as permitted under these guidelines, an educational institution should simultaneously conduct the process of seeking permission to retain and use the images. Where the rightsholder is unknown, the institution should pursue, and is encouraged to keep records of, its reasonable inquiry (see Section 5.2). Rightsholders and others who are contacted are encouraged to respond promptly to inquiries.

5.2 Reasonable Inquiry

A reasonable inquiry by an institution for the purpose of clearing rights to digitize and use digital images includes, but is not limited to, conducting each of the following steps: (1) checking any information within the control of the educational institution, including slide catalogs and logs, regarding the source of the image; (2) asking relevant faculty, departmental staff, and librarians, including visual resource collections administrators, for any information regarding the source of the image; (3) consulting standard reference publications and databases for information regarding the source of the image; and (4) consulting rights reproduction collectives and/or major professional associations re-presenting image creators in the appropriate medium.

5.3 Attribution and Acknowledgment

Educators, scholars, and students should credit the sources and display the copyright notice(s) with any copyright ownership information shown in the original source, for all images digitized by educators, scholars, and students, including those digitized under fair use. Crediting the source means adequately identifying the source of the work, giving a full bibliographic description where available (including the creator/author, title, publisher, and place and date of publication) or citing the electronic address if the work is from a network source. Educators, scholars, and students should retain any copyright notice or other proprietary rights notice placed by the copyright owner or image archive or collection on the digital image, unless they know that the work has entered the public domain or that the copyright ownership has changed. In those cases when source credits and copyright ownership information cannot be displayed on the screen with the image for educational reasons (e.g., during examinations), this information should still be linked to the image.

5.4 Licenses and Contracts

Institutions should determine whether specific images are subject to a license or contract; a license or contract may limit the uses of those images.

5.5 Portions from Single Sources Such as Published Compilations or Motion Pictures

When digitizing and using individual images from a single source such as a published compilation (including but not limited to books, slide sets, and digital image collections), or individual frames from motion pictures or other audiovisual works, institutions and individuals should be aware that fair use limits the number and substantiality of the images that may be used from a single source. In addition, a separate copyright in a compilation may exist. Further, fair use requires consideration of the effect of the use on the potential market for or value of the copyrighted work. The greater the number and substantiality of images taken from a single source, the greater the risk that the use will not be fair use.

5.6 Portions of Individual Images

Although the use of entire works is usually not permitted under fair use, it is generally appropriate to use images in their entirety in order to respect the integrity of the original visual image, as long as the limitations on use under these guidelines are in place. For purposes of electronic display, however, portions of an image may be used to highlight certain details of the work for educational purposes as long as the full image is displayed or linked to the portion.

5.7 Integrity of Images: Alterations

In order to maintain the integrity of copyrighted works, educators, scholars, and students are advised to exercise care when making any alterations in a work under fair use for educational purposes such as criticism, comment, teaching, scholarship, and research. Furthermore, educators, scholars, and students should note the nature of any changes they make to original visual images when producing their own digital images.

5.8 Caution in Downloading Images from Other Electronic Sources

Educators, scholars, and students are advised to exercise caution in using digital images downloaded from other sources, such as the Internet. Such digital environments contain a mix of works protected by copyright and works in the public domain, and some copyrighted works may have been posted to the Internet without authorization of the copyright holder.

Interlibrary Loan

St. Charles Community College
St. Charles Community College Library
St. Peters, Missouri

Document Delivery and Interlibrary Loan

Interlibrary loan activities are subject to copyright restrictions due to the fact that rights to publications are not purchased or transferred to the requestor. The House and Senate subcommittees made an interpretation of these restrictions in 1976 through an interpretation of 17 U.S.C. Section 108 (g)(2). The commission considers the guidelines, which follow to be a workable and fair interpretation of the intent of the law.

A few guidelines include:

> During a calendar year, a library may borrow 5 articles from a periodical title newer than 5 years old.

> All interlibrary loan requests must bear a symbol of compliance.

> The requesting library must keep borrowing records for 3 calendar years. Exceptions to this "Rule of 5" include when the title is on order, that issue is missing, the item is at the bindery, or the issue was damaged or not available.

The alternatives include borrowing the entire volume or issue, using a document delivery or full text service, which includes copyright fees, obtaining permission from the copyright holder directly or joining a copyright clearinghouse. Libraries that choose not to subscribe to such a service may simply keep track of their borrowing and lending habits and stop borrowing when their need necessitates purchasing the title directly. Most document delivery services factor the cost of copyright permissions into their fee. (Source: Handbook of Federal Librarianship. http://lcweb.loc.gov/flicc/hbfl/chap7.html)

Mohawk Valley Community College
Mohawk Valley Community College Libraries
Utica, New York

Interlibrary Loan

The National Commission on New Technological Uses of Copyrighted Works (CONTU) Guidelines limit the Libraries to no more than five requests a year for copies of any article or articles published in a given periodical within the past five years. This limitation is imposed so that libraries do not use photocopying as a substitute for purchasing a periodical subscription.

The Interlibrary Loan Librarian is responsible to review records of interlibrary loan photocopy requests to determine that they meet the CONTU Guidelines and the fair use provisions of the Copyright Law.

Material for Library—Reserve Use

Albion College
Albion, Michigan

Copying for Library Reserve Use

Photocopying for library reserve use is not mentioned specifically in the Copyright Act. In an attempt to offer guidance to faculty and libraries, the American Library Association issued a recommendation to libraries regarding photocopying for reserve shelf activities. This model policy has been adapted for use by the College's Library and is reproduced below. See also Appendix C.

At the request of a faculty member, the library may place on reserve photocopied excerpts from copyrighted works in its collection in accordance with guidelines similar to the guidelines for classroom copying for face-to-face teaching found in Appendix B. The College believes that these guidelines apply to the library reserve shelf to the extent that it functions as an extension of classroom readings or reflects an individual student's right to photocopy for his/her personal scholastic use under the doctrine of fair use. In general, the library may use photocopied materials for reserve shelf use for the convenience of students both in preparing class assignments and in pursuing informal educational activities which higher education requires, such as advanced independent study and research.

If the faculty request asks for only one copy to be placed on reserve, the library may place a photocopy of an entire article, an entire chapter from a book, or an entire poem. Requests for multiple copies on reserve should meet the following guidelines:

1) the amount of material should be reasonable in relation to the total amount of material assigned for one term, taking into account the nature of the course, its subject matter and level;
2) the number of copies should be reasonable in light of the number of students enrolled, the difficulty and timing of assignments, and the number of other courses which may assign the same material;
3) the material should contain a notice of copyright;
4) the effect of photocopying the material should not be detrimental to the market for the work. (In general, the library should own at least one copy of the work.)

For example, a faculty member may place on reserve, as a supplement to the course textbook, a reasonable number of copies of articles from academic periodicals or chapters from books. A reasonable number of copies will in most instances be less than six, but factors such as the length or difficulty of the assignment, the number of enrolled students, and the length of time allowed for completion of the assignment may permit more in unusual circumstances.

In addition, a faculty member may also request that multiple copies of photocopied copyrighted material be placed on the reserve shelf if there is insufficient time to obtain permission from the copyright owner. For example, a professor may place on reserve several photocopies of an entire article from a recent issue of *Time* or *The New York Times* in lieu of distributing a copy to each member of the class.

Please keep in mind: If there is any doubt as to whether a particular instance of photocopying can be considered fair use in the reserve shelf context, the copyright owner's permission should be sought. (See Appendix A for advice on how to obtain permission.)

Materials placed on reserve will be returned to the faculty member at the end of each semester.

Material for Classroom Use

Mohawk Valley Community College
Mohawk Valley Libraries
Utica, New York

Classroom Use

Books and Periodicals

A faculty member may distribute photocopied materials to students in a class, without obtaining prior permission to make multiple copies from the copyright owner, provided all conditions listed below are met:

General rules

- distribution of the same material does not occur every semester
- only one copy is distributed to each student and that copy is the student's property
- the material includes a copyright notice on the first page of the photocopied material
- no charge is made beyond the actual cost of reproduction

Additional requirements:

Brevity

- for prose: in its entirety if less than 2,500 words. Otherwise, the copy should not exceed 1,000 words, or 10% of the work, whichever is less
- for poetry: 250 words
- for illustrations: 1

Spontaneity and cumulative effect

- the copying is at the instance and inspiration of the faculty member
- the decision to use the material for maximum teaching effectiveness does not allow sufficient time to request permission prior to its use.
- the copying of the material is for only one course
- the copying is not done repeatedly from the same materials
- there are not more that nine separate instances of such multiple copying for one course during one class term.

Duplication which always requires copyright permission:

Repetitive copying. The classroom use of photocopied materials in multiple courses or in successive semesters will require advance permission from the copyright owner;

Consumable works. The duplication of works that are consumed in the classroom, such as exercises and workbooks, require permission from the copyright owner;

Anthologies. Copying used to create or replace or substitute for anthologies, compilations, or collective works. However, if copies of various works or excerpts are cumulated or reproduced and used separately, then they may not need permission;

Media software. Duplication of media software requires prior advance permission of the copyright holder.

Hamilton College
Burke Library
Clinton, New York

Photocopying

Copying for Classroom Uses

Primary and secondary school educators have, with publishers, developed guidelines which allow a teacher to distribute photocopied materials to students in a class, without the publisher's prior permission, upon compliance with these and other conditions:

1. The distribution of the same photocopied materials does not occur every semester.
2. Only one copy is distributed for each student, which must become the student's property.
3. The materials include a copyright notice on the first page of the portion of material photocopied.
4. The students are not assessed any fee beyond the actual cost of the photocopying.

University of Pittsburgh
Pittsburgh, Pennsylvania

Copies for Teachers for Classroom Use

Single Copying for Teachers. A single copy may be made of the following by or for a teacher at his individual request for scholarly research or use in teaching or preparation to teach a class:

- A chapter from a book
- An article from a periodical or newspaper
- A short story, short essay, or short poem, whether or not from a collective work
- A chart, graph, diagram, drawing, cartoon or picture from a book, periodical, or newspaper

Multiple Copies for Classroom Use. Multiple copies (not to exceed in any event more than one copy per pupil in a course) may be made by or for the teacher giving the course for classroom use or discussion, provided that:

- The copying meets the tests of brevity, spontaneity and cumulative effects, as defined in Procedure 10–04–01, Copying Copyrighted Material
- Each copy includes a proper notice of copyright

Multiple Copies

University of New Hampshire
University of New Hampshire Library
Durham, New Hampshire

Multiple Copies

For one-time distribution in class to students, a faculty member may make, or have made, multiple copies if he or she:

- makes no more than one for each student;
- includes the notice of copyright (writes it on the first sheet or copies the page on which it appears);
- is selective and sparing in choosing poetry, prose and illustration;
- makes no charge to the student beyond the actual cost of the photocopying.

The right to make multiple copies is strengthened if the copying will not have a significant effect upon the potential market for the work (this is probably the most important factor), or if there is insufficient time to seek permission from the owner of the copyright.

Music

St. Charles Community College
St. Charles Community College Library
St. Peters, Missouri

Music

An instructor may copy and use 10% or up to 30 seconds (whichever is least) of music without copyright permission.

University of Pittsburgh
Pittsburgh, Pennsylvania

Musical Works

Copying music scores for the purpose of performance is not permitted. However, exceptions may be made in emergencies:

- To replace University-owned copies which for any reason are not available for an imminent performance
- Providing purchased replacements are substituted in due course

Single Copies

A single copy may be made of an entire performable unit by or for a teacher for research or other academic purposes (other than performances) providing:

- It has been determined by a written statement from the copyright owner that the work is out of print
- The unit is unavailable except in a larger work

A single copy may be made of an entire recording of a performance by students for evaluation or rehearsal and the copy is retained by the teacher or the University.

A single copy may be made of an entire sound recording of a musical work, providing the original is a sound recording owned by the teacher or the University.

- The copying must be only for the purpose of constructing aural exercises or examinations
- The copy (e.g., tape or cassette) is retained by the teacher or the University

Multiple Copies

Multiple copies may be made of excerpts from copyrighted work providing the copying constitutes a non-performable unit.

(For additional policies, please see the accompanying CD-ROM.)

Personal Research

SUNY
Cortland Memorial Library
Cortland, New York

Personal Research Use

At the very least, faculty may make a single copy of any of the following for scholarly research or use in teaching or preparing to teach a class:

a. a chapter from a book;
b. an article from a periodical or newspaper;
c. a short story, short essays or short poem whether or not from a collective work;
d. a chart, diagram, graph, drawing, cartoon or picture from a book, periodical, or newspaper.

These examples reflect the most conservative guidelines for fair use. They do not represent inviolate ceilings for the amount of copyrighted material which can be photocopied within the boundaries of fair use. When exceeding these minimal levels, however, faculty and staff should consider the four factors listed under the discussion of fair use on pages 5 and 6 of this handbook to make sure that any additional photocopying is justified. The following demonstrate situations where increased levels of photocopying would continue to remain within the parameters of fair use:

- the inability to obtain another copy of the work because it is not available from the library or another source or cannot be obtained within your time constraints;
- the intention to photocopy the material only once and not distribute the material to others;
- the ability to keep the amount of material photocopied within a reasonable proportion to the entire work (the larger the work, the greater amount of material which may be photocopied).

As a general rule, most single-copy photocopying for individual use in research—even when it involves copying a substantial portion of a work—may well be considered fair use.

Mohawk Valley Community College
Mohawk Valley Libraries
Utica, New York

Personal Research Use

Faculty may make a single copy of any of the following for scholarly research or use in teaching or preparing to teach a class:

- chapter from a book
- article from a periodical or newspaper
- short story, short essay, or short poem
- chart, diagram, graph, drawing, cartoon or picture

Photocopies and Reproductions

University of Pittsburgh
Pittsburgh, Pennsylvania

Photocopying/Reproduction

Only a single copy of a copyrighted article or a minor part of a work may be made for personal use, unless written permission to do otherwise has been secured from the copyright holder by the person who makes the copy or requests copying service. See Procedure 10–04–01, Copying Copyrighted Material.

- The copy or copies of the copyrighted work becomes the property of the person who requested it.

It is not permissible to copy an entire issue, volume or complete work. However a copy may be made for replacement purposes if:

- The item has been lost, stolen, or damaged, and
- It has been determined that a copy is not available through normal trade sources at a fair price.

All the privileges of copying under Section 108 of the Copyright Act require that the copy:

- Be made without the purpose of direct or indirect commercial advantage,
- Be made by a library or archives that is open to the public or at least a non-affiliated researcher "doing research in a specialized field,"
- Include a proper notice of copyright.

(For additional policies, please see the accompanying CD-ROM.)

Public Domain Material

University of Pittsburgh
Pittsburgh, Pennsylvania

Public Domain

Almost everything copyrighted in 1905 or previously is now in the public domain and multiple copies may be made.

- In rare instances a private law has been passed by Congress to provide extended copyright protection for a title.

While some materials since 1906 have come into the public domain, the University and its libraries are not equipped to perform copyright searches to identify those materials which are no longer protected.

- The patron may have the U.S. Copyright Office perform a copyright search at an hourly charge.
- A written statement from the U.S. Copyright Office that a work is in the public domain is acceptable proof that multiple copies may be made.

Multiple works that are produced by the publisher without a copyright notice are not protected by Copyright. In those instances, the Copyright Act does not apply.

Syracuse University
Syracuse, New York

Copyright protection is granted for a specific number of years. When this term of copyright expires a work enters the public domain and can be freely used without further restrictions. Under the current law the term is the life of the author plus fifty years. There are, however, ongoing discussions to increase this to life plus seventy years. For some works where copyright is not held by an individual, the period is seventy-five years from publication. The copyright status of any work published since 1922 should be determined before use. The earliest of these will not enter public domain until the year 2003. Works published in the United States before 1922 were covered under the earlier 1909 copyright law and are no longer protected by copyright.

Works published by the U.S. government may not be copyrighted. All works published by the federal government are in the public domain and may be reused without further permission. Works created under federal grant or contract may or may not be protected depending on the provision of the grant or contract. Works published by state governments or the governments of other countries may be subject to copyright under the U.S. Copyright Law or the laws of the country in which the work was published.

Publication Procedures

Georgia State University
Georgia State University Library
Atlanta, Georgia

Publication Procedures

1. We request that citation be written as follows:

[collection name or book title], [name of curatorial unit, such as "Southern Labor Archives" or "Georgia Women's Collections"], Special Collections Department & Archives, Georgia State University Library.

The curatorial units are : Southern Labor Archives; University Archives; Popular Music Collection; Georgia Government Documentation Project; Women's Collections; Rare Book Collection.

(A) In publications it is preferred that the credit line appear on the same or facing page as the illustration. When possible, each individual item should be credited where it appears.

(B) With media projects (including films, documentaries, and mixed media products), include credit with other sources of materials

(C) With exhibitions, credit within exhibition area, preferably with each item that is used

2. The researcher agrees not to reproduce copies as dust jackets, or end papers, or to use in an advertisement or any commercial use of a similar nature, nor to mass reproduce, unless specifically authorized by Special Collections & Archives.

3. Special Collections & Archives requests one complimentary copy of the work in which the copies appear.

Please contact the Head of Special Collections with any questions concerning these procedures.

Single Copies

University of New Hampshire
University of New Hampshire Library
Durham, New Hampshire

Single Copies

For teaching, including preparation and for scholarly research, a faculty member may make, or have made, a SINGLE copy of:

- one chapter from a book (up to 10% of the book);
- one article from a journal, periodical or newspaper;
- one short story, essay or poem;
- one diagram or picture in any of those works.

University of California Policy on the Reproduction of Copyrighted Materials for Teaching and Research

Single Copying for Teachers

A single copy may be made of any of the following by or for a teacher at his or her individual request for his or her scholarly research or use in teaching or preparation to teach a class:

A. A chapter from a book;
B. An article from a periodical or newspaper;
C. A short story, short essay or short poem, whether or not from a collective work;
D. A chart, graph, diagram, drawing, cartoon or picture from a book, periodical, or newspaper.

Software

University of Texas System
Austin, Texas

Copyrighted software may be copied without the copyright owner's permission only in accordance with the Copyright Act. Section 117 of the Act permits making an archival back-up copy. Most software, however, is licensed to the user and the terms of the license agreement may give the user permission to make copies of the software in excess of the archival copy permitted by the Copyright Act. Each software license agreement is unique. As a result, the user's rights to copy licensed software beyond that permitted under the Copyright Act may only be determined by reading the user's license agreement. Any copying or reproduction of copyrighted software on System or component institution computing equipment must be in accordance with the Copyright Act and the pertinent software license agreement. Further, faculty, staff and students may not use unauthorized copies of software on System or component institution owned computers or networks or computers housed in System or component institution facilities.

University of Minnesota Duluth
UMD Library
Duluth, Minnesota

Software

The library will ensure that computer software installed on library equipment will comply with the licensing for that software. Library staff will be responsible for complying with the license for personal software they install on library equipment.

Albion College
Albion, Michigan

Albion College negotiates site licenses with software vendors whenever possible for software products that are selected for extensive use. These arrangements provide the college community with efficient access to computer programs that support the curriculum while assuring the copyright owner a fair royalty. Check with Information Technology to determine the availability of particular software and the license restrictions that apply.

Other products may be licensed on an individual or limited basis. However, copying is strictly limited except for backup purposes. The Copyright Act allows the purchaser of software to:

- make one and only one copy of software for solely archival purposes in case the original is destroyed or damaged through mechanical failure of a computer. However, if the original is sold or given away, the archival copy must be destroyed.
- make necessary adaptations to use the program.
- add features to the program for specific applications. These improvements may not be sold or given away without the copyright owner's permission.

Printed documentation is covered by copyright as indicated inside each volume of documentation.

In many cases, software may be lent but only for temporary use, not for copying. If the borrower transfers the software to a hard disk, the program must be deleted when the borrowed item is returned. Check the software license for restrictions. Circulating software in the Library's collection must include, and computer labs and other public facilities must post, the following warning to caution against illegal copying of software:

Software Copyright Warning

Software is protected by the copyright law. In general, software may not be copied without the copyright owner's permission. Read the software license for further restrictions that may apply.

The College strictly prohibits the illegal copying of software. You will be held liable for damages from the illegal duplication of software. Violators will be referred to the College's judicial process.

Copyright law presently is acknowledged to be inadequate in relation to the complexities of software use. EDUCAUSE, a nonprofit organization that supports the use of technology in education, launched the EDUCOM Software Initiative, which developed a statement of principle intended for use by individual colleges and universities and which is endorsed by Albion College.

The EDUCOM Code

Software and Intellectual Rights

Respect for intellectual labor and creativity is vital to academic discourse and enterprise. This principle applies to works of all authors and publishers in all media. It encompasses respect for the right to acknowledgment, right to privacy, and right to determine the form, manner, and terms of publication and distribution.

Because electronic information is volatile and easily reproduced, respect for the work and personal expression of others is especially critical in computer environments. Violations of authorial integrity, including plagiarism, invasion of privacy, unauthorized access, and trade secret and copyright violations, may be grounds for sanctions against members of the academic community.

Software Classifications

The EDUCOM Code defines four broad classifications of software and applies different principles to each classification as follows:

Commercial Software—software for which a license has been purchased allowing use. Minimally, the license will stipulate that the software is covered by copyright; one backup copy of the software may be made, although it cannot be used unless the original package fails or is destroyed; and modifications to the software are not allowed. Other restrictions may apply; read the license for specific limitations.

Shareware—the copyright holder specifically allows you to make and distribute copies of the software, but demands payment if, after testing the software, you adopt it for use. In general, all license restrictions for commercial software apply. Selling software as shareware is a marketing decision and does not change the legal requirements with respect to copyright.

Freeware—the conditions for freeware are in direct contrast to generally understood copyright restrictions. Although the software is covered by copyright, the license allows for free use, modification, and distribution of the software as long as the purposes are not for profit and credit for the original work is given to the copyright holder.

Public Domain—software for which the copyright holder has explicitly relinquished all rights to the software. It must be clearly marked as "Public Domain." Since March 1, 1989, all works assume copyright protection unless the "Public Domain" notification is stated.

Washington and Lee University
Leyburn Library
Lexington, Virginia

Guidelines for the Use of Computer Software

A. Use of Copyrighted Computer Programs (Software)

Copying not only entails duplicating software but includes transferring a program from one medium (CD, floppy, hard disk for example) or transmitting over a local area network, or a long distance line.

Unauthorized reproduction, distribution, or adaptation of computer programs is governed by the same rules as other end-uses and will be considered infringement unless it constitutes fair use under §107 of the Copyright Act or is exempted under §117 which is explained below.

Please note that the guidelines for classroom copying in not-for-profit educational institutions are explicitly limited to books and periodicals, and do not encompass other types of copyrighted works, including computer programs.

1. Copying

A University department purchasing a program may adapt the program so it can be used on the office machines. This use qualifies for the §117 exemption; the owner of a lawfully acquired copy of a computer program is permitted to make an adaptation of a computer program "as an essential step in the utilization of the computer program in conjunction with the machine and it is used in no other manner."

A department may not obtain a single machine license for a program and then make it available via a department network or through the campus-wide computer system that any number of students, faculty, and staff may access simultaneously either on or off campus. Despite the non-commercial purpose of such distribution, because the entire program is reproduced, there is a serious commercial effect caused by lost license fees and pirated copies.

2. Lending

Under §109(b)(2)(A) of the Copyright Act, a computer program may be loaned for non-profit purposes by nonprofit libraries. All copies that are loaned by a library must contain a warning of copyright in accordance with the requirements prescribed by the Register of Copyrights.

A library may lend a book with the supplemental software on a disk in the book pocket, so long as this is lent for a non-profit purpose and the library affixes to the book or the disk the required copyright warning.

3. Archiving Copies

Under §117 of the act, libraries and schools may lawfully make one copy under the following conditions: One copy is made, the original copy is stored. If the possession of the original ceases to be lawful, all copies must be destroyed. Only the number of copies purchased or licensed may be in use at any given time.

4. Licensing

Many computer programs are acquired under licenses rather than purchases.

License agreements govern many of the activities that a user of a computer-related work may conduct. These agreements are contracts between the owner or vendor of the copyrighted work and the user of the work. Contracts are governed by state law. The terms of the license agreement may broaden or narrow the rights that a user has under the Copyright Act. Such agreements usually specify restriction on the user's rights to copy the software, to access electronic information, to download information. It may specify what constitutes legitimate uses of information. If the University licenses rather than purchases a computer program, then the user should refer to the license agreement or contact the copyright owner before making an adaptation.

5. Areas of Caution

   a. Use of software may be restricted to a particular computer at a particular site. You should not assume that simultaneous use of a server copy of software is permitted under single copy license restrictions.

   b. Employees may not make copies of software licensed or owned by the University for their personal use except where explicitly allowed by the software vendor. (Check with University Computing.)

   c. If the University supplies licensed software to students in the course of instruction in a classroom, then sufficient licenses must be held by the University.

   d. Shareware is easily identifiable through explicit statements and software documentation. Unless the explicit statements identify the software as shareware, the user should assume that it may NOT be duplicated. Like other information, software not containing a copyright notice is not necessarily in the public domain.

Special Collections

University of Central Florida
University of Central Florida Libraries
Orlando, Florida

UCF Libraries may provide reproductions of Special Collections items under certain circumstances and in accordance with applicable law (including fair use). By providing reproductions, the UCF Libraries do NOT grant permission to publish or exhibit. Reproductions are provided for academic research purposes only. They may not be copied or distributed. Written permission to publish must be obtained from copyright and/or literary rights owners and from Special Collections for any publication or commercial use of copies. Fees may be charged at the discretion Director of the UCF Libraries. Write to: [contact info].

Unpublished Material

Albion College
Albion, Michigan

Manuscripts, letters, and other unpublished materials are likely to be protected by copyright regardless of age, even if they lack a notice of copyright. Unpublished works created before January 1, 1978 are protected through December 31, 2002, or life plus 70 years, whichever is greater. But, if the unpublished work is published before December 31, 2002, then it will be protected for life plus 70 years or until December 31, 2047, whichever is greater.

Unpublished works that belong to the Library Archives may be reproduced in facsimile format for preservation purposes or for deposit for research use in another library or archives. Copies may usually be made for individual researchers under the law's Fair Use provisions. Ownership of the physical object does not signify ownership of intellectual property rights. Beyond individual fair use, permission must be granted.

Syracuse University
Syracuse, New York

Unpublished works such as letters and journals are protected under the Copyright Act of 1976. Although the doctrine of fair use applies to these works it has been applied in a more restrictive manner, especially in relation to any use of quoted excerpts in a document which is then distributed to others. Many unpublished works are further restricted by license or donor restrictions. All use of unpublished materials requires documentation on the use that will be made of the information from the faculty member or researcher.

Web Pages

University of Minnesota Duluth
UMD Library
Duluth, Minnesota

Web Pages

Library Web pages comply with the University of Minnesota World Wide Web Publishing Guidelines, the University of Minnesota policy for Publishing Information on the World Wide Web and the ITTS guidelines Creating, Storing, and Linking Pages to the UMD Web Site.

Graphics used on the Library site will be originally created for the site, purchased, supplied with software packages the library owns, or graphics that are in the public domain.

The Web team will make links to Web sites that are relevant to the information presented on the library site and will request permission to link to sites that require permission in the copyright statement.

Permission will be requested prior to duplicating or modifying a site or page for use on the UMD Library site. Appropriate credit will be given to the original creator.

Washington and Lee University
Leyburn Library
Lexington, Virginia

Copyright and the Web

Copyright law applies equally to works electronically available on the Web. The fact that you can view, download or print text and graphics does not mean that the material is unprotected. Nor does it mean that you are free to disseminate that work to others either electronically or in hard copy.

1. Reading, Watching or Listening

There is controversy at the moment about the extent to which you can read, watch or listen to a copyrighted work without permission and/or royalties and whether fair use applies.

If a work is copyrighted and you have authorized access, you are free to read, watch or listen. There are some convincing arguments that fair use applies even if your use is not authorized.

2. Downloading

When you download material to your computer you make an electronic copy. Unless your copy falls within fair use, you may not make this copy without authorization of the copyright owner. The owner may have given permission to download.

You may be searching a commercial database that charges a fee for searching and may also authorize you to download or print the material. Such authorization is usually limited to a single copy for your personal use.

3. Home Pages

a. You may put your own created text, graphics, audio or video on your Web page.

b. If you use an item created by someone else whose copyright has not expired, then you should seek permission.

c. By creating a Web page you probably have given implied permission to others to link to your Web page. You may link to another URL because links are like street addresses and may not be copyrightable. However, a list of links may be copyrightable under a compilation copyright and if you copy the entire list to your Web page, it probably is a copyright violation.

Copyright Infringement and Enforcement

Hamilton College
Burke Library
Clinton, New York

Penalties for Infringement

Substantial penalties are provided for infringement of a copyright:

An injunction to stop the infringement is most likely to be the first action.

Payment of actual damages for financial loss suffered by the copyright owner may be required.

Statutory damages, for which no actual damages need be proved, may be assessed. If the court determines there is an infringement, it must award between $500 and $20,000.

An exception to the statutory damages is made in the case of teachers, provided the teacher believed and had reasonable grounds to believe that it was fair use. In this case the teacher may be found guilty but the damages do not have to be paid. This gives the teachers some special consideration under the law, but it also requires that they be thoroughly familiar with what might be considered reasonable fair use practices.

FORMS

Copyright Permission Sample Letter Form

St. Charles Community College
St. Charles Community College Library
St. Peters, Missouri

Copyright Permission Sample Letter

Date

Copyright Holder/Publisher [This portion to be filed out by LRC staff]

Street Address

City, State Zip

Attn: Copyrights and Permissions Department

Dear Sir or Madam:

Regarding the following title and information, I would like permission to retain a copy the following material on reserve in the library at St. Charles Community College.

[This portion to be filled out by instructor or requesting department.]

Author or Editor: _____

Article or Chapter: _____

Periodical or Book Title: _____

For Periodical: Volume #_____ Issue Date: _____ Pages: _____ ISSN: _____

For Book: Copyright date: _____ Pages: _____ ISBN: _____

Number of copies to be placed on reserve: _____

Time item will remain on reserve until: _____

The copy will be used exclusively for educational purpose, with no direct or indirect commercial advantage, and will include a notice of copyright for students enrolled in my class.

Thank you for considering my request; I am looking forward to your reply. If you have any questions, contact Gwen Bell, Secretary for Learning Resources at the address listed below, by phone at 636-922-8470, or by email gbell@stchas.edu.

Sincerely,

[Signature of instructor]

Sample Letter to Copyright Owner Form

University of California
San Diego, California
Policy on the Reproduction of Copyrighted Materials for Teaching and Research

The following is a sample letter to a copyright owner (in this example a publisher) requesting permission to copy:

Date

Material Permissions Department
Academic Book Company
200 Park Avenue
New York, New York 10016

Dear Sir/Madam:

I would like permission to copy the following for use in my class (name of class) (next semester) or (next semester and subsequent semesters during which the course is offered.)

Title: Ethics and the Law, Second Edition

Copyright: Academic Book Co., 1965, 1971

Author: John Smith

Material to be duplicated: Chapter 9 (photocopy enclosed)

Number of Copies: 50

Distribution: The material will be distributed to students in my class and they will pay only the cost of the photocopying

Type of reprint: Photocopy

Use: The chapter will be used as supplementary teaching materials

I have enclosed a self-addressed envelope for your convenience in replying to this request.

Sincerely,

Faculty Member

TEACH Act Checklist Form

University of Texas System
Austin, Texas

Use this handy checklist to see whether you are ready to use the TEACH Act:

_____ My institution is a nonprofit accredited educational institution or a governmental agency

_____ It has a policy on the use of copyrighted materials

_____ It provides accurate information to faculty, students and staff about copyright

_____ Its systems will not interfere with technological controls within the materials I want to use

_____ The materials I want to use are specifically for students in my class

_____ Only those students will have access to the materials

_____ The materials will be provided at my direction during the relevant lesson

_____ The materials are directly related and of material assistance to my teaching content

_____ My class is part of the regular offerings of my institution

_____ I will include a notice that the materials are protected by copyright

_____ I will use technology that reasonably limits the students' ability to retain or further distribute the materials

_____ I will make the materials available to the students only for a period of time that is relevant to the context of a class session

_____ I will store the materials on a secure server and transmit them only as permitted by this law

_____ I will not make any copies other than the one I need to make the transmission

_____ The materials are of the proper type and amount the law authorizes:

_____ Entire performances of nondramatic literary and musical works

_____ Reasonable and limited parts of a dramatic literary, musical, or audiovisual works

_____ Displays of other works, such as images, in amounts similar to typical displays in face-to-face teaching

_____ The materials are not among those the law specifically excludes from its coverage:

_____ Materials specifically marketed for classroom use for digital distance education

_____ Copies I know or should know are illegal

_____ Textbooks, coursepacks, electronic reserves and similar materials typically purchased individually by the students for independent review outside the classroom or class session

_____ If I am using an analog original, I checked before digitizing it to be sure:

_____ I copied only the amount that I am authorized to transmit

_____ There is no digital copy of the work available except with technological protections that prevent my using it for the class in the way the statute authorizes

Fair Use Worksheet

University of Minnesota Duluth
UMD Library
Duluth, Minnesota

Fair Use Worksheet

1. The worksheet below is a tool to aid in applying the four fair use factors to the use of copyrighted materials. (The four fair use factors are from the United States Code Title 17 Copyrights Chapter 1 Sec 107.)

2. With the particular use in mind, read each section and check the appropriate boxes.

3. See how the balance tips with each answer.

4. Make a judgment about the final balance: overall does the balance tip in favor of fair use or in favor of getting permission?

5. Retain a copy of this form in connection with each possible "fair use" of a copyrighted work for your project.

Thanks to the Indiana University–Purdue University Indianapolis Copyright Management Center for providing the basis for this worksheet.

Name: _____ Date: _____

Project: _____

Purpose (1) the purpose and character of the use, including whether such use is of a commercial nature or is for nonprofit educational purposes

Favors Fair Use

_____ Teaching (including multiple copies for classroom use)

_____ Research Scholarship

_____ Nonprofit Educational Institution

_____ Criticism

_____ Comment

_____ News reporting

_____ Transformative or productive use (changes the work for new utility

_____ Restricted access (to students or other appropriate group)

_____ Parody

Favors Getting Permission

_____ Profiting from the use

_____ Entertainment

_____ Bad-faith behavior

_____ Denying credit to original author

Nature (2) the nature of the copyrighted work

Favors Fair Use

_____ Published work

_____ Factual or nonfiction based

_____ Important to favored educational objectives

Favors Getting Permission

_____ Unpublished work

_____ Highly creative work (art, music, novels, films, plays)

_____ Fiction

Amount (3) the amount and substantiality of the portion used in relation to the copyrighted work as a whole

Favors Fair Use

_____ Small quantity

_____ Portion used is not central or significant to entire work

_____ Amount is appropriate for favored educational purpose

Favors Getting Permission

_____ Large portion or whole work used

_____ Portion used is central to work or "heart of the work"

Effect (4) the effect of the use upon the potential market for or value of the copyrighted work. The fact that a work is unpublished shall not itself bar a finding of fair use if such finding is made upon consideration of all the above factors.

Favors Fair Use

_____ User owns lawfully acquired or purchased copy of original work

_____ One or few copies made

_____ No significant effect on the market or potential market for copyrighted work

_____ Lack of licensing mechanism

Favors Getting Permission

_____ Could replace sale of copyrighted work

_____ Significantly impairs market or potential market for copyrighted work or derivative

_____ Reasonably available licensing mechanism for use of the copyrighted work

_____ Affordable permission available for using work

_____ Numerous copies made

_____ You made it accessible on Web or in other public forum

_____ Repeated or long term use

Chapter 30

PRIVACY

ADMINISTRATIVE GUIDELINES

General Privacy Policy Statements

Indiana University Bloomington
Indiana University Libraries
Bloomington, Indiana

Introduction

Privacy is essential to the exercise of free speech, free thought, and free association. The Indiana University Libraries define the right to privacy as the right to open inquiry without having the subject of one's interest examined or scrutinized by others. Confidentiality exists when a library is in possession of personally identifiable information about users and keeps that information private on their behalf.

The courts have recognized a right of privacy based on the Bill of Rights of the U.S. Constitution. The state of Indiana guarantees privacy in its constitution and statutory law (See www.in.gov/pac/statutes/ or www.ilfonline.org/IFC/inlaw/confidentiality.htm). IU Library's privacy and confidentiality policies are intended to comply with applicable federal, state, and local laws, as well as with any IU policies on privacy, including the IU Policy on Privacy of Information Technology Resources (www.itpo.iu.edu/IT07.html).

User rights—as well as our institution's responsibilities—outlined here are based in part on what are known in the United States as the five "Fair Information Practice Principles." These five principles outline the rights of Notice, Choice, Access, Security, and Enforcement.

Our commitment to our users' privacy and confidentiality has deep roots not only in law but also in the ethics and practices of librarianship. In accordance with the American Library Association's Code of Ethics:

"We protect each library user's right to privacy and confidentiality with respect to information sought or received and resources consulted, borrowed, acquired, or transmitted."

Duke University
Duke University Libraries
Durham, North Carolina

Introduction

One of the cornerstones of librarianship is respect for the privacy of library users. Duke University Libraries recognize the importance of protecting your privacy and the confidentiality of the information that you share with us when you use our web sites or other library services. Described below is our policy on the collection, use, disclosure, maintenance and protection of personal information that you provide to us.

Syracuse University
Syracuse University Library
Syracuse, New York

The Syracuse University Library is committed to protecting the privacy of its users. Our policies conform to the Code of Ethics of the American Library Association, which states: "We protect each library user's right to privacy and confidentiality with respect to information sought or received and resources consulted, borrowed, acquired, or transmitted." Syracuse University Library does gather data about system and resource use for administrative purposes, however we do not track personal information unless users elect to provide that information, for example by submitting a question, requesting an item, registering for a service, etc. Syracuse University will not release personal information gathered or collected by the Library except to the extent required by law. For the purposes of this policy, personal information is defined under New York State Technology Law as "any information concerning a natural person which, because of name, number, symbol, mark, or other identifier, can be used to identify that natural person."

University of Illinois at Urbana-Champaign
University Library
Urbana, Illinois

The UIUC Library formally recognizes:

That all records identifying the names, social security numbers, or I.D. number of library patrons are confidential in nature;

That such records are not to be revealed to anyone other than the patron in question without either the express written permission of the patron in question or the adherence to proper legal and University procedures regarding required access to such information:

That library employees are encouraged not to keep records with personally identifiable information, unless that information is necessary, and to destroy such records as soon as possible.

That the confidentiality of patron records requires that such records should be consulted by library employees only for LEGITIMATE purposes such as locating or recalling library materials, processing overdue notices and fines, adding or deleting names to the database, making collection development decisions, resolving billing matters, or investigating violations of Library circulation policies, including but not limited to, the following:

- expired I.D. number with overdue items still charged
- patrons who repeatedly claim to have returned books
- patrons who have manipulated the system to set their own due dates outside the Library's established patron loan periods
- patrons with outstanding Library accounts who have been referred to collection

Library employees may not be view patron records for such purposes as idle curiosity, personal interest, or general monitoring.

Special requests for confidential information to be used for research purposes shall be addressed to the University Librarian.

Information Collected

Duke University
Duke University Libraries
Durham, North Carolina

What information is collected and how it is used

When you use this website, our web server collects certain technical information from your web browser, including your browser type, operating system type, internet address, and the web address of the page from which you linked to our site. In some cases our web server may use browser "cookies" or other technologies to maintain session and preference information or to provide other complex functionality. You may adjust your Internet browser to disable the use of cookies and other web technologies; however, some features of this website may not function properly if you block these technologies. Any information that we automatically collect via this web site is only used internally for technical troubleshooting, to improve the usability of our website, and to track aggregate statistical trends. Except for information that you choose to submit to us (through web forms, e-mail messages, chat sessions, or other communication), we do not collect any personally identifiable information (such as your name, address, phone number, age, gender, ID numbers, etc.) on our website. If you do choose to submit personally identifiable information to us, that information is used only for the purpose for which you submitted it, and will not be used for other purposes. Information from other sources is not combined with the information that we collect. While we may disclose information about use of our web site in aggregate (such as server use statistics) we will not disclose to third parties any information that could be used to identify individuals or their use of Library resources, except as required by law or appropriate law enforcement procedures.

The Library does maintain personally identifiable information for library accounts of valid library users. If you are affiliated with Duke University, the library automatically receives personally identifiable information to create and update your library account from the Registrar's Office (for students) or Human Resources (for employees). If you purchase borrowing privileges, we must obtain certain information about you in order to provide you with a library account. We will maintain confidentiality of information sought or received, and materials consulted, borrowed or acquired, including database search records, reference interviews, circulation records, interlibrary loan records, and other personally identifiable uses of library materials, facilities, or services. The Library maintains several web-based management tools, such as forms related to renewing books, asking reference questions, saving search histories or resource preferences, requesting materials, etc. The personally identifiable information collected through these tools and stored in the library's computer systems will only be used to maintain your library account and provide services to you and is not made available to any other entity outside the Library except as required by law or appropriate law enforcement procedures.

Syracuse University
Syracuse University Library
Syracuse, New York

Information Collected Automatically

Syracuse University Library information systems gather and store certain information automatically when users browse the Web site, read pages, or download information. We use this information to track site usage, monitor site performance, and generate aggregate statistics. We do not track or record information about individuals. Examples of information collected include:

1. Internet domain (.edu for educational accounts, .com for commercial accounts) and the IP address;
2. Type of browser and operating system used;
3. Date and time of access;
4. Pages visited; and
5. Referring URL, if applicable.

Rights and Responsibilities of Staff and Users

Patron-Supplied Information

Yakima Valley Community College
College Library
Yakima, Washington

What We Collect If You Volunteer Information

If during your visit to our web site you participate in a survey, send an email, or perform some other transaction on-line, the following additional information will be collected:

- The email address, and contents of email, for those who communicate with us via email.
- Information volunteered in response to a survey.
- Information volunteered through an on-line form for any other purpose.
- The information collected is not limited to text characters and may include audio, video, and graphic information formats you send us.

We use your email to respond appropriately. This may be to respond to you, to address issues you may identify, to further improve our web site, or to forward the email to another agency for appropriate action.

Section C. Personal Information and Choice

You may choose whether to provide personal information on-line. "Personal information" is information about a natural person that is readily identifiable to that specific individual. Personal information includes such things as an individual's name, address, and phone number. A domain name or Internet Protocol address is not considered personal information.

We collect no personal information about you unless you voluntarily provide it to us by sending us email, participating in a survey, or completing an on-line form. You may choose not to contact us by email, participate in a survey, or to provide any personal information using an online form. Your choice to not participate in these activities will not impair your ability to browse YVCC's web site and read or download any information provided on the site.

If personal information is requested on the web site or volunteered by the user, state law and federal laws may protect it. However, this information is a public record once you provide it and may be subject to public inspection and copying if not protected by federal or state law.

If you believe that your personal/private information is being used for a purpose other than what was intended when submitted, you may contact the Registration and Records office or email registration as shown in the Contact Information Section of this statement.

YVCC's web site is a general audience site, and we do not knowingly collect any personal information from children. Users are cautioned that the collection of personal information requested from or volunteered by children on-line or by email will be treated the same as information given by an adult and may be subject to public access.

Highline Community College
Highline Community College Library
Des Moines, Washington

Personal Information and Choice

You may choose whether to provide personal information online.

Personal information is information about a person that is readily identifiable to that specific individual. Personal information includes such things as an individual's name, address, and phone number. A domain name or Internet Protocol address is not considered personal information.

We collect no personal information about you unless you voluntarily provide it to us by sending us e-mail, participating in a survey, or completing an on-line form. You may choose not to contact us by e-mail, participate in a survey or to provide any personal information using an online form. Your choice to not participate in these activities will not impair your ability to browse the Highline Community College Web site and read or download most information provided on the site.

Choosing not to participate in these activities may impair your ability to use on-line student services, participate in surveys, and participate in on-line instructional activities. On-line student services may be conducted using Touch-tone registration, mail, or telephone, as described in the section below on that specific service. Information about participating in surveys is available by contacting the office sponsoring the survey (identified on each individual survey), though some surveys will not be available off-line. Information about participating in instructional activities off-line is available by contacting the instructor, though some instructional activities may not be available off-line.

If personal information is requested on the Web site or volunteered by the user, state law and the federal Privacy Act of 1974 may protect it. However, this information is a public record once you provide it, and may be subject to public inspection and copying if not protected by federal or state law.

If you believe that your personal information is being used for a purpose other than what was intended when submitted, you may contact the Public Records Officer as shown in the Contact Information section of this statement.

Highline Community College web site is a general audience site and we do not knowingly collect any personal information from children. Users are cautioned that the collection of personal information requested from or volunteered by children online or by e-mail will be treated the same as information given by an adult, and may be subject to public access.

Protection of Patron-Supplied Information

Indiana University Bloomington
Indiana University Libraries
Bloomington, Indiana

Introduction

Privacy is essential to the exercise of free speech, free thought, and free association. The Indiana University Libraries define the right to privacy as the right to open inquiry without having the subject of one's interest examined or scrutinized by others. Confidentiality exists when a library is in possession of personally identifiable information about users and keeps that information private on their behalf.

The courts have recognized a right of privacy based on the Bill of Rights of the U.S. Constitution. The state of Indiana guarantees privacy in its constitution and statutory law. (See www.in.gov/pac/statutes/ or www.ilfonline.org/IFC/inlaw/confidentiality.htm.) IU Library's privacy and confidentiality policies are intended to comply with applicable federal, state, and local laws, as well as with any IU policies on privacy, including the IU Policy on Privacy of Information Technology Resources (www.itpo.iu.edu/IT07.html).

User rights—as well as our institution's responsibilities—outlined here are based in part on what are known in the United States as the five "Fair Information Practice Principles." These five principles outline the rights of Notice, Choice, Access, Security, and Enforcement.

Our commitment to our users' privacy and confidentiality has deep roots not only in law but also in the ethics and practices of librarianship. In accordance with the American Library Association's Code of Ethics:

"We protect each library user's right to privacy and confidentiality with respect to information sought or received and resources consulted, borrowed, acquired, or transmitted."

Duke University
Duke University Libraries
Durham, North Carolina

Introduction

One of the cornerstones of librarianship is respect for the privacy of library users. Duke University Libraries recognize the importance of protecting your privacy and the confidentiality of the information that you share with us when you use our web sites or other library services. Described below is our policy on the collection, use, disclosure, maintenance and protection of personal information that you provide to us.

Syracuse University
Syracuse University Library
Syracuse, New York

The Syracuse University Library is committed to protecting the privacy of its users. Our policies conform to the Code of Ethics of the American Library Association, which states: "We protect each library user's right to privacy and confidentiality with respect to information sought or received and resources consulted, borrowed, acquired, or transmitted." Syracuse University Library does gather data about system and resource use for administrative purposes, however we do not track personal information unless users elect to provide that information, for example by submitting a question, requesting an item, registering for a service, etc. Syracuse University will not release personal information gathered or collected by the Library except to the extent required by law. For the purposes of this policy, personal information is defined under New York State Technology Law as "any information concerning a natural person which, because of name, number, symbol, mark, or other identifier, can be used to identify that natural person."

University of Illinois at Urbana-Champaign
University Library
Urbana, Illinois

The UIUC Library formally recognizes:

That all records identifying the names, social security numbers, or I.D. number of library patrons are confidential in nature;

That such records are not to be revealed to anyone other than the patron in question without either the express written permission of the patron in question or the adherence to proper legal and University procedures regarding required access to such information;

That library employees are encouraged not to keep records with personally identifiable information, unless that information is necessary, and to destroy such records as soon as possible;

That the confidentiality of patron records requires that such records should be consulted by library employees only for LEGITIMATE purposes such as locating or recalling library materials, processing overdue notices and fines, adding or deleting names to the database, making collection development decisions, resolving billing matters, or investigating violations of Library circulation policies, including but not limited to, the following:

- expired I.D. number with overdue items still charged
- patrons who repeatedly claim to have returned books
- patrons who have manipulated the system to set their own due dates outside the Library's established patron loan periods
- patrons with outstanding Library accounts who have been referred to collection

Library employees may not be view patron records for such purposes as idle curiosity, personal interest, or general monitoring.

Special requests for confidential information to be used for research purposes shall be addressed to the University Librarian.

Staff Responsibilities

Vanderbilt University
Central Library
Nashville, Tennessee

No library employee shall reveal the identity of a borrower to any requestor.

Except in accordance with proper judicial order and with permission of the designated administrative officer(s) of the University, no person shall make known in any manner any information contained in such records listed above. In the absence of such judicial orders or University administrative permission, those to whom information will be denied include, but are not limited to, faculty, staff (including library staff except in the pursuit of their assigned duties), parents, students, campus security, police, FBI agents, and military personnel.

Library staff are to refer all requests for the above information to the appropriate Division Director or to the Office of the University Librarian. Those offices will contact the University General Counsel's Office.

University of Texas at Arlington
University Libraries
Arlington, Texas

Staff Responsibilities

Except in the provision of library services through contracts with third parties or in accordance with federal and Texas state laws, no Libraries' employee shall make known any information contained in the records listed above. Library records will only be released in accordance with a proper judicial order and with permission of the designated administrative officer of the University.

Library staff shall refer all requests for the above information to the Vice President for Administration and Campus Operations.

Users' Right to Know

University of Texas at Arlington
University Libraries
Arlington, Texas

Users' Right to Know

Users are entitled to know what information the UTA Libraries collects about them. State law, with a few exceptions, gives a user the right to be informed about the information UTA collects about the user. It also gives a user the right to request a copy of that information and to have the University correct any part of the information that is incorrect. This should be done by contacting the University's Vice President for Business Affairs and Comptroller. Procedures are set forth in UT System BPM # 32–12–01. The laws are found in sections 552.023 and 559.002 through 559.004 of the Texas Government Code.

Personal information received on faculty and staff comes from the Office of Human Resources Management and Development. Student information comes from the Office of the Registrar. The University does its best to ensure the security and accuracy of confidential information. Faculty and staff with an UT EID can check and update personal information such as their mailing address and e-mail address at UT Direct. Students can view some of their personal information at . . . and can change their address online and request other changes through the Office of the Registrar. Confidential information cannot be shared with external third parties.

Links to other sites from the UTA Libraries' web site, including, but not limited to, databases and electronic journals that the Libraries have licensed for use by UTA students, faculty, and staff, are covered by the other web sites' privacy practices. UTA Libraries are not responsible for the privacy practices of other web sites.

Data Security and Integrity

Highline Community College
Highline Community College Library
Des Moines, Washington

Security

Highline Community College, as developer and manager of the Highline Community College Web site, has taken several steps to safeguard the integrity of its data and prevent unauthorized access to information maintained by Highline Community College. These measures are designed and intended to prevent corruption of data, block unknown or unauthorized access to our systems and information, and to provide reasonable protection of private information in our possession.

This information should not be construed in any way as giving business, legal, or other advice, or warranting as fail proof, the security of information provided via Highline Community College's Web sites.

Indiana University Bloomington
Indiana University Libraries
Bloomington, Indiana

Data Integrity & Security

The data we collect and maintain at the library must be accurate and secure. Although no method can guarantee the complete security of data, we take steps to protect the privacy and accuracy of user data in the following ways:

Data Integrity: We take reasonable steps to assure data integrity, including: using only reputable sources of data; providing our users access to their own personally identifiable data; updating data whenever possible; utilizing middleware authentication systems that authorize use without requiring personally identifiable information; destroying untimely data or converting it to anonymous form.

Data Retention: We regularly review and purge personally identifiable information once it is no longer needed to manage library services. Information that is regularly reviewed for purging includes, but is not limited to, personally identifiable information on library resource use, material circulation history, and security/surveillance tapes and logs.

The IU Libraries are committed to investing in appropriate technology to protect the security of personally identifiable information while it is in the library's custody. The IU Libraries follow university policy for the retention of data, and access to data is restricted to a small number of authorized university computing personnel. The IU Libraries post announcements about the choice users make in signing up for customized or personalized services related to web and database services.

Services that Require User Login: In-library computers allow guest use of most library resources without logging in. Use of the full resources of the World Wide Web and of the full power of some subscription databases requires that a user log on to the workstation, either with his/her network ID and password or with a special guest account the user obtains from the library. Data about which users were connected to which machine is collected, in accordance with University policy, and kept for a limited time with very limited access by staff. Users of electronic resources that require authorization for their use are also asked to log in when they connect from outside the university IP address ranges. The data kept from these transactions does not include information linking the user to the resources to which the user connected or about searches completed and records viewed.

Cookies: Cookies are used by IUCAT to maintain the persistence of a default library search limit. These cookies are session cookies and are removed when the user exits the catalog and closes the browser. Some licensed databases also use cookies to remember information and provide services while the user is online. Users must have cookies enabled to use these resources.

We are committed to working with vendors of library resources to find solutions that respect the user's privacy and we include a review of the privacy policy espoused by the vendor in purchasing decisions. We provide users with information about the risks of providing personally identifiable information so that they can make reasonable choices about use of personalized services from vendors of electronic library materials. We discourage users from choosing passwords or PINs that could reveal their identity, including Social Security numbers. We regularly remove cookies, web history, cached files, and other use records from library computers and networks.

Security Measures: Our security measures involve both managerial and technical policies and procedures to protect against loss and the unauthorized access, destruction, use, or disclosure of the data. Our managerial measures include internal organizational procedures that limit access to data and prohibit those individuals with access from utilizing the data for unauthorized purposes. Our technical security measures to prevent unauthorized access include encryption in the transmission and storage of data; limits on access through use of passwords; and storage of data on secure servers or computers that are inaccessible from a modem or network connection.

Staff access to personal data: We permit only authorized Library staff with assigned confidential passwords to access personal data stored in the Library's computer system for the purpose of performing library work. The IU Libraries will not disclose any personal data collected from users to any other party except where required by law, to report a suspected violation of law or University policy, or to fulfill an individual user's service request. We do not sell or lease users' personal information to commercial enterprises, organizations or individuals.

University of California San Diego
University Libraries
San Diego, California

Site Security

To guard against unauthorized access, maintain data accuracy, and promote the correct use of information, we have implemented physical, electronic, and managerial procedures to safeguard and secure the information we collect online.

However, while we consider these measures reasonable, no guarantee can be given that they will always prevent or protect against invalid access or improper activity. For this reason, we avoid keeping information beyond the term of its primary use and, where possible, encrypt or delete data elements that might cause activities to be linked to individual users.

Staff Access

Eastern Michigan University
Bruce T. Halle Library
Ypsilanti, Michigan

Staff access to personal data: We permit only authorized Library or ICT staff with assigned confidential passwords to access personal data stored in the Library's computer system for the purpose of performing library work. We will not disclose any personal data we collect from library patrons to any other party except where required by law or to fulfill an individual user's service request. The Library does not sell or lease users' personal information to companies, universities, or individuals.

PROTECTION OF RECORDS

Library Records

University of California San Diego
University Libraries
San Diego, California

In order for the UCSD Libraries to provide services to UCSD students, faculty, staff, and public patrons, the Libraries maintain a patron record database based on information that you provide. The information we collect may include your name, address, telephone number, form of identification (e.g., driver's license), university affiliation, e-mail address, library barcode number, and an encrypted form of your self-established PIN, which allows you to view your patron record online and to request items through the San Diego Circuit.

The Libraries also collect information in conjunction with Library Express, Interlibrary Loan, or San Diego Circuit patron requests submitted via Roger or Melvyl, to allow us to complete the requested service transaction for you.

In the course of providing you with Web-based services, the UCSD Libraries collect and store certain information automatically through our Web site. It includes the date and time you access our site and the type of browser and operating system you are using. It also includes your IP address and Internet domain (.edu, .com, .org, etc), as well as the Internet address of the site from which you link to our Web site. We use this information on an aggregate basis to maintain, enhance or add functionality to our Web-based services.

University of Texas at Arlington
University Libraries
Arlington, Texas

Library Users' Records. These records include any information the Libraries requires users (faculty, staff, students, and guests) to provide in order to become eligible to access or borrow materials. Such information may include addresses, telephone numbers and UTA identification numbers, which is often the individual's social security number. This data primarily comes to us from other university records and is maintained indefinitely. Guests provide addresses, telephone numbers and identification information, which is often the individual's social security number, directly to Libraries staff.

The Information We Collect. This notice applies to all information collected or submitted to the Auburn University Libraries. For those who are affiliated with our university, the library automatically receives personally identifiable information to create and update your library account from the Registrar's Office or Human Resources. Other community user groups not directly affiliated with our university may also submit personally identifiable information. The types of personal information that may be collected may include, but are not limited to: Name, Address, E-mail address, Phone number, Fax number, Library card number, Record of circulation/interlibrary loan/document delivery transactions, University status, Credit card number, Financial obligations current and past, Online reference transactions, Internet IP addresses.

Indiana University-Purdue University Fort Wayne
Walter E. Helmke Library
Fort Wayne, Indiana

Confidentiality of Library Records

In keeping with ALA's Policy on Confidentiality of Library Records (1986) and Policy Concerning Confidentiality of Personally Identifiable Information About Library Users (1991), Helmke Library staff will not respond to any informal request by a third party for personally identifiable information about any library user. Such information includes database search records, reference interviews, e-mail requests for information, circulation records, interlibrary loan records, and other personally identifiable uses of library materials, facilities, or services.

Personally identifiable information may be released only to a law enforcement agency after presentation of an order by a court of competent jurisdiction issued in proper form (a legal subpoena or search warrant) that shows good cause based on specific facts.

Circulation Records

University of Illinois at Urbana-Champaign
University Library
Urbana, Illinois

Examples of Requests for Library Information That Is Confidential and Must Not Be Honored

This list is intended to provide examples of possible violations of confidentiality of library information and is by no means inclusive. Any request for confidential information from patron records coming from a law enforcement officer or investigative agent of the state or federal governments, MUST be referred to the University Librarian.

Circulation and Patron Records

- A request for the circulation records of a faculty, student, staff or other library card holder by someone else.
- A request by a faculty member for the identity of students who borrowed reserve items.
- A request to review the circulation records of a student suspected of plagiarism.
- A request to see interlibrary loan borrowing records.
- A request for addresses, phone numbers, I.D. numbers or other personal information contained in the borrower database.
- A request to see a list of individuals who are not members of the university community but who have been granted library borrowing privileges.
- A request by a parent for information such as fines or other fees by the library to Students Accounts Receivable without the student's permission.

Other Examples

- A request for the name of the person who has signed out a particular item.
- A request to review the identity of persons who have used a study room, listening room, study carrel or CD-ROM workstation.
- A request to reveal the nature of a library user's reference request or database search.
- A request for the names of persons who have used audio-visual materials.
- A request for a list of items photocopied for or faxed to a particular Library user.
- A request for a list of suggested acquisitions submitted by a particular Library user.
- A request from law enforcement authorities for the identity of anyone conducting research on a particular subject.

California State Polytechnic University Pomona
Cal Poly Pomona University Library
Pomona, California

Circulation

The Library does not reveal the names of individual borrowers nor reveal what materials are charged to any individual, except as required by law. The Library does not keep a permanent ongoing record of borrowing for any individual: However, the Library catalog's back-up files may retain borrowing information for up to a week after an item is returned. When the catalog retains the checkout history of an item, that information remains confidential within the Library. The Library PIN/Password is encrypted. Access to "My Library Account" is a secured login. For your protection, you will be asked to come to the Library in person and to present identification if there are problems with your Library PIN/Password.

Humboldt State University
Humboldt State University Library
Arcata, California

Circulation

The Library does not reveal the names of individual borrowers nor reveal what materials are charged to any individual, except as required by law. The Library does not keep a permanent ongoing record of borrowing for any individual, however the Library catalog's back-up files may retain borrowing information for up to three months after an item is returned.

Interlibrary Loan Records

University of Iowa
University of Iowa Libraries
Iowa City, Iowa

Interlibrary Loan/Document Delivery

Requests for interlibrary loan and document delivery services are confidential. Information about requests is shared in some cases with other libraries' staff for collection development purposes; it remains confidential within the Libraries. Documentation of requests may be retained as necessary for the Libraries to comply with auditing, copyright or other regulations.

California State Polytechnic University Pomona
Cal Poly Pomona University Library
Pomona, California

Document Delivery/Interlibrary Loan

Documentation of requests is retained as necessary for the Library to comply with auditing, copyright or other regulations. Because of the software the Library uses this documentation will include names of borrowers. Personal information provided in order to request ILL service might be forwarded on to other library lenders. In some cases, information about requests may be shared with other library staff for collection development and fine collection purposes; however, it remains confidential within the library.

Humboldt State University
Humboldt State University Library
Arcata, California

Interlibrary Loan/Document Delivery

Documentation of requests is retained as necessary for the Library to comply with auditing, copyright or other regulations. Because of the software the Library uses this documentation will include names of borrowers. Personal information provided in order to request ILL service might be forwarded on to other library lenders. In some cases, information about requests may be shared with other library staff for collection development purposes; however, it remains confidential within the library.

Donor Records

California State Polytechnic University Pomona
Cal Poly Pomona University Library
Pomona, California

Donor Privacy

Gifts and contributions make an important contribution to building and shaping the Library's collections. These donations can be made in an anonymous or private manner if so desired.

Requests for Purchase Records

University of Texas at Arlington
University Libraries
Arlington, Texas

Requests for Purchase or Special Materials Handling. Purchase or processing requests linked to individual users are not shared outside the Libraries. User names, telephone numbers, or e-mail addresses are attached to internal records and shared among library staff to facilitate follow-through and responding to the requester.

University of Iowa
University of Iowa Libraries
Iowa City, Iowa

Collection Development and Resource Management

Comments, purchase recommendations, gifts-in-kind, and special requests from users make an important contribution to building and shaping the Libraries' collections. Purchase, transfer, and related collection management requests linked to individual users are confidential reader information and not shared outside the Libraries without permission. Within the Libraries, user names are temporarily attached to internal records and shared among relevant staff to facilitate notification of library actions and follow-through.

Library Surveys Records

University of Iowa
University of Iowa Libraries
Iowa City, Iowa

Library Surveys and Assessments

The Libraries or its units may obtain information and data through surveys (group or individual interviews or other means) assessing services, collections, facilities, resources, etc., or in support of research related to library and information services. This information and data is confidential and will not be shared without permission except in aggregations which protect the privacy of individual participants.

California State Polytechnic University Pomona
Cal Poly Pomona University Library
Pomona, California

Library Surveys/Assessment Projects

Information and data obtained by the Library through surveys or other means, whose intended use it to provide assessment of services, collections, facilities, etc., are considered confidential and will not be shared except in aggregations, to protect the privacy of individual participants.

PROTECTION OF PRIVACY GUIDELINES

Reference Service Notes and Materials

University of Rochester
University of Rochester Libraries
Rochester, New York

Reference Services

In accordance with the principles laid forward in the American Library Association code of ethics, we make every effort to preserve the confidentiality of reference interactions with patrons. If you choose to contact us via email or telephone, it may be necessary to request minimum personal information in order to respond to your question, and depending on the complexity of your inquiry, it may be necessary to refer your question to one of our colleagues.

University of Iowa
University of Iowa Libraries
Iowa City, Iowa

Reference/Research Consultations

Reference and research consultation services are confidential and information about individuals using these services will not be shared outside the Libraries. Libraries' staff will not reveal the identity of library users, the nature of their inquiries, nor the information or sources they consult.

Anonymous data about reference or research consultations may be recorded for management or assessment purposes or to compile information on frequently asked questions.

Humboldt State University
Humboldt State University Library
Arcata, California

Reference/Research Consultations

Consultation services are confidential and information about using these services will not be shared outside the Library. Library staff will not reveal the identity of library users, the nature of their inquiries, nor the information or sources they consult.

University of Michigan
University of Michigan Libraries
Ann Arbor, Michigan

Reference Privacy Policy

The University Library maintains a high level of respect for the confidentiality of patrons and the questions that they ask. Data that is collected in the course of reference service that could identify specific individuals will not be shared outside University of Michigan libraries, except with the patron's permission or as required by law. University of Michigan libraries include any of the following:

University Library units

Independent UM libraries such as Law, Kresge Business, Bentley, Clements, UM Flint and UM Dearborn libraries

The University Library keeps general statistics about reference service and research consultations. These statistics do not include patron identification data. The data is used for assessment purposes and completion of statistical reports.

Information about the types of questions asked, as well as the content of responses to questions, may also be retained for "frequently asked question" files or "difficult to answer" question files. This type of data does not include patrons' names, addresses, phone numbers, or other identifying information.

The information from reference transactions is retained long enough to complete the request. Data will not be kept for more than three months after a reference transaction is closed, unless the patron has granted permission to do so, with the exception of requests made to the University Library's Special Collections Library.

In the course of typical reference service, a University Library employee may forward patron information to other University Library or other campus library staff members in order to answer questions efficiently and thoroughly. In such cases, the patron will be copied on the forwarded message.

Special Collections Materials

University of Texas at Arlington
University Libraries
Arlington, Texas

Special Collections. Users must fill out an application form in order to access research materials in Special Collections. This application asks for the user's address, telephone number, and a form of identification that may include a driver's license number. Research materials are provided to the user following completion of a request form. The request form includes the user's name, signature, and a description of the item or items to be viewed.

University of Michigan
University of Michigan Libraries
Ann Arbor, Michigan

Because reference questions addressed to the Special Collections Library are often complicated, multipart, and stretch over months or years, staff in Special Collections strive to preserve the privacy of individuals while keeping records that enable complicated inquiries to move forward without repetition of information. Written reference queries in these areas are excepted from the general reference privacy policy as stated in this document, but Special Collections Library staff will follow these procedures:

Inform patrons that some queries or requests for copies and the relevant answers are kept on file.

Give patrons the option of having their identities obscured in such files.

Remove identifying information from retained correspondence and replies when patrons have requested anonymity.

Third-Party Partners Information Collected

Eastern Michigan University
Bruce T. Halle Library
Ypsilanti, Michigan

Third Party Security: We ensure that our library's contracts and licenses reflect our policies and legal obligations concerning user privacy and confidentiality. Should a third party require access to our users' personally identifiable information, our agreements address appropriate restrictions on the use, aggregation, dissemination, and sale of that information, particularly information about minors. In circumstances in which there is a risk that personally identifiable information may be disclosed, we will warn our users. When connecting to licensed databases outside the library, we release only information that authenticates users as "members of our community." Nevertheless, we advise users of the limits to library privacy protection when accessing remote sites.

PROTECTION FOR ELECTRONIC RESOURCES USE

Chat Reference Notes and Materials

Drake University
Cowles Library
Des Moines, Iowa

Computer Trespassers
Law enforcement or federal agency surveillance or tracking of computer networks or Internet use may be authorized by a designated officer of Cowles Library, without a warrant or court order, when the

target of the surveillance is a computer trespasser. A computer trespasser is a person who accesses a protected computer without authorization and thus has no reasonable expectation of privacy in any communication transmitted to, through or from the protected computer. A person who has an existing contractual relationship with the owner or operator of the computer for access to all or part of the protected computer is not a computer trespasser.

Tracking Users

Eastern Michigan University
Bruce T. Halle Library
Ypsilanti, Michigan

Tracking Users: We remove links between patron records and materials borrowed when items are returned and we delete records as soon as the original purpose for data collection has been satisfied. Billing and fine information is retained as long as necessary. We permit in-house access to information in all formats without creating a data trail. Our library has invested in appropriate technology to protect the security of any personally identifiable information while it is in the library's custody, and we ensure that aggregate, summary data is stripped of personally identifiable information. We do not ask library visitors or Web site users to identify themselves or reveal any personal information unless they are borrowing materials, requesting special services, registering for programs or classes, or making remote use from outside the library of those portions of the Library's Web site restricted to registered borrowers under license agreements or other special arrangements. We discourage users from choosing passwords or PINs that could reveal their identity, including social security numbers. We regularly remove cookies, Web history, cached files, or other computer and Internet use records and other software code that is placed on our computers or networks.

Installation of Cookies

Syracuse University
Syracuse University Library
Syracuse, New York

Cookies

Cookies are small pieces of data sent by a Web server and stored by the Web browser. Cookies are often used to remember information about preferences and pages visited. You can refuse to accept cookies, can disable cookies, and remove cookies from your hard drive. In Netscape Navigator, choose Edit and Preferences to manage your cookie settings, in Internet Explorer, select Tools and Internet Options.

Some Syracuse University Web servers use cookies so you will not have to repeatedly enter a user name and password when you link to different parts of the Web site. Other University Web servers may also use cookies to retain user preference information. It is against University policy to share this information with external third parties.

Eastern Michigan University
Bruce T. Halle Library
Ypsilanti, Michigan

Cookies: Users of networked computers will need to enable cookies in order to access a number of resources available through the library. A cookie is a small file sent to the browser by a Web site each time that site is visited. Cookies are stored on the user's computer and can potentially transmit personal information. Cookies are often used to remember information about preferences and pages visited. The patron can refuse to accept cookies, can disable cookies, and remove cookies from their hard drive. Our Library servers use cookies solely to verify that a person is an authorized user in order to allow access

370

to licensed library resources and to customize Web pages to that user's specification. Cookies sent by our Library servers will disappear when the user's computer browser is closed. We will not share cookies information with external third parties.

E-Mail Reference Notes and Materials

University of California Santa Barbara
University Libraries
Santa Barbara, California

Online or Email Reference

The information we collect via our ASK email or online chat reference services is kept in the strictest confidence and helps us provide and improve these services. All access to and use of personal information is restricted to performing library business. While answering your question, we may refer you to web sites that are not maintained by the UCSB Library. When linked to another site, you are subject to the privacy policy of the new site—which may differ from the UCSB Library policy.

University of California Davis
University Library
Davis, California

Privacy Awareness Notice for E-mail Reference

The UC Davis General Library is committed to protecting the privacy of individuals who use our collections and services. The information we collect via our Email Reference Service form is kept in the strictest confidence and helps us provide and improve these services. All UC Davis General Library staff follow the American Library Association Code of Ethics, which states that "we protect each user's right to privacy and confidentiality with respect to information sought or received and resources consulted, borrowed, acquired or transmitted."

The Email Reference Service form collects limited personal information for several reasons. We may need to ask additional questions to clarify your request, or to send you materials in response to your query by mail or e-mail. Some resources are licensed by the University for faculty, staff and students only, so we need to know whether you are affiliated with the University. We retain information on UCD affiliation for statistical purposes.

While answering your question, we may refer you to web sites that are not maintained by the UC Davis General Library. Examples include full-text online journals, article indexes and web sites for other UC Davis departments. Please note that these sites may have different privacy policies and that the General Library has no control or responsibility for these policies.

While we do whatever we can to protect your privacy, please be aware that information or files transferred via the Internet or stored on Internet-accessible computers may be vulnerable to unscrupulous users. We urge you to use caution and follow accepted Internet safety guidelines. See the National Infrastructure Protection Center (www.nipc.gov/warnings/computertips.htm) for basic tips, or the Privacy Rights Clearinghouse (www.privacyrights.org/fs/fs18–cyb.htm) or CERT (www.cert.org/tech_tips/home_networks.html) for more detailed information. In addition, the Library may be required to disclose private information in response to a court-ordered warrant or subpoena. The USA PATRIOT Act [pdf] (http://frwebgate.access.gpo.gov/cgi-bin/getdoc.cgi?dbname=107_cong_public_laws&docid=f:publ056.107.pdf), passed by Congress (Public Law 107–56) expands the types of records that can be sought without a court order.

Based on UC Irvine Library "Ask a Librarian" privacy statement (www.lib.uci.edu/services/ask/askprivacy.html) (accessed 1/6/03).

Eastern Michigan University
Bruce T. Halle Library
Ypsilanti, Michigan

The Halle Library respects the privacy of our patrons. This policy is intended to let users know what information is collected by the e-mail and chat services and how this information is used.

What information is collected and why?

We ask for a name, e-mail address, the subject of the question being asked, your status, whether you would like a brief answer or suggestions for resources to explore, and the sources you have already consulted.

We use the following information for the following purposes:

Name: We need a name to identify a chat session and in communicating with you during that session. While a name is required, it does not have to be a full name or a real name. Names are stored in session transcripts.

E-mail address: An e-mail address is required so that we may send you a transcript of the chat session, and/or follow up on your reference question. E-mail reference requires an e-mail address so that we can respond to you.

All other information requested—subject, status, whether you would prefer a brief answer or suggestions for resources to explore, sources already consulted—will be used by the librarian in order to answer your question more efficiently.

We also use the above information, as well as transcripts of chat sessions, to help us determine appropriate staffing level, train librarians for this service, and improve the overall quality of the service.

Who has access to this information?

This information is only accessible to librarians and staff associated with the Ask A Librarian service.

Who does the library share the information with?

We do not share the information with anyone outside of the Library. Statistics generated from chat logs or e-mails, as well as anonymous excerpts, may be used for reports or publications. Information about specific individuals (e.g. e-mail addresses, names, etc.) will not be shared unless ordered by a court of law or by subpoena under the USA PATRIOT Act.

What choices do users have about the collection, use, and distribution of their information?

If you would like, we can delete the history of your questions from the Ask A Librarian database. Please e-mail with your name and e-mail address, as well as the date, so that we can identify the exact chat transcript or e-mail to delete.

University of Rochester
University of Rochester Libraries
Rochester, New York

"Ask a Librarian Online" Live Reference Service

In order to provide this service, only your email address is currently required. At the end of the session, a transcript is provided to you via the email address you have supplied, and will include the interaction between you and the librarian as well as the links to any web pages used during the session.

If your question is complex or highly technical, we may contact another librarian who specializes in the subject for assistance answering your question, or refer you to that librarian for follow-up.

The software used to provide the "Ask a Librarian" service is licensed from a third party (LiveAssistance); a transcript of your session is held on LiveAssistance's servers and is deleted after a limited period of time, according to the Library's agreement with them. Our contractual agreement with LiveAssistance states that they will not sell, share, or rent patron information to any outside parties.

An electronic copy of your transaction (with any personally identifiable information removed) is also retained for training and statistical purposes on the Library's server for a limited time.

PATRIOT ACT, LAW ENFORCEMENT, AND DISCLOSURE GUIDELINES

PATRIOT Act Compliance, Law Enforcement and Courts, and Disclosure

Indiana University Bloomington
Indiana University Libraries
Bloomington, Indiana

Enforcement & Redress

The IU Libraries will not make library records available to any agency of state, federal, or local government unless required to do so under law or to report a suspected violation of the law. Nor will we share data on individuals with other parties including faculty, staff (including library staff except in the performance of their assigned duties), parents, students, campus security, and law enforcement personnel, except as required by law or University policy or as needed to perform our University duties.

Library staff are to refer all requests for confidential user records to the appropriate Library Dean or Director or their designate. Only the Library Dean/Director or designate has authorization to receive and respond to requests from law enforcement or other third parties. The Dean/Director will forward all requests from law enforcement or other government officials, all requests under applicable "open records" laws, to University Counsel, and will consult with counsel regarding the proper response. Each library within Indiana University will develop written procedures to comply with this policy.

We conduct regular privacy audits in order to ensure that all library programs and services are enforcing our privacy policy. Library users who have questions, concerns, or complaints about the library's handling of their personally identifiable data should file written comments with the director of the library in question. We will respond in a timely manner and may conduct a privacy investigation or review our policy and procedures.

Georgia State University
Georgia State University Library
Atlanta, Georgia

Procedures for Law Enforcement Visits and Court Orders

Notice Regarding The U.S.A. PATRIOT Act

The Uniting and Strengthening America by Providing Appropriate Tools Required to Intercept and Obstruct Terrorism Act of 2001 ("USA PATRIOT Act") was passed by Congress on October 26, 2001. Although confidential library records have always been subject to disclosure pursuant to lawful process, the USA PATRIOT Act expands the authority of local, state and federal law enforcement to gain access to educational and library records, including stored electronic data and communications.

The Georgia State University Library recognizes that its circulation records and other records identifying the names of library users with specific materials and/or internet use are confidential in nature. No such confidential information shall be made available to any individual or office of the university, agency of state, federal or local government, or to any individual not specifically authorized by the University Librarian for legitimate business purposes, except where the person whose confidential information is to be released consents or pursuant to such process, order, warrant or subpoena as may be authorized under the authority of, and pursuant to, federal, state, or local law relating to civil, criminal or administrative discovery procedures or legislative investigating power.

An exception to this policy provided for by the USA PATRIOT Act allows voluntary disclosure for emergency situations, which are likely to be rare in the library. Should a staff member, in the course of business reasonably believe he has accessed information about an emergency involving immediate danger of death or serious physical injury, s/he should contact the university police immediately; then contact the Library Administration Office (LAO), or (if after regular business hours) any member of the Library Administrative Group (Lib Admin) and the supervisor in the unit.

Procedures for Law Enforcement Visits and Court Orders

1. Procedures if approached by law enforcement with identification and a court order in the form of a SEARCH WARRANT:

Staff should immediately ask for identification and a court order if they are approached by an agent or officer. If the agent or officer has no identification or court order with them, follow the steps outlined in #4 below.

A search warrant is executable immediately, unlike a subpoena. The agent or officer may begin a search of library records as soon as a library employee is served with the court order.

Before the search begins, the employee should ask if s/he can call his/her department head, who will contact the LAO, who will then contact Legal Affairs in order to allow Legal Affairs an opportunity to examine the search warrant and to assure that the search conforms to the terms of the search warrant. The officer may or may not agree to the request because, legally, the search may begin immediately.

If the visit occurs outside regular business hours, the employee should contact his/her supervisor at home. If the supervisor is not available, the employee should contact the department head at home. If the department head is not available, the employee should contact the University Librarian at home. If nobody is at home, the employee should contact legal counsel at home.

The employee should cooperate with the search to ensure that only the records identified in the warrant are produced and that no other users' records are viewed or scanned.

2. Procedures if the court order is a SEARCH WARRANT issued under the Foreign Intelligence Surveillance Act (FISA) (USA PATRIOT Act Amendment):

The employee should follow the procedures for a regular search warrant listed above. However, a search warrant issued by a FISA court also contains a "gag order." That means that no person or institution served with the warrant can disclose (outside the chain of command elaborated above) that the warrant has been served or that records have been produced pursuant to the warrant. However, the employee should still contact his/her supervisor, department head, or University Librarian when served with the court order.

The library and its staff must comply with this order. No information can be disclosed to any other party, including the patron whose records are the subject of the search warrant.

The gag order does not change a library's right to legal representation during the search. The library can still seek legal advice concerning the warrant and request that the library's legal counsel be present during the actual search and execution of the warrant. The officer may or may not agree to the request because, legally, the search may begin immediately.

3. Procedures if approached by law enforcement with identification and a court order in the form of a SUBPOENA:

The employee should give the subpoena to the department head, who will deliver it to the LAO. LAO will be responsible for contacting Legal Affairs.

If the visit occurs outside regular business hours, the employee should give the subpoena to the supervisor as soon as possible during the next regular business day. The supervisor should give it to the department head who will deliver it immediately to the LAO. The LAO will be responsible for contacting Legal Affairs.

4. Procedures if approached by law enforcement WITHOUT IDENTIFICATION OR A COURT ORDER:

If the agent or officer does not have a court order compelling the production of records, the staff member should inform the agent or officer that library users' records are not available except when a proper court order in good form has been presented to the library.

Without a court order, neither the FBI nor local law enforcement has authority to compel cooperation with an investigation or require answers to questions, other than the name and address of the person speaking to the agent or officer.

If the agent or officer persists, or makes an appeal to patriotism, the staff member should explain that, as good citizens, the library staff will not respond to informal requests for confidential information, in conformity with professional ethics, First Amendment freedoms, and state law.

The staff member should inform his/her supervisor about the visit. The supervisor should inform the LAO and the Office of Legal Affairs that such a visit took place.

Drake University
Cowles Library
Des Moines, Iowa

Procedure for Compliance with Requests for Confidential Information

When the Library receives an order, warrant, subpoena or other request for confidential information or surveillance, the request will not be handled by student or temporary staff. The request will be referred to the Dean of Libraries or, in his or her absence, the Acting Dean. The Dean shall request a copy of the document specifying what records are requested and will comply with any and all requests in a timely manner. The Dean may consult with legal counsel prior to the release of information.

On weekends, legal holidays, or other times outside of normal university business hours, any request for confidential library information will be referred to the Librarian on duty. The Librarian shall request a copy of the document specifying what records are requested and will comply with any and all requests in a timely manner. The Librarian may consult with legal counsel prior to the release of information.

Cowles Library will document all costs incurred in complying with a records request. If the costs of providing the requested information are more than a nominal amount, the Library will document, and request reimbursement for, the expenses incurred in complying with the request. The failure of the requesting party to pay such expenses, however, will not be used as a reason for the Library to refuse to comply with any request unless a statute, court order or regulation requires reimbursement of expenses prior to compliance with the request.

Cowles Library will inform the person whose confidential information has been requested or obtained, unless doing so would violate any statute, court order, warrant or subpoena. If the Library provides information to the government pursuant to a USA PATRIOT Act request, the Library cannot notify anyone, including the person whose confidential information is being provided. The same is true if a non-USA PATRIOT Act warrant, subpoena or other process forbids the Library to disclose any information about the request. Cowles Library cannot disclose to third parties the fact that confidential information has been requested or obtained on an individual unless the individual consents or the Library is compelled to make the disclosure by order, warrant, subpoena or other process.

Cowles Library reserves the right to voluntarily disclose any circulation records to any person or entity where the Dean of Libraries reasonably believes that an emergency involving immediate danger of death or serious injury justifies the disclosure.

Chapter 31

ETHICS

GENERAL GUIDELINES

Codes of Ethics for Librarians

Lane Community College
Lane Community College Library
Eugene, Oregon

Code of Ethics for Library Employees

The statement which follows sets forth the ethical obligations of individuals as LCC Library staff members.

1. To maintain the principles of the ALA Library Bill of Rights and the Freedom to Read Statement.
2. To maintain the principles of the LCC Library mission statement and unifying principles.
3. To understand and execute the policies of the College and Library, and to express in a positive manner any concern or objection with the policies, philosophy or programs of these institutions.
4. To maintain an objective and open attitude of understanding, courtesy, and concern for the patrons' needs.
5. To protect the essential confidential relationship which exists between a library user and the library.
6. To serve all patrons equally according to their needs.
7. To make the resources and services of the Library known and easily accessible to all current and potential users.
8. To avoid any possibility of personal financial gain at the expense of the employing institution.
9. To be aware of the obligations of employment and of what constitutes abuse of working conditions and benefits.
10. To acknowledge the importance of the work done by all staff in all divisions of the Library.
11. To maintain a sense of loyalty, respect, and cooperation in our relationships with fellow staff.
12. To carry out assignments so that fellow staff members need not assume added responsibilities, except in times of emergency.
13. To share knowledge, experience, and expertise with others.
14. To use the resources of the Library and College in an efficient and economical manner, consistent with the best service to the library user.
15. To use care and discretion to distinguish between private actions and speech, and those actions and speech which are taken in the name of the institution. This policy should be interpreted as consistent with the rights of an individual to take part in public debate, and to engage in social or political activity.

Rutgers University
Rutgers University Libraries
Newark, New Jersey

Code of Ethics—All information transactions between library staff and clients, regardless of whether they take place at a formal service point or in some other context, will be governed by the standards articulated in the American Library Association's Code of Ethics. A copy of the Code is attached.

Part IX
Information Literacy and Library Instruction

Chapter 32

LIBRARY INSTRUCTION

ADMINISTRATIVE GUIDELINES

Mission Statement

New Mexico State University
New Mexico State University Library
Las Cruces, New Mexico

Mission Statement:

The mission of the New Mexico State University (NMSU) Library Instruction Program is to foster the development of NMSU students, faculty, and staff as information literate people who determine when information is needed; access information in all formats; evaluate information and its sources; and use information effectively and ethically.

Core Values:

We recognize library instruction—both formal and informal—as central to the mission of today's libraries.

We are committed to library instruction that fosters life-long critical thinking skills.

We are committed to providing multiple modes of library instruction to meet the needs of diverse student learning styles and life situations.

We encourage course faculty to collaborate in the design, delivery, and assessment of library instruction.

We value course-integrated and curriculum-integrated instruction as the ideal for the NMSU library instruction program.

We work in concert with other campus and community groups in promoting information literacy skills.

We rely on specified goals and objectives to evaluate and assess the outcomes of library instruction in accordance with NMSU policies on academic freedom.

We recognize that library personnel providing instruction require continuous training and support.

We seek to broaden the pool of library instructors.

We value the contributions of personnel outside the reference unit to library instruction.

We seek to have library instruction more highly valued at New Mexico State University.

We are dedicated to developing a library-based team under the leadership of the Instruction Coordinator to address instruction issues on a continuing basis.

Fundamental Assumptions:

Library instruction can be both formal (occurring in classrooms, via the Web, etc.) and informal (occurring at the reference desk and other service points). Only formal instruction falls within the scope of the Library Instruction Program.

Students need more than factual/content knowledge to be successful professionally and personally. People encounter excessive amounts of information in everyday life in the "Information Age."

NMSU is a minority-majority institution; the numbers of non-traditional and distance education students are increasing.

NMSU faculty members share the Library Instruction Program's commitment to producing life-long learners and critical thinkers.

Course- and curriculum-integrated LI offers the best opportunity to develop higher-level and discipline specific information literacy skills.

The Library is a recognized leader on campus, and NMSU plays a similar role in southern New Mexico.

The Instruction Program cannot justify its existence by the number of sessions or students taught. Specific goals and objectives for performance outcomes must be developed and assessed in accordance with NMSU policies on academic freedom.

Many librarians and library staff come to NMSU without training or experience in teaching and consequently find LI uncomfortable.

Demand for LI is increasing: the number of LI sessions increased from 219 to 341 between 1999–00 and 2000–01, and 2001–02 seems likely to exceed earlier numbers.

Library personnel within and outside the reference unit will continue to be key to the provision of library instruction at NMSU.

Tallahassee Community College
Tallahassee, Community College Library
Tallahassee, Florida

The TCC Library Instruction Program supports the educational mission of the College to assist students "in developing the ability to think critically, creatively, and reflectively; and to prepare them for productive and satisfying lives" (Mission Statement, Tallahassee Community College). Our program's mission is to develop and foster information literacy skills within our college community.

Information literacy skills include the ability to identify, locate, evaluate, and effectively use information and to understand the legal, social, and ethical aspects of information use. Our program is aligned with the "Information Literacy Competency Standards for Higher Education" (Association of College & Research Libraries, 2000) and strategic Library planning.

To achieve this mission, we will:

- Collaborate with faculty to provide instruction that meets information literacy objectives.
- Utilize teaching strategies and methodologies that reflect the diversity of our learning-community, various learning styles, educational levels, and locations of our users.
- Continually evaluate and update programs, services and instructional skills.

Niagara University
Niagara University Library
Niagara University, New York

Niagara University Library's reference librarians train students to use Library resources to their fullest. Through personal attention and professional training, students learn to conduct research themselves and solve research problems.

To schedule a training session, please fill out a Library Instruction Request Form.

Mission Statement

The Library Instruction program attempts to:

- Foster information literacy skills in students, including the ability to locate, evaluate, and use information effectively.
- Support faculty by providing their students with the research skills needed to successfully complete specific assignments and coursework.
- Foster campus productivity by making faculty and staff aware of information resources and providing training in the use of those resources when necessary.

Assumptions

The Library commonly provides information literacy training to groups but also considers every reference interaction to be a teaching opportunity where students are encouraged to think critically and analytically about their research.

Successful learning is active and participatory. Therefore group training sessions should be hands-on and include problem solving and critical thinking exercises. Large classes need to be broken down into smaller classes, and the length of time allotted for training should to be sufficient to allow for interactivity.

Group Instruction should be tied to actual course work. Research assignments should be a precursor to the Library Instruction session. The presence of the faculty member at the training session is crucial for the collaborative process to work well.

Niagara University Library adheres to the standards and guidelines developed by the Association of College and Research Libraries:

>   Guidelines for Instruction Programs in Academic Libraries

>   Information Literacy Competency Standards for Higher Education

>   Objectives for Information Literacy Instruction: A Model Statement for Academic Librarians

Goals and Objectives

University of South Florida
Jane Bancroft Cook Library
Sarasota, Florida

Library Instruction Mission and Goals

Statement of Purpose

The ongoing mission of the University of South Florida Tampa Library is to support the teaching, research and service endeavors at the University of South Florida. The goal of the USF Tampa Library instruction program is to foster information literacy, through a variety of educational approaches and methods that accommodate different needs and learning styles of individuals. The information literate individual is able to recognize an information need and has the ability to locate, evaluate and use effectively the needed information. The instruction program, alone and through partnership with other university departments, is committed to providing individuals with the necessary information literacy skills essential for lifelong learning.

Program Goals

To ensure that students, faculty and staff are aware of the USF Tampa Library and its resources.

Benchmarks:

- Knowledge of the existence and location of the USF Tampa Library
- Awareness of the USF Libraries catalog and online resources
- Knowledge of different information formats available in libraries, including print, electronic, microform, audio and video
- Knowledge of reference services

Actions:

- Appropriate signage
- Distribution of flyers and brochures
- Development of an online video tour of the library
- Engage in marketing activities, such as mass mailings and sponsoring events promoting the library
- Participate in university events, such as Showcase of Services and New Faculty Orientation

To ensure that students, faculty and staff understand how the Library's collection is organized and accessed and that they are aware of and understand how to use library services.

Benchmarks:

- Knowledge of the physical organization of the libraries
- Ability to identify specific locations, collections and service points within the library
- Knowledge of specific library services and ability to use them. Services include reference, circulation, interlibrary loan, reserves.
- Ability to use USF Libraries catalog to find materials by title, author, subject or keyword
- Ability to recognize and interpret the elements of a catalog record, including author, title, call number, location, holdings and status of item

Actions:

- Signage
- Development of an online video tour of the library
- Point of use assistance at public service desks, phone, e-mail and chat
- Distribution of user aids at public service
- Scheduled "drop-in" library orientation sessions
- Instruction to classes on faculty request
- Self guided instruction such as online tutorials

To ensure that students, faculty and staff are aware of the resources available through the USF Libraries website.

Benchmarks:

- Knowledge of the existence and Internet address of the USF Libraries website
- Knowledge of the organization of the USF Libraries website
- Ability to locate USF Libraries catalog on the USF Libraries website
- Ability to identify resources by source, reliability and appropriateness of information
- Knowledge of and ability to use specific online library services available on the USF Libraries main page, including reference, ILL, electronic reserves, hold/recall, and renewal

Actions:

- Point of use assistance at public service desks, via phone, e-mail and chat
- Distribution of user aids at public service desks and electronically through the USF Libraries website
- Scheduled "drop-in" library orientation sessions
- Instruction to classes on faculty request

To ensure that students, faculty and staff are able to access particular resources, both print and electronic.

Benchmarks:

- Ability to locate a specific resource, either online or in print
- Ability to determine the content and coverage of the resource
- Understand the arrangement of the resource
- Perform a satisfactory search of the resource
- Ability to interpret citations and retrieve the full-text (if applicable) of the document

Actions:

- Point of use assistance at public service desks, via phone, e-mail and chat
- Distribution of user aids at public service desks and electronically through the USF Libraries website
- Scheduled "drop-in" library orientation sessions
- Instruction to classes on faculty request
- Self guided instruction such as online tutorials or web-pages developed for Classes

To ensure that students, faculty and staff understand the structure and format of information resources and their impact on the mechanics of searching.

Benchmarks:

- Knowledge of how information is formally and informally produced
- Knowledge of the general information provision role of books, journals, magazines, newspapers, government publications, audio/visual materials and online data sources
- Ability to construct a library search plan, which includes appropriate access tools
- Ability to identify and use appropriate search language
- Ability to use Boolean logic and truncation effectively
- Ability to identify related materials while researching
- Ability to refine search strategies as needed

Actions:

- Point of use assistance at public service desks, via phone, e-mail and chat
- Distribution of user aids at public service desks and electronically through the USF Libraries website
- Scheduled "drop-in" library orientation sessions
- Instruction to classes on faculty request
- Self guided instruction such as online tutorials or web-pages developed for Classes

To ensure that students, faculty and staff develop the skills to allow them to analyze and critically evaluate information.

Benchmarks:

- Ability to evaluate information based on standard criteria, including authority, appropriateness, accuracy, relevance, timeliness, point of view, publisher and medium
- Ability to determine whether an information resource is scholarly, popular, peer reviewed, a trade/professional publication, etc.
- Ability to recognize the difference between primary and secondary sources in determining their relevance to an information need
- Ability to determine whether the information retrieved satisfies the research need

Actions:

- Point of use assistance at public service desks, via phone, e-mail and chat
- Distribution of user aids at public service desks and electronically through the USF Libraries website
- Scheduled "drop-in" library orientation sessions
- Instruction to classes on faculty request
- Self guided instruction such as online tutorials or web-pages developed for Classes
- Partner with Library Science to teach LIS undergraduate and graduate classes

To collaborate with faculty to make effective use of Library/Classroom partnerships.

Benchmarks:

- Program in place for continual communication of instruction opportunities to each department by a librarian liaison
- Propose a collaboration to major departments to have at least one library/faculty partnership for teaching information literacy

Actions:

- Course integrated instruction though credit courses and initiatives, such as the Learning Communities
- Partner with Library Science to teach LIS undergraduate and graduate classes
- Instruction to classes on faculty request
- Web pages and user aids developed for classes on faculty request
- Orientation and training to individual faculty or workshops to departments

- Provide assistance to faculty in creating library assignments
- Development and distribution of model library assignments
- Work with campus partners, including VITAL, CTE and Academic Computing in their faculty outreach program

To engage in continuous assessment of the instruction program to determine its effectiveness in teaching students, faculty and staff information literacy skills.

Benchmarks:

- Develop a program to analyze written evaluations by students and faculty
- Develop a user needs assessment program

Actions:

- Pre- and post-tests given in selected class settings
- Develop a satisfaction survey
- Investigate a variety of assessment techniques

Florida International University
Florida International University Libraries
Miami, Florida

Information Literacy Goals and Objectives

The information literate student will:

Goal 1: Recognize and articulate the need for information.

- Objective 1: Formulate questions based on the information need
- Objective 2: Define or modify the information need to achieve a manageable focus
- Objective 3: Identify key concepts and terms that describe the information need
- Objective 4: Recognize the need for information in creative and analytical thinking

Goal 2: Understand how information is designed, stored, and organized.

- Objective 1: Define sources of information
- Objective 2: Delineate formats of information
- Objective 3: Describe the organization of information

Goal 3: Identify and select the most appropriate investigative methods or information retrieval systems.

- Objective 1: Determine what kind of information is needed (e.g., statistical data, narrative)
- Objective 2: Select the most appropriate research tool

Goal 4: Develop and implement effective search strategies.

- Objective 1: Formulate an effective search strategy
- Objective 2: Conduct the search using appropriate research tools
- Objective 3: Evaluate search results and revise search strategy as necessary

Goal 5: Identify, locate, and retrieve information.

- Objective 1: Record relevant information and its sources
- Objective 2: Determine location of information
- Objective 3: Use information in various formats
- Objective 4: Access and use information ethically and legally

Goal 6: Analyze, evaluate, and synthesize the information.

- Objective 1: Examine the content and the structure of the information
- Objective 2: Articulate and apply criteria for evaluating both the information and its sources
- Objective 3: Synthesize information to construct new concepts

Goal 7: Use information effectively to accomplish a specific purpose.

- Objective 1: Integrate new and prior information in the creation of a product
- Objective 2: Communicate the product effectively to others
- Objective 3: Acknowledge the use of information sources

Goal 8: Assess the information seeking process and product.

- Objective 1: Reflect on successes, failures and alternative strategies
- Objective 2: Evaluate the process and product within the context of the information need

Kansas State University
Kansas State University Libraries
Manhattan, Kansas

Library Instruction—Goals & Objectives

Offer learning opportunities for all at K-State (students, faculty, librarians, staff) to ensure a baseline of library and information literacy knowledge and skills that can then be built upon through coursework and librarian taught learning sessions:

- Walk-in library classes, e.g. Basic Library Class Tour, Basic Science Class, DED 075 (College of Education Orientation), How to Find a Journal Article, RefWorks
- Topic Research and Web Searching
- Short Cuts, a weekly undergraduate research newsletter
- Online tutorials, e.g., Assignment Calculator, assignment toolbox (for faculty and librarians)
- Faculty workshops
- Librarian workshops
- Offer tours and instruction to K–12 groups

Work with appropriate parties to create optimum learning environments:

Online/virtual:
- Tutorials
- Assignment Calculator

Physical:
- An adaptable learning space with necessary technology with space for at least 50–60 students
- General study and research space within the Libraries

Provide or collaborate with appropriate staff (below) to meet learning needs:

- Instructors for walk-in classes
- Designers and programmers for online resources
- Content creators for tutorials, Assignment Calculator, workshops and classes
- Support services for technology and program administration
- Continuously develop and administer assessment:
- Information Literacy—campus wide
- SAILS
- ETS ICT
- Effectiveness of walk-in classes, online tutorials, Assignment Calculator, etc …

CLASSROOM AND TEACHING GUIDELINES

Instructional Plans

Boston College
Boston College Libraries
Boston, Massachusetts

Instructional Plan and Objectives

The basic plan of instruction is outlined below. The plan includes specific learning objectives for the program.

I. Introduce incoming students to the availability of library resources and services through general orientation sessions conducted for the First Year, transfer, international, graduate, College of Advancing studies students, and other department specific orientations

> Objective A: Gaining awareness of resources and services available through the library.
> Objective B: Acquiring and understanding the library's role in the college experience.

II. Offer a variety of instructional tools, of both print and media format, to support the program.

> Objective A: Understanding how the library organizes and arranges its collections.
>
> Objective B: Acquiring and understanding the library's role in the college experience. Navigate the library's primary bibliographic tools.
>
> Objective C: Conceptualizing library research as a systematic process of learning.
>
> Objective D: Discovering the reference materials most appropriate for solving specific problems.

III. Provide instruction in basic research by designing learning sessions for the appropriate core courses.

> Objective A: Applying the research process to a specific information problem.
> Objective B: Learning the skill of developing a working bibliography.
> Objective C: Understanding the structures of knowledge and its classification.

IV. Provide instruction in advanced research techniques for specific disciplines as requested.

> Objective A: Acquiring advanced skills in bibliography development.
> Objective B: Learning methods of evaluating specific sources.

V. Offer independent training sessions on database search skills.

> Objective A: Developing proficiency in basic search functions.
> Objective B: Gaining awareness of advanced search functions.

Canisius College
Andrew L. Bouwhuis Library
Buffalo, New York

5.1   At the freshman level, most students are not aware of locations or services available to them in the Library. Internal library instruction during the first year is a valuable asset to the student which will ease the burden of research at a later date. The Bouwhuis Library seeks to play an active role in the academic process by providing and encouraging the use of library instruction. Introductory lectures, individualized student instruction, and advanced subject specialty classes in various disciplines are presently available to faculty members and their students.

5.2   Completion of one or more sections of library instruction in one or more disciplines should enable the student to think carefully about his/her information needs and provide basic skills necessary for requesting and finding information for curricular or personal purposes, by:

> 5.2.1   making the student feel physically and emotionally comfortable in the Library,
>
> 5.2.2   giving the student a logical map to follow in developing a search strategy,

5.2.3 making the student aware of the reference librarian as a main source of information access and a partner, with the academic faculty, in his/her endeavor,

5.2.4 making the student aware of the diversity, volume, and complexity of retrieving information, and how such characteristics affect information needs,

5.2.5 teaching the student how to locate information regardless of format (i.e., hard copy, software, etc.), and

5.2.6 informing the student of the differences between types of libraries (e.g., public, academic, etc.) and what kinds of materials each institution is likely to provide.

5.3 As a result of library instruction, the Reference Department seeks to teach the following skills:

5.3.1 Students should know the physical layout of the Library, particularly the location and function of the various service departments (Circulation, Periodicals, Reference).

5.3.2 Students, especially freshmen, should recognize that it is always appropriate to ask for help in finding material.

5.3.3 Students should understand the purposes and uses of a library reference collection and when to consult its sources.

5.3.4 Students should be able to use the catalog to its full potential. They should be able to access the catalog through title, author, subject and keyword approaches, and should know how to use subject tracings.

5.3.5 Students should know how to locate books in the Library collections by call numbers and location designators.

5.3.6 Students should know how to use periodical indexes and how to determine whether or not the Bouwhuis library owns the periodicals they need.

5.3.7 Students should know how and when to use local CD-ROM databases, online database searching, and other electronic sources (e.g., CanInfo, CARL, other Internet sources).

5.3.8 Students should know how to locate articles in locally held periodicals, whether in current issues, bound volumes, microform, or full-text databases.

5.3.9 Students should be able to use the Western New York Union Catalog, BISON, Sherlock, etc., to locate materials the Library does not own.

5.3.10 If the Library does not own needed materials, students should know how interlibrary loan works.

5.4 The program will be administered by the Coordinator of Bibliographic Instruction (a member of the Reference Department), whose major duties include: meeting with faculty to schedule instructional classes, collecting and organizing statistics, preparing and annual report on orientation/instructional activities, and scheduling the division of teaching responsibilities among all the reference librarians.

5.5 The Reference Department of the Library will offer bibliographic instruction independent of any academic department or other group.

Electronic Classroom Use

Suffolk University
Mildred F. Sawyer Library
Boston, Massachusetts

Usage of the Library's Instruction Lab

The Sawyer Library's Instruction Room is primarily for the use of classes being instructed by library staff in research methods and information resources.

Because library classes are scheduled (sometimes at short notice) at the request of the academic faculty throughout the semester, no courses can be scheduled in the room on a regular, recurring, basis. The room is kept locked when not in use.

The room may be reserved for instructors occasionally requiring specialized electronic resources by calling the Reference Department.

University of Maryland Baltimore County
Albin O. Kuhn Library
Baltimore, Maryland

I. Primary Use

The Library Instruction Room 259, is made available for the purpose of providing librarian-mediated instruction to students, faculty and staff on how to access library and electronic resources.

II. Additional Supported Use

The Library Instruction Room is available for librarian-sponsored events including professional meetings and exceptional uses approved by the Reference Department. Exceptional events should not conflict with potential use of the room during the semester and summer sessions. Usage for these events should be kept to normal class times in duration. Use of the room on these occasions should involve librarians working in an integral way with the program presented.

III. Scheduling

Room 259 is scheduled by contacting the Coordinator of Bibliographic & Electronic Instruction in person, by phone or email. In his/her absence, other designated staff in Reference should be contacted. As a general rule, no fewer than five (5) business days are necessary to reserve the room for an event. Requestors are encouraged to make use of the 'free period' on Monday, Wednesday and Fridays, from 1:00 p.m. to 2:00 p.m. No significant reconfiguration of room furniture or equipment is available. The room must be used as presented. Requestors must provide a date and time, including beginning and ending times of the event when making a reservation. Assignment of a "pending status" is available only for librarian-mediated and faculty-librarian team instruction.

IV. Prohibited Use

Room 259 is not available as a campus classroom, or as a location for regularly scheduled business meetings.

V. Food and Drink

Food or drink is not permitted in this room except by prior arrangement.

Course Evaluation

Boston College
Boston College Libraries
Boston, Massachusetts

Evaluation

Formal library instruction sessions are evaluated at the time of instruction by the instructor and students. Additional evaluation of the program is received from general student surveys.

Procedures for Subject Instruction Classes

Fullerton College
William T. Boyce Library
Fullerton, California

Subject Instruction Sessions

Instructors are encouraged to request an instruction session for specific classes. A librarian will tailor the session to the needs of these students. The instruction session on "How to Prepare a Works Cited Using

MLA," as noted above, can also be scheduled for a specific class. All instruction sessions must be scheduled one week in advance. Instructors should call the Library Administrative Assistant to arrange a session, or stop by the Library to fill out the Instruction Session Request form.

Procedures for Research How-To Classes

Fullerton College
William T. Boyce Library
Fullerton, California

Library Research Class (1unit)—CSU/UC/Degree Credit

Please consult a current class schedule for dates/times offered.

a. Library 100—Introduction to Research

This class is designed to introduce students to traditional and electronic methods of research including the Internet. Students learn to locate, evaluate, and correctly cite the information selected for use in a bibliography. This class is of special value to those students intending to transfer to a four-year institution.

b. Library 100H—Honors Introduction to Research

This is an enhanced course designed to introduce honors students to traditional and electronic methods of research including the Internet. The course is of special value to those students intending to transfer to a four-year institution.

University of California Davis
University Library
Davis, California

Using the Library: Catalogs and Services

Find books and journal articles at UC Davis and in all the UC libraries using the Harvest: UC Davis Library Catalog and the Melvyl Catalog. Learn how to start your research and use effective search strategies.

Using the Library: Finding Articles and Journals Online

Having a hard time finding the article you want? Is it available in electronic form in one of our full-text sources? This class will guide you through the process of identifying appropriate databases and electronic journals available through the Library web site.

EndNote for Research Papers

Learn to format bibliographies easily and automatically using this special bibliographical management tool. You will be taught how to download and export citations from catalogs and databases.

Searching the Agricultural Literature: CAB & Agricola Databases

Learn to search efficiently for farm animal (including veterinary), entomological (pest), fruit and vegetable crop, farming systems and human nutrition areas. Using UC eLinks and cross-searching both databases will be covered.

Searching the Animal/Wildlife Sciences Literature

Dependent on the subject interests of attendees, bibliographic databases and library resources on the appropriate animal-related Subject guides will be presented. Potential subject guides to be covered are: Animal Sciences, Entomology, Fisheries and Aquaculture, and Marine Biology. Database searching strategies covered include: topic/keyword, title and author searching; using the wildcard and limits; and using the thesaurus, index, and search history features. How to use UC-eLinks will also be discussed.

Searching the Biological Literature: BIOSIS & PubMed Databases

BIOSIS and PubMed are general databases for nearly all biological topics and are especially important for the molecular and cellular sciences. Database searching strategies covered include: Topic/keyword, title and author searching; using the wildcard and limits; and using the thesaurus/MeSH terms, and search history features. How to use UC-eLinks will also be discussed.

Searching the Ecological & Environmental Sciences Literature

Dependent on the subject interests of attendees, bibliographic databases and library resources on the appropriate ecological/environmental sciences related Subject guides will be presented. Potential subject guides to be covered are: Ecology and Conservation Biology; Environmental Sciences; Marine Biology; and Toxicology. Database searching strategies covered include: topic/keyword, title and author searching; using the wildcard and limits; and using the thesaurus, index, and search history features. How to use UC-eLinks will also be discussed.

Procedures for Special Faculty Services

University of California Davis
University Library
Davis, California

Library Resources for Instructors Library Instruction Services

The Library Instruction Services Department offers services designed to support classroom teaching and enhance student learning. Contact us for more information.

Tours/Orientations

The University Library provides tours of all its facilities throughout the year upon request. They are designed to introduce users to the libraries and their services. Drop-in Workshops Each quarter, the library holds a number of free workshops that highlight library resources and services. Popular topics include 'Using the Library: Catalogs and Services' and 'Finding Articles and Journals Online.' Please see our complete listing and schedule.

Library Instruction Sessions

Librarians are available to instruct your students on how to find, use and evaluate print and electronic information sources. Presentations are tailored to meet the specific requirements of your course, and prove especially effective when arranged to coincide with a term paper or research assignment. Sessions may be held in your classroom or in the Shields Library Instruction Lab, equipped with 25 computer workstations.

Individual Consultations Librarian Subject Specialists and Instruction

Librarians will gladly assist you in the creation of bibliographies or reading lists to meet your course needs. We are also available to help craft assignments that utilize library resources and develop students' critical thinking and research skills.

Print & Online Guides Incorporate information literacy into the curriculum using the tutorials, movies and pedagogical resources available from the 'Resources for Instructors' page.

Guidelines for High School Students

Henderson State University
Huie Library
Arkadelphia, Arkansas

Bibliographic instruction is provided for:

- Henderson State University courses
- Area high school classes 10th grade and above. No more than 25 students per session and there must be at least two adults with the group.
- Groups not falling within the above parameters will be considered on an individual basis

Arrangements for Bibliographic Instruction must be made at least one week in advance and receive approval from the Instructional Services Librarian or another Reference Librarian. If possible, high school orientations will take place very early in the semester during the week of classes public schools are in session before college courses resume. This period is usually around August 19th to the 25th in the Fall and the first full week of January in the Spring.

High school students may check out two books each on their teacher's library account. The teacher must have an ID/library card and his/her account must be in good standing. Books may be checked out for 28 days. No renewals.

University of Arkansas
University of Arkansas Libraries
Fayetteville, Arkansas

Guidelines for Visits by Non-University Groups

The University of Arkansas Libraries welcome those who wish to use our resources, particularly high school students working on specific assignments and college students or faculty members from other institutions. However, to get the most benefit from your visit and help ensure that all our patrons enjoy an environment conducive to study, please follow these guidelines.

Making Arrangements: Please make ADVANCE ARRANGEMENTS at least seven days prior to your visit. Contact Reference Department.

We suggest that secondary school groups limit their visits to half-day sessions, preferably in the mornings. We have found that students find a full day of library research difficult.

We usually provide an orientation session as the first hour of a group's visit in classrooms in Mullins Library. This program will describe the basic access points of the Libraries' collection as well as the physical layout of Mullins Library. You may look at the Libraries' home page and in particular, at the research help page, for online instruction.

As there is more and more competition for computers in the Libraries and a limited number of guest logins available, we suggest that students begin to search the InfoLinks online catalog and gather call numbers for materials before the visit.

Student groups are better able to make the most of their time here if they have assignments to research when they arrive, both to make immediate use of the skills taught in the library orientation, and to focus their time while in the library. When you schedule a visit, please supply information about the students' assignments or research projects so the program can be tailored to the students' interests.

Although we offer tours to groups of junior high/middle school students on a limited basis, our experience has shown that our resources and environment are not best matched to their needs. If you wish to bring a group of students below the ninth grade to the Libraries, please call us far in advance to discuss your plans and the objectives of the visit. Adequate chaperonage is crucial for these tours.

FORMS

Form for Student Evaluation of Library Instruction

Weber State University
Stewart Library
Ogden, Utah

Library Course/Instructor Evaluation Form

Course Name: [   ]

Section: [   ]

Semester: [   ]

Year: [   ]

Instructor: [_____]

Answer each question by marking the letter according to above scale

1. The course objectives were met [_____]

2. The course materials were helpful in meeting course objectives [_____]

3. Assignments contributed to student understanding of the subject matter [_____]

4. This course added to my knowledge of the subject [_____]

5. The objectives of the course were clearly stated [_____]

6. The instructor was organized [_____]

7. The instructor presented course content effectively [_____]

8. The instructor encouraged student discussion and participation [_____]

9. The instructor was enthusiastic about the subject of the course [_____]

10. The instructor was available for consultation with students [_____]

11. The instructor treated students with respect [_____]

12. Work was graded according to announced guidelines [_____]

13. The instructor used class time effectively [_____]

14. The instructor stimulated a desire for further learning [_____]

15. The instructor used different methods to interest and involve students in learning [_____]

16. Overall, this was an effective instructor [_____]

17. Overall, this was an effective course [_____]

Please complete the additional items below. These are very important for helping the faculty improve this course.

List two things that made this course work for you

[   ]

List two things that would improve the course

[   ]

List two things the instructor did well

[   ]

List two things the instructor could do better

[   ]

Thank you! Please verify all answers, then click the *submit* button.

[Submit Survey]

Xavier University
Xavier University Library
Cincinnati, Ohio

Student Library Instruction Evaluation   Monday, June 12, 2006
                                                          Hours Today: 8am to 10pm

Please evaluate the class you have just experienced.

Date of the class:

Who are you?

What Course and Section are you in?

Who is your Instructor?

Who was the Librarian that taught the class?

Comment on the quality of instruction for session:

Please rate...	strongly disagree	disagree	neutral	agree	strongly agree
The instruction was clear and understandable	○	○	○	○	○
The instruction helped me locate library resources for my assignment.	○	○	○	○	○

Comment on what was useful about this session:

Please rate...	Not useful	Somewhat useful	Very useful
Database searching	○	○	○
Xtreme subject guides	○	○	○
Overview of Library Home Page	○	○	○
AllCard	○	○	○
Help for users	○	○	○
XPLORE	○	○	○
OhioLINK	○	○	○
Document Delivery	○	○	○
My Library Record	○	○	○
E-mail notification	○	○	○
XuTutor	○	○	○

Other comments?

Library Instruction Request Form

University of Arkansas
University of Arkansas Libraries
Fayetteville, Arkansas

Request Library Instruction Class or Individual Consultation

University of Arkansas faculty members, instructors, researchers, or students who desire assistance from the reference department may use the form below in order to:

○ Request a library instruction class

OR

○ Request an individual consultation with a subject specialist in your area of interest.

You may also call (479-575-6645; toll-free 866-818-8115) or come by the Reference Desk in the main library to inquire about a class or consultation.

Please fill in and send the form.

Most of the boxes accept more text than their size suggests.

Designates a required field.

Your Info

*Your first name:

[   ]

*Your last name:

[   ]

*Your complete email address:

[   ]

*Campus (or other) phone number:

[   ]

Campus address:

[   ]

Requesting a Research Consultation?

Please provide a description of the class and the assignment or the subject area of interest (i.e., Marketing assignment, teeth whitening products, looking for market demographics and revenues):

[   ]

Requesting Class Instruction?

Class name along with the number of sections and each class size (i.e., Comm 1313, 4 sections, 30 students per section):

[   ]

What is their assignment?

[   ]

Any special needs or requests for topics?

[   ]

When would you like the class? (day, date, and an alternate):

[   ]

What time is the class held?

[   ]

Your request will be routed to the appropriate reference librarian and you will be contacted as soon as possible.

[Send the Request]

[Clear the Form]

Colorado State University Pueblo
Colorado State University Pueblo Library
Pueblo, Colorado

Library Instruction Request Form

If you would like to request a library instruction class, please complete and submit this form at least one week ahead of the date requested. The request will be sent directly to Karen Pardue, Instructional Technology Librarian.

Before you fill out the form, check the Library Instruction Lab (L214A)—Schedule for availability.

Today's Date: Professor's Name:
[   ]   [   ]

Department: Campus Phone:
[   ]   [   ]

Home Phone: E-Mail:
[   ]   [   ]

Level of students: ○ Undergraduate
                                       ○ Graduate
                                       ○ High School
                                       ○ Other

Course Name/Number: Number of students:
[   ]   [   ]

Preferred Librarian/Instructor: [   ]

Preferred Dates and Times: Date   Time

                       First: [   ]   [   ]
                       Second: [   ]   [   ]
                       Third: [   ]   [   ]

Please indicate the content you wish to cover in your session. Check all that apply.

○ Library Catalog   ○ Boolean Logic
○ Periodical Indexes   ○ Primary Sources
○ Internet Searching   ○ Interlibrary Loan
○ Reference Sources   ○ Other [   ]

397

General Description of the purpose of the instruction:

Please provide a description:

Please describe related student research activities or topics:

Will the classroom instructor be present at the library instruction?

○ Yes   ○ No

Other comments:

Columbia College Chicago
Columbia College Library
Chicago, Illinois

Library Instruction Request Form

Please provide the following information as indicated. This form must be submitted at least one week prior to the earliest date requested. Instruction Sessions are not available during last two weeks of the term. Thank you for your cooperation.

If you are teaching multiple sections of a class, you may use this form.

This form is NOT a confirmation. You will receive phone or e-mail verification stating the date/time of your session. If you have specific questions, please call the Reference Desk at 312-344-7153.

ALL fields are REQUIRED

After completing the form, scroll to the bottom and click on the "Submit" button.

Name:

Dept:

Phone: _____ (Home)
_____ (Work)

Email:

Course Title:

Academic Level: ○ 1st/2nd year   ○ 3rd/4th year   ○ Graduate

How many sections are you teaching?   ○ 1   ○ 2   ○ 3

Number of Students: First Section   Second Section   Third Section

Library Instruction should be done while students are working on an assignment/paper. Please describe the assignment/paper.

(Please note: You should provide us with a copy of the related assignment. You may either send the assignment via email to libraryinstruction@colum.edu or leave a copy at the Reference Desk.)

```
┌──────────────────────────┐
│                          │
│                          │
│                          │
│                          │
└──────────────────────────┘
```

Desired Date and Time:

(Please provide two separate possible dates for EACH section.)

INSTRUCTOR MUST ATTEND

First Section   Second Section   Third Section

```
┌──────────────┐    ┌──────────────────┐    ┌──────────────────┐
│              │    │                  │    │                  │
│              │    │                  │    │                  │
│              │    │                  │    │                  │
│              │    │                  │    │                  │
└──────────────┘    └──────────────────┘    └──────────────────┘
```

Additional Notes:

```
┌──────────────────────────┐
│                          │
│                          │
│                          │
│                          │
└──────────────────────────┘
```

```
┌──────────────┐
│   Submit     │
└──────────────┘
```

Fullerton College
William T. Boyce Library
Fullerton, California

William T. Boyce Library, Fullerton College

Library Instruction Session Request Form

Instruction will take place, unless requested otherwise, in the New Fullerton College Library's Bibliographic Instruction classroom, rm. 827, which is equipped with 33 computer research stations. It is our intent to provide the best possible bibliographic instruction for students, and to respond to the research needs of specific courses.

Following the librarian's instruction session, there may be time allocated for students to do research. It would be helpful for the librarian preparing an instruction session to know the instructor's expectations.

Please submit this completed form to the Library Administrative Assistant (ext. 27061) or the staff at the Information or Reference Desk at least one week before the desired date of the instruction session.

We ask that instructors select one of the following sessions:

○ General Overview—for an understanding of basic library tools.

○ Subject Specific—for an understanding of more specialized research tools.

Today's Date: _____

Instructor and dept.:_____

Instructor's Ext./Home phone/E-mail:

_____

Course title/number as it appears in the class schedule:

_____

Number of students in class: _____

Date(s) instruction desired: _____

Please note: At least one week's notice is required.

Alternate date(s) if first choice is unavailable: _____

Time(s) instruction desired: _____

Please note: Instruction begins on the hour. Sessions are for 50 minutes. If your students need additional instruction, please schedule a second session.

Type of Library Instruction: (check one, either General Overview or Subject Specific)

_____ General Overview (50 minutes)

Fullerton College Library's Homepage, Online Catalog, Internet, and Online Databases will be discussed.

Which would you prefer? (check one)

_____ hands-on library worksheet
_____ no worksheet/allow time for students to begin research on a class assignment
_____ neither of the above/librarian may instruct the full 50 minutes

_____ Subject Specific (50 minutes)

Specific research tools and materials will be discussed.

Which would you prefer? (check one)

_____ hands-on library worksheet
_____ no worksheet/allow time for students to begin research on a class assignment
_____ neither of the above/librarian may instruct the full 50 minutes

If you requested a Subject Specific instruction session, what specific research tools would you like discussed? (Example—online databases, Internet, reference books, or other)

_____
_____
_____

Additional Questions:

1. Please provide examples of student research topics; attaching a copy of the assignment would be helpful:

_____
_____
_____

2. What subjects or materials do you NOT want included?

_____
_____
_____

3. Would you like a tour of both floors of the library, including the Circulation and Reserve desk?

Yes _____ No _____

Would you like a tour of the Reference area only? Yes _____ No _____

Librarian preferred: _____

Instructor's signature: _____

Please note: It is the expectation that the instructor will attend.

_____
_____

Library Use Only

Date Received: _____ Librarian assigned: _____

Lake Sumter Community College
Lake Sumter Community College Libraries
Sumterville, Florida

Library Instruction Request

This form is designed for instructors requesting library instruction for LSCC classes. Reference librarians are available to conduct instructional sessions tailored to individual class needs. In order that we may accommodate all requests, please submit this form a minimum of **one week prior** to the desired date. **Please submit separate forms for each class session.** A librarian will respond to confirm your class session.

Instructor Information

Name: ☐

Phone Number: ☐

Best Time of Day to Contact: ☐

E-mail: ☐

Class Information

Course Name: ☐

Course Number: ☐

Campus: ☐

Number of Students: ☐

Requested Date

Day of week: ☐

Date (mm/dd/yy): ☐

Time: ☐ ○ A.M. ○ P.M.

Content for Session
(check all that apply):

○ General orientation   ○ Research assignment   ○ Choosing topics
○ Search techniques   ○ Full-text journals   ○ Online library catalog

Databases (check all that apply):

○ LINCC   ○ LUIS   ○ Internet Search Engines
○ Government Sites   ○ Academic ASAP   ○ Academic Search Premier
○ Business Source Elite   ○ CINAHL   ○ CQ Researcher
○ Criminal Justice Periodicals Index   ○ Custom Newspapers   ○ ERIC

[Complete list of available databases]

○ FactSearch   ○ FirstSearch   ○ netLibrary (e-books)
○ Health & Wellness Resource Center   ○ Hoover's Online   ○ Literature Resource Center
○ Medline   ○ NewsFile   ○ SIRS Researcher
○ WilsonSelect   ○ Other

Briefly describe the class assignment and any other library materials or resources you would like covered:

☐

Northern Arizona University
Cline Library
Flagstaff, Arizona

Request Course Support

Fields preceded by an asterisk (*) are required.

* Instructor Name: [_____]

* Instructor Phone: [_____]

* Instructor E-mail: [_____]

Course(s) Needing Support (ex: ECI 350): [_____]

* **Main Subject Area** (choose one):

○ Arts and Letters
○ Business
○ Consortium of Prof. Schools
○ Education
○ Engineering & Natural Sciences
○ Social & Behavioral Sciences
○ NAU Yuma

I am interested in learning more about: (check all that apply)

○ Using Electronic Reserves
○ Having a resource specialist provide one-on-one assistance to my students
○ Partnering with a resource specialist to plan research assignments
○ Integrating primary resources from Special Collections and Archives into my course
○ Inserting relevant resources into my syllabus or course
○ Scheduling a customized course session for my class
○ Cable Channel Delivery

How else can we help you?

[   ]

Library Instruction Evaluation for Faculty Form

Xavier University
Xavier University Library
Cincinnati, Ohio

Faculty Library Instruction Evaluation   Monday, June 12, 2006
Hours Today: 8am to 10pm

Please evaluate the class you have just experienced.

Date of the instruction:

[_____] [_____] [_____]

Course: [_____]

Section: [_____]

Your Name:

[_____]

Who was the Librarian that taught the class?

[   ]

Comment on the quality of instruction for session:

Please rate...	strongly disagree	disagree	neutral	strongly agree
The instruction was clear and understandable	○	○	○	○
The instruction helped my students locate library resources.	○	○	○	○

Comment on what was useful about this session:

Please rate...	Not useful	Somewhat useful	Very useful
Database searching	○	○	○
Xtreme subject guides	○	○	○
Overview of Library Home Page	○	○	○
AllCard	○	○	○
Help for users	○	○	○
XPLORE	○	○	○
OhioLINK	○	○	○
Document Delivery	○	○	○
My Library Record	○	○	○
E-mail notification	○	○	○
XuTutor	○	○	○

Comments...

[   ]

| Send It | Start Over |

Chapter 33

INFORMATION LITERACY

ADMINISTRATIVE GUIDELINES

Benefits of Information Literacy

Neumann College
Neumann College Library
Aston, Pennsylvania

Why Is It Important?

Students have always needed to know how to find and use information, and instructors have always taught these skills. Now, however, because of the Internet, students have access to more information than ever before. For instance, the Neumann College Library subscribes to about 400 print periodicals, but provides access to almost 10,000 online periodicals via databases. Google indexes over 4 billion Web pages!

Formal instruction in information literacy helps students deal with the deluge of information, and according to the Association of College and Research Libraries, "Information literacy forms the basis for lifelong learning." Because of its importance, accrediting bodies now expect colleges and universities to establish and assess information literacy standards.

University of Iowa
University of Iowa Libraries
Iowa City, Iowa

Why Is Information Literacy Important?

It has become increasingly clear that students are in need of skills to filter through the vast amount of information in their lives. Information literacy equips students with the skills they need to be thoughtful and efficient users of information. Information literacy skills also help students become independent, lifelong learners by enabling them to analyze and evaluate the information they find.

Integrating Information Literacy into the Classroom

The best way for students to become truly information literate is for information skills and concepts to be integrated into course goals as well as into the University's curriculum. We invite all faculty and teaching staff to consider implementing an information literacy component in their course to improve student learning.

Librarians are available to meet with faculty and TAs to discuss course goals and information literacy skills that can be emphasized in the course. They then collaboratively design the approach that best suits the course goals. For more information on integrating information literacy into the classroom, see Course-Related Instruction. The examples presented below are not "either-or." Many times a librarian and instructor work together on an assignment, and a librarian will provide an in-class presentation as well as a resources page for the course Web site.

ACRL Standards

Illinois State University
Milner Library
Normal, Illinois

Information Literacy Competencies/Standards

Know

- decide what is required to answer this question/what is required to do the assignment/what the question, assignment, etc. means to you

Access

- select appropriate search tool(s) and information source(s)
- design search strategy(-ies)
- implement search strategy(-ies) to find information
- assess and select search results/found information
- manage and record relevant search results/found information
- refine search strategy(-ies), if necessary, by repeating "know" and/or "access" process(es)

Evaluate

- recognize and summarize main ideas from search results/found information
- identify/create evaluation criteria
- assess search results/found information with evaluation criteria
- judge in comparison to existing knowledge
- refine search strategy(-ies) and/or evaluation criteria, if necessary, by repeating "know," "access," and "evaluate/incorporate" process(es)

Use/Incorporate Ethically/Legally

- apply new information ethically and legally
- integrate and synthesize new and existing information ethically and legally into paper, project, performance, etc.
- acknowledge new information used in paper, project, performance, etc. without plagiarizing and by appropriately attributing and citing sources
- share paper, project, performance, etc. with others using appropriate communication medium, format, technology, etc.

Neumann College
Neumann College Library
Aston, Pennsylvania

What Are the Standards?

Each institution can devise its own standards. The Association of College and Research Libraries recommends five basic standards, which can be broken down into various performance indicators and outcomes.

The information literate student determines the nature and extent of the information needed.

The information literate student accesses needed information effectively and efficiently.

The information literate student evaluates information and its sources critically and incorporates selected information into his or her knowledge base and value system.

The information literate student, individually or as a member of a group, uses information effectively to accomplish a specific purpose.

The information literate student understands many of the economic, legal, and social issues surrounding the use of information and accesses and uses information ethically and legally.

Mission Statement

Tallahassee Community College
Tallahassee, Community College Library
Tallahassee, Florida

Our mission is to provide an information literacy program that fosters the development of lifelong learning skills. Information literate individuals have the "ability to recognize when information is needed and have the ability to locate, evaluate, and use effectively the needed information" (American Library Association, 1989). These skills contribute to the ability to think critically and use information ethically and legally. Our information literacy program supports the Library's mission of providing resources and services necessary to support the excellence in teaching and learning objectives of the College.

We support this mission by:

- Collaborating with the College community to integrate information literacy across the curriculum in all academic programs
- Promoting the use of library resources in all formats
- Providing instruction formally or informally, in person or via technology
- Continually evaluating programs and methods and updating our skills to reflect best practices

Stetson University
duPont-Ball Library
DeLand, Florida

Library Instructional Services Mission Statement

The instructional mission of the Library is to initiate and support opportunities for faculty and students to develop technological, evaluative, and critical thinking skills in pursuit of lifelong information literacy.

Using a variety of methodologies, we will provide these initiatives in support of and in conjunction with the curricular and research needs of the University. We do this in the context of the Information Literacy Competency Standards of the Association of College and Research Libraries and the University's mission which embraces the value of "the centrality of knowledge, examined ideas, and independent judgment in the life of an educated person."

Florida International University
Florida International University Libraries
Miami, Florida

Information Literacy Mission Statement

The pursuit of knowledge is the foundation of the University. Providing access to the world of knowledge, imparting knowledge through excellent teaching, fostering creative expression and encouraging the creation of new knowledge through research are at the core of the University's mission.

Information literacy enhances the pursuit of knowledge at the University by preparing students to think critically and use information for their academic, professional and personal lives. The information literate individual can recognize the need for information, can locate it using a variety of media and technologies and can evaluate information in order to use it effectively. Information literate students have the flexibility to take these skills from their formal education and use them throughout life as citizens and professionals and as a means toward continued learning.

Colleges, schools, programs and the libraries share the responsibility for helping students develop information literacy skills. Successful implementation of information literacy goals is achieved by integration across the curriculum and depends on active participation of all parties.

The Libraries seek to promote information literacy by educating students to understand the organization of knowledge, to gather data of all kinds using both print and information technology resources and to evaluate the relevance and authority of information in all its forms. The Libraries provide resources and services in an environment that fosters free and open inquiry and serve as a catalyst for the interpretation, integration, and application of knowledge in all fields of learning.

Goals and Objectives

California State University, Los Angeles
John F. Kennedy Memorial Library
Los Angeles, California

(Policy copyrighted by California State University Los Angeles 2006. Used with permission.)

The goals of the John F. Kennedy Memorial Library Information Literacy Program are:

Goal One

Transform the current, traditional, teach-on-demand bibliographic instruction model to an information literacy program model.

Create a systematic Library Liaison program that supports the development of information literacy pedagogy for classroom faculty.

Further develop a tiered instructional program that develops information literacy skills incrementally from general education courses to graduation, with special emphasis on unique department- or discipline-based needs.

Expand the librarian liaison program by identifying and contacting special groups on campus.

Enhance off-campus outreach by extending information literacy and orientation efforts to local high schools and community colleges.

Create a web-based information literacy tutorial capable of general and specific use, accessible from the Library Web and classroom management software.

Develop an assessment process for both programmatic and class level review.

Encourage the professional development of librarians and staff through training in information literacy concepts, standards and teaching methods.

Goal Two

Create instructional programs for identified general education courses.

Ensure that every section of the college-based Introduction to Higher Education courses, and English 102 courses, attend an information literacy session with a librarian.

Create content, materials and instructional methods.

Ensure even distribution of teaching responsibilities for these classes among User Services librarians.

Goal Three

Participate in and support the accreditation and program review process.

Ensure that the Program Review Subcommittee annually notifies the Library of programs under review.

Assist in program reviews by providing appropriate statistics and other documentation.

Meet with external reviewers/evaluators.

Goal Four

Oversee the LIBR 150, Information Literacy and Research Skills course.

Create content, materials and instructional methods.

Incorporate use of the new information literacy tutorial.

Establish uniform learning objectives.

Develop learning outcome assessment tools.

Develop a depository for class materials.

University of Alaska Anchorage
Alaska Pacific University
Consortium Library
Anchorage, Alaska

Information Literacy Goals and Outcomes

1. Recognizes and articulates the need for information. Competencies/Learning Outcomes:
    a. Formulates questions based on the information need.
    b. Identifies key concepts and terms that describe the information need.
    c. Uses background information sources effectively to gain an initial understanding of the topic.
    d. Recognizes that assistance is available from librarians.

2. Understands how information is organized. Competencies/Learning Outcomes:
    a. Describes differences between and demonstrates appropriate use of general and subject-specific information sources.
    b. Identifies research sources, regardless of format, that are appropriate to a particular discipline or research need.
    c. Recognizes the format (e.g., book, book chapter, periodical article, website) of a reference from its citation.
    d. Identifies characteristics of information that make an item a primary or secondary source in a given field.
    e. Identifies the purpose and audience of potential sources (e.g., current vs. historical, popular vs. scholarly,).
    f. Understands the differences between freely available Internet search tools and websites and subscription- or fee-based databases.
    g. Describes when different types of information (e.g., primary/secondary, background/specific) may be suitable for different purposes.

3. Develops and implements an effective process or search strategy to meet the information need. Competencies/Learning Outcomes:
    a. Selects appropriate resources (e.g., indexes, online databases, books, primary sources) to research a topic.
    b. Understands the content and period of time covered by the resources selected.
    c. Chooses relevant keywords, synonyms, and related terms for the information needed, recognizing that different resources may use different terminology for similar concepts.
    d. Formulates and uses search strategies appropriate to the resources, whether they be print or electronic.
    e. Constructs a search strategy using appropriate commands (e.g., Boolean operators, truncation, proximity, limiting, field searching) when an electronic information retrieval system is used.
    f. Limits or expands searches by modifying search terminology or logic.
    g. Identifies when and where controlled vocabulary (e.g., descriptors, subject headings, assigned terms) is used in a bibliographic record, and successfully searches for information using that vocabulary.

4. Locates, retrieves, and selects appropriate information. Competencies/Learning Outcomes:
    a. Uses appropriate print and electronic resources (e.g., bibliographies, databases, indexes, search engines) to retrieve information in a variety of formats.
    b. Uses various classification schemes and other search strategies to retrieve appropriate information.
    c. Identifies the basic elements of different kinds of citations

    d. Examines footnotes and bibliographies from retrieved items to find additional sources.

    e. Understands methods for obtaining information not available in the library (e.g., interlibrary loan, community resources, document delivery).

    f. Selects information that provides evidence for or relates to the topic.

5. Evaluates the information and the effectiveness of the search. Competencies/Learning Outcomes:

    a. Reviews the initial information need and clarifies, revises, or refines the question as necessary.

    b. Gathers and evaluates information and appropriately modifies the research plan as new insights are gained.

    c. Assesses the quantity, quality, and relevance of the search results and identifies gaps in the information retrieved.

    d. Narrows or broadens questions and search terms in response to results to retrieve an appropriate quantity and quality of information.

    e. Describes the differences in results when searching with a library-provided tool (e.g., web-based library catalog, full-text electronic journal, web-based article index) and a general web search engine (e.g., Alta Vista, Google).

    f. Examines and compares information from various sources to evaluate reliability, validity, accuracy, authority, timeliness, cultural context, and bias.

6. Organizes and synthesizes the information and uses it appropriately. Competencies/Learning Outcomes:

    a. Understands the basic ethical, legal, and socio-economic issues (e.g., fair use, copyright, digital divide) involved in information and information technology.

    b. Demonstrates an understanding of what constitutes plagiarism.

    c. Understands that different disciplines may use different documentation styles (e.g., APA, MLA, CBE).

    d. Selects an appropriate documentation style and uses it correctly and consistently.

EVALUATION AND TESTING

Surveys

University of Maryland Baltimore County
Albin O. Kuhn Library
Baltimore, Maryland

The UMBC Information Literacy Survey contains 51 items and takes approximately 34 minutes to complete. The survey is automated and will be deployed via the UMBC portal, my.UMBC.edu. Survey participants will use a Web browser to access my.UMBC.edu. Once logged in they will select the AOK Information Literacy Survey link and follow the instructions to complete the survey. The survey will only be available during the month of September, 2003.

The majority of the questions on the survey have no right or wrong answers. These questions are designed to solicit student perceptions about information and the use of information.

Participating faculty will receive a list of the unique usernames of the students who have completed the survey as of Sunday, September 14th on Monday, September 15th. A final roster of those who have completed the survey will be distributed to participating faculty by Friday, October 3rd.

In addition to the assessment the Task Force will be developing and promoting the Faculty Awareness Project, to promote information literacy awareness, assist faculty, and provide support for integrating information literacy standards, objectives, and competencies into the classroom and across the curriculum at UMBC.

The Information Literacy Task Force believes that focusing Information Literacy Awareness efforts on Faculty will greatly benefit students. To that end, additional material has been developed for faculty to use in campus initiatives including the First Year Success Course. This material is also recommended for use in the First Year Seminar courses as well.

University of Maryland Baltimore County
Albin O. Kuhn Library
Baltimore, Maryland

The results of the Information Literacy Survey include no personal identifying information. However, results may be reported based on other demographic elements such as academic department.

The complete survey results (raw data) are available.

An executive summary has been prepared for the entire population, organized by the five ACRL Standards and other major areas of data collection. The summary includes key principles of the Standards which will then be mapped to indicators/results.

Reports of the results (based on data from participating students enrolled in departmental courses) were made for the following academic departments:

- English
- Biology

Participating teaching faculty will be able to request additional data about their individual classes upon request at the end of the semester.

The sections written by the Task Force are:

Standard I—The information literate student determines the nature and extent of the information needed.

The survey includes questions about the types of sources that exist for doing research and asks students to select those sources with which they are familiar. For example, one question has a list of sources that include some commonly used materials, such as magazine and journal articles, and some less commonly used, such as conference proceedings, dissertations, and manuscripts.

Standard II—The information literate student accesses needed information effectively and efficiently.

Included in the survey are questions that investigate students' abilities to select appropriate resource tools, develop successful search strategies, and extract needed information from their results. For example, one survey question asks students to specify how frequently they use search strategies such as Boolean operators, truncation, and proximity operators.

Standard III—The information literate student evaluates information and its sources critically and incorporates selected information into his or her knowledge base and value system.

The survey includes questions about students' capabilities in evaluating materials and selecting those most appropriate for a specific purpose. For example, one question asks students to specify how they select the best articles from a list of results in an article database.

Standard IV—The information literate student uses information effectively to accomplish a specific purpose.

Included in the survey are questions that will gather data regarding students' abilities to synthesize gathered information to produce a final product, such as a research paper. For example, a series of questions in the survey asks students to specify whether or not they've had the opportunity to present their research using various methods such as PowerPoint, visual projects, personal Web pages, etc.

Standard V—The information literate student understands many of the economic, legal, and social issues surrounding the use of information and accesses and uses information ethically and legally.

Questions in the survey regarding this Standard examine students' views and understanding of issues of copyright, plagiarism, and fair use. For example, one question offers specific writing scenarios (such as re-wording someone else's information and using it without giving credit to the author) and asks students to indicate whether or not they consider it plagiarism.

Relationship with Faculty—A very important element of information literacy involves students' relationships with their instructors. The survey contains a number of questions that investigate student/faculty relationships—whether or not a student is comfortable asking his or her instructor for assistance, whether or not a student has participated in directed research with a faculty member, among others.

Attitudinal Responses—A number of questions on the survey gather information regarding students' attitudes about doing research. Students are asked to indicate their comfort levels with working with various types of resources, and seeking information from a variety of sources, such as the Library homepage.

Demographics—The survey gathered a great deal of demographic data regarding the participants. Participants are asked to specify: gender, age, race, academic status, ethnic heritage, country of citizenship, native language, and academic history.

The Task Force will host two Brown Bag(s) during the month of November. They will take place Tuesday, November 18th from 12–1, and Monday, November 24th from 1–2, in the Albin O. Kuhn Library & Gallery, 3rd floor, Administration Suite, conference room. The focus of these sessions will be:

- Creating solutions to provide students with information literacy skills instruction;
- The role of the faculty in participating and supporting this effort;
- Obtaining meaningful feedback from students on information literacy efforts.

Assessment

University of California Davis
University Library
Davis, California

Resources For Instructors Library Instruction Assessment:

Minute Paper:

What was the most important thing you learned during the class today?

What important questions remain unanswered?

What would you change about this class?

Pre- & Post-Class Quiz:

Create a quiz that addresses the areas you will cover during the session.

Copy it on both sides of a sheet of paper.

At the beginning of the session, have students take the quiz. When they are done, tell them to set it aside.

At the end of the session, ask students to turn the sheets over and take the same quiz again. [They will immediately be able to see what they learned, and so will you when they pass it in.]

Save time to go over the correct answers during class. If you do not have time, make sure that students are given a handout or a follow-up email with the correct answers.

University of Maryland Baltimore County
Albin O. Kuhn Library
Baltimore, Maryland

The following are elements of the Information Literacy Program to be developed for faculty and students based on findings of the survey:

For Faculty:

Develop workshops for faculty on:

- Developing information literacy-friendly assignments;
- Integrating information literacy Standards into a course;
- Other topics determined relevant based on specific survey findings.

Further development of Faculty Focus Web Site to include additional information about the survey findings. The survey will be rewritten to include narrative and background information on the nature of the question and what we were attempting to ascertain. Faculty and Students will be referred to this Web site for additional information on the survey and its purpose. Refer to Information Literacy Survey Results Dissemination for more details.

Additional programs will be developed based outcomes of the Brown Bag sessions.

For Students:

- Individualized one-on-one sessions, upon request, with librarian to discuss results and develop a plan for future instruction needs.
- Develop factoids slide show to advertise on the Commons Commonvision based on findings from the survey.

Past programs offered:

Brown Bag Discussion—Plagiarism in the Classroom

The Faculty Development Center and the Albin O. Kuhn Library & Gallery are co-sponsoring a brown bag discussion on plagiarism in the classroom. Participants will be provided with two brief articles to read ahead of time in order to facilitate discussion. This session will take place Thursday, June 17th from 1:00 to 2:00 in the Library Administration Conference Room (Library 353). Light refreshments will be served. RSVP to sullivan@umbc.edu to reserve your spot.

Assignment Design Workshop I: Integrating Information Literacy Skills into Your Assignments

In April 2004, the Faculty Development Center and the Albin O. Kuhn Library & Gallery co-sponsored a workshop on assignment design. The workshop focused on integrating information literacy skills (based on the ACRL Information Literacy Competency Standards) into assignments. The PowerPoint presentation is available online.

Copyright and Fair Use Workshop: What Faculty and Students Need to Know

In March 2004, the Faculty Development Center and the Library co-sponsored a workshop on copyright and fair use. The workshop featured David McDonald, Special Assistant for Academic Affairs, Towson University. David's handout is available in PDF format. The workshop also included an update on the campus Intellectual Property Policy.

Sample Quiz

University of California Davis
University Library
Davis, California

Library Research Skills Quiz

1. Which of the following are effective strategies for choosing search terms?
    A. Write out your topic in a few sentences
    B. Highlight the main terms and phrases
    C. Brainstorm synonyms and different terms
    D. Check a subject encyclopedia for words and concepts
    E. All of the above

2. Which of the following would you use to search for books at the UC Davis University Library:
    A. LexisNexis
    B. UCeLinks
    C. Harvest

3. You can search for articles using Harvest.
    A. True
    B. False

4. Which of the following links from the UC Davis Library homepage offers the best help when you need to select appropriate article databases for your topic?
   A. Library services
   B. Electronic databases
   C. Subject guides
   D. Melvyl UC Catalog

5. Citations that include volume and issue numbers are for:
   A. Essays in edited books
   B. Articles in journals
   C. Documentary film series
   D. Different versions of the same Web site

Examine the citation below and answer the following 2 questions:

Kelly, W. E., Kelly, K. E., & Clanton, R. C. (2001). The relationship between sleep length and grade-point average among college students. College Student Journal, 35(1), 84–86.

6. What piece of information from the citation above will you use to search Harvest to find this item?
   A. The article title
   B. The publisher
   C. The journal title
   D. The call number

7. Identify the different parts of the citation above:
   A. Title of the article
   B. Title of the journal
   C. Author
   D. Volume number
   E. Issue number
   F. How many pages long is this article?

Class Assignments

University of Iowa
University of Iowa Libraries
Iowa City, Iowa

Development of Assignments

In one approach, a librarian and a faculty member or TA can work together to develop assignments that focus on information literacy skills while enhancing the learning of ideas and concepts for the course. Sample assignments may include finding primary source material, finding pro and con opinions, or creating a list of scholarly articles to be included in a bibliography.

Class Sessions

In another approach, a librarian can present a class session to teach students strategies for finding and evaluating information specific to the needs of the course. In preparation for such a class session, the librarian will consult with the faculty member or TA in order to design a class session to meet the course goals and instructional objectives. Instruction is most effective when students are able to immediately apply the material presented and when the presentation is directly tied to a course assignment.

Web-based Resources

Sometimes the collaboration between faculty member and librarian results in the development of a resources page for the course Web site including links to UI subscription databases and explanations of how to evaluate information found on the Web. A librarian could also provide a brief sample search strategy to help guide students.

Part X
Interlibrary Loan and Document Delivery

Chapter 34

INTERLIBRARY LOAN PROCEDURES

ELECTRONIC REQUESTS

Lynchburg College
Knight-Capron Library
Lynchburg, Virginia

Electronic requests may be made in three ways:

FirstSearch databases—Click on "ILL" button, fill out onscreen form and transmit.

Cambridge Scientific Abstracts databases—Click on "locate document," fill out onscreen form, click on "send form to your library," click on "send the request."

Click here to access the library's ILL form online—you will be given an onscreen form to fill out and submit.

Questions about any of these procedures should be directed to the Interlibrary Loan office.

University of Idaho
University of Idaho Libraries
Moscow, Idaho

How do I submit a request for a book or other returnable item?

Request a UI, North Idaho College or Lewis and Clark State College library book by finding the item in the UI catalog and placing a hold. The book will be retrieved the next day (Monday through Friday) and you will receive email notification to pick the book up at the circulation desk. If you are off campus or are Moscow campus faculty or staff the material will be sent to you through U.S. mail or campus mail.

Submit your request through WorldCat. When you locate the item in this database and it is not in the UI Library, click the "ILL" icon and fill in your personal information. Then click "submit" to complete your request.

Use the electronic form [click here] for books. This form has required fields and will be returned if the information is incomplete or unverifiable.

NUMBER OF REQUESTS ALLOWED

Neumann College
Neumann College Library
Aston, Pennsylvania

How many items can be requested?

While there is no limit on the amount of items requested, only 10 items per day per person will be processed.

Lake Sumter Community College
Lake Sumter Community College Libraries
Sumterville, Florida

Number of Requests

Students may submit a maximum of five requests per research project. The requested materials should be related to their course of study.

Faculty, staff and Board members may submit an unlimited number of requests.

The borrowing library is responsible for conforming to the copyright law and guidelines. Therefore, the library must adhere to the "5 in 5" rule. When the maximum of five periodical requests from a title of a periodical has been reached, any additional requests from that title will be denied or may require copyright clearance fees.

Macon State College
Macon State College Library
Macon, Georgia

Number of items requested—Students are limited to five (5) book requests at any one time. There is no limit on the number of journal articles requested; however, consultation with a librarian may be suggested to assist with selection of appropriate articles.

RUSH REQUESTS

Lake Sumter Community College
Lake Sumter Community College Libraries
Sumterville, Florida

Rush Requests

Rush requests are done at the discretion of the Interlibrary Loan Librarian. Some libraries will fax a periodical article depending on the length of the article and other related factors.

SUMMER REQUESTS

Kalamazoo College
Upjohn Library
Kalamazoo, Michigan

Summer Requests

During the summer, items will be ordered for current students who reside locally, and for current faculty and staff who are in the area to pick up items at the Circulation Desk. Unfortunately, we cannot send ILL items off campus; all ILL items must be picked up at the Circulation Desk. If you will be off campus and need to interlibrary loan an item, please consult your local public library.

Connecticut College
Charles E. Shain Library
New London, Connecticut

During the summer, books will be ordered for current students who live on campus (must provide extension), for faculty and staff who will be in the area to retrieve the item (please return all books before leaving for vacation).

Chapter 35

INTERLIBRARY LOAN ELIGIBILITY

USER ELIGIBILITY REQUIREMENTS

University of South Alabama
University Libraries
Mobil, Alabama

Eligible Users

USA faculty, staff and currently registered students may request research materials not owned by any of the USA Libraries. The University Library does not borrow textbooks and/or required reading for students through Interlibrary Loan.

Undergraduates are limited to 5 requests in process at one time.

Graduate students are limited to 20 ILL requests in process (only 10 will be input each day.)

Non-USA Courtesy Card holders are limited to 5 requests in process at one time (see fee chart below.)

When the "requests in process limit" is reached, patrons can turn in one more request as soon as one request is filled.

Lake Sumter Community College
Lake Sumter Community College Libraries
Sumterville, Florida

Interlibrary Loan Users

The library provides interlibrary loan services for the following individuals at all LSCC campuses:

- LSCC faculty
- LSCC staff
- LSCC students (currently enrolled)
- Dual enrollment students (currently enrolled)
- University 2+2 students (currently enrolled)
- LSCC Board of Trustees members
- LSCC Foundation Board members
- Any patron requesting a government document
- Community patrons and students enrolled in Continuing Education non-credit classes are NOT eligible to request interlibrary loan materials. It is recommended that these individuals seek the services of a local public library.

Chapter 36

CHARGES AND FEES FOR INTERLIBRARY LOANS

FAILURE TO PICK UP MATERIAL

University of South Carolina Beaufort
USC Beaufort Library
Beaufort, South Carolina

Charges for Failure to Pick Up Materials

Failure to pick up an interlibrary loan book will result in a charge of $2.00 being added to the requester's library record.

Failure to pick up a photocopied item will result in a charge of $1.00 plus copy charges being added to the requester's library record.

GUIDELINES FOR CHARGES AND FEES

Lynchburg College
Knight-Capron Library
Lynchburg, Virginia

Costs

The patron is responsible for any copying or lending fees charged by the lending library. Most in-state loans and copies are free. Most out-of-state locations have fees or copying charges. The patron should indicate on the Interlibrary Loan form the maximum they are willing to pay.

Neumann College
Neumann College Library
Aston, Pennsylvania

Fees

Students are charged 50 cents per item. This fee is payable at the time of the request. As a courtesy, full and part-time faculty members are not charged fees for Interlibrary Loan materials. Requests returned unfilled will not be refunded. Neumann College Library will not pay fees charged by loaning libraries for copying articles or loaning books. Students/Patrons will be notified of such fees and can opt whether they still wish to receive the request. The patron would be responsible for this payment, which will be charged to their patron record.

GUIDELINES FOR CHARGES AND FEES FOR OVERDUE OR LOST ILL MATERIAL

Henderson State University
Huie Library
Arkadelphia, Arkansas

Lost Items
Patrons are responsible for all charges accruing from lost Interlibrary Loan materials.

Unpaid bills will be sent to the HSU business office, at which time an additional $5.00 billing fee will be added.

University of South Carolina Beaufort
USC Beaufort Library
Beaufort, South Carolina

Lost ILL Materials

The borrower will pay all costs assessed according to the regulations of the lending library.

In addition, the borrower will pay a $5.00 processing fee and any overdue fines accrued up to the time the library is notified that the material has been lost.

LENDING CHARGES

Boston College
Boston College Libraries
Boston, Massachusetts

Charges

There are no charges for filling requests for Massachusetts non-profit libraries and/or libraries that are members of the cooperating groups in the section below.

- Non-profit libraries—loan or photocopy, $10
- For profit libraries—loan or photocopy, $15
- National Network of Libraries of Medicine
- Loan or photocopy, $11

Henderson State University
Huie Library
Arkadelphia, Arkansas

Charges for ILL

Most interlibrary loan requests are processed without any charge to the patron.

Student will pay the first $5 of the lending fee per request. The library will pay $50 for any additional fees per student in a fiscal year.

The library will pay $50 for lending fee per faculty/staff in a fiscal year.

Article rush requests are frequently faxed and are more likely to accrue charges.

Books may be FED EXed at the patron's expense.

Payment of ILL charges is due whether or not the patron picks up the item.

University of South Alabama
University Libraries
Mobil, Alabama

Costs

The patron is financially responsible for any royalty fees as well as for any charges assessed by the lending library for loans, copies, fines, damages or lost items. No charges are incurred for materials borrowed within Alabama. Most out-of-state libraries will loan books at no charge (except for dissertations) but will charge for photocopies—typically a $5.00–$10.00 minimum.

If materials cannot be received by the deadline date, patrons can make a choice. They can decide to cancel the request and not be liable for any charges, or they can accept the material and any charges.

Non-USA Courtesy Card holders are charged a $7.00 fee per request in addition to any charges assessed by the lending library.

Courtesy Card Holder Types

No Request Fee Required	Teaching Assistants	Retired Faculty	Adjunct Faculty	Continuing Ed Faculty & Students	ASMS Faculty & Students	English as a Second Language	Odyssey
$7.00 Fee per Request	USA Faculty Spouse & Children	UM, SHC, BSCC, FSCC Faculty	Active Alumni Association Member	Visiting Faculty	Purchaser	Murphy High School International Baccalaureate Program	National Science Foundation

Chapter 37

Interlibrary Loan Borrowing Guidelines

Materials from Available Lender

Rutgers University
Rutgers University Libraries
Newark, New Jersey

Eligible Materials

The Libraries reserve the right to restrict the loan period of, or refuse to lend, any circulating material that is fragile, in demand, or that may otherwise need special restriction.

Requests will normally be filled for the following material:

- Books in the circulating collections, including master's theses and doctoral dissertations.
- Photocopies of any material that would not be damaged in the process or that are restricted by copyright regulation.
- Bound periodicals, if the item to be photocopied is over 50 pages and permission is granted from appropriate library staff. Individual issues of periodicals circulate to SHARES libraries only.
- Microfilm or microfiche, except for negatives. Up to 12 reels of microfilm may be loaned at one time for a single request and up to 50 duplicated microfiche for a single request.
- In-process materials to SHARES libraries only.
- Art Library books to SHARES or academic libraries only.

Boston College
Boston College Libraries
Boston, Massachusetts

Eligible Material

In general, a loan or a copy of any material may be requested from another library, although the lending library will decide in each case whether or not a particular item can be provided.

Interlibrary loan requests will be accepted from Boston College users for material:

- not owned by the libraries
- listed on Quest as "missing"
- which has been recalled and not returned within 10 days
- long overdue and billed for replacement
- at the bindery

If an item is held at BC, but is unavailable, please note this on the form.

Henderson State University
Huie Library
Arkadelphia, Arkansas

What may be borrowed?

The patron may request journal articles and books not held by Huie Library. Circulating items may also be requested. The library will not process requests for items held by OBU's library; students may check items at OBU using their student identification.

The library will process requests for dissertations and theses, although many libraries will not loan these materials.

Items that are difficult and sometimes impossible to obtain include rare or valuable books; videotapes; bulky or fragile material; recently published books; and materials with local circulation restrictions, such as reference or reserve items.

MATERIALS UNAVAILABLE TO BORROWER

Boston College
Boston College Libraries
Boston, Massachusetts

Ineligible Material

Interlibrary loan requests will not be accepted from Boston College users for items:

- in the reference collection or on course reserves at a Boston College library
- in process that have been received to place on course reserve
- items that are checked out; these should be recalled through Quest
- items that we own in microform
- in the reference collection
- items in Quest with an "in process" status
- no language tapes for languages that are taught at Boston College

Manatee Community College
Manatee Community College Library
Bradenton, Florida

The following types of materials cannot normally be requested or loaned:

- Reference Books
- ERIC documents
- Dissertations
- Rare or valuable manuscripts
- Reserve materials
- Audiovisual materials

University of South Alabama
University Libraries
Mobil, Alabama

Materials Not Available Through ILL

Materials generally not available on interlibrary loan:

- Books owned by the USA Libraries but charged out. These can be recalled at the Circulation Desk or online (see www.southalabama.edu/univlib/scathelp.htm#holds) for instructions.
- Unique copies of theses or dissertations. Most dissertations can be purchased by the patron from University Microfilms.
- Newspapers or manuscripts, unless available in positive microfilm.
- Textbooks currently being used for USA courses.
- Whole volumes or issues of journals.
- Records, tapes, films, software, and other fragile materials.
- Materials for class reserve or group use.
- Archival, genealogical, and local history materials.

- Items of unusual value or rarity.
- Recreational reading titles.
- Journals in Storage; to retrieve these use the Storage Retrieval Request.

DIFFICULT MATERIALS TO BORROW

Kalamazoo College
Upjohn Library
Kalamazoo, Michigan

Libraries rarely or never lend:

- Rare or valuable materials
- Fragile materials
- Reference books
- Manuscripts
- Materials from special collections
- Complete issues of periodicals

Georgia State University
Georgia State University Library
Atlanta, Georgia

What cannot be borrowed?

Requests for articles available via the Library's online databases or within the general collection will not be processed.

GSU course textbooks available through the GSU Bookstore will not be requested unless the bookstore's supply is exhausted. Then ILS staff will attempt to locate a copy to borrow short-term but no renewals will be allowed. The University Library views the purchase of textbooks as part of the student's expected cost of pursuing a degree in higher education.

Entire volumes or issues of journals are rarely lent; photocopies will be requested instead. Generally, the Library cannot obtain genealogical research material; audio-visual materials; computer software; maps; newspapers in the original; rare books; original manuscripts; archival material; recently published items and current best sellers; and reference or non-circulating materials.

Requests that violate copyright law will not be processed. Inter-Library Services must monitor compliance with copyright clearance requirements.

ITEM-ARRIVAL NOTIFICATION

Boston College
Boston College Libraries
Boston, Massachusetts

Notification/Delivery Options

Books

You will be notified by e-mail when book loans arrive. Please bring a copy of your email notification with you when you come to pick up your material. Loans can be picked up at the O'Neill Circulation desk and charged out with your Boston College ID. Loans must be returned to the Circulation desk or to the ILL office by the due date. Your item will be returned to the lending institution ten days from the day it was received if you do not pick it up.

Photocopies

The fastest delivery option is e-mail, so we have made this our standard delivery option. Photocopied material will be e-mailed directly to your Boston College e-mail address indicated on the form as an attachment. In some cases we may have to mail items.

E-mail

Desktop Document Delivery Guidelines

Documents are deleted from the delivery queue after 48 hours. View received documents within 48 hours and within that time frame notify the O'Neill Document Services Center if documents are not legible or need retransmission for other reasons.

Understand and agree to abide by copyright regulations as outlined on the Interlibrary Loan page.

Understand that we make every effort to use BC email accounts only.

Do not print more than one copy.

Do not forward received documents on to other users.

Receiving and Reading Documents Requested via E-mail

You will receive an e-mail from the O'Neill Library with the subject "article delivery—CAUTION—DO NOT USE WEBMAIL TO OPEN". The article you requested will be attached to the e-mail message usually as a PDF file. Please understand that we make every effort to use BC email accounts only.

Storing Image Files

Image files can consume considerable space in your mail. Once you have read and/or printed received documents it is best to delete them from the University's mail server. You may move them to a local folder in your mail or save them to a file on your hard drive if you wish to retain them on your computer.

TURNAROUND TIME

Neumann College
Neumann College Library
Aston, Pennsylvania

Length of Time to Fill a Request

It generally takes a week to 10 days to receive requested materials. Patrons may inquire about the status of an outstanding request by calling the library circulation desk or the ILL desk. In most cases, the library staff will not call you unless there is a problem with your request. Note: Some requests can take up to thirty calendar days to be filled. Please keep this in mind, so you can plan ahead.

Henderson State University
Huie Library
Arkadelphia, Arkansas

How long does it take?

Most requests are processed within 24 hours.

Articles usually take 2 to 10 business days. Length of time depends upon the lending library and its turnaround time.

Turnaround time for books cannot be determined exactly as each lender treats requests differently; in addition, there may be few lenders available. Please allow for at least 2 weeks.

RENEWALS

University of Iowa
University of Iowa Libraries
Iowa City, Iowa

Renewals

Renewals may be requested if "NON-RENEWABLE" is not stipulated as a restriction on the book band. Such requests should be made a few days before the due date by the online form located at www.lib.uiowa.edu/forms/ill_renew.html, in person at the Interlibrary Loan Office, by phone at or by e-mail. Once you have contacted us about a renewal, you may keep the book until our office sends you a message approving the renewal or denying the renewal. If approved, materials must be returned to our office before the new due date provided.

Lansing Community College
Library at Lansing Community College
Lansing, Michigan

May I renew ILL requests?

Yes, however, the lending library may deny a renewal request. If the lending library chooses not to renew an item, you must return it by its due date. Renewals must be requested at least three days before the due date by phoning the ILL office.

LOAN PERIODS

Niagara University
Niagara University Library
Niagara University, New York

How long can I keep ILL Material?

Photocopies of journal articles and purchased dissertations and theses are yours to keep. The due date for books, audiovisual materials and borrowed dissertations and theses is determined by the lending library, not NU, and is usually between 2–4 weeks. Books, audiovisual materials and borrowed dissertations and theses must be returned to the Circulation Desk on or before the due date or you will be charged overdue fines of $1.00 per day. Renewals will be requested in unusual situations only (at the ILL Librarian's discretion) and must be requested before the due date. Many libraries do not allow any renewals, so plan your research accordingly.

Georgia State University
Georgia State University Library
Atlanta, Georgia

Length of Loans

The lending library determines the length of the loan (on average, 2–3 weeks). Lenders may also place certain restrictions on usage, such as "IN LIBRARY USE ONLY" or "NO PHOTOCOPYING." Any restriction will be honored.

RECALLS

Rutgers University
Rutgers University Libraries
Newark, New Jersey

Recalls

All materials loaned are eligible for recall by Rutgers primary borrowers. The Interlibrary Services staff will place the recalls. Recalls will be transmitted to the borrowing library by the fastest method possible.

Kalamazoo College
Upjohn Library
Kalamazoo, Michigan

Recalls and Conditions

Items borrowed through Interlibrary Loan are loaned through the courtesy of other libraries and governed by their loan rules. The lending library may set conditions on use or recall items at any time. Conditions, such as "no renewal" or "in library use only," are indicated on the identification band around each item.

BORROWING AND RETURNING ITEMS FROM LENDER

Lansing Community College
Library at Lansing Community College
Lansing, Michigan

Where do I pick up my requests? Where do I return them?

Photocopies of articles or a chapter in a book (non-returnable items) will be mailed to you. Returnable items such as books requested by students, employees, retirees or alumni need to be picked up at the Library Checkout Desk. For students andemployees who are taking courses off-campus, returnable items can be mailed to a home address provided the faculty or student agrees to return the item(s) to the LCC Library at his/her own expense.

Students and faculty at the Star Institute, Livingston Center (Howell), or Wilson Center (St. Johns) will have courier service to deliver returnable items to them. When it is time to return the items, the same courier service will be used to get the materials back to the LCC Library.

Users who have ILL materials to return and who are on campus need to put the loaned material(s) in a book return drop box (outside of the TLC building or on the 2nd floor in the Library), or give the loaned material(s) to someone at the Checkout Desk.

University of Idaho
University of Idaho Libraries
Moscow, Idaho

How should I return the material?

Return materials by mail, with the slip attached to the front of the book to: Interlibrary Loan office: University of Idaho Library P.O. Box.

Return materials in person, with the slip attached to the front of the book to the University of Idaho Library Circulation desk.

PERIODICAL ARTICLES AVAILABLE TO BORROWER

Kalamazoo College
Upjohn Library
Kalamazoo, Michigan

For Articles:

Check the Electronic Journal Finder. If the article is available in any of Kalamazoo College's Full Text databases, the Electronic Journal Finder will give you links to those databases.

Check the library catalog (Ariadne) to see if the item you need is available.

If a Kalamazoo College Library item is not on the shelf, please ask at the Circulation Desk. It may have been returned recently or it may be missing.

If a Kalamazoo College Library book is checked out, it may be recalled under certain circumstances. Please ask at the Circulation Desk.

Check WestCat, Western Michigan University's online catalog. If the material is available at one of Western Michigan University's libraries, you cannot request it through interlibrary loan; you must go to Western to retrieve it (see Directions to Western's Libraries). Kalamazoo College students and faculty have borrowing privileges at Western Michigan University's libraries upon presentation of a valid Kalamazoo College identification card (see Borrowing Privileges at WMU).

Be sure you have a complete bibliographic citation of the item(s) you wish to request.

Connecticut College
Charles E. Shain Library
New London, Connecticut

Journal Articles supplied through ILL

To expedite orders for copies of journal articles, please provide all of the information requested on the ILL Journal Article Request Form. Delays in ordering the item by the ILL office or delays in processing by supplying libraries can arise from the lack of volume number, page numbers, article title, etc. Providing your source of information can be of help to the ILL staff if the citation is inaccurate and needs to be checked. If you need help interpreting citations from various indices and databases, please ask a reference librarian.

According to copyright restrictions, institutions reserve the right to refuse copying orders. Please read the copyright notice on the ILL journal article request form before submitting your requests.

To request an article, log on to the ILL System.

BORROWING THESES AND DISSERTATIONS

University of South Alabama
University Libraries
Mobil, Alabama

Dissertations

A. Borrow through ILL: Some libraries will loan their dissertations if they have a circulating copy. Their loan charges vary from $5.00–$20.00. Delivery could take several weeks.

B. Purchase from UMI

Ask the ILL office to order a copy through UMI Dissertation Express.

Estimated Cost: $28.00. Your library account will be billed. Delivery will be 3–4 days.

Call University Microfilms International at (800) 521-3042 or (800) 521-0600 ext. 3781, or fax them at (800) 308-1586.

Estimated cost: Photocopy $41.00, Film $37.00. Rush delivery is extra. Have your charge card ready. Delivery within 14 working days to 3 weeks.

Order online from UMI. Locate the title on Dissertation Abstracts/Digital Dissertations database on the library's homepage (Available on campus and remotely with USA ID.)

Cost: See UMI's price list for hard copies at www.umi.com/hp/Support/DServices/order/

Some dissertations can be ordered from UMI in PDF format (indicated by a icon next to the record) and downloaded to your computer. When you order a digital dissertation, UMI sends you an e-mail giving the address from which to download your dissertation and a PIN that identifies your order. This PIN is not restricted by IP address or by computer, so you can order from a library computer and then go home or to your office and download the dissertation. The price of a dissertation in this format is calculated when you add the dissertation to your shopping cart. It can always be removed if you decide the cost is too much. Dissertations from the University of South Alabama are free for USA faculty, staff and students.

Chapter 38

DOCUMENT DELIVERY

DOCUMENT DELIVERY POLICY

University of Arizona
The University of Arizona Library
Tucson, Arizona

What Is Express Documents?

Express Documents is a service that provides delivery of UA-owned materials.

Articles, book chapters and books are delivered for all current UA-affiliated customers.

Articles and book chapters can be delivered for customers not affiliated with the University of Arizona.

Express Documents Fees

Express Documents fees are as follows:

Current UA-affiliated customers:

Articles and book chapters delivered via desktop delivery: $6.00 for the first 15 pages and $0.25 for each additional page per article.

Articles and book chapters delivered by mail: $6.00 for the first 15 pages and $0.25 for each additional page per article, plus shipping and handling.

On-campus delivery of books: $6.00 for the first book, $2.00 for each additional book.

Off-campus delivery of books: $6.00 for the first book, $2.00 for each additional book, plus shipping and handling.

NOTE FOR UA SOUTH FACULTY, STAFF AND STUDENTS: Currently, the fee for delivery of articles and books to UA South faculty, students and staff is covered by the UA South Campus.

Other customers:

Articles delivered via desktop delivery: $6.00 per item for the first 15 pages. 25 cents for each additional page.

Articles by mail: $6.00 (plus shipping and handling) per item for the first 15 pages. 25 cents for each additional page.

NOTE: Book delivery is not available for customers not affiliated with the University of Arizona.

Items Available for Request

Express Documents can provide the following material:

- Books (current UA-affiliated customers only)
- Articles
- Theses and Dissertations (current UA-affiliated customers only)
- Microforms (case by case basis). Please contact us for more information. (distance users only)
- Book Chapters
- Reports
- Maps (copies only)
- Reference material (copies only)

We cannot provide the following types of material:

- Special Collections items (photocopies of select material MAY be possible)
- Media (Videos, DVD, Laserdiscs, etc.) NOTE: If you are a faculty member and need a media item for instructional use, please contact us.
- CCP Rare Books
- Main or Science Reserves
- Music Closed Stacks
- Eligible Customers

All University of Arizona faculty, staff, graduate students, undergraduate students and visiting scholars with a valid CatCard are eligible to request material through Express Documents.

Library customers who are not affiliated with the University of Arizona are currently only eligible for the Express Documents article service.

Average time to fill a request:

Articles will be delivered electronically within 24 hours of the initial request.

Books will be shipped to the patron's address via Federal Express and should arrive within 3 to 4 days.

How long can items be used?:

Initial lending periods for books are the same as books checked out in person at the UA Library. Click here for information regarding loan periods.

Articles will remain accessible for 3 weeks through your Express Documents page.

Connecticut College
Charles E. Shain Library
New London, Connecticut

Commercial Document Delivery

There are commercial suppliers of journal articles that offer the delivery of articles to individual customers for a fee. There are always costs associated with the services provided by these companies but they can tailor services to your specific needs. Commercial suppliers can receive requests directly from you by various methods. Usually the companies can supply the articles (if they own the journal) within 48–72 hours by fax or they can mail the article to you.

By using commercial suppliers directly, you are bypassing the Interlibrary Loan Office and its services. The ILL Office will not assume any responsibilities for any transactions. You are assuming all financial obligations and any questions or problems should be resolved directly with the companies. Although the ILL Office occasionally uses commercial suppliers to fill requests, this office is not endorsing any particular company.

Grand Valley State University
Zumberge Library
Allendale, MI

First Time User Registration for Document Delivery

To request an item through Document Delivery, you must first identify yourself to the library's Document Delivery system. To do this you fill out a registration form using your Web browser. Registration has three purposes:

Entering your personal information into the Document Delivery system means you will not have to supply the information again when making future requests.

Having your e-mail and regular mail addresses on file with the Document Delivery system enables us to notify you promptly and deliver materials accurately when your request arrives in the library.

By logging in with your Username and Password, you will have secure access to information about your requests. You will also be able to review the list of items you have requested in the past.

About Your Username and Password

This is a Grand Valley State University service so you will log in with your GVSU Network Username and Password. This is the same username and password required by Blackboard, computer labs, and office computers.

Forgot your password? Instructions for: GVSU Students, Faculty & Staff.

Important Copyright Information

Warning Concerning Copyright Restrictions

The copyright law of the United States (Title 17, United States Code) governs the making of photocopies or other reproductions of copyrighted materials.

Under certain conditions specified in the law, libraries and archives are authorized to furnish a photocopy or other reproduction. One of these specified conditions is that the photocopy or reproduction is not to be "used for any purpose other than private study, scholarship, or research." If a user makes a request for, or later uses, a photocopy or reproduction for purposes in excess of "fair use," that user may be liable for copyright infringement.

This institution reserves the right to refuse to accept a copying order if, in its judgment, fulfillment of the order would involve violation of copyright law.

Chapter 39

FORMS

ILL REQUEST FORM

Columbia College Chicago
Columbia College Library
Chicago, Illinois

Interlibrary Loan Book/ERIC Document/Dissertation Request Form

Use this form to submit a request to borrow books, ERIC Documents, or Dissertations from other non-I-Share member libraries. Your request will be sent to and processed by the Interlibrary Loan Office. Requests generally take between 7–14 days to be filled. Consult the Borrowing From Other Libraries page for more information.

Stop by the Reference Desk (2nd floor) for assistance in completing this form or your book citation.

Interlibrary Loan Book Request Form

*REQUIRED FIELDS

After completing the form, please scroll to the bottom and click on the "Submit" button.

Your Name: (Last name, First name)* _____

Address:* _____

Street Line 1: _____

Street Line 2: _____

City: _____ State: _____ Zip: _____

Telephone: (please include area code)* _____

Email Address:* _____

How would you prefer to be contacted?* Email _____ Phone _____ US Mail _____

Columbia College Chicago Status: * Student _____ Faculty_____ Staff_____

Book/Dissertation/ERIC Document Title:* _____

_____

_____

Author: (last name, first name)* _____

Edition: _____

Publisher:* _____

Date:* _____

OCLC Number: _____
(if available)

ERIC Document Number:_____
(if applicable)

Where did you find this citation? _____
(i.e. in the MLA database, in a bibliography, etc.)

Need by Date (mm/dd/yyyy):* _____

Note: The "Need by Date" will not affect the time it takes to receive Interlibrary Loan materials. Instead, the date entered in this field indicates at what date we should stop searching for an item because it will no longer be of use to you.

COPYRIGHT NOTICE: The copyright law of the United States (Title 17, United States Code) governs the making of photocopies or other reproductions of copyrighted material. Under certain conditions specified in the law, libraries and archives are authorized to furnish a photocopy or other reproduction. One of these specified conditions is that the photocopy or reproduction is not to be "used for any purpose other than private study, scholarship, or research." If a user makes a request for, or later uses, a photocopy or reproduction for purposes in excess of "fair use," that user may be liable for copyright infringement. This institution reserves the right to refuse to accept a copying order if, in its judgment, fulfillment of the order would involve violation of copyright law.

Lake Sumter Community College
Lake Sumter Community College Libraries
Sumterville, Florida

Interlibrary Loan Request

Interlibrary loan services are available to faculty, staff and LSCC students currently enrolled in credit classes. Requests must be related to LSCC course work. All requesters must provide a valid ID card number. If you do not have a validated ID card, contact the library at 365-3563. Submit one request for each item.

- Check the LINCC Catalog to be sure LSCC does not own the item.
- We attempt to borrow from libraries which DO NOT CHARGE a fee. You will be notified if a fee is required. If charges are accepted, you will be responsible for payment upon arrival of the material.
- Students may request 5 items per research project.
- Average time to fill requests is 6–7 days. Some requests may take up to 3 weeks.
- Do not request reference books or audiovisual materials.
- You will be notified by telephone or e-mail when the item arrives. Please pick up the item promptly.
- For further information, call 365-3527 or 365-3563.

Requester's Information

Name:	ID Barcode #
Address:	E-Mail:
City:	Home Phone:
State:	Work Phone:
Zip:	Fax:
Not Needed After:	Campus:
Status:	Where you wish to pick up the item:

Course for which
material is needed:

Book Request

Title:	[ ]	Author:	[ ]
Publisher:	[ ]	Publication Year:	[ ]
ISBN (if known):	[ ]	This edition only: ○Yes ○No	

Article Request (do not abbreviate titles)

Periodical Title:	[ ]	Author:	[ ]
Article Title:	[ ]	Volume:	[ ]
No:	[ ]	Date:	[ ]
Pages:	[ ]	ISSN (if known):	[ ]

Source of citation (if FirstSearch, provide title of database): [ ]

Copy of online citation (if from an electronic database, please copy and paste complete citation)

[ ]

Copyright Restrictions

The copyright law of the United States (Title 17, U.S. Code) governs the making of photocopies or other reproductions of copyrighted material. Under certain conditions specified in the law, libraries and archives are authorized to furnish a photocopy or other reproduction. One of these specified conditions is that the photocopy or reproduction is not to be "used for any purpose other than private study, scholarship, or research." If a user makes a request for, or later uses, a photocopy or reproduction for purposes in excess of "fair use," that user may be liable for copyright infringement. This institution reserves the right to refuse to accept a copying request if, in its judgment, fulfillment of the order would involve violation of copyright law.

By submitting this request I verify that I have read the above copyright restrictions and agree to comply.

[Submit Request]

DOCUMENT DELIVERY FORM

Xavier University Library Document Delivery

Journal Article and Conference Proceedings Request Form

Before requesting a journal article or conference proceeding please search the Electronic Journal Locator for electronic holdings and then the for print, microfiche and microfilm holdings. If you do not find what you need in the Electronic Journal Locator or XPLORE Library Catalog, complete the form below. Required information is marked with an asterisk (*). Requests may take 2 weeks or more for ordering, shipping and processing, so please plan ahead. Need more information? View instructions for filling out this request form, call the document delivery office or contact the librarian at the reference desk

Author	[ ]
Article Title*	[ ]
Journal Title*	[ ]
Date Published	[ ]
Volume	[ ]
Issue	[ ]
Pages	[ ]

Cited In [   ]

Comments [   ]

ISSN [   ]

OCLC# [   ]

Cancel if not filled by [   ] [   ] [   ]

The copyright law of the United States (Title 17, United States Code), governs the making of photocopies or other reproductions of copyrighted material. Under certain conditions specified in the law, libraries and archives are authorized to furnish a photocopy or other reproduction. One of these specified conditions is that the photocopy or other reproduction is not to be "used for any purpose other than private study, scholarship, or research." If a user makes a request for, or later uses, a photocopy or reproduction for purposes in excess of "fair use," that user may be liable for copyright infringement. This institution reserves the right to refuse to accept a copying order, if, in its judgement, fulfillment of the order would involve violation of copyright law.

SEARCH THE LIBRARY CATALOG FOR THIS ITEM

For example, type "Jane Smith" and then press the TAB key.

Your Name: [   ]

For example, type "312312" and then press the TAB key.

Barcode (numerals only) [   ]

SUBMIT THIS REQUEST

DOCUMENT DELIVERY FROM REMOTE STACKS FORM

Document Delivery Services: Remote Stacks   Monday, June 12, 2006

Journal Request   Hours Today: 8am to 10pm

Use the request form below to request a journal from remote stacks. Requested journal(s) will be available for pick-up by the next business day at the circulation desk.

Name: [   ]

Email: [   ]

Phone: [   ]

Status: Undergraduate ○   Faculty/Staff ○

       Graduate ○   Other ○

Journal Title: [   ]

Volume: [   ]

Issue: [   ]

Date: [   ]

Comments:

[   ]

Submit

Clear

Part XI
Internet and Electronic Resources

Chapter 40

INTERNET AND ELECTRONIC RESOURCES ADMINISTRATIVE GUIDELINES

ACCESS TO ELECTRONIC RESOURCES

Lane Community College
Lane Community College Library
Eugene, Oregon

Electronic Database Searching

LCC Library provides access to many electronic databases as part of its reference services. This policy is intended to provide the fairest and broadest access to these services for our patrons, consistent with efficient use of the resource.

1. LCC Library undertakes to make database searching freely and equally available to all LCC students, staff, and public patrons.
2. Electronic database searching is free of charge to LCC students, staff, and public patrons.
3. Any search for which LCC Library incurs a database searching charge shall be performed by designated Library staff only. Searches which are free or which incur a minimal charge may be performed by the patron.
4. LCC Library may, at the discretion of the Library Director, perform database searching for outside organizations, businesses, and individuals. These patrons must be a resident or based in the LCC service area. LCC Library reserves the right to regulate the volume of such searches and to charge a reasonable fee to recover costs.
5. LCC Library reserves the right to regulate database searching to ensure efficient and economical use of the resource, consistent with the best possible service to students, staff, and public patrons.

Tulane University
Howard-Tilton Memorial Library
New Orleans, Louisiana

Computing Environment

Computers in the first-floor Reference area are equipped with Internet access and the Microsoft Office XP suite (including Word, Excel, Access and Power Point), and are for use by Tulane students, faculty and staff. These computers require a login using a Tulane RS6000 (Webmail) user ID and password. Members of the Tulane community may use these computers for any academic purpose including library research and writing.

In addition, a limited number of computers are available throughout the library for use without a Tulane login. These computers are equipped with a Web browser only, and are intended for academic research purposes such as library catalog and database searching, Internet searching, or brief e-mail.

Guests (Non-Tulane Library Users)

Guests may access the non-login computers for academic research only. Use of library computers by guests for non-academic purposes (i.e., recreation) is expressly prohibited, and guests may be asked to verify that they are using a computer for academic research purposes only. Tulane students, faculty and staff have priority over guests in cases where an insufficient number of computers are available in the library. We reserve the right to limit the amount of time that a guest may occupy a computer; normally this should not exceed two hours per day.

ACCESS TO LIBRARY SUBSCRIPTION DATABASES

Suffolk University
Mildred F. Sawyer Library
Boston, Massachusetts

Alumni Access to Licensed/Subscription Library Databases

Because of copyright licensing agreements with the information vendors, these databases are available only to current students and faculty of the College of Arts and Sciences and the Sawyer School of Management.

Syracuse University
Syracuse University Library
Syracuse, New York

Policy on Access to Licensed Web Resources

Syracuse University, on behalf of its Library, licenses a variety of research materials (databases, electronic journals and books, and other Internet and web-accessible resources) for online access through the Internet and Web. Anyone using a campus library or workstation may access these resources on site. However, only currently enrolled Syracuse University students, faculty, and staff are eligible to access licensed resources from off-campus locations. Access control (authentication) is required and specified in our contracts with the vendors of these resources.

Syracuse University affiliation is maintained and tracked in University systems such as the ID card system and PeopleSoft. Patron records for SU-affiliated users in the Library's online system are derived from University systems and include name, address, SU ID number, status, and an expiration date. The system deployed by the Library to provide authentication for remote access uses the SU ID number as the login ID. For this reason, it is incumbent upon all users to keep this number confidential and to report missing or stolen IDs as soon as possible.

The Library takes seriously its legal responsibility to comply with contracts and abide by current copyright law and is diligent in maintaining its database of eligible users. The Library works closely with other University units to resolve status and classification problems for eligible users. The Library is also contractually obligated to investigate reported misuse of licensed resources. The consequences of willfully breaching contracts could be significant for the University community, including the loss of campus access to library supported research databases. Violators of this policy may be subject to University disciplinary policies, criminal prosecution, and/or be liable for damages to the fullest extent provided by law.

Rockefeller University
Rockefeller University Library
New York, New York

Guidelines for Use of Licensed Electronic Resources

To provide access to electronic resources, the Rockefeller University Library is required to agree to the terms and conditions detailed in the license for each of those resources. As set forth in the Rockefeller University Code of Conduct and the Computing and Electronic Communications Policy, the community's responsible use of campus resources, and compliance with applicable laws, regulations and contractual obligations that affect them, is essential to the operation and reputation of the University.

The use of licensed electronic resources is restricted by agreements made with the producers of these materials or any element thereof (collectively "Materials"). Users of electronic resources are subject to the same copyright laws that govern the use of print materials. Use of electronic resources is governed by both U.S. copyright law AND terms and restrictions of the license agreements, as negotiated and accepted by the Rockefeller University Library on behalf of the RU community. Some common restrictions are:

> The Materials may be used for scholarly, educational and/or scientific research purposes; any selling, distributing, licensing, or renting of Material for commercial uses is prohibited.

> The Materials may be used by or made available to only authorized users. Authorized users are faculty, students, and staff of the Rockefeller University and those who have been allowed access to the library's computers.

> The Materials may not be systematically downloaded, electronically copied, distributed (including, but not limited to, mounting any part of the Materials on any electronic network, bulletin board, Web sites), or archived. Only a reasonable number of records, articles or chapters may be downloaded for personal use in the conduct of the Authorized user's research. Use of web crawlers, robots, or any other software packages or systematic searching tools or programs is forbidden.

> The proprietary and/or copyright notices, author attribution or disclaimers on the Materials may not be deleted or modified.

Users are expected to comply with terms and conditions of site licenses, and any copyright infringement or misuse of the electronic materials may result in the termination of access to those materials for the entire RU community.

Complete text of the U.S. Copyright Law is available at: www.copyright.gov/title17/

If you have any questions regarding e-resources licenses or restrictions please contact [staff info].

University of Iowa
University of Iowa Libraries
Iowa City, Iowa

Access to Commercial Databases by People Not Affiliated with the University

The University of Iowa Libraries provides access to not only the UI Libraries online catalog, but to many other online and electronic resources as well. Most of these resources—bibliographic and/or full text databases—are commercial products for which the UI enters into a licensing agreement with the business provider. This license agreement, for which the Libraries pays a fee, permits access to the commercial product for students, faculty, and staff of the

University of Iowa and, for some resources, to onsite users of a campus library. Therefore, the UI Libraries is not legally able to provide access to alumni, independent scholars, contributors or Iowa citizens where a commercial product has a license agreement that restricts access to specific authorized users, or to those who are physically in a campus library. It is important for alumni and others with ties to the University to understand that we are unable to provide open access to these commercial products that are produced and licensed to many markets (e.g., health care professionals, businesses, other academic institutions, etc.) for a profit. Everything that is on the Internet is definitely not free and those electronic resources that have greatest value to a research institution are often very costly.

University at Buffalo
University at Buffalo Libraries
Buffalo, New York

Electronic Resources Access and Restrictions

Access to electronic journals and article databases is available both in-library and from off-campus locations for UB faculty, staff and currently registered UB students. Guests and alumni may access electronic resources by applying for a courtesy Workstation Access Card or a Guest Borrower Library Card. Due to licensing restrictions, guests and alumni are limited to in-library access to electronic resources. Additional information can be found at the University Libraries Policy for Use of Online Information.

GOALS AND OBJECTIVES OF WEB SITES

Golden Gate University
Golden Gate University Library
San Francisco, California

Goals and Objectives—GGU University Library Web Site

Through the GGU University Library web site and other GGU programs and services, the University Library staff strive to provide research and information support for the GGU University community, including faculty, students, staff, and alumni. Please let us know your suggestions for how we can better address your needs.

Goal of the GGU University Library web site is to provide faculty, students, staff, alumni, and other users with starting points and search strategies they can use effectively even as the universe of information resources continues to evolve. GGU University library staff see the web site as a teaching tool to help faculty and students at all GGU campuses develop search strategies that will take advantage of the wealth of resources available in many formats. We work closely with faculty to develop research strategy guides and web sites to support their courses. We want to help our students learn to research effectively, evaluate information astutely, and document their sources clearly, as we use the web site to further the mission of the University Library.

The GGU University Library web site draws on the work of many here in the University, and tries to tap the wealth of resources created by others for Internet researching. We have high ideals, but a limited staff, and a pragmatic approach. We are learning as we go. We want to make the site as useful as possible, while we learn. We have begun with some macro links to great directories such as the Virtual Library and the Social Science Information Gateway. We are also putting in specific links so students and faculty can go quickly to resources they want. We are less concerned at this point with hierarchical relationships and exhaustive listings than with providing research strategies and starting points that will help users navigate the ever changing universe of information resources. We rejoice in the opportunity to be redundant, referring to sites as often and in as many places as we think may be useful.

Library staff monitor professional conferences and current alert services such as Scout Report, Librarian's Index to the Internet, New at Yahoo, etc. for resources that may be of use to students, faculty, and staff at GGU, and to the larger academic and business community. Librarians welcome the opportunity to work with faculty, identifying resources for their courses. Work with students, staff, and other web site users also leads to great discoveries.

As we go, we hope to find better ways to organize and format individual pages, and we especially want to integrate in guides to print sources in a way that does not discourage our clientele but rather encourages them to take full advantage of the broad spectrum of resources available. What else should we strive for, and how can we best achieve our goals? Send your suggestions to the Eclectic Strategist. She needs all the help she can get!

Library Web Development outlines GGU University Library's current process of reviewing and revising goals, objectives, structure, content, design, style, procedures and maintenance. What follows is a description of the early development of this web site.

While teaching Internet search strategies workshops and working with faculty and students in classes or at the Reference Desk, I noticed that many were "skimming the Net" using search engines to search web sites, but were not pulling up some of the deeper, richer resources on the Web. I heard one faculty member exclaim "there must be a better way to search than web search engines!" Actually, there are many ways. But how do we make those ways easy to use for faculty and students? And how do we make the non-Internet resources that are still essential to research easy to access, as well?

I also heard complaints from students and faculty such as "I have to click and click on one page after another before getting to content."

In developing the GGU University Library Web Site, we are trying to address the challenges and frustrations faculty and students have, and also make some of the deeper resources of the Internet—and other formats—easily available.

Georgia State University
Georgia State University Library
Atlanta, Georgia

Purpose: The purpose of the The University Library Web site is to support the Mission of The University Library by providing Web services that support the teaching, learning, research, service, and informational needs of the Georgia State University community. The University Library Web site supports this purpose by:

Providing electronic access to library resources, selected web sites, librarian-produced content, and other appropriate information

Providing electronic access to library services that support remote users, specifically through Web applications and forms that provide interactive, transactional, or communication capabilities

Providing intellectual access by serving as an instruction and learning tool

Promoting the full and effective use of library services and resources

Providing information about services, resources, policies, and activities of The University Library.

Compliance: The University Library Web site is an official publication of the organization. All Web pages contribute to the organizational "voice" of our institution and reflect on our institution's professionalism and credibility. Anyone publishing, editing, or contributing content to the Web site must follow this Policy and the associated Web Development Standards and Procedure Manual. Any page(s) not in compliance will be removed from the site per the procedures found in the Web Development Standards and Procedure Manual.

Design, Development, and Content Policies: To support the highest standards of academic library Web development, it is the policy of those that create and maintain the library Web site to:

Provide well designed Web page interfaces, navigation menus, and pages that download and work effectively for user Web devices

Provide Web content that is current, accurate, and has link integrity. Content created should be minimal in its use of academic, library, or technical jargon, but not unnecessarily over-simplified. All content should have identifiable authors, editors, or contributors embedded in the page to establish credibility and a contact point for the content in question

Provide a Web presence that supports current development and protocol standards from W3C and is compliant with Priority 1 and 2 levels of the W3C Check-list. This practice will bring us in compliance with Section 508 (www.section508.gov)

Provide a Web presence that displays on the most commonly used Web browsers and display resolutions and degrades gracefully on older browsers

Provide Web services designed around usability studies and evidence-based research to ensure that our Web presence is user-centric

Provide Web content contributors and authors with standards, procedures, and guidance through the availability of a Web Development Standards and Procedure Manual

Provide Web content contributors and authors with development support and training which incorporates the Web Development Standards and Procedure Manual

Provide a Web presence that complies with organizational standards and technical specifications by vesting oversight and management of the Web Development Standards and Procedure Manual in the Technology Planning Committee

Provide those who create and maintain the library Web site with the means to petition for changes to the Web Development Standards and Procedure Manual through the Technology Planning Committee.

Use of Images on the Library Web Site: All images used in the library Web site that are not created or owned by Georgia State University (GSU) Library or Georgia State University are believed to be in the public domain. Any image that is not in the public domain, created by GSU Library or GSU, or that has not been cleared with permission for use on the site will be removed immediately.

All images not created or owned by GSU Library or GSU that are used in library pages must either be in the public domain or used with the written permission of the copyright holder. Each image must be properly cited and include information such as where it was obtained, its copyright status, and any permission obtained regarding its use. If the author cannot verify that an image is in the public domain or get permission from the copyright holder, then that image cannot be used on the library Web site.

The use of images and graphics taken randomly from the Internet is not within fair use guidelines, and as such is an infringement of copyright, are not lawfully acquired, and do not fit within the limited distribution guidelines required for fair use.

Florida International University
Florida International University Libraries
Miami, Florida

The purpose of Internet/World Wide Web access in the FIU Libraries is to make available Internet resources that will support and enhance the educational, instructional, and research activities of the University Community on and off campus.

The University Libraries seek to protect First Amendment Rights, including freedom of access to information, for users; also, the individual right to privacy. However, those using the Internet must be sensitive to the fact that workstations are in public areas and screen images may be viewed by others. Also, electronic media do not afford privacy in communication, especially with respect to agencies other than the library indispensable for electronic communication.

FIU library staff offer assistance and instruction in the use of the Internet as a research and information resource. They do not censor access or protect patrons from information that they may find offensive.

As with other library resources, parents, legal guardians, or care providers are responsible for their children's use of the Internet and for intentional or inadvertent viewing or reading of other patrons' screens by accompanying children.

Materials obtained or copied on the Internet may be subject to copyright laws that govern making reproductions of copyrighted works. A work protected by copyright may not be copied without permission of the copyright owner unless the proposed use falls within the definition of "Fair Use." Patrons are responsible for compliance with all international, national, and state laws governing copyrighted materials.

Under no circumstances will the FIU Libraries have any liability for lost profits or for any direct or indirect special, punitive, or consequential damages, or any liability to any third party (even if the Libraries are advised of the possibility of such danger) arising from use of its connection to the Internet.

Consistent with the above, the FIU Libraries adhere to the ALA Library Bill of Rights. Internet users should, however, be aware of applicable University regulations governing display of sexually suggestive materials in the workplace as well as in public areas of the library and be reminded, once again, that the purpose of providing Internet access is to further the instruction and research mission of the University and those who comprise its community.

DISCLAIMER FOR LIBRARY INTERNET SITE

University of California Berkeley
University of California Berkeley Libraries
Berkeley, California

Disclaimer

Library websites developed by staff include selected links to Internet sites. Choosing to link to a website does not imply editorial or other control over linked-to websites and is not an endorsement of the website. The Library cannot warrant that its website, the server(s) that make it available, or any links from its site to other websites are free of viruses or other harmful components.

University of Alaska Anchorage
Alaska Pacific University
Consortium Library
Anchorage, Alaska

Disclaimer

The Internet, a global electronic network with a highly diverse user population, is one resource available through the Consortium Library. The Library does not monitor and has no control over information accessed through the Internet and cannot be held responsible for its content. Not all sources on the Internet provide accurate, complete, or current information. Users need to be good information consumers, questioning the validity of the information found. Comments on the contents of any Web page should be directed to the appropriate page authors.

The Consortium Library upholds the principle of the Freedom to read and adheres to the Library Bill of Rights. The Library is committed to providing an atmosphere that promotes learning, research, and intellectual freedom; encourages access to knowledge; challenges censorship; and allows sharing of information.

USE OF LIBRARY SUBSCRIPTION DATABASES

University of Alaska Anchorage
Alaska Pacific University
Consortium Library
Anchorage, Alaska

Database Restrictions

Many of the databases accessible through the Consortium Library are governed by subscription and license agreements to which the Library and its users are legally bound. These agreements identify who may use the databases, for what purposes they may be used, what uses are prohibited, what copyright restrictions may apply, and what the vendors are not responsible for. The following briefly summarizes the main points governing database use. Please be aware that by using any of the databases you agree to abide by these conditions.

Anyone may access the Library's databases from within the Library itself. For information on who is authorized to connect to which databases by remote access, go to the Database listing page for information on each database.

In general, authorized users may:

Use the databases for educational, research, scholarly, and/or personal purposes.

Search the databases, as well as retrieve, display, download, and print results.

Make one copy of any search output in electronic form to be used for editing or temporary storage only.

Make a limited number of hard copies of any search output that does not contain a significant portion of a database.

Download, email to self, and/or print single copies of individual works.

Users may not :

Use the databases for commercial purposes.

Use the databases in any way to offend or harass others.

Perform mass mailings of full-text articles or other search results.

Post full-text articles or other search results to websites or listservs.

Users have the responsibility to :

Abide by copyright laws.

Cite the source where they obtained the material.

Be aware that if the databases contain abstracts, they should consult the full-text material (the actual article or document) before reaching or suggesting conclusions.

Please note that neither the Library nor the database suppliers guarantee the authority, accuracy, or comprehensiveness of the information.

Chapter 41

GUIDELINES FOR USE OF INTERNET RESOURCES

ACCEPTABLE USE OF ELECTRONIC RESOURCES

Henderson State University
Huie Library
Arkadelphia, Arkansas

Internet Policy

Internet access is available to HSU/OBU students, faculty, and staff as well as to the community. Priority of use will be given to members of the HSU community. Community patrons may be asked to vacate terminals if HSU patrons are waiting.

If you are affiliated with Henderson State University, login using your computer account. Otherwise, a librarian will log you on to a computer. Failure to logout will allow others access to your computer account.

Terminals are provided for the community and may be used for an unregulated time period. Community patrons may be asked to vacate these terminals if other patrons are waiting. Priority use will be given to members of the HSU community.

Student email accounts provided by Henderson State University and web-based email access is available on specific computers.

Huie Library does not censor its resources, regardless of format. The library is responsible only for the content of those pages bearing its name. The library is not responsible for the accuracy of information found on the Internet. Patrons should evaluate sites for content and accuracy. Selected resources may be offensive to some patrons; parents are responsible for their children's use of the Internet.

Note: In compliance with Arkansas Act 1533 of 2001, patrons under the age of 18 will have Internet privileges suspended if using public terminals to access sexually explicit websites. Repeat offenses will result in revocation of Internet privileges.

The library's Internet resources are limited; use of these resources must support educational research. Chat, Games, and/or FTP are prohibited.

Misuse of Internet terminals may result in revocation of Internet privileges. Misuse includes:

chat

games

attempting to reconfigure workstations

loading additional software

destruction of or damage to equipment, data or software

violation of computer system security

unauthorized use of accounts or network identification assigned to others

unauthorized copying of copyright-protected material

disruption or unauthorized monitoring of electronic communication

violation of software license agreements

harassment of others

violation of another's privacy

Printing is available at the Reference Desk at a charge of $.05 per page.

Due to the emerging nature of this service, policies are subject to change without notice and at the Library's discretion.

Binghamton University
Binghamton University Libraries
Binghamton, New York

Acceptable use of Electronic Resources

All "BU only" resources are library subscriptions that are accessible only from the Binghamton University network or from an Internet Service Provider using the library proxy server. Access and use is restricted by license agreements to purposes of research, teaching, and private study by current BU faculty, staff, and students. The following are strictly prohibited: all commercial use; copying or tampering with any software or code used to display and/or run the resources; the systematic downloading, copying or distributing of information (including for use in course packs); and removing or altering copyright notices. Misuse of these resources violates the terms of BU's license agreements. Violation of a licensing agreement could result in termination of the resource to the entire campus community. See also Binghamton University Copyright Policy

Acceptable Use of Library Computers and the Network

Access to information technology is essential to the Binghamton University Libraries mission to provide leadership to the University community in accessing and using information resources for teaching, learning and research. The preservations of that privilege by the full community requires that each faculty member, staff member, student, and other authorized user comply with institutional and external standards for appropriate use.

East Carolina University
Joyner Library
Greenville North Carolina

Electronic Resources Use Guidelines

To provide access to subscription databases and electronic journals, Joyner Library is required to sign licenses agreeing to certain terms and conditions regarding the use of the information or data. The guidelines below provide a general outline of acceptable and non-acceptable uses of our electronic resources. Many publishers are aware of the technological potential for violating license restrictions and may monitor the use of their products to ensure that the terms of the agreement are being followed. If these restrictions are violated the provider may terminate access to the database or journal to the entire University.

Authorized users are:

- Currently enrolled full or part-time ECU students
- ECU faculty (full or part-time)
- ECU staff (full or part-time)
- Walk-in library users, while in the building

Off campus/remote use is:

- Available for most Web-based electronic resources
- Limited to ECU students, faculty and staff with current ECU e-mail accounts
- Available to authorized users through Joyner library's proxy server
- Is not available to users with Area Resident or Educator cards

Acceptable uses:

- Print one copy of an article for personal use (scholarly, educational, or non-commercial research)
- Download one copy of an article for personal use (scholarly, educational, or non-commercial research)
- Send one copy of an article to an authorized user
- Fulfill interlibrary loan requests as permitted under negotiated contracts

Prohibited uses:

- Systematic copying or downloading (i.e., downloading/printing/copying all the articles in a journal issue)
- Removal or alteration of the copyright notice on any licensed materials
- Sending a copy of licensed material to an unauthorized user either in print or in electronic format (this includes sending licensed material to a listserv or mass e-mail)
- Making licensed material available through an unsecured Internet server
- Adapting, abridging or altering the licensed materials
- Selling, distributing or otherwise commercially profiting from use of licensed material

All use of licensed materials is subject to copyright law (title 17, U.S. Code). Any questions regarding specific licenses should be directed to the Head of Acquisitions.

PROHIBITED USES OF ELECTRONIC RESOURCES

Colorado State University Pueblo
Colorado State University Pueblo Library
Pueblo, Colorado

Definition

For purposes of this policy statement, electronic communications includes but is not limited to electronic mail, Internet services, voice mail, audio and video conferencing, and facsimile messages that are sent or received by faculty, staff, students, and other authorized users of university resources.

Policy

Ownership of Electronic Communication and Permissible Uses

The University provides various forms of electronic communications for the purposes of conducting academic pursuits and other university business. The records created are the property of the University, not of the individuals sending or receiving such messages. Authorization to utilize electronic and voice mail is established by the Computer Center with right of appeal to the Office of the Provost. Individuals who are authorized to use electronic and voice mail may make incidental and occasional personal use of these facilities when such use does not generate a direct cost to the University. In doing so, users acknowledge the organization's ownership of the systems and its rights with regard to use.

Prohibited Uses

Prohibited uses include but are not limited to:

Commercial purposes or other personal gain.

Use of electronic communications to send copies of documents in violation of copyright laws.

The transmission of information, access to which is restricted by laws or regulations.

Use of electronic communications to intimidate, threaten, or harass other individuals, or to interfere with the ability of others to conduct university business.

The forging of communication so it appears to be from someone else.

Obtaining or attempting to obtain access to data, files, other electronic communication, etc. other than that for which one has proper authorization. Any attempt to breach security measures to access or acquire any electronically stored information one is not authorized to obtain is prohibited. These acts are prohibited regardless of methods utilized.

The term "access" includes reading, deleting, moving, changing access privileges, or affecting files, data, etc. in any unauthorized manner.

Use of chain letters.

Electronic communications conduct is expected to meet the standards of conduct, laws, regulations, etc. published in official University, State or Federal documents including but not limited to the CSU-Pueblo catalog, the Faculty Handbook, Colorado State Employees Handbook, etc.

Union College
Jones Learning Resource Center
Barbourville, Kentucky

Sharing Information and Communicating with Computers

Computers are particularly valuable resources for the sharing and communicating of programs, data, and texts. Thus, it is a serious matter when computer users take inappropriate advantage of the ease of communication that computers provide.

The sharing/serving of copyrighted materials such as software, music, movies, etc. is covered by the Copyright Law of the United States of America and Related Laws contained in Title 17 of the United States Code, including the Digital Millennium Copyright Act. Each network user will be held responsible for the material transmitted on the campus network and are subject to any repercussions of such transmission.

The use of computers and their associated communication equipment to abuse, harass, or offend others is improper. All computer users should realize that abusive, offensive, and harassing messages communicated or shared through computer resources are no different than similar conduct carried out in person, by telephone, or by mail.

What is considered obscene, abusive, offensive, or harassing when communicated in person, by mail, or by phone is also considered to be obscene, abusive, offensive, or harassing, when communicated by computer resources.

For the sake of clarity, the following are examples of things that should not be done with computers:

Place obscene materials on electronic bulletin boards.

Share files in your accounts that are obscene or contain harassing or abusive messages.

Send obscene material to anyone.

Send abusive messages to other computer users.

Make racially or sexually harassing remarks on electronic bulletin boards or send them to specific users.

Start or extend chain letters.

Using Computer Networks

Through the Union College computer system, users can access computers and networks outside the College. When accessing outside computer resources, all Union College users should know that they are representatives of the College. Users accessing outside computer systems become guests in someone else's home, and all of the rules of being a good guest apply to use of their computer systems.

Union College computer users have the responsibility to know and to follow regulations of the computer system accessed. Ignorance of the rules is no excuse for violating them. For example, users should be careful to log on and log off outside computers in the manner required by the outside computer system.

Computer users should be responsible for all charges incurred while linked to outside computer systems.

Access to other computer systems via campus and remote networks is restricted to properly registered individuals. No one should attempt to circumvent these restrictions.

Policy Related to the Union College Website and Homepage Development

The Union College Website may be edited, altered, or updated by authorized personnel only. Additional pages, sections, or substantive changes added to the Union College Website must be reviewed by public relations and receive administrative approval prior to posting or uploading.

Any faculty, staff, or administrator that posts an educationally or professionally related page must notify the system administrator prior to posting.

Future Policy Development

Due to the ongoing developments in computer technology, the College reserves the right to develop and distribute interim policies pending official approval.

PATRON VIEWING OF PORNOGRAPHIC MATERIAL

Phoenix College
Phoenix College Library
Phoenix, Arizona

Pornography Statement

In keeping with the ALA Code of Ethics, PC librarians "protect each library user's right to privacy and confidentiality with respect to information sought or received and resources consulted, borrowed, acquired or transmitted." Therefore, it is not the Library's practice to monitor the content being viewed on computer workstations.

The MCCCD has established Technology Resource Standards that prohibit certain behaviors. The viewing of pornography might fall within two of these standards:

Activities that would constitute a violation of any policy of Maricopa's Governing Board, including (but not limited to) Maricopa's non-discrimination policy and its policy against sexual harassment.

Transmitting, storing, or receiving data, or otherwise using computing resources in a manner that would constitute a violation of state or federal law, including (but not limited to) obscenity, defamation, threats, harassment, and theft.

Therefore, a librarian may ask a library user to cease viewing pornography, especially in cases where a complaint has been made. If the library user fails to comply with this request, the librarian may call Security. If the librarian is in a fearful situation and is unable to call Security, the panic button should be used.

The librarian must contact Security, who will call the Police, if someone is viewing child pornography.

CONSEQUENCES OF UNACCEPTABLE BEHAVIOR

Union College
Jones Learning Resource Center
Barbourville, Kentucky

Enforcement

The College considers any breach of the Union College Code for Computing and Communications to be a serious matter. Violations may result in loss of access privileges and/or possible disciplinary action. A violation of these rules resulting in a loss of privileges is an independent action from disciplinary action pursuant to College policy. Other disciplinary sanctions will be issued through appropriate College channels.

Appeal of sanctions will be handled according to established College Policy through appropriate College channels.

Monroe County Community College
Monroe County Community College Library
Monroe, Michigan

This acceptable use policy does not attempt to catalog or exhaustively enumerate all required or pro-scribed uses or behavior. The Vice President of Student and Information Services may at any time make determinations that particular uses are or are not consistent with the purposes of the MCCC computer network.

Infractions of this policy, when accidental in nature, will typically be handled internally by the appropriate administrator. More serious violations of this policy shall subject users to the regular disciplinary processes and procedures of the College for students, staff, administrators, and faculty. Illegal acts involv-ing College computing resources may also subject violators to prosecution by local, state, and/or federal authorities.

University of California Berkeley
University of California Berkeley Libraries
Berkeley, California

Enforcement

Penalties may be imposed under one or more of the following: University of California regulations, UC Berkeley regulations, California law, or the laws of the United States.

Minor infractions of this policy or those that appear accidental in nature are typically handled informally by electronic mail or in-person discussions. More serious infractions are handled via formal procedures. In some situations, it may be necessary to suspend account privileges to prevent ongoing misuse while the situation is under investigation.

Infractions by students may result in the temporary or permanent restriction of access privileges, notifi-cation of a student's academic advisor and/or referral of the situation to the Student Conduct Office. Those by a faculty or staff member may result in referral to the department chairperson or administra-tive officer.

Offenses which are in violation of local, state, or federal laws may result in the restriction of computing privileges, and will be reported to the appropriate University and law enforcement authorities.

Part XII. University Repositories

Chapter 42

UNIVERSITY REPOSITORIES ADMINISTRATIVE PROCEDURES

MISSION STATEMENT

New York University
New York University Libraries
New York, New York

I. Introduction

The New York University Archives serves as the final repository for the historical records of New York University. Its primary purpose is to document the history of the University and to provide source material for administrators, faculty, students, alumni, and other members of the University community, as well as scholars, authors, and other interested persons who seek to evaluate the impact of the University's activities on the history of American social, cultural, and intellectual development.

II. Core Mission

The core mission of the University Archives is as follows:

- To appraise, collect, organize, describe, make available, and preserve records of historical, legal, fiscal, and/or administrative value to New York University
- To provide adequate facilities for the retention and preservation of such records
- To provide information services that will assist the operation of the University
- To serve as a resource and laboratory to stimulate and nourish creative teaching and learning
- To serve research and scholarship by making available and encouraging the use of its collections by members of the University and the community at large
- To promote knowledge and understanding of the origins, aims, programs, and goals of the University, and of the development of these aims, goals, and programs
- To implement records management by formulating policy and procedures that will ensure the collection and preservation of archival materials.

Texas Tech University
Southwest Collections/Special Collections Library
Lubbock, Texas

Mission Statement

The University Archives serves as the institutional memory for Texas Tech University by collecting, preserving and making accessible to researchers such materials as administrative and faculty records, publications, photographs, video and audio materials. These materials document the legal, historical, fiscal, administrative and intellectual aspects of the university, as well as the cultural and social aspects of student life.

TRANSFER GUIDELINES

Iowa State University
University Libraries Special Collections
Ames, Iowa

Procedures:

A. Transfer of Records—The transfer of University records to the University Archives must be in accordance with the "Iowa State University Schedule for Records Retention and Disposition." The University Archives will accept University records which are scheduled for permanent retention only. It will not accept records which are scheduled for destruction. University records considered for transmittal to the University Archives for permanent retention must be reviewed and appraised by the Head, Special Collections, prior to transfer acceptance. All transfer of records must be placed in acid-free records cartons (supplied by the University Archives) and accompanied by a listing of the contents. Please consult the University University Archives' Policy and Procedure for Transfer of University Records for procedure explanation and compliance.

B. Deed of Gift/Transfer of Records Forms—The University Archives will not accept materials without a legal transfer of title through a deed of gift, deposit agreement, transfer of records form, or other official acknowledgement. All transmittal forms must be signed by the Head, Special Collections, and the donor/official from the transferring office.

C. Loans and Deposits—Materials loaned or deposited with the University Archives will be accepted when the conditions for acceptance are favorable to the University Archives and the Iowa State University Library.

D. Closed Collections—The University Archives will not accept materials that are closed to the public in perpetuity.

E. Deaccessioning—Duplicates and materials that do not reflect the University Archives' collecting areas or do not possess sufficient archival value may be deaccessioned, subject to the documented terms of acquisition, University regulations, and state and federal laws.

F. Revision of Policy—The University Archives reserves the right to amend its collection development policy at any time.

Texas Tech University
Southwest Collections/Special Collections Library
Lubbock, Texas

Transferring Materials to the University Archives

All university records should adhere to the records retention schedule. Once records become inactive, only those that have been determined as having permanent value should be transferred to the University Archives. All others should be disposed of according to the manner cited in the records retention schedule. When in doubt, don't throw it out but rather call the University Archivist for help.

When sending items to the University Archives, records should be kept in their original order and folder [i.e., never loosely dumped], boxed in a sturdy container, and have attached a sheet stating who is the sender/department, a contact phone number and a listing of what records are enclosed. Preferably, materials should not to sent without first making contact with the University Archivist.

Donors not currently affiliated with Texas Tech, such as alumni, should contact the University Archivist directly.

Indiana University Bloomington
Office of University Archives and Records Management
Bloomington, Indiana

Transfer guidelines for personal papers of faculty and staff

The Office of University Archives and Records Management is the repository on the IU Bloomington campus primarily responsible for collecting the personal papers of prominent Indiana University faculty and staff. The personal papers of faculty and staff provide a rich source for historical research. If you are interested in discussing the transfer of your papers, please contact...

The following guidelines will assist faculty and staff in identifying those portions of their files that are appropriate for transfer to the Archives. This list is by no means definitive or exhaustive. It is intended as a general approximation of materials that reflect and illuminate the careers of Indiana University faculty and staff members. Materials not specifically cited below that contribute toward documenting faculty and staff careers are, of course, welcome.

Papers commonly transferred to the Archives include, but are not limited to, the following materials:

Biographical material

Resumes, vitae, bibliographies, biographical and autobiographical sketches, chronologies, genealogies, and newspaper clippings

Correspondence

Official: outgoing (copies and/or drafts) and incoming letters and memoranda generated in the course of conducting university business

Professional: outgoing and incoming letters relating to all facets of one's academic career, including correspondence with colleagues, publishers, professional organizations and students

Personal: letters to and from friends, relatives and business associates

Diaries, notebooks and appointment calendars

Classroom material

Lecture notes, overheads, slides, syllabi, course outlines, reading lists, examinations, and student papers

Research files

Outlines, research designs, raw data, notes, analyses and reports of findings

Departmental and committee records

Agenda, minutes, reports, correspondence and related material

Drafts and manuscripts of articles, books, reviews and speeches

Published articles and monographs

Audiovisual material

Tapes, videotapes and films documenting personal and professional activities and/or Indiana University events or subject matter

Photographs

Prints, negatives, slides and digital images documenting personal and professional activities and/or Indiana University events or subject matter.

Memorabilia

Documents which generally should not be transferred without prior consultation with the Archivist include:

Detailed financial records, canceled checks, and receipts

Non-personally addressed mail and routine letters of transmittal and acknowledgment (i.e., "Junk Mail")

461

Duplicates and multiple copies of publications, course materials; all other duplicate material: transfer only the original and heavily annotated copies

Reference collections of books, research papers, journal articles, and reprints written by other persons

However, any of these publications that contain your annotated remarks or notes should be transferred to the Archives.

WHEN IN DOUBT, PLEASE DO NOT THROW IT OUT! CONTACT THE UNIVERSITY ARCHIVES!

Chapter 43

UNIVERSITY REPOSITORIES COLLECTION DEVELOPMENT

COLLECTION PROCEDURES

New York University
New York University Libraries
New York, New York

III. Collection Development

The University Archives was designated the "official repository for all non-current records of the University" in August, 1977. Its collections policy is based on the Society of American Archivists' Guidelines For College and University Archives (1983), and on the recommendations of the Archives Advisory Council, a committee of University faculty and administrators established in 1977 to advise the Archives on policy and procedures, and to oversee its growth and development. In 1978, the Advisory Council issued a policy statement calling for the preservation of University records for the purposes of:

- maintaining a clear account of University life and achievements, administrative policy and actions and educational programs

- reinforcing an image of the University that stimulates financial support and encourages an appreciation of the University's past and its role in the history of American higher education among students, faculty, and alumni

- making available a body of records useful for student, casual, and scholarly research in history and other disciplines.

The records of New York University are voluminous. In the absence of systematic records management, the Archives must rely on the cooperation and support of administrators, deans, directors, faculty, students, and alumni to ensure that materials of historical value are collected and preserved. The University Archives will promote university-wide records management and collect material in the following categories from all administrative and academic units of the University with the exception of the Medical and Dental Centers, which maintain separate archival collections:

Official Records, Papers, and Publications of New York University

Official records encompass the records or papers generated or received by the various administrative offices of New York University in the conduct of their business. These records will include:

- Minutes, memoranda, correspondence and reports of the Board of Trustees

- Records of the Office of President, including correspondence, administrative subject files and reports

- Correspondence, subject files, and reports of the Office of Academic Affairs

- Correspondence, subject files and reports of the offices of central administration, including: Administration, External Affairs, Finance, General Counsel and Secretary of the University, Student Affairs, University Relations

- Correspondence, subject files and reports of deans, directors and administrators of the schools, colleges, divisions, programs and institutes of the University

- Minutes, memoranda and reports of all major academic and administrative commissions, councils and committees including the University Senate and its committees

Departmental records, including: minutes, reports, correspondence, and syllabi

Accreditation reports and supporting documentation

Annual budget and audit reports

Records of the Registrar, including timetables, class schedules, enrollment reports, graduation rosters and other reports issued on a regular basis

Alumni records, including minutes of the alumni associations

Reports of the Admissions Office

Records of student organizations

All publications, newsletters and booklets distributed in the name of New York University, including catalogs, special bulletins, yearbooks, student newspapers, University directories and faculty/staff rosters, faculty and administration newsletters and publications, alumni publications and ephemeral material

Photoprints, negatives, slides, audio and video film, tapes, and reels, oral history interviews, and optical and compact discs documenting the development of the University

Security copies of microfilm reels containing vital records

Maps, prints and architectural drawings documenting the physical changes and development of the University

Reports of research projects, including grant records

Artifacts relating to the history of New York University

Electronic records.

The official administrative records of New York University (correspondence, reports and subject files) designated as archival should be inactive and no longer used in the current activities of the originating office. Records should be forwarded to the Archives according to schedule after consulting with the archivist for the orderly transfer of non-current materials. An inventory of records transferred should accompany accessioned material. The originating office may place restrictions on access to non-current records in addition to the restrictions on administrative, Board of Trustees, employee and student records described in the Access Policy statement, Appendix.

Personal and Professional Papers of New York University Faculty

The University Archives seeks to acquire, organize and provide access to the personal and professional papers of New York University faculty as a means of documenting the internal life and culture of the University community. Space and staff restraints in the University Archives and the size of the New York University faculty requires limits the volume of faculty papers that can be accessioned. In appraising and soliciting faculty papers the following criteria are suggested:

National or international reputation in a respective academic field

Record of service with New York University and contribution to its growth and development

Service on the faculty of a recognized area of excellence within New York University

Service and contribution in community, state and national affairs.

The University Archives seeks documentation of the careers of the New York University faculty in the following formats:

Correspondence: official, professional and personal.

Biographical material: resumes, bibliographies, biographical sketches, chronologies, genealogies, newspaper clippings, and personal memoirs

Photoprints and graphic materials

Tape recordings of lectures, speeches and discussions

Lecture notes and syllabi

Research files

Departmental or committee minutes and records

Drafts and manuscripts of articles and books

Diaries, notebooks, appointment calendars and memorabilia.

The University Archives recognizes the rights of faculty and private donors to impose reasonable restrictions on materials to protect privacy and confidentiality. Restrictions on access should be for a fixed term and determined at the time of donation. The Archives encourages minimal access restrictions consistent with the legal rights of all parties.

Special Collections

The University Archives will solicit and collect records and papers which are neither official University records or faculty papers, but which relate to the history of New York University. Examples include:

Professional and personal papers of the members of the University Council/Board of Trustees if associated with University business

Professional and personal papers of eminent alumni relating their New York University experiences

Papers or records dealing with the history of Washington Square and University Heights as they relate to the growth and development of the University

Papers, records and published items on New York University and its role in the history of higher education

Papers, records and published items pertaining to New York University as a major urban institution.

Texas Tech University
Southwest Collections/Special Collections Library
Lubbock, Texas

Acquisition Policy

University records are documents created, received or accumulated during the conduct of Texas Tech University business. Records sought for the University Archives include those that demonstrate the university's activities in teaching, research, student development, cultural enrichment, and campus growth. Also collected are non-official records pertaining to the history of the university. This includes faculty papers, organizational records, and student organizational records.

The types of records deemed worthy of permanent preservation are, in part, determined by the university's records retention schedule. Routine fiscal documentation such as purchase orders and travel receipts are not accepted as they are considered short-term records. Also, student academic records are not housed in the University Archives but rather reside with the Registrar's Office.

Materials not fitting the University Archives collecting scope can either be rejected, deaccessioned or disposed. Due to limited space, only a small number of duplicate materials are kept at any time, unless the item(s) prove to be very rare and/or unique.

All University Archives materials are non-circulating and can only be used in the Holden Reading Room. Use of University Archives materials are covered under the Policies of the Reading Room.

SELECTION CRITERIA

Iowa State University
University Libraries Special Collections
Ames, Iowa

II. Criteria

The University Archives seeks to document the Iowa State University community, which includes the administration, faculty, students, alumni, and staff. In assessing records appropriate for permanent retention, the University Archives attempts to collect the documentation produced from the conduct of University business. There are seven functions common to the operations of most academic institutions: convey knowledge; advance knowledge; confer credentials; foster socialization; maintain and promote culture; sustain the institution; and provide public service.

[Varsity Letters: Documenting Modern Colleges and Universities, Helen Willa Samuels, The Society of American Archivists and the Scarecrow Press, Inc., 1992. pp.19–23.]

Chapter 44

University Repositories Formats and Types of Material Collected

Faculty Papers

Iowa State University
University Libraries Special Collections
Ames, Iowa

The Papers of Iowa State University Faculty

As an important part of its mission of documenting the life of the Iowa State University community and placing it in a broader social context, the University Archives actively seeks to acquire, organize, and make available the personal and professional papers of the Iowa State University faculty. Faculty papers offer insight into the history and operation of the University that otherwise may be lost by relying only on official administrative records. They reveal professional interests and opinions that frequently clarify matters mentioned in the official records of the central administration. Faculty papers document the academic life of the University and relate one's academic career to his or her total interests, thereby constituting an important record. Personal viewpoints expressed in personal correspondence and documentation resulting from service on academic committees may provide a better basis for understanding the University than official records from administrative offices alone. Without a broad range of faculty papers available for consultation, the University Archives cannot provide a full compliment of perspectives regarding the historical activities of Iowa State University.

Types and Formats

The following types of documentation reflect and illuminate the careers of the Iowa State University faculty and are sought by the University Archives: official, professional, and personal correspondence; biographical material; photographs; tape recordings; class lecture notes and syllabi; research files; departmental or committee minutes and records; drafts and manuscripts of articles and books written; and diaries, notebooks, and memorabilia.

The Iowa State University Archives is committed to preserving selected faculty papers and to making them available for research as soon as possible. At the same time, it has an obligation to guard against invasion of privacy and to protect the confidentiality in its records in accordance with law. Therefore, every private donor has the right to impose reasonable restrictions upon his or her papers to protect confidentiality for a reasonable period of time. Restrictions on access are for a fixed term and are determined at the time of donation. The University Archives does not accept agreements that restrict access to material in perpetuity or does not supply a specific date releasing the restriction. It encourages minimal access restrictions consistent with the legal rights of all concerned.

Texas Tech University
Southwest Collections/Special Collections Library
Lubbock, Texas

Acquisition of Faculty Papers

The University Archives acquires, processes and makes available for patrons the personal and professional papers of Texas Tech faculty, several of whom are also senior administrators within the organization.

The decision to accept faculty papers into the University Archives holdings is determined by the size and extent of the collection and the faculty member's:

- reputation and output as a scholar
- involvement in the academic, social and administrative life of the university
- involvement in related discipline organizations and institutions
- willingness to allow unrestricted access to the papers

Below are the types of materials sought after in each faculty collection. Please note that only 1 copy is needed of each type:

- Curriculum Vitae and other forms of biographical information
- Research and personal diaries and notebooks
- Final research results and reports
- Oral history interviews and other forms of sound recordings
- Off-prints and other scholarly publications produced by the faculty member, including speeches, presentations, technical reports, and unpublished articles
- Correspondence with colleagues
- Documents relating to the faculty member's professional and research organization involvement
- Grant proposals
- Teaching materials written by the faculty member such as lecture notes, course outlines, course syllabi, guidelines for research papers, lab manuals, and workbooks
- Photographs of the faculty member, including those of his colleagues, campus activities, research activities and equipment
- Memorabilia such as news clippings, scrapbooks and videos documenting the faculty member's professional and community work
- Committee and departmental meeting minutes and agendas

Below are the types of materials NOT sought after in each faculty collection, due to limited storage space and retention times set by the university's records retention schedule:

- Raw research data [consult the University Archivist first before disposal]
- Personal financial records such as bank statements and cancelled checks
- Travel vouchers and receipts
- Time sheets
- Student grades of any kind
- Medical records
- Trophies and plaques [consult the University Archivist first before disposal]
- Junk mail
- Miscellaneous reference materials such as popular magazines and newspapers [unless there is an article on or written by the faculty member]
- Faculty Papers in the University Archives

Currently, there are several collections of faculty papers residing in the University Archives. Most are listed under the name of the donor, which is generally the faculty member. Click here to go to the manuscript finding aids.

468

Artifacts

Iowa State University
University Libraries Special Collections
Ames, Iowa

Artifacts or Three-Dimensional Objects

The University Archives seeks to collect artifacts that further the Department's mission to identify, select, preserve, create access to, provide reference assistance for, and promote the use of rare and unique research materials that support major research areas of Iowa State University. This includes rare and unique objects pertaining to Iowa State University, agriculture and rural life, science, and technology. The Department will consider for inclusion in the collection artifacts that contain well-documented provenance (1) and are in fair and original condition The Department will limit collecting to items that can be reasonably preserved, cared for, stored, and made accessible for research and exhibit purposes.

[1] Provenance includes where, how, and by whom the item was created, acquired, and/or used; how the donor came to possess the artifact; and any other pertinent information regarding the object.

Official Records

Iowa State University
University Libraries Special Collections
Ames, Iowa

Official Records, Papers, and Publications of Iowa State University

These records (which give evidence about the functions, policies, and decisions of the University) include among many different forms correspondence, reports, minutes, directives, announcements, publications, architectural and building plans, machine-readable files, and any other material produced by the University in pursuance of its functions. Faculty and professional & scientific personnel records are retained by the Provost's Office. The disposition of student records will be at the discretion of the Deans and the Registrar's Office. The University Archives also collects all publications, newsletters, or booklets distributed by Iowa State University including catalogs, yearbooks, student newspapers, University directories and faculty/staff rosters, faculty and administrative newsletters and publications, and alumni publications. Audiovisual records documenting the development of the University such as photographic prints and negatives, slides, motion picture film, oral history interviews, audio and video tape, discs, and recordings are solicited as well as dissertations and theses. Machine-readable data files generated for conducting University business will be considered for permanent retention as well. The University Archives may maintain security copies of microfilm produced by any vital records program. Maps, prints and drawings documenting the physical growth and development of the University form an important part of the collection and will be collected as well. The University Archives will consider retaining selected artifacts relating to the history of Iowa State University.

Student Organization Papers

Indiana University Bloomington
Office of University Archives and Records Management
Bloomington, Indiana

Indiana University Student Organizations

Guidelines on types of records to send to the University Archives

The primary mission of the Office of University Archives and Records Management is to collect, organize, make accessible and preserve records documenting Indiana University's origins and development and the activities and achievements of its officers, faculty, students, alumni and benefactors. Documenting IU student organizations/student life is a major objective of the Archives.

The following guidelines will assist student organizations in identifying those portions of their files that are appropriate for transfer to the Archives. Records commonly transferred to the Archives include, but are not limited to, the following material:

1. Constitutions and by-laws, minutes and proceedings, transcripts, lists of officers;
2. Office Files: correspondence and memoranda (incoming and outgoing) and subject files concerning projects, activities and functions;
3. Historical files documenting policies, decisions, committee and task force reports and proceedings, questionnaires;
4. Publications: three record copies of all newsletters, journals, brochures, monographs, programs, posters, and announcements issued by the organization or its subdivisions; the Archives should be placed on organization's mailing lists to receive all future publications;
5. Audio-visuals: photographs, digital images, films, and sound and video recordings;

Note: All information formats (e.g., published, typescript, audio-visual, and electronic data, such as computer disks and files) are appropriate for consideration for transfer. For documents in formats requiring any form of machine intervention, such as videotapes and all computer files, consideration should be given to converting the documents to a format accessible to the Archives' users. Early consultation with the Archivist is strongly encouraged for all such materials.

Records which generally should not be transferred but scheduled for disposal after consultation with the Archivist include:

1. Records of specific financial transactions;
2. Routine letters of transmittal and acknowledgment;
3. Non-personally addressed correspondence;
4. Requests for publications or information after the requests have been filled;
5. Replies to questionnaires if the results are recorded and preserved either in the Archives or in a published report.

These lists are intended as general guides. If there are questions about records not listed here or questions about the retention or disposal of specific record series, please e-mail the Archives at archives@indiana.edu.

When ready to transfer records, please review and follow the procedures outlined in the Procedures for Transfer of University Records.

WHEN IN DOUBT, PLEASE DO NOT THROW IT OUT! CONTACT THE UNIVERSITY ARCHIVES!

ADMINISTRATIVE PAPERS

Indiana University Bloomington
Office of University Archives and Records Management
Bloomington, Indiana

Office records of campus administrative and academic units

Guidelines on types of records to send to the University Archives

The Office of University Archives and Records Management is the official repository for the records of Indiana University that have long-term historical, legal, fiscal and administrative value. The mission of the Archives is to manage and make accessible these information resources in support of administration, teaching, research and service. When ready to transfer records, please review and follow the procedures outlined in the Procedures for Transfer of University Records.

The following guidelines will assist administrators, faculty and staff in identifying those portions of their files that are appropriate for transfer to the Archives. Records commonly transferred to the Archives include, but are not limited to, the following material:

- Constitutions and by-laws, minutes and proceedings, transcripts, lists of officers of University corporate bodies;
- Office Files: correspondence and memoranda (incoming and outgoing) and subject files concerning projects, activities and functions;
- Historical files documenting policies, decisions, committee and task force reports, questionnaires;
- Publications: three record copies of all newsletters, journals, brochures, monographs, programs, posters, and announcements issued by the University or its subdivisions; the Archives should be placed on college, department, and office mailing lists to receive all future publications;
- Audio-visuals: photographs, digital images, films, and sound and video recordings; Personal papers of students, faculty, and staff that relate to the University's work.

NOTE: All information formats (e.g., published, typescript, audio-visual, and electronic data, such as computer disks and files) are appropriate for consideration for transfer. For documents in formats requiring any form of machine intervention, such as videotapes, kinescopes, and all computer files, consideration should be given to transferring the equipment needed to access the documents or, preferably, converting the documents to a format accessible to the Archives' users. Early consultation with the Archivist is strongly encouraged for all such materials.

Records which generally should not be transferred but scheduled for disposal after consultation with the Archivist include:

- Records of specific financial transactions;
- Routine letters of transmittal and acknowledgment;
- Non-personally addressed correspondence such as "Deans and Directors" memoranda (except for one record copy from the issuing office)
- Requests for publications or information after the requests have been filled;
- Replies to questionnaires if the results are recorded and preserved either in the Archives or in a published report.

These lists are intended as general guides. If there are questions about records not listed here or questions about the retention or disposal of specific record series, please e-mail the Archives at archives@indiana.edu.

IF RECORDS ARE NOT LISTED ON A RECORDS DISPOSITION SCHEDULE, DO NOT THROW THEM OUT! PLEASE FIRST CONTACT THE UNIVERSITY ARCHIVES!

Web Sites of Contributing Libraries

Albion College
Stockwell-Mudd Libraries
Albion, Michigan
www.albion.edu/library/copyright2/main.htm
May 2007 Copyright 2006

Atlanta University
Robert W. Woodruff Library
Atlanta, Georgia
www.auctr.edu/libraryinfo/policies.html
April 2006 Copyright 2005

Auburn University
Auburn University Libraries
Auburn University, Alabama
www.lib.auburn.edu/askref.html
May 2007 Copyright 2006
www.lib.auburn.edu/hum/humweb/procedures.html
May 2007 Copyright 2006
www.lib.auburn.edu/dean/privacy_policy.pdf#
    search=%22%22Auburn%20University%22%
    20%22privacy%20policy%22%20library%22
May 2007 Copyright 2006

Augustana College
Thomas Tredway Library
Rock Island, Illinois
www.augustana.edu/Library/About/public-use.html
May 2007 Copyright 2006
www.augustana.edu/Library/About/Strategic/
    objectives.html#materials
May 2007 Copyright 2006

Ball State University
Ball State University Library
Muncie, Indiana
www.bsu.edu/library/services/maincirc/
    maincircfinecos/
July 2006 Copyright 2006

Barton College
Willis N. Hackney Library
Wilson, North Carolina

http://library2.barton.edu/libraryinformation/
    circulation.asp
August 2006 Copyright 2006

Baylor University
Moody Library
Waco, Texas
www.baylor.edu/lib/circ/index.php?id=30414
August 2006 Copyright 2006

Bergen Community College
Sidney Silverman Library
Paramus, New Jersey
www.bergen.edu/pages/2251.asp
May 2007 Copyright 2007

Bethel College
Bethel College Library
North Newton, Kansas
www.bethelks.edu/services/library/giftspolicy.php
August 2006 Copyright 2003

Binghamton University
Binghamton University Libraries
Binghamton, New York
http://library.lib.binghamton.edu/webdocs/
    circ.html#grad
May 2007 Copyright 2007
http://library.lib.binghamton.edu/webdocs/
    policies.html
May 2007 Copyright 2007
http://library.lib.binghamton.edu/webdocs/circ.html
May 2007 Copyright 2007

Boston College
Boston College Libraries
Boston, Massachusetts
www.bc.edu/libraries/services/interlibrary/
May 2007 Copyright 2007
www.bc.edu/libraries/services/ref-instruc/s-mission/
May 2007 Copyright 2005
www.bc.edu/libraries/services/document/
    s-docdelivery/
May 2007 Copyright 2005

www.bc.edu/libraries/services/circulation/#requests
May 2007 Copyright 2006

Brock University
James A. Gibson Library
Saints Catharines, Ontario, Canada
www.brocku.ca/library/reference/codcon.htm
May 2007 Copyright 2006
www.brocku.ca/library/areas.htm
May 2007 Copyright 2006
www.brocku.ca/maplibrary/general/policies.htm
May 2007 Copyright 2006
www.brocku.ca/library/reference/food.htm
May 2007 Copyright 2006
www.brocku.ca/maplibrary/default.html
May 2007 Copyright 2006

Brown University
Brown University Library
Providence, Rhode Island
www.brown.edu/Facilities/University_Library/
depts/acq/gifts.html
May 2007 Copyright 2000

Buena Vista University
University Library
Storm Lake, Iowa
www.bvu.edu/library/policy.html
May 2007 Copyright 2006

California State University Long Beach
University Library
Long Beach, California
www.csulb.edu/library/donors/giftpolicy.html
May 2007 Copyright 2004
All of the University of California and California State system schools' work is copyrighted and is used with their permission

California State Polytechnic University Pomona
Cal Poly Pomona University Library
Pomona, California
www.csupomona.edu/~library/about/privacy_
policy.html
September 2006 Copyright 2005
All of the University of California and California State system schools' work is copyrighted and is used with their permission

California State University, Los Angeles
John F. Kennedy Memorial Library
Los Angeles, California

www.calstatela.edu/library/infolit/il_mission.htm
May 2007 Copyright 2006
All of the University of California and California State system schools' work is copyrighted and is used with their permission

Central Oregon Community College
Central Oregon Community College Campus
Library
Bend, Oregon
http://campuslibrary.cocc.edu/Library+Services/
Circulation/default.aspx
May 2007 Copyright 2007

Central Washington University
Brooks Library
Ellensburg, Washington
www.lib.cwu.edu/info/policies/challenged
materials.html
September 2006 Copyright 2006

Centre College
Grace Doherty Library
www.centre.edu/web/library/information/
acquisitions.html
May 2007 Copyright 2006
www.centre.edu/web/library/information/
intellectual_freedom.html
May 2007 Copyright 2006
www.centre.edu/web/library/information/gifts.html
May 2007 Copyright 2006

Christopher Newport University
Captain John Smith Library
Newport News, Virginia
http://library.cnu.edu/policy.html
April 2006 Copyright 2001

College of Charleston
College of Charleston Libraries
Charleston, South Carolina
www.cofc.edu/~library/admin/pol8.html
April 2006 Copyright 2006
www.cofc.edu/~library/admin/pol16.html
April 2006 Copyright 2006
www.cofc.edu/%7Elibrary/admin/pol27.html
April 2006 Copyright 2006
www.cofc.edu/~library/admin/pol13.html
April 2006 Copyright 2006

The College of Saint Catherine
College of Saint Catherine Libraries
Minneapolis, Minnesota

http://library.stkate.edu/techserv/collpol.html
July 2006 Copyright 2005

Colorado State University Pueblo
Colorado State University Pueblo Library
Pueblo, Colorado
www.colostate-pueblo.edu/its/policies/Electronic
    Policy.asp?lnb=about
May 2007 Copyright 2007
http://library.colostate-pueblo.edu/circpolicy.asp
May 2007 Copyright 2007
http://library.colostate-
pueblo.edu/bi/instruction.asp
May 2007 Copyright 2007
http://library.colostate-pueblo.edu/copypolicy.pdf
May 2007 Copyright 2007

Columbia College
Columbia University in the City of New York
New York, New York
www.college.columbia.edu/privacy/
September 2006 Copyright 2006

Columbia College Chicago
Columbia College Library
Chicago, Illinois
www.lib.colum.edu/learn/services/
    illbookform.htm
May 2007 Copyright 2007
www.lib.colum.edu/services/inprocess.php
May 2007 Copyright 2007
www.lib.colum.edu/learn/services/
    purchaserequestform.htm
May 2007 Copyright 2007
www.lib.colum.edu/services/forms/
    purchaserequest.php
May 2007 Copyright 2007
www.lib.colum.edu/about/
    ecollectiondevelopment.php
May 2007 Copyright 2007
www.lib.colum.edu/services/forms/
    instructionrequest.php
May 2007 Copyright 2007
www.lib.colum.edu/learn/faculty/
    avreservesform.htm
May 2007 Copyright 2007
www.lib.colum.edu/learn/policies/
    collectiondevelopment.htm
August 2006 Copyright 2006
www.lib.colum.edu/learn/services/
    reqmaterialsinprocess.htm

August 2006 Copyright 2006
www.lib.colum.edu/learn/services/
    reqmaterialsinprocess.pdf

August 2006 Copyright 2006
Columbia University
Columbia University Health Sciences Library
New York, New York
http://library.cpmc.columbia.edu/hsl/disabilities
    .html
May 2007 Copyright 2005

Columbia University
Columbia University Libraries
New York, New York
www.columbia.edu/cu/lweb/services/preservation/
    dlpolicy.html
August 2006 Copyright 2005

Connecticut College
Charles E. Shain Library
New London, Connecticut
www.conncoll.edu/is/info-resources/ill/policy.shtml
July 2006 Copyright 2006

Cornell University
Cornell University Libraries
Ithaca, New York
www.library.cornell.edu/Admin/goals/goals-print.html
April 2006 Copyright 2002
www.library.cornell.edu/about/policyProtection.html
April 2006 Copyright 1998-2006.
www.247ref.org/portal/247priv.htm
April 2006 Copyright 1998-2006
www.library.cornell.edu/colldev/giftpolicy.html
December 2005 Copyright 2004

Crichton College
Crichton College Library
Memphis, Tennessee
www.crichton.edu/documents/
    materialsselectionpolicy.pdf
May 2007 Copyright 2007

Dartmouth College
Dartmouth College Library
Hanover,, New Hampshire
www.dartmouth.edu/~bakerref/Help/storage
    _ugrb.shtml
August 2006 Copyright 2006
www.dartmouth.edu/~cmdc/cdp/electronic.html
August 2006 Copyright 1999

www.dartmouth.edu/~libcirc/lockers.shtml
August 2006 Copyright 2003

Drake University
Cowles Library
Des Moines, Iowa
www.lib.drake.edu/site/aboutCowles/
    policies-specialEvents.php
May 2007 Copyright 2006
www.lib.drake.edu/site/aboutCowles/
    policies-confidentiality.php
May 2007 Copyright 2006

Duke University
Duke University Libraries
Durham, North Carolina
http://library.duke.edu/about/privacy.html
September 2006 Copyright 2006

East Carolina University
Joyner Library
Greenville North Carolina
www.ecu.edu/cs-lib/accesssrv/circulation/
    circpolicy.cfm
May 2007 Copyright 2005
www.ecu.edu/cs-lib/music/circpolicy.cfm
May 2007 Copyright 2006
www.ecu.edu/cs-lib/policies/
    electronic-resources.cfm
May 2007 Copyright 2005

Eastern Michigan University
Bruce T. Halle Library
Ypsilanti, Michigan
www.emich.edu/halle/collection_devleopment
    _policy_essentials.html
August 2006 Copyright 2006
www.emich.edu/halle/faculty_study_rooms.html
August 2006 Copyright 2006
www.emich.edu/halle/askalibrarian_privacy
    _policy.html
August 2006 Copyright 2006
www.emich.edu/halle/privacy_policy_university
    _library.html
August 2006 Copyright 2006

Emory and Henry College
Emory and Henry College Department of Library
and Information Services
Emory, Virginia
www.library.ehc.edu/statement.html
May 2007 Copyright 2007

Ferris State University
Ferris Library
Big Rapids, Michigan
www.ferris.edu/library/policy/reference.htm
July 2006 Copyright 2002
www.ferris.edu/library/policy/displays.htm
July 2006 Copyright 2004
www.ferris.edu/library/faq/lostfaq.html
July 2006 Copyright 2006

Florida Atlantic University
S.E. Wimbrely Library
Boca Raton, Florida
www.library.fau.edu/policies/pubpol/docpol
    .htm
May 2007 Copyright 2007

Florida International University
Florida International University Libraries
Miami, Florida
www.fiu.edu/~library/ili/goals.html
May 2007 Copyright 2000
http://library.fiu.edu/Services/
    LaptopBorrowingPolicy.aspx
May 2007 Copyright 2006
http://library.fiu.edu/Services/InternetAccessPolicy
    .aspx
May 2007 Copyright 1998
http://library.fiu.edu/Services/
    RetiredFacultyServicesandPolicies.aspx
May 2007 Copyright 2006
http://library.fiu.edu/files/services/av/avtable.html
May 2007 Copyright 2006
www.fiu.edu/~library/ili/mission.html
May 2007 Copyright 2000

Framingham State College
Henry Whittemore Library
Framingham, Massachusetts
www.framingham.edu/wlibrary/about/
    policies.htm
May 2007 Copyright 2005
www.framingham.edu/wlibrary/services/
    purchase_form.htm
May 2007 Copyright 2004

Franklin and Marshall College
Franklin and Marshall College Library
Lancaster, Pennsylvania
http://library.fandm.edu/friends.html
July 2006 Copyright 2005

Fullerton College
William T. Boyce Library
Fullerton, California
http://library.fullcoll.edu/orient.pdf
May 2007 Copyright 2005
http://library.fullcoll.edu/orient.htm
May 2007 Copyright 2006

Georgetown University
Georgetown University Library
Washington, D.C
www.library.georgetown.edu/dept/access/
    ced/index.htm
May 2007 Copyright 2003
www.library.georgetown.edu/dept/access/
    ugrad/index.htm
May 2007 Copyright 2003
www.library.georgetown.edu/dept/access/
    postdoc/index.htm
May 2007 Copyright 2003
www.library.georgetown.edu/dept/access/
    alumni/index.htm
May 2007 Copyright 2003

Georgia State University
Georgia State University Library
Atlanta, Georgia
www.library.gsu.edu/about/pages.asp?IdID=68&
    guideID=282&ID=3253
August 2006 Copyright 2006
www.library.gsu.edu/about/pages.asp?IdID=68&
    guideID=282&ID=3650
August 2006 Copyright 2004
www.library.gsu.edu/about/pages.asp?IdID=68&
    guideID=282&ID=2797
August 2006 Copyright 2005
www.library.gsu.edu/about/pages.asp?IdID=68&
    guideID=282&ID=2788
August 2006 Copyright 2001
www.library.gsu.edu/about/pages.asp?IdID=68&
    guideID=282&ID=2794
August 2006 Copyright 2002
www.library.gsu.edu/about/pages.asp?IdID=68&
    guideID=282&ID=2793
August 2006 Copyright 1999
www.library.gsu.edu/about/pages.asp?IdID=68&
    guideID=282&ID=2790
August 2006 Copyright 2004
www.library.gsu.edu/about/pages.asp?IdID=68&
    guideID=282&ID=2786
August 2006 Copyright 2003

www.library.gsu.edu/spcoll/avcoll/
    Duplication Serv.htm
November 2006 Copyright 2004
www.library.gsu.edu/spcoll/avcoll/cpyfrm2.htm
November 2006 Copyright 2006

Golden Gate University
Golden Gate University Library
San Francisco, California
www.buraphalinux.org/~twatchai/OLDWEB/
    hotel/facsup.html
April 2006 Copyright 2000
www.buraphalinux.org/~twatchai/OLDWEB/
    hotel/goals.html
April 2006 Copyright 2000

Gonzaga University School of Law
Chastek Library
Spokane, Washington
www.law.gonzaga.edu/Library+and+Technology/
    About+Chastek+Library/Policies/Food+and
    +Beverages.asp
May 2006 Copyright 2006
www.law.gonzaga.edu/Library+and+Technology/
    About+Chastek+Library/Policies/Noise.asp
May 2006 Copyright 2006

Goucher College
Julia Rogers Library
Baltimore, Maryland
www.goucher.edu/x10570.xml
August 2006 Copyright 2006

Grand Valley State University
Zumberge Library
Allendale, MI
www.gvsu.edu/forms/library/Donations.pdf
August 2006 Copyright 2006
http://gvsu.hosts.atlas-sys.com/illiad/firsttime.html
August 2006 Copyright 2006

Guilford College
Hege Library
Greensboro, North Carolina
www.guilford.edu/about_guilford/services_and
    _administration/library/policies/collection.html
April 2006 Copyright 2006
www.guilford.edu/about_guilford/services_and
    _administration/library/policies/patron.html
April 2006 Copyright 2006

Hamilton College
Burke Library

Clinton, New York
www.hamilton.edu/library/departments/circulation
    _and_reserves.html
July 2007 Copyright 2007

Henderson State University
Huie Library
Arkadelphia, Arkansas
http://library.hsu.edu/info/library_policy.htm
May 2007 Copyright 2003

Highline Community College
Highline Community College Library
Des Moines, Washington
www.yvcc.edu/about/privacy.asp
September 2006 Copyright 2006

Hofstra University
Joan and Donald E. Axinn Library
Hempstead, New York
www.hofstra.edu/Libraries/Axinn/axinn_libdepts
    _circulation_txtbk_reserve.cfm
May 2007 Copyright 2007

Hood College
Beneficial-Hodson Library
Frederick, Maryland
www.hood.edu/library/services.cfm
August 2006 Copyright 2006

Horry-Georgetown Technical College
Horry-Georgetown Technical College Library
Conway, South Carolina
www.hgtc.edu/library/LRCmission.htm
April 2006 Copyright 2005

Houston Community College System
Houston Community College Libraries
Houston, Texas
www.hccs.edu/system/library/pandp/odue.html
May 2006 Copyright 2006
www.hccs.edu/system/library/Policies/pol23.htm
May 2006 Copyright 1999

Hudson Valley Community College
Dwight Marvin Library
Troy, New York
www.hvcc.edu/lrc/policies/about_lib.html
May 2006 Copyright 2005

Humboldt State University
Humboldt State University Library
Arcata, California
http://library.humboldt.edu/ppolicy.html
September 2006 Copyright 2002

Illinois College
Schewe Library
Jacksonville, Illinois
www.ic.edu/library/policy.asp
May 2006 Copyright 2006

Indiana University Bloomington
Indiana University Libraries
Bloomington, Indiana
www.libraries.iub.edu/index.php?pageId=1137
September 2006 Copyright 2006
www.libraries.iub.edu/index.php?pageId=3355
October 2006 Copyright 2006
www.libraries.iub.edu/index.php?pageId=3293
October 2006 Copyright 2006
www.libraries.iub.edu/index.php?pageId=3291
October 2006 Copyright 2006

Indiana University–Purdue University Indianapolis
University Library
Indianapolis, Indiana
www.ulib.iupui.edu/printing/printing.html
November 2006 Copyright 2005
http://kb.iu.edu/data/atvs.html#paper
November 2006 Copyright 2006

Indiana University-Purdue University Fort Wayne
Walter E. Helmke Library
Fort Wayne, Indiana
www.lib.ipfw.edu/1557.0.html
May 2007 Copyright 2004
www.lib.ipfw.edu/682.0.html
July 2006 Copyright 2004

Indiana University South Bend
Franklin D. Schurz Library
South Bend, Indiana
www.iusb.edu/~libg/about/displays.shtml
August 2006 Copyright 2006

Iowa State University
University Libraries Special Collections
Ames, Iowa
www.lib.iastate.edu/spcl/arch/document/colldev.html
October 2006 Copyright 2006

Johnson State College
Johnson State College Library
Johnson, Vermont
www.johnsonstatecollege.edu/library/
    1749.html
May 2007 Copyright 2002

Kalamazoo College
Upjohn Library
Kalamazoo, Michigan
www.kzoo.edu/is/library/ill/index.html#recall
July 2006 Copyright 2006

Kansas State University
Kansas State University Libraries
Manhattan, Kansas
www.lib.ksu.edu/depts/libinst/goals.html
April 2006 Copyright 2006

La Sierra University
La Sierra University Library
Riverside, California
www.lasierra.edu/library/info_serve/circulation
    -policies.html
May 2007 Copyright 2006
www.lasierra.edu/library/medias/page5.html
May 2007 Copyright 2006

LaGuardia Community College
LaGuardia Community College Library Media and
Resources Center
Long Island City, New York
www.lagcc.cuny.edu/library/forms/ask.htm
July 2006 Copyright 2006

Lake Sumter Community College
Lake Sumter Community College Libraries
Sumterville, Florida
www.lscc.edu/library/coldev.htm#TYP
July 2006 Copyright 2006
www.lscc.edu/library/govdocs.htm#POL
July 2006 Copyright 2006
www.lscc.edu/library/libraryforms/lib_instructor
    _rqst.htm
July 2006 Copyright 2006
http://lscc.edu/library/illpol.htm#BOR
July 2006 Copyright 2006
http://lscc.edu/library/libraryforms/lib
    _interlibrary_rqst.htm
July 2006 Copyright 2006

Lane Community College
Lane Community College Library
Eugene, Oregon
www.lanecc.edu/library/about/princip.htm#purpose
July 2006 Copyright 2006
www.lanecc.edu/library/suggest/concern.htm
July 2006 Copyright 2006

Lansing Community College
Library at Lansing Community College

Lansing, Michigan
www.lcc.edu/library/about-the-library/collection
    -development-policy.htm#nonprint
July 2006 Copyright 2006
www.lcc.edu/library/library-instruction/guides/
    ILLGuidelines.pdf
July 2006 Copyright 2006

Los Angeles Valley College
Los Angeles Valley College Library
Valley Glen, California
www.lavc.edu/Library/facultyguide.htm
June 2006 Copyright 2004
www.lavc.edu/Library/loans.html
June 2006 Copyright 2006

Lynchburg College
Knight-Capron Library
Lynchburg, Virginia
www.lynchburg.edu/x3569.xml
June 2006 Copyright 2006

Macon State College
Macon State College Library
Macon, Georgia
www.maconstate.edu/library/FaxPol.aspx
August 2006 Copyright 2005
www.maconstate.edu/library/IllPol.aspx
August 2006 Copyright 2005

Manatee Community College
Manatee Community College Library
Bradenton, Florida
www.mccfl.edu/pages/314.asp
August 2006 Copyright 2004

Marlboro College
Rice-Aron Library
Marlboro, Vermont
www.marlboro.edu/resources/library/policies/
    documents/Artdisplayspolicy-PDF.pdf
June 2006 Copyright 2006
www.marlboro.edu/resources/library/policies/
    lockerspolicy.pdf
June 2006 Copyright 2004
www.marlboro.edu/resources/library/policies/
    lockerspolicy.pdf
June 2006 Copyright 2004
www.marlboro.edu/resources/library/policies/
    circulation.php
June 2006 Copyright 2004

Milwaukee Area Technical College
Milwaukee Area Technical College Library

Milwaukee, Wisconsin
www.matc.edu/library/policies.html
June 2006 Copyright 2006

Mohawk Valley Community College
Mohawk Valley Community College Library
Utica and Rome, New York
www.mvcc.edu/library
November 2006 Copyright 2006

Monroe County Community College
Monroe County Community College Library
Monroe, Michigan
www.monroeccc.edu/library/askalibrarian.htm
July 2006 Copyright 2006
www.monroeccc.edu/library/acceptableuse.htm
July 2006 Copyright 2006

Neumann College
Neumann College Library
Aston, Pennsylvania
www.neumann.edu/academics/library/
    infolit.asp
May 2007 Copyright 2007
www.neumann.edu/academics/library/
    policies_ill.asp
May 2007 Copyright 2007
www.neumann.edu/academics/library/
    policies_facreserves.asp
May 2007 Copyright 2007

New College of Florida
Jane Bancroft Cook Library
Sarasota, Florida
http://lib.sar.usf.edu/policies/policyADA.htm
August 2006 Copyright 2006

New Jersey City University
Congressman Frank J. Guarini Library
Jersey City, New Jersey
www.njcu.edu/guarini/Forms/forms.htm
August 2006 Copyright 2005

New Mexico State University
New Mexico State University Library
Las Cruces, New Mexico
http://lib.nmsu.edu/instruction/about/mission&
    values.PDF
August 2006 Copyright 2006

New Mexico State University Alamogordo
David H. Townsend Library
Alamogordo, New Mexico

http://alamo.nmsu.edu/library/nwcolldevpolicy.pdf
June 2006 Copyright 2001

New York University
Bobst Library
New York, New York
http://library.nyu.edu/about/facpols.html
May 2007 Copyright 2006
http://library.nyu.edu/about/stupols.html
May 2007 Copyright 2006
http://library.nyu.edu/about/code.html
May 2007 Copyright 2003
http://library.nyu.edu/collections/policies/fales_dwn
twn.html
May 2007 Copyright 2006
http://library.nyu.edu/collections/policies/archive
    .html
May 2007 Copyright 2003

Niagara University
Niagara University Library
Niagara University, New York
www.niagara.edu/library/affil.html
May 2007 Copyright 2005
www.niagara.edu/library/illweb.html
May 2007 Copyright 2005
www.niagara.edu/library/li.html
May 2007 Copyright 2006

Northern Arizona University
Cline Library
Flagstaff, Arizona
http://library.nau.edu/information/donations.html
July 2006 Copyright 2006
http://library.nau.edu/services/request/proxycard.html
July 2006 Copyright 2006
http://library.nau.edu/services/request/course
    support.html
July 2006 Copyright 2006

The Ohio State University
The Ohio State University Libraries
Columbus, Ohio
http://library.osu.edu/sites/circulation/circservpol.php
July 2006 Copyright 2004

Oklahoma State University Center for Health
Sciences
Medical Library
Tulsa, Oklahoma

www.healthsciences.okstate.edu/
medlibrary/policies.htm
May 2007 Copyright 2007

Oklahoma State University Tulsa
Tulsa Okalahoma
www.osu-tulsa.okstate.edu/academics/srr/
conduct11.asp
September 2006 Copyright 2004

Olin College
Olin College Library
Needham, Massachusetts
http://library.olin.edu/faq.php#shelves
June 2006 Copyright 2005
http://library.olin.edu/policies.php#D
June 2006 Copyright 2005

Palo Alto College
Alamo Community College District
George Ozuna, Jr. Learning Resource Center
www.accd.edu/pac/lrc/evaluatn/eval-cd.htm
August 2006 Copyright 2005

Phoenix College
Phoenix College Library
Phoenix, Arizona
www.pc.maricopa.edu/library
    .php?page=2196&subpage=3800&sublink=5413
May 2007 Copyright 2007
www.pc.maricopa.edu/library
    .php?page=2196&subpage=3800&sublink=29727
August 2006 copyright 2005
www.pc.maricopa.edu/library
    .php?page=2196&subpage=3800&sublink=26057
May 2007 Copyright 200&
www.pc.maricopa.edu/library
    .php?page=2196&subpage=3800&sublink=5417
May 2007 Copyright 2007

Princeton University
Princeton University Library
Princeton, New Jersey
http://library.princeton.edu/hr/forms/forms.html
November 2006 Copyright 2006
http://library.princeton.edu/hr/forms/LibIncident
    Rept.doc
November 2006 Copyright 2005
www.princeton.edu/hr/policies/conditions/523.htm
November 2006 Copyright 2006
http://library.princeton.edu/hr/forms/PULAPerf
    App/PerfAppraisalForm.doc
November 2006 Copyright 2006

Queens College CUNY
Rosenthal, Library
Flushing, New York
http://qcpages.qc.cuny.edu/Library/info/support.html
August 2006 Copyright 2006

Rockefeller University
Rockefeller University Library
New York, New York
www.rockefeller.edu/library/about/
    guidelines.php
May 2007 Copyright 2004–2005

Rutgers University
Rutgers University Libraries
Newark, New Jersey
www.libraries.rutgers.edu/rul/about/
    pub_serv_policies/pspm_06.shtml
May 2007 Copyright 2006
www.libraries.rutgers.edu/rul/about/
    pub_serv_policies/pspm_02.shtml
May 2007 Copyright 2007
www.libraries.rutgers.edu/rul/about/
    pub_serv_policies/pspm_04.shtml
May 2007 Copyright 2003

Saint Philips College Learning Resource Center
Alamo Community College District
San Antonio, Texas
www.accd.edu/spc/lrc/LRCINFO/policies/
    collectdel.htm
May 2007 Copyright 2007

Santa Monica College
Santa Monica College Library
Santa Monica, California
http://library.smc.edu/about/libpolicies.html
May 2007 Copyright 2006

Southeastern Louisiana University
Linus A. Sims Memorial Library
Hammond, Louisiana
www2.selu.edu/Library/ServicesDept/circ/
    reserve.htm
August 2006 Copyright 2005

Southern Illinois University Edwardsville
Lovejoy Library
Edwardsville, Illinois
www.library.siue.edu/lib/about_lovejoy_library/
    preservation_policy.htm
August 2006 Copyright 2006

State University of New York Cortland
Memorial Library
Cortland, New York
http://library.cortland.edu/policies/reference
    _policy.asp#mission
July 2006 Copyright 2002
http://library.cortland.edu/policies/reference
    _policy.asp#prior
August 2006 Copyright 2006

Stetson University
duPont-Ball Library
DeLand, Florida
www.stetson.edu/library/colldevref.html
August 2006 Copyright 2005
www.stetson.edu/library/instructmission.html
August 2006 Copyright 2005
www.stetson.edu/library/colldevweb.html
August 2006 Copyright 2006

Syracuse University
Syracuse University Library
Syracuse, New York
http://library.syr.edu/information/forms/recall.htm
June 2006 Copyright 2006
http://libwww.syr.edu/policies/photo/index.html
June 2006 Copyright 2006
http://libwww.syr.edu/information/circulation/
    circpol.htm
June 2006 Copyright 2006
http://libwww.syr.edu/policies/licensed.htm
June 2006 Copyright 2006
http://library.syr.edu/policies/privacy.html
September 2006 Copyright 2005

Tallahassee Community College
Tallahassee Community College Library
Tallahassee, Florida
www.tcc.cc.fl.us/dept/library/mission.htm
April 2006 Copyright 2006

Texas Tech University
Southwest Collections/Special Collections Library
Lubbock, Texas
http://swco.ttu.edu/University_Archive/
    uacollections7.html
October 2006 Copyright 2006
http://swco.ttu.edu/University_Archive/mainpage
    .htm#Transferring%20Materials%20to%20
    the%20University%20Archives
October 2006 Copyright 2006

Towson University
Albert S. Cook Library
Towson, Maryland
http://cooklibrary.towson.edu/eres/fac/
eresGuidelines.cfm
October 2006 Copyright 2006

Tulane University
Howard-Tilton Memorial Library
New Orleans, Louisiana
http://library.tulane.edu/about_the_library/library
    _policies/cell_phone_use.php
July 2006 Copyright 2006
http://library.tulane.edu/about_the_library/library
    _policies/computer_use.php
July 2006 Copyright 2006
http://library.tulane.edu/about_the_library/library
    _policies/quiet_study_area.php
July 2006 Copyright 2006
http://library.tulane.edu/about_the_library/library
    _policies/index.php
July 2006 Copyright 2006
http://library.tulane.edu/about_the_library/library
    _policies/borrowing_from_the_library.php
July 2006 Copyright 2006
http://library.tulane.edu/about_the_library/
    departments/collections/digital_collections
    _policies.php
July 2006 Copyright 2006

Union College
Jones Learning Resource Center
Barbourville, Kentucky
www.unionky.edu/DLIS/ITUsagePolicy.asp
July 2006 Copyright 2005

University at Albany
University Libraries
Albany, New York
http://library.albany.edu/dewey/referencepolicy.htm
July 2006 Copyright 2004
http://library.albany.edu/subject/cdp/reference
    _ulib.html
August 2006 Copyright 2006

University at Buffalo
University at Buffalo Libraries
Buffalo, New York
http://ublib.buffalo.edu/libraries/asl/services/refer-
ence-policy.html
July 2006 Copyright 2005

http://libweb.lib.buffalo.edu/aslstaff/ENotebook2/
    ReferenceServicesPolicyStatement.htm
July 2006 Copyright 2006

University of Alaska Anchorage
Alaska Pacific University
Consortium Library
Anchorage, Alaska
http://lib.uaa.alaska.edu/about/policies/
    acceptableuse.php
August 2006 Copyright 2005
http://lib.uaa.alaska.edu/research/instruction/
    outcomes.php
August 2006 Copyright 2005
http://lib.uaa.alaska.edu/about/policies/restrict.php
August 2006 Copyright 2006

University of Arizona
The University of Arizona Library
Tucson, Arizona
www.library.arizona.edu/services/docdel/policy.html
August 2006 Copyright 2006

University of Arkansas
University of Arkansas Libraries
Fayetteville, Arkansas
http://libinfo.uark.edu/info/studypolicy.asp
August 2006 Copyright 2006
http://libinfo.uark.edu/webdocs/info/facultystudy.pdf
August 2006 Copyright 2006
http://libinfo.uark.edu/reference/visitors.asp
August 2006 Copyright 2006
http://libinfo.uark.edu/reference/requestclass.asp
    ?prefix=neciap&name=Necia%20Parker-Gibson
August 2006 Copyright 2006

University of California Berkeley
University of California Berkeley Libraries
Berkeley, California
www.lib.berkeley.edu/Staff/PS/PSM/autoblck.html
July 2006 Copyright 2001
www.lib.berkeley.edu/AboutLibrary/visitor
    _information.html
July 2006 Copyright 2006
www.lib.berkeley.edu/services/comp_use.html
July 2006 Copyright 2006
http://itpolicy.berkeley.edu:7015/usepolicy.html
July 2006 Copyright 2006
www.lib.berkeley.edu/AboutLibrary/filming.html
July 2006 Copyright 2004
www.lib.berkeley.edu/AboutLibrary/values.html
July 2006 Copyright 2004

www.lib.berkeley.edu/services/library_privileges.html
August 2006 Copyright 2006
http://arch.ced.berkeley.edu/resources/gift/deed
    _of_gift.htm
August 2006 Copyright 2006
All of the University of California and California State system schools' work is copyrighted and is used with their permission

University of California Davis
University Library
Davis, California
www.lib.ucdavis.edu/dept/instruc/classes/
    descriptions.php
August 2006 Copyright 2006
www.lib.ucdavis.edu/dept/instruc/files/resources
    forinstructors.pdf
August 2006 Copyright 2006
www.lib.ucdavis.edu/dept/instruc/instructors/
    assessment.php
August 2006 Copyright 2006
www.lib.ucdavis.edu/dept/instruc/files/samplequiz.pdf
August 2006 Copyright 2006
www.lib.ucdavis.edu/dept/instruc/classes/
    descriptions.php
August 2006 Copyright 2006
www.lib.ucdavis.edu/ul/help/forms/ask/#policy
August 2006 Copyright 2006
www.lib.ucdavis.edu/ul/about/policies/privacy.php
August 2006 Copyright
All of the University of California and California State system schools' work is copyrighted and is used with their permission

University of California San Diego
University Libraries
San Diego, California
http://libraries.ucsd.edu/services/privacy.html
August 2006 Copyright 2004
All of the University of California and California State system schools' work is copyrighted and is used with their permission

University of California Santa Barbara
University Libraries
Santa Barbara, California
www.library.ucsb.edu/services/policies/privacy.html
August 2006 Copyright 2006
All of the University of California and California State system schools' work is copyrighted and is used with their permission

483

University of California Santa Cruz
University of California Santa Cruz University
Library
Santa Cruz, California
http://library.ucsc.edu/internal/personnel/
strategic/mv.html
April 2006 Copyright 2002
http://library.ucsc.edu/suggest/responses.html
August 2006 Copyright 2006
http://library.ucsc.edu/services/pubcomputing/
November 2006 Copyright 2006
All of the University of California and California State system schools' work is copyrighted and is used with their permission

University of Central Florida
University of Central Florida Libraries
Orlando, Florida
http://library.ucf.edu/Administration/Policies/
default.asp
August 2006 Copyright 2006

University of Colorado at Boulder
University Libraries
Bolder, Colorado
http://ucblibraries.colorado.edu/collection
development/map.htm
August 2006 Copyright 2006

University of Idaho
University of Idaho Libraries
Moscow, Idaho
www.lib.uidaho.edu/access_services/borrowing
_policies.htm
August 2006 Copyright 2005
www.lib.uidaho.edu/reference/ask_a_librarian.htm
August 2006 Copyright 2005
www.lib.uidaho.edu/access_services/reserve/
ereserve.shtml
August 2006 Copyright 2005
www.lib.uidaho.edu/donations/
August 2006 Copyright 2006

University of Illinois at Chicago
University Library
Chicago, Illinois
http://uic.edu/depts/lib/admin/personnel/forms/
August 2006 Copyright 2006

University of Illinois at Urbana-Champaign
University Library
Urbana, Illinois
www.library.uiuc.edu/administration/services/

policies/patron_conduct.htm
July 2006 Copyright 2004
www.library.uiuc.edu/administration/collections/
policies/gifts_policy.htm
July 2006 Copyright 2004
www.library.uiuc.edu/circ/policies.htm
July 2006 Copyright 2005
www.library.uiuc.edu/administration/collections/
policies/retention_in_digital_age.htm
August 2006 Copyright 2001
www.library.uiuc.edu/prescons/policy_statement.htm
August 2006 Copyright 2006
www.library.uiuc.edu/circ/policies.htm
September 2006 Copyright 2005

University of Illinois at Urbana-Champaign School
of Law
Albert E. Jenner, Jr Memorial Law Library
Champaign, Illinois
http://library.law.uiuc.edu/sub/circserv.html
August 2005 Copyright 2003

University of Indianapolis
Krannert Memorial Library
Indianapolis, Indiana
http://kml.uindy.edu/aboutus/policies.php#patron
July 2006 Copyright 2006

University of Iowa
University of Iowa Libraries
Iowa City, Iowa
www.lib.uiowa.edu/govpubs/documents/
collectionpolicy.pdf
July 2006 Copyright 2006
www.lib.uiowa.edu/ref/documents/fyidisab.pdf
July 2006 Copyright 2006
www.lib.uiowa.edu/ill/services.html
July 2006 Copyright 2006
www.lib.uiowa.edu/about/policies/media.html
July 2006 Copyright 2006
www.lib.uiowa.edu/about/policies/circulation.html
July 2003 Copyright 2006
www.lib.uiowa.edu/about/policies/access
commercial.pdf
July 2006 Copyright 2003
www.lib.uiowa.edu/preservation/
August 2006 Copyright 2006
www.lib.uiowa.edu/about/policies/userprivacy.pdf
August 2006 Copyright 2006

University of Maine Off Campus Library Services
University College

Augusta, Maine
www.learn.maine.edu/ocls/eref_policy.html
July 2006 Copyright 2005

University of Maryland Baltimore County
Albin O. Kuhn Library
Baltimore, Maryland
http://aok.lib.umbc.edu/reference/BI/roompol.php
July 2006 Copyright 2001
http://aok.lib.umbc.edu/reference/information
    literacy/program.php
July 2006 Copyright 2005
http://aok.lib.umbc.edu/reference/information
    literacy/results.php
July 2006 Copyright 2005

University of Michigan
University of Michigan Libraries
Ann Arbor, Michigan
www.lib.umich.edu/policies/reference.html
September 2006 Copyright 2005
www.lib.umich.edu/policies/reference.html
September 2006 Copyright 2005

University of Michigan Flint
Frances Willson Thompson Library
Flint, Michigan
http://lib.umflint.edu/govdocs.html
August 2006 Copyright 2004

University of Minnesota Duluth
www.d.umn.edu/lib/copyright/policy.htm
October 2006 Copyright 2001
www.d.umn.edu/lib/admin/library-
copyright.htm#reserveelectronic
October 2006 Copyright 2006

University of New Hampshire
The University of New Hampshire Library
Durham, New Hampshire
www.library.unh.edu/about/polreg/copyright.shtml
August 2006 Copyright 2005

University of North Carolina Wilmington
William Madison Randall Library
Wilmington, North Carolina
http://library.uncw.edu/web/policies/reference.html
July 2006 Copyright 2005
http://library.uncw.edu/web/policies/faculty.html
July 2006 Copyright 2006
http://library.uncw.edu/web/policies/exhibits.html
July 2006 Copyright 2005
http://library.uncw.edu/web/policies/theses.html

July 2006 Copyright 2003
http://library.uncw.edu/web/policies/honors.html
July 2006 Copyright 2005
http://library.uncw.edu/web/policies/preservation.html
July 2006 Copyright 2002
http://library.uncw.edu/web/policies/preservation.html
August 2006 Copyright 2005

University of Pittsburgh
Pitt Digital Library
Pittsburgh, Pennsylvania
www.library.pitt.edu/reference/
July 2006 Copyright 2002
www.library.pitt.edu/services/reserves/
July 2006 Copyright 2002
www.library.pitt.edu/uls/GE/main_ge.html
August 2006 Copyright 2002

University of Rochester
University of Rochester Libraries
Rochester, New York
www.lib.rochester.edu/index.cfm?PAGE=242
September 2006 Copyright 2006

University of Scranton
Weinberg Memorial Library
Scranton, Pennsylvania
http://academic.scranton.edu/department/wml/
    wmlinfo_2.html#ask_a_librarian
July 2006 Copyright 2006
http://academic.scranton.edu/department/wml/
    printfrm.html
July 2006 Copyright 2006
http://academic.scranton.edu/department/wml/
    fhome.html
July 2006 Copyright 2006
http://academic.scranton.edu/department/wml/
    distance_learning_info.html#general
July 2006 Copyright 2005
http://academic.scranton.edu/department/wml/
    wmlinfo_3.html#dlservices
July 2006 Copyright 2006
**The University of Scranton's web site is
changing and policies will be separated
from information on the updated sites.**

University of South Alabama
University Libraries
Mobil, Alabama
www.southalabama.edu/univlib/forms/database.html
July 2006 Copyright 2005
www.southalabama.edu/univlib/illforms.htm

July 2006 Copyright 2006
www.southalabama.edu/univlib/info/circ.html
July 2006 Copyright 2005
www.southalabama.edu/univlib/info/
   collectionman.htm
July 2006 Copyright 2004

University of South Carolina Beaufort
USC Beaufort Library
Beaufort, South Carolina
www.sc.edu/beaufort/library/pages/policies/
   reservespol.shtml
July 2006 Copyright 2004
www.sc.edu/beaufort/library/pages/policies/
   acqpol.shtml
July 2006 Copyright 2004
www.sc.edu/beaufort/library/pages/policies/illpol.shtml
July 2006 Copyright 2006
www.sc.edu/beaufort/library/pages/policies/
   theftpol.shtml
July 2006 Copyright 2004
www.lib.uiowa.edu/instruction/info_literacy.html
July 2006 Copyright 2006

University of South Florida
Jane Bancroft Cook Library
Sarasota, Florida
http://lib.sar.usf.edu/policies/policyADA.htm
August 2006 Copyright 2006
www.lib.usf.edu/ref/instruction/goals.html
August 2006 Copyright 2004

University of Southern California
University Libraries
Los Angeles, California
www.usc.edu/libraries/services/ask_a_librarian/terms/
August 2006 Copyright 2006

University of Texas at Arlington
University Libraries
Arlington, Texas
http://library.uta.edu/policies/circulation/userTypes
   Policy.jsp
August 2006 Copyright 2006
http://library.uta.edu/policies/circulation/media
   ReservesPolicy.jsp
August 2006 Copyright 2006
http://library.uta.edu/borrowing/parentalConsent.pdf
August 2006 Copyright 2006
http://library.uta.edu/policies/circulation/youth
   AccessPolicy.jsp
August 2006 Copyright 2006
http://library.uta.edu/policies/collections/elect

ResourcesPolicy.jsp
August 2006 Copyright 2006
http://library.uta.edu/policies/facilities/lostFound
   Policy.jsp
August 2006 Copyright 2006
http://library.uta.edu/policies/privacy/
August 2006 Copyright 2006

University of Texas at Austin
University of Texas Libraries
Austin, Texas
www.lib.utexas.edu/vprovost/policies/guidelines
   -for-reference-and-information-services.html
August 2006 Copyright 2006
www.lib.utexas.edu/services/reference/faq.html
August 2006 Copyright 2006
www.lib.utexas.edu/vprovost/policies/pres_policy.html
August 2006 Copyright 2005
www.lib.utexas.edu/services/reserves/policy.html
August 2006 Copyright 2005
www.lib.utexas.edu/admin/cird/policies/subjects/
   replacement.html
September 2006 Copyright 2006
www.lib.utexas.edu/admin/cird/policies/subjects/
   framework.html
September 2006 Copyright 2006

University of Texas at El Paso
University Libraries
El Paso, Texas
http://libraryweb.utep.edu/policies/policies.cfm
   ?page=commusers
July 2006 Copyright 2006
http://libraryweb.utep.edu/policies/policies.cfm
   ?page=elecreserves
July 2006 Copyright 2006
http://libraryweb.utep.edu/policies/policies.cfm
   ?page=general
July 2006 Copyright

University of Texas at Brownsville
Arnulfo L. Oliveira Memorial Library
Brownsville, Texas
http://library1.utb.edu/policies/studyrooms.htm
August 2006 Copyright 2006

University of Texas San Antonio
University Library
San Antonio, Texas
www.lib.utsa.edu/Services/Multimedia/policies.html
August 2006 Copyright 2006
www.lib.utsa.edu/Services/General/courier.html
August 2006 Copyright 2006

University of Vermont
Graduate College
Burlington, Vermont
www.uvm.edu/~gradcoll/rights.html
September 2006 Copyright 2002

University of Washington
University of Washington Libraries
Seattle, Washington
www.lib.washington.edu/services/borrow/lib38.html
July 2006 Copyright 2006
www.lib.washington.edu/about/StrategicPlan
   2002-2005.html
July 2006 Copyright 2003
www.lib.washington.edu/support/types_of_gifts.htm
July 2006 Copyright 2006
www.lib.washington.edu/services/borrow/visitor.html
August 2006 Copyright 2006
www.lib.washington.edu/services/course/test/
   reservefaq.html
October 2006 Copyright 2006

University of West Georgia
University Library
Carrollton, Georgia
www.westga.edu/~library/depts/ref/RefCollDev
   Policy.shtml
August 2006 Copyright 2005

University of Wisconsin Green Bay
Cofrin Library
Green Bay, Wisconsin
www.uwgb.edu/library/policies/spc.html
May 2007 Copyright 2006

University of Wisconsin Madison
Memorial Library
Madison, Wisconsin
http://memorial.library.wisc.edu/photocpy.htm
November 2006 Copyright 2005

University of Wisconsin River Falls
Chalmer-Davee Library
River Falls, Wisconsin
www.uwrf.edu/library/info/policies/rdeskpol.php
July 2006 Copyright 2006

Vanderbilt University
Central Library
Nashville, Tennessee
www.library.vanderbilt.edu/central/reserves_and
   _electronic_reserves.shtml
August 2006 Copyright 2006
www.library.vanderbilt.edu/access/confidentiality.shtml

September 2006 Copyright 2003
www.library.vanderbilt.edu/central/reserves_and
   _electronic_reserves.shtml
October 2006 Copyright 2006

Ventura College
Evelyn and Howard Boroughs Library
Venture, California
www.venturacollege.edu/accreditation/2004/
   standard-2c-1.htm
June 2006 Copyright 2006

Virginia Tech
Virginia Tech University Libraries
Blacksburg, Virginia
www.lib.vt.edu/services/circ-reserve/docdel.html
July 2006 Copyright 2005
http://sslweb.lib.vt.edu/forms/fine_appeal_form.php
July 2006 Copyright 2004
www.lib.vt.edu/help/instruct/facserv.html
July 2006 Copyright 2004
http://sslweb.lib.vt.edu/forms/Library_Material
   _Search.php
July 2006 Copyright 2004
www.lib.vt.edu/services/circ-reserve/docdel.html
August 2006 Copyright 2005

Washburn University
Mabee Library
Topeka Kansas
www.washburn.edu/services/mabee/policies/art
   _policy.html
August 2006 Copyright 2006

Washington and Lee University
Leyburn Library
Lexington, Virginia
http://library.wlu.edu/copyrightpolicy.html
August 2006 Copyright 2006

Weber State University
Stewart Library
Ogden, Utah
http://library.weber.edu/libadmin/lppm/prep
   _faculty.cfm#Reference%20Service
July 2006 Copyright 2004
http://library.weber.edu/libadmin/lppm/gift_in
   _kind.cfm
July 2006 Copyright 2006
http://library.weber.edu/libadmin/lppm/friends
   _constitution.cfm
July 2006 Copyright 2004
http://library.weber.edu/libadmin/lppm/reference.cfm

July 2006 Copyright 2006
http://library.weber.edu/il/team/assessment/
 studenteval.asp
August 2006 Copyright 2006

Wellesley College
Wellesley College Library
Wellesley, Massachusetts
www.wellesley.edu/Library/pol-gift.html
August 2006 Copyright 2006

Western Illinois University
Western Illinois University Library
Macomb, Illinois
www.wiu.edu/library/units/access/surrogate
 _checkout_form.pdf
August 2006 Copyright 2006

Williams College
Williams College Libraries
Williamstown, Massachusetts
www.williams.edu/library/vision.php
May 2007 Copyright 2006

Windward Community College
Windward Community College Library
Kaneohe, Hawaii
http://library.wcc.hawaii.edu/mission.html
May 2007 Copyright 2007

Xavier University
Xavier University Library
Cincinnati, Ohio
www.xavier.edu/library/evaluation/

evaluation_student.cfm
May 2007 Copyright 2006
www.xavier.edu/library/evaluation/
 evaluation_faculty.cfm
May 2007 Copyright 2006
www.xavier.edu/library/circulation/limits.cfm
May 2007 Copyright 2006
www.xavier.edu/library/askus.cfm
May 2007 Copyright 2006
www.xavier.edu/library/document_delivery/
 remote_journal.cfm
May 2007 Copyright 2006
www.xavier.edu/library/document_delivery/
 remote_stacks.cfm
May 2007 Copyright 2006
www.xavier.edu/library/education/research
 _consultations.cfm
May 2007 Copyright 2006

Yakima Valley Community College
College Library
Yakima, Washington
www.yvcc.edu/about/privacy.asp
May 2007 Copyright 2007

York College
Schmidt Library
York, Pennsylvania
www.ycp.edu/library/4591.htm
November 2006 Copyright 2005

INDEX

About the Author

Rebecca Brumley has worked as a librarian in both academic and public libraries. She worked for many years in the Humanities Division at the Dallas Public Library, Dallas, Texas, where she was the religion, philosophy, and paranormal selector. She currently works as a librarian at the Navarro College Library at the Waxahachie and Midlothian campuses in Texas.

Brumley has also worked as an information literacy workshop instructor for Dallas Independent School District teachers. She has served on the board of the Desoto Public Library in Texas and as a consultant to small libraries and communities interested in updating policy and procedure manuals.

Brumley received her Master's in Information Science from University of North Texas. She is the author of three other books, *Public Library Managers Forms, Policies, and Procedures Handbook with CD-ROM*, *The Reference Librarian's Policies, Forms, Guidelines, and Procedures Handbook with CD-ROM*, and *Neal-Schuman Directory of Public Library Job Descriptions with CD-ROM*. In her free time, she supports the efforts of Frisco Humane Society by fostering cats and kittens.